Emotional Cutoff
Bowen Family Systems
Theory Perspectives

HAWORTH Marriage and the Family
Terry S. Trepper, PhD
Executive Editor

Couples Therapy, Second Edition by Linda Berg-Cross

Family Therapy and Mental Health. Innovations in Theory and Practice by Malcolm M. MacFarlane

How to Work with Sex Offenders A Handbook for Criminal Justice, Human Service, and Mental Health Professionals by Rudy Flora

Marital and Sexual Lifestyles in the United States. Attitudes, Behaviors, and Relationships in Social Context by Linda P. Rouse

Psychotherapy with People in the Arts: Nurturing Creativity by Gerald Schoenewolf

Critical Incidents in Marital and Family Therapy A Practitioner's Guide by David A. Baptiste Jr.

Clinical and Educational Interventions with Fathers edited by Jay Fagan and Alan J. Hawkins

Family Solutions for Substance Abuse: Clinical and Counseling Approaches by Eric E. McCollum and Terry S. Trepper

The Therapist's Notebook for Families: Solution-Oriented Exercises for Working with Parents, Children, and Adolescents by Bob Bertolino and Gary Schultheis

Between Fathers and Sons: Critical Incident Narratives in the Development of Men's Lives by Robert J Pellegrini and Theodore R Sarbin

Women's Stories of Divorce at Childbirth: When the Baby Rocks the Cradle by Hilary Hoge

Treating Marital Stress. Support-Based Approaches by Robert P. Rugel

An Introduction to Marriage and Family Therapy by Lorna L. Hecker and Joseph L. Wetchler

Solution-Focused Brief Therapy: Its Effective Use in Agency Settings by Teri Pichot and Yvonne M. Dolan

Becoming a Solution Detective: Identifying Your Client's Strengths in Practical Brief Therapy by John Sharry, Brendan Madden, and Melissa Darmody

Emotional Cutoff. Bowen Family Systems Theory Perspectives edited by Peter Titelman

Welcome Home! An International and Nontraditional Adoption Reader edited by Lita Linzer Schwartz and Florence W. Kaslow

Creativity in Psychotherapy: Reaching New Heights with Individuals, Couples, and Families by David K. Carson and Kent W Becker

Understanding and Treating Schizophrenia. Contemporary Research, Theory and Practice by Glenn D. Shean

Family Involvement in Treating Schizophrenia Models, Essential Skills, and Process by James A. Marley

Transgender Emergence: Therapeutic Guidelines for Working with Gender-Variant People and Their Families by Arlene Istar Lev

Family Treatment of Personality Disorders: Advances in Clinical Practice edited by Malcolm M. MacFarlane

Emotional Cutoff
Bowen Family Systems Theory Perspectives

Peter Titelman, PhD
Editor

The Haworth Clinical Practice Press
An Imprint of The Haworth Press, Inc.
New York • London • Oxford

Published by

The Haworth Clinical Practice Press, an imprint of The Haworth Press, Inc. 10 Alice Street, Binghamton. NY 13904-1580

TR 11 19 03

Cover design by Marylouise E. Doyle

Library of Congress Cataloging-in-Publication Data

Emotional cutoff : Bowen family systems theory perspectives / Peter Titelman, editor
    p. cm.
Includes bibliographical references and index.
    ISBN 0-7890-1459-9 (hc)—ISBN 0-7890-1460-2 (sc)
    1. Family psychotherapy 2. Bowen, Murray, 1913- 3. International relations. I Titelman, Peter
    RC488 5 E47 2003
    616 89'156—dc21

                                                                    2002012075

Dedicated to my Aunt Lee, Cousin Edna (1902-2001),
cousins Joy and Lani, and to the whole Titelman family

CONTENTS

About the Editor	**xiii**
Contributors	**xv**
Foreword	**xix**
Michael E. Kerr	
Acknowledgments	**xxiii**
Introduction	**1**
Peter Titelman	

PART I: THEORY

**Chapter 1. Emotional Cutoff in Bowen Family
Systems Theory: An Overview** — **9**
Peter Titelman

Introduction	9
The Origin and Evolution of the Concept of Emotional Cutoff in Bowen Theory	10
The Theoretical Context for the Concepts of Fusion and Cutoff	19
The Concepts of Emotional Fusion and Emotional Cutoff in Bowen Theory	21
The Relationship Between Emotional Cutoff and the Other Concepts in Bowen Theory	29
Symptom Formation and the Continuum of Emotional Cutoff	38
Bridging Emotional Cutoff	52
Summary	65

**Chapter 2. Lone Wolves and Rogue Elephants:
Emotional Cutoff Among Animals** — **67**
Anthony J. Wilgus

Introduction	67
Solitary Behavior in the Animal World	68
Conclusion	76

Chapter 3. Emotional Cutoff and the Brain   **83**

Priscilla J. Friesen

Introduction   83
The Human Brain   84
Emotional Cutoff and Brain Development   89
Emotional Cutoff and Brain Functioning   91
Clinical Example   99
Emotional Cutoff in Clinical Work   106
Summary   107

PART II: THE THERAPIST'S OWN FAMILY

Chapter 4. Efforts to Bridge Secondary Emotional Cutoff   **111**

Peter Titelman

Introduction   111
A First Cousin Once Removed: A Resource
    for Multigenerational History and the Discovery
    of Cutoff in the Family   115
Bridging Emotional Cutoff with an Aunt   117
Beginning Efforts to Bridge Cutoff with Two First Cousins   125
Conclusion   134

**Chapter 5. Toward Undoing Cutoff: A Twenty-Five-Year
Perspective**   **139**

Brian J. Kelly

Introduction   139
Mr. A's Family History As Known in 1976   142
Mr. A's History Through the Lens of Theory   143
Initial Steps to Undo Cutoff   144
Summary and Conclusion   156

**Chapter 6. Bridging Cutoff with Divorced Relationships
and with Family**   **159**

Roberta M. Gilbert

Early Experience with Bowen Theory   159
A First Attempt to Put Theory to the Test   160
Bridging Cutoff with My Own Family   164

Results of Family Cutoff Work   168
Work for the Future   171

Chapter 7. Managing Cutoff Through Family Research   **173**
    Alice Eichholz

Shift from Individual to Systems Thinking   174
Researching the Cutoffs   175
Identifying Successful and Unsuccessful Approaches
    to Cutoffs   191
Identifying Variability in Functioning   192
Summary: Principles and Benefits of Managing Cutoff
    Through Family Research   194

PART III: RESEARCH AND CLINICAL APPLICATIONS

**Chapter 8. Toward Understanding and Measuring
    Emotional Cutoff**   **199**
    Selden Dunbar Illick
    Gail Hilbert-McAllister
    Susan Ewing Jefferies
    Charles M. White

Introduction   199
Emotional Cutoff Rooted in Evolution and Emotional
    Reactivity   200
Research Instrument   206
Development of the Scale   210
Validity and Reliability   213
Summary   215

**Chapter 9. Marital Functioning and Multigenerational
    Fusion and Cutoff**   **219**
    Phil Klever

Parent-Child Fusion and Separation—The Prelude
    and Backdrop to Marriage   219
The Effects of Cutoff on Marriage   224
Clinical Work with Emotional Cutoff   230
Conclusion   242

Chapter 10. Reproduction and Emotional Cutoff   **245**

Victoria Harrison

Introduction   245
Bowen Theory and Emotional Cutoff   246
The Study of Bowen Theory and Reproduction   249
Family Examples from Research and Clinical Practice   257
Conclusion   269

**Chapter 11. The Impact of Cutoff in Families
Raising Adolescents**   **273**

Anne S. McKnight

Introduction   273
Concepts from Bowen Theory   276
Outline of a Study   278
Some Considerations and Conclusions   284

**Chapter 12. The Continuum of Emotional Cutoff
in Divorce**   **289**

Stephanie J. Ferrera

The Complexity of Divorce   290
The Perspective of Bowen Theory   301
Emotional Cutoff and Divorce   310
Concluding Comment   312

**Chapter 13. Depression: A Symptom of Cutoff
in Relationship Processes**   **315**

Pamela R. Allen

Introduction   315
Bowen Theory and the Therapist's Own Emotional
    Functioning   316
Clinical Case   326
Conclusion   336

Chapter 14. Emotional Cutoff and Domestic Violence   **337**

Douglas C. Murphy

Introduction   337
Defining Terms and Processes   338

Bowen Theory and Its Relevance for Understanding
    Domestic Violence   340
Clinical Case Examples   344
Summary and Conclusion   349

**Chapter 15. Emotional Cutoff and Family Stability:
Child Abuse in Family Emotional Process**   **351**
    Walter Howard Smith Jr.

Introduction   351
Definitions and Background Ideas   352
Threats and Family Stability   360
Cutoff and Family Emotional Regression   366
Managing Cutoff and Family Emotional Regression
    in Professional Settings   371
Summary   374

PART IV: SOCIETAL APPLICATIONS

**Chapter 16. Emotional Cutoff and Societal Process:
Russia and the Soviet Union As an Example**   **379**
    Katharine Gratwick Baker

Introduction   379
Definitions of the Concepts   380
The Relationship Between the Concepts of Emotional
    Cutoff and Societal Process   385
An Example of Emotional Cutoff at the Societal Level:
    Russia and the Soviet Union   389
Can the Concept of Emotional Cutoff Provide a Generic
    Way of Understanding Societal Disruptions?   399

Chapter 17. Migration and Emotional Cutoff   **401**
    Eva Louise Rauseo

Introduction   401
Animal Studies   402
From Animals to Humans   405
Emotional Cutoff   406
Migration and Emotional Cutoff   409
Family Examples   410

Bowen Theory, the Relationship System, and Patterns
   of Migration   418
Conclusion   421

**Chapter 18. Emotional Cutoff and Holocaust Survivors:
Relationships and Viability**   **425**
   Eileen B. Gottlieb

Introduction   425
Emotional Cutoff and Holocaust Survivors   428
Case Histories   429
Conclusion   440

**Chapter 19. Israeli-Palestinian Relations: A Bowen
Theory Perspective**   **443**
   Fran Ackerman

Introduction   443
Bonner's Concepts of Integration and Isolation   444
Bowen Concepts That Are Relevant to Israeli-
   Palestinian Relations   445
Israeli and Palestinian Perspectives   451
Application of Bowen Theory   453
Israeli and Palestinian Textbooks and Societal Process   456
Conclusion   467

Appendix: A Key for the Family Diagram Symbols   **477**

Index   **479**

ABOUT THE EDITOR

Peter Titelman, PhD, maintains a private practice in clinical psychology, specializing in Bowen family systems therapy, consultation, training, and supervision in Northampton, Massachusetts. Dr. Titelman consults to family and closely owned businesses as a principal in LaForte & Titelman Associates, also based in Northampton. He is the editor of *The Therapist's Own Family: Toward the Differentiation of Self* (Aronson, 1987), in which he and the other contributors illustrate the application of Bowen's concept of differentiation of self to the therapist's own family as a means of working toward personal and professional responsibility. Dr. Titelman is the editor of a second book, *Clinical Applications of Bowen Family Systems Theory* (Haworth, 1998), in which he and the other contributors apply Bowen theory to a variety of clinical issues. He is a founding member of the New England Seminar on Bowen Theory. Dr. Titelman is an adjunct faculty member at the Union Institute in Cincinnati, Ohio. He has taught and supervised graduate students in several New England graduate and professional schools. He is an American Association of Marriage and Family Therapy approved supervisor. Dr. Titelman has given presentations and training events nationally and internationally, teaching Bowen family systems theory at the Society of Family Consultants and Psychologists in Moscow, Russia. His current research interests, in addition to emotional cutoff, include sibling leadership in family business, and emotional triangles in the human family.

CONTRIBUTORS

Fran Ackerman, MSW, is an instructor at Hebrew University School of Social Work, Jerusalem, Israel. She is on the faculty of Neve Family Institute, Jerusalem, Israel, and is in private practice in Jerusalem.

Pamela R. Allen, LCSW, is a private contractor in Topeka, Kansas, who provides training, supervision, and clinical services.

Katharine Gratwick Baker, DSW, is a senior consultant with the Metropolitan Group, Tenafly, New Jersey. She has taught Bowen family systems theory at the Society of Family Consultants and Psychologists in Moscow, Russia, and also has a private practice in Williamsburg, Massachusetts.

Alice Eichholz, PhD, CG, is a professor at Vermont College of Norwich University, where she directs independent studies in psychology and family history. Dr. Eichholz has twenty-five years of experience as a genealogist and has often lectured at national and regional conferences. Current research interests include Vermont families and the multigenerational patterns in families.

Stephanie J. Ferrera, MSW, is a faculty member at the Center for Consultation, Chicago, Illinois, and is in private practice in Oak Park, Illinois.

Priscilla J. Friesen, LCSW, has a clinical practice working with individuals and families incorporating the use of neurofeedback (EEG biofeedback) with Bowen theory. On the faculty at the Bowen Center for the Study of the Family, Washington, DC, she coordinates the Postgraduate Training Program on Bowen family systems theory and its applications. She lectures nationally and internationally on the brain and the family.

Roberta M. Gilbert, MD, is the founder and director of the Center for the Study of Human Systems in Arlington, Virginia, which offers training in Bowen family systems theory for clergy and executives. She is on the faculty of the Bowen Center for the Study of the Family in Washington, DC. Dr. Gilbert is the author of two books: *Extraordinary Relationships* (John Wiley & Sons, Inc., 1992) and *Connecting with Our Children* (John Wiley & Sons, Inc. 1999). She is a national and international speaker.

Eileen B. Gottlieb, MEd, LMFT, is the director of the Family Center in Delray Beach, Florida, where she has practiced psychotherapy for twenty-two years. She also serves as education director for the Florida Family Research Network, a nonprofit organization that provides Bowen theory training conferences and seminars for Florida-licensed mental health professionals and nurses. Ms. Gottlieb has written and presented papers on aspects of Bowen theory at scientific meetings nationwide.

Victoria Harrison, MA, is the director of the Center for the Study of Natural Systems and the Family in Houston, Texas, where she also conducts a clinical practice in psychotherapy and biofeedback based upon Bowen theory. She is on the faculty of the Bowen Center for the Study of the Family, Washington, DC. She is currently researching the impact of reactivity in the family on the development of endometriosis and polycystic ovarian disease.

Gail Hilbert-McAllister, DNSc, is professor emerita at The College of New Jersey, Ewing, New Jersey.

Selden Dunbar Illick, LCSW, is the director of the Princeton Family Center for Education, Inc., and is in private practice at the Princeton Family Center for Psychotherapy, Inc. Both centers are based on Bowen family systems theory and are located in Princeton, New Jersey.

Susan Ewing Jefferies, LCSW, is in private practice in Princeton, New Jersey.

Brian J. Kelly, EdD, is in private practice in Fairfield, Connecticut.

Phil Klever, LCSW, LMFT, is in private practice in Kansas City, Missouri. He has written "The Study of Marriage and Bowen Theory" in *Family Systems: A Journal of Natural Systems Thinking in Psychiatry and the Sciences* and "Marital Fusion and Differentiation" in *Clinical Applications of Bowen Family Systems Theory* (The Haworth Press, 1998). In 1995 he began a twenty-year research study on marriage, including fifty-one couples.

Anne S. McKnight, PhD, LCSW, is a faculty member, Bowen Center for the Study of the Family, Washington, DC; a staff member, Arlington County Bureau of Substance Abuse, Arlington, Virginia; and is in private practice in Arlington, Virginia.

Douglas C. Murphy, LCPC, is the clinical director of the Family Crisis Center of Baltimore County, a family violence service program. He is a faculty member of the Bowen Center for the Study of the Family, Washington, DC, and a member of the editorial board of the journal, *Family Systems: A Journal of Natural Systems Thinking in Psychiatry and the Sciences.* He also maintains a private practice in Towson, Maryland.

Eva Louise Rauseo, RN, MS, CS, is a faculty member, Bowen Center for the Study of the Family, Washington, DC; a board member, Center for the Study of Natural Systems and the Family, Houston, Texas; and program director. El Paso Educational Programs in Bowen Theory, a part of the Center for the Study of Natural Systems and the Family, El Paso, Texas. Her clinical and research interests are clinical studies of emotional cutoff and the ongoing study of families in the midst of migration.

Walter Howard Smith Jr., PhD, is the executive director of Family Resources, a large child abuse prevention treatment organization in Pittsburgh, Pennsylvania. He is a licensed psychologist in private practice and holds adjunct associate professor positions at both Duquesne University and the University of Pittsburgh. He is a founding member of the Western Pennsylvania Family Center in Pittsburgh, an organization providing educational resources in Bowen systems theory.

Anthony J. Wilgus, ACSW, is an associate professor of social work at the University of Findlay, in Findlay, Ohio. He has presented papers at both the annual Georgetown Family Center Symposium and the Midwest Family Systems Symposium in Chicago.

Charles M. White, LCSW, CADC, is a social work PhD student and a research associate in the Center for Social and Community Development, Rutgers University School of Social Work, New Brunswick, New Jersey.

Foreword

Peter Titelman has worked tirelessly for many years to make Bowen family systems theory accessible to people. In the two books that he edited previously, he challenged himself and others to do their best thinking about the theory and its applications, and to write clearly about their ideas. Dr. Titelman has again assembled a gifted group of Bowen theorists, this time to grapple with the concept of emotional cutoff. Each writer approaches the concept with different observations and experiences, but they stand on common theoretical ground.

Bowen theory assumes that all people have some degree of unresolved emotional attachment to their original families and that a lack of resolution has a huge impact on a life course. An unresolved attachment is associated with a level of chronic anxiety. For example, a mother feels unrealistically responsible for her adult son's life problems and he feels excessively dependent on her emotional support; consequently, their encounters often provoke anxiety. He vents his distress to her but feels diminished by her excessive advice giving; she wants to listen but feels troubled and unsettled that she cannot help her son.

The mother and son limit contact with each other to avoid the anxiety associated with their interactions. The emotional cutoff reduces the anxiety potentially generated by their interactions, but it does not resolve their vulnerabilities to each other. Cutoff only makes the intensity of the attachment grow dormant. The son cuts off with the hope of finding a better relationship elsewhere. Predictably, he picks women more like his mother than he would like to admit and replicates the unresolved attachment (the female plays out the opposite side) in a series of intense but short-lived romantic relationships. The mother carries a mix of feelings. She misses her son, in whom she has been deeply invested; she is angry with him for being distant; and she is anguished about his unhappiness.

My contact with Murray Bowen's ideas began in the late 1960s. He talked early on about how people distance from their families to avoid dealing with the emotionally difficult relationships. Like many of the authors in this book, the idea hit me like a ton of bricks. I saw that I had begun to distance from my original family and at the same time realized that I did not want to do that.

I soon discovered that not everyone responded to Bowen's ideas about cutoff in the way that I had. About eight months later, in the aftermath of a suicide in my family of origin, I was meeting with one of my child psychiatry supervisors. I had told him about the suicide. He thought I would benefit from individual psychotherapy, where I could address my reactions to what had happened. I told him that I was not in conventional therapy, but that Dr. Bowen was helping me deal directly with my family.

I was not prepared for what happened next. My supervisor leaped up from his chair and, looking truly shocked, burst out, "You can't deal with your family directly; it's too difficult! You must deal with your feelings in the protective setting of a therapist's office."

As I drove away from my supervisor's office that day, it sunk in how much courage and conviction Murray Bowen must have had to buck the tide in psychiatry. My supervisor's reaction alerted me to how baffled and even frightened conventional psychiatry is of the family. The attitude that permeated the mental health world was that the family caused the problem, so people need to escape their families to heal.

Bowen's dealing with his own family and suggesting that others could do the same required, of course, more than courage and conviction. It required a new theory to guide the way through the treacherous web of family relationships. Moreover, Bowen's new approach of working directly to resolve the *original relationships* with one's parents and larger family produced a therapeutic result that was superior to resolving a transference relationship with a psychoanalyst. The radical approach moved therapy out of the therapist's office, out of the therapeutic relationship, and into the real world of one's family. The therapist became a "coach."

Brain researcher Paul MacLean dates the origin of the family to the evolution of mammals about 180 million years ago. His work is relevant to understanding the forces that promote emotional cutoff. The evolution of maternal care was a major innovation, a significant departure from the reptiles. The infant's separation cry coevolved with nursing and other nurturing behaviors by mammalian mothers. A consequence of the fine-tuning of sensitivities between mother and offspring is the marked suffering triggered by social separation and isolation. The emotional response to isolation is truly painful. It is a more powerful emotional response than that triggered by more obvious threats to survival.

A paradox of emotional cutoff is that it is a consequence of how evolution has shaped our emotional investment in and sensitivity to one another. Excessive reactivity to separation cries and isolation, and intense yearnings to connect through nurturing behaviors, can make comfortable contact difficult to maintain. The problem is too much of a good thing.

I will make one last comment before turning the reader over to the fine authors in this book. It relates to differentiation of self, the antidote to emotional cutoff. Among the more frightening things about the world in which we live is that people adhere to strong beliefs based on incredibly few facts and that people are easily persuaded by the poorly supported views of others. The essence of the process of differentiation of self is improving one's ability to think for oneself and to act consistently with that thinking. There is no better arena for learning to do this than in one's family. Bridging cutoffs depends on a person addressing his or her part in the unresolved emotional attachments. It involves separating facts from feelings and learning to think for oneself about the family. An important aspect of this process is that an increased ability to think for oneself in the family predictably extends to thinking for oneself in the larger society.

History will treat Bowen family systems theory favorably. This is because science will increasingly support the accuracy of applying natural systems thinking to human behavior. People do not have to wait, however, for science to prove the theory. They can prove it to themselves through a disciplined study of their own families. This is much more than an intellectual undertaking; it is also an emotional one. Bowen led the way with his theory and his effort to live the theory. This book describes the varied efforts of those who have followed. They have not followed blindly but have made the theory their own.

Michael E. Kerr, MD
Director, Bowen Center
for the Study of the Family
Washington, DC

Acknowledgments

The contributors deserve thanks for their willingness to put forth their best thinking about emotional cutoff in writing, often a challenging process carried out in the midst of having to fulfill other primary professional activities.

Acknowledgment is due to Michael E. Kerr, Selden Dunbar Illick, and Randall Frost for sharing their thoughts about emotional cutoff and clarifying my understanding and presentation of the material in the first chapter of this book.

The editorial care and patience of Peg Marr, Dawn Krisko, Jennifer Durgan, and Yvonne Kester at The Haworth Press need to be acknowledged.

Special thanks are offered to my wife, Katharine G. Baker, for her sustained willingness to read and offer constructive criticism of this manuscript. Her presence during the voyage of writing and editing this book was invaluable, both intellectually and emotionally.

Introduction

Peter Titelman

This book highlights emotional cutoff, one concept in Bowen family systems theory. It must be understood in the context of the eight interlocking concepts that constitute Bowen theory. I refer the reader to the original writings of Bowen (1978), Kerr and Bowen (1988), and Papero (1990) for excellent renderings of Bowen theory in its full breadth.

The concept of emotional cutoff is one of the most important but least understood of the Bowen concepts; therefore it is deserving of more clinical and research attention. The concept of emotional cutoff describes the way people, using physical or internal emotional distancing, handle their unresolved emotional attachment to their parents, expressed through specific issues. According to Bowen (1978), "The concept deals with the way people separate themselves from the past in order to start their lives in the present generation" (p. 382). Emotional distance is one way to handle attachment and dependency on one's parents or other family members when there is an emotional "allergy" to closeness. Running away from home and never leaving home are both ways that the allergy to emotional closeness is expressed.

Bowen (1978) went on to describe why he chose the term *cutoff,* as opposed to a term with less emotional intensity:

> Much thought went into the selection of a term to best describe this process of separation, isolation, withdrawal, running away or denying the importance of the parental family. However much *cutoff* may sound like informal slang, I could find no other term as accurate for describing the process. (p. 382)

All of the contributors in this book share the same conceptual frame of reference, Bowen theory, but the reader should be aware that the contributors present their own ways of understanding and articulating Bowen's concept of emotional cutoff. Although the definitions and descriptions of cutoff vary, to some degree, among the chapters, the authors are rooted in their shared commitment to Bowen theory. Each contributor brings his or her own perspective on Bowen theory to bear on his or her understanding and application of cutoff.

Of all the eight concepts in Bowen theory, cutoff was least fleshed out by Bowen. This presented both difficulties and opportunities. On one hand, the road map for navigating the complex terrain of cutoff was not clearly laid out by Dr. Bowen in his writings. On the other hand, this lack of total clarity regarding the meaning of cutoff provided an opportunity to add something of value to the understanding, explication, and application of the concept.

The contributors to this book all had the opportunity to learn Bowen family systems theory through direct contact with Murray Bowen. They have spent many years studying the theory and applying it clinically, in organizational and societal settings, in teaching, and in research.

The book is divided into four parts: Theory, The Therapist's Own Family, Research and Clinical Applications, and Societal Applications.

Part I, Theory, includes three chapters. In Chapter 1, I provide an overview of the concept of cutoff in Bowen theory from my own vantage point. The origin of the concept of cutoff in Bowen's research on schizophrenia and the development of the concept are discussed, as are the theoretical context for the concepts of fusion and cutoff; the relationship between the concept of emotional cutoff and other concepts in Bowen theory; symptom formation and the continuum of emotional cutoff; and bridging emotional cutoff. In Chapter 2, Anthony J. Wilgus describes how emotional cutoff is situated in human evolutionary heritage. This chapter explores evidence of emotional cutoff within the nonhuman world, particularly among species that have complex social organizations. Natal philopatry, emigration and immigration, ostracism, and isolation are presented as descriptions of this process within the nonhuman sphere. The author includes descriptions of the behavior of lone wolves and rogue elephants. In Chapter 3, Priscilla J. Friesen addresses the concept of emotional cutoff through the physiology of the brain. The author hypothesizes that decreased social complexity in one generation will produce a more constrained brain development in the next generation. Observed in the fields of neurofeedback and sensory integration, a less neuronally integrated brain perceives the environment as more of a threat more of the time, and the outcome is a limit to life options. Bowen suggested bridging cutoff to decrease symptoms in individuals and to increase the viability of present relationships. Friesen suggests that this behavior of moving toward knowing the reality of the past changes the basic organization of the brainstem and limbic system influenced early in development. In addition, for the brain to change at these most automatic levels, addressing the anxious "solutions" of previous generations is essential.

Part II of the book, The Therapist's Own Family, includes four chapters. These present the efforts of three systems therapists and one genealogist to understand and bridge cutoff in their own families. In Chapter 4, I describe my efforts to bridge secondary cutoff. Whereas primary cutoff takes place in the parental-child relationship, secondary cutoff takes place between an individual and a sibling, grandparent, aunt or uncle, or cousin. This form of cutoff takes place in the context of secondary triangles that are interlocked with the primary parent-child triangle. My efforts to bridge cutoff with an aunt and with cousins are described as a part of the attempt to modify unresolved attachment to my parents. This work described part of an effort to differentiate a self within one's family. In Chapter 5, Brian J. Kelly describes a twenty-five-year history of one person's efforts to reconnect himself after a six-year period of no contact with a single relative. The author describes the cutoff, its history, the initial understanding of it, the initial efforts at making contact, the idea of working for a broader perspective through family history, defining a self through work and deed, positioning oneself to benefit from nodal events, and working toward greater neutrality within the family. In Chapter 6, Roberta M. Gilbert describes an effort to bridge cutoff with divorced relationships and the family of origin. She describes her efforts to bridge cutoff with the parents of her former husband, with her ex-husband, and with members of her family of origin. In Chapter 7, Alice Eichholz, based on her experience as a genealogist with training in Bowen theory, explores the benefits and challenges of working toward managing emotional cutoffs through family history research on one family across four generations. The research covered over 100 years in the life of the author's family.

Part III of the book, Research and Clinical Applications, includes eight chapters. Three of them focus on research and five on clinical applications. One chapter is solely on research and two chapters focus on research and contain clinical material. In Chapter 8, Selden Dunbar Illick, Gail Hilbert-McAllister, Susan Ewing Jefferies, and Charles M. White, the Princeton Family Center Research Team, describe the theoretical and research background that went into creating a research instrument for measuring emotional cutoff. In this chapter emotional cutoff is described as being rooted in emotional reactivity and evolution. There are sections on the emotional cutoff construct and the development of an emotional cutoff research instrument. Examples from an instrument, the Family-of-Origin Survey (FORS-2), are presented. In Chapter 9, Phil Klever describes marital functioning in terms of the interrelationship between fusion and cutoff. He describes his research on the effects of cutoff on marital functioning, using both a qualitative and a quantitative analysis. Klever describes the effect of cutoff on marital process, and he ends his chapter by describing clinical work with marital reactivity and emotional cutoff. In Chapter 10, Victoria Harrison discusses emotional cutoff and reproduction through the lens of Bowen theory and the study of evolution. She provides examples from her research illustrating her findings of the presence or absence of contact between family members. This factor correlated with variation in ovulation in her study of reactivity and reproduction. Part III, Research and Clinical Applications, continues as Anne S. McKnight describes in Chapter 11 a research study she undertook on the impact of parents' cutoff from their families on raising teenagers. Sixty families with teenagers who sought evaluations or therapy were interviewed. In the statistical analysis, the level of cutoff of the parents was correlated with the level of impairment in the teenager. Several case studies are provided to illustrate and describe how cutoff of the parents from their own families impacts their parenting.

In Chapter 12, Stephanie J. Ferrera describes the continuum of emotional cutoff in divorce. This chapter discusses the intensity surrounding divorce, leading many to assume that the wisest resolution is emotional cutoff. The author offers ideas using Bowen theory that can help divorcing spouses and their families steer their way through the period of high intensity and beyond to a period of calmer, more stable relationships. In Chapter 13, Pamela R. Allen explores depression as a symptom of cutoff and other relationship processes. She describes her own efforts to understand and manage the symptoms of depression. She also describes her attempts to be more of a self within the family, her efforts to work toward reducing cutoff, and how this has the potential of not only reducing the symptoms within the individual but also decreasing anxiety within the entire system. Allen also presents a clinical case example of a fifty-year-old male which illustrates how the emotional process involving anxiety and cutoff led to his symptoms of depression and the therapeutic interventions undertaken, using Bowen theory as a guide. In Chapter 14, Douglas C. Murphy places domestic violence within the context of the multigenerational family emotional system and offers an additional hypothesis about the occurrence of domestic violence by utilizing the concept of emotional cutoff. He illustrates the place of emotional cutoff in domestic violence with two clinical case examples. In Chapter 15, Walter Howard Smith Jr. describes how and when cutoff and distance are predictable ways for families to cope with stresses and threats. In the short term, cutoff increases stability and decreases relationship conflict in stressed families. However, over longer periods of time this cutoff increases the risk of aggression emerging as a symptom and problem. Preventing and treating child abuse always entails bridging the use of distance and cutoff to manage conflict, threats, and stress. Clinical examples and clinical issues are presented and integrated into the description of ideas.

Part IV, Societal Applications, includes four chapters. In Chapter 16, Katharine Gratwick Baker explores emotional cutoff as it is manifested both at the level of individual families and at the level of societal process in the former Soviet Union. Findings from a research study conducted by Baker exploring the impact of the 1930's Soviet political purges on three generations of Russian families are described. These findings validate the hypothesis that functioning in the grandchild generation is adversely affected by cutoff from the grandparent generation. It was also found that emotional cutoff was a more significant factor than the political purges, World War II, or other traumas in affecting grandchild functioning. The chapter includes in-depth presentations of two adult grandchildren whose grandparents were purged in the 1930s. In Chapter 17, Eva Louise Rauseo's focus is migration and emotional cutoff. This chapter describes some observations about migration that shed light on the process of emotional cutoff as a means of managing relationship tension or challenge. The author explores the following areas: (1) migration or dispersal as a process grounded in nature; (2) emotional cutoff as a process grounded in nature, as a problem for future generations, and when emotional cutoff is related to migration; (3) human emigration and emotional cutoff; and (4) Bowen theory, the relationship system, and patterns of migration.

In Chapter 18, Eileen B. Gottlieb explores the relationship between emotional cutoff and human viability as manifested in the functioning of Holocaust survivors. Bowen family systems theory is utilized as a guide for understanding the variable presence of emotional cutoff and the long-term variation in human viability in this population. In Chapter 19, Fran Ackerman explicates a natural systems perspective for understanding cutoff between Israeli Jews and Palestinian Arabs. She describes how human distancing includes at one end of the continuum a cutoff that is respectful of the "other." At the other end of the continuum, the cutoff is characterized by a demonizing and dehumanizing of the "other." Society has a strong influence on the manner in which its members express cutoff, and likewise individuals shape societal process. Conditions within society have a significant influence on the process, for example, increased population density and a decrease in basic resources such as water raise the level of anxiety of individuals as well as society.

The clinical case material presented in this book has been modified in order to protect the confidentiality of these families. The editor and contributing authors have, for the most part, referred to themselves in the third person in an effort to decrease subjectivity in their theoretical and personal writing.

It is the my hope that this set of essays on cutoff are in line with Murray Bowen's thinking about the concept. Although each contributor has his or her own way of viewing the concept, I believe that the book in its entirety expresses the spirit of Bowen's thinking.

REFERENCES

Bowen, M. (1978). *Family Therapy in Clinical Practice.* Northvale. NJ: Jason Aronson, Inc.

Kerr, M.E. and Bowen, M. (1988). *Family Evaluation: An Approach Based on Bowen Theory* New York: W.W. Norton and Company.

Papero, D. (1990). *Bowen Family Systems Theory.* Boston: Allyn and Bacon.

PART I:
THEORY

Chapter 1

Emotional Cutoff in Bowen Family Systems Theory: An Overview

Peter Titelman

INTRODUCTION

This chapter provides a historical and theoretical overview of the concept of emotional cutoff in Bowen family systems theory. It presents a description of cutoff and its place in Bowen theory. In the 1950s, Bowen's research on families with schizophrenic offspring provided a unique description of the emotional process of separation between the adolescent and his or her parents, culminating in the failure of the schizophrenic offspring to leave home. In retrospect, this early research provided the understanding of how "cutting off" provides a pseudosolution for the adolescent or young adult who is unable to manage the unresolved attachment to his or her parents.

From the late 1960s, Bowen (1978) used the term "emotional cut-off" or simply "cut-off" to refer to emotional distancing (p. 535). In 1975, emotional cutoff became the last of the eight concepts (differentiation, triangles, nuclear family emotional process, family projection process, multigenerational transmission process, sibling position, societal process, and emotional cutoff) that Bowen (1978) formally added to his family systems theory after being a "poorly defined extension of other concepts for several years" (p. 382). At that time, Bowen wrote:

> It [emotional cutoff, now spelled as one word, dropping the hyphen] was accorded the status of a separate concept to include details not stated elsewhere, and to have a separate concept for emotional process between the generations. The life pattern of cutoffs is determined by the way people handle their unresolved attachments to their parents. All people have some degree of unresolved attachment to their parents. The lower the level of differentiation, the more intense the unresolved attachment. The concept deals with the way people separate

9

themselves from the past in order to start their lives in the present generation. Much thought went into the selection of a term to best describe this process of separation, isolation, withdrawal, running away,
or denying the importance of the parental family. (1978, p. 382)

This chapter illustrates two perspectives that informed Bowen's understanding of emotional cutoff: (1) the continuum of cutting off within the
framework of the emotional process of separating between the adolescent or
young adult and his or her parents and (2) the continuum of cutoff in the
emotional process between the generations. This expresses the way individuals handle their unresolved attachment to their parents through their life
patterns. Both these frameworks are based on understanding cutoff as embedded in multigenerational family emotional processes.

This chapter is divided into the following sections: (1) The Origin and
Evolution of the Concept of Emotional Cutoff in Bowen Theory; (2) The
Theoretical Context for the Concepts of Fusion and Cutoff; (3) The Con-
cepts of Emotional Fusion and Emotional Cutoff in Bowen Theory; (4) The
Relationship Between Emotional Cutoff and Other Concepts in Bowen
Theory; (5) Symptom Formation and the Continuum of Emotional Cutoff;
(6) Bridging Emotional Cutoff; and (7) Summary.

THE ORIGIN AND EVOLUTION OF THE CONCEPT
OF EMOTIONAL CUTOFF IN BOWEN THEORY

The Origin of the Concept

Bowen's first papers describing schizophrenia and the family were presented and originally published between 1957 and 1961. Every concept and
idea that eventually crystallized in Bowen theory can be found, at least in its
nascent or embryonic form, in his early research and writing. Very early on,
Bowen seemed to have a preliminary sense of most of the form his full-
blown theory would ultimately take. His earliest papers contain harbingers
of what would become the final concept in Bowen theory: emotional cutoff.
These papers are collected in the first section of *Family Therapy in Clinical
Practice* (Bowen, 1978), Part I. Schizophrenia and the Family. The following papers provided the clues for understanding wherein the roots of cutoff
can be traced: "Treatment of Family Groups with a Schizophrenic Member"
(1957), "The Role of the Father in Families with a Schizophrenic Patient"
(1959), "Family Relationships in Schizophrenia" (1959), "A Family Concept
of Schizophrenia" (1960)," Family Psychotherapy" (1961), "Outpatient Fam-

ily Psychotherapy" (1961), and one additional chapter from Part II: Family Systems Theory, "Interfamily Dynamics in Emotional Illness" (1965).

Drawing from these early papers, this section documents that emotional cutoff was already an implicit part of how Bowen understood family functioning prior to the thematic development of the concept of cutoff at the end of the 1960s and in the early 1970s. Using other terms and other concepts, he described the process and variation through which people "separate themselves from the past in order to start on their lives in the present generation" (Bowen, 1978, p. 382). This chapter also documents how the concept of cutoff is derived from the nascent concepts of the triangle and multigenerational emotional process.

In his work at the National Institute of Mental Health, 1954 through 1959, Bowen started by hospitalizing the schizophrenic patient and the mother, then moved to hospitalizing the schizophrenic patient, both parents, and the nonsymptomatic sibling. The observations and conclusions regarding these families served as forerunners of Bowen's later conception of emotional cutoff, as it refers to the immature emotional process of separation between the generations. Following are a summary of some of Bowen's observations:

1. Schizophrenia is an outcome of a multigenerational process, taking at least three generations to develop (later Bowen revised it to many generations).

2. The parents of the schizophrenic have lower levels of differentiation than, for the most part, their respective siblings.

3. The parents' are characterized by what Bowen termed *emotional divorce*, his description of the emotional distance between the parents. There exists a prerequisite overadequate-inadequate reciprocity between the spouses, with the mother usually being in the overadequate position and the father in the passive inadequate position both in regard to issues between themselves and as parents.

4. The symbiotic relationship between the mother and the schizophrenic offspring includes an intense projection process. In this process the mother's anxiety is transferred to the schizophrenic child and the mother then becomes an overfunctioning caretaker. Simultaneously, the patient is taking care of his or her mother by being functionally helpless so that the mother can take care of her or him in order to be less anxious.

5. The mother, father, and schizophrenic child function as an *interdependent triad* (this was the early term for triangle).

6. In adolescence or young adulthood the patient "tears self away" and creates a "pseudo self" by going through a "pseudo separation" and then often collapses into psychotic withdrawal when having to return home, a form of internally cutting off.

Later Bowen would see the characteristics of families with a schizophrenic offspring in all families, with a range of intensity based on variation in level of differentiation.

In 1957, Bowen (1978), in a paper titled "Treatment of Family Groups with a Schizophrenic Member," characterizes the unresolved symbiotic attachment between the schizophrenic offspring and the mother in the following statement:

> . . . the process is initiated by the emotional immaturity of the mother who uses the child to fulfill her own emotional needs. The mother feels guilty about this use of the child. While she covertly does things to block the child's development, she simultaneously tries to force the child to achievement. The child, once entangled, tries to perpetuate the symbiosis along with the opposite effort to grow up. The father passively permits himself to be excluded from the intense twosome and marries his business or other outside interests. Symbiosis was seen as developmental arrest which at one time was a normal state in the mother-child relationship. (p. 4)

Bowen (1978) offers many descriptions of *emotional divorce* or emotional distancing (which involve some of the reactive behaviors such as withdrawal and isolation that would be a part of the later developed concept of emotional cutoff) which he observed between the parents of the schizophrenic patient and the father's functioning in this triangling process. In 1959, in "The Role of the Father in Families with a Schizophrenic Patient," Bowen writes:

> The family members, particularly the father and the mother, function in reciprocal relation to each other. They are separated from each other by an emotional barrier which, in some ways, has characteristics of an "emotional divorce." Either father or mother can have a close emotional relationship with the patient when the other parent permits. The patient's function is similar to that of an unsuccessful mediator of the emotional differences between the parents. (1978, p. 22)

Bowen (1978) describes how the family functioning can change to allow the schizophrenic patient to separate and grow away from the family in the following passage:

> When the parents can maintain a closeness in which they are more invested in each other than either is invested in the patient, then the patients have made rapid gains. When either parent becomes more invested in the patient than in the other parent, the psychotic process becomes intensified. (p. 21)

In the paper, "Family Relationships in Schizophrenia," originally published in 1959, Bowen notes that the emotional divorce between the parents of the schizophrenic can involve either or both physical and emotional distance: "Most parents use combinations of controlled positiveness and physical distance" (1978, p. 27). Bowen uses the term *controlled positiveness* to describe a form of internal distancing.

Bowen (1978) went on to describe how working with the hospitalized family brought about change that reflects his incipient understanding of the process of emotional cutoff:

> The emotional divorce was resolved [the father was able to take and maintain an I-Position in the presence of the wife's anxiety and the latter subsided] and the father and mother were as devoted to each other as a teen-age couple in love for the first time. They were so much invested in each other that neither was overinvested in the patient. Both were then able, for the first time, to be objective toward the patient. At this point, the schizophrenic daughter began some significant changes toward more adequate functioning. (p. 29)

Bowen's (1978) early description of the course of outpatient psychotherapy with a schizophrenic patient and the family provides an example of the way he implicitly understood how emotional cutoff operates, how one generation separates from another and attempts to moves into the future.

The family consisted of two parents in their fifties. An elder daughter, in her twenties, had been overtly psychotic for six years. There was a second daughter, three years younger than the first daughter. The father was completely involved in his business, and the mother devoted herself to her children and the home. The mother's functioning position was that of an overadequate decision maker, while the father's functioning position placed him on the periphery of the family's life. The older daughter's functioning position was that of the "helpless inadequate one." The other daughter had been more outside the emotional projection process. She had separated smoothly after college and made a good adjustment to independent life.

During the pregnancy the mother had worried about her baby, the identified patient. She worried about birth defects and stillbirth. Her worries would decrease when she was emotionally closer to her husband. The mother's overinvestment in her firstborn daughter continued over the years. The other sibling was freer of the projection process. The father and mother became increasingly distant from each other. When the identified patient became a teenager she tried to be "grown up." She looked forward to college and living away from home as a way of gaining emancipation from the family. She was vaguely aware of her dependence on her mother. This girl had her first psychotic break while she was away at college. This was the beginning of six years of active psychosis (pp. 30-32).

Bowen's description of this psychotic daughter and her parents' relationship suggests the following four steps in the evolution of emotional cutoff and the failure of separation between the generations:

1. Symbiotic dependence between the daughter and her mother
2. Pseudoindependence from the parents when the daughter went away to college
3. The outbreak of psychosis as a way of expressing the severe unresolved attachment to the mother
4. A return to the family when the separation could not be maintained

In a paper, "A Family Concept of Schizophrenia," originally published in 1960, Bowen described the continuum of unresolved attachment, the outcome of varying levels of differentiation, that lead to varying forms and varying degrees of intensity in the separation process between the generations. He would later incorporate this process into the term *emotional cutoff:*

> I believe that unresolved symbiotic attachment to the mother can vary from the very mild to the very intense, that the mild ones cause little impairment, and that schizophrenic psychoses develop among those with the most intense unresolved attachments. There are a number of ways in which the individual with an intense attachment may find some solution to his dilemma. Certain individuals are able to replace the original mother with mother substitutes. The functional helplessness may find expression in somatic illness. The person with a character neurosis can use a flight mechanism to deal with the helplessness. The patients in our families attempted to find distant relationships. The psychotic collapse is seen as an effort at resolution that failed. (1978, p. 66)

In "Out-Patient Family Psychotherapy," originally published in 1961, Bowen (1978) described the range of differentiation and how this has an impact on the development of schizophrenia as a multigenerational process. He described how the process of separation between the generations varies along a continuum that leads to an autonomous self at one extreme. It can also lead to a high degree of unresolved attachment in which the individual *tears way* to become a *pseudo self* in the middle range. And at the lowest end of the continuum, the individual often has a psychotic collapse in the first effort to function independently.

Bowen described the parents of schizophrenic offspring as individuals who have low levels of differentiation, but who manage to function adequately in their life adjustments. Unlike more highly differentiated individuals they do not, according to Bowen, *grow away* from the *family ego mass* (Bowen's early term for the fusion that characterizes the togetherness forces of the nuclear family emotional system) to the same degree as their siblings. The parents of schizophrenic offspring tear themselves away from their own parents after adolescence, creating pseudoselves in order to function through a pseudoseparation from the fused family ego mass. Bowen describes different mechanisms they use to achieve this pseudoseparation. Some achieve it with a facade of independence while living at home with their parents. Others achieve it with denial and physical distance. Bowen (1978) describes their adjustment as being maintained by emotional distance. By staying away from close emotional relationships, they can function quite well academically and in the world of work: "The young adult who runs away from home never to see his parents again may have more basic attachment to his parents than other siblings who continue to live with their parents" (p. 109). They marry at equally low levels of differentiation. The relationship is characterized by emotional fusion, in which their individual boundaries are obliterated. Bowen points out that the same process occurs between spouses with higher levels of differentiation of self, but it is not as intense as in couples with lower levels of differentiation.

Bowen (1978) describes the emotional process in couples with lower levels of differentiation as eventually being characterized by emotional divorce, a response to fusion gone awry (p. 93). These couples develop a "triadic involvement of one child" that is similar to families with a psychotic child, except the difference is one of degree.

Bowen conveyed his effort to help parents make a "project" out of themselves in his outpatient family psychotherapy and how this effort had a positive effect on the process of separation between the generations: "In every family in which parents could continue the focus on themselves, the teenage child would give up 'tearing himself away,' and establish a new emotional closeness with the family and then proceed to a more orderly 'growing up' and 'growing away' from the family" (p. 96).

In summary, Bowen's early descriptions of the variation in the emotional process of separation between the generations, and the variation in the outcome of becoming a separate self—from growing away at the highest level of functioning, tearing away at the middle level of functioning, and cutting off and collapsing at the lowest level of functioning—illustrated both the process and degree of intensity that would later be partly included in the concept of emotional cutoff.

It is clear that the origins of the concept of cutoff are rooted in Bowen's parallel early understandings of differentiation, triangles, the nuclear family emotional process, the family projection process, and multigenerational transmission process. The way in which all of the other concepts in Bowen theory interlock will be discussed later in this chapter.

Evolution of the Concept

The early harbingers of the concept of emotional cutoff evolved in Bowen's thinking, teaching, and clinical practice from the end of the 1960s, particularly in relation to his increasing understanding of interlocking triangles. The latter became clearest to him through his own efforts to differentiate a self in his family of origin, as described in the paper titled, "On the Differentiation of Self" (Bowen, 1978), first presented in 1967, and originally published anonymously in 1972 (Framo, 1972).

During the course of Bowen's efforts to explore and differentiate a self in his own family of origin in the late 1960s, he provided a hint of his growing awareness of and interest in the process of emotional cutoff. In the course of his work on person-to-person contact with his mother and his effort to explore his own multigenerational history, Bowen (1978) discovered an interesting segment of cutoff in his maternal family:

> In my work on past generations I had discovered a whole segment of her side of the family that she did not know existed. It covered a period from 1720 to 1850 when this segment had moved west. The family name was well recorded in the area and there were cemeteries where they were buried, churches where they worshiped, lands they had owned, houses they had built, and other items of personal and family interest. (p. 502)

Bowen (1978) also alluded to the issue of emotional distance in his father's family describing an interesting event that occurred in 1969. In the course of gathering multigenerational family history, Bowen discovered, in a nearby county, "a whole segment of my father's family that he had never known about. I arranged two trips to go with him alone to see the land they had owned and the houses where they had lived" (p. 517). Bowen's second brother, Jess Jr., thanked Bowen for making the effort to find that segment, or cutoff branch, of their father's family. Bowen quoted his brother as saying:

> "Dad is ten years younger now than he was when you started this effort." . . . My view of the situation was slightly different. I believe that I had done something to change my relationship with my father, which in turn changed his relationship to all he contacted. I do think, however, that the work on his family was the issue around which the relationship changed. (p. 517)

It is interesting that Bowen found a striking similarity in both the families of his mother and father. Each had a whole segment of their extended families that they did not know existed. These cutoffs, Bowen was to discover, commonly existed in all families. This author assumes that, like so much of Bowen theory, his personal experience and research in his own family regarding cutoff were two factors in the development of the concept.

When Bowen shifted his focus from the nuclear to the extended family, from a focus on differentiation in the context of marital fusion to differentiation in the context of an individual's unresolved attachment to his or her family of origin, the significance of emotional cutoff became clearer. By deepening his understanding of the impact of the multigenerational emotional process, he was able to see that emotional stuck-together fusion and emotional cutoff constitute an intertwining process. In Bowen theory, fusion can evolve into cutoff, which inevitably evolves back to fusion, followed by cutoff. Figure 1.1 illustrates this process. (At the end of the chapter the reader will find an appendix, "A Key for the Family Diagram Symbols.")

In Figure 1.1, F. was fused with his parents, A. and B. When the degree of stuck-together fusion in conjunction with the degree of anxiety became too great, behavior manifested in a high degree of conflict. F. and his parents, A. and B., moved toward cutoff as a means of binding anxiety. E., the sister of F., was outside of the family projection process and achieved a somewhat higher level of differentiation. She was subject to a significantly lesser degree of fusion and cutoff with her parents in comparison with her brother. A parallel process occurred with G. and her sibling H. in relation to their parents, C. and D. When F. and G. married, their level of differentiation was relatively low and subsequently their degree of marital fusion was high. A comfortable degree of closeness existed between the couple until the arrival of children. Emotional distance grew as the balance of emotional invest-

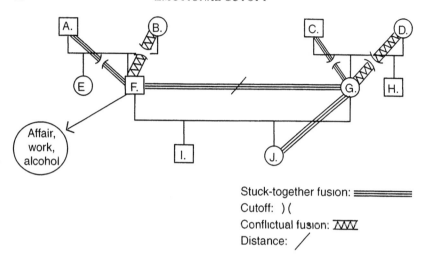

Stuck-together fusion: ≡≡≡≡
Cutoff:) (
Conflictual fusion: ⅄⅄⅄
Distance: ╱

FIGURE 1.1. Multigenerational interlocking of emotional fusion and emotional cutoff.

ment in each spouse was disrupted and the emotional equilibrium was altered. The youngest child, J., became the recipient of the greatest amount of the family projection process, with the greatest degree of emotional fusion existing between the mother, G., and the daughter, J. The mother's primary emotional investment now resides in her daughter, J., and not her husband, F. At the same time, F.'s emotional energy is now being invested in an affair, work, alcohol, or a combination of those pursuits. It is important to realize these are not cause-and-effect outcomes but rather they are circular, interlocking emotional processes. More discussion of how the triangles interlock with cutoff will be presented in a later section of the chapter. The process described in Figure 1.1 will predictably continue over time and through successive multiple generations. The fusion between J. and her mother, G., may very well become too intense when J. tries to separate from her parents as a young adult, evolving into cutoff as a means of automatically controlling the anxiety of the loss of self associated with the mother-daughter fusion.

On the videotape, "The Nuclear Family Emotional System," Bowen (1970) clearly described how individuals "tear self away" from their families of origin to start new families. He spoke of individuals attempting to get away by "running away" and by becoming "refugees from life." According to Bowen, no one ever successfully handles an emotional system by running away from it. He spoke of the interlocking process of cutting off from fusion in the family of origin and then reproducing it in a subsequent marital fusion. This process reduces anxiety in the moment but duplicates the original problem of past generational fusion in the future.

From the end of the 1950s, Bowen understood that the emotional process in the nuclear family was a fragment of a larger process involving young adults leaving their families of origin through variations of cutoff. That roughly correlated with the degree of undifferentiation as expressed by the intensity of the unresolved attachment to the family of origin, specifically the parents.

Following Bowen's breakthrough efforts during the 1960s, to define himself in his own family of origin with his newly acquired knowledge of the interlocking triangles illuminating multigenerational emotional process and the interlocking patterns of fusion and cutoff, he began teaching and applying his newly expanded theory clinically. Bowen (1978) came to understand, "It is not possible to differentiate a self in any single triangle without a method for dealing simultaneously with the interlocking triangles" (p. 531). His own experience in his family and in working with psychiatric residents between 1967 and 1969, in which coaching focused on their relationships in their families of origin, led to a clinical focus on the differentiation of self in one's family. The concept of emotional cutoff was formally added to Bowen theory in 1975.

THE THEORETICAL CONTEXT
FOR THE CONCEPTS OF FUSION AND CUTOFF

It is important to locate the concepts of fusion and cutoff in the context of Bowen's view of the family as a multigenerational emotional unit. The concepts of the emotional and relationship systems, differentiation, and anxiety are discussed in this regard. The other concepts in Bowen theory will be discussed as they relate to the concept of emotional cutoff in a subsequent section of this chapter.

The *emotional system* is a product of several billion years of evolution. It is the driving force of the family and other relationship systems. The concept of the *relationship system* is a *description* of what happens among family members, their communications and interactions, whereas the concept of the emotional system is an *explanation* of what happens. The emotional system refers to what "energizes" the family system, and includes those aspects that humans have in common with other forms of life. It includes automatic, instinctual mechanisms such as finding food, fleeing from enemies, reproducing, rearing young, and other aspects of social relationships. Bowen (1978) postulated that the emotional system is governed by the interplay of two counterbalancing "life forces," *individuality* and *togetherness,* which are rooted in biology. The individuality force propels an organism to follow its own directives, to be an independent and distinct entity. The togetherness force propels an organism to follow the directives of others, to be a dependent, connected, and indistinct entity.

Bowen theory postulates two main variables in human functioning: *anxiety* and *differentiation*. His theory makes the distinction between *acute* and *chronic anxiety*. Acute anxiety occurs in response to real threats and is time limited. Chronic anxiety generally occurs in response to imagined threats and is not experienced as time limited. Acute anxiety is fed by fear of what is; chronic anxiety is fed by fear of what might be (Kerr and Bowen, 1988, p. 113).

Differentiation is a natural, automatic process through which the human individual develops from being symbiotically attached to the mother, in the context of the parental unit, to being an emotionally separate self in relation to family and others. Differentiation of self also describes a process whereby an individual intentionally seeks to define a self, become more of a separate self in relation to his or her family, usually with a coach grounded in Bowen theory who has an understanding of the process.

Differentiation of self can be described as the way an individual manages the interplay of the individuality and togetherness forces within a relationship system (Kerr and Bowen, 1988, p. 95). Differentiation of self can also be described as the ability to act for oneself without being selfish and the ability to act for others without being selfless. Differentiation involves the ability to be an individual while simultaneously functioning as part of a team (Kerr and Bowen, 1988, p. 63).

At the level of the individual, the concept of differentiation defines people according to the degree of separation, or lack thereof, between emotionally reactive and thoughtful, goal-directed functioning. Individuals reside on a continuum constituted by this universal characteristic. Bowen developed a descriptive "scale of differentiation" on which anxious, reactive, automatic togetherness responses characterize those at the lower end of the scale, and calm autonomous responses characterize the functioning of those at the higher end of the scale.

At the level of marriage in a nuclear family, differentiation of self refers to a continuum consisting of the ways the marital partners maintain self—the degree to which the couple are emotionally separate from each other. Conversely, undifferentiation refers to a continuum in the ways partners borrow or lend self to each other, expressed in the reciprocity of over- and underfunctioning leading to a dysfunction in one spouse. At the level of the nuclear family with children, differentiation describes the variation in the degree of emotional separateness among the members of the family. Conversely, undifferentiation, at the level of the nuclear family, refers to a continuum along which family members are "emotionally stuck-together." At the level of the family of origin, differentiation describes the degree to which family members have open, one-to-one relationships with one another. Conversely, undifferentiation at the level of the family of origin describes the degree of unresolved attachment between an individual and his or her parents through overcloseness or cutoff.

THE CONCEPTS OF EMOTIONAL FUSION AND EMOTIONAL CUTOFF IN BOWEN THEORY

Emotional stuck-together fusion and emotional cutoff are interrelated expressions of undifferentiation. Bowen (Kerr and Bowen, 1988) chose the terms *fusion* and *cutoff* in order to describe processes in the human family that would fit, when appropriate, with concepts from biology: "[They] describe the ways cells agglutinate and the way they separate to start new colonies of cells" (p. 362). The greater the degree of stuck-together fusion in a family, the greater the degree of cutoff that will follow. This interlocking process continues through the multigenerational history of the family. However, at any given time in any family it may be easier to see a pattern of multiple generations of emotionally stuck-together fusion or it may be easier to see a pattern of emotional cutoff in one or multiple generations. According to this author's understanding of Bowen theory, when a pattern of fusion exists in one segment of a family, nuclear, family of origin, or extended, there is an equivalent degree of cutoff in the same or another segment of the family as a multigenerational system. This follows the idea in systems thinking that change in one part of a system elicits compensatory change in another part of the multigenerational family system.

The Concept of Emotional Fusion

Fusion is defined as the emotional oneness or emotional stuck-togetherness between family members. Stuck-together fusion refers, primarily, to a continuum of closeness or bond between a child and his or her parents within the nuclear family. Secondarily, fusion exists between an individual and his or her sibling(s), members of the extended family, and significant nonfamily others. Stuck-together fusion can take the forms of "conflictual fusion" or "warm fusion." Fusion refers to the ways that people borrow or lend self in relation to one another.

The function of fusion is to ensure that the individuals within the nuclear family will remain attached to the emotional nucleus, usually the parents. It is like the magnetic force of gravity. It keeps all members of the family from falling away from the emotional nucleus, to which their survival necessitates attachment.

The degree of emotional fusion is equal, primarily, to the degree of emotional attachment to one's parents. The degree of fusion with one's siblings, spouse, other members of the family of origin, and larger extended family is secondary to the degree of emotional attachment between a child and his or her parents.

The behavioral patterns that function automatically to control the intensity of the emotional fusion and anxiety within the nuclear family are the following: the over-underfunctioning reciprocity between spouses, the projection process, triangling, and conflict or distancing between spouses. There are innumerable specific expressions of fusion, including the following: (1) acting as if one can read the other's mind; (2) speaking or acting for the other; (3) automatically expressing emotional, social, or physical responses that are reactions to expressed or unexpressed behavior or feelings of another family member; and (4) adopting or living out, automatically, a family belief, tradition, or lifestyle choice.

The Concept of Emotional Cutoff

Emotional cutoff is defined as the emotional process between the generations through which "people separate themselves from the past in order to start their lives in the present generation" (Bowen, 1978, p. 382). Emotional cutoff is emotional distance that regulates the discomfort of emotionally stuck-together fusion between the generations. It expresses the unresolved emotional attachment of an individual to his or her parents. In this context, the term *emotional attachment* is synonymous with *emotional fusion*. The term *unresolved attachment* refers to a universal continuum of parent-child fusion, along which all individuals fall. It encompasses the degree to which an individual has been unable to be a self, separate from his or her parents. Being a self means being able to act based on one's own beliefs and principles separate from those held and expressed by one's parents. When the emotional fusion between parent and offspring is too intense, chronic anxiety rises and an individual can act as if the parental family is not important. The specific, emotionally reactive distancing behaviors that can serve to control this anxiety include running away or flight, isolation, withdrawal, and collapse. Cutoff is expressed through a range of behaviors from little to extreme emotional distance, manifested internally or geographically. Cutoff is an automatic, emotional, behavioral reaction, and at times it includes an intentional effort to distance from situations involving extreme conflict, fear. and anxiety. Cutoff, insofar as it is an emotional process, is rooted in evolutionary processes that are instinctive and automatic. Cutoff functions to control and reduce anxiety generated by intense contact—stuck-together fusion—with the family of origin. It controls or wards off acute anxiety in the short run by reducing fear of loss of self and a variety of emotional allergies, but at the same time it can augment chronic anxiety and impede its resolution in the long run. The degree of cutoff is a more intense and prolonged emotional response when the level of differentiation is lower and the level of anxiety is higher and more chronic.

Emotional cutoff, the emotional process between the generations, refers primarily to an individual's relationship with his or her parents after leaving home; in other words. the emotional process of separation between an individual and his or her parents when an individual starts a new nuclear family or otherwise sets up an independent living situation.

Cutoff is not created or sustained by a single individual. It takes two or more individuals to sustain a cutoff. In addition, it takes at least one parent and a child for a process of cutoff to occur. However, cutoff is integrally related to the process of the parent-child triangle, as well as the emotional immaturity that resides in the parents and their relationships to their own parents. In short, cutoff is rooted in the emotional process of the family as a multigenerational unit. The child's future effort to become a separate individual in relation to the parents and others depends on the way the parent-child triangle unfolds. When the parents have a fairly direct and open relationship with each other, and each has the same with the child, then the child when grown to a young adult can eventually leave the parents at home with their stable relationship, go out into the world, and proceed to be a relatively autonomous individual. In contrast, when the parent-child triangle is fraught with an intense projection process toward the child and emotional divorce between the parents, undergirded by lower levels of differentiation and higher levels of anxiety in the family, the outcome of the separation between the generations often leads to emotional cutoff. The family projection process occurs when a parent maps his or her own anxiety onto the child and then the child automatically lives out the parent's anxiety.

In addition, cutoff refers to many variations of emotional distancing that occur among individuals both within and outside their family systems. In this regard. Bowen (Kerr and Bowen, 1988) wrote that cutoff can "describe the immature separation of people from each other" (p. 346). This author understands Bowen's use of the phrase "separation of people from each other" to indicate that the phenomenon of cutoff can refer to a process between an individual and others besides his or her parents. The degree and intensity with which cutoff occurred for an individual in relation to parents is the degree to which that individual will cut off from others in the present and future generations.

An important dimension of the concept of cutoff is the unfolding process of emotional separation between the adolescent or young adult and his or her parents. This process runs along a hypothetical continuum. At the highest level of functioning the process can be characterized in terms of an individual growing away from his or her family of origin, leading to the development of an autonomous self. At the middle level of functioning, the process can be characterized in terms of an individual tearing away from his or her family of origin to become a pseudo self. At the lowest level of functioning the process can be characterized by an intense degree of cutting off or distancing. This is followed by collapsing, in which, for example, a psychotic individual emotionally collapses in the first effort to function independently, returns home, and then retreats into an internal cutoff as a way of denying the emotional attachment between self and parent(s).

Growing away, the more highly differentiated end of the continuum, is characterized by minimal distancing, withdrawal, isolation, and collapse. The individual maintains relatively open communication and relatively direct one-to-one relationships with his or her parents. Tearing away, characterized by a midlevel degree of differentiation, involves distancing behavior that leans more in the direction of cutoff than those whose higher level of differentiation places them in the growing away range. These individuals have relationships with their parents that are characterized by the absence of direct, if any, communication. The relationships are closed and so distant as to be experienced as nonexistent. The distance may be internal, involving severe emotional withdrawal or collapse. However, the adolescent who rebels or runs away and the adolescent or young adult who stays or returns home but withdraws or collapses both have an intense amount of unresolved attachment to their parents. The functioning at this range of the emotional process of separation is characterized by the term cutting off.

The emotionally distancing behavioral patterns of cutoff (emotionally reactive responses to unresolved attachment) including emotional isolation, withdrawal, flight, collapse, and geographical distancing, are expressed in many other subtle and not so subtle behaviors. The following are just a few examples of various forms of cutoff that occur along the continuum:

1. A young adult (or any family member) not communicating with other family when geographically distant, particularly avoiding communicating bad news
2. Being conflictual with a family member prior to embarking on a separation from that person

3. An individual's polarizing his or her position with a parent in order to gain emotional distance
4. Forgetting or choosing not to acknowledge important family events or milestones such as birthdays, anniversaries, graduations, or achievements
5. The absence of or refusal to make eye contact with the other
6. The absence or avoidance of verbal communication with the other
7. Not referring to the other by name
8. Not initiating contact, but responding to it, or not initiating and not responding to contact from the other

Primary and Secondary Emotional Cutoff

From this author's perspective, emotional cutoff can be either *primary* or *secondary* (in other words, derivative of the primary cutoff). It can be direct or indirect. Although Bowen did not use the terms *primary* and *secondary* to describe cutoff, he did refer to the mother-father-child as the primary triangle, thereby suggesting that the other triangles involving siblings and other family members were secondary to or derivative of the original, primary triangle. They follow and interlock with the primary triangle. In writing about the concept of cutoff, Bowen described the immature side of the emotional process of separation between the generations, referring to the unresolved attachment to the parents as being the primary unit from which cutoff follows. He refers to cutoff as the immature separation of people from one another, suggesting cutoffs do not solely occur between parent(s) and a child. It thus appears to this author that there is theoretical and useful justification to introduce the terminology of primary and secondary or derivative cutoff.

A primary or direct cutoff takes place within the primary triangle, an individual in relation to one or both of his or her parents. A secondary or derivative cutoff takes place between an individual and a sibling, grandparent, uncle or aunt, or cousins. This form of cutoff takes place within secondary triangles that spin off from or are interlocked with the primary parent-child triangle. Secondary cutoffs, based on interlocking triangles, can be described as indirect or "inherited," and are based on multigenerational emotional process. Some cutoffs are inherited in the sense that an individual has had no direct face-to-face contact with a particular individual. For example, a son may be cut off from his aunt solely because his parents are cut off from her. They may be cut off from her because of issues involving the parents, aunt, and grandparents that led to a cutoff between an individual's parents and his aunt. The son goes along with the family emotional "party line." However, insofar as the secondary cutoffs are based on interlocking triangles, the origination of these, and thus the priority, is the emotional cutoff, the immature, unresolved attachment that exists between the parents and child.

A Case Example of Primary and Secondary Cutoffs

A forty-eight-year-old married woman. Mrs. A.. living in western Massachusetts with three teenage sons, presented with the symptom of depression, focused on feeling sensitive and rejected by recent and longtime friends. She had an "allergic reaction" to perceived rejection. Conflict with her sons, particularly her youngest, led her at times to vow that she was no · longer going to have any contact with him. After a few days she would again begin interacting with him.

During the initial evaluation, Mrs. A. provided a family history with clear examples of what this author described as both primary and secondary emotional cutoffs. Mrs. A. described herself as having a tendency to "burn my bridges" with friends and family. The primary cutoff resided between Mrs. A. and her father, whom she described as an alcoholic. Her parents divorced when Mrs. A. was sixteen years old. after her father had had several affairs. including involvement with one of her teenage friends. From then on Mrs. A. and her father had infrequent and emotionally distant contact. Mrs. A. did make an effort to relate to her stepmother. The client had been and continued to be devoted to her seventy-nine-year-old mother, who never remarried. Figure 1.2 is a family diagram that illustrates the presence of primary and secondary cutoff involving at least three generations on the maternal side of the family. Primary and secondary cutoffs had been and continued to be present between Mrs. A.'s mother and Mrs. A.'s maternal grandmother and between Mrs. A.'s mother and Mrs. A.'s maternal aunts. respectively.

This vignette will focus on Mrs. A.'s family of origin. Although the interlocking process between the extended family and the family of origin will not be discussed, it can be hypothesized that the emotional cutoff between Mrs. A.'s mother and grandmother as well as between her mother and two aunts, interlocked with the cutoffs involving herself and her father and her brother. In terms of the primary triangle, Mrs. A. was overly close with her mother and extremely distant from her father. Mrs. A. described her father as "an empty suit." He never sought contact with her or his grandchildren. The cutoff came to a head in early 1987, when the father initiated but failed to show up for a visit with Mrs. A.'s children, shortly following the birth of the youngest. From that point forward, Mrs. A. never initiated or received any contact from her father. He died ten years later.

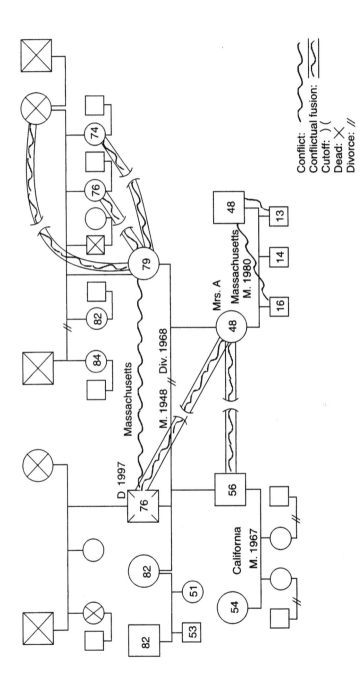

Conflict: 〜
Conflictual fusion: 〜〜
Cutoff:)(
Dead: X
Divorce: //

FIGURE 1.2. Primary and secondary cutoff.

27

Mrs. A. was involved in what might be described as a secondary, derivative cutoff with her only sibling, a fifty-six-year-old married, retired, naval officer. The latter lived in California and had two daughters who were each divorced; one was remarried. Mrs. A. described herself as always having a somewhat distant relationship with her older brother. In his primary triangle growing up he was closer to his father, with the mother in the outside position. After their parents' divorce, the brother did not keep in good touch with his father. Nevertheless, when their father died in 1997 he played a significant part in his funeral, much to the chagrin of Mrs. A., who merely attended the funeral. In 1990 the distance between brother and sister escalated into a full-blown cutoff in response to Mrs. A.'s perceiving that her brother was not paying enough attention to their mother. For example, he planned to visit his mother in western Massachusetts for only one day to attend a special seventieth birthday party that Mrs. A. had arranged for her. Mrs. A. was involved in a conflictual phone call with her sister-in-law a couple of weeks prior to the party. The brother came home, heard his wife and sister talking on the phone, and told his wife to hang up. Mrs. A. and her brother had no contact in the subsequent ten years. Mrs. A.'s children got together with their uncle on one occasion, at his request at their grandmother's home, but Mrs. A. was not present. Figure 1.3 illustrates the primary and secondary triangles in Family A.

In summary, this vignette illustrates primary cutoff between Mrs. A. and her father that developed over time. This cutoff was embedded in the primary triangle of Mrs. A. Mrs. A. was close to her mother and distant from her father. After her father and mother divorced when Mrs. A. was an adolescent, fusion increased between mother and daughter, distance increased between father and daughter, and mother and father were legally and emotionally divorced. Later, a severe cutoff between Mrs. A. and her father crystallized, ending with the father's death.

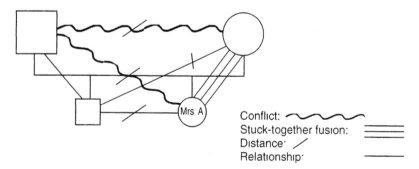

Conflict:

Stuck-together fusion:

Distance·

Relationship·

FIGURE 1.3. Primary and secondary triangles.

As a child, Mrs. A.'s brother's primary triangle involved emotional distance between him and his mother, emotional closeness between him and his father, and emotional distance between his sister, Mrs. A., and himself. After their parents divorced his primary triangle shifted. Greater distance developed between himself and both of his parents. When he left for the Navy a moderate degree of cutoff developed between each of his parents and himself.

Mrs. A.'s fusion with her mother was interlocked with her cutoff from her father, and the strengthening of that process intensified the cutoff between Mrs. A. and her father. In addition, there was an interlock between this process and the increase of her brother's distancing from his mother and Mrs. A. The primary triangles of Mrs. A. and her brother interlocked with the triangle involving their mother and themselves: Mrs. A. being fused with her mother and very distant from her brother, and her brother and mother being very distant. Over time, and spurred by the nodal event of the brother's lack of involvement in their mother's seventieth birthday party, a secondary or derivative cutoff emerged between Mrs. A. and her brother. Figure 1.4 illustrates the interlock of primary and secondary triangles with primary and secondary cutoff.

It should be clear from the preceding description that the primary and secondary cutoffs and the primary and secondary triangles of which they are a part are interlocked. The depression Mrs. A. experienced and her tendency to be oversensitive regarding rejection in social relations with friends also appeared to be derivative and related to the significant level of emotional cutoff in her life, primarily with her father and secondarily with her brother, in conjunction with the fusion with her mother.

THE RELATIONSHIP BETWEEN EMOTIONAL CUTOFF AND THE OTHER CONCEPTS IN BOWEN THEORY

This section briefly describes how the concept of emotional cutoff interlocks with the other seven concepts that constitute Bowen theory: differentiation, triangles, nuclear family emotional process, family projection process, multigenerational transmission process, sibling position, and societal emotional process. All eight concepts fit together to describe the functioning of the family as a multigenerational emotional unit or system. In addition, the concept of anxiety, the forces of togetherness and individuality, and the concepts of the relationship system and the emotional system are other important aspects of the theory. Bowen theory must be understood as a whole. Each concept is integrally related to all the others, and an individual's behavior must always be understood in the context of the multigenerational

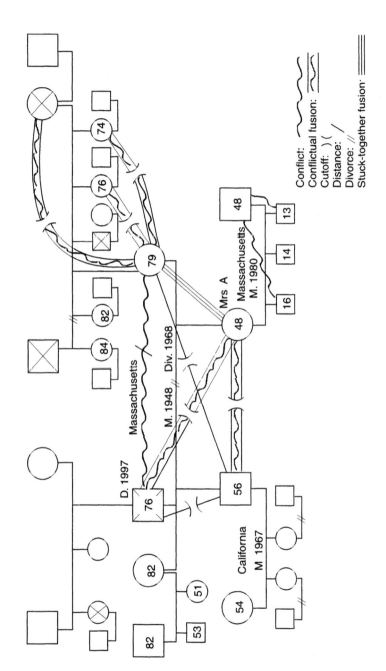

FIGURE 1.4. The interlock of primary and secondary triangles with primary and secondary cutoff.

family emotional system of which he or she is a part. All behavior in the system can fully be understood only by viewing it in terms of the interrelatedness of the eight concepts of Bowen theory. The reader is referred to Bowen (1978), Kerr and Bowen (1988), and Papero (1990) for a comprehensive articulation of Bowen theory that is beyond the scope of this book.

As the reader will remember from the second section of this chapter, The Origin and Evolution of the Concept of Emotional Cutoff in Bowen Theory, Bowen already had an incipient understanding of the process and significance of emotional cutoff for understanding family functioning in the 1950s, when he was studying and treating hospitalized schizophrenics and their families at the National Institute of Mental Health.

Drawing from Bowen's observations of inpatient and outpatient cases of researching and treating schizophrenia, the following interlocking of cutoff with the other concepts that constitute Bowen theory can be seen in its nascent form. The concept of differentiation is drawn from Bowen's descriptions of the functioning of parents of the schizophrenic and can be extrapolated to apply on a continuum to all people. The parents have more unresolved attachment to their parents, for the most part, than do their siblings. They marry at the same level of maturity or differentiation. Their marriage is characterized by a high degree of fusion and a reciprocal over-underfunctioning process in which the mother usually is in the overadequate position and the father in the passive, inadequate position. As they begin a new nuclear family, a low level of differentiation, stress, and increasing anxiety eventually can lead to distance or emotional divorce between the couple. The arrival of children marks the onset of triangles. One child is, usually, involved in the most intense symbiosis with the mother and the father is, usually, in the outside position in this triangle. The undifferentiation and anxiety in the nuclear family emotional system is bound by emotional distance between the spouses and impairment of a child or (children), in which the child is the recipient of the parental anxiety. One child usually receives the greatest amount of the family projection process. In this process the anxiety of the mother is directed toward and is taken up by or transferred to the child in a symbiotic fashion. In this process the mother's anxiety is transmitted to the child. Simultaneously, the child takes care of his or her mother by being functionally helpless in order to relieve the mother's anxiety. Often the child who develops the greatest impairment by receiving the brunt of the projection process is in the firstborn or last-born sibling position. The firstborn child often receives the expectations and/or anxiety of the same-sex parent. The youngest child is often vulnerable to functioning in a dependent position.

The process that leads to emotional cutoff involves a multigenerational transmission process whereby the unresolved attachment of children to their parents is followed by fusion in the child's marriage and distance from parents. When fusion in the marriage cannot sufficiently bind anxiety, the distance between the marital partners, or parents, is a part of the triangling process with the child who receives the highest degree of projection. That child is fused with the mother, or both parents, and in growing up is unable to grow away in an orderly fashion. Instead he or she goes through a process of emotionally tearing away from his or her parents through denial of the importance of the parental family, expressed through the emotionally reactive distancing behaviors of withdrawal, freezing, or collapsing.

In the following sections the concept of emotional cutoff is related, individually, to each of the other seven concepts that make up Bowen theory.

Emotional Cutoff and Differentiation

The continuum of emotional cutoff is intertwined with the process of differentiation. The process of differentiation includes the issues of attachment and separation at the levels of both the nuclear and extended families, and refers to an individual's management of relationship components that express the interplay of two life forces: individuality and togetherness. It is a process that accounts for the balance between being an individual and being a team player in a family. In the nuclear family the issues of attachment and separation involve being highly stuck-together fused or distantly fused at the lower end of the continuum of differentiation, and more separate but connected at the higher end of the continuum. In the family of origin, the low end of the continuum of differentiation can be manifested in either a high degree of cutoff or overcloseness. The higher end of the continuum of differentiation can be manifested in the capacity to be both separate and connected.

At the immature level on the continuum of undifferentiation to differentiation, the separation between the generations leads to the unresolved attachment between an offspring and his or her parents being expressed through pseudo separation, or emotional cutoff. Emotional cutoff is one automatic response to fusion. In the presence of a low level of differentiation and a high degree of anxiety, the fusion cannot contain or bind it and the relationship can shift toward cutoff.

Emotional Cutoff and Triangles

Bowen described the triangle as the smallest stable unit in an emotional system. It involves three people, with two in a closer relationship and the third more distant. When the system is calm, the preferred position is in the close relationship, with the outsider seeking to get into a closer relationship with the other two. In an anxious system the preferred position is on the outside. The automatic reaction of an anxious individual is to draw in a third person, issue, or activity. When the anxiety in a family or any "emotional system" cannot be contained by a single triangle, interlocking triangles will develop.

Kerr (2000) places cutoff in the context of triangles. When a child is growing away from his or her parent, emotional cutoff is the behavior that develops in response to the intensity in the parental triangle. Cutoff can be described as part of an interlocking process of fusion and cutoff between the generations (see Figure 1.1).

In another example, Mr. W., who was emotionally fused with his mother and distant or cutoff from his father, may eventually become allergic to the emotional intensity with his mother. He may manage the intensity with his mother by distancing behavior. Eventually he will marry and become emotionally fused with his wife and emotionally cutoff from his mother. The mother and her daughter-in-law may predictably be in conflict. In this description of interlocking triangles, Mr. W. starts out in the fused position with his mother, while his father is in the outside position. Then, in the next interlocking triangle, Mr. W. is emotionally fused with his wife, with his mother emotionally cutoff from him and in a conflictually distant relationship with her daughter-in-law. Examples of the relationship between primary and secondary cutoffs and their connection to primary and secondary triangles were described in a previous section (pp. 25-29).

Emotional Cutoff and Nuclear Family Emotional Process

The concept of the nuclear family emotional process is defined as the relationship process between marital partners and eventually with their children. This concept deals with the intensity that develops in the emotional fusion or "we-ness" of the marital relationship. It includes four automatic mechanisms or patterns in response to emotional fusion: distance, marital conflict, dysfunction in one spouse, and transmission of the problem to a child. Each of these mechanisms for managing fusion in the presence of anxiety can eventually lead to cutoff. Clearly, distance and/or marital conflict can escalate to a point where cutoff between the spouses can occur.

A social dysfunction in a spouse, such as alcoholism, involves a triangling process in which the symptomatic, underfunctioning spouse is in the close position with the alcoholic substance and its effects, while the overfunctioning, nonsymptomatic spouse is in the outside position. Over time, one development of such a process can be cutoff between the alcoholic and nonalcoholic spouses. Other forms of physical dysfunction in a spouse, such as cancer or diabetes, can lead to severe distancing that culminates in emotional cutoff. Also, emotional dysfunction in a spouse, such as depression, can lead to a distancing process that culminates in emotional cutoff between spouses. In addition, the process of distancing or cutoff between spouses can be a factor in one spouse investing or binding his or her undifferentiation in a social symptom, such as another relationship.

The mechanism of impairment or projection of anxiety onto a child in conjunction with the triangling process can also lead to cutoff. When the parents are in a close relationship and the child is in the outside position, or if one of the parents, more often the mother, is in an overly close relationship with a child and the other parent is in the outside position, emotional cutoff can evolve. For the individual in the outside position, parent or child, eventually the reciprocal process of cutting off and being cutoff may occur.

Emotional Cutoff and the Family Projection Process

In the family projection process the parent maps his or her own anxiety or inadequacies onto the child and then the child automatically lives out the parents' anxiety and inadequacies. In this emotional reciprocity the child, in order to adapt to the parent, lives out the position of functional helplessness and the parent lives out the position of functional strength. The term *functional position* indicates that the child and parental behaviors are not constitutional but rather are determined by the automatic, reciprocal emotional dance that exists among members of the family unit.

The child (or children) who receives the greatest brunt of the family projection process is the most impaired. This process, in which the parental undifferentiation impairs one or more of the children, operates within the father-mother-child triangle. Whether the nuclear family emotional process is more focused on marital conflict or on dysfunction in the spouse, there is always some family projection in which anxiety drips down from the parents, usually an anxious mother and a father who goes along with the mother, and is lived out by the child. Over a period of time the anxiety can be initiated either by the parent or the child, with the other responding in a similarly anxious fashion.

The projection process that exists between an anxious mother and the most vulnerable reciprocating child (one who may be the oldest male or female, an only child, one with a physical disability, or some other special feature) becomes fully activated in conjunction within an "emotional divorce" between the parents. The latter is defined as emotional distance between the father and mother, with the father's position becoming secondary and distant from the mother-child dyad. Therefore, the family projection process is intertwined with the process of emotional cutoff, and cutoff can be intensified by a projection process.

Emotional Cutoff and the Multigenerational Transmission Process

The concept of the multigenerational transmission process involves the naturally occurring repetition of the family projection process over multiple generations, running as long as the family exists. Individuals marry spouses of similar levels of differentiation and reproduce a family line characterized by decreasing levels of differentiation in individuals who are the primary object of the projection process over multiple generations. Children who have been freer from the projection process marry and reproduce and their children emerge with higher levels of differentiation over multiple generations.

Over eight to ten generations, the level of differentiation of the most impaired individual in each succeeding generation decreases. This process provides the possibility for the emergence of a level of impairment that can lead to severely compromised functioning, for example, schizophrenia. As Bowen (1978) described it, schizophrenia is "a natural process that helps to keep the race strong. The weakness from the family is fixed in one person who is less likely to marry and reproduce and more likely to die young" (p. 385).

Likewise, there is in each succeeding generation a process that includes emotional distancing or emotional divorce, which is part of the phenomenon of emotional cutoff. One of the outcomes of the multigenerational transmission process is the natural occurrence of cutoff in one line and between many lines of a multigenerational family. This is expressed as emotional distance or cutoff between individuals in a given extended family and between individuals and entire branches across lines of a family. It is not unusual for an individual seeking to learn about his or her family to find that there is not only little contact between certain relatives, but often there has been little or no knowledge transmitted from the parents about previous generations, going back into the distant past.

Emotional Cutoff and Sibling Position

The concept of sibling position, drawn from Toman (1969) and adapted by Bowen (1978), describes the characteristics of oldest, youngest, and middle siblings. It also describes how these positions relate and are determined by their interaction with their parents and with siblings who hold other reciprocal positions. Sibling position also describes how spouses and parents will reciprocally interact, based on the birth positions of the individuals involved. The level of differentiation will determine how rigidly or flexibly these positions will be lived out.

For example, when the projection process is focused on an oldest, that individual may, if he or she is severely impaired, function like a dependent youngest. Or if his or her level of impairment is moderate, he or she may function as an autocrat. The oldest may be abrasive to siblings, and this may play into a process of cutoff between siblings that relates to their competitive struggles within the context of the parental triangle.

Emotional Cutoff and Societal Emotional Process

The concept of societal emotional process is based on Bowen's effort to extend his understanding of the family as an emotional system to an understanding of society as an emotional system. He believed that the triangle exists in all living systems, not just the human family. Bowen (1978) portrayed societal emotional process as follows:

> The societal concept postulates . . . that we are in a period of increasing chronic societal anxiety; that society responds to this with emotionally determined decisions to allay the anxiety of the moment; that this results in symptoms of dysfunction; that the efforts to relieve the symptoms result in more emotional band-aid [sic] legislation, which increased the problem; and that the cycle keeps repeating, just as the family goes through similar cycles to the states we call emotional illness. (p. 386)

The following vignette involving emotional cutoff and societal emotional process illustrates how these concepts interlock. This vignette highlights the origins of societal violence in its relationship to emotional cutoff in family emotional process. In this family history, two half brothers, Isaac and Ishmael, ended up in an emotional cutoff so intense that 160 generations later their descendants not only fail to acknowledge one another as kin, but perceive one another as the ultimate Other: different in race, religion, and nationality.

Family History

The family vignette, found in the Bible's book of Genesis, starts with a married couple, Abraham and Sarah, who apparently were infertile. Being unable to conceive a child, Sarah suggested to Abraham that he have a child with Sarah's maid, Hagar, an Egyptian slave woman. When Hagar became pregnant, Sarah paradoxically became angry with Abraham, since she was in the outside position of the triangle, with Abraham and Hagar in the inside positions. Abraham dealt with the conflict by telling Sarah that she owned her slave and should do with her as she pleased. Sarah sent Hagar away from their home. A powerful figure, God, whose existence in this context is viewed as a functional fact, convinced Hagar to return to the home of Abraham and Sarah and put up with Sarah's anger. God informed Hagar that she would have a son named Ishmael. God's prophecy was that Ishmael would become a strong and dominating leader who would "dwell over against all his kinsman" (Genesis 16: 12, KJV).

When Ishmael was thirteen, God promised to help Abraham find a solution to Sarah's infertility. He promised that Sarah would have a son named Isaac. God also promised to make Isaac a very powerful man and promised to be a generous benefactor to all of Isaac's descendants.

After Isaac's birth, Sarah tolerated the presence of Hagar and Ishmael in her home for a time, but her anxiety and anger were triggered by seeing Ishmael and Isaac playing together and possibly beginning to develop a sibling bond. Sarah told Abraham that she wanted to throw the slave woman out with her son, Ishmael, because she did not want him to be an heir with her son, Isaac.

Abraham consulted his benefactor, God, and in a triangling move complained about Sarah's demand that he abandon his own son, Ishmael. As a "family consultant," God recommended that Abraham accommodate Sarah's demand. In return, Isaac and his future descendants would be provided for. Likewise, the consultant-benefactor would make Ishmael into an equally important figure in an adjoining nation. Abraham was triangled between the mothers of his sons, Sarah and Hagar, and also caught in the interlocking triangles that involved God, Sarah, and himself and himself, Hagar, and God. He opted to follow God's direction and go along with Sarah's pressure to cut off from Ishmael and Hagar. Abraham gave provisions to Hagar and Ishmael and sent them away into the wilderness. When it looked as though Hagar and Ishmael could not survive, God intervened and gave them resources and emotional support. Ishmael lived in a very remote, unpopulated area. Hagar found him a wife from the land of Egypt.

Implications

A family conflict involving the cutoff of two half brothers, Isaac and Ishmael, when taken to its multigenerational historical and metaphorical conclusion, led to the ossification of a cutoff between two whole branches of a family: Israelis and Egyptians, Jews and Muslims.

The evolutionary pressures of asymmetrical kinship and undifferentiation in the face of anxiety, generated by the external stressors of scarcity, infertility, lack of food and material resources for survival, and lack of territorial security, can lead to a cutoff in kinship, to a point where one's kin are perceived as foreign, as the enemy, the "evil other" that must be annihilated.

This mythical/historical case illustrates that emotional cutoff in the family can, in some cases, lead to intense societal violence through the multigenerational emotional transmission process. It can begin in one triangle in a nuclear family and spiral through a process of interlocking triangles. The societal emotional process involving the violence expressed in Arab-Jewish conflict today took 160 generations of conflict oscillating with cutoff to evolve to its current fratricidal intensity.

SYMPTOM FORMATION
AND THE CONTINUUM OF EMOTIONAL CUTOFF

The variation in intensity and severity of emotional cutoff as it relates to a variety of emotional, social, and physical symptoms will be illustrated by several case vignettes. Emotional distance or cutoff can lead to, or exacerbate, a variety of symptoms. Bowen (1978) spoke of the "relationship nomad" as a person who under tension may go from one marriage to another or from one short relationship to another, always "cutting emotional ties to the past and investing self in the present relationship" (p. 536). Bowen also described how some individuals use internal mechanisms to express emotional cutoff. These individuals are more prone to symptoms of depression, alcoholism, and physical dysfunction. Specific examples of the relationship between emotional symptoms, such as depression; physical symptoms involving chronic disease, including physical trauma; and social dysfunction such as domestic abuse and child abuse will be illustrated in separate chapters later in this book. In addition, the reader is referred to the discussion earlier in this chapter of how the concept of emotional cutoff was embedded in Bowen's research on schizophrenia.

There is a spectrum of ways adult individuals deal with emotional cutoff in relation to the emotional process between the generations. The degree and intensity of the symptoms depend on the level of differentiation in conjunction with the degree of chronic anxiety. In general, emotional cutoff between the extended and nuclear families intensifies all forms of symptoms. Without solid contact between the generations, anxiety and fusion increase in the nuclear family. Differentiation decreases and inflexibility in coping with life's problems increases.

Several clinical examples of cutoff in relation to symptom formation—including depression, physical illness, sexual abuse, and alcoholism—are presented. The examples describe the range of cutoff from milder tearing away to more intense expressions of cutting off.

Vignette 1: Growing Away to Tearing Away

The first vignette describes an individual, Ms. D., whose level of cutoff from her family is in the milder range, characterized by a process that includes both dimensions of growing away and tearing away accompanied by symptoms of anxiety.

Presenting Problems

Ms. D., a thirty-three-year-old, single social worker came to therapy because she was experiencing mild anxiety, an adjustment reaction, after moving back to western Massachusetts to take a job in a clinic, close to where her parents live and where she grew up. She was "dealing with the pros and cons" of whether she had made a mistake by moving back to her home territory. She was also wondering whether she should "get away from her parents and the whole area." In addition, Ms. D. was experiencing issues in her relationship with her boyfriend. She was professionally competent, attractive, and had hobbies and friends.

Family History

Ms. D. has a younger sister who is age twenty-eight, a chemist, engaged to be married, and living in a large southern city. Her father, age fifty-five, is a landscaper at a local college, and her mother, age fifty-three, is a florist. Both parents have less education than the levels attained by both daughters. The members of the nuclear family are described as caring for one another but they have difficulty expressing emotional closeness. However, Ms. D. was seeing her family at least once a week and speaking with them on the phone between visits. Figure 1.5 presents the D. family diagram.

Within a year prior to entering therapy, Ms. D., who had figured out several years prior that she was conceived before her parents were married, had a discussion with her mother in which the latter acknowledged this fact to be true. Ms. D. believed that her mother had been frustrated about not continuing in college after her birth and that the circumstances surrounding her

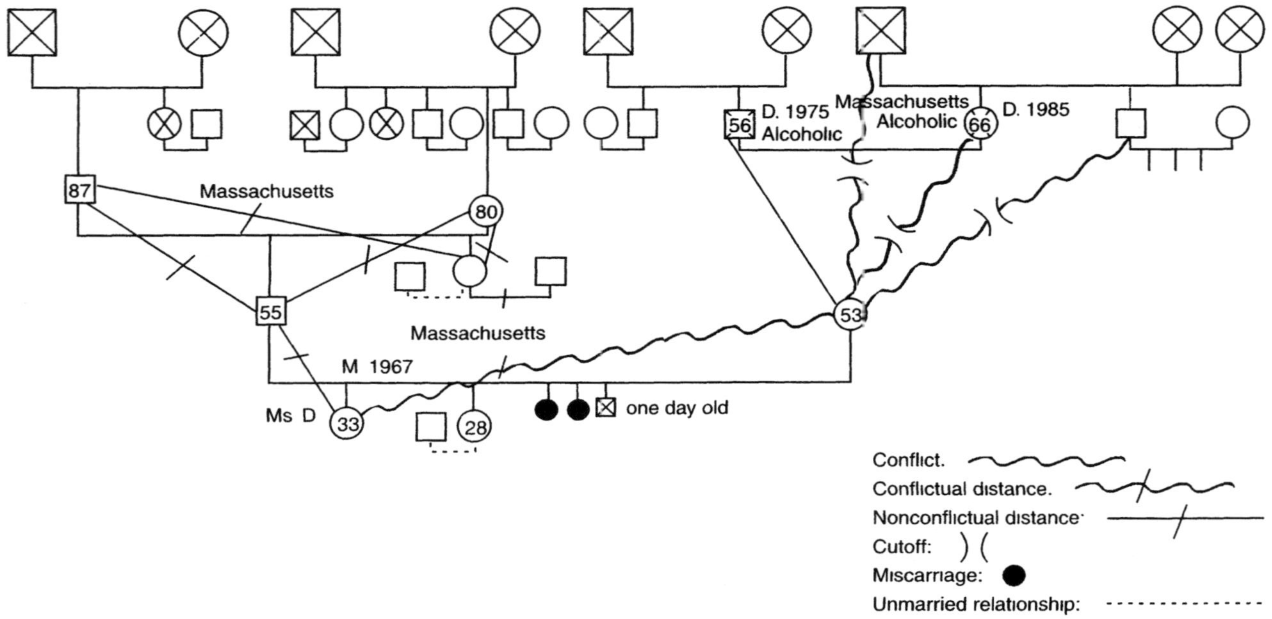
87
Massachusetts
80
55
Massachusetts
M 1967
Ms D
33
28
one day old
56
D. 1975
Alcoholic
Massachusetts
Alcoholic
66
D. 1985
53
Conflict.
Conflictual distance.
Nonconflictual distance·
Cutoff:
Miscarriage:
Unmarried relationship:

FIGURE 1.5. D family diagram.

birth were a part of the distance she experienced in her relation with her mother. Ms. D.'s mother was a homemaker and later worked as a teacher's aide before she became a florist. Ms. D. perceived her mother as being closer to her sister, with herself being in the outside position in that triangle. Ms. D. described feeling closer to her father than to her mother, and often defended her father when she felt her mother was browbeating him. Mr. D. was described as caring but emotionally inexpressive. He was unable to have his own relationship with his daughter separate from his wife, which left Ms. D. feeling distant from him and wishing she could be emotionally closer to him.

In the maternal extended family, Mrs. D. was an only child from an Irish family. Her father died from alcoholism when he was in his fifties. Their relationship was described as being good. Mrs. D.'s relationship with her mother deteriorated after the death of her father, when her mother began drinking. Eventually, there was complete cutoff between Mrs. D. and her mother following the death of Mrs. D.'s son one day after he was born. According to Ms. D., she frequently heard her mother say, "I got no support from my mother when my baby died." Mrs. D. also had two miscarriages prior to the death of her one-day-old son. The miscarriages and premature death occurred subsequent to the birth of Ms. D. and her sister. Ms. D.'s mother was also emotionally cutoff from her maternal grandfather who remarried quickly after her grandmother's death. Following the cutoff between Mrs. D. and her mother, Ms. D. never again saw her grandmother.

Mr. D. has a younger sister and both of his parents are still alive. They are in their eighties. Mr. D.'s family of origin is described by Ms. D. as aloof and distant. She describes her father as being distant from his father and having a mildly close relationship with his mother. His sister lives at the other end of the state and is somewhat cutoff from their parents. Ms. D. describes her nuclear family as having had very ritualized and distant relationships with her paternal grandparents. They lived only fifteen minutes away when she was growing up.

This vignette illustrates a relatively mild degree of cutoff between Ms. D. and her parents. The emotional distance between the daughter and both her parents, particularly her mother, is in the range between growing away and tearing away, consonant with a relatively low level of chronic anxiety and a level of differentiation in the moderate range. There is a continuous history of relating with both parents that is indicative of contact with a mild to moderate degree of emotional distancing, and the unresolved attachment between Ms. D. and her parents is in the mild to moderate level. Ms. D. "inherited" the primary cutoff that existed between her mother and maternal grandmother, insofar as she had very little contact with her grandmother and she believed the many negative things about her grandmother that she had heard from her mother. In addition, to some extent she also is involved in a mild secondary cutoff with her paternal grandparents that interlocks with both of her parents' moderate cutoff with the paternal grandparents. Here again, she had infrequent contact with her grandparents and she believed the somewhat disparaging comments and views her mother held about her paternal grandparents.

Vignette 2: Tearing Away to Cutting Off

The second vignette depicts an individual, Mr. E., whose level of cutoff from his family is in the midrange, characterized by a process of tearing away accompanied by moderate physical symptoms, career uncertainty, and relationship difficulties.

Presenting Problems

Mr. E., a twenty-seven-year-old male who is an art teacher in a secondary school, presented for psychotherapy with concern about his relationship with his girlfriend of one year, somatic complaints (including irritable bowel and asthma), uncertainty about the direction of his career as an artist, and concern about the emotional distance between himself and his father.

Family History

Mr. E. was an only child. His parents' marriage ended in divorce when he was one year old. Mr. E. lived with his father and paternal grandmother in Connecticut until he was twelve, and had little contact with his mother or her side of the family. Mr. E.'s father was a sound-recording engineer who was alcohol and drug dependent. Mr. E. moved with his father to Montana and then to Idaho in an effort to overcome his father's drug dependency. Mr. E. got along well with his father, but he was often his caretaker and spent much time alone. Father's moves were precipitated by the endings of disappointing relationships with girlfriends. At the age of fourteen Mr. E., after experiencing much loneliness and feeling overwhelmed with his father's problems, went back to the East Coast to a boarding school with the help of his grandmother. From the time Mr. E. moved back to the East Coast he saw his father on only a couple of occasions. In 1981, Mr. E.'s father remarried and had two sons with his new wife. Mr. E. had seen his father only a couple of times between 1981 and 1992, when Mr. E. came to therapy. Mr. E. felt that he was the pursuer in his relationship with his father, which consisted of irregular phone calls in which his father complained about his new family and his serious hepatitis. Eventually, Mr. E.'s father became a candidate for and he did receive a liver transplant. By that time he was back living near Mr. E and his mother. The father's second marriage went downhill, and he and his wife divorced. The two sons moved to the West Coast with Mr. E.'s stepmother.

Mr. E.'s mother had moved to the Southwest and he only saw her on rare occasions when she came back to visit her extended family. She remarried and had another son whom Mr. E. had never met. She had a couple of relationships following her divorce from her second husband.

Mr. E.'s father was also an only child. His parents divorced when he was a toddler. Mr. E.'s grandmother remarried and had five children with that husband. The stepfather was a musician and composer, and he was alcoholic and abusive toward Mr. E.'s father. Mr. E.'s father got along well with his half siblings and maintained reasonable contact with them and his mother. Mr. E. had a good relationship with an aunt who was the middle one of the five half siblings.

Mr. E.'s mother's family lived in Massachusetts. Mr. E.'s mother had six siblings, four sisters and two brothers. One sister committed suicide. Mr. E.'s mother told Mr. E. that there were many generations of divorce and suicide in her family. Mr. E. had a minimal relationship with his maternal grandfather during his adolescence. The grandfather was providing him with some financial support at the boarding school. However, Mr. E. found him to be an unemotional man who dealt with relationships through possessions and money.

Figure 1.6, the E. family diagram, depicts the cutoffs that existed at the time Mr. E. began therapy in 1992.

Mr. E. was cutoff from his father, mother, stepmother, and stepbrothers. All of the primary cutoffs were initiated by his parents and the secondary cutoffs with his half siblings were "inherited"; they were interlocking cutoffs spinning off of the primary ones in that Mr. E.'s cutoff from his half siblings followed from his being cutoff from both of his parents, expressed primarily through physical distance. Even though there was so much cutoff in this family, including Mr. E. from his own father, and his father from his father before, Mr. E.'s moderate level of differentiation, lack of high chronic anxiety, and his desire and willingness to work on his cutoff relationships accounts for the characterization that his level of unresolved attachment to his parents is described as tearing away rather than cutting off.

Vignette 3: Cutting Off

The third vignette depicts an individual, Mr. N., in whom severe dysfunctional emotional symptoms are present. Severe cutting off characterizes his family relationships.

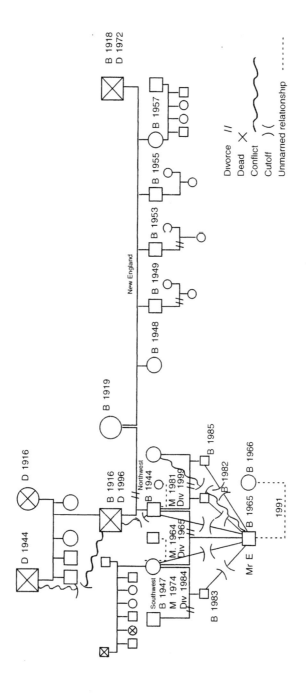

FIGURE 1.6. E. family diagram.

44

Presenting Problems

Mr. N.. a forty-nine-year-old, single, Jewish, social service professional, presented for therapy complaining of an anxiety disorder with panic attacks and stating that he suffered from post-traumatic stress disorder resulting from the near death of his beloved cat eight years prior. Mr. N. believed his cat had kept him alive during periods when he experienced suicidal ideation. He stated that he had stayed alive in order not to abandon his cat, Mr. Felix. The client had been in psychotherapy for approximately three years in the early 1990s. At that time Mr. N. was isolated and depressed, dissociated from his own body and feelings, and described himself as dysthymic. He had been on high doses of antidepressant medication for the past six or seven years. Mr. N. was in a long-term relationship with Ms. B. He met her in 1974, and they had been dating since 1991. She was a physical therapist, also Jewish, and had never married. Ms. B. wanted Mr. N. to live with her. For Mr. N. the issues between him and Ms. B. were money (Mr. N. was in considerable debt), where the couple would live, and most difficult was the dislike Ms. B. had for Mr. Felix. The triangle involved Mr. N. and Mr. Felix in the close relationship, with Ms. B. in the outside position. Mr. N. described himself as being worried that Ms. B. would abandon him. Mr. N. reported that Ms. B. felt that he had "an old man's energy."

Family History

Mr. N. was the youngest of three brothers. His oldest brother was sixty-eight, married, with a married daughter who had one child, a daughter. He was a salesman and lived in another state. There was a severe emotional cutoff between Mr. N. and this brother. They never saw or talked with each other, and this had gone on for several years. The second brother, age sixty-five, was divorced and had an eighteen-year-old son. He taught college mathematics. Mr. N. had infrequent contact with this brother and his son. Figure 1.7 presents Mr. N.'s family diagram.

Mr. N.'s father was born in 1901 and died in 1996. He dropped out of grade school and joined the Navy, and later became a manual laborer. The mother was born in 1905, and had been in a nursing home for five or six years. The parents were both born in London of Polish parents. Each parent left England and moved to Connecticut, where they met, and later settled in Pennsylvania. Their relationship was described as conflictual. The parents refused to tell their birthdays and refused to tell Mr. N. and his siblings any information regarding their grandparents and other members of their ex-

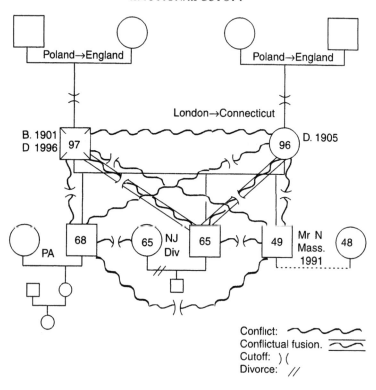

FIGURE 1.7. N. family diagram

tended family. Both parents were completely emotionally cutoff from their own families.

Mr. N. had few memories of his childhood. He described his parents as being "crazy." He remembered, for example. digging holes for his father in the backyard and then filling them up. They never socialized outside the family. Mr. N. and his brothers were never allowed to invite anyone in, and they never were allowed to visit any other children. Mr. N. describes being physically abused by both parents.

This vignette illustrates an intense version of emotional cutoff, involving physical and emotional distancing from the parents' families and in the family of origin. It appears that his symptoms of depression, isolation, difficulty socializing, and difficulty maintaining intimate relationships were closely related to the heightened emotional cutoff his family had experienced before he was born and the emotional process of the nuclear family of which he was a part. This intense emotional cutoff took the form of extreme geographical and internal distancing, in a family with a very low level of differentiation of self. The client's symptoms of depression can be more fully understood by placing them in the context of his and his family's extensive emotional cutoff from one another.

Vignette 4: Cutting Off

The fourth vignette describes a couple, Mr. and Mrs. B., for whom severe cutting off interlocks with intense marital and individual dysfunction, including severe emotional and physical symptoms.

Presenting Problems
.

Mr. B. was a fifty-one-year-old Caucasian with a severe case of multiple sclerosis. He was a retired social service professional and entrepreneur. Mrs. B. was a fifty-two-year-old Puerto Rican teacher with a master's degree in fine arts. They came to therapy together. They had a fifteen-year-old daughter who was free of symptoms, receiving little of the projection process. The majority of the anxiety in the family was bound in a combination of marital conflict and marital distance. Clearly the management of Mr. B.'s medical problems and the attendant difficulties were impacting the emotional, social, and physical functioning of both members of this couple. Although neither husband nor wife complained about the burdens of coping with the husband's continual deterioration from multiple sclerosis, he was angry and depressed about the limitations created by his physical illness.

Family History

Mr. and Mrs. B. became a couple in 1983 while living in Boston. They married in 1988, when their daughter was three. Mr. B. wanted more children, but Mrs. B. did not. When Mr. B. was thirty-seven he broke his hip, and four or five years later he went into further physical decline. Figure 1.8. presents the B. family diagram.

Both Mr. B. and Mrs. B. were extremely cutoff from their respective families of origin. Mr. B.'s parents were in their seventies and lived in a metropolitan center about 100 miles away. He never saw or spoke with them. Mrs. B. and their daughter had never met Mr. B.'s parents. The surface issue was that his parents disapproved of his having married a Puerto Rican. However, Mr. B. had had no contact with his parents for several years before he met his wife. Some years ago the B. family moved to Oklahoma and lived in the same city as Mr. B.'s brother. After a couple of years they moved back east,

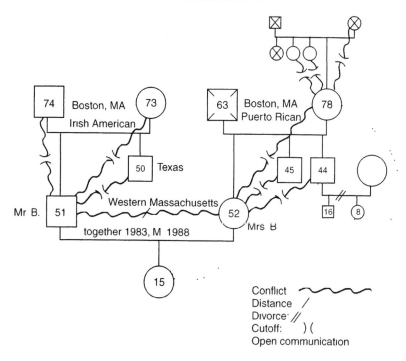

FIGURE 1.8 B. family diagram

to western Massachusetts, and had no further contact with Mr. B.'s brother. The intense and pervasive emotional cutoff that existed between Mr. B. and his family was matched by the same degree of cutoff between Mrs. B. and her family of origin.

Mrs. B.'s father died fifteen years before therapy began, about the time she connected with Mr. B. Her mother was always negative about Mr. B. because, according to Mrs. B., he was Caucasian and physically disabled. Deeper issues of conflict that existed between mother and Mrs. B. involved the mother being perceived by her daughter as very controlling, self-centered, and very "bourgeois and snobbish." Mrs. B. was very cutoff from her forty-five-year-old, single brother and from her forty-four-year-old, divorced brother who had two children: a son sixteen and a daughter, age eight. Interestingly, the B.'s daughter had contact with her maternal grandmother, one of the uncles, and his two children (her cousins). The daughter was the freest of emotional, physical, and social symptoms.

This vignette illustrates how the choice of a spouse of a different racial background, or any significant difference from an individual's own family background, may in part be an expression of cutoff from one's parents and a form of reactive distancing. It goes without saying that it is not the inter-racial marriage that caused emotional cutoff in both families. The cutoff is a function of a long-term emotional "allergic reaction" on the part of each spouse to conflictually unresolved attachments to each one's respective parents. The intensity of marital conflict had increased in tandem with the escalation of Mr. B.'s multiple sclerosis with its physical disability. The couple is more interdependent than ever, as they have no contact or social support from either of their extended families. This in turn leads to an increasing spiral of conflict interspersed with distance and withdrawal from each other. Mr. B. and Mrs. B. are a family with a history of a high degree of emotional cutoff in their respective relationships with their families of origin. The latter interlocks with the initial heightened fusion and subsequent high level of emotional distancing between the spouses. Both spouses fall into the "cutting off" category in regard to the severity of unresolved attachment from their respective parents, as reflected in the high degree of cutoff present in the relationships both spouses have with their parents and other members of their families of origin.

Vignette 5: Cutting Off

The fifth vignette depicts another individual, Ms. C.. in whom severe cutting off is accompanied by severe social and emotional symptoms.

Presenting Problem

Ms. C. was a thirty-nine-year-old divorced mother of two preteenage children. She had been a recovering alcoholic for over sixteen years. She was a social worker. Ms. C. took antidepressant medication and tranquilizers. She sought psychotherapy for "transference issues" with men, managing her depression, and issues left over from a divorce that had occurred four years ago. She described being hurt by her adoptive father, her husband, and other men.

Family History

Ms. C. was married in 1989. Her former husband, age forty-one, was a carpenter and a recovering alcoholic who was addicted to pornography. He was sexually abused by two baby-sitters while he was a young child. Their older daughter was ten and the younger was seven. The children lived with Ms. C. Figure 1.9 presents the C. family diagram.

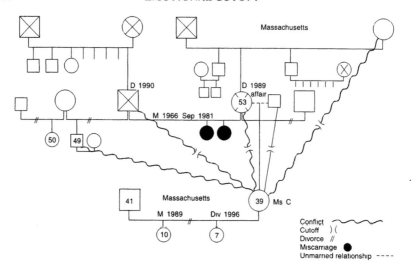

FIGURE 1.9. C. family diagram.

Ms. C.'s parents married in 1966 and separated in 1981. Ms. C. was
adopted by her stepfather. She discovered as a teenager that her biological
father was Asian, and he was married and having an affair with Ms. C.'s
mother when she was conceived in 1961. That relationship took place at a
Navy base. Ms. C. knew nothing about him. No one in her family had, or
would share, information regarding her biological father. Ms. C.'s adoptive
father had an adopted daughter from a previous marriage and a biological
son from that marriage. Those siblings were fifty and forty-nine, respectively.

Ms. C. reported that her adoptive father had been sexually inappropriate
with her for many years. When Ms. C. was thirteen her father French kissed
her while her mother was in the next room. She remembers she psychologically "disappeared," internally cutoff from shame and disgust. She was
shocked by her father's behavior. She felt ashamed and she blamed herself.
Ms. C. began running away from home in seventh grade. At age fourteen her
father got drunk frequently and was more sexually inappropriate. She ran
away to a large city where she was brutally raped twice, in the span of two
days. She had been a virgin. The two rapists were grooming girls for prosti-
tution. Ms. C. escaped from the apartment where she was being held, ran
through the streets, and boarded a bus back to western Massachusetts. Following several statutory rapes, Ms. C. stated that drinking saved her life, because when she drank she told people to stay away from her.

Ms. C. had difficulty sustaining intimate relationships. She was just beginning a new relationship. When she kissed her boyfriend, she felt herself cutting off internally. She did feel somewhat safer with him because he was also a recovering alcoholic and she believed he shared similar feelings of shame and embarrassment with her.

At age twenty-eight, Ms. C. disclosed the sexual abuse behavior to her mother. The day she and her mother were going to talk more about it, her mother died. Ms. C. described feeling that she had killed her mother. Her mother was a diabetic, had had a stroke, and died of a heart attack at age fifty-three. Ms. C.'s adoptive father was angry at her having disclosed the sexual behavior that had occurred between him and Ms. C. Ms. C. saw her adoptive father only a couple of times after her mother's death. He died from alcoholism in 1990. Ms. C. not only lost her mother, but she cut off and was cut off from her adoptive father and her stepsiblings. She described having had positive relationships with the latter until her father turned them against her for telling her mother about his inappropriate sexual behavior. Ms. C. reported that her inheritance was taken away by her adoptive father and stepsiblings in retaliation against her disclosing the sexual abuse.

Ms. C. had been sober for sixteen years. It appeared that her history of depression and alcohol abuse was, at least in part, both an outcome of and a reaction to the emotional distance and cutoff position she occupied in her family system. She had been cutoff from her entire paternal extended family for the previous eleven years. Her paternal grandparents were dead, and she had no contact with any of her seven paternal uncles and aunts. Nor did she have any contact with her stepsiblings. Ms. C. had only one living grandparent, her maternal grandmother, whom she described as very cold and unwilling to share anything about the family. She had contact with one maternal uncle whose wife is dead, but she had no contact with the other uncle or his family.

The vignette of Ms. C. is another example of a high level of cutting off and a high degree of unresolved attachment in relation to her parents.

As can be seen in these vignettes, this author's clinical experience supports the view in Bowen theory that physical, emotional, or social symptoms emerge and are intensified in a family emotional system in which emotional cutoff prevails. The lower the level of differentiation and the higher the level of chronic anxiety, the more emotional cutoff can emerge and intensify in the variety of symptom types—emotional, social, and physical. The vignettes included from among innumerable examples from the author's clinical practice were chosen to demonstrate the continuum of cutoff—from growing away, to tearing away, to cutting off.

BRIDGING EMOTIONAL CUTOFF

This section of the chapter explores the interventions for bridging emotional cutoff in the family. The following topics are explored: (1) bypassing the nuclear family and (2) developing an open system.

Bypassing the Nuclear Family

Before specifically looking at the theory and methods for bridging cutoff, it is important to describe how bridging emotional cutoff became the central focus for clinical applications of Bowen family systems therapy. In the early 1960s Bowen shifted from a clinical focus on loosening the fusion in the nuclear family to a focus on the marital or parental fusion, with the therapist replacing the child in the triangle. In a final shift in clinical focus, Bowen's efforts were directed to modifying interlocking triangles involving the nuclear and extended families, including emotional cutoffs and functioning positions transversing many generations. Bowen (1974) described this shift in his thinking and clinical direction in a seminal paper, "Toward the Differentiation of Self in One's Own Family."

Following Bowen's breakthrough efforts to define himself in his own family of origin, with his newly acquired knowledge of the interlocking triangles expressing multigenerational emotional process and the interlocking patterns of fusion and cutoff, he began teaching and applying his newly expanded theory clinically. Bowen (1978) came to understand that, "It is not possible to differentiate a self in any single triangle without a method for dealing simultaneously with the interlocking triangles" (p. 531). His own experience in his family and his experience working with psychiatric residents between 1967 and 1969, in which coaching focused on their relationships in their families of origin, led to a clinical focus on the differentiation of self in one's family of origin. This approach replaced the primary focus on the marital relationship. He continued to intersperse work on differentiation of self in the family of origin with work on differentiation between the spouses. However, Bowen (1978) came to the following conclusion in 1974:

> *families in which the focus is on the differentiation of self in the families of origin automatically make as much or more progress in working out the relationship system with spouses and children as families seen in formal family therapy in which there is principal focus on the interdependence in the marriage.* [Bowen's italics] (p. 545)

It is necessary to describe what Bowen (1974) meant by differentation of self as the context for understanding the idea of bridging cutoff. The concept deals with the following:

the degree to which a person becomes emotionally 'differentiated' from the parent. In a broad sense, the infant is physically separated from the mother at birth. The process of emotional separation is slow and complicated, and at best incomplete. Originally, it has to do more with factors in the mother and her ability to permit the child to grow away from her, than with factors in the infant. In the background are a number of other factors, including the degree to which the mother has been able to "differentiate" herself from her parents, the quality of her relationships with her husband and her parents and all other people important to her, the number of reality stresses at the time, and her ability to deal with stresses. The degree of the child's involvement with the father has to do with the quality of the mother's relationship with the father. . . . The term "differentiation of self" was chosen as the one that most accurately describes this long-term process in which the child slowly disengages from the original fusion with his mother and moves toward his own emotional autonomy. (p. 74)

As has been described earlier in this chapter, Bowen's definition of differentiation shifted focus to the issue of unresolved attachment to parents, moving away from a focus on the emotional stuck-togetherness in the nuclear family or marital fusion. He moved his theoretical and clinical focus to the relationship between an individual and his or her family of origin.

Open versus Closed System

Bowen made a distinction between a relatively open relationship system and an emotional cutoff. An open system is one in which all family members have a modicum of emotional contact with one another—that is to say, a reasonable degree of one-to-one open communication with one another. There are of course wide variations in the level of contact and quality of contact of relationships in cutoffs and in openness. A system characterized by openness is the opposite of a system characterized by cutoff. The latter involves the absence of open, one-to-one contacts.

Bowen (1978) believed that relative openness or contact does not increase differentiation, but it does lower anxiety. When anxiety continues to be low, motivated family members can begin to make efforts to achieve a higher level of differentiation, including bridging emotional cutoff. When there is high sustained anxiety in a family, undifferentiation in the family will gradually increase.

Bowen described the value of increasing contact between family members in the following way:

> Any successful effort that goes toward improving their frequency and quality of emotional contact with the extended family will predictably improve their family's level of adjustment and reduce symptoms in the nuclear family. This is most striking in the families with more complete cut-offs with their extended families. The level of adaptability to stress is lower, anxiety is higher, and the family is extremely vulnerable to all kinds of human problems. To attempt family therapy that focuses directly on problems within the family can be long-term and non-productive. (1978, pp. 537-538)

In order to bridge emotional cutoff, not just make perfunctory or formalized contact with family members from whom one is cut off, one must define self in the extended family using three main principles and techniques: (1) working toward person-to-person relationships; (2) becoming a better observer and managing one's own emotional reactiveness; and (3) detriangling self in emotional situations.

Working Toward Person-to-Person Relationships

Gathering family history, meeting unknown family members, expanding contact and visits with extended family members and members of the family of origin, and attending important family events such as weddings, funerals, and graduations, among others, are important ways of lessening cutoff.

The open, person-to-person relationship consists of being able to speak about self as a person to one's parents or to other family members. Bowen (1978) wrote that it is very difficult to communicate openly and directly in a relationship for more than a few minutes at a time. When anxiety occurs, one or both family members become silent, talk about external things, or invoke a triangle. In addition, many individuals have a fairly well developed person-to-person relationship with one parent and a rather formal and distant relationship with the other (p. 236). A person-to-person relationship "is conceived as an ideal in which two people can communicate freely about the full range of personal issues between them" (p. 499). A person-to-person relationship consists of two people communicating directly with and to each other and showing mature respect for each other. It takes a fair amount of differentiation to accomplish this kind of relating. If one can develop a person-to-person relationship with each living individual in one's extended family, it goes a long way toward overcoming cutoff and working toward an open family system (Bowen, 1978, p. 540). Calmness and living out long-accepted functioning positions in communicating with family is not the same as what transpires in a person-to-person relationship. In the latter all the emotional foibles and issues the parents have in their own relationship and that existed in their own families of origin are revealed (p. 540).

Bowen believed that if an individual develops a person-to-person relationship with each living person in his or her extended family it will help him or her "grow up" more than anything else in life. Being "present, and accounted for" was a phrase Bowen often used, referring to the process of being with the family in a differentiated way when the family is going through a significant event or transition.

The quality and intensity of the cutoff will determine how difficult it is to bridge a cutoff. Of course, cutoff is a reciprocal process. An individual may begin to make contact with a family member and the latter may not respond in kind. However, it also takes two to cut off. If an individual continues to stay in contact with a person from whom he or she is cutoff, without getting reactive, eventually the other party may begin to reciprocate.

Becoming a Better Observer and Managing One's Own Emotional Reactiveness

Becoming a better observer, gaining more neutrality, and controlling one's own emotional reactivity are reciprocal processes. As an individual becomes a better observer of how the family operates as an emotional system, as opposed to blaming and being angry, he or she begins to gain the ability to be more emotionally neutral, to see the bigger picture. When this occurs an individual is better able to respond to family members with less automatic, emotional reactivity. When there is less reactivity there is an ability to better see the part that self plays in the problem, as well as the part played by the other family members. If one can be more neutral, there is less need to automatically distance or cut off from a family member to whom one is reactive. As Bowen (1978) put it:

> One never becomes completely objective and no one ever gets the process to the point of not reacting emotionally to family situations. A little progress on this helps the trainee [or family member] to begin to get a little "outside" the family emotional system, and this in turn helps the trainee [or family member] to "know" a different view of the human phenomenon. (p. 541)

Detriangling Self from Emotional Situations

According to Bowen (1978), the efforts to develop person-to-person relationships, becoming a more neutral observer while learning about the family, and controlling reactivity "help to create a more 'open' relationship system, and to reactivate the emotional system as it was before one's own cut-off from it" (p. 542). It is at this point, in terms of differentiation efforts, that an individual can see the triangles he or she grew up in, and can attempt to function differently in them. The effort is to be involved with important family members while dealing with an emotional issue, remaining neutral, and neither attacking nor defending. Differentiation cannot be accomplished through contact, observation, and the management of reactivity alone. It must involve relating to the family around a real, emotional issue. When the family is calm, the emotional issues are submerged and therefore work on differentiation cannot take place. The effort to deal with an emotional issue in the family is always unsuccessful if emotional confrontation takes place, rather than dealing with an emotional issue directly in a calm, objective, nonblaming manner.

Cutoff is related to the triangling process insofar as it involves an intensity with the parent(s), followed by a reactive distancing, and often a movement toward an intense fusion with a spouse. To reconnect with the cutoff parent there has to be a recognition of the fusion in the marital relationship. It takes an effort to move back toward the parent(s) with whom one once moved from fusion to a position of reactive distance in order to develop a relationship characterized by a reasonable degree of separateness with contact.

Bridging emotional cutoff involves detriangling insofar as the cutoff developed from an individual's having been fused with one parent and distant or cutoff from the other parent. Cutoff emerges from the primary mother-father-child triangle. The distance in the parents' marriage goes hand in hand with the emergent stuck-together fusion between one parent and a child. Eventually, when the youth enters the stage of separating from the parental generation, there is a reactive distancing that can be described as cutoff, with all its specific variations and behavioral manifestations. Therefore, it takes detriangling efforts, in conjunction with person-to-person contact, based on becoming a more neutral observer of oneself and one's family system, to fully modify a cutoff. Making contact will lead to functional change in the relationship, but it takes a systematic detriangling effort to make a basic change in overcoming a cutoff. Detriangling is the process, around an emotional issue, in which defining self occurs.

Bowen (1978) has described at length the process of detriangling as the basic method for defining self in depth. As has been described earlier in this chapter, cutoff is closely interlocked with the projection process and triangling. If reactive distancing behaviors have led to an emotional cutoff, the effort to reverse that process, to bridge cutoff, in the service of defining or differentiating a self, involves detriangling. Bowen (1978) defines the latter in the following way:

> When there is finally one who can control his emotional responsiveness and not take sides with either of the other two, and stay constantly in contact with the other two, the emotional intensity within the twosome will decrease and both will move to a higher level of differentiation. Unless the triangled person can remain in emotional contact, the twosome will triangle in someone else. (p. 480)

There are many forms that detriangling takes: expressing neutrality-objectivity, humor, reversal, systems questioning, and avoiding fusion by "putting the other together with the other" or "phantom other" (Titelman, 1998, pp. 39-45). A variety of efforts to work on bridging emotional cutoff will be described in other chapters in this book.

Bridging cutoff is accomplished by specific efforts to make contact with members of the family from whom one has either been internally isolated or physically distanced. Such an effort is most effective when it is part of a systematic effort to differentiate a self in one's own family—in the nuclear family, in the family of origin, and in the wider extended family. Such an effort is best undertaken in the context of individual or group coaching with someone who has been trained in Bowen theory and who has made a serious effort to define himself or herself in his or her own family.

Vignette: Efforts to Bridge Cutoff

An illustration of an effort to bridge cutoff draws upon the efforts of Mr. E., whose vignette, describing tearing away (moderate-level cutoff) was presented previously in this chapter (see pp. 42-44). The family diagram, Figure 1.6, illustrated cutoffs that existed between Mr. E. and his mother, him and his father, him and his stepmother, and him and his half siblings at the time he began psychotherapy. Rather than describe the entire course of the psychotherapy to date, the focus is on Mr. E.'s efforts to bridge cutoff in his family of origin and the ramifications of his efforts. The principles of bridging cutoff—working toward person-to-person relationships, becoming a better observer, managing one's own emotional reactiveness, and detriangling self from emotional situations—are illustrated in the description of Mr. E.'s efforts in the course of being coached.

When Mr. E. began therapy in 1992, he had seen his father only a couple of times in the previous ten years following his choice to go to a boarding school. He had a minimum of contact between age fifteen and his early twenties. Eventually, with the aid of coaching, Mr. E. (who had sporadic phone contact with his father) was able to begin to engage with him. He had to become less reactive to his father's tendency not to reciprocate contact. Gradually, Mr. E. was able to communicate his disappointment regarding his father's lack of involvement without being so reactive. The father was able to hear his son's wish to be involved with him, and over time they began to share more about themselves with each other. The coach asked questions of Mr. E. throughout this period to elicit more thoughtful responses that might help Mr. E. be more realistic about what he might expect from his father. The coach also asked questions regarding what Mr. E. expected from his father and what his response would be if his father did not fulfill his expectations. Other questions were geared to elicit thoughtful, rather than emotionally reactive, responses from Mr. E. about his functioning position in his family, the functioning position of the significant other members of his family, and how his position was located within a multigenerational emotional field. During the first two years of the coaching, the seeds of understanding cutoff were planted. Many years of hard work took place before Mr. E. began to build a bridge across cutoff. Throughout the coaching process the coach would seek to be neutral, not viewing Mr. E. as a victim of cutoff but an individual with choices and opportunities to work on the cutoff in his family.

In 1994, after a two-year break in the therapy when Mr. E. was planning to get married, he redoubled his efforts to be in better contact with his father and to begin to be in contact with his mother, whom he had not seen for several years. Both parents were invited to and attended the wedding. Much effort went into Mr. E.'s planning how he could spend some one-to-one time with each parent surrounding this event. His father came a couple of days before the wedding, and Mr. E. was able to spend individual time with him walking and talking about shared interests and the direction of Mr. E.'s life. At the wedding Mr. E.'s mother was able to be a part of the event, and there was some relatively comfortable interaction between his long-divorced parents. The coach's effort was to ask questions about what Mr. E. expected of his parents, how he would keep his expectations of them reasonable, and how he might have personal one-to-one time in the context of the emotional intensity of the ritual of marriage, in which considerable forces of togetherness are understandably evoked.

In 1995, Mr. E. continued his effort to bridge cutoff with his father. Mr. E. described it in the following way:

Eventually I got him to talk on the phone every Sunday night. We'd talk about music mostly, and he was supportive about my musical projects. In a rare moment of generosity, he sent me a harmonica microphone and subscription to a blues magazine for my birthday in May, 1995.

Eventually, in 1996, Mr. E. made a visit across country to visit his father, stepmother, and half brothers for ten days. The function of the coach was to ask questions. encouraging Mr. E. to reflect on what would it take to enhance the possibility of having a more direct, personal relationship with his father. Discussion of the usefulness of getting his father to share his vast experience in recording and producing music and the possibility of playing music together came up. Before going on the trip, coaching also focused on what the potential triangles would be, involving the stepmother and his half brothers in his relationship with his father. The coach reviewed with Mr. E. the pitfalls of the previous visit with his father and second family. Alternative ways of handling the intensity, conflict, and distance were elicited and reviewed. Compared to the visit of many years prior, before he started coaching, in which Mr. E. experienced a high level of tension and conflict with his stepmother and an inability to have a personal relationship with his father, Mr. E. was able to have meaningful one-to-one time with his father. They shared their interest in music (both played the guitar) and painting. They also were able to talk about the difficult times that had taken place when Mr. E. was an adolescent living alone with his father, who was then depressed and abusing substances. Mr. E. visited his old house and school. He was able to share his feelings of guilt at leaving his father when he was an adolescent, as well as his own feelings of abandonment. This is not to say that the visit was free of tension. Mr. E.'s father spent a good deal of time criticizing his wife. Mr. E. went on an overnight trip with his father during the course of the visit. It was the first time they had been alone together since 1980. Mr. E. described how his father dealt with the triangle of himself, his wife, and his son, Mr. E.:

> On our trip he told me that, because his wife and I didn't get along, he had felt he needed to choose. He said that he chose to focus on her and their new family. I then asked him if he would meet me halfway for some kind of short vacation together sometime. He said, "Oh, I could never take time off and not spend it with my family here." I don't think he realized how heavy these things were to hear. I could only respond with persistence—words of hope that we could connect more.

Mr. E. worked hard to stay detriangled by not taking the bait to criticize his stepmother and by trying to keep the focus on the relationship between himself and his father.

The visit was only a start at renewing and developing his relationship with his father and getting to know his two half brothers. Mr. E. had to continue to deal with a father whose hepatitis had left him seriously disabled. Mr. E. sought to maintain regular phone calls with his father. These had their ups and downs. It took a great deal of effort for Mr. E. to sustain contact when his father would slack off. Often he felt if he were to express his disappointment with his father, it would cause too much pain for the latter and he . would withdraw further from him. Gradually, he was able to understand his part, as well as his father's part, in the emotional distance between them. He began to understand that after he went away to boarding school his disappointment led him to play a part in the reciprocal process of cutoff with his father. He came to understand that his caretaking attitude and worry about his father's physical and mental well-being kept him from being more direct in the style and substance of contact with his father. He would submerge his own feelings and concerns when it came to dealing with his father.

In 1997 Mr. E. learned that his father was very ill. The Sunday night phone calls became fewer, but father and son continued to communicate. In addition to being present and accounted for during his father's illness, and for various family events and rituals. Mr. E. embarked on an effort to find his paternal grandfather, whom he had only seen once, as a five-year-old child, and whom his father had only seen one time after his parents divorced when he was a small child. Mr. E.'s father's subsequent stepfather was an abusive alcoholic. Mr. E. described his effort to search for his lost grandfather, a man of Latino descent:

> My grandmother knew some about his early life, so I started to try and construct a portrait of him. It took one and a half years, but I learned he had died in Texas two years before. He had moved there in the 1970s with his wife and he taught Chicano literature at a university. I wrote to his nurses, his colleagues, and his students for information. I got photos, stories, papers from his office (mostly dirty limericks written in Spanish). He died from Alzheimer's disease. I felt an unexpected sadness. I linked our stories—his, dad's, my own. All men who left home around fifteen and felt estranged from their fathers. I showed my dad what I found. He didn't seem moved but was happy that the mystery of his dad was solved. I started making a family tree and contacted a great-aunt in California.

The search for his grandfather helped Mr. E. to understand more about how his father was cut off from his grandfather and his stepgrandfather, and also how his grandfather was cut off from his father, by understanding the context for the cutoff. It was embedded in the multigenerational history of cutoff in his family.

In 1998, Mr. E.'s father, whose liver was not functioning, was in need of a liver transplant due to deterioration from hepatitis and moved back to New England without his wife to await a transplant and to be closer to his son and extended family. Mr. E. and his wife offered to take care of him. They helped connect him with a transplant team in Boston and took care of him. Mr. E. reported, "I felt good that he and I would have time together. He was so sick, however, that I could play only a parental role, and I felt disappointed." Shortly afterward, his father's wife and his half brothers joined his father in New England. Mr. E.'s effort was to relate to his father, his illness, and potential death with care, but without being overresponsible and without overfunctioning in a way that had characterized his position in relation to his father while he was growing up. This effort was complicated by the conflict, eventual separation, and divorce of Mr. E.'s father and his stepmother. Mr. E.'s adolescent half brothers, whose lives were not being structured by their parents, began to act out. Mr. E. worked hard not to get triangled in the relationship between his father and his stepmother, and in the relationships between his half brothers, his father, and his stepmother. Eventually, in 1999, Mr. E.'s father had a liver transplant and is still surviving, although he continues to struggle with low energy, depression, and short-term memory loss.

In March of 2000, Mr. E. organized and participated in an art exhibit consisting of his own work and that of his father, and also of a paternal uncle. At the opening of the show Mr. E.'s maternal aunt and his maternal grandmother read poetry, and he and his uncle were present. Mr. E.'s father was too ill to attend. At this time Mr. E. was feeling distant from his father once again, and his coach suggested he deal directly with his father about his upset at the lack of contact. Mr. E. describes it in the following way:

> I wrote him a letter at some point, asking, as I had many years earlier, that he make more of an effort to reach out. I still barely hear from him, but every once in a while he'll surprise me. Sometimes it's just a quick thinking-of-you call. But sometimes he'll have clarity, and we'll really share things deeply. I hang on to those moments.

At Christmastime, 2001, his two half brothers came from the West Coast, where they live with their mother, to visit their father. Mr. E. described their contact in the following way:

They were in such better shape! We had a nice time together, and they even came up to Vermont to go out to lunch with me. It's amazing the difference in my mind-set compared to ten years ago. Although we don't have much contact, I feel that I have three brothers out there. I wonder if we'll ever be closer?

While one of the foci of several years of coaching was directed at Mr. E.'s effort to bridge the cutoff with his father, intermittent attention was also paid to the minimal contact Mr. E. had with his mother. She was much more elusive than his father and the cutoff between mother and son was far greater than that between Mr. E. and his father. Following his wedding in 1995, Mr. E. did not initiate or receive contact from his mother for three years. In 1998, they started to have a minimal amount of contact through e-mail. Over the following three years Mr. E. continued to be in contact with his mother, who lived in the Southwest. They were able to share more information and began to have regular e-mail contact, exchanging what they were doing in their respective lives. Their relationship became more personal as they shared difficulties each was having and had experienced. At Christmastime in 1999, in Connecticut, Mr. E. got together with his mother and half brother. He experienced his mother as being his mother, fundamentally and biologically. He reported that they were very similar to each other in their physical appearance and in some of their ways of thinking. Mr. E.'s mother reported that she had married and divorced her fourth husband, who had Lou Gehrig's disease.

During the same visit, Mr. E. got together with his mother, half brother, father, paternal grandmother, and aunt. He felt as if it were the first time he had ever been with his parents together. Mr. E. took pictures of them together. Mr. E. described the dinner with both of his parents and his half brother in the following way:

> I joined her for a dinner at my [paternal] grandmother's house. Actually, her son was with her, and it was a very powerful evening. Both my parents were there together, and obviously shared a lot of love. I hadn't seen Alan since he was a baby, and now he was a college-bound guy; it was great to meet him. I was really struck that night with a feeling of Mother that I had never felt—that there was some ineffable bond there between me and my mom that was powerful. I also felt a kinship with Alan. From that night, we continued sporadic e-mail contact.

In August 2001, Mr. E. made his first visit in ten years to see his mother and half brother in Arizona where they now lived. They spent a week together. They talked; his mother really listened to him; and he felt she was supportive of him. For Mr. E. the connection with his mother was "magical, a beautiful presence and distance." Mr. E. described his response to his new stepfather and the continuing development of his relation with his half brother:

I got to know her husband a bit. He's a man's man, a law enforcer at a reservation, a fireman, a cowboy—but we found common ground. We're actually the same age! I also had time to bond with my half brother. It was really cool to notice our many similarities—body, temperament.

Mr. E.'s mother described how she had recently changed her first name, modifying her given name, in order to get separate from her own mother. The author would see the mother's name change more as unresolved attachment to her mother than as an effort to be more differentiated from her mother. Mr. E.'s mother described herself as being the most sane of her sisters and brothers. There were five girls and two boys. His mother described many generations of divorce and suicide in her maternal family. She described her mother as a very unreliable, abstract person. Communication between Mr. E. and his mother has continued following this trip.

Figure 1.10 illustrates the outcome of Mr. E.'s nine-year effort to bridge emotional cutoff in his family. It illustrates that he has more open, one-to-one relationships between himself and his mother, father, stepmother, and half siblings.

This type of effort is never finished or set in stone. He continues to develop a more open relationship with each parent. In what ways did Mr. E.'s effort to bridge cutoff in his family enhance his overall functioning? Besides having a better understanding of both his parents and himself and being less lonely and isolated from his family, Mr. E.'s sense of confidence and competence in his work and his art continued to grow, as did his professional accomplishments.

This vignette outlines his effort over a long period. Other issues were dealt with in the course of therapy. Initially he was working on distance in a relationship with a girlfriend that eventually ended. Later, in 1993, he began dating another woman. They married in 1995, separated in 1999, and divorced in 2001. This was a painful loss for Mr. E., although he played his part in the marital difficulties; he did not cut off from his ex-wife but has stayed in contact with her. Mr. E. has made many gains in dealing with his unresolved attachment to his parents, expressed by the work he did on bridging cutoff from them, but the fact that his intimate relationships, particularly the one with his wife, have been difficult indicates that the issues of fusion and cutoff are far from resolved. Nevertheless, Mr. E.'s capacity to initiate contact, observe and modify his own emotional reactivity, and work

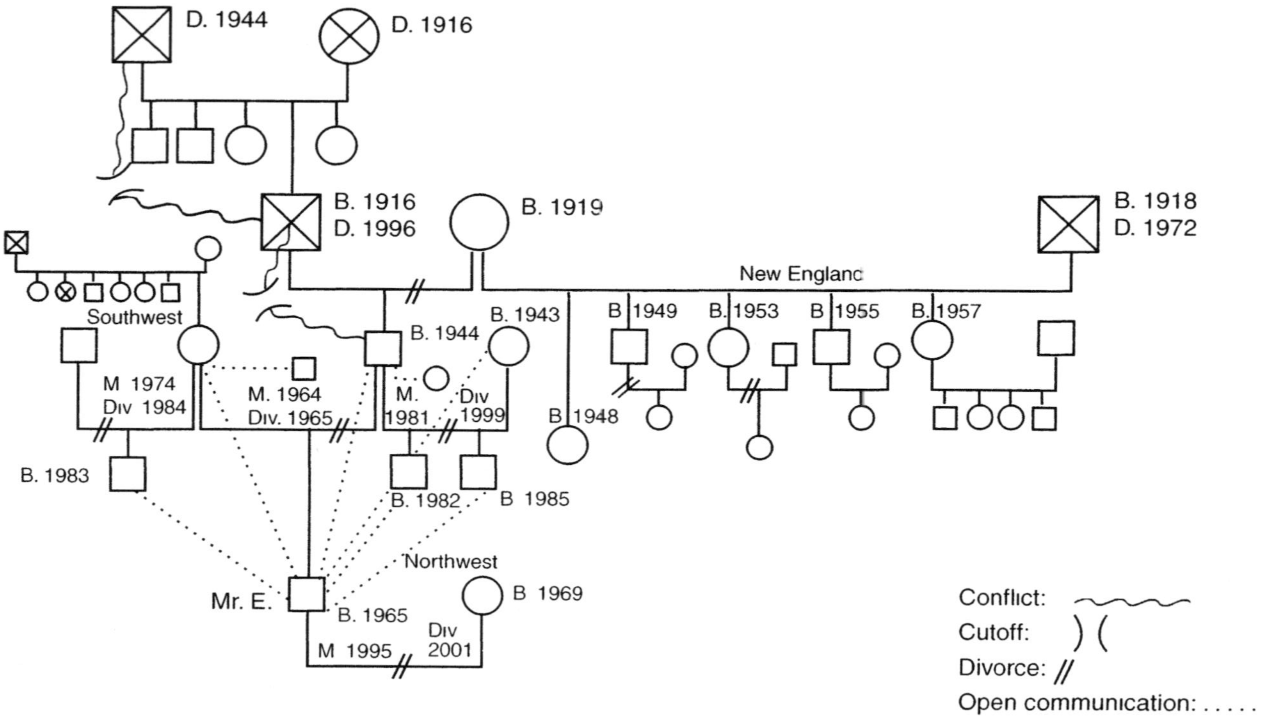

FIGURE 1.10. Brdging cutoff.

B. 1918
D. 1972

New Englanc

B. 1957

B. 1955

B. 1953

B. 1949

B. 1948

B. 1919

B. 1943

B. 1944

B. 1985

B 1969

Northwest

M. 1981
Div 1999

B. 1982

B. 1965
M 1995

Div
2001

D. 1916

B. 1916
D. 1996

M. 1964
Div. 1965

B. 1944

Mr. E.

Southwest

M 1974
Div 1984

B. 1983

Conflict:
Cutoff:
Divorce: //
Open communication: ......

64

to be detriangled suggests a higher level of emotional maturity or differentiation than that of either of his parents. How can that be accounted for? His basic level of differentiation seems to be not only somewhat higher than that of his parents but also the level of his chronic anxiety seems to be lower. In addition, he seems to have been subjected to less severe external environmental stressors than were either of his parents. Mr. E. was fortunate to have not been in the middle of a direct, or indirect, triangling process involving himself and his parents. The fact that he was nurtured to a great extent by his paternal grandmother and members of his paternal extended family (one paternal aunt and one paternal uncle) contributed to making a difference in his level of differentiation. When Mr. E. was asked how he accounted for his higher level of functioning in comparison to his father (who had drug addiction, physical illnesses, multiple divorces, severe career difficulties), he described his father as a "victim" and said that he had greater willpower and a clearer vision of his path than did his father. His coach would add that his efforts were aided by his tendency not to blame the other, his capacity to take responsibility for self, his curiosity and ability to observe and be neutral about how his family system operates, and his capacity to initiate and persevere in making contact with his parents, as well as others in the family, in the face of their tendency to cut off.

SUMMARY

In this chapter the author has provided a historical and theoretical overview of the concept of emotional cutoff in Bowen family systems theory. The chapter began by tracing the origin and evolution of the concept of emotional cutoff. This was followed by delineating the concepts of emotional cutoff and fusion in Bowen theory. The author then portrayed the link between the concept of emotional cutoff and each of the other seven concepts that constitute Bowen theory. The next section described the relationship between symptom formation and emotional cutoff, and, finally, the chapter dealt with bridging emotional cutoff.

REFERENCES

Anonymous (M. Bowen) (1972). "On the Differentiation of Self." In J. Framo (Ed.) *Family Interaction: A Dialogue Between Family Researchers and Family Therapists* (pp. 111-173). New York: Springer Publishing Company, Inc.
Bowen, M. (1970) *Nuclear Family Emotional System.* Videotape produced by the Georgetown Family Center, Washington, DC.

Bowen, M. (1974). "Toward the Differentiation of Self in One's Own Family." In F.D. Andres and J.P. Lorio (Eds.), *Georgetown Family Symposia*, Volume 1 (1971-1972) (pp. 70-86). Washington, DC: The Georgetown Family Center.

Bowen, M. (1978). *Family Therapy in Clinical Practice*. Northvale, NJ: Jason Aronson, Inc.

Framo, J. (Ed.). (1972). *Family Interaction: A Dialogue Between Family Researchers and Family Therapists* (pp. 111-173). New York: Springer Publishing Company, Inc.

Kerr, M.E. (2000). "Comments on Emotional Cutoff." Research Workshop Sponsored by the Georgetown Family Center, Washington, DC June 17 and 18

Kerr, M.E. and Bowen, M. (1988). *Family Evaluation*. New York: W.W. Norton and Company.

Papero, D. (1990). *Bowen Family Systems Theory*. Boston: Allyn and Bacon

Titelman, P. (1998). *Clinical Applications of Bowen Family Systems Theory*. Binghamton, NY: The Haworth Press, Inc.

Toman, W. (1969). *Family Constellation*, Second Edition. New York: Springer Publishing Company, Inc.

Chapter 2

Lone Wolves and Rogue Elephants: Emotional Cutoff Among Animals

Anthony J. Wilgus

INTRODUCTION

The human being is a social organism. In the United States today, there are estimates that the average person devotes 6.75 hours daily to interactions with members of the same species (McGuire and Raleigh, 1986). Despite this orientation toward "the other," individuals within *Homo sapiens* dwell on the fringes of this social interplay. Fictional characters such as Norman Bates or such real persons as Jeffrey Dahmer, John Hinkley, Jr., and Ted Kaczynski display degrees of isolation that are extreme. Their solitary lifestyles and bizarre behaviors carry a certain fascination for the general populace, who view these men as aberrant and sick. Consequently, they remain objects for scrutiny by both social scientists and tabloids.

Less dramatic examples are those people who function at the periphery of society. Lest humans believe that this phenomenon is a deviant occurrence restricted to the homeless, mentally ill, or segments of the prison population, Bowen theory posits the notion of emotional cutoff. The concept of emotional cutoff describes the ways in which the human attempts to distance self both internally and physically from unresolved attachments with the family of origin. As a consequence of this posture, and coupled with a climate of chronic anxiety, a variety of symptomatic outcomes emerge that encompass the physiological, emotional, and social arenas. Furthermore, this process operates within *all* humans in varying degrees of intensity (Bowen, 1978, p. 382).

It is the thesis of this chapter that these phenomena are not restricted to *Homo sapiens*. A review of animal behavior illustrates the evolutionary sub-

Presented at The Midwest Symposium on Family Systems Theory and Therapy, Chicago, Illinois, May 9, 1992.

strates for such functioning within the human. In the body of the chapter, there is an examination of solitary behavior among animals that live in groups and display some complexity in their social organization. The next segment of the chapter explores some of the significant variables associated with these behaviors, followed by a discussion of the consequences of isolation and emigration to the individual and to the group. Finally, the chapter relates these studies to the human condition and to the concept of emotional cutoff.

SOLITARY BEHAVIOR IN THE ANIMAL WORLD

Basic Concepts

Any discussion of solitary behavior must encompass not only a review of intraspecific interaction but also the spatial context in which these behaviors happen. Thus, it is important to examine concepts that relate to the territory occupied by the animal group under study. Waser and Jones (1983) define natal philopatry as "an individual's continued use of its natal home range past the age of independence from its parents" (p. 356). They also point out that female philopatry is a common characteristic in the primate world, in which the females of the group inhabit ranges that overlap.

Juxtaposed with the notion of natal philopatry is the process of dispersal, which Bekoff (1977) defines in the following manner: "Movement of an individual from its natal site and out of the home range of its parent(s) to another site at which it breeds, or at least attempts to pair with a conspecific of the opposite sex for purpose of a breeding" (p. 715). McFarland (1981) provides a broader context for this activity in his description of dispersion: "The dispersion pattern of a species is the distribution in space of individuals within their natural habitat" (p. 131). He goes on to note that two key variables impacting upon this process include not only interaction between group members but also topological factors. Related concepts include emigration (the departure from the home site) and immigration (the entrance into the home site of another).

In his classic study of lions, Schaller (1972) distinguishes between residents and nomads. Those identified as residents will live for more than one year or perhaps their entire lives in a specific area, whereas nomads will roam widely. Depending upon a variety of factors, these categories are mutable and not fixed (pp. 64-82).

A multidisciplinary conference in 1984 explored the concept of ostracism from a biological and social perspective (Gruter and Masters, 1986). For the purposes of this chapter, the definitions of this phenomenon are particularly relevant. Gruter and Masters define ostracism as "the general process of social rejection or exclusion" (p. 2), while Raleigh and McGuire (1986) view it as the "forced or involuntary exit from a desired social group or setting" (p. 55). Lancaster (1986) situates ostracism within the framework of the reproductive process and its concomitant competition for critical resources that suggests a broad continuum of behaviors for study: "If we define ostracism as socially induced exclusion from vital resources necessary for life and reproduction, then it becomes obvious that infanticide and intraspecific killing are immediate and final acts along a continuum that includes partial or complete exclusion from estrous females, safe sleeping sites, water and food" (p. 68). Consequently, ostracism is a process along a continuum of behaviors that may range from simple avoidance mechanisms, such as the aversion of eye contact, to acts of homicide, the ultimate exclusion from the group. Given these concepts, what are the manifestations of solitary behavior or emotional cutoff within the animal world?

Examples

Among animals that organize themselves in groups, there are situations in which an individual or group of individuals will leave that group either voluntarily or involuntarily. The sampling of species discussed is not meant to be comprehensive but rather illustrative of some of the processes of exclusion.

In their longitudinal studies of baboons, the Altmanns (1970) describe occurrences of isolation of individual members from the group. The isolated baboons fall into two categories: (1) those who are physically unable to maintain contact with the mobile troop and (2) those who are physically capable but do not appear to be part of any particular troop at the time of observation. Moreover, they detected a pattern of behavior with regard to the emigrating males who fall into the latter category: "The emigrant male had lost a fight—either with the most dominant male of the group or with a coalition of other males—several days before his departure. Yet in none of the observed cases were there any conspicuous wounds" (p. 57).

In his study of wolves, Lawrence (1986) highlights the characterization of the "lone wolf," noting that at certain times the individual will require solitude (p. 20) resulting in departures from the pack. He also observes situations in which females are driven from the group during the breeding season (p. 25). Likewise, Peterson (1979) reported the expulsion of a lower-ranking female by pack members after she had disturbed the hierarchical structure by mating with the alpha male. Schaller (1972) compiled a great deal of data on solitary lions over a three-year period. During that time, he identified 330 solitary lions, which represented 10 percent of the total population observed. He reports:

> Of 330 lions seen alone, 47 percent were adult males, 22 percent were subadult males, 27 percent were adult females, 3 percent were subadult females, and 1 percent were large cubs. When compared to the population composition . . . these figures show that adult males are alone nearly twice as often as expected, and subadult females much less frequently so. (p. 65)

In a study of emigration of subadult lions (i.e., ages twenty-five to forty-eight months), Hanby and Bygott (1987) concluded that the emigration of all subadult males and some subadult females corresponded with the takeover of a pride by a new adult male.

Among brown hyenas in the southern Kalahari, Mills (1983) finds that the loser in an agonistic interaction was the individual to emigrate from the group. Also, aggression by adult females toward younger females resulting in their departure seems related to the maximum number of females that the group would tolerate.

Jane Goodall (1986b) relates three behavioral contexts in which "social rejection," "exclusion," or "shunning" occurred among chimpanzees. The first instance included competition among members of their own group. An example of this behavior was the attack of Evered by two brothers, culminating in Evered's avoidance and withdrawal from the group. In another instance, a female chimpanzee, Skosha, whose mother and "foster mother" died, was the recipient of severe attacks by juvenile and adolescent males.

The second context in which exclusion occurs, according to Goodall, is the interaction that involves members of different communities. Hence, resident females may attack strange females (Tutin, 1975; Pusey, 1977) or adult males will exhibit violent behavior toward a strange mother and/or her offspring, occasionally resulting in the death of some or all parties (Bygott, 1972; Goodall et al., 1979). In addition, Goodall (1986a) described in vivid detail the obliteration of one chimpanzee community by another over a five-year period (pp. 503-513).

Finally, Goodall recounted the phenomenon she calls "shunning," in which chimpanzees in a group avoid the abnormal behavior of other members. An illustration of this process was the avoidance of two individuals within the troop who had contracted poliomyelitis (1986b).

Moss (1988) depicted the situation of a "loner elephant calf" who left the group to remain near a feeding and watering area, thereby conserving her strength and resulting in her survival (pp. 59-60). Examples of solitary individuals may also be found among the white-handed gibbon (Delaney,

1982), as well as the gorilla (Caro, 1976; Fossey, 1983). In his observations of chimpanzees at the Arnhem Zoo, Frans de Waal (1989) described the predicament of an excluded member:

> In view of their extreme territoriality, male chimpanzees may almost be regarded as captives in their own group; they cannot leave their home range without running into great trouble. A feral male suddenly finding himself . . . in a very uncomfortable position can only move to the periphery of the community range. In this no-man's-land he will have to keep one eye on his groupmates and the other on the boundary patrols of his neighbors. . . . Their fate has been characterized as "going into exile." (p. 72)

Based upon these descriptions, several characteristics of the individuals ostracized from the larger group emerge. Losers in a fight seem particularly at risk for emigration (Altmann and Altmann, 1970; de Waal, 1989; Mills, 1983) and, in many instances, reproduction appears to be a key element in these contests. Rank is another feature of some significance, as Wynne-Edwards (1962) emphasizes in his discourse on animal dispersion: "the individuals expelled are . . . usually the same, being the junior fraction of the hierarchy" (p. 483). Studies of the mountain gorilla (Harcourt, 1978) and gelada baboons (Dunbar and Dunbar, 1975) concur that lower-status females having difficulties in raising progeny will leave the group in an attempt to improve their reproductive opportunities. And de Waal (1989) recounts an incident in which an adult male chimpanzee apparently died at the hands of two other male chimpanzees as a result of shifting hierarchical coalitions within the Arnhem group (pp. 61-69).

Strangers also carry a vulnerability to exclusion that can sometimes erupt into the extremes of ostracism, namely infanticide, cannibalism, and homicide (Goodall, 1986a). The old and infirm also may experience isolation from the group, as Darling (1937) notes in his research on red deer:

> Sometimes an old stag will become anti-social and, either alone or with a fellow of like inclinations, will keep low all through the summer. . . . The solitary or semi-solitary old male is a common figure in many of the higher animal communities from the elephant and the cattle kind to man. (p. 80)

Another particularly intriguing dimension within a relationship context is the observation that loners seem to gravitate toward other loners, as suggested in Darling's account of solitary red deer just described. Again, Lawrence (1986) tells of the similarity among breeding pairs of wolves, among which it is not uncommon to find combinations of lone males and lone females. Schaller (1972) also reported an attraction between nomadic lions: "Generally a companion of the same age and sex is preferred, and a solitary individual possibly is accepted by another lone one more readily than by a group in which social ties already exist" (p. 68). In addition, a female gorilla lower in the hierarchy who has not had offspring may leave her natal group to mate with a lone silverback (Fossey, 1983).

Although these behaviors are interesting in and of themselves, the researcher must take into account the context in which they occur. Are certain environmental conditions more favorable to ostracism? Is there a particular phase in the life cycle of the group in which an animal is more vulnerable to exclusion? What are the relationship factors driving this process?

Ecological Variables

Environmental stressors play a significant role in the onset of social disintegration within various groups. Mark and Delia Owens (1984) described group fragmentation and "enforced isolation" of male lions from the pride during periods of drought in the Kalahari. Under similar conditions, elephant mothers with newborn calves engage in the unusual behavior of leaving the group, leading Moss (1988) to hypothesize that this departure was an attempt to avoid competition for limited resources.

Population density is another factor that precipitates dispersion and exclusion. As described previously, female brown hyenas will drive out other females when the maximum number of females in the group is attained (Mills, 1983). There is a slight variation in this process among lions: "population density of lions can affect emigration, particularly that of females, a greater proportion leaving permanently when the area, rather than the pride itself, is crowded" (Hanby and Bygott, 1987, p. 167).

Insufficient food supplies have an impact upon the social behavior of animals. Messier (1985) found a correlation between a low prey base and an increase in solitary living among adult wolves. Within this same species, Zimen (1976) reported that the stress of an inadequate food supply would result in an increase in hostility toward females by males, which would at times culminate in their departure from the pack. Among captive wolves, the withdrawal of food led to the emigration of low-ranking adults and juveniles, both of their own volition and as a result of the harassment by higher-ranking group members (Zimen, 1976).

Finally, Wynne-Edwards (1962) describes the interrelationship between food supply and population density, which then influences the processes of emigration and exclusion:

In general, the fluctuations in animal numbers tend to reflect the swings in available food-supplies so that optimum densities where possible shall not be exceeded and resource-damage be avoided. . . . When food supplies are fortuitously removed or fail to materialize, a local emergency of overpopulation results; and . . . this can be immediately relieved by emigration. (p. 482)

These ecological aspects are just a small sample of elements that can contribute toward the separation of an animal (or group of animals) from other group members. Some of the data suggest that rank is a factor in accounting for how the individual animal fares under the conditions of environmental stress. Consequently, an understanding of the process of exclusion and isolation cannot be divorced from a study of the interplay between the demands of the habitat and the relationship process within the group.

Relationship Variables

In order to survive, living organisms must reproduce. Little wonder then that a substantial amount of ostracizing behavior occurs not only at the time of reproduction but also in the service of ensuring progeny. The intensity of the timing of these behaviors is apparent in Messier's (1985) description of this phase among wolves: "The higher social stress within packs prior to and during the breeding season . . . likely explains the increasing tendency of some individuals to leave their pack during this period" (p. 244). Both Lawrence (1986) and Peterson (1979) note that exclusion of group members coincides with the mating season among wolves; Peterson also found that there is a penalty for not adhering to the hierarchy, inasmuch as the mating of a lower-ranking female with the alpha male resulted in her expulsion from the group on two occasions.

Additions of members, particularly the entrance of a new male into a group, can result in the emigration of both males and females as Hanby and Bygott (1987) report in their study of lions: "We conclude that take-overs by new adult males are an effective trigger for the emigration of subadult males, and also for subadult females under certain conditions of age and population density" (p. 164). Schaller (1972) observed that there was a general hostility by lionesses within a pride toward nomadic females and males except when the female (either within the pride or outside of it) was in estrus.

Lancaster (1986) would view reproductive activity as the main lens through which she would examine the processes of isolation:

Regardless of the benefits of "optimal outbreeding" and the natural expansion and contraction of regional populations in marginal habitats, the crux of ostracism and group transfer in primate society rests on understanding the specifics of reproductive competition. (p. 70)

From her perspective, females engage in competition for resources that will ensure the survival of their offspring, whereas male competition focuses upon the opportunity to mate.

Despite Lancaster's assertion, other relationship factors outside of the breeding event apparently contribute to this process. In an intriguing finding, Bekoff (1977) found that among canids, those individuals within a litter ' who interacted least with their siblings were the ones most likely to leave the group. On somewhat of a larger scale, after observing the breakup of elephant families, Moss (1988) concluded there were a variety of factors at play:

In each of these six cases there seems to be a different combination of factors accounting for the lack of family stability: the death of a matriarch, the size of the family, the strength of the bonds among the members, the presence of floaters in the family, the physical condition of an important member, and the attempted immigration of a stranger. (p. 216)

Regardless of the degree of significance that Lancaster attaches to reproduction as it relates to ostracism, it is clear that these behaviors have a relationship orientation. Whether it is the selection of a mate, the expulsion of a potential rival, or the death of the matriarch, the common thread is that of interaction among members of the same species.

Consequences of Exclusion

If the behaviors that result in isolation, ostracism, and exclusion have persisted in a variety of species over long periods of time, the inference may be that they serve specific functions. Raleigh and McGuire (1986) highlight some of the positive outcomes: "This forced dispersal may result in range extension, outbreeding, population density regulation, and the spread of learned traditions. Thus, from the point of the species as a whole there may, in fact, be many beneficial consequences of ostracism" (p. 56). Similarly, Archer (1970) comments upon the relationship between population density, aggression, and emigration:

Aggression spaces out individuals. The aggressive behavior of a given species is related to a certain range of population densities and the ecological conditions under which the species normally lives. As density increases, the reaction is an increase in aggression, so that surplus animals tend to be driven out to less densely populated areas. (p. 198)

This dispersion of the population can lead to enhanced opportunities for mating (Fossey, 1983; Lancaster, 1986; Lawrence, 1986) and to the settlement of sparsely populated areas (Hanby and Bygott, 1987). Wynne-Edwards (1962) provides a cogent summary of the beneficial impact of these strategies:

It can be concluded that two distinct biological functions are served by emigration. One is the "safety-valve" function, to give immediate relief to overpopulation; and the other is the "pioneering" function, to expand and replenish the range of the species as a whole and provide for gene-exchange. (p. 483)

There is another side to this equation that nature always provides. Consideration of the costs of exclusion are clear when examining the benefits of natal philopatry. The mortality rates for red foxes and water voles is lower for those who are philopatric than for those who disperse (Storm, 1972; Leuze, 1980). Black bears and rabbits that remain in their habitat of birth grow more quickly than those who leave their home range (Rogers, 1977; Mykytowycz, 1960). Lancaster (1986) also points out the evidence for increased mortality and morbidity among those extruded from the group, and Hanby and Bygott (1987) note that solitary lionesses have significantly diminished reproductive outcomes. In a comparison of dispersing and nondispersing foxes, Woolard and Harris (1990) found that " four of the nine foxes tracked during their dispersal period died when less than a year old, whereas all the non-dispersers survived for at least 12 months" (p. 719).

Obvious disadvantages also arise when engaging in even the basic functions of food acquisition. The lone wolf and the solitary lion will have access to very different kinds of prey than the entire group and must resort to strategies different from those available to their connected counterparts (Lawrence, 1986; Schaller, 1972).

Biology may not be destiny, but isolation certainly impacts that aspect of the organism, as McGuire and Raleigh (1986) note:

A number of biological processes, including those associated with hypothalamic-pituitary-adrenal, serotonin, and catecholamine function appear to be particularly responsive to forced isolation from social settings . . . experimental investigation indicates that ostracism exacts a substantial biological price. It is accompanied by reduced immune function and altered brain activity. (pp. 47,65)

Hence, when macaque monkeys are separated from their mothers, researchers have chronicled changes in the following functions: sleep patterns, heart rate and rhythm, circadian rhythms, body temperature, and immunological functioning (Reite and Short, 1978; Reite et al., 1978, 1981, 1982).

Similarly, Sapolsky (1994) found that baboons varied in their physiological responses to stressful events. Those with diminished social affiliations had higher stress hormone levels than their counterparts who were "most capable of developing friendships" (p. 264). Again, when he observed elderly members of the troop being extruded at a time when group living was most beneficial, the critical variable was the long-term ability in maintaining affiliative relationships:

> When I compared males who, in their later years, remained in the same troop with those who left, the former were the ones with the long-standing female friendships—still mating, grooming, being groomed, sitting in contact with females, interacting with infants. These are the males who have worked early on to become part of a community. (Sapolsky, 1997, p. 171)

Within the complex social structure of chimpanzee society, the outcomes of fractured relationships can have dire consequences, as de Waal (1989) eloquently describes: "Males have good reason to restore disturbed relations; no male ever knows when he may need his strongest rival. Holding grudges may cause isolation which within the coalition system amounts to political suicide" (p. 53). Finally, the costs of exclusion may include the life of the individual organism itself. Incidents of infanticide, homicide, and cannibalism—all of which are the extreme forms of exclusion—are now familiar within the literature of animal behavior (Goodall, 1986a; de Waal, 1989; Fossey, 1983).

CONCLUSION

Emotional cutoff describes the ways in which humans manage the intensity in their relationships via physical distancing or emotional withdrawal (Bowen, 1978; Kerr and Bowen, 1988). Among animals, it is fairly simple to conceptualize a continuum of spatial relationships that would range from natal philopatry at one end; dispersal and migrations in the midrange; entailing some overlapping of home ranges among conspecifics; and pioneering at the other extreme, involving an absence of contact with the area of birth. It would be possible to situate humans within a similar context, measuring the physical distance of the individual from the identified "home range" of a particular family unit. However, the spatial context is only one dimension that may or may not reflect the nature of the relationship process.

Another critical variable for animals and humans alike is the relationship process that can sometimes be manifest when examining the physical distance of an organism from its kin and/or home range. Thus, a relationship continuum that measures the nature of the interaction between members of the same species could range from individuals who remain within the group at one end, to individuals within the group who are shunned or avoided by some (or who themselves avoid certain group members), to those who remain peripheral to the group, to solitary animals (physical injuries, losers in a fight), and to those animals who are permanently excluded from membership through homicide or infanticide. The superimposition of this relationship continuum upon the spatial continuum would afford an opportunity to examine the way in which relationship factors operate within a framework of physical distance. One of the dilemmas with such a scheme is its inability to measure internal distancing mechanisms, which are a part of the human repertoire.

Homo sapiens is not immune from the ecological variables which affect relations of both individuals and groups of animals. The depletion of essential resources can have a significant impact upon an individual's capacity to function within a group. For example, researchers have documented a correlation between the unemployment rate and a variety of behaviors that result in exclusion. Hence, in difficult economic times, the crime rate increases with an accompanying rise in the incarceration rate—the exclusion of individuals from the larger group (Sviridoff and Thompson, 1983). Also, social problems such as homelessness (those without a home base) and suicide (another extreme distancing mechanism) increase during periods of deprivation (Hagen, 1987; Hamilton, 1989).

Another ecological component is that of the population density of a species. Within the animal world, it is evident that increases in population are a catalyst for individual and wholesale emigrations. As the numbers of *Homo sapiens* continue to grow geometrically with a concurrent exhaustion of natural resources, will there be similar types of responses that have been observed in nonhumans? Is it possible to view the growing fragmentation of nation-states and the flare-up of ethnic antagonisms as manifestations of this process?

There also are parallels between the relationship variables that have an impact upon both animals and humans. The addition and subtraction of key members within a group can result in the extrusion and isolation of certain individuals. The entrance of a "strange male" can not only result in the departure of subadult males within a lion pride but can also contribute to an adolescent running away from home in a remarried family. The death of a family matriarch within an elephant herd can result in the fissioning of that group just as the death of a clan leader among humans can contribute to the scattering of its members to varying geographic locales. The array of activities that occur around the reproductive act including competition, aggression, and violence is not unfamiliar to either the ethologist or the social scientist.

Moreover, the human is not exempt from the consequences of both isolation and migration. Stewart Wolf's study of the relationship networks in Roseto, Pennsylvania, found a higher incidence of physiological problems in those who emigrated from the region than from the family members who remained within the community (Wolf, 1966; Egolf et al., 1992). Volkart, Dittrich, and colleagues (1983); Volkart, Rotherfluh, and colleagues (1983); and Volkart (1983) studied the impact of solitary confinement among prisoners, finding a 50 percent increase in the incidence of psychotic behavior as well as significantly higher rates of depression and suicide among the isolated population. An impressive array of research now links decreased social networks in the human population with compromised immune functioning, higher levels of stress, poorer disease prognosis, and shorter life expectancy (Sapolsky, 1994, pp. 151-152, 326-327).

At the same time, there are benefits to the removal of self from an intense relationship system. Is there, in fact, a "safety-valve" function that operates among all forms of life in the distancing process, as Wynne-Edwards (1962) suggests for animals? Conflict reduction, increased opportunities for reproduction, and access to more plentiful resources are some of the potential byproducts of a distancing venture.

As humans vary in the degrees in which they emotionally cut off from those with whom they are connected, so also is there a range of responses to the relationship systems within the animal world as Schaller (1972) observed among lions: "Some animals tend to remain solitary, others associate casually for varying periods, and still others form companionships that persist for years" (p. 64).

Based upon the research within this chapter, it is proposed that the evolutionary roots for emotional cutoff can be found through careful scrutiny of the mammalian world. Any explanation of emotional cutoff in humans as well as nonhumans needs to account for the complex interplay of relationship factors within the group and the environmental context surrounding these organisms. "One" may indeed be the loneliest number that you'll ever know, and the roots for that singularity can best be understood within the context of human evolutionary heritage.

REFERENCES

Altmann, S. and J. Altmann (1970). *Baboon Ecology.* Chicago: The University of Chicago Press.

Archer, J. (1970). Effects of Population Density on Behaviour in Rodents. In Crook, J. H. (Ed.), *Social Behaviour in Birds and Mammals* (pp. 169-210). New York: Academic Press.

Bekoff, M. (1977). Mammalian dispersal and the ontogeny of individual behavioral phenotypes *American Naturalist* 111. 715-732.

Bowen, M. (1978). *Family Therapy in Clinical Practice.* New York: Jason Aronson, Inc.

Bygott, J. D. (1972). Cannibalism among wild chimpanzees. *Nature* 238: 410-411.

Caro, T. M. (1976). Observation on the ranging behaviour and daily activity of lone silverback mountain gorillas *(Gorilla gorilla beringei). Animal Behaviour* 24: 889-897.

Darling, F. F. (1937). *A Herd of Red Deer.* London: Oxford University Press.

Delaney, M. J. (1982). *Mammal Ecology.* London: Blackie and Son Limited.

de Waal, F. B. M. (1989). *Peacemaking Among Primates.* Cambridge, MA: Harvard University Press.

Dunbar, R. I. M. and E. P. Dunbar (1975). Social dynamics of gelada baboons. In Kuhn, H., W. P Luckett, C. R. Noback, A. H. Schultz, D. Starck, and S. S. Szaley (Eds.), *Contributions to Primatology* (pp. 1-157). Basel, Switzerland: Karger.

Egolf, B., J. Lasker, S. Wolf, and L. Potvin (1992). The Roseto Effect: A 50-year comparison of mortality rates. *American Journal of Public Health* 82: 1089-1092.

Fossey, Dian (1983). *Gorillas in the Mist.* Boston: Houghton Mifflin Co.

Goodall, J. (1986a). *The Chimpanzees of Gombe.* Cambridge, MA: The Belknap Press of Harvard University Press.

Goodall, J. (1986b). Social rejection, exclusion, and shunning among the Gombe chimpanzees. In Gruter, M. and R. D. Masters (Eds.), *Ostracism: A Social and Biological Phenomenon* (pp. 79-88). New York: Elsevier.

Goodall, J , A. Bandora, E. Bergmann, C. Busse, H. Matama, E. Mpongo, A. Pierce, and D. Riss (1979). Intercommunity interactions in the chimpanzee population of the Gombe National Park. In Hamburg, D. A. and E. R. McCown (Eds.), *The Great Apes* (pp. 13-53). Menlo Park, CA: Benjamin/Cummings.

Gruter, M. and R. D. Masters (1986). Ostracism as a social and biological phenomenon: An introduction. In Gruter, M. and R. D. Masters (Eds.), *Ostracism: A Social and Biological Phenomenon* (pp. 1-10). New York: Elsevier.

Hagen, J. L. (1987). The heterogeneity of homelessness. *Social Casework* 68: 451-457.

Hamilton, J. (1989). The first Canadians. *Canada and the World* 54: 29.

Hanby, J. P and J. D. Bygott (1987). Emigration of subadult lions. *Animal Behaviour* 35: 161-169.

Harcourt, A. H. (1978). Strategies of emigration and transfer by primates, with particular reference to gorillas. *Zeitschrift fur Tierpsychologie* 48: 401-420.

Kerr, M. and M. Bowen. (1988). *Family Evaluation*. New York: W. W. Norton.

Lancaster, J. (1986). Primate social behavior and ostracism. In Gruter, M. and R. D. Masters (Eds.), *Ostracism: A Social and Biological Phenomenon* (pp. 67-77). New York: Elsevier.

Lawrence, R D. (1986). *In Praise of Wolves*. New York: Holt and Company.

Leuze, C. C. K. (1980). The application of radio tracking and its effect on the behavioral ecology of the water vole, *Arvicola terrestris* (Lacepede). In Amlaner, C. J. and D. W. MacDonald (Eds.), *A Handbook on Biotelemetry and Radio Tracking* (pp. 361-366). Oxford: Pergamon Press.

McFarland, D. (Ed.) (1981). *The Oxford Companion to Animal Behavior* Oxford: Oxford University Press.

McGuire, M. T. and M. J. Raleigh (1986). Behavioral and physiological correlates of ostracism. In Gruter, M. and R. D. Masters (Eds.), *Ostracism: A Social and Biological Phenomenon* (pp. 39-52). New York: Elsevier.

Messier, F. (1985). Solitary living and extraterritorial movements of wolves in relation to social status and prey abundance. *Canadian Journal of Zoology* 63: 239-245.

Mills, M. G. L. (1983). Behavioural mechanisms in territory and group maintenance of the brown *Hyaena brunnea*, in the southern Kalahari. *Animal Behaviour* 31: 503-510.

Moss, C. (1988). *Elephant Memories*. New York: Fawcett Columbine.

Mykytowycz, R. (1960). Social behavior of an experimental colony of wild rabbits, *Oryctolagus cuniculus* (L.). *Commonwealth Scientific and Industrialized Research organization: Wildlife Research* 5: 1-20.

Owens, M. and D. Owens (1984). *Cry of the Kalahari*. Boston: Houghton Mifflin.

Peterson, R. O. (1979). Social rejection following mating of a subordinate wolf. *Journal of Mammalogy* 60: 219-221.

Pusey, A. E. (1977). "The physical and social development of wild adolescent chimpanzees." Doctoral dissertation, Stanford University.

Raleigh, M. J. and M. T. McGuire (1986). Animal analogues of ostracism: Biological mechanisms and social consequences. In Gruter, M. and R. D. (Eds.), *Ostracism: A Social and Biological Phenomenon* (pp. 53-66). New York: Elsevier.

Reite, M., R. Harbeck, and A. Hoffmann (1981). Altered cellular immune response following peer separation. *Life Science* 29: 1133-1136.

Reite, M., C. Seiler, T. J. Crowley, M. Hydinger-Macdonald, and R. Short (1982). Circadian rhythm changes following maternal separation in monkeys. *Chronobiologia* 9: 1-11.

Reite, M. and R. Short (1978). Nocturnal sleep in separated monkey infants. *Archives of General Psychiatry* 35: 1247-1253.

Reite, M., R. Short, and C. Seiler (1978). Physiological correlates of separation in surrogate reared infants: A study of altered attachment bonds. *Developmental Psychobiology* 11: 427-435.

Rogers, L. C. (1977). "Social relationships, movements, and population dynamics of black bears in Northeastern Minnesota." Doctoral dissertation, University of Minnesota.

Sapolsky, R. (1994). *Why Zebras Don't Get Ulcers*. New York: Freeman and Co.

Sapolsky, R. (1997). *The Trouble with Testosterone.* New York: Touchstone.

Schaller, G. B. (1972). *The Serengeti Lion.* Chicago: The University of Chicago Press.

Storm, G. L. (1972). "Population dynamics of red foxes in north central United States." Doctoral dissertation, University of Minnesota.

Sviridoff, M. and J. W. Thompson (1983). Links between employment and crime: A qualitative study of Rikers Island releases. *Crime and Delinquency* 29: 195-227.

Tutin, C. E. G. (1975). "Sexual behaviour and mating patterns in a community of wild chimpanzees *(Pan troglodytes schweinfurthii)*." Doctoral dissertation, University of Edinburgh.

Volkart, R. (1983). Einzelhaft: Eine Literaturubersicht. *Revue Suisse De Psychologie Pure et Appliquée* 42. 11-24.

Volkart, R., A. Dittrich, T. Rothenfluh, and W. Paul. (1983). Eine kontrollierte Untersuchung uber Psychopathologische Effekte der Einzelhaft. *Revue Suisse de Psychologie Pure et Appliquee* 42: 25-46.

Volkart, R., T. Rotherfluh, W. Kolbert, A. Dittrich, and K. Ernst (1983). Einzelhaft als Visikofaktor für psychiatrische Hospitalisierung. *Psychiatria Clinica* 16: 365-377.

Waser, P. and W. Thomas Jones (1983). Natal philopatry among solitary mammals. *Quarterly Review of Biology* 58: 355-390.

Wolf, S. (1966). Mortality from myocardial infarction in Roseto. *JAMA* 195: 186.

Woolard, T. and S. Harris (1990). A behavioural comparison of dispersing and non-dispersing foxes *(Vulpes vulpes)* and an evaluation of some dispersal hypotheses. *Journal of Animal Ecology* 59: 709-722.

Wynne-Edwards, V. C. (1962). *Animal Dispersion in Relation to Social Behaviour.* New York: Hafner Publishing Co.

Zimen, E. (1976). On the regulation of pack size in wolves. *Zeitschrift für Tierpsychologie* 40: 300-341.

Chapter 3

Emotional Cutoff and the Brain

Priscilla J. Friesen

INTRODUCTION

The concept "emotional cutoff" in Bowen family systems theory describes the mechanism for managing anxiety related to the connection with one's original family. Emotional cutoff is manifested in physical distance, internal distance, or a combination of both in order to create a life of one's own. Bowen observed these patterns in the behavior and psychology of individuals (Bowen and Friesen, 1988). The interplay between emotional cutoff and physiological functioning can be considered the underpinnings of behavior and psychology from the point of view of Bowen family systems theory.

This chapter addresses the concept of emotional cutoff at the level of physiology of the brain. One measure of the brain's functioning is through the mechanism of neurofeedback. Neurofeedback measures and relays specific patterns of electrical activity in the brain to the individual via a system of electrodes connected to a computer. Neurofeedback is also known as electroencephalograph (EEG) biofeedback as developed by Sterman and Friar (1972), Lubar (1991), Green, Green, and Walters (1970), and Peniston and Kulkosky (1989).

For the clinician using neurofeedback in the context of Bowen family systems theory, variation in these electrical patterns between people and within one person over time raise some interesting questions: How can these variations be understood? What are these patterns of the brain responding to? Can the patterns of the "individual" brain reflect the patterns of relationships? How do the processes Bowen described in the family relate to the in-

My appreciation goes to numerous colleagues who have engaged with me in the synergy of ideas over the past twenty-five years. I would like to thank Dr. Joan Lartin-Drake for her generous and tenacious assistance in editing this chapter, Elizabeth Utschig for producing the graphics, and the subject of the clinical case for her interest and willingness to contribute her experience for others to learn.

dividual brain? How do brain patterns within the individual relate to emotional cutoff between the generations?

The purpose of this chapter is to address these and other questions that are a natural consequence of using this technology in a clinical setting. This chapter posits a fundamental assumption that the structures and functions of the human brain are a culmination of the coevolution of social units/systems and the brain itself. In other words, the electrical patterns seen in an individual brain on neurofeedback probably reflect an evolutionary interplay with the relationship environment (i.e., family) that has been essential for its survival in the human. In order to explore this thesis, the evolutionary development of the brain in the context of the family will be described.

In addition, information about electrical patterns in the brain is described. Some observations, questions, and preliminary conclusions about ways in which emotional cutoff is manifested in neurofeedback are presented and then illustrated in a clinical case.

THE HUMAN BRAIN

Evolution

In his book, *Evolving Brains* (1999), Allman describes the evolution of the human brain. His thesis is that the complexity of the human brain evolved in conjunction with the development of the extended family as the social group. The complexity of the human brain can be seen as a by-product of a three-generation social unit.

Allman cites a difference in the size of the brains of those primates that have a multigenerational social unit and those that have a dyadic social unit. Humans, bonobos, and chimpanzees raised in three-generation social groups have a larger cortex than species that are raised in a dyadic social group such as gibbon, orangutan, and siamang. In looking at the variables of the generational character of the reproductive unit and brain size, there is no overlap between the groups (Allman, 2000, personal communication).

A three-generation reproductive unit means that there is knowledge of and association with at least three generations. In the dyadic reproductive unit, the group of association is the same generation of peers raising their young. In the human, reproductive units may have varied association with three generations, but three generations are typically known. The range of the human reproductive unit's association patterns includes three or more generations relating closely with one another to three generations that are known but have little or no contact. It is the author's suggestion that this variation in association patterns among generations within the human species is linked to the concept of emotional cutoff as a mechanism regulating the attachment among the three generations.

The size of the cortex corresponds to the number of neural connections present. The connections create an expanded adaptive capacity needed in a multigenerational context. The ability of the brain to have an increased variety of choices for survival-related decisions can be linked with the presence of a social unit that is both multigenerational and more dependent for a longer period of time. A human infant requires eighteen to twenty-one years of potential development and dependence upon the social group for its survival and maturity (Hannaford, 1995). This prolonged period of development allows for remarkable levels of diversity in adaptation. The next section explores this thesis, namely, that the brain can be thought of as a "relationship organ."

Brain Development

Physical and emotional development in individuals within each generation provides a window to observing how each generation varies and what the mechanisms are for transmission of patterns from generation to generation. It might be possible to look step by step at the development of the brain and the coinciding processes present in the family. This may allow for an understanding of the mechanisms present that produce variations in the individual brain and how those variations are passed from one generation to the next.

Development takes place within an environmental context. Our genes, cells, senses, and muscles require the environment to develop. What is the "environment"? At the earliest point, it is the uterine environment of the mother. The physical and emotional condition of the mother is the environment of the developing fetus. The fetus experiences the mother primarily through her changing hormonal state. This hormonal state is regulated by her experience of her life moment to moment—how glad is she to be pregnant; how does the pregnancy affect her marriage? If she is not married, how does she experience her situation? Does she have a mother and extended family? What is her relationship with them?

Science is discovering more about the effects drugs, malnutrition, and trauma have on stages of uterine development, thus having a long-term impact on the life course of a developing individual (Hofer, 1981). These are the more gross observations. In addition and perhaps more fundamentally, I suggest a more subtle level of impact. The development of the sensory experience of the fetus and infant is primarily influenced by the mother's experience of her own world. The mother's own anxiety level, and her relationship position and functioning mold the basic sensory development of the child. The mother's experience of her own mother and father's marriage is reflected in her emotional experience and therefore is communicated in her hormonal reactions. As she experiences the ebb and flow of increased or decreased arousal levels in response to her life, that too is communicated to the fetus. These reactions have an impact on the mother's own relationship with the child's father, and the fetus responds to that interaction long before it is aware of the parents' interaction per se. This is how fundamental the relationship nuances are and how they are built into our brains.

The way we experience the world is highly variable. The way we develop our senses, how they are organized and related to each other, and the way we interpret the information are all variations that are relationship dependent. The environment in which these variations occur is the relationship system.

Bowen Theory and Brain Development

From a Bowen theory point of view, there are three factors affecting a child's brain development:

1. The level of differentiation of the family unit in which the child is developing
2. The level of anxiety present during different developmental stages
3. The position of the developing individual in the anxiety regulation of the family or the extent to which the child is absorbing anxiety— related to the family's methods of anxiety regulation

Level of Differentiation

The level of differentiation of the family is a composite of the functioning of its members. The more emotionally dependent family members are on one another, the more reactive they are to one another. These family members are physiologically organized to be highly reactive and responsive to one another. They heavily rely on mechanisms such as social or emotional distance, conflict, adaptation of a spouse, and projection of anxiety to manage this anxiety. Thus, these families have the most relationship problems and emotional, social, and physical problems expressed by individual members. From a sensory integration point of view, the perception of the environment by the individuals in this kind of family is constrained and limited as the individuals organize automatically for survival.

Individuals in families at higher levels of differentiation function more independently of each other. During anxious periods, they are able to optimize the benefits of cooperation that a family unit affords and manage the anxiety with more resilience. Individuals and families at higher levels of differentiation rely less on anxiety-regulating mechanisms, such as physical or emotional distance, to manage themselves in their families. The sensory perception of the environment is more considered and less survival oriented.

For a child developing in these varying ranges of functioning, the basic brain structures and functions are developing in concert with similar levels of brain organization as his or her parents. That is, the way the parents' experience the world and respond is the primary influence upon the child's own development. These patterns of experience and response can be observed in the organization of the brain. These patterns are an aspect of levels of differentiation.

Emotional cutoff corresponds to level of differentiation. Emotional cutoff occurs more at lower levels of differentiation, providing a current solution but exaggerating the problem in the next generation. People with higher levels of differentiation have more viable connections with the generations present, providing more flexibility in managing the challenges life presents. The more relationships present, the more flexibility in functioning for the individual. People with lower levels of differentiation have less multigenerational connection, producing more dependence on the present generation. That is, the more rigid the patterns of intergenerational relationships, the fewer relationship options are available and a decrease occurs in the individual's functioning.

Level of Anxiety Present During Individual's Development

The level of acute anxiety present in every family varies over its life course. How individuals and families experience anxiety varies with different levels of differentiation. The higher the level of differentiation, the more a member of a family has the ability to perceive or experience the environment with more options and less reactivity, and can manage anxiety while developing fewer symptoms.

At lower levels of differentiation, life is experienced as a threat more of the time. Life presents challenges. A child born when there is a high level of family life challenge will be impacted differently than a child born during a less challenging period of time. The earlier in the child's development the family challenge occurs, the greater is the lifelong impact.

For example, a child is developing during the second trimester of pregnancy when her maternal grandmother suddenly dies. The child, a girl, is born three months later, on what would have been her grandmother's birthday. This child, as an eight-year-old, displays a high level of social anxiety as well as learning difficulties related to the intense fusion with her mother.

The child was in the womb and born in the midst of a challenging period in the life of the family.

The grandmother had experienced forced immigration due to war during her young adulthood, leaving her with minimal contact with her original family in her adult life. She raised her own children without grandparents and with minimal extended family. To the extent the grandmother was cut off from previous generations, she invested her life energy more intently into her children.

The pregnant mother in this case is vulnerable to a disruption in the relationship with her own mother. The grandmother's death during the pregnancy affects the mother's own emotional well-being. The emotional state, primarily transmitted through the hormonal state of the mother, is the environment for the final stages of sensory organization and integration during the third trimester. The birth of the child on the birthday of her deceased grandmother seals the association between the disruption of the relationship with the grandmother in her death and the newborn. The young mother describes the time between the death of her mother and the early years of her daughter's life as a blank. A disorganized, distracted mother provides a disorganized environment for a developing child.

The mother and her offspring inherit a degree of intensity between them. The intensity between the pregnant mother and her own mother is a product of the grandmother's investment in her children as she dealt with her own disconnection. The intensity is also related to the disruption in the mother-grandmother relationship with the grandmother's death as the next generation is born. This intensity is transmitted into the next generation with a resulting heightened arousal level in the child that can be observed with persistent cold hands and high levels of distraction in her EEG patterns on the biofeedback machine.

This family is highly educated and otherwise high functioning. The child's level of social anxiety and academic problems are unusual for the family. Had the grandmother died when the granddaughter was thirteen years old, the death would have had a different impact on the daughter. It may have then had more of an impact on a different aspect of the granddaughter's development, such as her experience of maturing and becoming more independent, rather than her basic sensory organization, which affected her ability to learn and her state of well-being in relationships.

Position of the Child in the Anxiety Regulation of the Family

The position that the developing child plays in the anxiety management of the family is related to the impact of life challenge upon the development of the brain. In the family just described, the family worried about the well-being of the child born at this important time. The anxiety related to the sudden loss of the grandmother was exaggerated when the birth occurred on the birth date of the grandmother three months after her death. The child was a girl, the same sex as her grandmother, and in the tradition of the family the child was named for the grandmother. All this contributed to an increased focus on the child. Perhaps the anxiety would have been a bit less had the child been a boy. Had the anxiety been "managed" in the marriage with increased marital conflict leading to a divorce, the child's functioning would have been differently impacted. Had the death of the grandmother occurred as the granddaughter was entering adolescence, it might have activated something different in the mother. The mother had had a difficult time with her own mother at that time in her life and so the death then might have funneled anxiety into the relationship between the mother and granddaughter. This pattern often results in acting-out behavior on the part of an adolescent daughter.

These three factors—level of differentiation of the family, level of anxiety present during different developmental stages, and the position of the developing individual in the anxiety regulation of the family—provide a framework for seeing the remarkable capacity our species has for adaptation. The way a family adapts to challenges during the development of its members sets the stage for adaptability into the next generation. It sets in motion both the potential for adaptation and constraint in the next generation.

EMOTIONAL CUTOFF AND BRAIN DEVELOPMENT

The human species has one of the longest periods of offspring dependency on the parent; the time the human offspring responds to the family unit in its potential development is twenty-one years (Hannaford, 1995). With a genetic underpinning also influenced by the environment, the structure and functioning of each individual brain, mind, and body occurs as the individual brain develops in the interaction with its family and social environment. I suggest that the developing individual brain adapts to the influences of the multigenerational family and is the basis for individual differences in functioning.

The concept of emotional cutoff will be discussed within the context of these assumptions about the brain. How is sensitivity to the previous generation passed to the next? It is hypothesized that emotional withdrawal from one generation in order to create the next generation is not only a behavioral phenomenon. In order to move into his or her own life and reproduce, an individual may respond with distance from his or her parents. This response or emotional cutoff has a physiological as well as emotional and behavioral substrate. It is the physiological reactivity present in the individuals constituting the new parental unit that sets the stage for the reactivity in the next generation. A mother's way of dealing with the acute and chronic anxiety in her own family lives in her physiology. Beginning in utero, the reactivity of the mother and her relationship to her family is communicated primarily at the hormonal level, influencing the development of the senses and their organization and the basic patterns of reactivity, all of which influence the ability of the infant to survive.

Emotional cutoff describes a pattern of reactivity that requires distancing oneself emotionally and/or physically in order to act on one's behalf into the future. Emotional cutoff may refer to actually putting physical distance between self and one's family. There may be an optimal distance. For example, six hours distance may seem optimal as long as it is on the same continent or each sibling unit has his or her own city. What is considered a comfortable distance from family varies. Another individual might consider it incomprehensible to live anywhere other than the town where his or her parents are buried.

Individuals may disregard or be unaware of the impact their families have on them. They may say they do not like their family and see no reason for continuing contact with them; they have "moved on." Emotional cutoff may also be more internal. Individuals may live in the same town or house and be emotionally disconnected from one another. In this case, individuals may lose energy or shut down in the presence of family, or focus on the baseball team, or complain about others. All of these stances serve to separate individuals from one another. This process of moving away from relationships reduces complexity and diversity in the short run. It produces more rigidity or a predictably patterned response that can be observed not only in behavior but also in the psychology and physiology of the individual.

At higher levels of differentiation, the process of moving away from the family of origin into one's own life is natural and smooth. Families with more anxiety require some emotional cutoff to make the transition to the next generation. The term *emotional cutoff* refers to a mechanism that happens in all families to some degree as generations develop and configure new family units. This chapter addresses how the intensity of this process is passed from generation to generation.

A clinical case that illustrates the ideas of emotional cutoff and the individual's behavioral, emotional, psychological, and physiological functioning, as well as the family relationships, is presented. It describes how functioning, particularly when significant emotional cutoff is present, can be observed in the family and in an individual's brain and physiology with biofeedback. Bowen hypothesized that if a person can move into meaningful contact with previous generations, there is a decrease in anxiety in the present generation and an increase in functioning. The author believes that a change in the relationships is correlated with a change in the brain. Bridging cutoff changes the adaptability of the brain and physiology of the bridging individual.

To understand this in relationship to the concept of emotional cutoff, a brain that develops with more contact between more generations may develop more intrinsic ability to discriminate the input from the senses with a wider range of possible associations and behaviors. A brain that develops within a more limited relationship system has more reliance on fewer individuals. The individuals they are dependent upon have fewer resources themselves and are more vulnerable to a heightened experience of threat. The sustained increased experience of threat can be transmitted to the developing individual in the next generation. The more the experience of heightened threat, the more the individual will react to the threat for survival. The short-term solution is protective, but as a long-term solution withdrawal builds less resilience and fewer alternatives into the brain, physiology, and behavior of the next generation.

The ability of an individual to evaluate new situations and make decisions is essential for optimal adaptation. In the human species, it appears that the brain develops within a social structure that requires at least three generations for optimal adaptation.

Bridging cutoff also changes relationships. Theoretically, bridging cutoff not only changes the individual initiating the behavior but affects all in the emotional unit. The clinical case illustrates this.

The human brain is a product of the evolution of the human family. It has developed within the set of relationships necessary for survival. These interdependent relationship patterns have led to the development of our complex and adaptive brains. As the next section elaborates, perhaps a broad and connected extended family matrix provides the most functional potential for raising the next generation.

EMOTIONAL CUTOFF AND BRAIN FUNCTIONING

Allman discusses the importance of the *anterior cingulate gyrus* (Allman et al. 2001). This structure of the brain is considered a part of the cortex; it is located deep within the cortex, close to the subcortical portion of the brain. Allman describes the anterior cingulate gyrus as the focal structure for evaluating new situations and making decisions. This structure is important because of its linkage between the subcortical areas of the brain and the cortex. The subcortex is the deeper, survival-oriented portion of the brain. This linkage is made early in human development, with neuronal migration between subcortical and anterior cingulate gyrus beginning within days of birth (Allman, Hakeem, and Watson, 2001).

The first fruits of the ability to decipher basic sensory information and to build in the ability to respond to it with cortex potential has profound resonance with Bowen's concept of differentiation (Bowen, 1978). It can be inferred from this knowledge of early brain development that the difference in social structures or the number of individuals present in the social system of an infant *is* the basis for the connection between the lower parts of the brain (survival or automatic functions) and the cortex. That is, the early neuronal pathways developing the basis for the functioning of the anterior cingulate gyrus are established in the early family relationships. This variation in the functioning of the anterior cingulate gyrus is associated with the three-generation family.

Allman (2000, personal communication) also suggests that multigenerational interdependence might be a better criterion for social complexity than simply the actual numbers of individuals present in a social group. For example, individuals in a social group based upon three generations of family may have more neuronal pathways between the subcortical regions of their brains and the anterior cingulate gyrus in the cortex. This means that an individual's ability to evaluate and consider possible reactions to a situation is based upon the multigenerational complexity of his or her relationships and is reflected in brain functioning. In addition, this may be more relevant to complexity and variation in the brain than the presence of a large, unrelated social group.

Bowen described an individual's ability to distinguish the automatic "feeling" reactions from the "thinking" ability as fundamental to differentiation. This psychological description may be consistent with the function of the anterior cingulate gyrus. It may relate not only to brain functioning but also to the complexity of the multigenerational family in which the individual brain develops. This may be one function of the brain relating to the level of differentiation.

To extend this idea further to the concept of emotional cutoff, this author suggests that there is a relationship between the complexity of the extended family into which one is conceived, born, and nurtured and the structures and function of the brain. The more limited the relationship connection with multiple generations of a family, the more constrained the adaptation of an individual brain.

Bowen's concept of emotional cutoff describes the nature of relationships from one generation to the next. This concept also describes the trend toward decreased social complexity as anxiety increases. The outcome of decreased complexity is a constraint in the flexibility of functioning in subsequent generations. Knowledge of the brain may illuminate how solving relationship issues by increased emotional distance between the generations is a physical response on the part of the organism itself—one that seems to produce an internal constraining experience as well as a behavioral one.

The evolutionary nature of the brain also provides a context for understanding a broader range of human social potential. What is optimally possible for the human? Does this evolutionary basis provide the ability to form even larger, more complex adaptive social groups, such as businesses, churches, and organizations, to cooperate for the greater good of individuals, even beyond nuclear and extended families?

Bowen theory describes the emotional processes that occur in human social groups and the ways in which these processes can build in flexibility over the generations. His theory looks at the family over many generations and describes the patterns that are transmitted. One aspect of those patterns is the way in which each generation organizes itself in relationship to the previous generation. Bowen describes the variation in the human family that evolves over at least three generations to create the diversity that optimizes the family's ability to survive.

Biofeedback, Neurofeedback, and the Family

For more than twenty years, the author has observed many individuals' physiological responses via biofeedback technology. Using this technology, individuals simultaneously receive information through sight and sound about their brain waves, blood pressure, heart rate, vascular blood flow (hand temperature), muscle tension, respiration, and sweat response. This information is used to assist individuals to change their body's automatic responses through use of the mind, developing self-regulation. The clinician can also use the information to observe how it corresponds to emotional reactions as the individual is speaking about his or her life. Over time, one can see changes in the physiology related to relationship changes. Monitoring a person during consultation sessions supplies both an immediate feedback during conversation as well as information at the end of a session. One can also compare sessions over time.

Each individual has a physiological profile, or a consistent way that his or her body responds. Within this response pattern, an individual varies in the intensity and severity of the response. For example, the amplitude, the dominant frequency of a brain wave, as well as its synchrony with other waves constitute a given pattern. Another response pattern is the intensity of a muscle response and the ability to recover after a challenge. These physiological patterns correspond to level of differentiation, level of anxiety, and patterns of anxiety management in relationships.

Biofeedback and brain wave biofeedback (also known as neurofeedback) shows the physiological reactivity present in individuals. Biofeedback usually describes the process of self-regulation through the learned control of the autonomic nervous system, including muscle tension, hand temperature, sweat response, and heart rate. Electroencephalograph (EEG) biofeedback and neurofeedback refers to the process of learning control of the central nervous system or brain waves. For the purposes of this chapter, references to neurofeedback or biofeedback include both the central nervous system and the autonomic nervous system. Although immediate feedback may be focused on the central nervous system during training, the autonomic nervous system responses also are collected. All the physiological data is considered at the end of the session. In addition to training with the central nervous system, ongoing information from the autonomic nervous system displays the nuances of reactivity during talking, thinking, and training. From a training point of view, neurofeedback is quicker, but information from the physiology is invaluable in understanding the connections between one's relationships and reactivity at the level of physiology.

The underpinning of the response patterns is genetic. It is genetic that one individual reacts predominantly with a cardiovascular response and another tends to have a gastrointestinal response. However, the intensity, frequency, and duration of the individual's patterns of physiological response is developed in the context of the family and varies with the individual's differentiation. The ability to regulate oneself is at the core of differentiation. Biofeedback used with Bowen theory associates the individual's reactivity with relationships. Biofeedback is used to increase the ability to regulate oneself by seeing one's automatic patterns of response and associating them with one's position in the relationship processes. Developing more ability to regulate self through biofeedback can be a part of the process of differentiation of self.

Neurofeedback and the Central Nervous System

Neurofeedback or brain wave training involves the central nervous system (CNS). Neurofeedback measures brain waves with EEG (Figure 3.1). The electrical patterns measured on the surface of the head with neurofeedback technology are by-products of the chemical actions taking place within the brain. The measurement of the electrical patterns from the head is a gross measurement of the summary of electrical activity happening within the brain at a moment in time. The electrical patterns are a range of electrical

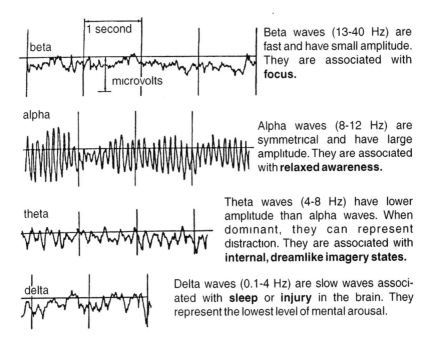

Beta waves (13-40 Hz) are fast and have small amplitude. They are associated with **focus.**

Alpha waves (8-12 Hz) are symmetrical and have large amplitude. They are associated with **relaxed awareness.**

Theta waves (4-8 Hz) have lower amplitude than alpha waves. When dominant, they can represent distraction. They are associated with **internal, dreamlike imagery states.**

Delta waves (0.1-4 Hz) are slow waves associated with **sleep** or **injury** in the brain. They represent the lowest level of mental arousal.

FIGURE 3.1 Brain wave patterns.

frequencies, measured in Hertz (Hz), that can be correlated with both subjective states and with the functioning of the organism. Twenty-three years of observing these electrical patterns during training, talking, and thinking has given this author an ability to correlate brain activity with family functioning.

There are many variables to consider as one interprets the brain wave patterns. Different brain wave frequencies are generated in different parts of the brain (Sterman, 1996). The importance of the origin of the brain wave is related to how to "read" the brain wave patterns that one sees. For example, theta brain wave frequency (4-8 Hz) is produced in the thalamic region of the brain, also known as the limbic region. This is the area of the brain that expands its development early in life and regulates the autonomic nervous system. This brain wave is essential for integration of new information into an individual's personal history. This brain wave carries the "emotional" character of one's life.

Beta waves (13-40 Hz), produced in the cortex, are correlated with focus and attention. If theta is overriding the faster brain wave patterns such as beta that are essential for attention in the moment, a person will be distracted, preoccupied, and unable to focus.

Different brain waves are optimally found in particular parts of the brain. If they are found in a part not usually associated with them, it may be an indication of symptoms. For example, alpha (8-12 Hz) is typically seen in the back of the brain with heightened amplitudes as eyes are closed. It is a state of relaxed awareness. Alpha in the left frontal lobe may be an indication of depression.

An optimally functioning brain has the ability to focus. This means that an individual can organize his or her intention to attend to a task. In the brain this can be seen as the inhibition of lower frequencies (theta) and the consistent presence of higher frequencies (beta). A person can have difficulty focusing or attending to the present when it is difficult to inhibit the activity of the deeper parts of the brain—the parts of the brain required for survival and automatic functioning. This is very basic in the ability to regulate oneself. This can be seen in the EEG patterns as dominant low-frequency brain patterns with little ability to produce high-frequency patterns. Or a brain may "try" very hard to get itself organized and produce repetitive thought patterns. This can be an EEG pattern of dominant high "beta" (30+ Hz), corresponding to effortful anxiety or persistent worry.

The optimal brain function is a flexible one, demonstrating the ability to produce a wide range of brain states as well as to produce a focusing state in the midst of high anxiety. It is possible to see via the neurofeedback the subtle ways in which thinking patterns are dominated by the emotional state. Often this subtlety is out of our awareness. Noticing the cluttered kitchen counters when anxious, but finding that the same cluttered counters are out of awareness when less anxious is an example of the subtlety of anxiety-driven experience.

When physical, emotional, and social symptoms are present, the brain wave patterns are less flexible. The lower-frequency waves (theta) are dominant more of the time. Or the high frequency (beta) patterns may be unrelenting.

In the author's experience, there are two general patterns of brain waves that seem to coincide with social systems that are emotionally cutoff. Both patterns coincide with high levels of emotional sensitivity and reactivity to relationships. Both patterns are present in individuals developing within a more isolated relationship system. Both patterns are less flexible than in individuals who are not cut off.

The first is a highly reactive behavior pattern that corresponds with high amplitude brain wave patterns. This means the amplitude or strength of the wave is greater than typical for the brain wave, indicating excessive activity. The detail of this pattern is described in the following clinical example.

The second is a constricted, inwardly oriented behavior pattern associated with low amplitude in the brain wave patterns. It is as if the individual is constraining his energy to adapt. Both are products of similarly anxious and cutoff families. Both have high levels of physiological reactivity—cold hands and high muscle tension. This pattern may also produce a "shutdown" sweat response, a sweat response that is below normal (10 µmhos).

The author associates high levels of chronic physiological reactivity with high levels of relationship sensitivity, more emotional cutoff, and lower levels of differentiation. More emotional cutoff is associated with more reliance on existing relationships, an increased relationship sensitivity producing heightened physiological response patterns, and less ability to regulate self.

Autonomic Nervous System and Self-Regulation

Although there is a genetic underpinning to physiological, psychological, emotional, and behavioral patterns, the details of functioning are fleshed out in interaction with the relationship environment generation to generation. The autonomic nervous system is a by-product of the central nervous system. The body's response system to threat is called the autonomic nervous system (ANS). It is the physiological regulation system that develops in response to what we have learned and is essential for survival. The autonomic nervous system provides the organism's ability to respond when it experiences a threat and to recover after the threat subsides.

The autonomic nervous system develops early in life. Schore (1994) describes the period of its development as occurring between the ages of ten and eighteen months. He describes this process as the development of the self, or the ability of the individual to learn to regulate the reaction to threat. Physiological self-regulation provides the underpinning for the development of emotional and psychological functioning. The ability for an individual to regulate physically is then an important marker of "self" for the individual. Self-regulation is an aspect of differentiation of self.

The autonomic nervous system is a counterbalancing system. An organism evaluates a threat, responds, and then returns to baseline. The sympathetic nervous system or the excitatory response develops between ten and twelve months. The parasympathetic system, or the inhibitory response, develops between sixteen and eighteen months. These response patterns develop in reciprocity with the parents. The parents' ability to be steady, consistent, and defined in relationship to a child promotes the ability of the child to develop this ability for himself or herself. A parent who is reactive and has little ability to self-regulate has an impact upon the child's ability to develop self-regulation (Gottman, 1997).

Variations on the theme of self-regulation emerge (Siegel, 1999). Patterns of response in the child vary with parental pattern. For example, a child who experiences a parent as emotional, inconsistent, and volatile during the development of self-regulation may develop a highly responsive, vigilant stance with an overexcited response pattern, becoming anxious and unable to calm down. Or a child with preoccupied parents may be wary of the environment, hesitant, and overinhibited in his or her actions. These behavioral patterns also have physiological manifestations.

Gellhorn (1969), a physiologist, describes this balancing of the excitatory and inhibitory responses as a "tuning" process. There are those individuals with response patterns that are dominantly excitatory, those whose are primarily inhibitory, and those who seem to employ both mechanisms. In these cases, there is a pronounced physiological double bind. It is like pressing the gas and the brake pedal at the same time. Both responses are activated in tandem, sustaining a chronic reactivity that may produce physical symptoms such as asthma or gastrointestinal symptoms.

Emotional cutoff exaggerates the perception of threat and decreases the ability to regulate self at the level of physiology. The greater the emotional cutoff between generations, the more intensely individuals within the family require one another. This "requirement" can be played out in a variety of relationship patterns, including what may appear as minimal responsiveness.

It is important to observe how a person recovers after being in a stressful situation or thinking about a difficult situation. How does an individual's body calm down after a challenge? Does it recover completely, and how long does it take? Often there is a sustained response that does not change. This reflects the chronic level of reaction. Some examples are a person who has cold hands all the time, an individual who sustains a high level of muscle tension, or a person who consistently worries. The more flexibility there is in a bodily or mental response, the more "flexible" a person is in recovering from a challenge. Symptoms are present when there is little flexibility and an individual is unable to recover from an aroused state. This highly sustained physiological arousal corresponds to an individual who experiences self in a chronic state of "threat."

A sense of threat as described earlier varies from individual to individual. What a person experiences as a threat and how intense that experience is depend upon the patterns and levels of anxiety in his or her nuclear and extended family during development. The earliest developmental context for threat is in the sensory development in utero and continues in response to his or her position in the family. This early experience varies from individual to individual and then manifests differently in patterns of the body, mind, and action of the individual. The physiology, psychology, and behavior develop within the family that an individual depends on for survival. These patterned responses guide the individual through a lifetime of adapting as he or she has learned.

CLINICAL EXAMPLE

A clinical example will illustrate the levels of physiological, emotional, perceptual, cognitive, and relationship reactivity that are present in individuals. The variation in an individual's reactivity corresponds to the variation in relationship sensitivity. The more emotionally cutoff, the more reactive an individual is to his or her present relationships. This reactivity can be observed in the physiological patterns (brain waves, muscle tension, hand temperature, and sweat response) as well as emotional, behavioral, and relationship patterns.

Mr. and Mrs. Bailey originally initiated consultation six years ago during the ending of their marriage. During the phone call before meeting, Mrs. Bailey reported that she feared for her and her husband's safety. They had been married for sixteen years. They had no children and worked together during their married life to establish a church. The intensity in this marriage corresponded to the level of isolation of the couple and emotional cutoff. Mr. Bailey had left India twenty-five years before to pursue education in the United States. He had no contact with his family or country of origin after leaving India. He built a successful life as a prominent spiritual leader. He had been married before and had a child from that marriage.

Mrs. Bailey was seventeen years younger and initially her husband's student. She was also committed to the development of the church and spiritual community. Until two years before consultation began, Mrs. Bailey had limited social contact beyond her husband and her immediate family. Mrs. Bailey's immediate family was present at the wedding, as was Mr. Bailey's child. However, the marriage between Mr. and Mrs. Bailey was a secret within the community, as was the existence of his first wife and child.

A number of factors affected the stability of the marriage. Secrecy permeated the relationship from the beginning. Although a constant challenge, the secrecy became intolerable to Mrs. Bailey later in the marriage when it supported Mr. Bailey's extramarital affairs. This became more evident and pronounced following the death of Mrs. Bailey's mother. Mrs. Bailey's mother died five years before consultation began. An inclination by Mr. Bailey toward affairs seemed to be in place from the beginning of the marriage, although nothing manifested until the death of Mrs. Bailey's mother. Mrs. Bailey spent a great deal of energy guarding against such an occurrence, at great cost to herself.

Both Mr. and Mrs. Bailey's anxiety-driven behaviors increased greatly with the death of Mrs. Bailey's mother. Mr. Bailey had great respect and affection for his mother-in-law. She may have been a suitable replacement for his mother. With the death of Mrs. Bailey's mother, his anxiety was evident. He had less enthusiasm and energy for life during the next five years, further fostering an emerging affair. Mrs. Bailey focused more on her marriage with more concern about Mr. Bailey's affairs.

Over the next five years, the intensity in the marriage increased. Two years before consultation, Mrs. Bailey finally confirmed her fears of other women in her husband's life. She described this as a turning point, at which she began to pursue a professional direction. At the same time she started school full-time, Mr. Bailey's mother died. He had not seen her for twenty-five years. Mr. Bailey experienced increased intense focus on Mrs. Bailey as she began expanding her relationships. The marriage became volatile, with threatened violence. Mrs. Bailey described this time as "dangerous, extremely unstable, and fearful." It was at this point that the couple sought consultation.

Mrs. Bailey had moderate contact with her family of origin and minimal contact with extended family. Her main priority was her husband and the church community they had created together, with her playing a background role. She was inclined to go along with others but at a cost to herself. She had circulatory disorder (constricted blood flow into hands and feet), erratic emotional states, and chronic insomnia. She had anxious energy and accomplished more than most could.

In the consultation with the couple, both described how they used meditative prayer to manage their personal levels of reactivity. But as Mr. Bailey described, the anxiety was too high for prayer to manage. Within three months of couple consultation, Mrs. Bailey began more consistent contact with her family. Mr. Bailey responded to his family in India about the news of his mother's death, eventually visiting his country for the first time in twenty-five years. During this very volatile time, the couple separated safely, albeit with the potential of violence at times. Mr. Bailey dropped out of consultation and Mrs. Bailey continued.

Contact with extended family in this case helped to decrease the high level of anxiety enough for the couple to separate without incident. Mrs. Bailey's achievement of more emotional stability through increased family contact, increased neutrality, and a broadening professional community helped avoid an unstable and dangerous outcome during the separation. They remained in contact with each other as they negotiated the financial and emotional details of divorce. They continue in cordial contact to this day. Mr. Bailey now maintains consistent contact with his family in India.

Early in the individual consultation, Mrs. Bailey began to use neuro-feedback to assist in managing her anxiety. The amplitudes of her brain wave patterns were high, particularly during conversation or thought. Initially she had difficulty becoming focused (inhibited theta and enhanced beta) on either side of her brain. Focusing means her ability to inhibit the emotionality enough to be present in the moment with thoughtful attention. Self-criticism or focus on others was a primary cognitive state during this period. Her hand temperature was consistently in the low 70s (°F), which indicates chronic physiological reactivity. Meditative prayer was an important natural adaptation for managing the high levels of emotionality present. Her years of meditative prayer could be seen with high levels of alpha waves on the right side of the brain.

In the early stages of consultation, Mrs. Bailey was unsure of herself in relationships. She selected a life out of college that focused her energy on prayer and spiritual practice. Her primary relationship was her teacher, who became her husband. Her move to pursue further education and a broader world of relationships became the arena for learning in the next part of her life (Figure 3.2).

Family History

Mrs. Bailey is the youngest of four with an older brother and two older sisters. Her parents divorced when she was in college. Mrs. Bailey described her mother as energetic, full of life, and dramatic, with little self-awareness, and her father as hardworking, reliable, and emotionally constrained. The father was thirteen years older than the mother. Mother was described as dissatisfied in the marriage and had affairs. Mrs. Bailey was born into the family when the marital relationship was beginning to establish this dissatisfied pattern. Mrs. Bailey initially viewed her father as inadequate with respect to the demands of her mother and her mother as a vibrant and dramatic handful.

Mrs. Bailey's mother's life had been turbulent, including a sexual assault as a child. It is reported that her family blamed and punished her for the event. After the divorce, Mrs. Bailey's mother did not remarry. She lived a dramatic life in the arts, traveling widely until she died fifteen years ago in South America.

Mrs. Bailey's father was a successful lawyer. Given the wide socioeconomic gulf that existed between her mother and paternal grandmother, Mrs. Bailey admired the respect and mutual acceptance they had for each other. Mrs. Bailey describes her father as successful in the world but clueless with

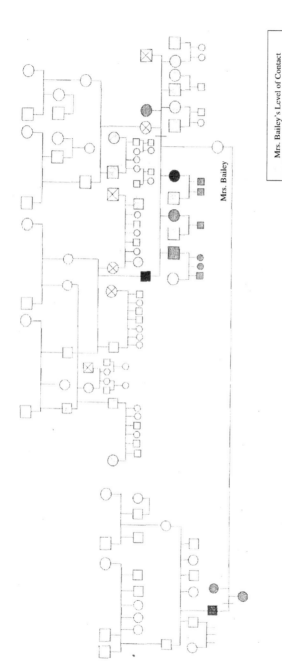

Mrs. Bailey's Level of Contact	
●	close communication
◐	consistent personal contact
◯◯◯	family/social functions
◯◯	no personal contact
✕	dead

FIGURE 3.2. Original family diagram with first husband initial consultation six years ago.

his wife, and attentive as a father. After the divorce, he remarried a widow with adult children.

Mrs. Bailey grew up in primary association with her maternal side. She knew her mother's only older brother and family well as a child. Superficial contact existed with the paternal side of the family. Grandparents were known but minimal personal relationship existed.

Consultation

During the eight years of consultation, Mrs. Bailey diligently used the neurofeedback and pursued knowledge of/and relationships with the broader family and other important family friends. Before Mrs. Bailey began consultation, she lived in an isolated world with her husband with some contact with her siblings and parents. The idea of more contact with the broader extended family made sense to her. She reestablished relationships with aunts, uncles, and cousins with whom she grew up but had contact only during family occasions, such as wedding and funerals, as an adult. She also pursued relationships with family members she did not know well, particularly on her paternal side. There were opportunities such as deaths, weddings, and birthday celebrations, at which she made a point of being present and an active participant. Developing these relationships allowed her to see her family and herself more neutrally (Figure 3.3).

After six years of consultation, she married her present husband. This marriage lives in the broader context of both families. She "uses" her relationships with her family and his family to counterbalance her tendency to focus on her spouse when anxious.

Mrs. Bailey used the neurofeedback consistently to improve her ability to think through emotional situations. She would think of difficult situations and work to maintain a neutrally focused brain state. This improved her ability to optimally think through an emotional dilemma.

Mrs. Bailey's improved ability to manage her emotional and physiological reactivity was particularly effective when she and her present husband discussed an issue while she was using neurofeedback. One time in particular, Mrs. Bailey experienced a "shutdown," as she describes it. In the exchange with her husband, Mrs. Bailey became overwhelmed, shut down, and could not speak. This corresponded to high levels of theta (above 15 [microVolts]) and low beta (below 3 mV) on the neurofeedback, cold hand temperature, and high muscle tension. This was the first time that she was able to consciously experience the shutdown state and put it into language that allowed her to reengage in the relationship with her husband. This was an important turning point for Mrs. Bailey. With the assistance of the neurofeedback, she de-

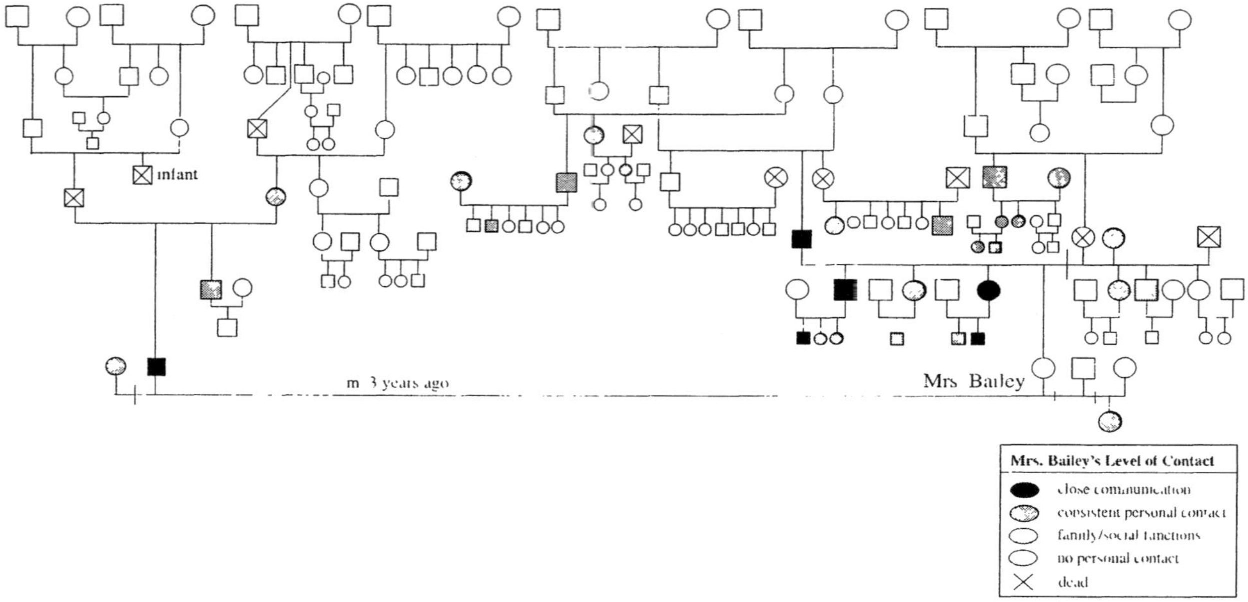

FIGURE 3.3. Family diagram with second husband at present.

scribed in a neutral fashion, an ability to experience the state that had previously overtaken her. This reactive state had previously compelled her to shut down. This was a familiar state that she formerly lived in for long periods of time.

Her brain patterns are more integrated with lower amplitude when she is calm. The theta and beta brain waves are closer together, producing a calmer, focused attention. When she is anxious, the previous patterns of high amplitude theta are present although not as sustained. In addition, her hand temperature is warmer and muscle tension is lower. Mrs. Bailey describes the process of neurofeedback and consultation as "loosening the knots or ruts of habit." She describes the process of consultation about herself in her family and relationships as amplified by the neurofeedback. The objectivity of the neurofeedback assisted her to see herself in her relationships more accurately and more quickly.

Over the past six years, Mrs. Bailey finished her education and successfully established herself in the field of medicine. She is teaching and is active in the broader professional community. After several years of exploring relationships, she developed a relationship with her present husband. She describes establishing relationships with her broader family and his family as having helped her loosen the focus on the current relationship, allowing it to be mutual and cooperative.

She is experiencing the fruits of her efforts. This past year included the death of two significant men in the older generation. Mrs. Bailey was an important part of these two family units during the period of dying. She was able to use her medical skill with the dying as well as with the surviving family members. She is an important part of each of these families. Rather than being experienced as the little sister, her opinions and thoughts are considered and acknowledged by her siblings and her father and stepmother. Her family is a resource to her and she to them. She is calmer, more thoughtful, and more present. She describes her life as having been transformed "like alchemy."

Change of this proportion takes time and determination. Moving into the past initially activates the anxiety that produced the cutoff. Learning to manage oneself despite the anxiety is essential to being able to change one's behavior and life patterns. Neurofeedback seems to provide a neutral reference point about anxiety and a vehicle to experience life differently. Bowen theory provides the grid to move in relationships differently.

The physiological changes correspond to the relationship changes. Changing the role one plays in the important relationships of one's history changes not only the relationships in the present but also one's physiology. These physiological changes may occur automatically as relationships change. There is also a learning process. Learning how to realistically see one's part in relationships brings a realization that the perceptions are constructed to promote the automatic reactions. When one can experience the part one plays in a situation, the relationship changes and the *brain* changes. Experiencing the part one plays is a complex brain integration. The automatic survival perception is to experience the impact others have on us and to focus on them. It is a different perspective to experience self through another's eyes.

EMOTIONAL CUTOFF IN CLINICAL WORK

In clinical work, the idea of emotional cutoff can be one of the most elusive concepts for individuals to grasp. Families living with high levels of cutoff often reject the idea that lack of contact is damaging or that knowledge of a broader extended family network is important for improving one's functioning. Individuals do not comprehend, or aggressively argue and disregard, that parts of the family are important: "I don't like them and they don't like me." "What do people I don't even know have to do with my life?" "I don't see how contact with them has anything to do with my marriage." Sometimes the response is more lethargic. Bridging cutoff may make sense, but it is difficult to find the energy to do anything. Some say they procrastinate, put off contacting individuals, and lose energy at even the thought. All of these responses reflect emotional cutoff and highlight the difficulty of pursuing the blind spots in perception.

There are reasons that emotional cutoff exists. It is important to respect its force. Moving back toward the known fears or the unknown produces anxiety. Neurofeedback provides a tool to engage the chronic anxiety of the individual. Knowledge of the past provides a framework for understanding one's reactions to the present. Bridging cutoff changes the basic patterns of perception built into the development of the brain and patterns of reactivity. Neurofeedback is a tool to assist in this process. It helps us to see how thought and responses out of our awareness are reactive responses developed to adapt to difficulties in our early relationships. The more the mechanism of emotional cutoff is present in the texture of the history of the family and in the individual, the less reality-based that individual's current perception will be. The individual will also perceive fewer choices. Neurofeedback can be a tool to increase "self" in relationships by experiencing the subtlety of anxiety-driven experience in a neutral environment, thus having more ability to respond with awareness, consideration, and choice.

Bridging the emotional cutoff present in a family is basic to differentiation of self. Bridging cutoff is not differentiation of self per se. It is, however, essential to building the functional basis upon which to be more of a self. Decreasing chronic anxiety allows one to be more of a self. Bridging emotional cutoff addresses the chronic anxiety present in a family. Although one may initially increase anxiety by moving toward an emotional cutoff, it increases the flexibility and promotes an increase in functioning and the potential to be more of a self.

SUMMARY

This chapter addresses the concept of emotional cutoff at the level of physiology and the brain. The functioning of an individual's brain is a product of the relationship system. The brain is a "relationship organ." The evolutionary nature of the brain is a culmination of the coevolution of social organizations and the brain itself. Adaptation occurs generation to generation. The variation in adaptation is transmitted through the development of individuals within a family adapting to the changing conditions of life. Bowen theory suggests three variables important in this variation in development: composite level of differentiation of the family; the level of anxiety present during different developmental stages; and the position of the child in the anxiety mechanisms of the family. Emotional cutoff is more prevalent at lower levels of functioning. Emotional cutoff, while solving the short-term anxiety, increases the long-term problem by decreasing the flexibility of functioning in the next generation, as well as the current generation over time.

The author has studied emotional cutoff in her clinical work applying Bowen theory with neurofeedback, a clinical technology that provides information about the brain functioning by measuring the electrical patterns of the brain. Brain patterns and physiological measures correspond to variations in emotional cutoff in families. A clinical case presented a description of an individual's physiological, cognitive, emotional, and relationship functioning; her multigenerational family history; the nature of the emotional cutoff; the course of consultation with neurofeedback and Bowen theory; as well as changes in the individual's functioning, including the brain wave patterns.

Emotional cutoff, the mechanism for managing the intensity of the connection with one's original family by distancing to create a life of one's own, can be observed not only at the level of behavior and experience of individuals, as described by Bowen, but also at the level of the brain and physiology.

REFERENCES

Allman, J. (1999). *Evolving Brains*. New York: Scientific American Library.
Allman, J., A Hakeem, J. Erwin, E. Nimchinsky, and P. Hof (2001). The anterior cingulate cortex: The evolution of an interface between emotion and cognition. *Annals of the New York Academy of Sciences* 935:107-117.

Allman, J., A. Hakeem, and K. Watson (2002) Two phylogenetic specializations in the human brain. *Neuroscientist* 8:335-345.

Bowen, M. (1978). *Family Therapy in Clinical Practice.* Northvale, NJ. Jason Aronson.

Bowen, M. and P. Friesen (1988). *Fusion and Physiology.* Videotape produced by Georgetown Family Center, Washington, DC.

Gellhorn. E. (1969). Further studies on the physiology and pathophysiology of the tuning of the central nervous system. *Psychosomatics* 10 (March-April):94-103.

Gottman, J. (1997). *The Heart of Parenting.* New York: Simon and Schuster.

Green, E., A. Green, and D. Walters (1970). Voluntary control of internal states: Psychological and physiological. *Journal of Transpersonal Psychology* 2:1-26.

Hannaford, C. (1995). *Smart Moves: Why Learning Is Not All in Your Head.* Arlington, VA: Great Ocean Publishers.

Hofer, M. (1981). *The Roots of Human Behavior: An Introduction to the Psychobiology of Early Development.* New York: W.H. Freeman and Company.

Lubar, J. (1991). Discourse on the development of EEG diagnostics and biofeedback for attention-deficit/hyperactivity disorders. *Biofeedback and Self-Regulation* 16:201-224.

Peniston, E. and P. Kulkosky (1989). Alpha-theta brainwave training and b-endorphin levels in alcoholics. *Alcoholism: Clinical and Experimental Research* 13: 271-279.

Schore, A. (1994) *Affect Regulation and the Origin of the Self: The Neurobiology of Emotional Development.* Hillsdale, NJ: Lawrence Erlbaum Associates.

Siegel, D. (1999). *The Developing Mind: Toward a Neurobiology of Interpersonal Experience.* New York: The Guilford Press.

Sterman, M.B (1996). Physiological origins and functional correlates of EEG rhythmic activities: Implications for self-regulation. *Biofeedback and Self-Regulation* 21:3-33.

Sterman, M.B and L. Friar (1972). Suppression of seizures in an epileptic following sensorimotor EEG feedback training. *Electroencephalography and Clinical Neurophysiology* 33:89-95.

PART II:
THE THERAPIST'S OWN FAMILY

Chapter 4

Efforts to Bridge Secondary Emotional Cutoff

Peter Titelman

INTRODUCTION

This chapter focuses on the author's efforts to bridge secondary emotional cutoff as part of his work on differentiating a self. In an earlier publication, "Reaction to Death in a Family" (Titelman, 1987) he described his work on fusion in his family of origin, particularly the fusion with his mother in the context of the parent-child triangle. The following is excerpted from the end of that chapter:

> By the time I wrote the paper in 1979, I perceived my family as fused, but less cohesive and containing more covert conflict than was indicated by the myth of family harmony. However, it was not until the last few years that I was able to see, based on a better understanding of family systems theory and increased acquisition of multigenerational data, that my fused family of origin was, in fact, a small splinter branch of an explosive family that was characterized by major emotional cutoff with the paternal extended family. . . . In this case I link the cutoffs within my paternal extended family to the cohesive, emotionally fused character of my immediate family of origin. (Titelman, 1987, p. 345)

The past twenty years involved a shift in the author's focus from the family of origin and the family of procreation to the family as a multigenerational emotional unit; from a focus on the primary triangle, parents and self, to a focus on interlocking triangles including the family of procreation, the family of origin, and the larger extended family; from a focus on fusion to a focus on the interlocking relationship between fusion and cutoff.

The author's effort to differentiate a self has roughly fallen into three phases: (1) efforts to differentiate a self in his family of origin: 1973-1977; (2) continuing efforts to differentiate a self with a focus on the death of the author's mother: 1977-1978; and (3) efforts to bridge cutoff in the paternal side of the extended family: 1978-2001.

The following is a summary of the first phase. Initially, in 1973, he collected basic genealogical and other family data from his maternal aunt (the author's aunt was a first cousin of the Titelmans, as was his mother). From 1974 to 1977, the effort was to work on the primary triangle of self and parents, in which the author was quite fused with his mother and his father was in the outside position. The work centered on understanding the functioning position of the author as the youngest, dependent on his mother in the context of the suicide of his maternal grandfather. On his maternal side, his mother was an underfunctioning youngest with an overfunctioning sister. The projection process involved men being perceived as weak. The nodal event was the suicide of the author's maternal grandfather. The author's mother took care of his father and worried that if she did not do so he would become suicidal. This at least may in part account for his mother's constant watchfulness and overprotectiveness of the father. And, finally, the author's mother's anxiety about the viability of males was directed at her son, the author.

On the author's paternal side, the projection process involved his father being the "spoiled" youngest of five brothers. An uncle reported that the author's father was the "sensitive emotional" one who needed to be protected. This author (Titelman, 1987) wrote the following:

> The projection process between my father and myself involved my father feeling more capable and less a "baby" by projecting his concern about being in that position toward me. Through the projection process, whereby I lived out my father's concerns regarding being the babied one, my father managed somewhat to extricate himself—or pretended to—from that position. My position of being fused with my mother was similar to my father's position of being fused with his mother. (Titelman, 1987, p. 330)

In the briefest terms, the author's effort during the first phase of his differentiation work was to use his understanding of the impact of the maternal grandfather's suicide to understand his mother's overprotectiveness and to open up that issue with his mother and maternal aunt—that is, to detoxify it. This seemed to have an impact on the mother's anxiety, freeing her to be less worried about her son, the author, and her husband, particularly in regard to the husband's depression and perceived suicidal potential. The author put effort into having a less intellectualized-fused relationship with his mother and was able to gain a little more separateness and a stronger connection with his father.

The second phase of the differentiation effort took place from 1977 to 1978. The focus was on the author's effort to define himself through taking an I-Position, and creating a ritual for dealing with his mother's death in the face of the rest of the family's preference for avoiding a ritual. (An I-position is an action stance on behalf of self that defines a solidly held principle or belief in the face of opposition of one or more family members or significant others.)

During the period of 1977 through 1988 the author experienced a great deal of marital conflict. Figure 4.1 illustrates the interlocking of the symptom development of marital conflict with emotional cutoff in the families of origin of both spouses. Though emotional distance between the author and his father, aunt, and sister decreased, cutoff between the author' wife and her parents and siblings did not decrease. The presence of that intense cutoff seemed to play a part in furthering conflict and distance between the author and his wife, culminating in a marital separation in 1988 and followed by divorce in 1989.

The remainder of the chapter describes one important aspect of the third phase. As he came to understand the presence of emotional cutoff in his

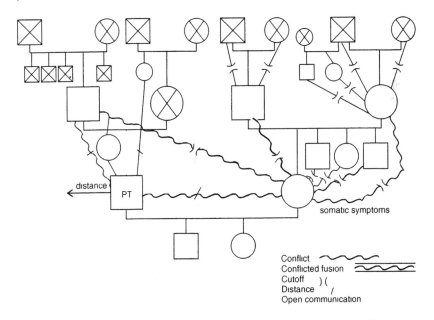

FIGURE 4.1. Marital conflict and distance and emotional cutoff.

family, he made an effort to bridge emotional cutoff with the paternal side. The choice to focus on the paternal side was based on two factors. The author's mother had only one sibling who never married or reproduced. A significant relationship existed between that deceased aunt and the author. The author's life course was lived within the bounds, for the most part, of his paternal family. Future effort may someday be directed to the maternal side of the family. Of course, efforts continue on differentiation of self, following the death of the author's mother in 1977 and the incipient development of his father's Alzheimer's disease in the early 1980s made a focus on the extended family a logical choice. In addition, Bowen (1984) pointed out that the primary triangle is embedded in the multigenerational extended family. Although theoretically it is possible to detriangle self from one's parents, from a practical perspective an individual is more than a product of his or her relationship with parents. One gets to know more about one's parents by getting to know more about one's extended family.

The efforts of this chapter deal with the relationship between fusion—unresolved attachment between the author and his parents—and the presence of cutoff of a secondary type. To refresh the reader's memory, a primary cutoff takes place within the primary triangle, an individual in relation to one or both of his or her parents. A secondary, or derivative, cutoff takes place between an individual and a sibling, grandparent, uncle or aunt, or cousins. This form of cutoff takes place within secondary triangles that spin off from, or are interlocked with, the primary parent-child triangle. Secondary cutoffs, based on interlocking triangles, can be described as indirect or "inherited," and are based on multigenerational emotional process. Some cutoffs are inherited in the sense that an individual has had no direct, face-to-face contact with a particular individual.

By 1980, the author (who previously had had a mix of some personal and some formal contact with a considerable number of his living uncles and aunts and their children, his first cousins and their children, and his first cousins once removed) began to slowly increase his contact with several of them. In 1983, he articulated a personal goal, which he knew was probably impossible to accomplish in one lifetime, of developing one-to-one relationships with as many of his cousins as possible. This goal was a blueprint based on Bowen's notion that developing an "open system"—a modicum of reciprocal emotional contact with all significant members of the family—would be one of the high roads for potentiating differentiation through being both responsible for self and being responsible to others in the family. Needless to say, such a goal is very idealistic and this author still has a long way to go to even get close to accomplishing it.

The author realized that he would not have the energy and time—given financial and geographical limits, as well as the limits of balancing selfhood, parenthood, and spousehood—to devote to developing personal, one-to-one relationships with all living members of his extended family. Following Bowen's suggestion to direct one's effort to all significant members of the family, the author decided to use the following rule of thumb: work to bridge cutoff with aunts (all uncles were dead), first cousins, and first cousin once removed, who fit into the following criteria:

1. Choose family members who add new knowledge about the extended family and specifically about cutoff in the family (who, what, when, and where) that provides a wider context for understanding the functioning of the family. This would allow for more understanding of the impact of the multigenerational extended family on the reactivity and choices made by one's parents and oneself. Bowen (1984) said: "the more you know about the past, the more you know about you . . . the feelings in the family, they are in all alive members." This research can be an important part of bridging secondary cutoff in the family.
2. Work on the relationships with family members from whom the parents were cutoff and who were closely tied to the parents' emotional system. This enables the differentiating one to revive the emotional system that individual inhabited with his parents. Work on the relationships that involve bridging secondary cutoffs inherited from cutoffs that existed between one's parents and significant other family members. This provides a rich opportunity to continue to differentiate or modify the unresolved attachment with one's parents around an emotionally intense and "alive" issue.

A FIRST COUSIN ONCE REMOVED: A RESOURCE FOR MULTIGENERATIONAL HISTORY AND THE DISCOVERY OF CUTOFF IN THE FAMILY

In the summer of 1978, the author received a letter from a family friend which contained the address of a distant cousin living in Hamden, New Jersey. The author wrote to him, and in the late fall of that year he exchanged letters and had a telephone conversation with a previously unknown third cousin, Robert Teitelman. The author began to get the idea that there were many family branches and members of whom he was unaware. That cousin provided the name of another distant cousin, a psychiatrist, living in New Jersey who was closer to the author's own branch. The author wrote him on a couple of occasions but never heard back from him, even though he was in a related field and at one time was scheduled to present papers at the same professional conference. They never met. Nevertheless, the phantom psychiatrist cousin passed the letter through his mother to Edna Hillman, a seventy-eight-year-old childless widow who the author learned was his first cousin once removed. In November 1980, he received a letter from cousin Edna. It would be the first of at least fifteen letters and many phone conversations over the next twenty-one years, he even made one trip to visit her in Maple Shade, New Jersey. She died at the age of ninety-nine in December 2001.

Cousin Edna's first letter was a real eye-opener about the relationship between the author's family of origin and the extended family. She provided missing information about the eleven surviving children, out of thirteen, of his great-grandfather Isaac (1842-1923) and his great-grandmother, Leah (1845-1911). The author's father had told him that he had only one paternal uncle and one paternal aunt. Also, he learned that nine of the eleven siblings in his grandfather's generation spelled their name one way, while the author's grandfather and his younger brother changed the spelling of their surname. This was when he began to key in on the cutoff that existed on this side of the family. Figure 4.2 illustrates the cutoff that existed in the author's paternal extended family between his grandfather and his eight older siblings.

Cousin Edna told stories of strife at family gatherings, and correspondence with Edna suggested several possible clues to the cutoff in this family:

1. According to Cousin Edna, "When there was a family function you always had to check who was not speaking to whom, so you did not seat them next to each other. Uncle Meyer [my grandfather's oldest sibling] was perpetually feuding, and some of the other cousins were at swords points."

2. Cousin Edna reported that females who married into the family were in severe conflict.

3. The author's grandmother was described as looking down on the grandfather's family, which may have led to more emotional distancing. Edna reported:

   Your grandmother was not very friendly with the other women of the family. I always had the feeling that she felt superior to them. I remember visiting at your grandmother's home in what was called "Strawberry Mansion," Philadelphia, and she made us take our shoes off before we could go into the house. Of course the Japanese and the Muslims do that, but seventy years ago it was not done in Jewish circles in this country . . .

4. Following the death of the author's grandfather, Israel Samuel, in 1934, at the early age of fifty-nine, and the moving of the family

sweater business from Philadelphia to Altoona, Pennsylvania, there was less communication with the extended family, according to cousin Edna.

5. Cousin Edna reported that the author's great-grandfather, Isaac, had four additional wives after Leah, the mother of the eleven siblings of which his great-grandfather was eighth. These marriages may have been a source of distance between these children and their father and his four new wives. Cousin Edna wrote that "he married four times after that, and when he finally died, I saw an old woman beating her head against the hearse. My mother was with me and I asked who the woman was. She replied, 'I never saw her before. . . .' "

6. As-yet unsubstantiated data that the author's great-great-grandfather had two marriages, each of which produced four children. Again, these multiple marriages may have been another factor in the splintering of the family at that time

7. There were a decreasing number of religious and family rituals in the author's branch of the family, in conjunction with an increase of assimilation, including moving away from the practice of Judaism on the part of the author's grandfather. A focus on business, professional life, the arts, and political involvement seems to have replaced involvement with the extended family and religion in the multigenerational process of the family. Cousin Edna's niece reported that her aunt spoke of some of the family envying the author's branch of the family because of the financial success of their sweater business.

BRIDGING EMOTIONAL CUTOFF WITH AN AUNT

During the 1980s, when the author presented material about his family in workshops on Bowen family systems theory, he would acknowledge being cutoff from Aunt Lee, the wife of the uncle who was closest in age to his father and the brother with whom his father had been closest. The author would say with a chuckle that someday he wanted to get to know her, but he acknowledged that somehow he had never gotten around to working on it. Years later, only after both his parents had died, he came to fully understand that his inability to work on his relationship with this aunt (who was the only living member of the older generation) was due to unresolved attachment to his parents. Specifically, he had taken on the negativity that existed between his parents and his aunt and the subsequent cutoff they had from her and was living out a secondary cutoff from her. The following is an account of the

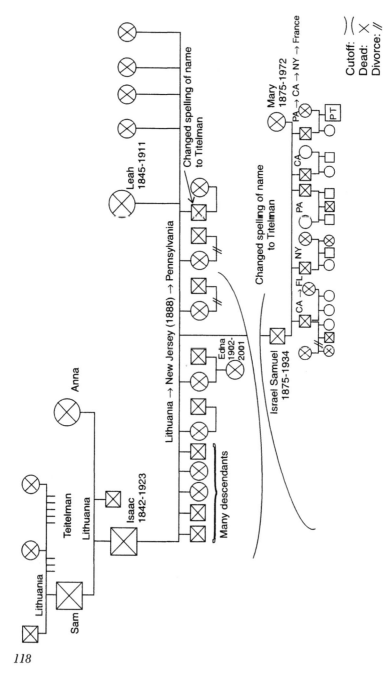

FIGURE 4.2. Cutoff in the paternal extended family.

118

author's effort to work on bridging the cutoff with his paternal Aunt Lee. The author uses the first person to describe his efforts in bridging the cutoff with his aunt.

In 1955 I moved from Los Angeles to Altoona, Pennsylvania, with my parents and sister. A few weeks before I left Los Angeles my father took me to see my Uncle Herb in a hospital, where he was recuperating from surgery for lung cancer. At that time I got the impression that I would never see my uncle again, although my father did not directly say that he was going to die. My uncle Herb died in 1956. Only my father went back to California for his memorial service.

During the years from 1973 to 1980, when I was focusing on my relationships with my parents and my own nuclear family, I paid little attention to my Aunt Lee, Uncle Herb's widow. My parents had always described her in negative terms. I was told that she did not like and was unfriendly toward my mother. Basically, I accepted their position and made no efforts to get in touch with her. After I left Los Angeles at age eleven I next returned there for two or three days in September 1977 at age 33. I visited with my cousin, Susie, the daughter of Aunt Lee and Uncle Herb. I spent a few hours with her and it never entered my mind to call Aunt Lee. Susie and her brother Russ were more accessible. I viewed them positively, as the extension of my Uncle Herb. The emotional cutoff was so ingrained, so much in place, that I gave no thought to seeing my aunt. Figure 4.3 illustrates the cutoff between my family of origin and Aunt Lee.

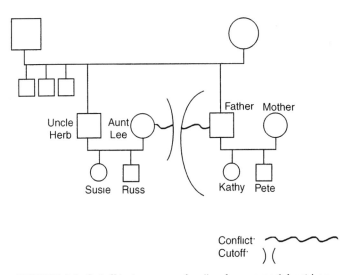

FIGURE 4.3. Cutoff between my family of origin and Aunt Lee.

When my father died on January 28, 1993, I wrote to Susie to tell her. She wrote me a warm letter about my dad and mentioned that her mother had heard about his death. I received a nice card from my Aunt Lee on March 3, 1993. She wrote the following:

> Dear Pete,
>
> I can't tell you how sad I feel about your father's death. It is difficult to think of any words of consolation—I suppose the Kaddish says it all.
> We mourn with you and know you will make it through this time of indescribable loss.
> If we can be of any comfort we are at your service.
>
> Love,
>
> Aunt Lee

My aunt's sweet condolence letter got the ball rolling. I wrote her back a thank-you letter. Then we began an exchange of holiday cards.

The following was my first letter back to Aunt Lee, written April 6, 1993.

> Dear Aunt Lee,
>
> Thank you for your kind words of sympathy regarding my father's death. I very much appreciate hearing from you, my only living aunt or uncle.* Over the last few years on several occasions I've thought about you and meant to contact you. I'm sorry it's taken so long. But better late than never. Since I moved from Los Angeles in 1955 I have seen Russ and Susie on a number of occasions. . . . I remember visiting Uncle Herb in the hospital not too long before he died. As you must know, Uncle Herb was my father's favorite and closest brother.
> I look forward to following up on our long-overdue contact.
>
> Love, Pete

I received the following letter, written April 24, 1993, from my Aunt Lee:

> Dear Pete,
>
> It was good to receive your letter, like a gift of love or life—while there is still time for us to get to know each other and enjoy the luxury of still being a part of [each other's life].

---

*Until February 1999, when I inadvertently ran into the name and address of my Uncle Manny's second wife, Thelma, I had completely put out of my mind any thoughts about having another living aunt. I had never met her, and my father had seen her only on a couple of occasions. Discussion of Aunt Thelma, Uncle Manny, and their daughters Joy and Lani will follow later in this chapter.

Your life sounds full and busy—we would like you to send us a picture of you and your family—as a starter . . .

Your Aunt Lee

On February 15, 1994, I had my first direct contact since seeing her in the spring of 1955, a phone call. Not only had emotional space been opened up by the death of both of my parents but also I was living alone with my two children following my divorce. Aunt Lee was warm, interested in me, picked up on my low-key mood, and was upbeat herself. Her voice reminded me of Susie's voice and had a familiar ring. The phone call was definitely a positive experience. It was the thawing of almost forty years of cutoff.

I had tried calling Aunt Lee on February 14, 1994, but could not reach her. Susie called me on February 15, 1994—a coincidence—telling me about a common relative we had never met named Gerry Aronson, a psychoanalyst, originally from Harrisburg, Pennsylvania; he was related to us through our paternal great-grandmother, Leah Aronson.

On February 26, 1994, I had lunch with my cousin Susie in New York City. During the lunch discussion, I told her that my father and hers had been best friends. I talked about visiting Herb in the hospital when he was dying of lung cancer. Susie talked about not knowing that her father was going to die. She cried. I held her hand and gave her a hug. I felt a close connection with Susie, through the deaths of our two closely related fathers and uncles and the unfortunate way with which her father's death was hidden.

On July 21, 1994, I had positive phone contacts with Susie and Lee. It was just nice to be in touch with them. Further phone and letter communication with Aunt Lee and Susie indicated that they were somewhat cut off from Aunt Lee's son, Russ. Susie and Lee occupied the inside positions of the triangle and Russ occupied the outside position. Lee asked me to send Russ, as a birthday present from her, a copy of my book, *The Therapist's Own Family*, because she thought the chapter on my family might be interesting and useful for him.

I received the following letter from Aunt Lee written on September 9, 1994.

Dear Pete,

Thank you for taking care of getting your book to Russ. He told me that he got it last week and was really pleased with it.

I think it will be an important factor in his search for who he is—therefore I think it was the perfect Birthday gift—so thank you, Pete.

Enclosed please find a check for your pains and the book. Couldn't have done it without you.

Thanks again—Hope all goes well for you—

Love,
Aunt Lee

I made plans to go back to Los Angeles the following spring, for only the second time since 1955. The previous trip involved a two-day stay in Los Angeles while looking for a new job in 1977, following the completion of my PhD. The occasion of this next trip was the fiftieth anniversary of the Westland School, an elementary school founded by my mother. I decided that this would also be a great opportunity to see my Aunt Lee, for the first time since the spring of 1955. I looked forward to this opportunity to see her face to face after a number of letters and phone calls taking place over the previous six years, and my goal was to continue to seek a one-to-one relationship with my Aunt Lee from whom I had been cut off for thirty-eight years, as an extension of the cutoff between my parents, particularly my mother and Aunt Lee.

My older sister also came to Los Angeles for the school anniversary. Plans were made for a dinner with some cousins we had never met, in addition to Susie, her husband, my sister, my wife and I, and Aunt Lee. We also planned a brunch with Susie, her family, Aunt Lee, mutual friends, and my sister, for the following Sunday.

When I told my sister Kathy that I would be getting together with Aunt Lee, her response was negative: "She's not a nice person. She wasn't nice to our mother. Don't waste your time." My understanding of my sister's negativity toward Aunt Lee was that she was speaking out of her sense of loyalty to our mother and father. In this sense she was defending our parents and perpetuating the cutoff.

On Thursday, March 4, Susie and I picked up Aunt Lee for dinner. Immediately I felt an easy rapport with her. We talked about my father. She said, "women were always running after him and he wasn't a very fast runner."

My sister sat next to Aunt Lee. They apparently had a pleasant conversation. My sister began to soften in her response to our Aunt Lee.

On Friday, March 5, my sister and I visited the school our mother had founded. During the time we spent together, my sister continued to question my interest in spending time with Aunt Lee. She couldn't understand why I wanted to get together with her the next morning. She continued to believe I was wasting time because of the negative relationship between her and our mother. I was able to resist being reactive or influenced by my sister's negativity and seeming desire to keep the cutoff going with our Aunt Lee.

On Saturday, March 6, I picked Aunt Lee up at the door of her apartment. We walked to a restaurant and spent two hours together. We talked about her relationship with Uncle Herb. She talked about how she and Uncle Herb and my parents had been "intellectual communists." Herb and my father worked for a radical union, the International Electrical Union, at the Douglas Aircraft plant. Lee talked about communism, and about Marx and Freud as being their religion. All of them were atheists.

I asked about Susie and Russ going to Westland, the school my mother founded. They had attended for one year. I asked why they had left. I assumed Aunt Lee took them out of the school because of conflict between her and my mother. However, Aunt Lee said that her reason for taking them out of Westland was because she believed in public education. She said if she could do it over, she would have kept them at Westland.

I did not want to rush headlong into a discussion about the relationship between Aunt Lee and my mother. I wanted to get to know Aunt Lee better and begin to build more of a one-to-one relationship. I did not want to put Aunt Lee on the defensive regarding her relationship with my mother. Also I sensed that at age eighty-three she was quite fragile, even though she had a pixie quality to her eyes and a great self-deprecating sense of humor.

Aunt Lee was born in 1916. Uncle Herb was born in 1905. Aunt Lee was married at the age of eighteen after knowing Uncle Herb only eleven days. They had been married twenty-two years when he died of lung cancer. At the time they met in the summer, in Wisconsin, she was moving to Los Angeles with her family. For a year or two after their marriage she traveled with Uncle Herb, who was a salesman for the family business, Puritan Sportswear. Her family had moved to Los Angeles, and she and Herb subsequently moved there permanently in 1935. My parents married in 1937 and moved to Los Angeles in 1942, in part to live near Uncle Herb.

I asked my aunt about her relationship with my paternal grandmother, Mary Titelman. She said, "Mary was a terror" regarding housecleaning, among other things. My grandmother was known as a "crumb detector." Everyone had to take their shoes off when they entered the front door of her house. According to Aunt Lee, other daughters-in-law did better with Mary than she did.

I asked about what my mother was like. She thought carefully about it. Finally, after a pause of a minute or two, in which it seemed as though she was seeking to find something positive to say about my mother, she said, "Very serious."

At the end of brunch, as we walked outside the restaurant, I said that it seemed my mother and she hadn't gotten along. I was factual and low key in my statement. Aunt Lee agreed. She said it was because my mother was such a strong person. Aunt Lee said she felt that she couldn't compete with her. She had only attended two years of college and my mother had started an important private elementary school. Since my mother was a first cousin of the Titelmans—my paternal grandmother and my maternal grandfather were siblings—Aunt Lee felt that my mother was favored by Mary, their mother-in-law. The triangle involved my aunt in the outside position and in conflictual relationships with my mother and my grandmother, who were closer and in the inside positions of the triangle. Actually, as I understand it, my mother was able to deal with my grandmother, but it was not a particularly close relationship.

Aunt Lee said that she felt the problem in the relationship with my mother was more her fault because of her defensiveness, her sense of competition, and her feelings of not being equal to my mother.

At the end of our meeting and our open talk about the cutoff, my Aunt Lee said it was so important that we talked. She described feeling transformed. I experienced a warm connection with my attractive, humorous aunt, no longer the "difficult one" as lived out through the processes of projection, interlocking triangles, and cutoff. We were forming our own relationship—outside of the emotional amalgam of my grandmother, parents, sister, and self.

The functioning position of the "bad one" or "difficult one" in a family system is best understood in terms of a reciprocally determined multigenerational process. The conflict between my mother and aunt seems best understood in terms of interlocking triangles. It was not based on the problems or personality of one person.

After I met with Aunt Lee in March 1999, I sent her a letter with a photo of herself and me and spoke with her on the phone several times. She was always glad to hear from me and, likewise, I enjoyed connecting with her.

Aunt Lee's memory was definitely fading. Nevertheless, I was glad to be getting the opportunity to know and relate to her. By developing a one-to-one relationship my perception of her changed from that of the "difficult one"—a view I "inherited" without questioning from my parents—to that of a warm, humorous, and multifaceted aunt.

Aunt Lee encouraged me to make contact with her son, Russ. According to his sister, Susie, Russ had been quite cut off from his mother and his sister. He saw his mother infrequently, while Susie was more present and more involved in her mother's care. In addition, my sister Kathy and her son Josh had been angry with Russ and had been cut off from him for more than a year.

On February 5, 2000, my wife and I went to visit Susie and her husband, who were in New York for business. The next day a friend organized a brunch including Susie, my wife and I, my sister Kathy, Josh, and Russ. I had suggested that our friend invite Russ, knowing that my sister and nephew did not want to have contact with him based on some recent disappointing experiences they had had with him. My sister and nephew did not know Russ was coming. I viewed this meeting as another opportunity to deal with cutoff. My view was that the cutoff that had been bridged with Aunt Lee was continuing to play itself out in the cutoffs between Susie, Russ, and their mother and between my sister, nephew, and Russ. Indirectly, there was also a cutoff between Russ and me.

When Russ arrived at the brunch, my sister and nephew were there and looked quietly surprised. I went right over and greeted Russ. Then my sister and nephew did the same. The ice was broken. My sister, nephew, and I all had direct one-on-one contact with Russ.

In June of 2001, I took another trip to Los Angeles, the purpose of which was twofold: (1) to visit Aunt Lee and Susie, her family, and the paternal cousins I had met two years prior; and (2) to meet and make contact with two paternal first cousins I had never met before. The latter is discussed in the next section of this chapter. The visit with Aunt Lee was a great pleasure. Between visits we spoke on the phone quite frequently. An ease of relating was present. In July she broke her hip and was in rehabilitation. In a phone call on July 24, 2001, Aunt Lee said: "Your visit was the highlight of the year." I would say likewise for myself. Our relationship continued to grow.

BEGINNING EFFORTS TO BRIDGE
CUTOFF WITH TWO FIRST COUSINS

In February 1999, while preparing for my first trip to Los Angeles to see my Aunt Lee, I ran across the name and address of my paternal Uncle Manny's second wife, Aunt Thelma. A bell rang in my head. Even though I had heard my parents refer to her and their daughters, Joy and Lani, I had never met them. Also, I had never met Uncle Manny's first wife, Aunt Sarah. She and Uncle Manny had divorced many years before I was born. She died of lung cancer in 1984, at the age of 89. Another cutoff. Uncle Manny married Thelma, who wasn't Jewish, in Mexico in 1933. Figure 4.4 is a family diagram that illustrates the cutoff of Uncle Manny from his parents, his four brothers and their families, his first wife, Sarah, and their children Lorry, Jack, and Joan.

I saw my Uncle Manny on only two or three occasions. He, the eldest of the five brothers; the middle brother, Frank; and my father were working in the family sportswear business. Uncle Manny, a traveling salesman, would come to Pennsylvania or New York where my father was sales manager, and I would see him briefly. He seemed nice but distant. I remember him with

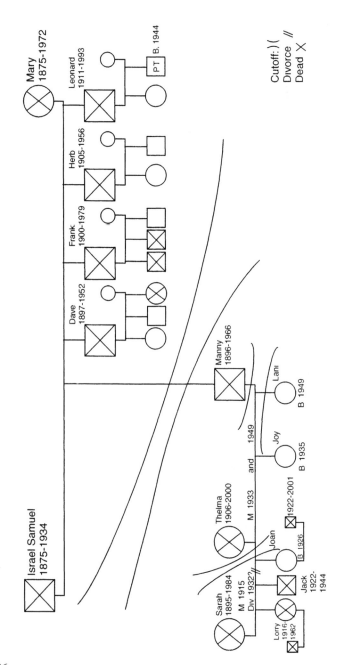

FIGURE 4.4. Cutoff between Uncle Manny and his family of origin and his nuclear families.

126

white hair slicked back, suntanned, wearing a cream-colored suit and speaking with a mildly southern drawl that surprised me. My parents described Uncle Manny as being an unreliable "playboy." He had had to be bailed out of jail on at least one occasion by the family. I was told that he did not receive a share of the family business as his four other brothers had, due to debts from gambling and drinking that his parents had helped him with. Family stories indicate a triangle in which Uncle Manny was the spoiled, doted-upon firstborn son of his mother, my grandmother. He was in a distant and conflictual relationship with his father, my grandfather. He was described by my parents, without rancor, as a kind of family outsider—another cutoff.

Uncle Manny and Aunt Sarah had three children. Their eldest child was my cousin Lorry, the firstborn grandchild of my paternal grandparents. She had lived in Los Angeles with her husband and two daughters. I had met her a couple of times before my family moved away from Los Angeles. She died from a brain tumor in 1962. There has been a cutoff with virtually no contact between her daughters Gail and Carole and their grandfather and their uncles and their cousins, including me. I have just begun to make contact with these two cousins once removed. This effort is too new to report in this chapter.

The second child of Uncle Manny and Aunt Sarah was Jack, a dashingly handsome youth who was killed in a Jeep accident on a military base during World War II. The youngest child was Joan, a beautiful young woman, who married another first cousin, Dick, the eldest son of Uncle Frank (the middle brother) and Aunt Rose. I lived close to my cousins Joan and Dick and their three sons for three years as a young adolescent and continued to see them over the years. Joan never spoke about her father.

I never questioned why we didn't see Uncle Manny, Aunt Sarah, Aunt Thelma, or Manny and Thelma's children, Joy and Lani. My parents occasionally mentioned Joy and Lani, but for the most part it seemed as if they didn't exist. This denial of their existence is typical of secondary cutoffs. It was during the bridging of my cutoff from Aunt Lee that I realized I had another aunt from whom I was cut off: Aunt Thelma. I tried calling Aunt Thelma in March of 1999, when I was in California. Ironically, she was living in elder housing in the same development as my wife's uncle and aunt, with whom we were visiting. My phone calls went unanswered. I was later to find out from her daughter, Lani, that she was hospitalized during that time. The following summer I tried reaching Lani, having gotten her telephone number from my cousin Joan, her half sister. Both times I called, Lani was not at home, but I did speak with her son Chris, a teenager, who filled me in on his family. I found out that my Aunt Thelma was living near them. I decided that I would wait to call her until I spoke with one of her daughters, thinking that she was very old and maybe it would be confusing to hear from me, a nephew she had never met.

In November 2000, I won two roundtrip airplane tickets in a raffle at the twenty-fifth anniversary of the Georgetown Family Center. I decided that I would use the tickets to go to Los Angeles to visit Aunt Lee and her daughter and family, and hopefully to make contact with my first cousins Joy and Lani as part of my effort to work on cutoff in my family. I tried reaching my Aunt Thelma at the nursing home. I found out that she had died the previous February 2000. I realized that I had lost the opportunity to speak with or see my aunt. A nurse did tell me that my aunt was a very nice person and that her daughters were equally nice and very caring children. I spoke with Lani, the younger sister, age fifty-one. She seemed interested in meeting with me. She suggested I talk with Joy, her older sister, and coordinate our getting together. I spoke with Joy and we arranged to meet on June 22, 2001, at her home in San Clemente.

When I arrived at Joy's house, I found that Lani lived right next door but was at work. She stopped in later in the visit. I sensed that Joy was somewhat anxious about meeting this strange cousin she had never seen before. We immediately began asking each other questions about our lives and our families. Figure 4.5 is a family diagram that illustrates the secondary cutoff between Joy and Lani and their families and the Titelman extended family.

Joy, age sixty-six, was warm and had a good sense of humor. Her husband also was affable and comfortable to be around. Both of them were retired. They have two sons, Brian, thirty-six, married, and Cameron, thirty-four, divorced with one son. I noticed that there were no photographs of my Uncle Manny, nor were there any photographs of my Aunt Thelma. Joy said that she had no pictures of either parent. According to Joy, Uncle Manny and Aunt Thelma met in Los Angeles and supposedly were married in Mexico, in 1933. She said that her parents may not actually have gotten married then because they got married again before Lani's birth in 1949. Joy told me about her childhood. After being born at the same hospital where I was born in Los Angeles, nine years before me, she moved with her parents and sister all over the country: Michigan, Rhode Island, Long Island, Chicago, and Texas. Finally, Uncle Manny and Aunt Thelma lived in Miami for ten years until his death. Joy described her father, my Uncle Manny, as being "abusive" to her mother, her sister, and herself. She described her mother as adaptive to her father and "helpless." Cousin Joy said that Aunt Thelma had been a beautiful woman who had appeared in twenty silent movies. But Uncle Manny kept her helpless in a trailer. She couldn't drive. My cousin described her as being "nominally Protestant." At the age of sixteen, Joy left

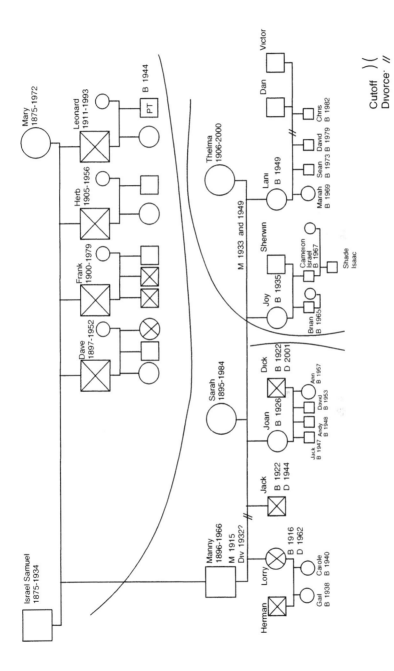

FIGURE 4.5. Secondary cutoff between Joy and Lani and their nuclear and extended families.

home because of severe conflict between her parents. She described feeling guilty about leaving Lani. Joy went to live with her maternal grandmother and stepgrandfather in Alexandria, Virginia. There, at the age of seventeen, she met Sherwin, and she converted to Judaism. They both went to George Washington University. Life was difficult because Sherwin had to go through eight hip surgeries due to a chronic, hereditary disease. Joy was only two courses shy of a master's degree in social work.

After I had visited with Joy for an hour or two, Lani joined us with her husband, Victor, whom she had recently married, following an earlier divorce. I was amazed at the resemblance between Lani and my cousin Joan, her half sister: their hair, smiles, skin color, and body build. Lani and Victor could stay only a short while as they had to attend a party. Later, Joy said that Lani was very nervous about meeting me. She told her sister she didn't think she should answer the door if I came to her house. Lani said to Joy that she should hide in her house. The power of cutoff? An association of fear with her father? They were afraid of me. I hadn't adequately prepared them for my arrival after a lifetime of being cut off. Nevertheless, Lani related warmly with me after she met me.

After pictures were taken of the three of us cousins, Lani and her husband left. Joy then told me how she had "hated the Titelman side" of her family. She felt rejected by the Titelmans. She never heard from or saw them. Joy reported that her father, Uncle Manny, never told any family stories. He cut off his family and they cut him off. She knew that he was thrown out of Penn State University. In describing her father she said that he had instant mood changes. Joy described Uncle Manny as having an impulse disorder, involving alcohol and gambling. He was the stereotypic traveling salesman. Joy described how her father, in 1963, had asked her to drive him to the hospital to see Lorry, her half sister, who was dying. But he would not let her come up and meet her half sister. This anecdote suggests the active part that Uncle Manny played in keeping Joy and Lani from getting to know the Titelman family. It is interesting that Joy gave her oldest son, Cameron, the middle name of Israel, which is the first name of our grandfather, without knowing that was his name. Joy's son Cameron gave his son, Shade, the middle name Isaac, which is the name of our great-grandfather. She also converted to Judaism, her father's and her husband's religion, even though she was very cut off from her father. Beneath the severe cutoff that existed between Joy and her father I suspect that attachment existed.

Cousin Joy and her husband took me to dinner at a magical restaurant on the ocean. She described our meeting as "spooky, a lot of ghosts I didn't even know existed." I left with the sense that I had begun a journey to know these two first cousins from whom I had been totally cut off. In the next six months I exchanged many e-mails with Joy and a couple with Lani. We also exchanged photographs.

On July 1, 2001, a few days after I returned home from my California visit, I sent the following e-mail:

Dear Joy,

The chance to meet and visit with you meant a lot to me. I apologize for arriving at your doorstep with so little preparation in terms of e-mail, letters, or phone calls. I am also sorry that I didn't get the opportunity to meet and know my Aunt Thelma. I wish I had followed up earlier to at least speak with her over the phone. I guess part of this, a big part, is the cutoff in our family. And while I have been trying to learn more about the Titelman family for almost thirty years, I am also subject to the anxiety about meeting family members I haven't been introduced to. Anyway, I am glad that we did meet and hope we will be in communication with each other . . . thank you and Sherwin for the enjoyable visit and the lovely dinner overlooking the sea.

Sincerely, Pete

In that e-mail I also asked if it would be okay to give her e-mail address to our cousin Susie, whom I had told about the visit. Also, I asked how she would feel if her half sister Joan wanted to contact her. In response, also on July 1, Cousin Joy wrote back: "I would be glad to be in touch with my cousins and half sister, but the family tree will really come in handy here because I can't seem to remember whose children are from which uncle. To be honest, there wasn't much in the way of contact with my mother's family, either, but at least Thelma would talk about them once in a while." She further wrote:

Thanks for sending the family tree and the wonderful letter from Edna Hillman. She must have worked very hard to compile such a detailed history of so many people. It was jarring to hear her ask about my father in 1980 when he had died so many years ago, in 1966. I am still bemused by all of this and don't quite know how to respond to the gift of a family whom I never knew, at this stage in my life. I know my children will also be interested to see all the information you have provided.

Later in the e-mail she asked if I would like to see a few pictures of my Aunt Thelma. She wrote:

If you had grown up around her, she would have taught you to recognize beauty in wildlife, flowers, and color. Toward the end of her life, she took art from noted teachers in Laguna Beach and became quite good (I think). She also had a great sense of humor which made her so much fun to be with.

Later the same day I spoke with my cousin Joan. She was interested in my visit with her half sister and I gave her Joy's phone number. I also sent copies of the photos of myself with Joy and Lani to each of our living first cousins with the idea of sharing my contact with our cutoff cousins. Joy later wrote the following:

> Speaking of guessing, guess who phoned me this afternoon? Joan Titelman called from Atlanta and will be visiting her son and daughter-in-law in Santa Barbara next week. On the way, she'll stay overnight in Los Angeles, giving Lani and our husbands a chance to have dinner with her on Tuesday night. She sounded very nice on the phone and mentioned that she thought it was sad that we had no contact all these years. This will be a year full of family surprises and I thank you. You're a good kid, Cousin.

> Love, Joy

Along with the above correspondence, Joy sent me a photo of my Aunt Thelma on the cover of a 1925 magazine. She was a stunning woman at the age of nineteen.

On August 8, 2001, Cousin Joy wrote me the following report about her meeting with her half sister Joan:

> Thank you again for being the prime mover in reuniting our family. Although Lani's husband and Ry weren't able to make it, we even got to meet Susan! Joan and all our "new" relatives are delightful. We had a great time taking pictures of one another and spent at least five hours talking. I'm only afraid that we must have tired Joan, who was on Atlanta time and had the long plane ride that same day. . . .

Cousin Joy then went on to speak of her negative feelings regarding her father, my Uncle Manny:

Basically, the more I learn about my father, the less I wish I knew, but neither Lani nor myself can be very surprised at anything revealed about him. We're just a little more disappointed in what a doctor friend of mine would call "piss-poor protoplasm" of the mental kind.

On August 11, 2001, I wrote to Joy asking her about some of the highlights of the get-together with her half sister, Joan, Joan's son, David, his wife, Lisa, and our cousin, Susie. Joy wrote the following in response to my request:

> Highlights of our first get-together, for me, included the amazing realization that it was so easy for us to meet and immediately begin to act like a family. I suppose this is due to the warmth and generosity of spirit that everyone was able to share with your having paved the way. It might not be so easy for other "disenfranchised" families to establish that sense of trust. There was no attempt to isolate the cause of the cutoff. It was merely dismissed as circumstances beyond all of our control. I wonder if it could have been possible to achieve reunion if any of the main characters in the drama were still living? It was interesting to me that Joan bemoaned growing up without a father, while I bemoaned growing up with one. I was very touched by the bond that seemed to blossom between Lisa and Sherwin (they both share the same hereditary disease). Their respect for each other and the challenges they face were so apparent. She is a little darling! I wish I had had the chance to talk to Susie for a longer time.

In conversations with my cousins Susie and Joan I got reports that their meeting with Joy and Lani was a warm and meaningful experience. Susie described the dinner as "wonderful." Both Joan and Joy shared the unfortunate bond of being angry and disappointed with their father, my Uncle Manny. Perhaps they may yet come to share a picture of their father that is more neutral, more balanced. It is my guess that while Uncle Manny was the "problem one" of his generation, and of the following generation, such a functioning position was reciprocally determined by his relationship with his parents—my grandparents—and his siblings—my father and four uncles. Stories about my grandfather, my father, and his brothers reveal that the characteristics attributed to Uncle Manny—being a playboy, irresponsibility, aggression, negativity, and sarcasm toward his spouses and children—were, to some degree, all characteristics of Titelman males. Yet Titelman males are also seen as being intelligent, entrepreneurial, handsome, and generous. I would suggest that Uncle Manny may have also had some of those positive qualities, as well as those characteristics that his family found reprehensible.

CONCLUSION

In retrospect, the author believes that he could have done several things differently in his efforts to bridge cutoff. First, rather than talk for many years about being cut off from his Aunt Lee while knowing that he was buying into his parents' biases and immaturities about her, he might have begun his effort to get to know her earlier. From this author's perspective, working on bridging cutoff can take many years. Actually, it is a lifelong endeavor, as is the larger effort to differentiate a self in one's family. It was only after both of his parents died and when his aunt initiated contact with him, at the time of his father's death, that the author began his effort. He would view that as a sign of his own immaturity, his continuing to "go along with" or be fused with his parents.

In the effort to bridge the cutoff with his cousins, Joy and Lani, the author believes he did not do enough preparatory communication through phone, e-mail, or letter before meeting them in person. Had more preparation been undertaken, the author believes his cousins might have been more comfortable when they met him. The effort to bridge cutoff with those two cousins is just in the beginning stage. Only time and continued contacts will indicate if this effort will be fruitful. However, the decision to present a beginning effort with the two cousins was undertaken because it provided another example of working on secondary cutoff. This can offer potential benefits to further work on differentiation, by being less a part of the "family herd" while at the same time being a more responsible member of the family as a whole.

The gains the author believes he has made from his still continuing effort to bridge cutoff with at least some members of his family, include the experience of taking more leadership within his extended family, taking on more responsibility to know his family and to be known by them, and being an available resource to them. This effort seems to have yielded not only a greater sense of personal confidence and integrity but also a growing respect for all members of the family, including those whose views or behavior may differ from his own.

The author's future goals to bridge cutoff include seeking to maintain and build his relationship with Aunt Lee, the only remaining member of the older generation. He will also seek to learn more about two of his other aunts by marriage who died without his ever meeting them. The author and his sister are two of fifteen first cousins. Of the five that have died, two he did not know at all, two he barely knew, and one he knew quite well, having had a fairly open, person-to-person relationship with him. The author will seek to get to know his other first cousins better. Another goal is the continuing effort to know and develop personal relationships with many first cousins once removed. The author will seek to learn about and have more contact with cousins who are from distant branches of the family. Bridging cutoff does not come about through one positive visit or a few e-mails. It is a long process that once begun needs to be tended over the course of one's life. Cutoff is a reciprocal process. The author assumes that efforts to bridge cutoff on his part will not always be met by other family members, who may not have the same motivation or interest. However, cutoff is a reciprocal process and if one continues to make contact with a cutoff relative, or with those family members in his or her network, such an effort, even if not pleasurable, can be part of an individual's effort to be both responsible to self and to others in the family.

In addition, it is his hope that by working to bridge cutoff in his family, the author's effort will accrue to his children. A by-product of this work may lead them to gain a fuller sense of who they are, as well as a potentially more available family network that can be an invaluable resource in their effort to be both responsible for themselves and to others.

In this chapter the author has illustrated the concept of secondary cutoff by describing his effort to understand and modify his own functioning in his family system. He has contextualized his understanding of cutoff between his family of origin and particular members, aunts, an uncle, and two first cousins, in his paternal family. This is not to say there are not other cutoffs that exist on both the paternal and maternal sides of the family. Rather, this is where the author directed his focus in his ongoing efforts toward the differentiation of self. The author began by describing how he came to understand that cutoff was alive and thriving over the course of the multigenerational emotional process with his paternal family. His growing discovery and understanding of the long-term history of cutoff, for example, the fact that his father and uncles were unaware of the existence of eight of their uncles and aunts, led him to focus on the presence of cutoff, embedded in undifferentiation, in relations between his family of origin and his extended family.

The author came to realize that the cutoff that existed between his parents and his aunt, which he "inherited" through his fusion with his parents, represented his own position in interlocking triangles that originated in the triangle involving his paternal grandmother, mother, and aunt. The latter triangle appears to have originated in the primary triangles involving the author's father and grandparents and the author's uncle and grandparents. In another case, the author's cutoff from two female cousins could be traced back to the interlocking triangles involving the grandfather, grandmother, uncle (with the uncle being in a fused position with his mother and a distant and conflictual relationship with his father), and interlocking triangles involving the uncle and his siblings, including the author's father.

This chapter provides examples of the following:

1. primary and secondary cutoff;
2. primary and secondary triangles and how they are interlocked over the course of multigenerational emotional process;
3. the place of the projection process whereby certain individuals occupy the functioning position of the "problem person." Particular forms of the family projection process are reciprocally determined rather than being "caused" by the problematic behavior of the designated individual. The perception of a family member as being "the problem" is based on a lack of understanding of the way the family system co-creates the "problem person." It is the presence of undifferentiation in family members that creates cutoff. Usually it takes many family members and multiple generations to create cutoff.); and
4. the place of undifferentiation (or fusion of self in the family) in conjunction with chronic anxiety, which underlies an individual's propensity to initiate and perpetuate cutoff that began earlier in the emotional process of the family.

There are two theoretical principles underlying the effort to bridge secondary emotional cutoff in the family:

1. Working on secondary cutoff is a continuation of the effort to detriangle self from the parental triangle, by reviving the original emotional system whether the parents are alive or dead. This provides an opportunity to deal with the unresolved attachment to one's parents by utilizing that which preceded and succeeded the parent-child triangle in the multigenerational family emotional system.
2. The effort and even the success of bridging cutoff do not create differentiation. Rather, decreasing cutoff by developing person-to-person relationships with family members and gaining more neutrality—by

becoming a better observer and controlling one's emotional reactiveness in response to family members—sets the base for being able to take I-Positions (defining self through action) in relation to family members. This in turn creates the possibility of increasing one's level of differentiation of self.

REFERENCES

Bowen. M. (1984). "Two Days with Murray Bowen, MD." Program sponsored by The Western Psychiatric Institute and Clinic, University of Pittsburgh, Pittsburgh. PA.

Titelman. P. (1987). Reaction to death in a family. In P. Titelman (Ed.). *The Therapist's Own Family* (pp. 317-347). Northvale. NJ: Jason Aronson, Inc.

Chapter 5

Toward Undoing Cutoff:
A Twenty-Five-Year Perspective

Brian J. Kelly

INTRODUCTION

This case study begins in 1976 when a thirty-five-year-old psychologist first encountered the concept of cutoff.* At the time he was living in the Los Angeles area of California, his marriage of more than six years was ending, his three children were very young, and his wife was planning to leave California for her family home in Mississippi. His father was dying of cancer and he had been out of contact with any relative for over three years. He was plagued with a fear of abandonment despite the fact that he was involved with another woman. Prior experience with therapy had indicated that his father was at fault and that he should move on and put this behind him. This was not a satisfying solution.

Mr. A, as he will be referred to in this chapter, was attending a lecture by Dr. Murray Bowen, and it was here that he encountered the concepts of cutoff and the multigenerational transmission process. What he heard was that when one is cut off from the significant emotional persons in life, especially those in one's family of origin, both parties are participating in those cutoff processes. As a result, the same tendencies toward cutoff became a part of every relationship. In essence, an individual is either perpetuating or reversing a cutoff. There is no in between. It is most unlikely that a person perpetuating a cutoff with his or her family of origin can become adept at managing other relationships differently. This is true because, while an individual is in the process of managing his or her most stressful relationships by avoidance and cutoff, it is such an automatic part of his or her life that no other options

---

*The author wrote this account in the third person in order to achieve a higher degree of objectivity in presenting a personal narrative.

139

will be available for reasoned consideration when any other relationship is anxious. Bowen theory postulates that all humans will respond in an automatic fashion when sufficient anxiety is present. Each person learns, in his or her formative years, to manage the anxiety within the family system in specific ways. The individual might develop an overresponsible, fix-it mentality, become a peacemaker by sacrificing self, or become a distancer and an avoider by withdrawing. People who cut off are in the last category. It is how they survive, physically and/or emotionally, in the face of their fears of rejection or control, and they will do it again and again when their fears well up in other relationships. Anxious humans are very predictable, for once a person's brain senses a threat (real or imagined) it will trigger the only survival response it knows. It is unrealistic to believe that any individual can continue to employ one method of managing fear and threat in important relationships and succeed in controlling the same tendencies in another relationship.

In addition, Mr. A learned from Dr. Bowen's lecture that the absence of viable contact with the significant formative relationships in life places one in a more anxious life situation. To be cut off from one's family of origin is to be in a very anxious position in life. New relationships become very intense, and new partners are monitored closely for signs of disapproval and abandonment. There is very little room for even the most legitimate differences to emerge and be pursued without strong emotional pressures to change. Furthermore, extreme cutoff of Mr. A's type was the product of several generations and, given that a family is a single emotional unit, cutoff cannot begin to be reversed without immediately approaching the most emotionally laden relations in the family of origin.

Writing on emotional cutoff in 1976, Bowen stated,

> the life pattern of cutoffs is determined by the way people handle their unresolved emotional attachments to their parents. The concept deals with the way people separate themselves from the past in order to start lives in the present generations. (Bowen, 1978, p. 382)

He also wrote that the intensity of the separation from the past increased the probability that the pattern of cutoff would be played out in the cutoff person's own history of marriage, as well as in the lives of his or her children. Bowen pointed out that an individual who runs away from his family is as emotionally dependent on the family as the person who never leaves home. People in these situations need closeness but are allergic to it. Even so, the one who stays on the scene has advantages over those who cut off because they have more emotional support. Basically, people who have cut off will most likely cut off again. People who continue the cutoff are vulnerable to a life pattern of impulsive marriages and serial relationships.

This view of a family as a single multigenerational unit is vital in any effort to reverse a cutoff from one's family of origin. It means that the initial efforts to reverse a lifelong pattern of distance. avoidance, blame, and cutoff can begin with manageable steps. Contact with the more emotionally peripheral members (uncles, aunts, cousins) of the extended family is, after all, contact with the system. Gathering information about earlier generations from genealogical sources such as wills, census records, and birth/death certificates. with an eye to learning about the facts of the family, is also a calming step during early efforts to reconnect with family. Calm contact with the emotional field of one's family is a positive step and a reversal of the patterns of avoidance. blame, withdrawal, and cutoff.

Mr. A reports that he was immediately aware, to some extent, of his participation in the cutoff with his family. It was because he believed his father had rejected him that Mr. A removed himself from the entire family, despite the knowledge that there were aunts, uncles, and cousins who would be willing to continue relationships with him. His reaction to his father was so intense that he believed all was lost; no other family member or group seemed significant. Such thinking is a product of the intensity of Mr. A's relationship with his father. Mr. A also thought he was powerless to do anything about what he saw as an intransigent father. So he gave up on family but sought approval and acceptance elsewhere, while being hyperreactive to disapproval in all relationships. What Mr. A heard that day struck him as an accurate description of his life experiences. It was much more than an explanation of a life course that was dissatisfying: it was a view of himself, not as a victim, but as someone empowered to do something. What had seemed hopeless now was viewed with the possibilities of making a difference in his rapidly changing personal life. The future seemed to be something that could be shaped more positively—because as an individual works toward an "open" relationship in the extended family, anxiety will be reduced. An open relationship system is the opposite of emotional cutoff. It refers to a family in which family members have a reasonable degree of emotional contact with one another. Relative openness in a family is not a cure in and of itself, but it reduces anxiety, and the lower level of anxiety allows motivated family members to begin slow steps toward better functioning. Any successful effort that goes toward improving the frequency and the quality of contact with the extended family will predictably improve the family's level of adjustment and reduce symptoms in the nuclear family. This is most obvious in the families with more complete cutoffs.

MR. A'S FAMILY HISTORY AS KNOWN IN 1976

Mr. A was born in Connecticut in 1940. His mother was twenty-five years old, suffering from both diabetes and tuberculosis, and an only child of her mother's second marriage. His father was twenty-three years old, a brakeman on the railroad, and the oldest of eight. Both sets of grandparents lived on the same street, one and a half blocks apart. Mr. A has no memory of his mother, who died in a sanitarium fifteen months after his birth. He lived with his father and maternal grandparents until he was six years old.

In 1946 Mr. A's father remarried, picked Mr. A up from school one day · and brought him to live with his new wife and her parents. Mr. A never saw his maternal grandparents again and did not visit his paternal grandparents, aunts, or uncles for several years. In 1948, when Mr. A was seven years old, a son was born to his father and stepmother. In 1952, upon returning from summer camp, Mr. A was informed that his father "no longer lived with the family." His father and he moved to a house in a nearby town and did not see his stepbrother, stepmother, or her parents again. Three months later, Mr. A was informed that his father was marrying a third time. Nine months later that union produced a baby girl, born in New Jersey, where they had settled after leaving Connecticut.

Mr. A reported that he was a poor, troubled student. He had intense, negative relations with his father, characterized by lack of conversation and physical discipline administered by his father and stepmother during his high school years (1954-1960). He had a positive relationship with his young half sister and with his stepmother's parents. He also had good relations with his paternal grandmother, aunts, and uncles.

In 1960, he graduated from high school. The family moved to Rhode Island and Mr. A enlisted in the Coast Guard. After boot camp, an incident occurred when Mr. A was late to a meeting with his parents because he chose to see his half brother for the first time in eight years. When he informed his father of his decision, his father announced that he would not wait the extra two hours, leaving Mr. A feeling disowned. Mr. A had no contact with his father during the next two years. Then a reconciliation did occur, and Mr. A had some contact with his nuclear family from 1963 to 1972. Those years also included the pursuit of a doctoral degree, a marriage, and the birth of three children. Minimal contact was maintained with the extended paternal family. No contact occurred with his half brother. Mr. A's father was out of touch with his own father and Mr. A did not feel free to risk contact with people his father had cut off (Figure 5.1).

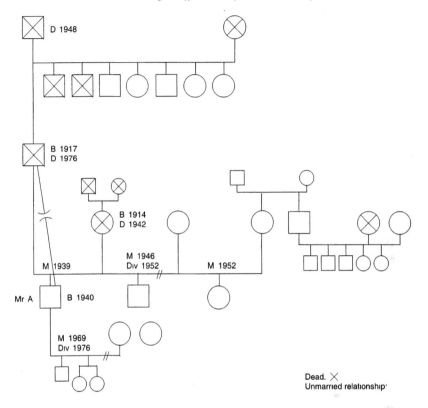

FIGURE 5.1. Mr. A's known family in 1976.

MR. A'S HISTORY THROUGH THE LENS OF THEORY

Bowen theory views relationships as mutually influencing, so one would want to understand Mr. A's own contribution to his isolation. It is an important question for him to answer if he is to be more than a helpless victim. It will also be important to raise questions about the role extended family played with Mr. A's father that aided the pattern of cutoff and extreme emotional distancing. Since Bowen theory looks to reciprocal functioning in relationships and sees all relationships as the product of the participation of all its family members, there is no blaming to be done. This family and all families are composed of people struggling to survive in a sea of anxiety. The indications in this family history point to a high level of anxiety. Note the early death of Mr. A's mother, serial marriages, and almost complete cutoff from the past on the part of his father. It would seem than Mr. A was born into a cutoff position in life. When Mr. A first heard of the Bowen concept of cutoff he had viewed himself as a victim of his father's anger and thought he was helpless to change the relationship. He also viewed lost family members with idealized thinking: "If only I had a mother, things would be different."

From the broader spectrum of Bowen theory, one must question what the characteristics and circumstances were that would cause a man to take himself and his son away from his maternal grandparents. Although we can only speculate at this point, speculation requires Mr. A to think differently about the situation. This is an important first step in beginning the task of undoing a cutoff.

Indeed, cutoff seems to produce rigid, polarized thinking and it is necessary to expand thoughtfulness and curiosity about alternate explanations for people's behavior. Dr. Bowen once asked, in reference to Mr. A's father, "What did you do to piss that good man off?" It was, according to Mr. A, a benchmark question. Mr. A took it seriously and sought answers to the question. It was the first step toward thinking differently about himself and his family of origin.

At all costs, one must avoid joining in the blaming process if therapy is to be successful. The task of the therapist is to remain neutral and curious about conditions that would account for emotionally charged behavior. Mr. A's divorce and pending loss of relationships with his young children were a powerful motivator. He was immediately struck by the tendency for patterns to repeat themselves from generation to generation. Dr. Bowen had stated that the intensity of cutoff increases with each generation. Mr. A did not want that for himself or his children. He also saw for the first time that his father was cut off from his family, and that fact was undoubtedly a major factor in the intense father-son relationship he and his father had.

INITIAL STEPS TO UNDO CUTOFF

April 1976-1981

Shortly after encountering Dr. Bowen and the concept of cutoff, Mr. A wrote his father a letter aimed at establishing calm contact, if that were possible. Mr. A's father did not read the letter and died within days of its arrival. However, others read it and Mr. A was notified of the death by his sister. He attended the funeral with the idea of reawakening as many relationships as possible. His plan was to visit and be friendly with as many people as possible. Mr. A, who was living in California, flew to Connecticut and was met at the airport by a cousin, the son of one of his father's brothers. During the week of the funeral he stayed with two of his father's brothers and met his half brother for the first time since 1960. He was able to have friendly visits with his father's siblings, who gathered together for the funeral. The next day he visited his stepmother and her parents, as well as his half sister. His stepmother reluctantly agreed to another visit in the future, as did his half sister and half brother. Upon returning from the funeral, Mr. A began at least monthly correspondence with each relative he had contacted. He also decided to commit to formal training with Dr. Bowen at the Georgetown University Family Center in Washington, DC. This would bring him east four times a year, so the mechanism was in place to visit his family with each trip. One uncle, Mr. A's father's youngest brother, flew to California for a visit. The strategy for all these contacts was to monitor himself and try to control any tendency to be critical or defensive and to avoid any polarization: "Just hang in there and try to be helpful if the opportunity presents itself." Other important moves were to make contact with his first stepmother and to gather facts about his biological mother's life and family.

To accomplish this, Mr. A began a record search, looking for data in old city directories, cemetery records, census records, and church records. Several visits to his mother's and his paternal grandparents' graves produced some data, but it was not until Mr. A got over his automatic assumption that his father owned the grave his mother was buried in that things happened. First, the grave belonged to a man he had never heard of before: his mother's half brother. Using the address on the register, he found that it included a phone number and address. Mr. A wrote a letter and, after six weeks, got a response from a cousin who was joyous and filled with information and an invitation to visit. The letter also included the address of two of three aunts, his mother's half sisters. When Mr. A visited this cousin he was asked to stay the night, slept in his mother's bed, and was presented with jewelry that had been held for him for thirty years.

Contact continued with other family members and the visits were less anxious. Mr. A was now in contact with twelve relatives on a monthly basis. Issues were not dealt with, but Mr. A kept all informed of his contacts with others as he monitored his reactions. He noted that when visiting his stepmother things were pleasant but formal. He developed the idea that nothing was going to change until there was a shift in the family. The two important steps were that his grandparents were in their nineties and he knew he would have the opportunity to contribute when death came.

In November of 1979, three and a half years into this process, Mr. A's stepmother's father died, and he flew to the funeral with the idea of lending a helping hand wherever possible and behaving as a responsible family member. This proved to be important. His helpful presence brought with it common experiences and appreciation. Through action, Mr. A defined himself as a family resource and barriers fell. He was now welcomed to spend the weekend, borrow the car, and was included in humorous tales of events surrounding the funeral. His stepmother once said, as she lent him her car, "I don't know why you are going to see those crazy people you think are your family." Then, in March 1981, Mr. A's stepgrandmother died. His half sister was out of the country so the primary task of helping by being a presence to his stepmother fell to Mr. A. At the conclusion of that visit, Mr. A was told, "I am glad your sister was not here for this, for it was good for us." From then on he was introduced as "my son."

Theoretical Comments

It is important to remember that one is either perpetuating a cutoff or working at bridging a cutoff. It is a fact that the quality of a human life is dependent on the quality of relationships once the necessities of food, shelter, and clothing are in place. Friendliness, curiosity, interest in the other, and a desire to be known characterize quality relationships. One can define oneself as a calm person by attempting to be a calm and thoughtful presence in the lives of others. If this does not exist with one's family of origin, it is not likely to exist on a lasting basis in other intimate relationships, since how one participates in relationships is repetitive and automatic when anxiety is present. Mr. A spent years staying in contact with his family. At one point he described a list of twenty-three monthly contacts (phone calls, cards, letters). He reported that he did not get many responses to his initiations, but the fact that he persisted changed the way he was received on visits. The family knew what he had been doing and responded with apologies for not writing back, rather than expressing awkward suspicion about why he was visiting after so many years. This points out that being in contact is much more important than focusing on who initiates the contacts. Mr. A also stated that it was significant to him that while visiting different "factions" of the family, he did not criticize or defend other factions. Indeed, to ally with one side against another would forbid the development of open relationships with everyone. Remaining neutral and curious about conflicts and resentments, and actively seeking other possible explanations for people's behavior is important. Finally, to succeed one must keep in mind that bridging is a lifelong process, or at least the objectives are long range. This requires patience and persistence along with a commitment to be present and accounted for at nodal events in the family (births, deaths, weddings, moves, and divorces). Emotional forces in a family are at times in transition, such as when nodal events are occurring (especially deaths) and openings to the family are available.

During these early years Mr. A focused on the effort to establish contact with as many relatives as possible. He knew that while the ultimate goal was to define a self, or to work at differentiation, these early years were aimed at just getting calmer through being in contact. An individual cannot define self in a relationship while the relationship is tenuous. Early efforts simply went toward easing the tension of being present in the lives of the people who had been part of a tumultuous history. It would be foolish to think that prior experience would not cause them to approach Mr. A with suspicion and anxiety, and Mr. A's own anxiety must also be considered. Indeed, Mr. A found it necessary to plan each contact prior to each visit, letter, and phone call. He learned that having an idea of what he would say and how he wanted to present himself fostered calm contact.

This is not only true of his contacts with his family of origin but also with his young children and their mother. Letters were, for the most part, kept humorous and light, and were factual reports on his life. Issues were not engaged in as Mr. A remained self-effacing as part of a plan to keep from being critical of others or defensive of self. Whenever he was caught off guard by an angry or critical comment, Mr. A would respond with, "I'm listening to you," "That's worth thinking about," or similar comments. Mr. A developed the habit of writing reflections on thought-provoking conversations to those with whom he had had those conversations. Once a topic was mentioned, it could always be returned to for further reporting of the thoughts and questions it had raised. To respond thoughtfully was a goal, and the swiftness of the response was not important. It is important to know how you want to be perceived by family members and to behave consistently with your desires. To be angry, resentful, impulsive and unreliable, or dishonest is not conducive to maintaining calm contact. As Mr. A phrased it, "It is important to remember that if you want to be understood you have the responsibility of creating an environment that is conducive to being understood."

Mr. A found his efforts to learn the facts about his ancestors were very helpful. The gathering of information gave him a sense of connectedness to the past that was calming. That he had made the effort to find the facts defined him to other relatives as being genuinely interested. He even began to be viewed as a resource for family information among his relatives.

It is important to note that without a theory to rely on as a compass for steering him in the right direction, all this work would not have been possible. Almost nothing came naturally. It was faith in the Bowen theory and the ability of coaches to guide and predict obstacles that kept him going. Another factor that was helpful was his ability to use Bowen theory in a formal way in his work environment. There he could see patterns of functioning and test the theory out. Work became a laboratory to practice Bowen theory and to learn things that could be applied with his family of origin. It was a great exercise in thinking theory and observing patterns of interactions.

Mr. A is quick to remind people that the effects of his efforts were not as rapid and as sweeping as he had hoped. During this first five-year period he divorced, married his second wife, divorced that wife, and almost immediately entered a third marriage. This happened despite all kinds of anxieties about the person that he married. These anxieties caused him to be overly focused on the behavior of his new wife. Change of the magnitude that differentiation involves does not come easily, quickly, or in huge chunks.

Mr. A recalls that one day he found himself feeling frustrated with his inability to move as quickly as he wanted with his relatives. Then a thought struck him: "I am 2,000 miles from my nearest relative, but there is a church down the street and I have cut myself off from it despite its importance to me for most of my life." With this thought he began to go back to church and to study religion, thinking that, if he were to call himself a Catholic again, he would need a very clear idea of just what that meant. Mr. A claimed that it is difficult to measure the impact of this move, but it was significant for him and a resource for calm and thoughtful ideas.

1981-1986

During this five-year period Mr. A, who was then living in Texas, stayed involved with all the relatives he knew. Some began to relate in a more reciprocal fashion. Visits to his brother, sister, and five paternal aunts and uncles were reciprocated. He was best man at his half brother's wedding, and gave his half sister away when she married. He attended or made his presence felt at all family gatherings. If he could not be present, he sent flowers so that his interest in the family would be known. He would also seek out family histories and spent considerable effort searching out documentation on the family using church records and state and local records such as census records, birth and death certificates, and probate records. Mr. A voiced a willingness to view his father in a more neutral, less negative light. To that end, he would ask people what they recalled of his father's strengths and what were things that his father might have liked to change in himself. In tracking down records, he noticed that cutoff ran throughout the families. His maternal grandfather was never known to have contact with or to mention a relative of his own. In his stepmother's family an uncle and his son were completely cutoff. The actions expressed the belief that "it was one's Christian duty to forgive and forget, so one must forgive people who offend and forget them." Another attitude often heard was if someone was a problem for you, cut him or her off. Mr. A gathered records on five generations of his paternal family of origin and diagramed the facts of the family (Figure 5.2).

While looking at his diagram he was shocked to see that for five generations the eldest son was the least involved with the family and that this lack of involvement increased with each new generation. Mr. A's father and grandfathers were barely on speaking terms at the time of the grandfather's death. The father had taken business away from his father's company and started a competing business some years earlier. Mr. A's grandfather was the only male

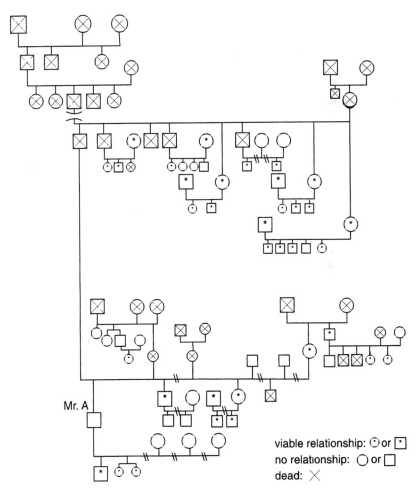

FIGURE 5.2. Mr. A's known family in 2001.

in the family to move out of the Boston area, though he kept up some contact with his siblings. Mr. A's great-grandfather had left the family business and struck out on his own, producing a split in the family that exists to this day. As Mr. A viewed the diagram, he was stunned to recognize, "My God, my father did not do anything to me. We were both caught up in a process that was bigger than we were." With the experience of that awareness came new freedom to be thoughtful about relationships and to develop a much less reactive, more neutral understanding of his father.

Theoretical Comments

Mr. A's actions during this period of time point to the importance of a persistent effort to stay in contact and focus on the facts of the family over time. Mr. A's genealogical research gave him a broader perspective when Bowen theory was imposed on the facts he had gathered. In addition, Mr. A, through contact with a wide range of relatives, encountered people as they struggled with their lives. As he viewed the intensity of others struggling with life, he started asking himself about the strengths he had inherited from his family of origin. He also became clearer about the fact that his own siblings had lived in at least as intense environments as he had and that the intensity had taken its toll on their lives. Mr. A began to believe that he might have escaped some of the intensity of focus. For example, the first six years of his life he was raised in an extended family of twelve people besides himself. Was it possible that the joint efforts of these people reduced some of the intensity that came with greater cutoff when his siblings were born? He knew that the intensity of parental focus, either positive or negative, can inhibit the development of maturity. It was very enlightening to see this in operation in his family.

This five-year period was an important time for increased efforts to define a self within the family. Important achievements during this time came with an increased ability to discuss emotionally charged issues. Most of these occurred with his stepmother, who he had discovered was the one person in the world with whom he was most reactive. During this period of time Mr. A moved from calm listening to telling her that he had a different view or memory of events. He consistently avoided seeking agreement while stressing that he had no claim to accuracy but was simply reporting on his thoughts and views. Another significant piece of self-definition was a continual expression of ideas and beliefs that came from Bowen theory. He made statements such as: "I've been thinking that all relationships are mutually influencing and so I wonder what part my father played in that." It was an interesting revelation to learn firsthand that Mr. A and his father were part of triangles with many relatives. Bowen theory (1978) states that the triangle, a three-person emotional configuration, is the molecule or the basic building block of any emotional system. The two person system may be stable as long as it is calm, but when anxiety increases, it immediately involves the most vulnerable other person to become a triangle. A triangle in moderate tension characteristically has two comfortable sides and one side in conflict. Since patterns repeat and repeat in a triangle, the people come to have fixed roles in relation to each other. (p. 373)

The task of managing self in a triangle is to keep relating to the other sides and not to be the focus or the absorber of the anxiety. In Mr. A's case, his history with his father would trigger an emotional response. If people had a positive view of the father, they would be critical of Mr. A, and if they held a negative view of the father, they would see Mr. A positively or not at fault. When this occurred, no one was seeing Mr. A as a separate individual. To buy into this would leave Mr. A defined by his parent. Either way, after a lifetime of feeling and thinking that he was a victim, the effort to manage self in these triangles required a concerted effort to be neither defensive nor critical. When he noticed people relating to him through their perception of his father, Mr. A would respond, "That is surely part of the truth, but I have been thinking there is more to it than that. Does that make sense to you?" Or "If my father were here, what do you think he would be saying?" All in all, the effort went toward creating some flexibility so that people could think in a less polarized fashion about Mr. A and his father. It is important to note that when a powerful emotional presence dies, that person is still present in the heads of those who were close to him.

Mr. A found that it was very helpful for him to spend time with his father's peers. These were much less intense relationships, and they proved to be useful practice fields for remaining neutral. An important development that bore much fruit during these years was evolving relationships with his siblings. Although Mr. A had to remain vigilant about being involved in his siblings' problems, these relationships were fun, playful, and rewarding. As his half brother and half sister reported positive, happy times with him, the older generation began to enjoy the knowledge of these developing relationships. An important point here is that when someone loved and valued by others reports positive experiences about a person, that person gains status in the eyes of those who value the one making the reports. In other words, not only do siblings provide for some much-needed playfulness, their reports to the older generation affect how a person is received and viewed by the older generations. Cousins can serve a similar function. Sometimes it is important to just be playful and enjoy relatives. Times of playfulness are part of the reward for the effort, and playfulness comes to those who are calm and not reactive.

Finally, during this period of time, as is always the case, thinking theory is vital to the effort. Bowen theory teaches that how you behave has much to do with how you are treated. As family members got more accustomed to Mr. A, he found that all contact did not require preparation, but significant contact always required preparation.

Mr. A's Children

Mr. A is convinced that the nature of his relations with his children benefited from his efforts with his family. No longer would they identify him as their lone connection to the paternal side of their family. They now had ten to twelve relatives on that side of the family with whom they could relate. They did not do much with it, but the awareness was there. Significantly, Mr. A was in all his relationships, monitoring his tendency to cut off and forcing himself to overcome initial reactions to withdraw. He was able to see in himself tendencies to want to give up on meaningful relations with others, including his children. Instead, he employed the same methods of staying in contact with them that he used with his family of origin. When one works on controlling oneself in the family of origin, one is forced to overcome destructive tendencies. The lessons learned have a profound impact on all significant relationships.

1986-1996

During the next ten years Mr. A continued to involve himself with his relatives. He moved to Connecticut in 1986 and began to involve his now-teenaged children in family life. He also involved himself with cousins who were members of his own generation. This allowed him to view firsthand how the extended family functioned and to observe how family dynamics had played out in other branches of the family. These were not uneventful years. After the move, Mr. A's third wife soon responded, "I thought that I had married an orphan, and all of a sudden this orphan is surrounded by relatives." It must have been quite a shock to have aunts, uncles, a sister and brother-in-law, and a variety of cousins knocking at the door. Life was further complicated by the arrival of his wife's two teenage children—the eldest fresh from a thirty-day psychiatric hospitalization. All in all, it was an influx of emotionally laden relationships that proved challenging. Being in New England did allow for greater participation at the Georgetown Family Center and helped with family research, both historically and through the observations of family patterns of interaction.

As may be typical of cutoff families, not much was known about the past. What was rumored was for the most part inaccurate. Mr. A, acting on family stories, searched for his paternal great-grandfather's death certificate in Massachusetts only to learn that he had died in Vermont. He scoured Massachusetts for birth certificates only to discover that the births were in Maine. This information became available through the developing relationship with a great-aunt, his grandfather's youngest sibling. This aunt was reluctant to talk until Mr. A gave her, as a gift, her father's death certificate. "Oh! That's why you are curious," she stated, as she showed him a box of old family photos and recalled that her father and uncles used to visit a cemetery in Portland, Maine. Suddenly Mr. A had access to five generations of family history and a happy, rewarding relationship with a great-aunt.

In 1988, Mr. A had a heart attack. One of the patterns that he had observed among his father's male relatives was that they were very active outside the home but accepting of most anything in their marriages. They preferred to "go along" at home rather than make waves, and for three generations none of them had seen their sixty-fifth year. Bowen theory suggests that physical dysfunction is a logical consequence of such actions. Mr. A was able to ask himself if that family pattern played a part in his heart attack. Further, he recognized a "devil-may-care" attitude toward death, as though it was beyond human influence. He did not believe this, but found himself automatically acting on an idea that ran contrary to his thinking. Mr. A recognized that he needed to make changes in relationships, especially with his wife, if he was not to surrender to an early death. Mr. A was able to do this with some success. The marriage was difficult. Mr. A reports that managing himself in the relationship with his wife and her children is very difficult for him. This insight contains some important understanding of his father and the cutoff from his maternal family. It too may have been a very difficult thing to for his father to handle.

Although the marriage ended in divorce, it lasted more than twice as long as any other relationship in Mr. A's life. Mr. A reports that he managed to emerge from that marriage more in control of himself than when he entered it. He also attaches some significance to the fact that he did not leave or stop trying to improve on his ability to be himself within that relationship. The end of the marriage did not result in panic or chaos, as had his earlier divorces. Mr. A was able to focus on himself and his responsibilities, rather than to blame or criticize any one person for the divorce. The transition to divorce was much smoother than it had ever been before.

Throughout these years, work continued as Mr. A clarified his thinking to important others, asking them about the facts of their lives that he thought would be difficult for them to discuss. He not only wanted to be known but also to know, so he committed himself to asking questions despite his fear of the reactions he might get.

Mr. A also knew by this time that the challenge was to confront his own fear and that when this was done the outcome would be positive. One such example had to do with asking his stepmother what her thoughts were on why his father had never mentioned his biological mother to him. Mr. A had never been able to comfortably speak about his mother and doing so seemed to be breaking a family taboo. Mr. A practiced this conversation in his head, approached it several times, and backed off until one day he simply said, "It has always confused me to have never been given any information about my mother. Don't you think it's curious that Dad never said anything to me?" "Son," was the response. "the easiest thing you could do is to make too much of that. I do not think it ever crossed your father's mind to discuss it with anyone." "Mom," he responded. 'I've probably made too much of it most of my life. I should have asked you years ago." They laughed and an old demon died. This is the kind of work that has slowly gone on over these ten years, along with continued family research and ongoing contact. Mr. A has made his presence known at family nodal events and social gatherings, and the cutoffs that exist among other members of his family have lessened, while the freedom to relate on a wide variety of personal issues has increased.

In the spring of 1992, Mr. A was ordained a deacon in the Roman Catholic Church. He invited every known relative to the ordination and to a party afterward. It was the first time that some of the representatives of branches of his family were in the same room. Mr. A's father's nieces. nephews. brothers, and sisters were there. For the first time Mr. A was together with his brother and sister simultaneously. The two had never spoken. At the end of the ceremony Mr. A and his brother were headed to the party. Mr. A said, "Well, you survived church without the building collapsing on you. I guess if I just keep you from your sister you will survive the party." "That won't be necessary," he replied. "You see, during the ceremony she kissed me and one hundred pounds fell from my shoulders." Mr. A reports that, as touching as that was for him, the best part was an increased openness with the important people in his life and the fact that he now thinks of himself as having one family. In twenty years he had moved from thinking he had no family to thinking he had separate families to thinking he had one family complex. but a family. Mr. A expressed it this way: "My whole life seems more integrated.

Theoretical Insights

While working at defining a self in a multigenerational family there are always difficult facts of family life to learn about. These facts are difficult because of their emotional attachments; they are not difficult in and of themselves. As Dr. Bowen repeatedly noted, facts are neutral, and if you can be neutral about them, you can discuss them with anyone. The ability to be calm in the face of emotionally charged situations is in fact what is developed within yourself as you continue to work at defining yourself within relationships. It is a lifelong process. That is the good news despite the fact that progress is not as fast or as dramatic as one would hope, given the fact that we live in a "quick fix" culture. Mr. A reports that, upon reflection, his efforts were more sporadic in these ten years than he would like to think. As a result of previous efforts he was more comfortable with his life than in the past. Yet the next event to disrupt the family never seemed far off, and those events served to activate his efforts to work on himself. The fact that Mr. A was a practicing psychologist also served as motivation and moved him out of his comfort zone. Whenever anxiety within the family rises, there is an opportunity to define oneself and resist the pushes and pulls of family members to have one ally oneself with a particular view in opposition to another's view.

1996-2000

These years represented a continued effort to be clear and nonreactive in the face of unending family issues. They also serve as a constant reminder that emotional cutoff is an extended family event. Mr. A and his father are not an isolated relationship. The tendencies to cut off physically and/or emotionally are common throughout the family system and exist in various degrees of intensity in the different branches of the family.

Mr. A has described the process of working on family cutoff as being analogous to painting the hull of a ship, as he did in his military service years. To get a raft between a dock and a ship you could move the ship gradually and imperceptibly by exerting steady pressure, but if you let up a little the ship would move back to its former position. Family can be like that. They will respond to a consistent effort, but when you withdraw the effort the family may close back in on you. Undoing cutoff is therefore a never-ending process. Mr. A recently stated, "I have learned so much about myself and about life through my efforts, and yet I still struggle to apply the knowledge I have gained in my relationships. There is so much that remains undone that one lifetime is not enough. I'm just glad I usually like the challenge."

Mr. A still has much work he would like to accomplish. He has met some cousins related to him through his biological mother, but he has not yet succeeded in establishing good relationships with that branch of his family. He still has no knowledge of his maternal grandfather and his family beyond having a copy of his grandfather's death certificate. No one on the paternal side of the family has any information about his grandfather's mother, other than the fact that she died from tuberculosis at an early age. An apparent split in the past between his paternal great-grandfather and his brother continues. Mr. A hopes to learn about that by establishing relations with relatives from that branch of the family. Indeed, there is much yet to do, but it must be accomplished while maintaining current relations.

SUMMARY AND CONCLUSION

When asked to reflect on what had been the result of his quarter century of effort, Mr. A responded, "I don't believe that anything has been as important as having something that I could dedicate my life's efforts toward. The pursuit of an enhanced quality of life, through a commitment to one theory as a road map for success, has given my life a consistent thread that has allowed for a more stable life course. I do not think that any other single factor has provided me with as much satisfaction. I believe that this dedication to a way of living is the foundation of all my good relationships and has given my life course a stability that otherwise would have eluded me."

By way of review, let us list the significant life knowledge mentioned in this chapter—what Mr. A gained as he minimized and undid cutoff in his life:

- Relationships are mutually influencing. If you are in a troubled relationship, you are a part of the problem.
- To be cut off from family places a person in a position of increased vulnerability to life's problems.
- Unresolved issues from the past infect the present.
- A family is a single multigenerational emotional unit. If you are cut off from it that fact will rule your life.
- There is always something that can be done to improve your participation in a relationship system.
- A gathering and searching for the facts of a family over time can be calming. A focus on the facts is helpful.
- Blaming, criticizing, and defensive posturing are anxious behaviors that hinder the quality of your life.
- If you participate in a problem, then you cannot legitimately claim to be an innocent victim.
- Searching and finding new ways to think about an old issue is very calming.
- To be different you must think differently so you can come to a new understanding.

- Toxic issues in families are a multigenerational phenomenon. Both the perceived persecutor and victim are part of a process that is much larger than the two of them.
- To be in contact with family is much more important than who makes the most effort to stay in contact.
- When in a cutoff position you either perpetuate it or work to undo it. There is no middle ground.
- Good relationships are open to new ideas. They stimulate thinking and they require thoughtful planning.
- Remaining neutral and curious about conflicts and resentments plus seeking other possible explanations is important.
- Times of significant loss through death and divorce are opportunities for progress in building meaningful family relationships.
- Efforts to reduce anxiety by controlling your own reactivity are significant.
- An anxious person adds anxiety, and anxiety is debilitating. Calm contact and thoughtful presence always improve a situation.
- Having a plan for anticipated anxious times and interactions is calming.
- If you want to be listened to, you must create an environment conducive for listening to take place.
- To be distant in a relationship or relationships is a function of emotion, not geography. Contact and interest do not require that you be geographically close.
- The intensity of the emotional investment parents make in a child is a major hindrance to development; whether the investment is positive or negative is not significant.
- When an individual who has been a powerful emotional presence dies, his or her presence lives on in the minds of those who were close to him or her.
- Have fun with your family no matter what. They can be enjoyed if you do not take the "craziness" seriously.
- Find a mental guidance system for your life that you can trust and rely on it until it is proven wrong. A theory can be the rudder that will keep you on a life course.

Here are Mr. A's final comments:

It should be noted that anyone who undertakes the task of undoing cutoff is engaged in a lifetime effort with many opportunities for serious mistakes. To proceed, one must be willing to change during this long-term effort. This effort requires an experienced coach. Like a sailor getting out to sea, one must be aware of how turbulent the sea can become and be prepared. Families, too, may become very stormy at unexpected moments. A knowledgeable coach is an important resource for navigating the storms and shoals that are a part of every family.

For myself, these last twenty-five years have been a quest for personal freedom, personal integrity, and the kind of stability that comes from living out a commitment to a belief. What I have gained is freedom and open relationships. I am much freer to be who I am now than I ever have been. I am much less likely to surrender myself to a relationship by complying or denying things that are important to me; I am much less likely to withdraw from a relationship to preserve myself. I demand less of others and like myself more than ever. I am satisfied with the results thus far, but the room for improvement is vast, and for that I am thankful. The efforts I have made with my family are the most satisfying achievement of my life despite the fact that I had foolishly hoped for more.

REFERENCE

Bowen, M. (1978). *Family Therapy in Clinical Practice*. New York: Jason Aronson.

Chapter 6

Bridging Cutoff with Divorced Relationships and with Family

Roberta M. Gilbert

EARLY EXPERIENCE WITH BOWEN THEORY

My naive first encounters with Bowen family systems theory at national meetings were probably similar to many professionals' then, in the 1970s, and now. I listened with curiosity and tried hard to understand. Failing to comprehend, yet intensely aroused by the talk of family relationships, I would linger afterward to try to get Bowen to see that my family problems were not covered by his remarks. My family was different. What could I do? His calm responses were even more frustrating. "I knew a guy with a family like that once. He tried very hard, but nothing much ever came of it." When psychiatrists get into a corner, they diagnose. My best assessment was that, obviously, Bowen was crazy, talking of a new theory. We did not need a new theory. We already had one—Freudian theory. Who did he think he was? Another Freud?

Still, I perceived that Murray Bowen was on to something. The new (to me) family systems approach made some kind of sense. "Cutoff" was the first of the theoretical concepts I heard. It might not work for my family, but I told my patients and later my teachers at the Menninger Clinic about cutoff. Teachers in those days showed no interest whatsoever. Patients, however, were different. Many of them recognized their cutoffs and began applying my neophyte guidance. The energy and groundedness they obtained from bridging their cutoffs with family were rather impressive.

By the time Dr. Donald Shoulberg, a serious student of Bowen, came to town and began to teach and coach interested professionals in Bowen family systems theory, I was ready to try harder to hear. The mental/emotional and relationship sectors of my life were falling apart exponentially, though I had been in a serious psychoanalytic effort for several years. No therapist or analyst with whom I had worked gave any evidence of knowledge that my difficulties might have to do with my cutoff with my family.

Many colleagues in psychoanalysis had warned me not to finish my analysis until I had "analyzed the transference," although they themselves had done just that! I didn't worry about it since I thought I had been engaged in analyses of my transferences all the way through. At any rate, when I began seriously to hear the concepts of Bowen family systems theory, I realized that here was a way of thinking and of working in therapy that was many orders of magnitude superior to anything I had been exposed to in psychiatric training. When that became clear, I announced to my analyst that I would be terminating, at least for now. I knew very well that termination is a process that usually takes months. My transference was probably far from completely analyzed. However, I could see no benefit in continuing with an inferior and extremely expensive pursuit. I was into my sixth year. When my analyst asked about the target date for termination, I forced out the words, "One week?" He thought it was the wrong way to terminate. I, however, thought it was about four sessions more than I actually needed. But I wanted to be as kind to him as possible.

A FIRST ATTEMPT TO PUT THEORY TO THE TEST

I never accepted anything, not even Bowen family systems theory, in the beginning. I would have to try it and see if it "worked" in real life. Since I had not found psychoanalytic theory all that useful in my own life or practice, I was skeptical. The only way to give it a fair test, I reasoned, would be to try to clear my thinking of all other theories, try as hard as I could to absorb all I could of Bowen theory, and then put it into life and practice as well as I was able.

After working with Dr. Shoulberg awhile, I began to commute to the postgraduate program at the Georgetown Family Center four times a year. This continued for five years. At the end of that time I moved to the Washington, DC, area to continue my study and work. All my coaches saw how cutoff I was long before I could see it.

Though unaware of the cutoff that existed between my family and me, I understood that my family relationships were not optimal. I also knew that I was cut off from some other people who had been important to me—the parents of my former husband. I thought it might be worthwhile to reestablish contact with them. But what would I say? What excuse would I use to get in touch after years of rebuffing their efforts at relationship?

At a feeling level, I was indebted to them. They had helped support my ex-husband and me through medical school. I decided on a letter. It began,

"Dear Mom and Dad, When I divorced your son I thought I had to divorce you, too." I was laboring under the illusion then that a proper divorce meant as little contact as possible—in other words, a cutoff. I had read the popular and professional literature prevalent then on divorce. I knew how important it was to "emotionally divorce." I went on, "But recently I have come to understand that I owe you a great deal. I would not be a doctor today if it were not for your assistance through school. At the present time my practice is flourishing and I would like to pay you back for the help you willingly gave. I do not know what your circumstances are, but for all I know, at this time in your lives, it might be useful if I made regular payments to you by way of trying in some way to compensate you for your aid to me."

I continued. "Further, you have never been in my home. I know Mom J. well enough to think that she would like to see where the children are living. The next time and every time you are in town I hope you will save some time for dinner or lunch here."

The response was prompt and warm. They assured me they were fine financially and had never expected any recompense. Their pleasure was to see the grandchildren grow up in a good environment, healthy and well cared for.

Soon I learned that they would be in town for a visit. At that time my children were nine and twelve. Their behavior, when it came to the finer points of etiquette, was sometimes not what I would have desired. I used the impending grandparent visit as an occasion for instruction. The visit worked some kind of magic. Both boys met the grandparents at the door and asked for their coats. Then they gave them a tour of the apartment. Grandma's chair was held for her at the table. Manners during the meal, as far as I remember, were perfect.

Thus began a relationship with my sons' grandparents that continued for some twenty years until they died. There were calls at regular intervals that became more and more meaningful to me. There were visits to Florida, where they lived, whenever possible.

Somehow this work with them eased the way for me to begin to reconnect with my former husband, who had remarried. Sometimes I called him or his wife, just to inform them of what was happening with the children. If one of the children was having a problem, I called a "family meeting" at my home where we all sat together to try to find some resolution. Sometimes this meant just agreeing on consistent discipline between the two households. Initially, his response to my overtures was not prompt and warm, as that of his parents had been. This changed over time. We were actually able to go through the weekend of our twenty-fifth reunion of medical school graduation together, during which we saw the house we had bought together as residents and met together with old friends, recalling old times.

He had become a famous surgeon by then, but when it was his turn to speak at the reunion about his life, he mentioned none of this. He spoke only of me and our children. Fortunately, I spoke later and was able to let our classmates know of his achievements.

All of this was especially meaningful because less than two years later my ex-husband died. He was only fifty-one, and although he had been quite ill and a patient for several weeks in the university hospital where he was a professor, it was not expected that he would die. The night before his death, we had talked for half an hour on the phone. As soon as I received the news of his death, I went to the city where he died to be with my sons. ages nineteen and twenty-two, for a week before the funeral.

His parents, in their eighties, had not traveled for some time. They sent word that they would be "unable" to come to the funeral. This I saw as another manifestation of the cutoff with which both our families struggled. It was clear to me, from my knowledge of Bowen theory, that their absence from the funeral of their son was not a good thing for them or for us. To me, Bowen theory dictated that they needed to be there to have this last connection with their son. If they were not going to come to the funeral physically, I determined to try to bring them in some way. I decided to call them every evening of the funeral week before retiring and walk them through the day's events.

They were extremely grateful. I was able to describe to them, in the initial days, how our oldest son, on a camping trip, could not be located. The youngest son, living a less responsible and even angry lifestyle, was the closest present relative to their dad. (My ex-husband had divorced from his second wife.) When it was time to make choices at the funeral home, the funeral director looked at the youngest son and opined, "Son, if you would rather wait until your brother is found, that is okay; we can wait." I realized someone must have talked to him about this son. There were many "take-charge" people hovering about all the events and they were all taking charge. At any rate, our youngest son thought a moment and replied to the undertaker. "No, when my brother gets here, he will have only just heard of our dad's death. He'll be in shock. I've had some time to recover. I'll make the choices now and then check them out with him." No anger or irresponsibility here. When it was time to go into the room where the choices would be made about the casket, burial, and related decisions, Dr. J's second wife, two of his close professional associates, and a few other people who loved Dr. J rose to go in also. My knowledge of Bowen theory guided me as I realized this was not really a group project. I said firmly, "My son and I will go in alone." We did.

His brother seconded all the decisions the next day, except for one minor change. The brothers worked together as a team in a way I had not seen before then. These and many other priceless memories I would describe every night of the funeral week to the elder Js. For example, how did our older son, with no coaching at all, know exactly what to do about informing people? He had worked for many years in his dad's lab, done research, attended meetings with him worldwide, and knew all of his colleagues. Often, I heard him calling surgeons and other colleagues of Dr. J. all over the world to tell them of his death. "No, I can't leave a message," I heard him say, over and over again. "I have to talk to Dr. X in person."

I explained to them about the outpouring of money, flowers, fruit, and kind acts that went on during those unforgettable days.

I described every detail of the funeral and the burial. The city's largest cathedral, where he had worshiped, was packed. People spoke of his life and his tremendous professional contributions. The little cemetery where he was buried was chosen by our youngest son as one where he sometimes used to ride his bike when growing up. The site of his grave overlooked a hospital. All this and more I went over with them every evening. This was my way of bringing the elder Js to the funeral.

My relationship with them only improved after that. The guiding principle that I worked out for myself during those years was to act as a sort of "stand-in" for their son who was gone. They seemed to recognize what I was doing and thanked me many, many times.

But after her son died, Mom J went slowly but steadily downhill. Then came the day, about a year and a half later, when Dad J called to say Mom was probably dying. He reassured me that everything was being done that could be and there was no need for me to come down. I said I wanted to be there. Again, he said it would not be necessary—cutoff. I pushed, "Let me put it this way. If I come down, would I be welcome?" "Of course," he said. I said my next call would be to let him know of my arrival time at the airport.

I sat with the two of them at Mom J's bedside for two days. Their oldest son called during the first day. "Do you think I should come?" Cutoff. "Well, the people I am working with believe it is extremely important to be with family at the time of death." He came down on the next plane. Though I had to leave after two days, the older son was there with his mother when she died. He thanked me many times later for my part in his being present at the time of her death. A few years later, when his father was dying, no one had to put out any suggestions for him. He was there before I got there, calling me to tell me what was happening.

Throughout these years, after moving to Washington, I was in regular coaching sessions with Dr. Bowen until he died. A sort of informal coaching took place with friends who had been involved in Bowen theory for many years. All of this served to help me continue to keep thinking systems.

Bowen theory guided me through the funerals of both, suggesting how to conduct myself, how to be present and accounted for, and how to be more connected with my sons at those times. These were priceless relationships that, were it not for Bowen family systems theory, I believe would have been inaccessible to me from the time of the divorce. I would have deprived myself of many years of two important friendships and being present at the end of their lives. All of this carries great meaning for me.

Further, I believe that this work with my former husband's family was somehow more possible, more accessible for me in the beginning, than the efforts with my own family. It went faster than that in my own family. It is hard to see one's own eyeball. But this I could see and it was a place to start. Further, I believe that the improvement in the quality of those relationships had the important effect of showing me something about what was lacking in my own family relationships. When those relationships actually became more open, more emotionally connected than any I had my own family, I could see, by comparison, more about what work needed to be done there.

BRIDGING CUTOFF WITH MY OWN FAMILY

Not long into the work with my divorced family, I began to perceive that I was also cut off from my family of origin. I had known the relationships were not ideal, but since I went back home for holidays and there were occasional phone calls, I had been in denial about the true state of affairs. Eventually, however, I realized that I was emotionally cut off from my family of origin.

I had no understanding of the connection between cutoff and three extremely red flags—my mental depression (lasting several years by then), my poor relationship history, and the difficulties my children were experiencing. My depression had necessitated psychotherapy for about ten years. Notwithstanding intense involvement in the "Cadillac" of treatments, psychoanalysis, with every passing year my symptoms seemed only to intensify.

It did not take my Bowen theory-trained coach long to point out that my relationships with my family of origin might benefit from some attention on my part. Encouraged by what I had already experienced in my divorced in-law family, I set to work. Many people heard what Bowen said about going back to one's family. Few people heard what he said to do when you got there. I was in that category in the beginning. I called my parents more frequently. I did not really know what to say. I was not in the habit of revealing myself or my life to them. It was enough then just to try to make more frequent contact.

I began to visit home more often. Then I remembered why I cut off in the first place. I was intensely reactive to being in the presence of my family. On the visits I would develop my allergic symptoms, withdraw into reading or long naps. What was I reacting to? Just my family. I was sensitive to everything about them—their food, their interactions, their religious devotion, their guiding principles. My next efforts included going home and staying more connected during the visit. In time, I was able to avoid excessive hours of reading or sleeping. Eventually, I got to the point that I was able to help Dad tend his roses without having allergic attacks.

As a trainee in the special postgraduate program at the Georgetown University Family Center in Washington, DC, I was able to hear Dr. Bowen lecture on a regular basis. One day in class I heard him say to another trainee, "When you get to the point where your parents are your best friends, you'll have it made!" This statement rang in my ears for many years to come. It was so far from where I was at the time, but friendship was a paradigm I could somewhat understand. It gave me a goal. The goal was far off, to be sure, but nonetheless there was a goal. I shrank, cringed, and wrestled with it. Finally, I picked up the gauntlet. Could my parents really become my best friends? Maybe.

I called them more often. I "shared" more of myself with them. I asked about their lives and concerns. Slowly, the gap was bridged. We were not cut off, but for a very long time, we were still not "best friends."

I was especially dissatisfied with a relationship pattern between my father and me. When upset by something I said that reminded him of my immaturity in general or my rebellion against the family religious beliefs, he had a tendency to become quite intensely critical. Then I would get extremely reactive and distance from him and my mother. My relationship with my mother, as an adult, was distant but fairly calm. Bowen theory notwithstanding, I had tried to change my father's tendency to criticize for a long time, to no avail. One day I realized that the relationship between my dad and me was suffering from my antitheoretical approach to the relationship. I had been focusing exclusively on his part of the relationship pattern, a part I had no power to change. I got clear enough to ask myself a useful question: "What would happen if I focused on my part of the relationship instead of my father's, and really did that part differently?"

What was my part? How could I even be said to play a part in my father's being so critical? It had begun when I was a young child. Be that as it may, upon further reflection, I realized that, at this point, my part was just as real, intense, and predictable as his. My part of the interaction after the critical episodes was that I would lose energy, be unable to think or say anything logical, and then become very depressed for several days or weeks. *I crawled under a rock.* "Wouldn't anyone though?" I defended myself. "No, not everyone would," I answered as I began to visualize a different way of being and "doing myself," should the interaction repeat itself. I thought it probably would. I rehearsed my part in my head many times. I knew I would need to "over-learn" my responses if I were to remember them under battle conditions. I scheduled more visits home.

The next time we began to enter our pattern, instead of getting defensive or interrupting him to argue, I just listened and watched him. I heard him out, all the way through. "This is what my father does when he gets anxious," I thought, "and it comes out of the generations of his (my) family." After some time, he ran down. I paused and then said firmly and as calmly as I could, "Dad, I know you see it that way. I don't see it that way." I was a little more reactive than when I rehearsed in my head, but not much. *And I refused to go under a rock!* That may not seem like much of an "I-position," not much of a defining statement, but for me it was miles from where I had always been in the relationship. I thought I would have a few more chances to practice this routine. I never did. The pattern never repeated. Incredibly, my father has never dumped criticism upon me again. Also, I have not been available for it. I suppose we both know that somehow, and now we relate more comfortably.

To roughly summarize the efforts I had made in my family of origin up to then: First, I struggled to just get better-connected relationships. Next, my efforts concentrated around staying more connected during visits. Then I worked on not becoming physically or mentally symptomatic (excessively allergic or depressed) around my parents.

Later, with more of an understanding of the generations that went before me, I could see my parents as people with their own heritage of strengths and weaknesses, doing the very best they knew how. I thought, for example, that my father's tendency to criticize grew out of the relationship he had with his fairly rigid mother. Further, I never had understood my mother's fascination with the male gender. She had been quite excited when her second child, my brother, was born. I always felt I took second place in her heart after that. This was quite irritating to me until, once, during one of my visits home, I studied her intently watching some men working on planting some trees on their property. She observed their work for what seemed like hours to me. Why was she not paying more attention to me? I had come so far to visit her and she stood transfixed by these men doing this inconsequential work. She wanted them to come inside so she and I could serve them lunch. I was irritated. In order to try to change my attitude, I scanned over her early years to see what I could find. I got a picture of her as a child, following her three older brothers around. She was never happier than when they would allow her to hunt or fish with them. I remembered Lorenz's work with the baby ducks. They followed the first thing they saw after hatching. This Lorenz called imprinting (Lorenz, 1965). My mother was absolutely imprinted on the male of the species. With the light that some understanding of the generations of the family provides, I have been able to calm down a great deal in my relationships with my mother and father. I accept that this is just how it was and is for them, and I do not particularly hold it against them. At that point, I was ready for friendship with my parents. It came about very slowly, over time.

Once my parents became my best friends, it was possible for me to take advantage of their years of accumulated wisdom. In rearing children, in my work dilemmas, in sometimes just being able to talk to them, they were now an advantage, a gold mine of experience that often was extremely useful to me.

I knew that my relationship with my parents had reached a better level one day while walking with my mother near the lake where they lived. I was tired of the single life, which had gone on quite a few years. Any attempts to bring up the subject with Mom and Dad had met with no comment—absolute silence on the other end of the phone. They were obviously against any attempt at remarriage on my part. I had finally told them, as one might a best friend, how much their great marriage had meant to me growing up, and how much I wanted to create a home like theirs for myself. This, apparently, they could hear. On the day of the walk, Mother had her own way of letting me know that any residual distance was definitely over and we were if not best friends then very close to it. "Dad and I are praying that you will find the right man," Mom said to me.

More recently my efforts have focused on being more present, accountable, and taking a little more initiative in the family at large. After all, I was an oldest child of five. I was not evidencing, in the family, the natural strengths that should have been my heritage in that position. So as well as working hard on my relationships with my parents, there have also been efforts over the years to have the same quality of friendship with each of my four siblings—not easy work and not short term, but most rewarding.

My next oldest sibling, my brother, adored by my mother, was also adored by me. I think I must have, at a very young age, reacted to the natural feelings of disappointment I had at the loss of my parents' undivided attention at his birth and, instead of admitting or dealing with them, simply mimicked my mother's excessive approval of him. As adults we had a wonderful relationship—wonderful, except for the fact that I had trouble being a self around him. So the work in that relationship centered around not simply being his chief listening post, but letting him know about me emotionally, as well. I also had to learn to not always thoughtlessly agree with him in a reflexive way but to say what I really thought.

My sister, ten years younger, had been more like a doll to me than a real person while we were growing up. Living in the same metropolitan area has afforded us the chance to develop our relationship as adults. This work with my sister has had a spin-off benefit of boosting my ability to be interested and engaged in meaningful friendships with women. This means that I am able to enjoy women's group meetings to a much greater degree since developing a relationship with my sister.

Each relationship with my siblings and their spouses and children has had its own quality and each one has demanded different work from my end, but all of it has been useful and rewarding for me.

RESULTS OF FAMILY CUTOFF WORK

The Family Calls on One for Important Tasks

My most recent efforts, learning to be someone the family could count on, have begun to produce results of note. In the past two years, when my parents have needed to change residences, they and the rest of my family have called on me to have the important conversations and to be there to help make the important decisions during health crises. Presently, medical and other questions are asked on a regular basis. The family seems to see me as a resource in a way it never has before.

Loss of Symptoms

Cutoff is one of three relationship postures associated with symptoms. (The other two are the focused child and the adaptive spouse [or under-functioning] positions.) In my case a depression that had been in place for around ten years lifted almost overnight when I began the work on connecting with my family of origin. In looking back I realized that the timing of the onset of the depression was coincident with the beginning of the cutoff from my family. Though I sometimes have my bad days, depression as such has never returned in the twenty years since I began the work. Subjectively, this phenomenon was striking and dramatic.

Having used Bowen theory as a guide for family and other relationships, and seeing positive outcomes through bridging cutoffs, has been an attention-getter for me. I became reactive toward the helping professions. I wonder how psychiatry has missed the important phenomenon of cutoff with its attendant symptomatic potential for so long. How many people, with the aid of a coach, would be able to discontinue their antidepressant medications if they made meaningful contact with their families? Further, cutoff seems to be a routine part of how people grow up and establish new families in the United States. One cannot help but speculate about the impact on our culture if the news about the deleterious impact of cutoff were to become a part of the national ethos.

Rewards

To summarize the rewards of the work I have done, the loss of a decade-long depression as a result of making meaningful contact with my family would have been reward enough, but it also served as a hook, spurring me on to further work on myself in the context of my family relationships.

In that way, bridging a cutoff in one's own family was only a first step in a long effort to become a more engaged, more responsible part of the family. That work is equally if not more important than the initial efforts. The changes in self from that type of work are just as dramatic and interesting to observe. For example, changing my part in the posture I took with my father greatly improved the relationship I had with him. The attack-and-slink-off pattern was gone. We were then in a position to become friends for the first time.

It also improved my ability to take a position with other people when needed. I found that I took other people's anxiety and sensitivities less personally. I became less sensitive. This makes it easier for me to hear them when they become intense and enables me to make an appropriate response. In other words, after the exercise with my father, I believe I became a little less reactive in general—with friends, with family, and with people seen in consultation.

The family has various ways of letting one know when one is on track. Some make positive comments directly. Others show it by wanting to be together more often. Still others seek me out to talk of their own personal dilemmas. They talk of their gratefulness at my being there as a resource for the family.

The Family Functions As a More Cooperative Group

Bowen theory postulates that when one's functioning increases, the functioning of others connected to that one will also go up, in time. My nuclear family's functioning has definitely increased over the years. Although there are a few symptoms in the family, most are doing well in their fields and in their marriages. There has been one divorce in the last few years among my siblings, but all the children of the youngest generation seem to be doing well.

One noticeable difference in the family is the interest they have in one another. Before I began this work, people were scattered around the country and rarely spent time together. In more recent years, people are interested in one another—vacationing together, e-mailing, and calling one another frequently.

At this writing, my parents are turning ninety years of age. Almost all their children, some of their grandchildren, and their two great-grandchildren plan to congregate for two separate birthday celebrations. It is far from a perfect family, but it does seem that my family of origin is functioning better as a family than before my work in Bowen family systems theory began.

Though some of the work described in this paper, and lived through in life, seems in retrospect to have achieved dramatic results, it all took place with a great deal of preparation and much effort. Most of my work in Bowen theory has not been of the dramatic variety; far more often results have been obtained gradually over a great deal of time with careful, even plodding, attention.

Shifts in My Thinking and Functioning

In addition to the benefits listed already, how has this work changed me? I am aware of several other shifts within myself. Of course, the predominant shift—that of a major paradigm shift—has meant that I developed a different way of thinking about my professional work. Once, when beginning to learn Bowen theory, I explained the concept of differentiation to a patient during a session. People were very patient during those years while I was making a paradigmatic change that was radically different. This person listened to my explanation, absorbed. When I finished, he said, "Dr. Gilbert, I have been seeing you for seven years. You have never told me anything this important before. Why not?"

I have had the sense all along that my involvement with Bowen theory has put me on a different trajectory—one that would not have been possible without it. The scale of differentiation is a never-failing indicator of where I am and where I need to head. I know that I will not necessarily get there overnight. The results of movement in a direction may not always be and have not always been as dramatic as some described here, but having the scale to point the way is quite a consolation in an uncertain world. I cannot always change my circumstances, but I can always work on myself. I can always focus on differently managing my contribution to the problem.

One interesting result that I notice is that I am much less tired after a day of work. The daily effort to stay out of the emotional intensities of other families, to be a neutral third person with the predominant mental set of curiosity, apparently is less exhausting than trying to empathetically take on the feelings of the families so as to understand them better. In psychoanalyt-ically oriented psychotherapy, the effort to explore feelings all day, using one's own feelings in the process, was incredibly draining. Going from cause-and-effect thinking to systems thinking means seeing how symptoms and problems develop within the context of the family. As people begin to think in this way they begin to get some resolution, in their own way. The burden is less on the therapist to know the answer or find a cure. The "re-search attitude" of a Bowen-trained therapist makes work interesting and gives energy. Also, I find it easier to make and sustain a connection with people in consultation than it was for me before I addressed the cutoffs in my own family.

Moreover, I have better-functioning family, friendship, and professional relationships than ever before. They are not perfect, or devoid of all reactiv-ity, but in general they are more connected, more satisfying, and freer of troublesome emotional problems. Although other people in my social and family circles do not always behave the way I would choose for them to, I find I have tools that enable me to be more prepared to handle whatever comes along.

I am still plagued with some physical symptoms (allergies that take the form of asthma and headaches), but for the most part they remain at a low and controlled level that interferes little with activities.

Although all lives have a certain amount of stress, I am quite aware of bringing fewer self-induced problems upon myself than I did on a regular basis before my engagement with Bowen theory. These effects have made it possible to be more productive in reaching life goals. With less relationship trouble and less intensity in general to deal with, there is more energy avail-able to do the work that I would like to accomplish. The attitude of skepti-cism with which I entered my work in Bowen family systems theory has, over the years, given way to one of gratitude.

WORK FOR THE FUTURE

Far from seeing my work on myself in my family relationships as com-pleted, I am well aware that, with my history of cutoff, I am at risk for revert-ing to my old patterns at any time. For me, constant vigilance is still needed to keep my hard-won connections in good working order. This reaching out and being present does not always come easily or naturally to me. But Bowen theory is always there, prodding, goading me to call someone I have not talked to in some time, or to e-mail, or to get on that plane even though I can think of seventeen other ways to spend my long weekend. As a part of a large family, I always have the sense that I am leaving several relationships not tended as well as they might be. I once expressed this sentiment to Bowen. He replied, "You just do what you can." So that gap between what could and should be, what time will allow, and how to prioritize it all constantly nags.

My work on connecting with my family, although dramatic and unbelievably useful in some respects, has not been a panacea. Many areas remain a reminder of an only modest level of differentiation. My physical symptoms remain a challenge that I work with constantly. Sometimes they are better and sometimes worse, but they seldom interfere with life.

Research, greatly needed, to validate and demonstrate what clinically seems to be so evident to so many, is still a life goal, but so far it is always just a little out of reach. For many who are acquainted with Bowen theory, research must be a high priority if theory is ever to graduate and become scientific fact.

REFERENCE

Lorenz, K. (1965). *Evolution and Modification of Behavior.* Chicago: University of Chicago Press.

Chapter 7

Managing Cutoff
Through Family Research

Alice Eichholz

What are the benefits and challenges of trying to bridge emotional cut-offs in a family? This is one of the questions that emerged when I first encountered Bowen theory (Bowen, 1978) and began to apply it toward understanding the concepts of emotional cutoff and multigenerational emotional process. For over twenty years, I had been researching both my own family and those of many others. Drawing my own family's diagram for the first time made clear to me why I found these two Bowen concepts so intriguing. It immediately became obvious that emotional cutoff was a prominent theme on both sides of my family. From that point on, the research became a laboratory for observing and comprehending the multigenerational process of emotional cutoff, as well as maintaining neutrality in an intense emotional system. Without previously realizing it, I learned that researching my family's history and managing my response to the facts as they emerged were also strategies I could develop—through trial and error—for bridging cutoffs.

The research process using the lens of Bowen theory includes the following:

- A shift from individual to systems thinking
- Comparison between psychoanalytic thinking implicit in the concept of abandonment and systems thinking implicit in Bowen theory
- Understanding the multigenerational process of chronic anxiety and emotional cutoff
- Use of family research as a vehicle for understanding emotional cutoff working through five generations in my family
- Identifying differing approaches to family cutoffs

- Identifying variability in functioning between branches of the family where cutoff was found to be intense and those where it had less of an emotional impact
- Assembling the facts of functioning across several generations and analyzing those differences in functioning between branches of the same family

SHIFT FROM INDIVIDUAL TO SYSTEMS THINKING

Abandonment fears are a common focus for those in psychoanalysis or psychoanalytic psychotherapy. In my seven years' work on this issue in analysis, I could not understand why this was such a difficult issue for me. My parents had always been present and had a long-term, stable marriage during which they both were reasonably productive at work and home. I was not literally "abandoned" by them, unless one counts the ten days my mother was in the hospital having my sister while my father and I stayed at my paternal grandmother's house. None of these experiences seemed enough to explain my angst or behavior around abandonment. As an adult I had a steady career track, generally good health, and a successful education, yet I kept gravitating toward situations in which the men I chose would end the relationship abruptly and become unavailable for any closure.

This continued to happen long after analysis apparently was finished. What could explain the pull toward emotional relationships with males who had this pattern of leaving relationships without closure? Where did the "lovemaps" (Money, 1986) come from in my family history so that I somehow sensed the ones who tended toward abandoning behavior and become involved with them?

In March 1990, after attending my first seminar on Bowen family systems theory, I drew a family diagram with the basic information on my family. Immediately, I had a new understanding about the origin of my abandonment fears (see Figure 7.1). During the several relationships with men who became abruptly unavailable, a good deal of my energy had been spent trying to get those men to connect to their families, particularly their fathers. My family diagram showed that a generation before me my paternal grandfather had abandoned his wife and children, including my father. A shift in my thinking began. Perhaps my abandonment fears were related to events and responses to them in the family's emotional process in previous generations.

My family diagram made it possible to look at the lives of both my mother and my father in the context of their families of origin, and as a partial explanation of their attraction to each other. Both were the eldest in their fami-

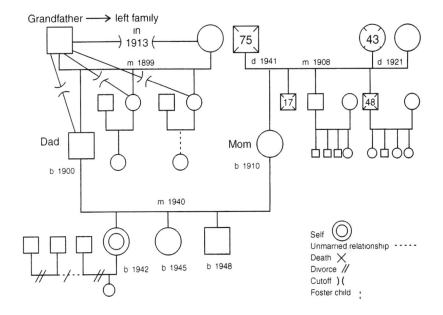

FIGURE 7 1. First family diagram, 1990.

lies. Each lost the same-sex parent during pre- or early adolescence—one the result of a traumatic death and the other the result of abandonment. Neither of them were sustained through their adolescent development by the same-sex parent. They were generally left to fend for themselves emotionally, even though the surviving/remaining parent tried to compensate for the loss.

RESEARCHING THE CUTOFFS

The family diagram became the basis for establishing a strategy for collecting the facts surrounding the cutoffs in order to better understand the family process and my part in it. It became clear that there were four major cutoffs in the previous two generations—two each on my maternal and paternal sides. Baker and Gippenreiter's (1996) research on cutoff and the Stalin purges suggested that descendants of people who were purged but able to pass on oral history about the "lost" generation alive functioned at a higher level than those people who had no knowledge of the lost generation. I wondered whether the level of functioning in several generations in my family could be documented to understand how different branches fared after the cutoff.

To explore the question of the impact the previous generations' cutoffs may have had on descendants, I needed to gather many more facts. Before exploring possible variables, it was necessary to identify all people and the basic facts surrounding the previous generations. Contacting present-day descendants in the cutoff and obtaining more facts about the nature of the cutoffs were essential. It quickly became apparent after some anxious attempts that this required a thoughtful strategy. A decision was made to try to maintain a neutral position in the context of these cutoffs through fact-gathering and making contact with the other parts of the family with the hope of learning to manage my own life choices, particularly around men, less anxiously.

Cutoff #1

On my father's side of the family, I discovered through several years of research (some before I knew about Bowen theory) that there were two cutoffs, both beginning in his adolescence. The first began when Dad was thirteen and my grandfather abandoned the family and neighborhood (see Figure 7.1). This much was known, until my research seventy-five years after this cutoff occurred revealed that within a five-year period my grandfather married another woman by whom he had two children, left that family, married a third woman, came back to the neighborhood, divorced my grandmother, and left the state again. My father was then eighteen. Research further revealed that my grandfather then had a son with the third wife, married a fourth woman, then divorced the third wife and had two additional children with the fourth wife (see Figure 7.2). My father knew nothing about these other family members. There was little to no contact between my grandfather and his first family after 1913, although a series of letters from him to my father in the 1920s emerged during the research process to indicate where grandfather was living at that time. Learning about this sequence of events took some effort and became a good lesson in learning about the problems of moving toward a cutoff too quickly and without a thoughtful plan.

My first attempt to bridge the cutoff with my grandfather's family was carried out in 1988 before I knew about Bowen theory or that grandfather had so many wives and children. After some research based on the letters from the area where he lived during the 1920s, I was able to locate a "second" family (which actually was the third, but no one knew that at the time). Social Security Administration forwarded a letter I wrote to members of this

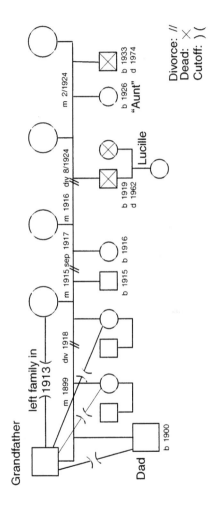

FIGURE 7.2. Discovering family secrets. third and fourth marriages discovered in 1988; second marriage discovered in 1999.

177

"second" family, asking for information. The son of this "second" family was no longer living, but his wife, Lucille, was (see Figure 7.2). She responded with a short note that said she understood I was looking for information about my grandfather. Lucille provided her phone number and I called immediately. She did provide basic information on herself and her only daughter and added information about what happened to my grandfather and the fact that he had another family (the "third") with two children. There was a strained relationship between them. She knew the "third" family, and when and where grandfather died. I obtained the death record, obituary, and probate record. None of these records acknowledged the earlier families. All of this was new information to my immediate family, illustrating the intensity of the cutoff operating in the family.

Without much thought, I wrote to the living daughter of this third family (Father's half sister), precipitously calling her "Aunt," without having any understanding about the nature of cutoffs and the potential for stirring up a hornet's nest. Two years after the letter was sent, there still was no response from her. A colleague of mine lived in that same city and knew someone who was acquainted with this living daughter. The mutual friend agreed to talk with the living daughter about my letter and my desire to have contact. However, the daughter had no intention of having any contact, and although she still had the letter after two years, she denied the validity of my relationship to my grandfather and indicated she did not want to hear from me again.

I quickly learned that I had moved too fast in my anxiety to bridge this cutoff. The emotional system moved in just as quickly to cut it off. It was during this time period that I began working from a Bowen theory perspective. As a result, I decided to approach this cutoff much more cautiously and simply sent an annual Christmas card to Lucille instead. It was a small beginning. After five years, I started receiving a card back and three years later, Lucille's daughter wrote me to tell me of Lucille's death. Lucille's daughter wanted to have contact with me, which we have continued.

Three months after that contact with Lucille's daughter began (and eight years after I started working on this cutoff), I heard from two other previously unknown relatives of my grandfather's. The first was a man who married into "Aunt's" family and had found the letter I had written her ten years previously. We exchanged pictures and family information through e-mail. He was about to set up a phone call between us when he broke off contact and has not responded to any contact since.

The second person who contacted me was *another* granddaughter from a previously *unknown* marriage that occurred during the years my grandfather had first disappeared—1913 to 1917. Her revelations renumbered the previously known families, making her a descendant from a second marriage of grandfather's. This made Lucille the daughter-in-law of the third wife and my "aunt" a descendant from the fourth family. This cutoff certainly proved to be even more complex than I initially understood.

Once I started approaching this cutoff from a systems perspective, a second approach involved going through calmer interlocking triangles. After the difficulty experienced in the first approach, I began to appreciate calm triangles. Rather than approaching my grandfather's descendants directly, I researched the previous generation to learn more about the emotional unit of the family into which he was born (see Figure 7.3). Not only did the facts of his parentage (born to an unmarried mother who two years later married his birth father when the birth father was dying and then married his stepfather) elucidate a broader perspective in his life, but they provided a different multigenerational group of people with whom to try to establish a connection and learn more about the emotional process in the family.

I worked with my grandfather's oldest grandchild, my cousin Shirley (see Figure 7.4), to locate the networks in the old neighborhood—people who had known my grandfather, including the descendants of his own siblings. Even seventy-five years after grandfather "disappeared" in 1913, we were able to still find people who had stayed in and around the original neighborhood and had had regular contact with his siblings and their descendants.

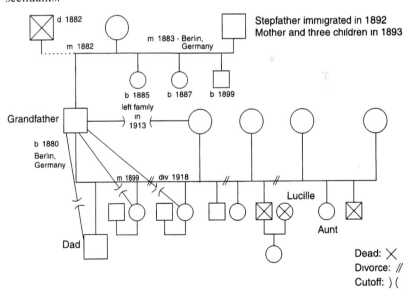

FIGURE 7.3. Grandfather's family of origin.

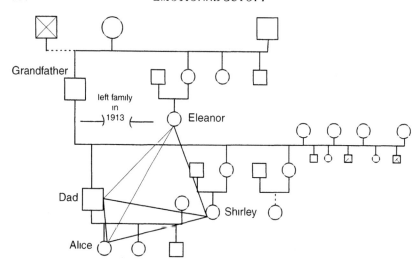

FIGURE 7.4. Calmer multigenerational triangles.

After several attempts Shirley and I finally located and contacted my grandfather's half sister's daughter, Eleanor (see Figure 7.4). She provided important information about the family's life before immigration and pictures of that family, including my great-grandparents, which we had never seen. Shirley, Eleanor, Dad, and I all got together before he died and made a videotape of their memories of grandfather, his siblings, mother, and stepfather. Eleanor was present at Dad's memorial service. The cutoff with some of grandfather's descendants might exist, but maintaining newly developed contact with some of the interlocking triangles in his family could also continue.

Cutoff #2

The second cutoff in my father's family occurred at the time of his parents' divorce in 1917. Within a few months not only was Grandma's marriage over, but her mother, her only sibling, and a nephew all died in the worldwide influenza epidemic, leaving her with no known, living immediate family besides her three children and an abusive, distant stepfather (see Figure 7.5). She withdrew from all social life, except that associated with the German Baptist church next door. At the time of her death sixty years later, she had not left her home for over twenty years. Her last trip away from home had been to attend her son's wedding out of state.

By the time I started approaching this cutoff, I had learned the lessons about moving too quickly and working, instead, through calmer interlock-

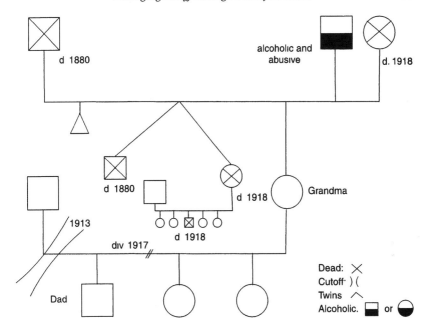

FIGURE 7 5. Cutoff from death and divorce of significant others.

ing triangles. My cousin Shirley and I worked collaboratively to determine whether there were other remaining people in grandmother's extended family that she might not have known.

Through census records, vital records, and Internet discussion groups, a number of people assisted in locating what turned out to be a wealth of information on the family (see Figure 7.6), none of which was known to my father, his sisters, or descendants of grandmother's sister who had died in the flu epidemic. A family of three siblings emigrated in 1871 from Hannover, Germany: my great-grandmother, Margaret (who died during the 1918 epidemic); her brother, Jacob; her sister, Mary, and Mary's five-year-old daughter. They arrived in Chicago shortly after the Great Chicago Fire. Mary apparently had a marriage already arranged to provide a family for her young daughter and immediately left for Montana.

Sisters Mary and Margaret maintained some contact with each other between Montana and Chicago for over twenty years. Both of Mary's daughters returned east to Margaret's home in Chicago to attend school. Then, the sisters apparently lost track of each other's lives. What became of the brother and who their parents were was not determined until five years after these initial discoveries of Mary's family.

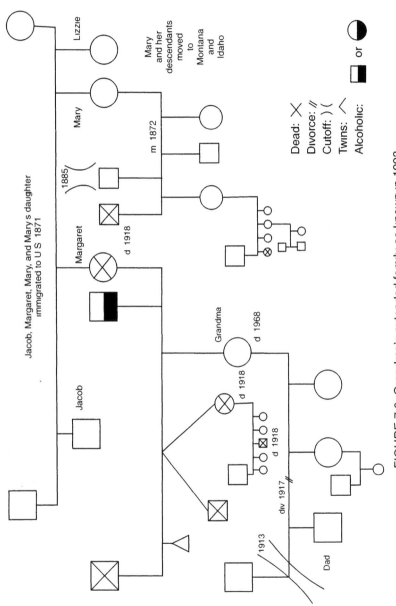

FIGURE 7.6. Grandma's extended family as known in 1993.

182

My cousin Shirley traveled to Montana and Idaho, taking pictures of the places where Mary's family lived and talking with neighbors and friends who knew them. In the process, a very different cultural adaptation between the two families was uncovered, in terms of occupation, social class, and religion, although there was similar longevity, with many members in both branches living into their nineties. Only Mary's oldest daughter, who emigrated with the family from Germany, produced any offspring. Some welcome contact was established with them.

Five years after this initial contact between the descendants of two sisters, Internet databases had become sophisticated enough to locate the brother who immigrated with them. This has led to new understandings about the nature of the family system in Germany. These were not the only siblings who immigrated. Others came later, including their father and several related families from the Stade region in Germany, all of whom settled in the same area of Minnesota (see Figure 7.7). Contact with these branches of the family has just been initiated through descendants who had been researching their lines for many years and knew nothing about Mary and Margaret. Their research may make it possible in the future to understand more about the purpose of their immigration and compare functioning between the branches after immigration.

Despite the fact that grandmother thought she was alone—having lost her husband, mother and only living sibling in 1917-1918, a fact which became a defining moment in her troubled life and that of her children—she had many other close relatives—aunts, uncles, and cousins—who lived only a few hours away. One wonders what her life course and that of her descendants might have been had the cutoff that occurred after immigration not been so complete.

Cutoff #3

As with Father's side of the family, Mother's side also had major cutoffs on both her paternal and maternal sides. As had my father's relationship with his same-sex parent, my mother's relationship with her mother tended to define the developmental issues of her life.

First, though, I explored the cutoff with my maternal grandfather's family. He died a year before I, the oldest of his grandchildren, was born. H.R. was a "larger-than-life," charismatic person, according to everyone I have known who met him. He was highly educated—an activist in women's suffrage and the first teachers' union. He raised all four of his children alone after his wife died. It seemed important to know how it was that two of this esteemed grandfather's siblings, a sister Julia and half brother R.B. Jr., became "estranged" (see Figure 7.8).

184

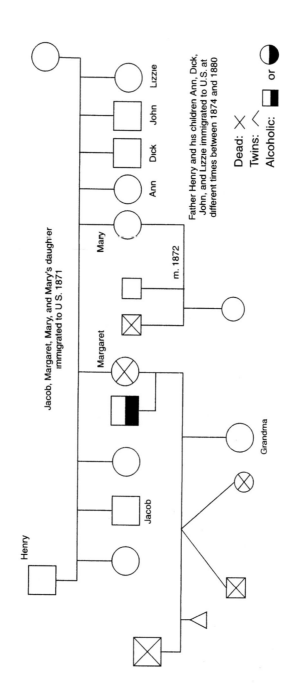

FIGURE 7.7. Grandma's aunts, uncles, and grandfather as discovered in 2000.

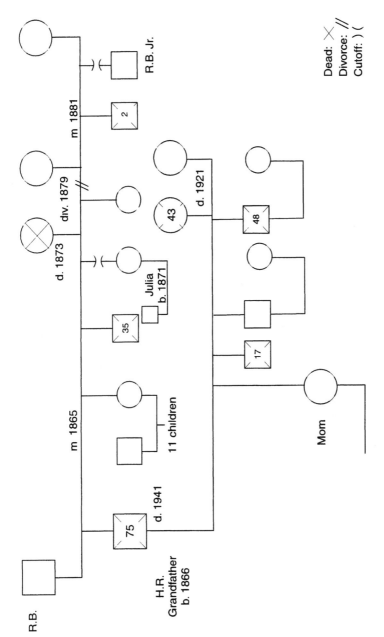

Dead: ✕
Divorce: //
Cutoff:) (

FIGURE 7.8. Two "estranged" siblings.

185

H.R. did not know what happened to them and asked in a letter to his sister (a schoolteacher and mother of eleven children) in Portland, Oregon, if she knew. She did not. It seemed especially important to understand the nature of this cutoff since, although at school and work in the East, he maintained a very close relationship with this sister who lived in Portland, where the rest of the family still lived. She, too, had no contact with Julia or R.B. Jr., even though living in the same vicinity.

Through Internet conversations, I found several people who assisted in on-site research in Portland, Oregon. Within a few weeks, the fate of his half brother, R.B. Jr., was discovered. After several felonies, he was jailed in the 1930s in federal prison in Washington for ten years for forging a twenty-two-dollar welfare check. He then returned to Portland, where he died ten years later of undetermined causes on a railroad trestle and was buried in an unmarked grave a few blocks from where the family had lived. Twice I visited his unmarked grave and even located the trestle where he died and talked with the medical examiner about the records of the death. A family he was living with at the time of this death put an article in the newspaper looking for relatives to claim the body, but no one was still living, then, who knew who those relatives were. The cutoff had been complete.

Grandfather's "estranged" sister, Julia, lost contact with the rest of the family about the same time as their half brother did. Research in vital, census, court, and medical records revealed the events and life course of those in this cutoff. Julia had a difficult divorce from an abusive husband. A guardian was appointed for her by the court because of mental problems. She lived a borderline existence, working in custodial jobs, and died in a state mental hospital in Washington. She had a son and a daughter, ten years apart, who also died in mental institutions, one after a stay of thirteen years. Neither had any children themselves (see Figure 7.9). Medical records and two sets of divorce records for the son document that his first wife abandoned him and a second sued because of an abusive relationship. While in Oregon, I visited the state hospitals, the neighborhood where the family lived, and the graves of Julia's son and daughter.

Clearly, the two siblings who were cut off from the rest of the family led difficult lives that were completely different from their highly functional brother and sister.

Cutoff #4

The second cutoff in my maternal side of the family was by far the most intense and geographically far-reaching in comparison with all the others. Working on understanding that cutoff has also been the most productive in terms of understanding the concept of emotional cutoff in Bowen theory. This cutoff illustrates what Bowen referred to as a "shock wave" in the emo-

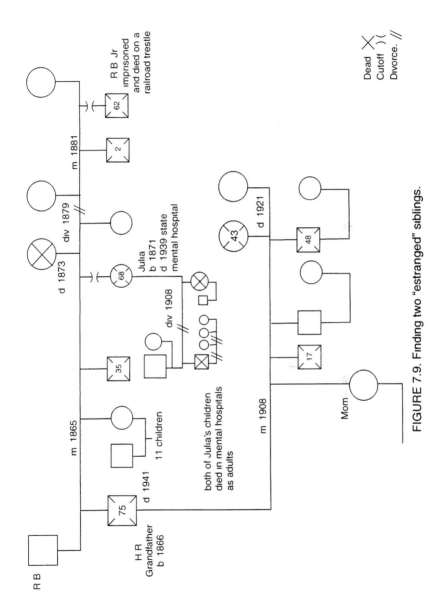

FIGURE 7.9. Finding two "estranged" siblings.

187

tional process (Bowen, 1978, p. 325). I have come to understand "shock wave" as a nodal event that sends the emotional system reeling from its more or less steady mooring for several generations. The explosiveness of this shock wave suggests that it may have influenced the early deaths, physical and mental illnesses, and suicides in several of the descendants. Before returning to this nodal event, some background concerning my grandmother and the maternal side of my family is relevant.

My maternal grandmother, Adele, died at age forty-three of breast cancer. All of her children stated that her death was a severe emotional trauma. Adele was the last of her parents' three children to be alive and the only one to produce offspring to the second generation. Adele's mother and brother died within six months of each other twenty years earlier; her sister had died ten years earlier. My mom thought she had cousins in England related to her grandmother, who she thought was named Josephine Louise. Since her grandmother died twelve years before Mom was born, and her own mother died when Mom was eleven, her knowledge of the facts was limited (see Figure 7.10).

Discovering the circumstances surrounding Adele's family of origin brought into sharp focus the issues of abandonment. The new facts helped

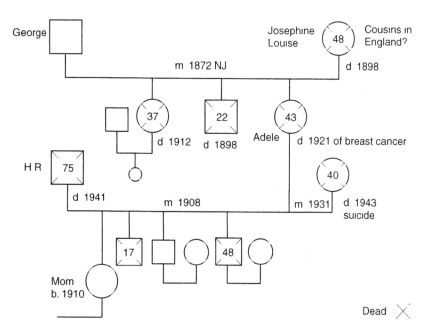

FIGURE 7.10. Adele's family of origin.

me to understand the intensity in her family and the complex multigenerational triangle in this part of the family that was my emotional heritage. At the time I discovered the events surrounding my great-grandparents' lives, neither of their living grandchildren, including my mother, knew anything about these events. My approach to handling the intensity of this multigenerational triangle has been to discover as much detail as I could about the lives of the individuals in the triangle before, during, and after the intense cutoff that my grandmother and great-grandmother experienced in 1887-1888 and then to work through the interlocking triangles to try to differentiate myself in this part of my emotional unit by carefully maintaining contact without increasing the intensity. In this cutoff, I discovered just how extensive interlocking triangles in an emotional unit can be.

The shock wave began with my great-grandfather, George, who was married to my great-grandmother Josephine, and father of three children, including the youngest, my grandmother Adele. A successful and controversial minister in Liberty Corners, New Jersey; Brooklyn, New York; Hamden, Connecticut; and Chicago, Illinois, he renounced his pulpit in 1882 and became a Shakespearean actor of much repute. Traveling through the United States and Canada in a touring company, he had a child in 1887 with his leading lady, Louise. Grandmother Adele, at age seven, was the only member of his first family to be part of the acting company, playing child roles when they were in the Chicago vicinity. When the discovery of the affair and the resultant child occurred, George took the new family and his touring company off to Australia and a tour of the Far East for four years. His first wife, Josephine, filed for and was granted a divorce. But a year before the divorce was filed, he had married Louise, making George a bigamist, much the same as my paternal grandfather. With his second wife George had a total of seven children. These were the "cousins" in England about whom my mother had heard (Figure 7.11).

When George abandoned his first family, he left my great-grandmother, Josephine, with three young children to raise in Chicago, isolated from her own family, which was still in New Jersey. Two weeks after the divorce became final in 1888, Josephine's father, her only living parent, died. Six months later she returned to New Jersey to live with her older half sister.

Contact between George and his children from the first family was nonexistent, except for what appears from research in family letters and memorabilia to be some clandestine contacts with daughter Adele eight years later when he returned to the Brooklyn, New York stage and twelve years after that during Adele's honeymoon trip to Europe, where George had finally settled with his second wife and remaining four children. Of his ten children, the three born to Josephine died young of appendicitis, kidney failure, and breast cancer. Only Adele, who died of breast cancer at age forty-three,

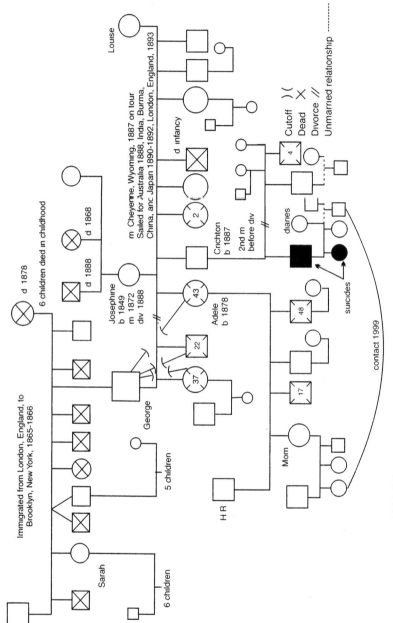

190

FIGURE 7.11. George's family before and after "shock wave" in 1887-1888.

produced descendants beyond one generation. It was her death that left an emotional void in my mother's life at age eleven. Of the seven children born to Louise, two died in infancy and two had lifelong illnesses and no children. One other child had no offspring. One of the two who did reproduce had children with challenging and difficult lives, including mental illness, suicide, and legal problems.

IDENTIFYING SUCCESSFUL AND UNSUCCESSFUL APPROACHES TO CUTOFFS

Uncovering the facts and understanding the emotional forces operating in my family has lessened the impact on me of those events that occurred over 100 years ago in 1887 and 1888. When the shock wave went through the family so fiercely, connection and contact between father and children was cut off. None of the original parties are living anymore. In fact, most died more than twenty years before I was born. No one who was alive that I knew after I was born was aware of the circumstances of the cutoffs or even that there had been several. Yet the impact of these cutoffs on the chronic anxiety passed on in the family were clearly felt by me on some level and might explain the anxiety I experienced with issues of abandonment.

After stumbling into the intense cutoff in my paternal grandfather's family (Cutoff #1) and not moving cautiously, I quickly learned to respect the emotional unit's adaptation to chronic anxiety from which the cutoff emerged. If I wanted to learn more about the emotional unit, I needed to become more neutral in the way I approached it. Rather than approaching the unit head-on, which was not only unproductive but also created an apparent hardening of the cutoff, working the interlocking triangles of relationships was more productive and helped to calm the system down as I tried to reconnect. For example, instead of "confronting" my paternal grandfather's daughter from the last marriage in Cutoff #1, I worked back to the previous generation and tried to gather information about his relationship within his family of origin from the people who knew them. This proved to be quite rewarding and provided a connection with a distant cousin I had not anticipated. Using that same approach, through less intense interlocking triangles, I attempted the same with my maternal great-grandfather's family. The hornet's nest of intimate relationships stirred up by both of these men's lives seemed to have a strong influence on my own "lovemaps."

With assistance from four people, all who had tangential connections to my great-grandfather, George, I was able to locate, contact, and visit George's descendants in England. The four people were not directly related to the family, but had knowledge of its emotional process. In many ways, they were enough removed from the intensity of its process but interested enough to have retained basic information. A description of the four people illustrates how far-reaching the ripples of this intense emotional cutoff were.

One was a man who married George's sister Sarah's granddaughter and had collected biographical material on Sarah's descendants. Letters emerged documenting Sarah's descendants' knowledge of George's affair and pictures verifying a brief relationship between Sarah's son's family and my mother when they lived in the same area of England in the 1930s, although Mother had forgotten how they were related.

A second person led to contact with two others. The second was a man who was working on his doctoral dissertation on popular culture's view of China at the turn of the twentieth century and was trying to understand Louise's life and prolific writings on China. He had discovered in a book that George and Louise's son, Crichton, born before George's divorce, was a writer of girls' stories.

The third was a man in England who had published the book on writers of girls' stories, providing basic information about Crichton. He also located a man he thought was George's great-grandson, Peter.

Peter was the fourth person who assisted in uncovering the facts. Although Peter carried George's surname, he was not his great-grandson. Instead, Peter was the son of George's great-granddaughter-in-law, Simone, from an affair after her husband committed suicide. Peter, curious about this family whose name he carried, worked with me in 1999 to document many critical pieces of information, and lent me his mother Simone's daily diaries, which she had kept for over thirty years.

Each of these people had their own interest in the lives of this family, even though they were not directly related. In fact, they held more information about the family than those who were part of it. It became a good lesson in the extent of the ripples left in the wake of a shock wave and the value of working through the interlocking triangles.

IDENTIFYING VARIABILITY IN FUNCTIONING

With the facts gathered as a result of the help from the interlocking triangles, it is possible to consider whether this emotional cutoff in 1887-1888 led to varying adaptations in the family between the branch in which cutoff occurred and one in which it did not. This is a very small piece of a much larger research project being undertaken by the Bowen Center for the Study of the Family in its Family History Database Project. That project is attempting to analyze the differentiation of self occurring over the course of multiple generations of several families. My attempt to understand the functioning in George's and Sarah's descendants describes only one possible variable in functioning—reproductive success in successive generations. To look at this, I also needed to understand the reasons for not reproducing, including mental and physical illnesses and early deaths. Were the early deaths in my grandmother's family typical in the family as a whole? Were mental illness and suicide typical in the family as a whole? These questions cannot yet be answered.

Enough facts were gathered to draw a comparison between George's descendants and those of his sister Sarah (work on their brother William's descendants continues). Their parents and four remaining children immigrated from London to Brooklyn, New York, in 1865. Sarah married and her family stayed in Brooklyn when George's moved to Chicago in 1881. In 1888 their paths diverged further, when George left the family for a tour around the world, re-emigrating to London. A theater engagement in Brooklyn brought George and his children and sister together again briefly. Sarah's family later moved to Chicago, so that years later the two siblings were again together in Chicago when George and Louise returned to sue Louise's mother over her father's estate. After that (1904), George and Louise returned to London. Louise never acknowledged George's first family.

Analyzing the Differences in Functioning

Considering one variable, reproductive history, here are the results for five generations of the two siblings 110 years after the cutoff.

Sarah Jean	George
6 children—4 who reproduced; 2 died in infancy	10 children—4 who reproduced; 2 died in infancy; 2 died as young adults; 1 died in middle age; 2 had lifelong illnesses and did not reproduce
8 grandchildren—6 who reproduced; 1 died as young adult; 1 died in middle age	8 grandchildren—4 reproduced; 1 died as a teenager; 1 died young; 2 died at middle age; (including 1 who committed suicide by jumping from a building)
8 great-grandchildren—5 who are known to have reproduced	17 great-grandchildren—11 were through 1 child, Adele; 9 reproduced; 1 died as a young adult; 1 committed suicide by jumping in front of a train

15 great-great grandchildren— 7 who have reproduced to date; 1 died in childhood	11 great-great grandchildren—2 who have reproduced to date
16 great-great-great grandchildren	6 great-great-great grandchildren

Since George started out with significantly more children, one would expect over the course of five generations a larger number of descendants reproducing. Instead, the majority of George's descendants come from one child, Adele, and a significant number of early deaths (including suicide) suggest they may illustrate the extent of chronic anxiety in the family, perhaps related to the cutoff. The question remains as to what other variables in functioning beyond reproduction might be illustrative of emotional cutoff, as well as whether these variables are significantly different from families without cutoff. Exploring these kinds of questions will be part of the Family History Database Project.

SUMMARY: PRINCIPLES AND BENEFITS OF MANAGING CUTOFF THROUGH FAMILY RESEARCH

As a result of these attempts at managing cutoffs that occurred in previous generations yet still are influencing my life today, I have developed several principles.

Principles

First, work on one cutoff at a time. This work can be personally overwhelming because the emotional field shifts both in reality and in perception as the facts emerge. When new understandings about relationships emerge, it becomes necessary to rethink one's sense of self, which had been predominantly formed in response to the cutoff in the emotional system before those understandings.

Second, stay calm and patient. Rushing in is usually less productive and stirs up the family like a hornet's nest. Not all people in a cutoff may want to acknowledge it, and some people may not be interested in being "found."

Third, cultivate useful triangles. People who are more distant from the intensity of the cutoff, such as neighbors, family friends, those who married into the family, and other researchers, can help form useful triangles. Such triangles can be sources of information but also make it possible to have some contact with the multigenerational emotional process, which might reduce levels of anxiety in the system.

Fourth, there are many ways to maintain contact. Maintaining contact does not necessarily mean seeing or visiting people directly nor confronting the people in the system. When the principle parties to the cutoff are no longer living, visiting places where they lived, worked, went to school, or died, or talking with those who knew them can make it possible to "maintain contact" with the emotional process in the system.

Fifth, cutoffs come in themes or arenas for conflict that are likely overlays of deeper emotional relationship processes. For example, immigration or migration may lead to cutoff, but there may be other themes underlying the reasons for immigration. Many families not only maintain contact after immigration but move with extended family and whole communities to a new location. Other themes or arenas for cutoffs in a family could be religious or political differences, or an inability to tolerate any differences. In the four cutoffs I have explored in my family, the most intense arena for cutoff that came to light gave a much richer understanding to what had appeared to me to be abandonment issues. The two most powerful cutoffs in my family originated between my mother and her mother through death and a cutoff from her mother's father, and my father and his father. In both of these cutoffs, bigamy, extramarital affairs, and abandonment represent the arenas for the conflict.

Sixth, share findings with family members. Sharing information can often bring new insight and understandings. However, not all members in an emotional unit may have an interest in personally knowing relatives across a cutoff. Because trying to engage family members involved in a cutoff can stir up the emotional process, it is important to move slowly and with a thoughtful plan. Researching the facts can be a way to move neutrally through the interlocking triangles in the emotional cutoff.

Benefits

First, from my own perspective, I know that I am much calmer and can take a broader outlook not only in my family but also at work and in my professional life. Since working to understand the cutoffs in my family, there have been numerous life challenges where managing interlocking triangles and not polarizing the situation have been essential. It is as if learning about the cutoffs in my family has been a proving ground for managing self in challenging circumstances both at home and at work.

Second, it has become possible to be more objective about my own part in the process of gravitating toward situations where cutoff might be inevitable. It became clear to me that the anxiousness I felt about relationships with men was not so much in my own psyche (which had been the focus of individual work in psychoanalytic psychotherapy) but part of a broader, chronic anxiety that could be related to the emotional process around issues of love relationships in the multigenerational triangles in my family. Learning about that emotional process has been liberating in the way it has afforded me a neutral position that allows me to stay in contact with the intensity in my family. In the past year, I have been able to reestablish valuable friendships with two of the men from whom I previously was cut off.

Third, there is no question that I have been able to be more present with my daughter's father's family. She was born out of a relationship between two people who were, at the time, in intense cutoffs—my former husband from his immediate family and I from a long-term relationship that had abruptly ended. Staying calm, present, yet as much as possible not in the middle between my daughter and former husband, I think has lessened what could have been a tumultuous emotional history of cutoff for her.

Fourth, the variation in behavior that can be found in families with emotional cutoff can be helpful in realizing that dealing with variation is an important part of human relations, both in families and the work environment.

The way for me to function around cutoffs is to continue to work on understanding the facts about the people who came before me. It keeps me in touch with the multigenerational emotional process in my family. When I look at that, it is possible to understand how our family has survived the challenges of the past, particularly given difficult and challenging circumstances.

The milieu I was born into included some intense multigenerational cutoffs around abandonment. I suspect that I will continue to struggle with the issues of cutoff throughout my life, but now I have a different and fuller understanding of the process involved.

REFERENCES

Baker, K.G. and Gippenreiter, J. B. (1996). The effects of Stalin's purge on three generations of Russian families. *Family Systems: A Journal of Natural Systems Thinking in Psychiatry and the Sciences* 3(1): 5-35.

Bowen, M. (1978). *Family Therapy in Clinical Practice.* Northvale, NJ: Jason Aronson.

Money, J. (1986). *Lovemaps: Clinical Concepts of Sexual/Erotic Health and Pathology, Paraphilia, and Gender Transposition in Childhood, Adolescence and Maturity.* New York: Irvington Publishers.

PART III:
RESEARCH AND CLINICAL
APPLICATIONS

Chapter 8

Toward Understanding and Measuring Emotional Cutoff

Selden Dunbar Illick
Gail Hilbert-McAllister
Susan Ewing Jefferies
Charles M. White

INTRODUCTION

Emotional cutoff is an instinctual process between generations in the behavior of living things. In humans, this emotional process deals with the way people separate themselves from the past in order to start their lives in the present generation. This process varies from person to person and family system to family system depending on the degree of unresolved emotional attachment one has to one's parents, and the degree of anxiety that comes from that unresolved emotional attachment. Variation of the emotional process between the generations lies along a continuum.

For the purposes of this chapter and of the research instrument, the previous paragraph constitutes a working definition of *emotional cutoff*. For years, Selden Illick has been seeking to understand and write about the concept of emotional cutoff in Bowen family systems theory. While she was lis-

The authors acknowledge the Delta Nu Chapter of Sigma Theta Tau International at the College of New Jersey for funding received for this research project. The authors also wish to acknowledge the thinking and influence of Michael E. Kerr, Daniel V. Papero, and John T. Bonner, along with Barbara Smuts, who also assisted in the development of the FORS. The authors also acknowledge Mark F. Schmitz for his valuable contributions to the development of the FORS. The authors gratefully acknowledge Hilary Selden Illick, Jane Wei-yueh Low, and Margaret Donley for their editorial contributions; Melanie T. White for her contribution to the graphic design of the instrument; Ona Cohn Bregman and Deborah J. Monahan for their assistance in the administration of the FORS; and Peter Titelman for the opportunity to publish a preliminary report on this project.

tening to Bowen talk about how the concept of emotional cutoff could be operationalized, she began to think about translating the mechanisms of emotional cutoff into a research instrument. The intention was (1) to have a way to measure the degree of emotional cutoff in any given individual or group, and (2) to find a way to do research on this concept that would speak to the broader scientific community. Since Bowen family systems theory is rooted in evolution and predicated on the belief that other forms of life have properties in common with humans (Kerr and Bowen, 1988), it is important to be able to communicate with those in the natural sciences by conducting valid and reliable research based on Bowen theory. Bowen himself carried out valid research, documenting data from the populations with which he worked, especially at the National Institute of Mental Health in the 1950s. The authors believe it would be useful for clinicians trained in Bowen family systems theory to continue Bowen's work by conducting research on the application of Bowen theory to the lives of their clients and themselves. The Family of Origin Response Survey (FORS), a research instrument being developed by Hilbert and colleagues (2000), is intending to further validate elements of emotional cutoff that the Illick believes Bowen observed in human families and social systems.

This chapter has two components. The first is an elaboration of Bowen family systems theory, with a focus on Bowen's concept of emotional cutoff as understood by Illick. The second part is a discussion by Hilbert of the research instrument being developed by Hilbert and colleagues (2000).

EMOTIONAL CUTOFF ROOTED IN EVOLUTION AND EMOTIONAL REACTIVITY

Introduction

Understanding the emotional process that runs in one's family is key to understanding oneself. Whether or not one considers one's family to be important, the family system is one of the most valuable resources a person has for understanding himself or herself. Knowing about how the family system operates and the impact that each person has on the others is essential to understanding how one functions in relationship to others. Bowen theory, by providing a lens through which to understand self in the broader context of the family system and in the even broader context of other life forms, adds dimension and scope to one's knowledge of oneself.

To learn systems thinking from a Bowen theory point of view, one can begin with any of the concepts in Bowen family systems theory. Because the theory is a system of eight interlocking concepts (Kerr and Bowen, 1988) any concept eventually will lead to all the others. Emotional cutoff has been the entry point for Illick, and has riveted her attention for a number of years, bringing her into a deeper understanding of the overall theory. She has seen emotional cutoff as an important variable in her work on differentiation of self.

A hypothesis in Bowen family systems theory is that the more cut off a person is from his or her family of origin, the more likely the person is to develop physical, social, or emotional symptoms (Bowen, 1978). When Illick first came across this idea, she found herself attaching value to not cutting off, until she realized that judging behaviors was not in keeping with systems thinking. In the rigorous challenge to think systems, the question is not, Is this good or bad? the question is, What is the function of the behavior? Illick came to see that cutoff does have a function. In the short term, cutoff can provide space, a way to back off from the intensity of a situation and reestablish contact with oneself. Yet although initially providing relief in the short term, in the long term cutoff can limit one's options, resources, and overall flexibility. Illick believes it is important to find a way to both see the function of emotional cutoff and at the same time endeavor to bridge cutoffs within herself and her family relationship system. This effort is a lifelong challenge.

In learning about cutoff, there have been a few guidelines that Illick found helpful. Using Bowen's own words and definitions has been critical. Her goal has been to do her best not to let her own subjectivity alter what Bowen defined and described. Another guideline has been to integrate what Illick intellectually understands about the theory with how she lives her life. She found herself going back and forth between learning the theory and applying it to her life. On one level, the theory makes intuitive sense and seems very simple. In trying to live it, however, the obstacles confronted in oneself and the effort to be responsible for one's own part in what goes awry in family and other important relationship systems pose significant ongoing challenges.

The endeavor to see emotional cutoff in the natural world has been a third guideline. Although Bowen focused on humans, Bowen theory posits that humans have much in common with all living things and are a part of evolution. If emotional cutoff were particular only to human beings, it would not be theoretically consistent with Bowen's view that what humans do is related to other forms of life. Illick has come to see that cutoff does exist, as far as she can tell, in other life forms.

Cutoff in Evolution

Bowen (1978), defining cutoff as "the emotional process between the generations" (p. 382), connects cutoff to the multigenerational picture as a part of evolution. The word *emotional* in Bowen theory refers to processes that are instinctive and automatic. All life forms have a process between the generations and all life forms with a brain have an emotional process between the generations that is instinctive. The cycle of development, reproduction, and survival to maturity is part of all life. Emotional cutoff addresses the process of the human moving from one generation to the next. Emotional cutoff is a natural step that has evolved between the generations.

One of the eight interlocking concepts in Bowen family systems theory is the multigenerational transmission process, in which Bowen observed how emotional process gets passed from one generation to the next. As in the evolutionary process, some aspects of human functioning advance in the succeeding generations and some aspects of human functioning regress in the succeeding generations. Also as in the evolutionary process, much of the behavior in our mammalian ancestors is driven by automatic and instinctive processes. Bowen (1978) wrote about this automatic instinctive process in humans. "According to my theory," Bowen wrote in 1976, "a high percentage of human relationship behavior is directed more by automatic, instinctual emotional forces than by intellect. Much intellectual activity goes to explain away and justify behavior being directed by the instinctual-emotional-feeling complex" (1978, p. 321). The elements of our evolutionary inheritance—namely, the instinctual-emotional-feeling complex—connects us to our mammalian ancestors and is what drives the multigenerational transmission process in humans. As Bowen saw it, a challenge for the human's highly developed cerebral cortex is to find a way to distinguish between what is emotionally driven versus what is thoughtfully directed. Thinking, instead of reacting automatically, is no small challenge, especially when one considers how recently developed the cerebral cortex is compared to other brain components, millions of evolutionary years in the making, that are guided by instinct and reactivity.

The Term Emotional Cutoff

Bowen (1978) added the concept of emotional cutoff to his theory in 1975. "After having been a poorly defined extension of other concepts," Bowen said, emotional cutoff "was accorded the status of a separate concept to include details not stated elsewhere, and to have a separate concept for the emotional process between the generations" (p. 382). Before that, in 1974, he used the term emotional "cut-off" to refer to emotional distancing "whether the cut-off is achieved by internal mechanisms or physical distance" (1978, p. 535).

In 1988, when he wrote about the development of the theory in "An Odyssey Toward Science," he stressed the importance of using terms that were found in biology. It was important "to avoid coining new terms, to use simple descriptive words when possible, and to make biological comparisons when appropriate" (Kerr and Bowen, 1988, p. 362). The terms *fusion* and *cutoff*, for example, were used in biology to describe "the way cells agglutinate and separate to start new colonies of cells" (p. 362). Bowen (Kerr and Bowen, 1988) then used the term *fusion* "to denote the ways that people borrow or lend self to another" (p. 346) and *cutoff* "to describe the immature separation of people from each other" (p. 346).

Illick believes that the essence of the focus of concept of emotional cutoff is on the distancing mechanisms in the process between the generations. In 1975, when Bowen (1978) accorded emotional cutoff "the status of a separate concept to include details not stated elsewhere," his description of emotional cutoff emphasized distancing mechanisms. Bowen further wrote, "Much thought went into the selection of a term to best describe this process of separation, isolation, withdrawal, running away, or denying the importance of the parental family" (1978, p. 382).

Emotional Cutoff in Humans

While separation, isolation, withdrawal, and running away are distancing mechanisms rooted in the primitive flight patterns found in evolutionary behaviors, the capacity to deny the importance of the parental family appears to be unique to the human.

Bowen (1978) states that "the person who runs away from his family of origin is as emotionally dependent as the one who never leaves home. They both need emotional closeness, but they are allergic to it" (p. 382).

Bowen talked about handling the attachment by intrapsychic distance, geographical distance, or a combination of both, with collapse into psychosis as an extreme form of intrapsychic distancing. Collapse can be placed on a continuum from mild episodes of inability to function to the more severe states of psychosis. All distancing mechanisms can be seen on a continuum or, as Bowen said, as gradations of emotional cutoff. "The more intense the cutoff," Bowen (1978) wrote, "the more [a person] is vulnerable to duplicating the pattern with the first available other person" (p. 383). Evidence for duplicating the pattern can be found in one's family, work, and social relationships.

The human infant begins life in an intense symbiosis with its mother. The symbiotic relationship between the infant and its mother is embedded in a triangle with the infant's father. The challenge is to move from an intense symbiosis or fusion with the mother and father toward a process of increasing independence. Two important variables—the level of differentiation of self and the level of anxiety or emotional reactivity in the system—profoundly influence the process toward increasing independence. Bowen (1978) wrote about the life pattern of cutoff being determined by the way people handle their unresolved emotional attachments to their parents: "All people have some degree of unresolved emotional attachment to their parents. The lower the level of differentiation, the more intense the unresolved emotional attachment" (p. 382). The degree of emotional cutoff in the human is directly linked to the degree of unresolved emotional attachment.

Unresolved Emotional Attachment

Emotional attachment begins in the original triangle with one's mother and father, or, in the absence of either, one's early caretakers. Attachment is a natural state of symbiosis between mother and infant, necessary for survival. Over time, how a person proceeds toward increasing independence depends on the level of chronic anxiety and undifferentiation in the family system. Other factors that influence this process include: the multigenerational transmission process, the patterns of emotional process in the family of origin, and how an individual handles life events and circumstances. These factors influence the process of moving from early degrees of symbiotic attachment to increasing degrees of maturity. According to Illick, the degree of symbiotic attachment that continues to be unresolved in the overlap between self and mother and self and father in the original triangle fundamentally influences the degree of unresolved emotional attachment one has. Unresolved emotional attachment represents the emotional degree to which a person is unable to move forward in the process toward increasing independence, unable to be a self and define a self in relationship to important others. The greater the emotional degree to which one is unable to be a self, the greater the degree of unresolved emotional attachment, and the greater the degree of anxiety (Bowen, 1978). In Illick's experience the greater the degree of both anxiety and fear that have gone along with the greater degree of unresolved emotional attachment, the greater the challenge to be a self.

Listening to seminars and training presentations (Papero 1995-1997) on the relationship between fear, anxiety, and physiology stimulated Illick's further thinking on the relationship between fear, anxiety, physiology, and emotional cutoff. Anxiety, as described by Kerr and Bowen (1988), is the "organism's response to a threat, real or imagined" (p. 112). Anxiety and fear are described by LeDoux (1998) "as closely related" and as "reactions to harmful or potentially harmful situations" (p. 228). Both responses have physiological components. Although one often can be aware of one's anxiety, anxiety also can be vague and not in one's awareness. People can feel agitated and uncomfortable and not know what is wrong, or can know something is wrong but be unable to name it. Whereas at least for Illick, fear is a very clear emotion with a direct and knowable stimulus, whether real or imagined. It is as though anxiety is part of a deeper emotional state, not always in one's awareness, and fear is in the more available feeling realm, and more in one's awareness.

It is interesting to note that according to Kerr, Bowen chose the term *anxiety* over *fear* when developing his theory. Bowen understood anxiety to be more rooted in biology and fear to be more embedded in psychological theories. "One of the most important things about Bowen theory," Kerr (2001) states, "is its recognition of the myriad manifestations of anxiety: beliefs, behaviors, feeling states, attitudes, fantasies, body states, rituals, and so on" (personal communication with Michael E. Kerr).

One manifestation of anxiety is fear, for example the fear that one perceives and experiences when one is afraid of being oneself. One way that people avoid this anxiety, and avoid the fear that is a manifestation of the anxiety, is cutoff. The distancing mechanisms of cutoff are driven by the anxiety that goes along with the unresolved emotional attachment. By emotionally distancing from relationships in which one finds it difficult or intimidating to be oneself, one can operate as though one is more independent than one really is. This pattern of emotional distance and denial begins in the original triangle with oneself and one's mother and father. In his 1974 discussion of cutoff, Bowen (1978) pointed out that the "principal manifestation of emotional cut-off is denial of the intensity of the unresolved attachment to parents, acting and pretending to be more independent than one is" (p. 536). Bowen's (1978) reference to having "the ability to see one's own family more as people than emotionally endowed images" (p. 531) is important. Seeing one's parents more as "emotionally endowed images" than as people is an indicator of the degree of intensity and the degree of anxiety in the relationship system. This perception is a marker of unresolved emotional attachment.

The degree of unresolved emotional attachment to one's parents and the anxiety that goes along with it fundamentally contributes to a person's inability to be a self in important relationships. The greater the degree of the unresolved emotional attachment, the more vulnerable one is to anxiety. The more vulnerable one is to anxiety, the greater the tendency to act more from emotional reactivity than from thought (Kerr, personal communication, 2001). The greater the tendency to act from emotional reactivity, the greater the tendency to emotionally distance, to cut off.

Anxiety

The first step in managing oneself, Bowen said, is to observe the level of anxiety that is present in self. Bowen (Bowen and Kerr, 1979) also described anxiety as "emotional reactiveness to a real or imagined threat." Emotional reactivity, because it manifests itself as a behavior in direct relationship to other people, is more readily observable than anxiety, which often can be vague and free-floating. That Bowen links these two entities is enormously helpful; when one finds oneself in an emotionally reactive state, one can be sure there is anxiety present. In Bowen's own words, "reactivity is a manifestation of the anxiety" (Bowen and Kerr, 1979).

All people have unresolved emotional attachment to their parents, but in varying degrees. The degree of unresolved emotional attachment is based on two important variables: the level of differentiation in the family system and in self, and the level of anxiety. "The lower the level of differentiation," Bowen (1978) wrote, "the more intense the unresolved emotional attachment" (p. 382). According to what Illick has observed in herself and others, this interrelationship proposed by Bowen has further implications: the lower the level of differentiation, the more intense the unresolved emotional attachment *and* the higher the level of anxiety. This pertains to the family system as well as to the individual. Level of anxiety is a key variable to observe when looking at human behavior through the lens of Bowen family systems theory. In 1974 Bowen wrote, "All things being equal, the life course of people is determined by the amount of unresolved emotional attachment, the amount of anxiety that comes from it, and the way they deal with this anxiety" (1978, p. 537).

RESEARCH INSTRUMENT

The Princeton Family Center Research Team (PFCRT) was formed in response to the April 1996 conference on variability held at the Georgetown Family Center and David Gubernick's challenge to those interested in Bowen theory to engage in further research, using accepted scientific methodology. Selden Dunbar Illick and Susan Ewing Jefferies, both clinical social workers, attended the Georgetown Family Center conference. Each independently was interested in pursuing research based on Bowen family systems theory. Illick had devoted years to understanding the concept of emotional cutoff and the mechanisms associated with it. Jefferies had developed and received approval to implement a research protocol that was to study the relationship between a genetic anomaly of the dopamine system and the behavior of overconsuming refined carbohydrates. Following the conference Jefferies became interested in including a component in her study that would measure Bowen theory concepts. Illick was interested in measuring Bowen's concept of emotional cutoff. Illick and Jefferies began to work together, a collaboration which evolved into PFCRT, the research team that is in the process of developing FORS, a research instrument designed to measure elements of emotional cutoff. Gail Hilbert-McAllister, a faculty member at The College of New Jersey and a nurse researcher with expertise in instrument development and knowledge of Bowen Theory, was invited to join the team. In 1998 Charles M. White, a social worker and DSW student with knowledge of Bowen theory and an interest in statistics and psychometrics, became the fourth member of the team as the data analyst. The goal of the team is to develop a valid and reliable research instrument that seeks to be consistent with Bowen family systems theory and to measure particular elements of the concept of emotional cutoff.

Based on the hypothesis that the degree of emotional cutoff can be measured by the degree to which one is emotionally reactive to one's mother and father, the PFCRT developed the FORS. As Bowen said, "the notion of reactivity gives us something we can get our hands on and see" (Bowen and Kerr, 1979).

There is a great deal of variation in the way people react to their parents and in the way they manage the process between the generations. Both Bowen (1978) and Kerr and Bowen (1988) have referred to a distinction between the more orderly process of separation versus the more automatic, more reactive process of separation. Bowen (1978) wrote about a "more orderly growing up" and "growing away" from the family versus a "tearing himself [or herself] away" resulting in a more "pseudo-self" with a more "pseudo-separation" from the family ego mass (p. 92). Kerr (Kerr and Bowen, 1988) wrote that growing away "depends on gaining more emotional objectivity" and that "most people who claim to be independent of their families have broken away from them rather than grown away from them" (p. 272). Seen on a continuum (Jefferies, 1998), tearing away would be on the end where there is more reactivity, lower levels of differentiation, and higher levels of anxiety. Growing away would be on the calmer end of the continuum, in which there would be increasing levels of differentiation, lower levels of anxiety, and less emotional reactivity. Emotional distancing describes a pattern that individuals use to deal with the anxiety present in the relationship. The term *emotional separateness* describes people's ability to move apart or together without acting out any anxiety that might be triggered by the change (Kerr, 1988).

In order to design a research instrument that could capture the mechanisms of emotional cutoff and differentiation that are consistent with Bowen family systems theory, the PFCRT decided to measure well-known evolutionary behaviors such as flight and freeze and the more recently understood process of triangles in nature as described by de Waal (1989) and Smuts (1997). These behaviors are exemplary of what is automatic and instinctual. As Bowen (1978) wrote, "emotional reactiveness operates like a reflex" (p. 322).

The PFCRT assigned Bowen's descriptors of emotional cutoff in humans to the broader evolutionary mechanisms that reflect emotional processes in other life forms. Bowen's descriptors are: separation, isolation, withdrawal, running away, and denying the importance of the parental family. The broader evolutionary mechanisms which reflect emotional processes in other life forms that were chosen for use in the research instrument are: flight, freeze, and triangle. The process of assigning Bowen's terms to the concepts being researched is challenging because in systems theory every component relates to every other component. The authors have made an effort to separate out and measure distinct components, to the extent that this is possible.

When the PFCRT uses the term *flight* in FORS, the authors are measuring separation, withdrawal, and running away. *Freeze* is used to measure momentary episodes of isolation and withdrawal. *Triangle* is used to measure the degree of distancing in the original triangle with one's mother and father. The authors are using degrees of flight, freeze, and triangle to represent the more emotionally reactive, less thoughtful process consistent with Bowen's conceptualization of degree of unresolved emotional attachment. In addition, a category called "think" was designed. The authors are using the degree of "think" to represent the more thoughtful, less emotionally reactive response that is consistent with Bowen's conceptualization of degree of differentiation of self and the process of growing up.

Bowen (1991) wrote,

> Every human infant starts life fully dependent on others, specifically on the family of origin. Growing up involves progressive development of individual characteristics, and aspects of increasing independence. The development of self occurs, in the case of each person, in and through networks of relationships with other members of the family system. (p. 89)

Literature Review

A search of the literature revealed that previous attempts to measure the concept of cutoff, as described in Bowen family systems theory, have been part of dissertation research. Two studies (Day, 1988; Lartin, 1986) measured cutoff in relation to other variables with which it was hypothesized to have significant relationships. Both researchers used small samples and reported only a partial range of validity and reliability measures. Another measure of cutoff (McCollum, 1986, 1991) was originally developed for a dissertation but was used in subsequent research, thus providing further validity and reliability data with a larger sample size. The fourth dissertation (Skowron, 1996; Skowron and Friedlander, 1998) focused solely on instrument development in order to measure multiple concepts from Bowen family systems theory, including cutoff. The Skowron study had an adequate sample size and demonstrated adequate validity and reliability.

Only the two instruments with adequate sample size, validity, and reliability will be discussed in depth in this literature review. McCollum (1991) developed the Emotional Cutoff Scale (ECS) with five items that were placed on a five-point Likert scale ("strongly disagree" to "strongly agree") and repeated for father and mother. An example of an item is, "I would prefer not to have much contact with my mother if I could avoid it." The ECS measures the cognitive component of cutoff, assuming a relationship between attitude and behavior. In developing the scale, content validity was determined by submitting a list of items to a panel of experts and calculating a content validity index. Only those items with adequate validity were retained. Adequate validity and reliability were then demonstrated in the three studies using the ECS. Alphas, as measures of internal consistency and reliability, were above .70 in all three studies. McCollum hypothesized that the scale would have two factors, "father" and "mother." This hypothesis was supported in that all items of the scale loaded on two factors, one of which had only the items pertaining to "mother" and the other of which had only the items pertaining to "father." The concurrent validity of the scale was supported by correlations with a variety of measures theorized to be related to cutoff. Convenience samples for the three studies of the ECS totaled 398. Although appearing to be a valid and reliable measure of cutoff, the ECS samples a small number of possible items that measure cutoff and does not attempt to tap into the complexity of those evolutionary components of cutoff consistent with Bowen theory: flight, freeze, triangle, and think.

The Differentiation of Self Inventory (DSI) (Skowron and Friedlander, 1998) is a forty-three-item multidimensional scale which measures four Bowen family systems theory concepts: emotional reactivity, I-position, emotional cutoff, and fusion with others. Items are placed on a six-point Likert scale ranging from "not at all true of me" to "very true of me." The emotional cutoff subscale consists of twelve items that measure the intrapsychic and interpersonal components of cutoff. The items reflect feeling threatened by intimacy and feeling excessive vulnerability in relationships with others. The stems do not pertain specifically to mother and father but rather use the terms *people, family, someone, spouse,* and *partner.* An example of an item is, "I have difficulty expressing my feelings to people I care for." The DSI was refined during testing of three iterations of the scale with a total nonclinical convenience sample of 509 adults, most of whom were employed at a large northeastern state agency. It is notable that the emotional cutoff subscale was developed as an empirically based measure after a series of factor analyses indicated that the previously theorized "reactive distancing" and "fusion with parents" subscales were conceptually weak. They were refined as "emotional cutoff" and "fusion with others," respectively. The emotional cutoff subscale was supported by factor analysis in the final test of the DSI. Subscales had low to moderate correlations, indicating that the theorized components of differentiation were, in fact, separate concepts, thus supporting the content validity of the scale. Overall, coefficient alphas were consistently above .80. As with the ECS, the DSI scale is valid and reliable but did not capture the complexity of cutoff by tapping into the evolutionary components consistent with Bowen family systems theory, as described in the first section of this chapter. Also, it does not measure cutoff in relation to mother and father, essential to the definition of cutoff proposed by Bowen (1978).

DEVELOPMENT OF THE SCALE

Introduction

Emotional cutoff described by Bowen (1978) has to do with the distancing mechanisms involved in the process between generations. The PFCRT developed items for the Family of Origin Response Survey (FORS) that measure aspects of emotional reactivity occurring in the process of separation between the generations, specifically between mother/father and offspring, consistent with Bowen's (1978) definition of cutoff. This reactivity was theorized to be an indicator of the degree of unresolved emotional attachment and the degree of accompanying anxiety in the relationship system with one's mother and father. The anxiety from this unresolved attachment fuels the process of emotional cutoff. It is thought to be manifested by emotionally reactive responses to interactions with one's parents in terms of flight, freeze, and triangle.

The team was also interested in information on the respondents' quality and quantity of contact with parents and extended family and their knowledge of family of origin, as described by Baker and Gippenreiter (1996). Items were developed to tap frequency and variability of emotional reactivity responses through the use of the Likert scale and three- to four-part options in responses to family scenarios. Frequency was determined by the respondent's choice of "always," "often," "sometimes," or "rarely," the descriptors on the Likert scale. Variability was captured through allowing respondents to indicate which situations described in the family scenarios applied to them. A decision was made early in the process to measure only the behavioral aspects of cutoff that could be observed and which are called emotional reactivity responses in this chapter.

Description of the Scale Items

The FORS consists of fifty-six items placed on a five-point Likert scale with the options of "always," "often," "sometimes," "rarely," and "never," plus an "undecided" option. Four of the fifty-six items are single statements. An example of this type of item is, "I am interested in knowing about past generations of my family." Four of the items are paired statements that have to do with how one responds when with family or apart from family, closeness/distance, and asking for help or being asked for help. Sixteen items have paired statements which differ only in that one contains "mother" and one contains "father." Examples of this type of question are, "If my father tells me stories about his life, I'm interested. If my mother tells me stories about her life, I'm interested" and "The contact I have with my father lacks spontaneity. The contact I have with my mother lacks spontaneity."

The remaining sixteen items are based on simple family scenarios, such as, "When my comments to my father are inaccurately repeated by him to another person(s)," and "When things get tense between my mother and me during one of our contacts." There are eight scenarios, each of which is repeated for father and mother. For each one there are three or four responses placed on the five-point Likert scale of "always" to "never" with the additional response option of "undecided." These responses contain various combinations of items that are hypothesized to measure flight, freeze, triangle, and think. Scenarios placed early in the questionnaire are thought to elicit less reactive responses than those placed later in the questionnaire, thus taking into consideration a continuum of intensity of emotional response.

To deal with the possibility that respondents do not experience all of the scenarios within their families, sixteen items were placed on a green sheet of paper that was inserted before the first scenario. A green sheet was used so respondents could more easily identify the page when referring back to it. Respondents indicate on the green page how often they encounter each scenario, using the Likert scale of "always" to "never" with the additional response item of "undecided." Before each of the items that relate to the scenario, respondents are told that if they answered "always," "often," "sometimes," or "rarely" to this situation on the green page, they should select response options for each of the three or four statements. If they answered "never" or "undecided," they should go to the next question.

Examples of Items That Measure Reactivity Responses and Think

Listed below are sample questions that illustrate the aspects of cutoff defined for the FORS—flight, freeze, triangle, and think. The words in parentheses indicate the type of response but do not appear on the actual questionnaire.

23. When my comments to my **father** are inaccurately repeated by him to another person(s),
   A. I stay away from him *(flight)*
   B. I calmly describe my point of view to him *(think)*
   C. I find myself unable to think *(freeze)*
   D. I attempt to find another family member who will talk to my father about what he said *(triangle)*

46. When I become uptight about things my **mother** is saying to me
   A. I have an urge to complain to another person about my mother *(triangle)*
   B. I distance from her *(flight)*
   C. I become paralyzed *(freeze)*
   D. I tell my mother that I need time to think *(think)*

54. When my **father** is arguing with another person in my presence
   A. I'm out of there *(flight)*
   B. I think about what is happening *(think)*
   C. I freeze *(freeze)*
   D. I take sides in the argument *(triangle)*

56. When my **father** criticizes my efforts to help him during one of our contacts,
   A. I complain about him to someone else *(triangle)*
   B. I tune him out *(flight)*
   C. I can't respond *(freeze)*
   D. I shut down *(freeze)*

Personal Data Form

The personal data form is highly detailed and integrated. There are twenty-eight items. Some responses are straightforward, such as, gender, age, current field of employment, and racial/ethnic identity. More complex data pertain to adoption, contact with adopted and/or biological parents, multiple marriages and relationship difficulties of parents and respondents, sibling ages, birth order, and respondent's health. Items that are likely to generate less reactivity (such as age) are placed first, and those likely to generate more reactivity (such as sexual orientation) are placed at the latter part of the questionnaire.

VALIDITY AND RELIABILITY

Content Validity

Content validity, a measure of the degree to which a scale actually measures the concept or construct being examined (Burns and Grove, 1993), was determined for sixteen family scenarios with three- or four-part responses, thirteen paired mother/father items, and twenty single items, using the method described by Lynn (1986). Items were sent to fourteen persons identified as theoretical and clinical experts in Bowen family systems theory. Seven responses were received. Experts rated each of the sixty-four items on relevancy to the purpose of the instrument on a four-point scale, ranging from not relevant to highly relevant. Only those items with 100 percent relevant and highly relevant responses were retained as originally written. Items with less than 100 percent response as relevant or highly relevant were either dropped or rewritten based on suggestions of the experts.

Sample

During the spring of 1999, questionnaires were administered to a sample of graduate students at four institutions of higher learning. A total of 116 questionnaires were usable. Due to the "undecided" response option for the family scenarios, the number of questionnaires that were usable for reliabilities and correlations ranged from thirty-seven to forty-nine. Ninety percent of the sample was female, with 68 percent of respondents from one institution. The average age was 34.4 with a mode of 24.

Reliability

Reliability is the accuracy and the consistency with which an instrument measures the attribute it is supposed to be measuring. One aspect of reliability is internal consistency, the degree to which all items of a scale measure the same concept. It is determined by coefficient alpha or Cronbach's alpha that can range from -1.0 to $+1.0$ (Polit and Hungler, 1987). The responses to the four cutoff modes of flight, freeze, triangle, and think formed four subscales each for "mother" and "father" responses. Coefficients of .70 and above are considered acceptable for new scales (Burns and Grove, 1993). Coefficient alphas for the reactivity responses of the "mother" subscales ranged between .892 and .903 for flight, freeze, and triangle. Coefficient alphas for reactivity responses of the "father" subscales were between .819 and .879 for flight, freeze, and triangle. The subscales "think related to mother" and "think related to father" fell below the acceptable level with .190 for father and .439 for mother. This may be due to the fact that those two subscales had only four items. Scales with more items have greater internal consistency (Light, Singer, and Willett, 1990).

Discriminant Validity

Correlation's were done among subscales for mother-referenced items and father-referenced items. Moderate correlations suggest discriminant validity, the degree to which subscales measure different but related concepts (Polit and Hungler, 1987). Correlations ranged from −.026 to +.689. It should be noted that the correlations with "think" were negative, indicating that the more respondents use this mode of response to family situations the less likely they are to use flight, freeze, and triangle. All of the correlations that were below .40 involved the "think" response. These findings suggest that the "think" mode of response does not relate conceptually to the other response modes. One must, however, keep in mind that the homogeneous composition of the sample and the small sample size does not warrant drawing conclusions about discriminant validity at this time.

Scoring

A total score for the FORS four- and five-part questions may be obtained by reverse scoring the think subscale, since think is a positive dimension of emotional reactivity, and summing the scores for the flight, freeze, triangle, and think subscales. It must be kept in mind, however, that individual respondents will choose varying numbers of scenarios to which they will respond and some will choose undecided for some of those scenarios to which they respond. Therefore, comparing total scores on the four subscales among respondents may not yield meaningful information for clinical purposes. It is more useful to look at variation in patterns of response for each individual in terms of which scenarios they encounter in interactions with father and mother and how they respond to each of the scenarios. For research purposes, there are methods that will allow scores on the three- and four-part questions to be statistically manipulated in order to obtain meaningful comparisons.

The responses to the twenty-four single and paired statements that are separate from the scenarios may also be totaled. In contrast to the scenarios, these scores may be used to compare individuals, since all subjects will answer the same number of questions.

Future Plans

The PFCRT has collected data from graduate students for test-retest correlations for scale items, using a twenty-eight- to forty-nine-day interval between testing. When these data are analyzed the results will be reviewed to determine which items have acceptable stability over time, a measure of reliability of the scale (Polit and Hungler, 1987). In addition to the test-retest sample, data will be collected from a clinical sample to determine whether those subjects are similar to or different from the student samples. The clinical sample will also provide more data from male respondents. Data collection will proceed until a sample size of five respondents per item on the exam is reached. When these steps are completed, all statistical data will be reviewed by the PFCRT with the goal of reducing the total items on the scale. Items that have test-retest correlations below .70 will be eliminated. When pairs of items that have correlations above .70 are identified, one of the items will be eliminated in order to decrease redundancy. Items with low item-to-total correlation (below .30) will also be eliminated in order to include only items that contribute to internal consistency of the scale, ensuring that all items consistently measure the same construct (Kerlinger, 1986).

After the revisions described have been implemented, the FORS will be a scale to measure emotional reactivity as an indicator of cutoff that has preliminary validity and reliability. It will be appropriate both for researchers wishing to measure the Bowen family systems theory concept of cutoff and clinicians who may use the FORS as a resource for clients wanting to explore their relationships with parents and levels of cutoff intensity in their lives.

SUMMARY

Broadly, this chapter has been an effort to outline an understanding of the concept of emotional cutoff in Bowen family systems theory. It has been important to understand emotional cutoff as rooted in evolution and emotional or instinctual reactivity. Beginning to operationalize some of the elements of the concept into a research instrument has also been essential, as has focusing on human behaviors that are observable.

The hope is that the instrument, when completed, will be a basis of communication with those in the broader scientific community, especially with the natural sciences. Of particular importance is the fact that both Bowen theory and biology are rooted in evolution, thus it has been important in the development of the research instrument to reflect the broader evolutionary distancing mechanisms found not only in humans but also in other life forms as well.

This instrument seeks to operationalize and reduce to simple observable behaviors only *some* of the elements of emotional cutoff. Efforts are being made to create a valid and reliable research instrument for others to use in conjunction with their own research on emotional cutoff. It is further hoped that clinicians will find these questions useful in helping to better understand the varying degrees of emotional cutoff in their clinical populations.

For further information on the preliminary version of FORS, please contact Selden Dunbar Illick: (1) by phone at the Princeton Family Center for Education, Inc., (609) 924-0514, or (2) through her e-mail address <seldendi@aol.com>. For further information about participating in data collection or on use of the completed version, contact Charles M. White: (1) through his e-mail address <cmwhite@comcast.net>), (2) through accessing Rutgers University's Online Directory using the Find People link at the Rutgers University Web site <www.rutgers.edu>, or (3) by contacting Rutgers University (732) 932-1766 and asking for the doctoral program office administrator at the School of Social Work (New Brunswick), who will have current contact information for Mr. White and may be able to forward messages to his attention.

REFERENCES

Baker, K. and J. B. Gippenreiter (1996). The effects of Stalin's purge on three generations of Russian families. *Family Systems* 3(1): 5-35.

Bowen, M. (1978). *Family therapy in clinical practice*. Northvale, NJ: Jason Aronson, Inc.

Bowen, M. (1991). Individuality and cooperative action. In Early, Joseph Edward (Ed.), *Diversity from unity*, (pp. 87-90). Washington, DC: Georgetown University Press.

Bowen, M. and M. E. Kerr (1979) "Anxiety and emotional reactivity in therapy." Videotape produced by the Georgetown Family Center, Washington, DC.

Burns, N. and S. Grove (1993). *The practice of nursing research*. Philadelphia, PA: W. B. Saunders.

Day, L. H. (1988). Intergenerational distancing and its relationship to individual, family and occupational functioning: A partial test of Bowen theory. *Dissertations Abstracts International* 49(08): 2407A. (University Microfilms AAT 88-19224).

de Waal, F. (1989). *Chimpanzee politics: Power and sex among apes*. Baltimore, MD: The Johns Hopkins University Press.

Hilbert, G. A., S. D. Illick, S. E. Jefferies, and C. M. White (2000). *The Family of Origin Response Survey*. Princeton, NJ: The Princeton Family Center Research Team.

Jefferies. S. E. (1998). "An attempt to understand cutoff." Bowen Center for the Study of the Family. Training presentation at the Georgetown Family Center. Washington. DC.

Kerlinger. F. N. (1986). *Foundations of behavioral research*. New York: Holt, Rinehart and Winston.

Kerr. M E. and M. Bowen (1988). *Family evaluation: An approach based on Bowen theory*. New York: W.W. Norton and Company.

Lartin. J. M. (1986). The relationship between emotional cut-off and symptoms in the nuclear family. *Dissertations Abstracts International* 46(07): 2088A (University Microfilms ATT 85-15399).

LeDoux. J. (1998). *The emotional brain: The mysterious underpinnings of emotional life*. New York: Touchstone Books.

Light. R. J.. J. D. Singer, and J. B. Willett (1990). *By design: Planning research on higher education*. Cambridge. MA: Harvard University Press.

Lynn. M. R. (1986). Determination and quantification of content validity. *Nursing Research* 35: 382-385.

McCollum. E. E. (1986). Bowen's concept of emotional connectedness to spouse and family of origin as a moderator of the relationship between stress and individual well being. *Dissertations Abstracts International* 47(05): 1895A (University Microfilms 86-17119).

McCollum. E. E. (1991). A scale to measure Bowen's concept of emotional cutoff. *Contemporary Family Therapy* 13(3): 247-254.

Papero. D. V. (1995-1997). Presentations at Bowen Family Systems Theory Seminars. Washington. DC. and Princeton, New Jersey.

Polit. D. F. and B. P. Hungler (1987) *Nursing research: Principles and measures*. Philadelphia. PA: J. B. Lippincott.

Skowron. E. A. (1996). The differentiation of self inventory: Construct validation and test of Bowen theory. *Dissertations Abstracts International* 56(10): 235-246.

Skowron. E. A. and M. L. Friedlander (1998). The differentiation of self inventory: Development and initial validation. *Journal of Counseling Psychology* 45(3): 235-246.

Smuts. B. (1997). "Cooperation and conflict in families of wild baboons." Presentation at the Princeton Family Center for Education. Inc. Princeton. NJ.

Chapter 9

Marital Functioning and Multigenerational Fusion and Cutoff

Phil Klever

Individuals or couples who seek consultation for marital problems often have a hidden or sometimes expressed hope that the therapy will change the spouse's problem behavior. A clinician guided by Bowen theory broadens the lens from this narrow focus on the other to the reciprocal influences in the marital and nuclear family relationships. The factors that are brought into consideration in understanding marital functioning are the level of dependence and individuality, the patterns of emotional reactivity and thinking, the amount of anxiety and stress, and how the marriage manages the togetherness pressures and stress within the nuclear family. Bowen theory also opens the window beyond the nuclear family to examine the reciprocal influences between the multigenerational families and the husband and wife. How the multigenerational members relate to one another and how each spouse relates to his or her parents, aunts, uncles, grandparents, and cousins affects how the husband and wife relate to each other. The aim of this chapter is to examine the influence of intergenerational fusion and cutoff on marital functioning. Murray Bowen's family systems theory (Bowen, 1978; Kerr and Bowen, 1988; Papero, 1990) provides the theoretical framework for this chapter The author presents his understanding of parent-child fusion as a prelude and backdrop to marriage, the effects of intergenerational fusion and cutoff on marriage, and the elements of addressing intergenerational cutoff in clinical work.

PARENT-CHILD FUSION AND SEPARATION— THE PRELUDE AND BACKDROP TO MARRIAGE

Mammalian life begins in a symbiotic relationship between the fetus and the mother. This togetherness is essential for the development of the fetus

---

All names used in clinical examples are pseudonyms to protect confidentiality.

and, after birth, for the survival of the offspring. Because this sensitivity is so essential to survival, it is wired into humans and other animals as well. The parents' and children's mutual responsiveness to sensory cues includes physiological reactivity, feeling states, cognition, and behavior. The mother's responsiveness helps to regulate the infant. In varying degrees, the baby's responsiveness helps the parent regulate his or her feelings, thoughts, and behavior. As the child develops and moves toward separation, parents and children vary in how much each depends on the other to regulate self and how reactive one is to the other. As a child moves through childhood and adolescence, a more symbiotic parent-child attachment may be characterized by highly interdependent emotional states. The parent and child are caught accommodating, avoiding, rebelling, or fighting. An inordinate amount of mental energy goes into thinking or worrying about the other or blocking out any thoughts of the other. Knowledge of self is underdeveloped or out of reach, and sensitivity to others is a guiding force in life. With greater resolution of the original symbiosis, the parent and child are more emotionally independent, self-regulated, less reactive, more open, and self-directed.

When the time comes for an adult child to go on with his or her life, varying degrees of independence have been reached between the parents and child. With the greatest degree of resolution of the attachment, the process of separation is orderly, with few symptoms and minor emotional reactivity. In this case, forming a pair bond and getting married often is a natural step in the adult's development.

Stuck-Together Fusion

At higher levels of parent-child fusion, the separation process is more difficult. The two most common ways to handle this greater fusion are to stay stuck together with varying degrees of emotional distance or to cut off overtly. The most extreme form of stuck-togetherness is the parent and child who seldom leave each other until their deaths. Attempts the adult child makes to be an independent individual fail. He or she is unable to consistently support himself or herself financially or to form a lasting companion relationship. In addition, he or she may feel suicidal or extremely anxious away from the parents. Because the individuality of the parent and child is so underdeveloped, they have little self-knowledge or real understanding of the other. The irony of the extreme closeness is the lack of a mature person-to-person relationship. The person's personality is often an accommodation or adaptation to the other. This inability to be two separate individuals creates a covert cutoff or an underlying emotional distance in the midst of the extreme togetherness.

When the parent and child are stuck together with slightly less fusion, the child may support himself or herself financially or receive partial help from parents. Often the child and parent live near each other and have daily or frequent contact. They also are vulnerable to a covert cutoff. They may avoid any difference for fear of disrupting the togetherness or report there are no differences between them—"We usually think and feel the same on all things." The pseudoselves, or the parts of self that are an adaptation to the relationship, may in fact maintain a sameness between them. They may report telling each other everything, which often reflects a dependent openness. As long as they can be there for each other, each may function relatively well. When the togetherness is threatened, an overt cutoff becomes more probable.

Overt Cutoff

Overt cutoff is another way unresolved attachment is handled. The stress of the emotional sensitivity in highly fused parent-child relationships can become too much to manage and cutoff seems the only way out. In its most extreme form the parent and child stop all contact with each other. One may even disown the other. Some move far away, so involvement is next to impossible. The other, not the relationship, is seen as the problem and the only solution is to get away from the toxic person. One woman reported in a clinical session, "I believe I would have died from depression or a health problem if I had kept subjecting myself to my mother's criticism and abuse. I had already been hospitalized once." Cutting off is an instinctual as well as learned reaction to intense emotional discomfort. It is one way for the child to go on with his or her life away from the parent. Although the symbiosis begins at conception, the distancing or flight response may begin at various points of the life cycle—before birth, during the child's development, or during adulthood. Engagement and marriage are common times in the life cycle when cutoff occurs.

When the cutoff occurs in a somewhat less extreme parent-child fusion, the cutoff is less severe or persistent. The parent and adult child may have cordial contact on duty visits, but the relationship is not open. One-to-one interaction between the adult child and his or her father and the adult child and his or her mother is minimal or nonexistent. Almost all of the interaction is in a family group with mother and father together and the adult child and his spouse, children, or siblings. They know little of what one another thinks and feels about personal issues. Families at this level often see the emotional distance as a sign of independence instead of cutoff. Expectations for more involvement often are absent. Differences or emotional issues are avoided. To do otherwise seems invasive. The wisdom of this distance is that highly fused families are limited in their ability to balance emotional reactivity with clear thinking and appropriate control. The distance appears to protect the family in the short run from emotional outbursts or upsetting interactions. In a clinical session one man said, "I don't talk about anything personal with my mother because I know I would lose control of my temper and say or do something I would regret. I have done that in the past."

The Primary Triangle

The fusion or stuck-togetherness between the mother and the child does not occur in a vacuum, but in a set of interlocking triangles or relationships. One factor that assists the mother and child in moving to greater separateness is involvement in a range of open, mature relationships in the family. Usually the most influential or primary triangle is the father, mother, and child. The togetherness between the mother and child is usually less fixed when the father has a steady, mature relationship with his wife and child. When the father is more on the outside in the primary triangle, the mother and child are more stuck with each other on the inside. But the father's involvement with his wife and child is not a certain counterbalance to the mother-child togetherness. When a father and mother join forces with an immature focus on the child, the symbiosis is reinforced and harder to resolve. This often takes the form of feeling sorry for or being overcritical of the child. Another less frequent configuration of the primary triangle is the father as the primary caretaker in the inside position with the child, while the mother is on the outside.

Extended Family

The interlocking triangles in the extended family relationships also influence the degree of autonomy that is possible for the parent and child. Bowen theory posits that each person's level of differentiation or separateness is formed in family relationships. The range of separateness or individuality that parents are able to promote in their offspring is dependent on how much fusion or individuality the parents have (or had) with their parents. This multigenerational process toward greater fusion or toward greater individuality provides both constraint and flexibility. The multigenerational process has flexibility in that a parent and child may achieve a somewhat greater or lesser degree of separateness than the parent did with his or her parents. This promotes change in maturity from one generation to the next. The process also has constraint, though, in that a parent and child are limited in how far they can go in resolving the original symbiosis based on the parent's own level of individuality. This orderly multigenerational process is the larger context in which the parent-child relationship is embedded.

A second way that extended family relationships influence the parent-child symbiosis is the degree to which the extended family members are a resource to the parents and child in managing anxiety and stress. Mature involvement with the extended family makes it less difficult to resolve the original symbiosis. When the parents have open, responsible, and personal relationships with their parents and extended family, the parent and child have a wealth of emotional resources available to them. These family members are resources by listening to the parent or child, playing together, providing family stories and information about emotional patterns in the family, being a part of life cycle events and transitions, respecting and discussing differences, and being interested in the parent and child's well-being. These relationships promote more thinking and reduce emotional reactivity between the parent and child. For instance, when a mother starts to worry about her daughter, the mother can talk with her mother, the grandmother, about her concern. The grandmother can listen and give her viewpoint. She may give a broader perspective by discussing what was similar and different about the mother when she was the age of her daughter. This discussion and the perspective gained from it may be useful to the mother in reducing her worry and developing a more reasoned response to her daughter. Other ways the extended family members may provide occasional help are with child care, moving, car or home repair, and financial planning, among others.

When the parent is in a more stuck-together fusion with his or her parents or other extended family members, the symbiosis is more difficult to resolve. Parent-child separation for these families has definite limitations. The extended family reinforces peace at any price and the values of harmony and sameness. But because this kind of togetherness is difficult to maintain in a family over a long period of time, the relationships are often vulnerable to periods of anxiousness, overreactivity, and cutoff. So the parent-child relationship is not only dealing with the pressure of sustaining a comfortable togetherness with one another but also doing this in a more anxious extended family environment. While some of these extended family members tend to be overinvolved with one another, there usually are other members of the extended family who are cut off.

When the parent is in a more overt cutoff with his or her parents and extended family, the parent and child are left in a cocoon that is difficult to escape. Without the resources of the extended family they tend to lose perspective, to be more emotionally reactive, and to be vulnerable to an overt cutoff from each other or to a covert cutoff while stuck together. Isolation from the extended family amplifies the parent-child symbiosis.

THE EFFECTS OF CUTOFF ON MARRIAGE

The Process of Attachment

Falling in love usually is one of the best times in life. In the midst of the intense emotions of attachment the couple is potentially learning about the other, self, and the relationship. Patterns are forming related to being open, managing differences, building trust, spending time together and apart, making decisions, and leading and following. How much thinking and objectivity are available to guide each individual is affected by the amount of fusion in the individual's relationships with his parents and extended family. The degree of fusion in the dating and married relationship is a reenactment of the same degree of fusion in the parent-child relationship. Research using attachment theory found a high degree of correlation between the nature of a parent-child relationship during childhood and the adult child's romantic and marital relationships (Feeney and Noller, 1990; Levy and Davis, 1988; Main, Kaplan, and Cassidy, 1985). Generally, secure parent-child attachments were associated with positive adult relationships, while avoidant or anxious parent-child attachments were associated with fearful or dependent adult attachments.

Bowen theory broadens the lens by seeing the current parent-child relationship as influential and by placing the parent-child relationship in the context of a multigenerational emotional process. The husband and wife are both wired with a degree of emotional reactiveness that is rooted in their relationships with their parents and extended family. The degree of emotional sensitivity between the husband and wife is the same as with their parents, but the patterns may be very different. For instance, a husband may have fought bitterly with his parents and is now devoted to his wife through accommodation and avoidance of differences to avoid repeating the bitterness he experiences with his parents (Klever, 1998).

The less fused a person is with his or her parents, the more that thinking and individuality counterbalance the flood of emotions and the push for togetherness in the new attachment. When parent-child fusion is greater, the dating relationship is guided more by the effort to sustain positive feelings and by reacting to the other rather than by internal principles. The reaction to the other may be overaccommodation, distance, conflict, or domination. With less fusion, more thinking is available to be objective about self and one's partner. In addition, standards or foundations for a good relationship and marriage have been developed. With more undifferentiation, foundations for strong relationships are lacking or are feeling- and other-focused. In premarital therapy this author often asks, "At the end of the day how would you know if you were being a responsible spouse?" Responses suggesting more undifferentiation are: "I have no idea," "If we feel love for each other," or "If I'm making my partner happy." A few responses suggesting more differentiation are: "If I were open and a good listener,. "If I were being a good friend and doing my part in the relationship," or "If my partner and I were each able to pursue our personal and common goals and keep good communication with each other." One couple who divorced reported in a clinical session that they were having so much fun dating in college that at the end of their senior year it just made sense to get married. In looking back they realized that neither of them thought about what were the important foundations of a good marriage and that they ignored the red flags during dating.

When one's underdeveloped self is more fused with one's parents, the self during dating can easily meld into the underdeveloped self of the other. The couple may report that they think alike and agree on almost everything and that the new relationship "completes" them and gives them a new feeling of security. When the more fused relationships with the parents have been tense or cut off, the new attachment seems like a warm blanket in a cold world. The belief and hope is that the new attachment can take the person away from the dysfunctional family, and that just finding the right person will remedy relationship problems. There is a lack of awareness of how the patterns of fusion and cutoff operate in the individual and in the new relationship.

When the parents and child have been stuck together, the new partner must blend in with the family togetherness or the dating relationship ends. Often the new partner comes from a family with a more overt cutoff, so the new family togetherness is welcome, and he or she is adopted into the fold. Mr. Lerner illustrates this arrangement. He reported his mother to be a nonstop talker. He and his father ignored her and kept an impersonal relationship with her. Mr. Lerner's father was often away from home with his work. When Mr. Lerner was a sophomore in college he met and within two months started to live with his future wife. Her family was very close and involved with one another. He said, "I was adopted into her family. I finally had a family that I never had. My wife and I spent much of our free time and holidays with her family."

Dating patterns usually are a sign of levels of fusion and cutoff in the parent relationships. At higher levels of parent-child fusion the individual may date earlier than most of the peer group, form an overly intense attachment, let dating become the main priority and ignore personal goals, and/or act impulsively in the dating relationship. The new attachment for some may provide the confidence to separate from the family. Others may avoid dating, want to date but have behaviors that keep others away, or show extreme caution or anxiety about closeness or commitment.

Increased Dependence and Focus on the Spouse

Everyone has some degree of fusion or unresolved attachment to his or her parents, and therefore some aspects of the self that are underdeveloped. The self is less developed with greater degrees of undifferentiation in the parent-child relationship. With less self the individual becomes more dependent on the other for direction, security, and well-being. Values, goals, and principles for self are lacking, are an unquestioned incorporation of the parents' values, goals, or principles, or are in opposition to the parents. In addition, one's self-concept is vague, dependent on the parents' approval, or in opposition to the parents.

The undeveloped parts of self with the parent become the dependent parts of self in the marriage. In marriage this is evidenced in a person having unclear, dogmatic, or waffling positions on important marital issues such as finances, parenting, communication, household responsibilities, physical affection, sex, religion, and leisure. With higher levels of fusion in the marriage one avoids addressing marital issues, depends on the spouse to take leadership and define the direction, depends on the spouse to follow or accommodate, or persistently opposes the spouse's ideas.

Another way cutoff increases dependence on the spouse is through the lack of supporting relationships. The self is developed and maintained in the matrix of the family emotional system. The stability and strength of these relationships make a significant difference in the stability of an individual. When a person has an open, personal relationship with his or her parents and extended family, he or she has a broad network of relationships, each of which provides a unique perspective on the family history and family system. With these perspectives and the varied experiences in these relationships the individual better understands his or her history and patterns of behavior and emotion. With more isolation the spouses turn more to each other. At higher levels of dependency the expectations of the spouse go beyond what is realistic. The spouse cannot be father, mother, sibling, aunt, uncle, cousin, or grandparent. Without the larger family system the self and spouse's patterns of behavior, thought, and emotion are difficult to know or understand. Eventually most marriages crack from the weight of this dependency, and the spouses are disappointed or angry that their needs are not being met. This often leads to increased marital distance.

At higher levels of cutoff the partners are more focused on each other, since one's well-being is more highly dependent on the spouse. During calmer times this dependence may show itself in a cozy togetherness with a positive focus on each other. Comments made during this time are, "He/She is so wonderful. I couldn't live without his/her love." "We are everything for each other." In times of higher stress, the spouse focuses on the partner's weaknesses or vulnerabilities and takes an overly critical or sympathetic stance. Often the criticism is about the shift in attention or involvement from the togetherness of the early marriage or dating. The view is that the *spouse* needs to change to make the marriage better. Comments made during this time are: "Our problem is that she/he won't express her/his feelings and talk to me." "Since we have had children, she/he isn't paying attention to me." Mr. and Mrs. Jones illustrated this dependence on each other. They reported being soul mates and "joined at the hip" during their dating and first year of marriage. But in the second year he had an affair after his wife got depressed and withdrew from him. He said, "I'm an attention hound. I've got to be getting lots of attention from a woman to feel OK about myself."

Increased Dominance of Emotional Reactivity

A key component of differentiation of self is the ability of the individual to have the internal resources of thinking and emotion or to think in the midst of emotions. At higher levels of differentiation thinking is less colored by feelings, and both are resources to guide the self. At lower levels of differentiation thinking is less available or at the mercy of the emotional system. Thinking and feeling are fused. The parent and child who are more fused with each other also have more thinking that is fused with feeling. When the parent and child are more dependent on each other for security or well-being, the emotional sensitivity between them increases with less thinking as a counterbalance. At higher levels of dependency the parent and child are more vulnerable to feeling threatened or hurt by the other. They have difficulty getting perspective on the tension, and distancing thoughts and behavior automatically emerge. Cutting off potentially reduces the parent's and/or child's discomfort, at least in the short term.

The more cut off a husband and wife are with their parents, the more emotionally reactive their marriage is. The marriage is guided more by feeling and less by thoughtfulness, values, and principle. Gottman's research (1994, 1999) on marriage illuminates the interplay between emotion and thinking within the marriage. His research has studied the effects of emotional reactivity on marital stability and cognitive functioning. One finding is that a couple's autonomic arousal—heart rate, pulse transit time, skin conductance, and activity level—while discussing a conflictual issue was a longitudinal predictor of marital satisfaction. The less reactive or aroused the couple was while discussing a conflictual issue, the more likely they experienced marital satisfaction. The more reactive the couple, the less likely they experienced marital satisfaction. Couples who were more aroused experienced more "physiological linkage" (Gottman, 1994) and regulated each other's physiological responses more. In other words, they had less ability to be physiologically separate individuals. This research also found that a couple's physiological state overwhelmed cognitive ability. With diffuse physiological arousal, the couple had reduced ability to process new information, increased reliance on overlearned behaviors and thoughts, and reduced ability to find a way out of fight-and-flight behaviors. When the physiological state became so predominant that the person was able to attend to little else, he or she experienced "flooding." Physiological flooding reduced one's ability to think clearly and act flexibly. Relationships with chronic negative affect that leads to flooding became "hypervigilant to threat and misattributed threat to relatively neutral or positive acts" (Gottman, 1994, p. 76). From the perspective of Bowen theory, physiological linkage and flooding appear to be markers for marital fusion and reflect the increased dominance of emotional reactivity. Bowen theory posits that a precursor to this marital process is a similar level of emotional sensitivity in the parent-child relationship.

Greater Instability with Stress and Change

During times of lower stress a couple with higher degrees of cutoff from their parents may function as well as a couple with less cutoff. However, as the marital togetherness changes with the birth of a baby, a move, a job change, increased work demands, children growing up, or an illness, the stability of a couple who is more cut off from parents is often threatened. At this time symptoms may emerge in the marriage, the spouses, or children.

Mr. and Mrs. Peel illustrated how symptoms emerged during stress when the marital and intergenerational fusion is high. Mr. and Mrs. Peel sought consultation because Mr. Peel was having an affair and had moved out of the home after eight years of marriage. Mr. Peel's relationships with his parents were superficial with steady contact. He said that he felt close to them, but he did not talk about anything personal. He had not talked with them about the affair or the separation. He had almost no contact with his aunts, uncles, or grandparents. Mrs. Peel and her mother were best friends. They could talk about anything. Mrs. Peel and her father had no contact with each other since her parents divorced when she was five years old. Her older brothers went to live with her father at that time and she lived with her mother. Mrs. Peel had a close relationship with her maternal grandmother, but no aunts and uncles. The couple reported the first five years of their marriage as being intensely loving. They did everything together. They spent all their time off work devoted to each other. When Mr. and Mrs. Peel had their first child in the fifth year of their marriage. Mr. Peel became more dissatisfied. He said, "She was busy with the baby and stopped paying attention to me. Whenever I would bring it up to her, she would get angry with me." They both saw the problem rooted in the other. Mrs. Peel thought her husband was immature in not accepting her need to attend to her child, and Mr. Peel thought that his wife was too involved with the child and became hard to talk to. Their focus on each other switched from positive to negative. The backdrop to this marital fusion was the intergenerational cutoff and fusion.

The relationships with one's parents and extended family provide a backdrop or foundation in which one lives. The more secure and stable those relationships are, the less chronic anxiety a person and marriage has to manage. The more emotionally reactive or absent those relationships are, the more chronic anxiety there is to handle. In a clinical consultation with a couple experiencing severe marital disruption, the wife reported always feeling unsteady and insecure because of the distance with her parents and family. She had frequent contact with her mother and father, who were divorced when she was a teenager, but she never experienced them as reliable or interested in her. She took on a caretaker role with them and her younger siblings. Her father was raised in an orphanage and her mother was cut off from her siblings and parents several years before the divorce. This wife saw her chronic insecurity and caretaking position as contributing to making a poor choice in a husband, who was a "compulsive gambler, alcoholic, unfaithful spouse, and habitual liar." She believed the only way to get a husband was to find one who needed her help.

Greater Vulnerability to Divorce

Although little research has been done on the relationship of cutoff and divorce, the author hypothesizes that people who are more fused with and cut off from their families are more vulnerable to divorce than those who are less cut off. With greater degrees of parent-child fusion and anxiety, the parent and child are more vulnerable to a covert or overt cutoff with each other. Divorce is a process that is similar to cutting off from one's parents. Marital fusion and anxiety leads to conflict and/or emotional distance, which are often precursors to divorce. Gottman's marital research describes in particular four marital behaviors that lead to divorce—criticism, defensiveness, contempt, and stonewalling (a form of emotional distance) (Gottman, 1999).

The laws of the triangle to some degree predict who in the nuclear family will end up on the outside or in a more cutoff position. As intensity in the primary triangle increases, pressure mounts to get away from the "bad" parent, child, or spouse. For instance, when the primary target of the projection process is the child, a cutoff between the parents and adult child is more predictable. But when the marriage or one of the spouses is the primary symptom bearer, the marriage is more vulnerable to distance and eventual divorce.

CLINICAL WORK WITH EMOTIONAL CUTOFF

Most couples in clinical consultation for marital difficulty are primarily concerned about how to change the marital relationship. The focus is usually on the dyad. But the most effective clinical work with a couple expands beyond the individual and dyad to the interlocking triangles of the nuclear and extended family and social network. When a couple is motivated to observe self in those relationships, addressing the cutoff almost always becomes a part of the clinical work.

Assessment of Cutoff

One of the areas of assessment for a clinician applying Bowen theory is the degree and nature of the cutoff between the person and his or her parents. The degree of cutoff is the amount of distancing that is used to handle the unresolved attachment and the current level of anxiety in the relationship. The nature of the cutoff is whether the cutoff is handled more through an overt or external cutoff, in which there is little contact with each other, or a covert or internal cutoff, in which there is involvement with little personal interaction. The following factors are used in assessing cutoff.

Frequency of Contact

One quick way to assess an overt cutoff is to inquire about frequency of contact between the person and his parents and extended family. If the contact is nonexistent or only once or twice a year, then the clinician can easily assume a cutoff exists. But as the contact increases, the level of fusion and cutoff is less clear and predictable from this measure only. For instance, while daily contact between a parent and child is probably an indicator of some dependence, this may not always be assumed. Daily contact between a mature parent and child may have little dependence, but instead be a reflection of responsible involvement in a more differentiated relationship.

Geographic Proximity

Part of clinical assessment is finding the geographic location of family members. As with contact, geographic proximity may give a partial indication of the degree of cutoff. When a parent or child reports moving to get away from the difficulty in the parent-child relationship, this indicates an overt cutoff. Mrs. Tate reported a very close relationship with her daughter during her childhood. Mrs. Tate said that of her two children her daughter seemed to have the hardest time with Mr. and Mrs. Tate's divorce and the father's alcoholism, so the mother felt sorry for her daughter throughout her childhood. When the daughter married, she became very upset with what she perceived as her mother's attitude toward the new husband. At this point the daughter cut off all contact and refused any letters or gifts from the mother. In order to get away from Mrs. Tate, her daughter and new husband moved to Australia and left no forwarding address or phone number. This type of cutoff is rooted in the myth that physical distance is a way to resolve the tension in the parent-child relationship. Often to their surprise, the emotional difficulty in attachment follows the child to whatever continent or state he or she goes.

Other than the move to explicitly get away from one's parents, geographic proximity by itself is not a reliable indicator of cutoff. Some parents and children live across the country and maintain steady, open contact through e-mail, phone, and regular visits. In reverse, some adult children never leave home, but the parent and child have no personal conversations with each other.

Degree of Openness

The most critical aspect of cutoff to assess is the degree of openness between the parent and child. Lower levels of cutoff are characterized by a steady, personal, one-to-one relationship with each parent. A broad range of personal and family issues are discussed, as well as an ability to address differences. This does not mean that conversations are always calm. Emotional reactivity is inevitable in open family relationships, but with less cutoff more thinking is available to help modulate the emotions and to guide the self. With more cutoff the range of personal issues that are discussed is narrow and differences are avoided. To assess the degree of openness I ask some of the following questions: "Do you talk with your mother/father about personal thoughts and feelings?" "How would you compare your level of openness with your parent as compared to your spouse?" "What are some of the issues or thoughts you avoid with each parent?" "Who in your family have you talked with about this problem?" "If you were more open with your parent, what do you think would happen?" With more cutoff the person reports not talking about personal issues and avoiding anything that would stir emotions.

Probably one of the most difficult kinds of cutoff to assess is the covert cutoff in a cozy togetherness. The parent and child report being open with each other about almost everything. Two possibilities exist when this level of openness is reported. First, in fact the parent-child relationship is a mature relationship embedded in a fairly differentiated family with low stress, and therefore the cutoff is quite low. A second possibility is the parent and child have an overaccommodating relationship in which differences are blurred or nonexistent. They may be open about what little self they have or hide any areas of conflict. The parent or adult child often does not know what she or he thinks or feels about important issues or opinions and feelings borrowed from the other. They lack self-awareness or have an internal cutoff. If the parent or child develops more self, differences emerge in the relationship. The clinical assessment of this type of cutoff often takes some time to clarify.

Several factors differentiate between a mature, open, parent-child relationship and a pseudo-open relationship. One is the awareness and discussion of differences and emotional issues. Sometimes this is not evident until months into therapy. For example, Mr. Smith initially reported having a close relationship with his mother. Four months into the therapy he reported having responsibilities taken away at work and being reprimanded for poor performance. When asked if he had talked with his mother about this problem, he said, "No. That would upset her and cause her to worry about me." This indicated that the relationship had more limitations on the degree of openness than first described.

Involvement with the Broader Family

Another factor that sheds light on the degree of cutoff is the nature of the parent's and child's relationships with the extended family. Assessing the frequency and openness of contact with the extended family gives a clearer picture of the interlocking triangles in which the primary triangle is embedded. Some parent-child relationships are more isolated from the extended family. An example of this is the person who has contact with his parents five times a week, but no contact with any of his aunts, uncles, cousins, or grandparents. This is in contrast to the person who has contact with his parents five times a week, and monthly or bimonthly contact with several aunts, uncles, cousins, grandparents, and a great-grandparent. In the former example the parent and his or her family members are more cut off from one another, which promotes an intense togetherness between the parent and child.

Greater levels of intergenerational fusion are expressed in more cutoff or stuck-together relationships with the extended family or some combination of the two. The triangles in these families have more people stuck on the outside in cutoff positions or on the inside in stuck-together positions. For example, a mother may be in an overt cutoff from her father, overinvolved with her mother, and in an overt cutoff with her adult daughter. Another example is a father who is practically cut off from both of his parents and stuck-together with his wife and dependent adult child. The cutoff and stuck-together positions are each expressions of fusion because both are emotionally driven responses to a lack of individuality and an oversensitivity to the other.

In families with more differentiation, third parties are less involved in one-to-one extended family relationships. When triangling does occur, it is more flexible. People can move more freely to be in an "in" or "out" position and therefore are not usually stuck in a cutoff position. Because of this the parent and child have more members of the multigenerational family with whom they relate. This promotes lower levels of anxiety and more people and pathways to manage the anxiety, relationship sensitivity, and physiological reactivity. This helps the individual to be less symptomatic and/or more able to handle symptoms responsibly and with greater resilience.

Family research supports the idea that involvement with the extended family is associated with less symptomatic functioning. Harrison (1997) found that ovulatory women and their mothers had contact with more family members than anovulatory women and their mothers. The latter pairs were more isolated from their families and are hypothesized to have exerted more pressure on each other than less isolated mother-daughter dyads. In the first three years of a longitudinal study Klever (1999) found in a sample of fifty couples that broader extended family contact was associated with fewer and/or less severe nuclear family symptoms. Husbands and wives in early marriage who had contact three times a year with a broader range of family members tended to have fewer and/or less severe nuclear family symptoms than husbands and wives who had contact with fewer extended family members.

The following two family diagrams derived from the longitudinal research study illustrate this point. The first diagram (Family A) is of a family with almost no physical, emotional, social, or marital symptoms. The second diagram (Family B) is of a family with physical (spastic colon, ulcers, overweight, and high blood pressure), emotional (major depression), and social (driving under the influence of alcohol and federal tax delinquency) symptoms. The diagonal lines for Family A and Family B represent each family member the husband and wife had contact with at least three times a year. The couple in Family A was in contact with nineteen family members at least three times a year. The couple in Family B was in contact with five family members at least three times a year (Figure 9.1).

Responsible Involvement with Family Events and Transitions

Another area for assessing the level of cutoff involves determining whether one is a part of important family events and transitions. Births, funerals, graduations, weddings, divorces, moves, and retirements are just some of the important life cycle events that potentially bring families together. One way to

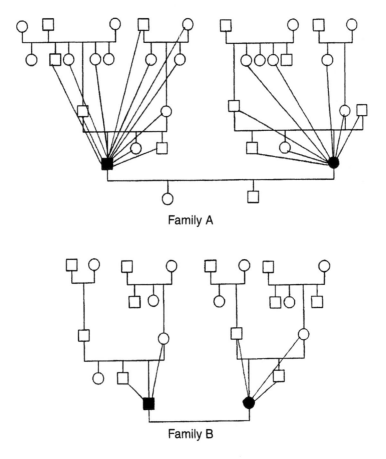

FIGURE 9.1. Family A and Family B: Contact with the multigenerational family.

assess the level of cutoff is to inquire about an individual's involvement in these transitions. Examples of some questions that assess this are, "Did you go to your uncle's funeral? What responsibility did you take on in moving your mother from her home to the nursing home? Did your parents attend your child's bar (bat) mitzvah?" During a clinical session with a woman working on her marital distance, she reported the death of her uncle. When I asked if she attended the funeral, she said that there was no funeral, memorial service, or family gathering. She saw this as a reflection of the distance in her family and the belief that each person should take care of himself or herself and not bother anybody. This confirmed for her the challenge she was facing in bridging a cutoff with her family and reducing the distance in her marriage.

Involvement at family events by itself is not a sure indicator of low fusion. In a highly fused family the expectation for involvement at family events may press on one's separateness. Some couples report that they are required to attend dinner at their parents' home every Sunday or to go to every birthday party for every extended family member. Family expectation supersedes the individual's thoughtful decision about which events to attend. This type of family involvement is part of the fusion and is not counterbalanced by individuality.

The Clinician's Own Cutoff

All clinicians have some degree of cutoff in their own families. If clinicians are not working on cutoff in their own families, they will be limited in how much they can help the client in bridging the cutoff in his or her family. All the principles, difficulties, and benefits of bridging a cutoff apply equally to helping professionals. Clinicians gain a respect for the function of cutoff and the challenge to be faced by observing it in themselves and their own families. Nothing teaches what is involved in working on family relationships as well as applying it to one's own family.

Addressing the Cutoff

One of the ways a person can work on developing a self and managing his or her reactivity in the marriage is to work on these issues in multigenerational relationships. In these relationships the self and the emotional patterns of attachment are formed and continue to be reenacted. When a person increases awareness of the multigenerational family and his or her part in it and develops a responsible involvement in the family, the marital relationship over time usually becomes less reactive. However, short-term anxiety is typical with a move toward greater differentiation. Bowen found that psychiatric residents who were studying their own multigenerational families seemed to do better than psychiatric residents in therapy who were primarily focused on their relationships with their spouses and children (Bowen, 1978). A person is limited in how far he or she can go in working on the marriage when the only focus is on self and the marital relationship. The following are some areas involved in addressing the cutoff clinically.

Level of Motivation and Interest

Addressing a cutoff requires a person to have an interest in his or her family and to see the family as a factor that contributes to individual and marital functioning. This is not a marital project but an individual effort. It requires commitment sustained over a lifetime. The more cut off a person is from his or her family, the less interest he or she has in the family, and the more he or she sees the family as irrelevant to addressing the marriage. The clinician's assessment of the client's level of motivation to look at the family relationship system is an important step. One of the ways to assess this is to ask a question that relates the client's presenting problem with the multigenerational family. For instance, "Is your marriage more or less distant than your parents' marriage?" or "Who in your family knows about your marital problems?" The response from a more cutoff person would be, "No one in my family knows about my marital problems. I don't talk with my family. Besides, it's none of their business. I'm better off if I stay away from them." Or in an irritated tone, "I don't know why you ask about my family. They have nothing to do with my marriage." Or in a proud way, "My family is great. We have a close relationship. They have no problems. But my spouse's family is really crazy." For the clinician to even inquire about the family challenges the mind-set in cutoff that the family is irrelevant or unimportant.

Others may describe the dysfunction in their family of origin as a main factor in the current marital problems, but they want to work on the problem away from their family. To engage with the family in any way seems overwhelming and unmanageable. Sometimes these people try to develop a substitute family through their church or synagogue, a recovery group, or group of friends.

The clinician's response to this lack of interest or motivation reflects his or her own level of differentiation. First, the client's areas of interest and the cutoff in any family should be respected. The cutoff is one adaptive response to relationship pressure. If a client does not want to address the cutoff or talk about his or her family, the clinician should defer to this boundary. It may be useful, though, for the clinician to develop an understanding of the client's viewpoint and to take an I-position on the topic. An I-position may involve the clinician defining how he or she sees the function and effects of the cutoff on the individual and marriage. This may involve respectfully defining the differences in viewpoints about the impact of the family on the marriage. However, when the professional takes a position that cutoff is dysfunctional and attempts to sell the client on the importance of bridging a cutoff, the clinician has crossed a boundary of respect for the client as the expert on self. This undifferentiated position of the clinician reflects a position of "I know what is best for you," and a lack of understanding about cutoff. Likewise, for the clinician not to define his or her position on this subject can sometimes be an undifferentiated stance as well.

Mr. and Mrs. Crane demonstrated the ambivalence and emotional intensity that can be stirred by clinically assessing family relationships with major cutoff. They came for consultation concerning marital tension after the husband's one-night stand while on a business trip. Their three-year marriage had been distant before the affair, but Mrs. Crane had withdrawn even further after contracting a sexually transmitted disease from her husband after his affair. They both reported constantly thinking about and missing the other and yearning to be together when the husband was away on business trips. However, when they were with each other, their thoughts became critical and they avoided each other. They reported being drawn to each other during courtship because they had an important area in common—they were both from "dysfunctional families" with whom they both had little contact. They provided each other a closeness that they had never felt before. They saw their marriage as an escape from their "sick" past. Because they presented this as an important part of their coming together, in the third session the author asked each of them what was dysfunctional about his or her family and what his or her family of origin relationships were like. In a matter-of-fact way they reported severe emotional problems, parental divorces, and considerable difficulty in sustaining a relationship with their parents. They failed to attend the next session. When they rescheduled and came for the fourth session, Mrs. Crane said that she had had a migraine that lasted for two days after the last session. She definitely believed the headache was triggered by discussing her family relationships. She said that she never wanted to do that again. She did not want to come back for therapy if she was going to have to talk about her family. They came for two more sessions, then Mrs. Crane stopped the consultations. She believed that the marriage was hopeless and that she should have known better than to think her husband would be any different than the unreliable men in her family.

Understanding the Emotional System

Effective clinical work with a couple helps the husband and wife to understand their patterns of interaction and how each influences the other. Likewise, one step for the husband or wife in bridging a cutoff is understanding their family system. This means examining how family members, including the client, influence one another's functioning. This moves the thinking from a blaming stance with "good and bad guys" to a systems view. The cutoff is seen in the matrix of the family and not as an inevitable response to a "sick" individual. This shifts the understanding of the cutoff, from "I had to get away from my overbearing mother," to the systems perspective of "I have not developed a strong enough self to hold my own when my mother tries to dominate. I get too upset to think when she gets that way. My father's distance from my mother and me adds to my mother feeling isolated and anxious. When she is anxious, she tries to control others. Also, my maternal grandmother's underfunctioning added to my firstborn mother's automatic tendency to take care of others." This individual's understanding of how the system works in turn helps him or her in taking a less reactive stance in the marriage, to be less overbearing or distant himself or herself.

People who attempt to naively bridge a cutoff without a systems understanding can make relationships more distant or tense. Pursuing the idea of an open relationship, people will confront the family members: "Mother, I'm really angry with you for being overbearing and trying to control my life. You have made my life miserable. I think you need to get counseling." When the mother responds defensively, denies the accusations, and refuses counseling, the child wonders why he or she even thought a relationship with his or her mother could be worked out. In fact, this person was open about his or her feelings and thoughts about the mother, but these feelings and thoughts are not based on a systems understanding of the family; they are based on cause-and-effect thinking. This is an example of how open communication can sometimes contribute to or perpetuate family regression. The child's openness kept the mother and child in an emotionally reactive pattern of blame and defensiveness.

In bridging a cutoff not all contact is intensely personal. In fact, too much emotionally laden personal interaction can promote a cutoff. Humorous, playful, and superficial interaction is a positive part of a healthy, open relationship. Beginning to bridge a cutoff usually begins with finding a comfortable connection with easy conversation or activity. Over time, as one has clearly shown a commitment and interest in being involved, more personal topics can be discussed.

One-to-One Personal Relationships

One characteristic of an effective marriage is the ability to have a one-to-one personal relationship. Building a more personal relationship with one's spouse is similar to bridging a cutoff with one's parents and family. An important component of bridging a cutoff is building one-to-one relationships with one's family of origin. A misguided attempt some make at bridging a cutoff is to bypass the one-to-one relationship and attempt to build relationships in the family group at the Thanksgiving dinner table, around the Christmas tree, at a birthday celebration, or at a family reunion. With greater cutoff, opening up personal issues in the family group is like throwing a match on gasoline. Instead, an individual is more successful at bridging cutoffs in one-to-one relationships and with an understanding of the important triangles. The effort is to be interested in and listen to the other, to be open about self, and to reduce the focus on the third party in the triangle. In the primary triangle this means sometimes having personal communication with father and mother separately. When one has laid the necessary groundwork in the one-to-one relationships, family gatherings can then more easily be the frosting on the cake.

The parent-child relationships are usually the most important relationships in bridging a cutoff and developing a one-to-one relationship because the child's dependency and fusion is usually greatest with the parents. But a person is limited in how far he or she can go in differentiating a self with a parent without also developing one-to-one relationships with other family members. For instance, an open relationship with a maternal aunt, grandparent, and/or cousin gives a broader perspective on the person's mother and the maternal family system. They often have a viewpoint that adds more pieces to the family puzzle and gives more objectivity. For example, Mrs. Tandy experienced a fair degree of anxiety about the stability of her marriage. She realized that some of her fears were not rooted in the marriage but in her family. Over half of her siblings, parents, aunts, uncles, grandparents, and cousins had been divorced at least once. She wanted to develop a better understanding of her parents' marriage and marriages in the larger family, but she found her parents to be closed to discussing their own marriage and divorce. So Mrs. Tandy developed a more personal relationship with a paternal aunt, a maternal uncle, and an older maternal cousin. Mrs. Tandy over time learned more about her mother and father's position in their families, her grandparents' negative reaction to her parents' marriage, and her parents' brief courtship. This knowledge helped her to understand her own anxiety better and led to more open discussions with her father about his marriage and divorce.

Clarifying the Goal

What is the goal in one's relationships with the extended family? One of the most common goals is to change the other. As in marriage, where one hopes the partner will change, the person working on his or her relationships with the family hopes the other will change, that the patriarchal father will be less dominating, or the distant mother will initiate contact. When this is the goal, the person is almost always met with resistance and ends up frustrated. Instead a more useful goal is to take responsibility for one's own part in maintaining a personal one-to-one relationship. In more cutoff families this goal may be only partially achieved at best. Some report that they can never be with their mother without the stepfather on the phone or in the room, or that any attempt to be mildly personal about oneself is met with tears, defensiveness, and further distance. A more realistic goal for beginning to bridge a cutoff in these families is to maintain steady contact, share an activity, or discuss safe issues.

Some have an initial enthusiasm and success in bridging the cutoff in their family relationship, but what often happens in more cutoff families is that a person's motivation wanes over time. Various factors influence this. The more automatic emotional response to ignore, not think about, or feel negatively about one's family may reemerge. Working on these relationships may be more difficult than originally thought. Father, mother, grandmother, or other family members may not change. Father may continue to be alcoholic, mother may continue to be critical, and grandmother still may never call or show an interest in the client. From this often emerges the question, "Why am I doing this?" or "What is the point of this anyway?" These questions, however, can lead to a reevaluation of one's motivation and a clarification of one's goal and the purpose of working on these relationships.

Management of One's Own Anxiety and Emotional Reactivity

As a person works on establishing more personal one-to-one relationships, inevitably his or her own anxiety and emotional reactivity emerge. The cutoff is a way of dealing with one's own emotional reactivity. With the cutoff the individual may seem calmer, but when the individual moves toward the parent, he or she eventually finds himself or herself wading in the waters of emotional intensity. One's awareness is clearer about the challenge of the parent's defensiveness, criticalness, dominance, quietness, nonresponsiveness, changing the subject, helplessness, poor listening, crying, fidgeting, worrying, nurturing, anger, addiction, or fiscal irresponsibility. However, it often is less clear how one's own mind-set and emotional and behavioral patterns add to the problem in the parent-child relationship. Questions that help to stimulate that awareness can be: "What is the challenge you present to your parent?" or "How do you affect your parent's behavior?" or "How does your anxiousness with your father affect his distance?" A person begins to make some headway in bridging a cutoff when he or she moves from blaming the cutoff on the parent's behavior to seeing how one's own emotional reactivity contributes to the cutoff. Sometimes the child sees his or her response as the only reaction possible to the parent's behavior.

Developing more flexibility in response to the parent and other family members usually is helpful. Several steps are involved in doing this. First, self and other awareness is required. This involves observing one's thoughts, feelings, and behavior in interacting with the other. For example, Mr. Brown observed that he instantly felt tense around his father and that his father seemed cool or aloof around Mr. Brown.

A second part of developing more flexibility is examining one's mind-set or way of thinking about the relationship. Often the person's inflexible response is rooted in an immature expectation or in blaming thoughts. Mr. Brown realized that he felt tense because he wanted his father's approval. He perceived his father's aloofness as a sign of disapproval. Others hold a blaming view of the parent, who is perceived to have caused the individual's problems because of inattention, overcontrol, excessive yelling or criticism, or irresponsibility. Mr. Brown blamed the distance with his father on his father's aloofness. When this mind-set was reexamined with a systems perspective, a more flexible response became possible. For instance, Mr. Brown developed a more systems-oriented view of his father's aloofness. He saw that his father's behavior was a response to being excluded in the tight togetherness between Mr. Brown and his mother and to Mr. Brown being on guard. In addition, his father handled his anxiousness in his family of origin with aloofness.

A third part of developing more flexibility is generating options for alternative responses. With a systems perspective, new ways of responding often emerge naturally. Other times the individual needs to plan different ways of responding. For instance, with a broader understanding of the relationship tension, Mr. Brown was less anxious with his father and was more able to be direct and playfully persistent with him. He saw his immaturity in needing his father's approval. He also realized the importance of his relationship with his mother in getting closer to his father. With Mr. Brown's mother he reduced his critical comments about his father and increased his neutral and positive comments about him and their marriage. In addition, he planned ways to have time with his father alone, away from his mother.

Mrs. Ford, who sought clinical consultation for marital problems, is another example of someone who worked on her own reactivity to her parent. She was motivated to examine her relationships with her family. Prior to therapy she had begun to work on her relationship with her mother, who had persistently been critical of Mrs. Ford. Her usual response was to pull away and keep a superficial relationship. Ten years before the clinical consultation Mrs. Ford realized that she wanted a different relationship with her mother. She knew she could not change her mother but that she could take more responsibility for her own goal in the relationship, which was to have a more personal relationship. So Mrs. Ford began to increase the frequency of her contacts and to tell her mother more of Mrs. Ford's personal thoughts and what was going on in her life. Mrs. Ford also knew that if she confronted her mother about her criticalness, her mother would get defensive and become even more critical. One of the most difficult parts of this project' for Mrs. Ford was managing her automatic emotional sensitivity to her mother. Mrs. Ford reported that she had been fairly successful in accomplishing her goal over the previous ten years. Her mother's behavior was also fascinating for Mrs. Ford to observe. During the first two years of this work, her mother maintained her critical behavior. But over the next six years Mrs. Ford noticed her mother gradually becoming less critical. In the last two years her mother almost never criticized Mrs. Ford. Changing her mother was not her goal, but was a welcome by product of her personal goal to change her own reactiveness with her mother.

CONCLUSION

Cutoff is a natural part of life. It is one way for a child to move on with his or her life in the midst of parent-child fusion. The levels of emotional sensitivity and underdeveloped self between the parents and child are replicated in the child's marital relationship. Application of Bowen theory to a marital problem widens the scope beyond the couple to the patterns of attachment in the primary and interlocking triangles. From this theoretical perspective an effort to improve emotional functioning in the marriage usually involves addressing the cutoff with the multigenerational family.

REFERENCES

Bowen, M. (1978). *Family Therapy in Clinical Practice*. New York: Jason Aronson.
Feeney, J. A. and P. Noller (1990). Attachment style as a predictor of adult romantic relationship. *Journal of Personality and Social Psychology* 58:281-291.
Gottman, J. M. (1994). *What Predicts Divorce?* Hillsdale, NJ. Lawrence Erlbaum Associates.
Gottman, J. M. (1999). *The Marriage Clinic*. New York: W.W. Norton and Company.

Harrison, V. (1997). Patterns of Ovulation, Reactivity, and Family Emotional Process. *Annals of New York Academy of the Sciences* 807 (January):522-524.

Kerr, M. and M. Bowen (1988). *Family Evaluation.* New York: W.W. Norton and Company.

Klever, P. (1998) Marital Fusion and Differentiation. In Titelman, P. (Ed.), *Clinical Applications of Bowen Family Systems Theory* (pp. 119-145). Binghamton, NY. The Haworth Press, Inc.

Klever, P. (1999). "Variation in Nuclear Family Functioning." Presentation at Georgetown Family Center Family Theory and Psychotherapy Symposium, Georgetown Family Center, Washington, DC, November.

Levy, M. B. and K E. Davis (1988). Lovestyles and attachment styles compared: Their relationships to each other and to various relationship characteristics. *Journal of Social and Personal Relationships* 5:439-71.

Main, M., N. Kaplan, and J. Cassidy (1985). Security in infancy, childhood, and adulthood: A move to the level of representation. Monograph. *Society for Research in Child Development* 50:66-104.

Papero, D. (1990). *Bowen Family Systems Theory.* Boston: Allyn and Bacon.

Chapter 10

Reproduction and Emotional Cutoff

Victoria Harrison

INTRODUCTION

Reproduction is a part of all life. Each form of life reproduces its genetic template, along with its biology, brains, and patterns of relationship with kin. The family itself, with various kinds of relationships between generations, between male and female, and with children, is part and product of reproduction. Each generation produces the next, similar to the past with slight differences.

Variation in reproduction is universal. Charles Darwin considered differential reproduction one of the fundamental facts of life. Every family has its own examples. In three generations of any family, there will be those who have children and those who do not. Some have one child; others have several. Some will want children and be unable to have them. Some have more children than they want.

Much of the variation in reproduction operates automatically, without choice or deliberation. The hormones and chemistry, the nervous system and reproductive systems react, for the most part, without choice or deliberation. A human female does not choose to delay ovulation any more than does the panda. Emotional reactions to relationships with kin and to the conditions of life, to food, and to family impact who does and does not reproduce, when reproduction occurs, and with what results in the natural world. This author believes the human family is no exception.

Bowen theory, a natural systems theory of the family, provides a conceptual framework for understanding the physiological impact of relationships in the family on reproduction. People usually recognize attraction or affection or conflict as reactions to relationships. People may not realize that reactions to relationships also alter physiology and brain chemistry. It is possible for any person to perceive reactivity more clearly and to recognize its impact on reproduction. Knowledge about the ways in which reactivity to

245

relationships affects human reproduction can inform difficult personal decisions and can be integrated into reproductive medicine, research, and clinical practice to address what many experience as distressing symptoms. There is some evidence that it is possible to modify reactivity and its impact on reproduction as well.

This chapter first introduces emotional cutoff as one of the central concepts in Murray Bowen's natural systems theory of the family. The second section summarizes twenty-five years of research on reproduction and family systems, in which emotional cutoff is a recurring variable. The third section outlines facts about reactivity to relationships, stress, and reproductive biology and examines the ways that contact and cutoff between generations of kin affect reproduction. Section four describes examples from research and clinical families. The chapter concludes with a discussion of ways that clinical practice and reproductive medicine can employ this knowledge.

Some will read only this far and react. Does this perspective blame the woman or the family for problems as vast as overpopulation or as disturbing as infertility? No one is to blame for biology. Bowen (1978) put it best when he wrote, "Systems [theory] therapy cannot remake what nature created, but through learning how the organism operates, controlling anxiety, and learning to better adapt to the fortunes and misfortunes of life, it can give nature a better chance" (p. 410). Women and families find more liberty than guilt as they begin to recognize how reactions to relationships in the family system have an impact upon their reproduction. They find that a wider range of choices about reproduction is possible.

BOWEN THEORY AND EMOTIONAL CUTOFF

While at Menninger Foundation from 1946 to 1954, Bowen began to develop a new theory of human behavior integrating what he considered scientific in the work of Freud with facts from evolution and the natural sciences. The years of family research that followed elaborated upon eight interconnected theoretical concepts that provide the foundation for research, teaching, and applications in diverse fields. Dr. Bowen came to Georgetown University in 1959 and founded The Family Center, now independent of the university, to be a center for research, study, and practice.

Emotional cutoff was not one of the first concepts defined as part of this natural systems theory of the family. Physical and internal distance were evident as background forces in any family, but Bowen added emotional cutoff as a separate concept in 1975 to specifically describe the emotional process between generations (Bowen, 1978). That one generation will separate from past generations is universal. The degree of emotional cutoff will vary, depending upon other facts and factors that are defined in Bowen theory.

Bowen theory is about the family emotional system and ways that people adapt to being an inherently social species, a family form of life. Two universal life forces, one for togetherness with others and one for independence from others, counterbalance to influence physiology, psychology, and behavior. A brain that is capable of recognizing reactions to relationships and of self-regulation provides the human with additional resources for adaptation.

Emotion, in Bowen theory, is the force behind responses of an organism to the natural and social environment. Emotional reactivity is built into biology and influences all internal states and behavior. Brain chemistry, cell growth, sperm production, hormones, nervous systems, ovulation, digestion, heart rate, and energy levels are all influenced by the emotional reactivity humans share with other living creatures. Reproduction is governed in large part by emotional reactions to relationships in the family, reactions that affect both the biology of reproduction as well as how we think and feel.

A large prefrontal cortex distinguishes human intelligence from other forms of life on earth. The ability to perceive emotional reactions, to evaluate them, and to alter them provides people with more choices. Human intelligence provides new ways to adapt to one another, to change, and to challenge. The exercise of intelligence not only produces civilization and technology but also regulates physiology and behavior. Education, particularly literacy for women, is associated with increased health and longevity, decreased birth rate, and decreased infant mortality (Sagan, 1987; Sen, 1993). Interactions between emotional reactivity and intellect vary within the population in ways that are not equivalent to intelligence quotient (IQ). Individuals have more or less ability to determine their own functioning related to family and to reproduction, depending on their level of differentiation of self.

Bowen (1978) developed the Scale of Differentiation to describe variation in the basic orientation of individuals and families toward emotional reactivity and intellect. According to Bowen,

> There are varying degrees of "fusion" between the emotional and intellectual systems in the human. The greater the fusion, the more life is governed by automatic emotional forces that operate. The greater the fusion between emotion and intellect, the more the individual is fused into the emotion of people around him. (1978, p. 305)

With greater fusion, one person will react to the emotions of others as if they are his or her own, within his or her brain and body. With greater differentiation of self, a person can distinguish his or her own internal states from those of others and reactivity is more under the influence of intelligence. Relationships and levels of differentiation of self govern the levels and patterns of reactivity and their impact on reproduction. Cutoff from past generations affects levels of fusion and reactivity within a family in ways that require more careful study.

Reactivity to relationships both constrains and supports individuals. We cannot live without relationships and it can be difficult to live with them. Tensions within togetherness generate reactivity that takes predictable shape. People adapt to one another through distance, conflict, development of symptoms (physical, psychological, social), reciprocal functioning, and projection of the problem onto another. These adaptive reactions occur in each and every family. Each of the mechanisms by which people adapt to one another operates in emotional triangles. Any two people react to each other in relation to a third. Father reacts to closeness between mother and child. Child reacts to the relationship between the parents. The closeness between mother and her mother shifts in response to the birth of a child.

Distance, conflict, reciprocal functioning, projection of the problem onto another, and development of symptoms occur within triangles, not just between the two most obviously involved people. Emotional cutoff occurs in triangles. Degrees of cutoff from one's own family often leave a person more comfortable in one set of relationships and more reactive in relation to others. It is more difficult for a person who is cut off from the past to perceive patterns of reaction in the family and to know facts behind the reactions stirred.

Anxiety, the perception of threat to self or to the system, stirs reactions in the effort to adapt to change and challenge. At lower levels of differentiation of self, people perceive threat more easily, experience anxiety more often, and are more likely to develop symptoms related to stress. With higher levels of differentiation, threat is experienced less often. Individuals are better able to counterbalance subjective reactions and govern themselves, their physiology, decisions, and actions with principles, knowledge, and facts. Conditions of life that threaten survival, as they do for much of humanity, can affect any level of differentiation. Responses, however, will vary. Degrees of emotional cutoff may occur.

Separation from past generations may occur as a product of life circumstance. Migration from Ireland or Norway or the villages of Brazil during famine may produce cutoff from past generations and intensify the dependence of one generation upon the next. Levels of differentiation will make a difference in how people adapt to the new set of circumstances. Some will maintain contact with the past through photographs, language, or memory of history. Others will quickly try to forget the past to deal with the demands at hand, and leave the next generation with less connection to the history of the family.

Reactions to the fortunes and misfortunes of life impact reproduction levels of reactivity, anxiety, and differentiation of self are transmitted across generations in every family. One generation will function at about the same level as the parents with slight variation in differentiation of self, and each generation reacts to the reactions of past generations of family. The impact of reproduction and birth order on nuclear family emotional process depends upon the level and patterns of reactivity operating across generations. Emotional cutoff does not stand alone but interacts with the other variables defined in Bowen theory to influence reproduction. Most of these influences occur automatically, without awareness and without choice.

The concepts in Bowen theory provide a framework for thinking that begins with what is known through careful observation and study. Murray Bowen attempted to describe the ways in which the human family is part of the natural world, the world of evolution, biology, and science. It is common for people initially to read Bowen theory as an extension of psychiatry or medicine, as a description of pathology or diagnoses. It is not. Bowen theory describes characteristics of human nature held in common with all of life, including the ways nature adapts to change and challenge. This theory provides a way to study the impact that relationships in the family system have on reproduction and a way to integrate knowledge from the natural sciences with clinical practice and original research.

THE STUDY OF BOWEN THEORY AND REPRODUCTION

Bowen taught and talked about the importance of science and evolution in the development of theory and to this new way of thinking. Using his teachings as a foundation, this author determined to study reproduction as a vehicle for building a base of knowledge in the impersonal facts of nature. In 1980, the study of reproduction and biology became a priority focus for my clinical practice, study, and research. Collaboration with Dr. Susan Atlas, a reproductive biologist who also studies family systems, furthered reading and research between 1980 and 1986. Dr. Roberta Holt chaired a biology study group at Georgetown Family Center and Dr. Bowen led an ongoing Monday night think tank that provided direction to this study. The biofeedback program at Georgetown Family Center, directed by Dr. Lilian Rosenbaum, provided ways to measure and study physiological reactions. I attended conferences and courses on reproduction, biology, and evolution and met Emil Steinberger, MD, director of the Texas Institute of Reproductive Medicine and Endocrinology (TIRME), at a Society for Menstrual Cycle Research meeting. He and the other directors of TIRME offered a six-month sabbatical in 1986, which afforded me opportunities for systematic study, consultation, and research with scientist physicians. Upon return to Washington, DC, I resumed clinical practice with a focus on reproduction and referrals related to infertility, high-risk pregnancy, and other difficulties related to bearing and rearing children.

The first research project was a clinical survey of fifty women who had not reproduced. Two distinct groups emerged with a common characteristic. One group of extremely capable women assumed a great deal of responsibility in their families and in their work. The other group of women had serious health or life symptoms and depended almost entirely upon their families for everything. The degree of dependence upon others in the family was the common thread. Both depending upon the family and being depended upon by the family, taken to an extreme, were associated with the absence of reproduction. Emotional cutoff from the broader family was a background factor producing the degrees of dependence that developed among a few family members.

This author's daughter's marriage and pregnancy, the birth of a granddaughter, and her own marriage, pregnancies, and miscarriages launched more detailed study of the interaction between stress reactions and reproductive biology. The family as the unit of influence over reproduction came into focus. If a woman's lap is full of family, there is less room for a baby.

A second major study organized years of family research to investigate facts about reproduction over eight generations of the author's own family. Three patterns related to emotional cutoff and contact between generations were evident. Relationships between generations appeared to be both resources and sources of stress (Harrison, 1990).

This study of reproduction and the family informed a decision in 1991 to move back to Houston, Texas, in order to be a local resource as mother and grandmother and in order to be more involved in the life of the family. Texas Institute for Reproductive Medicine and Endocrinology offered the opportunity to establish a clinical practice in their offices at Woman's Hospital of Texas. The research interests of the physicians permitted a study of reactivity and ovulation that included hormone assay, biofeedback measures of physiology, and facts about the family system. Contact and emotional cutoff emerged from this study as key to levels of reactivity and patterns of ovulation (Harrison, 1995).

Multigenerational family research and the study of ovulation and family emotional process indicate that contact between generations influences variation in reproduction. Increased numbers of children following migration, declining birth rate associated with an increased number of living generations in contact with one another, and infertility associated with the isolation of mother and daughter together indicate patterns consistent with observations about reactivity to relationships in the natural sciences. Contact and cutoff between generations influence biological states and behaviors that regulate reproduction.

Relationships, Reactivity, and Reproduction

Human biology, with emotional reactivity grounded in mammalian and primate evolution, provides for the counterbalance among (1) survival of the individual, (2) reactivity to relationships, and (3) reproduction. Reactions to generations of kin and individual metabolic stability depend upon each other but also compete with each other. Reproduction, relationships, and individual metabolism depend upon one another and compete with one another as well. Brain development is an additional variable for the human that depends upon and competes with relationships, individual metabolism, and reproduction. For example, digestion, stress, cognitive tasks, and sex coordinate and compete with one another for oxygen and energy. Blood flow shifts from the stomach and intestines to the brain and muscles to fuel responses to a demand or emergency. Oxygen fuels emotional reactivity at the expense of complex thinking. Reading and study require oxygen to fuel cortical activity. The chemistry of affection and closeness inhibits stress hormones. Attraction is a mix of stress and delight, excitement and anxiety. Adaptation to relationships and other realities of life involves a shifting dynamic of internal states and interactions. A large prefrontal cortex provides additional resources through the ability to recognize reactivity, to develop knowledge, and to perceive and make choices. The regulation of reproduction is influenced by both emotional reactivity to relationships and the exercise of intelligence.

In a life's work that spans fifty years of neuroscience research and evolutionary study, Paul MacLean (1990) outlines ways in which the human brain is built for reactions that maintain both relationships and survival of the individual. Neuronal activity in the brainstem, limbic system, and prefrontal cortex interacts to provide both the automatic emotional reactions required for survival and reproduction and the intellectual activity involved in increased knowledge and choice. The "triune brain" (MacLean, 1990) is built for the counterbalance and trade-off between reactivity to relationships, individual survival, and reproduction. Although Joseph LeDoux (1998) does not agree with the anatomical hierarchy described by MacLean, his research defines a fundamental variability in neuronal connections between the limbic centers of emotional reactivity and the prefrontal cortex. There are more connections upward, from the limbic brain to the intellect, than there are down, from the intellect to the limbic (Ledoux, 1998). John Allman and colleagues (2001) likewise describe another source of variability in the interaction between emotional reactivity and intellect. Specialized cells in the anterior cingulate gyrus, a collar of cells at the cusp of the limbic system and cortex, vary in number and functioning. Some people appear to maintain more cortical cell activity under stress than do others (Allman et al., 2001). Emotional reactivity is part of us all. What varies is the extent to which the influence of intellect is available for regulation of automatic physiology or for choices that accompany awareness and knowledge.

The chemistry of relationships, stress reactions, and hormones of reproduction arise within the limbic system and travel throughout the body. They interact and affect one another. Chemicals and hormones released within the limbic system travel via blood vessels and portals to endocrine glands and sex organs to regulate ovulation and sperm production.

Ovulation is regulated through hormonal interaction between the limbic system and ovaries. The female hypothalamus, located in her midbrain, begins to secrete regular ninety-minute pulses of gonadotrophin releasing hormone (GnRH), which stimulate pituitary production of follicular stimulating hormone (FSH). FSH travels through the bloodstream to the ovary and stimulates ovarian production of estrogen. Rising estrogen fuels the development of a cohort of oocytes in the ovary until one bursts from the ovary, releasing progesterone that stimulates pituitary secretion of leutinizing hormone (LH). Both progesterone and LH play a part in preparing the uterus for pregnancy. When the interaction of hormones occurs without interruption, menstruation occurs about every twenty-eight days and ovulation at about day fourteen in that cycle. The same hormones also regulate movement of the walls of the fallopian tubes, which carry the released egg and the sperm toward each other for fertilization. The same hormones are active in implantation, early cell division, and pregnancy (Hotchkiss and Knobil, 1994).

Male fertility is regulated by the interaction of brain hormones with gonads in sperm production. GnRH pulses stimulate FSH, which regulates the ability to produce sperm, and LH, which stimulates sperm production and testosterone levels. Male libido, the energy for sex, as well as sperm count, motility, and fertility are influenced by the interaction of brain and sex hormones with other metabolic states (Steinberger, Steinberger, and Sanborn, 1974; Steinberger, 1987).

Fifty years of stress research describe various pathways of hormonal and nervous system activity that interact to affect ovulation, fertility, and reproduction (Stratakis and Chrousos, 1995; Chrousos and Gold, 1992). Emotional reactivity stirs chemistry and hormones in response to experiences that are perceived as stressful. Corticotrophin-releasing hormone (CRH) is released by the hypothalamus when a threat is perceived. CRH has local effects in the limbic system on the hormones involved in ovulation and sperm production. If the precise timing of GnRH pulses is disturbed, ovulation is delayed or interrupted (Hotchkiss and Knobil, 1994; Schenker, Meirow, and Schenker, 1992). The local effects of CRH are brief and transient if a disturbance is mild or passing.

CRH also stimulates sympathetic nervous system activation, which rapidly travels through nerves that connect the midbrain and brainstem to all of the organ systems governing metabolism and reproduction. Sympathetic nervous system activity stimulates adrenal production of epinephrine and norepinepherine (catecholamines), which provide rapid responses, shifting oxygen and energy throughout the body to assure responses to the most immediate demands of life. Catecholamine levels alter the precise release of GnRH and interrupt or delay hormonal interactions that produce ovulation (Schenker, Meirow, and Schenker, 1992). Increased sympathetic nervous system activity changes the diameter and motility of smooth muscles that make up the walls of the blood vessels, digestive organs, fallopian tubes, uterus, and urinary tract. Constriction and dilation, patterns of movement, and seizure activity of these hollow vessels determine functions associated with survival and reproduction. For example, if life or relationships appear demanding or challenging, sympathetic nervous system activity will decrease blood flow to fingertips and feet and increase blood flow to the muscles or brain for fast action. At the same time, sympathetic enervation of the hollow vessels in the stomach, gastrointestinal (GI) system, and fallopian tubes interrupt digestion or ovulation or conception until the situation is more stable, less demanding. Biology is less likely to use energy for digestion and reproduction if there is a need for "flight," "fight," or "freeze" in order to deal with a challenge or threat. Para-sympathetic nervous system pathways provide counterbalancing responses that shift energy back toward digestion and reproduction, relaxation, or metabolic stability when a threat is successfully addressed or avoided.

Sustained production of CRH and rising levels of catecholamines (epinephrine and norepinephrine) stimulate pituitary production of adrenocorticotrophin hormone (ACTH), which travels through the bloodstream to the adrenal gland, where it stimulates production of cortisol. Rising cortisol levels travel back to the brain and inhibit further production of ACTH and CRH. Rising cortisol levels have an impact throughout the brain and body. Elevated cortisol is associated with increased heart rate and blood pressure, changes in GI activity, sleep disruption, immune system disruption and increased susceptibility to infectious diseases, depression, anxiety, and fatigue (Koob et al., 1994; Ridley, 2000).

Elevated cortisol and various symptoms produced affect reproduction in direct and indirect ways. Cortisol directly suppresses testicular production of testosterone and indirectly interrupts ovulation through suppression of hypothalamic GnRH and pituitary production of FSH and LH. Severe depression, chronic pain, and amenorrhea, associated with elevated cortisol, limit reproduction (De Bellis et al., 1994).

Cortisol influences immune system functioning, cytokine production, and lymphocyte and leukocyte function, and mediates inflammatory response (Costas et al., 1996; Flinn, 1998). Immune system disruption has direct and indirect effects on reproduction. The impact of elevated cortisol levels on suppression of the immune system is evident in studies of infectious disease, herpesvirus, cardiovascular problems, lupus, and diabetes, some of which threaten reproduction. Research on endometriosis, one of three symptoms most often diagnosed with infertility, suggests that immune suppression and disruption are involved when endometrial tissue implants outside the uterus (Kaider et al., 1999; Lucena and Cubillos, 1999; Migaki, personal communication, 2000).

The failure to produce cortisol under distress is a paradoxical stress response associated with symptoms that also impact reproduction. Decrease in right hemisphere activity and associated inhibition of sociability, empathy, and tolerance for others accompany low cortisol levels under certain stressful conditions (Henry, 1990). Severe and prolonged duress and generations of hardship are among the conditions in which cortisol production may be suppressed. Although cortisol levels have not been documented for women who have numerous children in harsh conditions, one study of reproduction suggests that the ability to inhibit reproduction through ovulation disruption or miscarriage is lost when stress is prolonged (Wassar and Barash, 1983).

Other chemical and hormonal reactions counteract and interact with stress responses. Prolactin, another hormone secreted by the pituitary, is associated with nurturing and caretaking. Elevated levels of prolactin support milk production and lactation and suppress the hormones of ovulation when nursing is vigorous and frequent. Prolactin may also rise as part of a cascade of stress reactions for women who are not nursing. Prolactin levels also rise around childbirth for a percentage of men and for males of other species when they are actively involved in care of the young (Storey et al., 2000). Allman and colleagues' research on longevity and care of young across primate species demonstrates a uniform increase in longevity for males who are active in the care of young. These researchers suggest that elevated prolactin serves as a protection against stress reactions associated with common causes of death (Allman et al., 2001).

Another chemical, a neurotransmitter called oxytocin, is secreted from the hypothalamus in the experience of closeness, warmth, nurturing, humor, friendship, and positive interactions. Oxytocin functions to suppress cortisol levels and other stress reactions through complex and varied interactions in the central nervous system (Insel, 1992; Carter, 1998; Lumpkin, 2002). Interaction between the chemistry of stress and the chemistry of closeness produces dynamic and shifting internal states that play a part in reproduction.

Although all studies do not measure stress reactions in the same way, the evidence for variation in levels and patterns of stress response is extensive. Sympathetic nervous system activity will be stirred for some; some may experience the simultaneous activation of sympathetic and parasympathetic nervous systems. Some will experience both elevated catecholamines and cortisol. Others will experience one without the other. Some people exhibit elevated cortisol without elevated ACTH. Some people will experience elevated prolactin under stress; others will not.

Variations in stress reactions are associated with differences in how brains and bodies function. Sensory information travels to different sites in the brain, stimulating neuronal activity throughout the brain and almost simultaneously stimulating responses throughout the body. Information about the environment and particularly about the social environment is evaluated very quickly for its personal significance as threat or resource, as food, friend, or foe. The limbic system, the amygdala and hippocampus, and the prefrontal cortex interact to determine responses, often in the space of a heartbeat. Past and previous experience play a large part in which responses are activated. Those that have been triggered in the past are the most readily triggered in the present: hence the inherently subjective nature of perception and emotional reactivity. Many of the studies of variation in stress response credit early experience—the levels of stress in utero and in the first few years of life—as influences over the levels and patterns of stress reaction in adulthood (Gunnar and Barr, 1998; Henry, 1977, 1990). The duration and frequency of stress reactions over time play their part in the level and pattern of reactivity present (Orchinik, 1998).

A survey of work in the natural sciences provides convincing evidence that relationships over generations of kin regulate reactivity and the physiology and behavior involved in reproduction. Emotional cutoff occurs within the context of the impact of relationships on reactivity. The research of Stephen Suomi (1999) at National Institutes of Health Comparative Ethology Lab and Brain Research Unit documents multigenerational transmission of levels of fearfulness, aggression, and cortisol in rhesus monkeys, primates with a brain and biology very similar to our own. Sons and daughters grow up to be much the same as their parents. Contact with a calmer adult caretaker can moderate the level of reactivity and tolerance for stress. The more fearful or shy males and females are likely to reproduce later in life than their more laid-back peers. The more aggressive males are more likely to be driven out of the troop too early to survive or they fail to successfully join a new troop at adolescence. Females with higher levels of aggression, however, will still reproduce and their offspring will carry levels of reactivity similar to their parents.

Additional research documents ways in which relationships between family members over the generations govern the levels and patterns of reaction to stress and to relationships. Early experience in relation to mother and the family "program the stress circuits of the central nervous system" and determine the magnitude and duration of stress reactions later in life (Gunnar and Barr, 1998, p. 1). Those individuals who are born into a family in which anxiety is high, in which the circumstances of life are harsh, or where relationships are a source of threat are likely to demonstrate adult stress reactions characterized by either elevated or blunted responsiveness to cortisol. They are likely to either avoid close relationships that stir threat reactions or pursue closeness as a cure for distress and have little inhibition of ovulation and conception.

Interaction between generations of kin regulates the experience of threat and reactions to threat that occur throughout life. In *Mother Nature* (2000), anthropologist Sara Blaffer Hrdy describes the human family as both a source of threat and the resource necessary for survival and reproduction. The demands of pregnancy, lactation, and prolonged dependence of young require supportive relationships between mother and mate as well as with other family members. The absence of grandmothers, older sisters, or aunts to assist at birth and in the early months of life increases the experience of stress for mother and infant. The absence of male support for protection and for food supply commonly put infant survival in jeopardy. The vast majority of problems related to reproduction, for both mother and infant, develop when the relationship resources are not sufficient to support survival and care of young.

Trevathan (1987), in *Human Birth*, describes the biological challenges inherent in human birth as a series of compromises struck in the trial-and-error trade-off between survival of the mother and development of dependent young with big brains. It is likely that the population stability over thousands of years of early human life was in part the result of deaths in childbirth. The size of the female cervix and circumference of large-brained babies along with the pelvic tilt that occurred with upright posture make birth a difficult maneuver. The assistance of family or mate during birth decreased the risk of death and improved survival for mother and young. Both the energy required for nine months of gestation and the energy requirements of lactation promote the mother's reliance on family. Reproduction, as important to humans as to any other form of life on earth, requires the resources of mother, father, and generations of family. When those resources are strained, reproduction itself produces stress reactions in the family.

Reactivity to relationships and the biology of reproduction interact. Relationships are necessary resources for reproduction and buffer stress reactions, supporting reproduction. Relationships also are a source of stress and thus produce reactions that hinder reproduction. Reproduction itself can be perceived either as a threat or a resource. Emotional cutoff is one way people deal with sensitivity to the forces of togetherness and individuality in the family. The following examples from research and clinical practice illustrate the evidence that contact and emotional cutoff between generations of family affect reactivity and reproduction.

FAMILY EXAMPLES FROM RESEARCH
AND CLINICAL PRACTICE

Multigenerational Study of Reproduction

The history of reproduction over generations in any family provides an opportunity to observe emotional cutoff, and reactions to relationships and the conditions of life through the facts of birth and death, migration, and education. The study of reproduction over eight generations in my own family afforded a perspective on the impact of contact and cutoff between generations on the regulation of reproduction itself. Ten years of genealogical research provided facts for 270 family units from 1789 to 2000. I counted the number who were born, the number who survived, and the number who reproduced for each family in each generation and noted geographical moves, migrations, and dates of births and deaths. Three patterns appeared (Harrison, 1990).

The first pattern was that those who left their family and country of origin had the largest number of children. Ten out of the eleven families who migrated from Norway, Ireland, and England had between seven and twenty-four children. Forty-six of the 270 families had larger families, between seven and twenty-four children. These larger families all occurred within two generations of migration and cutoff from past generations. In this pattern, one person becomes cut off from his or her parents and past generations of family through migration under duress. Figure 10.1 illustrates this pattern of reproduction in the generation that leaves family behind.

Andrea Olsdatter left her mother and father and family in Norway when she married Magnus Nielson. The young couple came to America in 1860

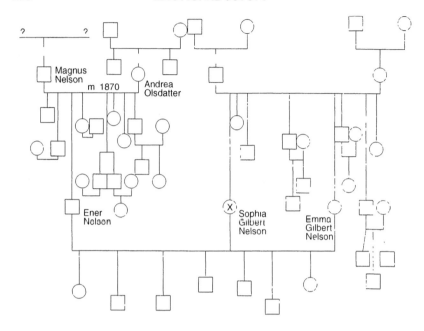

FIGURE 10.1. Emotional cutoff and family size.

and moved to Central Texas in 1870. Nothing is known about Mr. Nielson's family, but records at the Mormon family archive indicate that Andrea's two brothers in Norway had no children. The older brother stayed with the parents to manage the family land and married an older woman late in his life. The younger brother married in his late teens. His wife and child died in childbirth. Andrea and Magnus had no contact with past generations of family after moving to America in 1860. The family name changed to Nelson. This couple bore nine children between 1863 and 1882 (Harrison, 1990).

Not everyone born in a large generation reproduces. In fact, a percentage of children born into larger families die before reaching five years of age. For example, seven out of the ten children of Andrea and Magnus survived infancy; of those, only three reproduced. My ancestor, Ener Nelson, had four children with his first wife, Sophia. After Sophia died, he married her younger sister, Emma, with whom he had three more children.

The second pattern, related to the impact of relationships on reproduction, emerges as more generations survive and maintain contact with one another. For those families in which more generations are alive and in contact with one another, family size decreases. Increased contact between generations increases responsibility and reactivity between them. Each generation serves as a resource for the other. Investment in family is not measured by numbers of children alone, but by survival, education, and involvement in family land and businesses. Each generation also serves as a constraint or stressor for the others.

Ener Nelson, for example, established a mill and construction company in Waco, Texas, that provided income and work for his children. Andrea and Magnus followed their son to Waco and lived near him until their deaths in 1908 and 1911. Magnus and Andrea Nelson died before the birth of Ener and Emma's first child, leaving only two generations alive during the majority of child-rearing years. Ener and Emma survived, however, to see the birth of great-grandchildren. There were, for a time, four generations alive and in contact with one another.

Infant mortality also declines with increased number of generations alive and in contact with one another. In addition, infant mortality declines dramatically in smaller families. In the 146 families who had between one and three children, only one child died before adulthood. The investment between generations is also made from the present to the past. Children and grandchildren assume responsibilities for their parents and grandparents over time.

The third pattern, continued emotional cut off between generations, is associated with absence of reproduction. With contact comes reactivity that stirs difficulty and discomfort for some. Some individuals in each generation moved away or cut off from the larger family for various reasons. Most of those who are involved in multiple generations of cutoff or isolation from family have no children (Harrison, 1990). One ancestor married and moved out of state. Another ancestor became a drifter and lost contact with his family.

The impact of cutoff from past generations over high birth rate and infant mortality is exaggerated under harsh conditions, in an environment less fortunate than the Nelson family found in Texas. In *Death Without Weeping,* Nancy Scheper-Hughes (1992) describes the life history of women who leave their families in rural Brazil during times of drought and starvation to work in sugarcane-growing villages. Between 1964 and 1989, Scheper-Hughes, anthropologist and community health worker, came to know the lives and deaths of three generations of families. Reproduction occurred early and often. Women and men had multiple partners. Birth rate and infant mortality were high. Fragments of families tried to care for the children.

Certainly circumstances of life—poverty, poor nutrition, starvation, and terrible sanitation—play a part in mortality of infants and adults. Women return to work and work hard after giving birth. They do not nurse. Food is scarce and nutrition poor. Cutoff between generations of kin has another direct effect on mortality: children are left alone or in the care of strangers or other children, without the resources that generations of family may be able to provide. Cutoff from generations of kin and from those who assume responsibility for one another also appears to suppress the effect of cortisol, allowing reproduction to occur again and again, without the constraints of lactation and delay of ovulation, without counterbalance of responsibility for past generations of family and the stress reactions produced.

In these contrasting histories it is possible to see the difference that several generations of family can make in survival and future reproduction. When circumstances are somewhat more fortunate and family history somewhat more stable, more individuals survive and live longer, more generations are alive and in contact with one another. The number of children born decreases and the number who survive increases. Resources are available for education and intellectual development. The generations are a resource for rearing children and at the same time appear to constrain reproduction through reactivity produced in ordinary interactions of family life.

The study of family history, facts of genealogy, and family stories provide clues to the impact of contact and cutoff between generations on reproduction. Facts about reactivity in biology, however, are not available. Clinical observation, research studies, and participant observation research afford opportunities to "connect the dots" among the study of biological reactivity, relationships, and reproduction.

Examples from Research and Clinical Practice

The following families provide examples of various ways that reactivity to relationships, evident in contact and cutoff between generations of kin, regulates reproduction. These families are drawn from research, clinical practice, and family studies. They represent a variety of ways in which contact and cutoff among family members are active in regulating reproduction, not as pathology or problem, but as one of the facts of life.

One study of ovulation and reactivity was conducted between 1992 and 1995. Three groups of women were recruited for this study: one group of women without medical or mental health symptoms, a second group of women in psychotherapy for anxiety-related symptoms, and a third group of women in treatment for infertility. The study aimed to see if patterns of ovulation and reactivity were different for these groups. I predicted that facts about the family system would account for variation in reactivity and in ovulation. Physiological reactivity was measured with biofeedback equipment while each woman described her family history. Hormonal levels were measured for three months. Basal body temperature was taken daily for three months. Each woman completed a daily diary that included perceived level of stress along with life events and contact with family.

The study held some surprises. Reactivity associated with stress reactions was present for every woman in the study. Even the women who had no medical or mental health symptoms had elevated muscle tension, vasoconstriction evident of sympathetic nervous system activity, and elevated adrenal hormones while talking about family history. Their levels of reactivity shifted from stressed to relaxed, however, while sitting quietly. The women in psychotherapy for anxiety-related symptoms also experienced variation in reactivity measures. The women in fertility treatment, in contrast, sustained high levels of stress reactions while talking about their families and while sitting quietly.

Ovulation patterns were surprising. The majority of women in the study experienced delayed ovulation, a pattern associated with decreased fertility. The women in fertility treatment did not ovulate. One woman in the study ovulated near the fourteenth day of her cycle. The patterns of ovulation suggested that shifting stress reactions interrupted and delayed the hormonal interactions that produce ovulation. Sustained levels of stress reactions disrupted the hormones necessary for ovulation to the extent that ovulation ceased. Ovulation appeared to be regulated in response to the minute-to-minute, day-to-day shifts in reactivity that were evident in physiological measures and daily diary reports. The regulation of ovulation by reactivity occurred not as pathology but in coordination with the demands of overall family relationships.

The third surprise in this study was the discovery that levels of reactivity corresponded to levels of contact and cutoff among the women, their mothers, and the broader family. Those women who had sustained levels of stress reactions and did not ovulate were isolated with their mothers from the larger family. They had contact with few members of their family. Their mothers had contact with few members of the family. There was a great deal of emotional cutoff between generations, as measured by contact between family members. They did have intense contact with their mothers, often positive. These mothers and daughters were characterized by higher levels of emotional fusion with each other, each depending upon the other and experiencing the distress of the other as her own.

The women who experienced delayed ovulation—the majority of women in this study—had contact with a wide variety of family members as well as with their mothers. There was little cutoff between generations. Certainly some interactions were described as stressful or difficult. Some life events were stressful. Contact with a variety of family members over the generations, however, was associated with greater flexibility, a shifting dynamic of relationships and reactivity, each counterbalancing the other.

The one woman whose pattern of ovulation characterized optimal fertility had been working on connecting with various members of her family prior to the study. She will be introduced in the following section as Mrs. C.

The following families provide examples of relationships and the regulation of ovulation and reproduction. Contact and cutoff between generations are evident in the regulation of reproduction under ordinary circumstances as well as under conditions of duress. Each family diagram will present facts about three generations of family members. Family members who have contact with one another within a given year will be darkened. Facts about physiological reactions and the biology of reproduction will be described.

The A Family

Mrs. A volunteered to participate in the study of ovulation and reactivity as one of the families in the group without any mental health or medical problems. Each woman in the study described three generations of family history while her physiological reactivity was monitored with biofeedback equipment. Mrs. A was married and had three children. There had been no problems with fertility or with childbirth. There were no symptoms in the family. Mrs. A had contact with many members of her family, as did her mother and her husband. Contact could be stressful in one set of relationships and reassuring in another. A visit from her parents, for example, could be stressful, but at the same time, talking to past generations was a resource for dealing with the anxiety of her husband's temporary unemployment (Figure 10.2).

Mrs. A had elevated muscle tension, vasoconstriction, and elevated heart rate while talking about family history. Her physiology relaxed while she sat quietly for five minutes following the interview. This flexibility was also evident in the three months of hormone assay and daily ratings of stress (Table 10.1).

Physiological levels of stress varied over the three months of this study. Life events and contact with family, along with basal body temperature, were also recorded. Mrs. A reported variable levels of stress and one major life event during the study: her husband lost his job.

Ovulation occurred each month, but was delayed, indicating interruption of the hormonal interactions that produce follicular development. Elevated DHEA-sulfate and vasoconstriction suggest that both sympathetic nervous system and adrenal activity were involved in delay of ovulation during the months that stress reactions were stirred. Contact with a variety of family members provided resources for dealing with her husband's temporary unemployment and for modifying stress reactions stirred. At the same time, responsibilities as mother, wife, and family member involved mild and shifting reactions that played a part in the delay in ovulation.

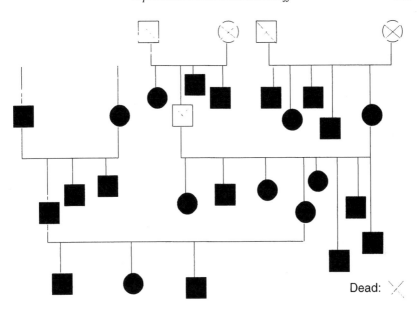

Dead: ✕

FIGURE 10.2   A family diagram (darkened circles and squares indicate family members who are in active contact).

TABLE 10 1. Physiological and Hormonal Measures of Reactivity for Mrs. A

Androgens		Physiological Measures			
DHEA-S (ug/dl)	T (ng/dl)	EMG (mv)		DST (F)	
79 9	10 2	Family History	Quiet	Family History	Quiet
79 8	11 2	12.0	6 0	68.0	**89.0**
89.3	5.6				

Key: Criteria for elevated DHEA-sulfate: >150 ug/dL; for elevated testosterone: > 40 ng/dL

Average of skeletal muscle activity (EMG) for 45 minutes of family history and 5 minutes of quiet, elevated EMG: > 8 mv/min

Average of digital skin temperature (DST) for 45 minutes of family history and 5 minutes of quiet, vasoconstriction· < 90 F

Numbers in bold: elevated according to criteria.

The B Family

This second example represents a contrast that makes it easier to see the impact of absence of contact between generations on reactivity that affects reproduction. In this family, absence of contact between generations of kin leaves two generations isolated from the larger family: a mother and daughter clinging to each other for dear life. This was the pattern present for those women who did not ovulate in the study of reactivity, relationships, and ovulation (Harrison, 1995). It is a pattern that may sustain elevated levels of reactivity for both mother and daughter, as they rely upon and react to each other day to day, without the advantage of other stabilizing relationships.

Mrs. B, an only child, was raised by her mother without contact with her father or her father's family. Her maternal grandmother lived in the household until her death when Mrs. B was five. There is no contact between Mrs. B's mother and any other members of the family. Mrs. B's mother dedicated herself to raising her daughter and to career development as a college professor. Mrs. B dropped out of college when she married. She and her husband attempted to reproduce for five years before Mrs. B took a job as receptionist in a fertility clinic where she received treatment. Mrs. B was diagnosed with ovulatory dysfunction and elevated androgens (testosterone and DHEA-sulfate), hormones produced by the adrenal gland that are clinically associated with various reproductive symptoms. She conceived and miscarried several times with hormonal treatment and in vitro fertilization before maintaining a pregnancy and bearing a daughter, premature but able to survive with the benefit of technology (Figure 10.3).

The tensions between Mr. and Mrs. B escalated during the first year of their daughter's life. Mrs. B began divorce proceedings and mother and child moved to live with the maternal grandmother. Mr. B stalled on divorce and maintained contact with his child and wife from a distance. Mrs. B had been separated ten years when she began to talk to me about depression, migraines, and obesity. During the first year of coaching, Mrs. B determined to resume her marriage and mother and daughter moved back into the household with Mr. B. She also determined to resume college to work on her own career plans. She maintained frequent contact with her mother and began to consider ways to contact more of the family she did not know.

Mrs. B's initial physiological measures indicated sustained levels of sympathetic nervous system arousal and digital vasoconstriction. Hormonal measures, obtained by her physician, indicated elevated androgens (testosterone and DHEA-sulfate), which are often present with obesity and depression. Mrs. B chose medication to treat reactivity and did not participate in biofeedback training. Physiological measures are not available to demonstrate change during family systems psychotherapy. The changes she made

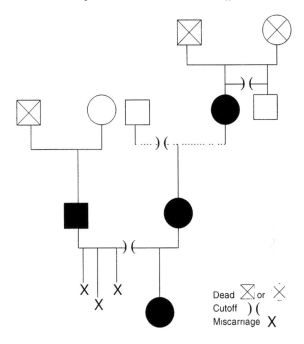

FIGURE 10.3. Mrs. B family diagram (darkened circles and squares indicate family members who are in active contact).

in her life and relationships are evident in increased contact with a few family members and increased tolerance for her husband while maintaining a relationship with her mother and a career of her own. The future will show whether these changes affect reproduction for her daughter.

The C Family

The third family example indicates ways that someone can use knowledge about reactivity and relationships to make a difference in her own attempts at reproduction. Mrs. C initially began to talk with me about tensions in her family that resulted in lack of contact between an older sister and her parents. As Mrs. C described the ways people reacted to one another in her family, she reported her own physical reactions to anxiety. At our third meeting she used the biofeedback equipment to measure reactivity while talking about family history and while sitting quietly. Mrs. C experienced sustained levels of skeletal muscle tension, vasoconstriction, and skin sweat response, characteristic of women in the ovulation study who had little contact with their family and who did not ovulate. Mrs. C in fact had contact with few members of her family. Mrs. C was not thinking about reproduction at this point. Hormone levels and ovulation patterns were not known until Mrs. C participated in the research project two years later (Figure 10.4).

Mrs. C is the youngest of three, with an older sister and middle brother. The firstborn sister was a difficult infant and child, born to parents who distanced from their families and became intensely involved in marriage and in working together. Mother was anxious and frustrated with her firstborn. Father sympathized and favored his daughter. The second child, the son, comforted mother and had a more distant relationship with his father and older sister. Mrs. C had more of her own relationship with each of her parents and siblings, but would feel herself pushed aside when tensions rose. She, watched her mother idealize her brother and her father protect and favor her older sister.

Mrs. C's family distanced from both sets of grandparents. Her father was the eldest of three, with a younger brother and a younger sister. His father was disabled and his mother was hospitalized for psychiatric symptoms when he was a teenager. At that time he assumed tremendous responsibility for his family. After he moved away to attend college, he married and became very involved in his career and rarely visited his family. He was "on call" for problems but did not maintain regular contact. Mrs. C's mother was

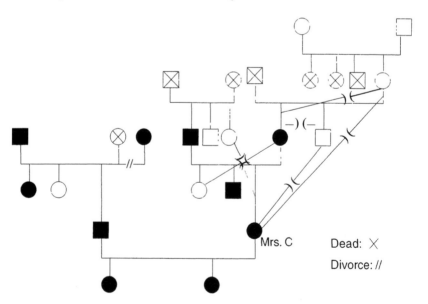

Mrs. C   Dead: ✕

Divorce: //

FIGURE 10.4. Mrs. C family diagram before family systems psychotherapy (darkened circles and squares are family members in contact with one another).

the older sister of a brother. She felt displaced by the adoring relationship that developed between her mother and brother. Her mother moved in with Mrs. C. following her father's death. During this time, Mrs. C experienced severe health problems, from which she eventually recovered. Turmoil in the family increased during this time. Her mother finally moved to live near her son and Mrs. C maintained dutiful contact for a time. When her mother was placed in a nursing home because of symptoms of senility, Mrs. C found it painful to visit. Four years had passed without contact between Mrs. C and her mother and also between her mother and brother.

Mrs. C left home to attend college, married there, and finished her degree. She and her husband volunteered for an overseas work placement and conceived their eldest daughter while living out of the country. Conception was planned and birth was routine. Mrs. C reflects upon this time as an exciting adventure with low anxiety about bearing or rearing her first daughter.

Mr. and Mrs. C returned to the United States and settled within minutes of his parents and family. Mr. C is the youngest of three siblings, with two older sisters. His mother died when he was in his twenties following several years of illness. Mr. C looked to his oldest sister as another mother. Mr. C preferred little contact with his family and became immersed in his work and marriage. Mr. and Mrs. C assumed leadership positions in an organization they direct together.

Mrs. C recognized that her cutoff from her maternal grandmother was a nagging source of anxiety. She also believed that relationships with her parents' families would provide her knowledge and resources if she were able to do her part to make and maintain contact with them. She drove north from Texas and across three states in the fall of 1993 to spend three days alone with her grandmother. Within a month, Mrs. C's mother also visited her mother and renewed contact with her brother. By the end of a year in family systems psychotherapy, Mrs. C had contact with a significantly increased number of family members, as did her mother (Figure 10.5).

The changes in physiological levels of reactivity were evident immediately. Mrs. C experienced warmer skin temperature and lower muscle tension, both indicators of a shift from stress reactions to stability. Mrs. C continued to expand her contact with family members and, when her grandmother died two years later, Mrs. C was able to organize a memorial service attended by many extended family members. Levels of physiological reactivity measured with biofeedback instruments indicated increased flexibility to shift between stress reactions and stability (Table 10.2).

Mrs. C also participated in the study of reactivity and ovulation for three months in 1994. By this time, she had begun to think about having a second child. During the study, Mrs. C's hormonal and physiological measures indicated varying levels of stress reactions. Her basal body temperature, how-

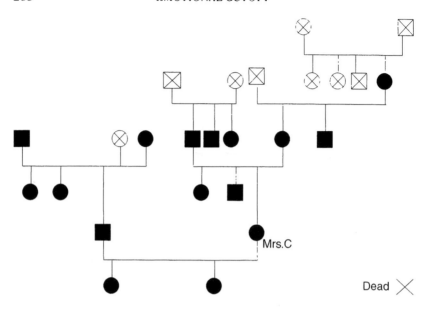

FIGURE 10.5. Mrs. C family diagram after one year of family systems psychotherapy (darkened circles and squares are family members in contact with one another).

ever, indicated a consistent pattern of ovulation considered optimal for conception. She and her husband could not, however, agree upon a decision and they avoided conception.

Mrs. C decided to do three things to better understand and address the anxiety around having another child. First, she spoke to her husband's oldest sister about Mr. C's hesitation to have more children. His sister voiced her blessing on more children and Mr. C decided that it was a good idea. Mrs. C also began to look at facts of family history to determine whether there had been problems around pregnancy or childbirth in her family. She discovered few, but she noticed that mothers often became symptomatic around the time that their daughters enter puberty. She began to talk to her extended family about their experiences regarding bearing and rearing children. Before she could draw any conclusions from these studies of anxiety and reproduction in her family, she conceived their second child in February 1995. Mrs. C's grandmother died in May 1995 and she organized a memorial service, held that summer. Pregnancy and the birth of her second child in November 1995 were routine, although increased stress reactions were evident in biofeedback measures and in health symptoms throughout the family during the first year of rearing a second child.

TABLE 10.2. Physiological and Hormonal Measures of Reactivity for Mrs. C Baseline Measures While Cutoff from Many Family Members

Androgens		Physiological Measures			
DHEA-S (ug/dl)	T (ng/dL)	EMG (mv)		DST (F)	
No measures		Family History	Quiet	Family History	Quiet
		9.08	3 54	**75.4**	**74.2**

Measures After One Year of Family Systems Psychotherapy with Biofeedback

Androgens		Physiological Measures			
DHEA-S (ug/DL)	T (ng/dL)	EMG (mv)		DST (F)	
109.3	46.8	Family History	Quiet	Family History	Quiet
79.3	11.0	**13.1**	**8.6**	**85.6**	**89.0**
127.3	14.6				

Key: Criteria for elevated DHEA-sulfate: >150 ug/dL; for elevated testosterone: > 40 ng/dL

Average of skeletal muscle activity (EMG) for 45 minutes of family history and 5 minutes of quiet, elevated EMG. > 8 mv/min

Average of digital skin temperature (DST) for 45 minutes of family history and 5 minutes of quiet, vasoconstriction: <90 F

Numbers in bold. Elevated according to criteria.

Mrs. C's older daughter just entered puberty and her younger child is now five. She has continued to observe reactivity in the family and to work on using her knowledge about family systems to guide her decisions as wife, mother, and family member. Mrs. C could write her own chapter about the complexity of cutoff and contact within this family and the reactivity stirred by each. The ability to perceive the part that relationship patterns play in reactivity and in symptoms provides additional resources for choices related to reproduction and for modifying one's own reactions for the benefit of others as well as oneself.

CONCLUSION

The study of contact and cutoff in the family as an influence over reactivity that governs reproduction provides a kaleidoscopic view of factors that interact over generations. Variation in ways that reactions to relationships regulate the biology of reproduction provides increased ability to adapt reproduction to the resources and stresses in relationships that are necessary for survival and for reproduction itself.

Every family holds examples of the impact of relationships on reproduction and of reproduction upon the family. Anyone can study facts about several generations of his or her family and learn about the impact of versions of emotional cutoff on reactivity and reproduction. Those who assume that contact between family members is "good" and cutoff is "bad," or vice versa, will be confused by facts that appear contradictory. Those who assume that oxytocin is good and cortisol is bad, or vice versa, will be confused by the complexity evident in their effects.

Bowen theory provides a conceptual framework for identifying factors that make a difference in the impact of cutoff between generations. Levels of differentiation will make a difference in the way that people adapt to the new set of circumstances. Some will maintain connections to the past through photographs, language, or knowledge of history. Others will quickly try to forget the past, dealing instead with the demands at hand and leaving the next generation with less connection to the past of the family.

Although research is slow to document and carefully examine how relationships between family members regulate physiology, brain function, and behavior, medicine and mental health can use Bowen theory and the growing body of knowledge in the natural sciences to guide diagnosis and treatment. Physicians and therapists can recognize levels of emotional fusion and realize that it is necessary to address the concerns of those who react to each other. It is possible to recognize relationships as both resources and sources of stress, to coach someone to be realistic about each. For example, a physician who knows that a patient has contact with no family other than her mother and sister can expect her to have greater reactivity during a time when her sister's health is failing and her mother is distressed. The physician may recommend contact with an aunt who is distant but concerned. When stability acquired through medication is disrupted, the doctor can recognize the impact of anxiety and maintain steady contact instead of accelerating treatment toward surgery or hospitalization. Her physician will know to wait until relationships stabilize to pursue expensive fertility treatment.

It is likely that the complexity that affords us the ability to juggle survival, relationships, and reproduction will probably elude simplistic study altogether. Bowen theory provides one way to extend knowledge about cutoff and contact between generations toward facts about biological reactivity and to inform those who must make and guide decisions about reproduction.

REFERENCES

Allman, J. (1999). *Evolving Brains.* New York: Scientific American Library.
Allman, J., Hakeem, A., Erwin, J. M., Nimchinsky, E., and Hof, P. R. (2001). The Anterior Cingulate Cortex: The Evolution of an Interface Between Emotion and Cognition *Proceedings of the New York Academy of Sciences* Volume 935:107-117.
Bowen, M. (1978). *Family Therapy in Clinical Practice.* New York: Jason Aronson.
Carter, S. (1998). Neuroendocrine Perspectives on Social Attachment and Love. *Psychoneuroendocrinology* 23(8):779-818.
Chrousos, G. P. and Gold, P. W. (1992). The Concepts of Stress and Stress Systems Disorders. *JAMA* 267(9):1244-1252.
Costas, M., Trapp, T., Pereda, M. P., Sauer, J., Rupprecht, R., Nahmod, V. E., Reul, J. M. H. M., Holsboer, F., and Arzt, E. (1996). Molecular and Functional Evidence for in Vitro Cytokine Enhancement of Human and Murine Target Cell Sensitivity to Glucocorticoids *Journal of Clinical Investigation* 98:1409-1416.
De Bellis, M. D., Chrousos, G. P., Dorn, L. D., Burke, L., Helmers, K., Kling, M. A., Trickett, P. K., and Putnam, F. W. (1994). Hypothalamic-Pituitary-Adrenal Axis Dysregulation in Sexually Abused Girls. *Journal of Clinical Endocrinology and Metabolism* 78:249-255.
Flinn, M. (1998). Family Environment, Stress, and Health During Childhood. In C. Panter-Brick and C. Wortham (Eds.), *Health, Hormones and Behavior* (pp. 105-138). Cambridge: Cambridge University Press.
Gunnar, M. R. and Barr, R. G. (1998). Stress, Early Brain Development, and Behavior. *Infants and Young Children* 11(1):1-14.
Harrison, V. (1990). "Family emotional process and reproduction over several generations." Presentation at the Georgetown Family Center Annual Symposium in Family Systems Theory and Therapy, Washington, DC, November.
Harrison, V. (1995). Patterns of Ovulation, Reactivity, and Family Emotional Process in the Integrative Neurobiology of Affiliation. In C. S. Carter, I. J. Lederhendler, and B. Kirkpatrick (Eds.), *Annals of the New York Academy of Sciences,* Vol. 807 (pp. 522-524).
Henry, J P (1977). *Stress, Health, and the Social Environment: A Sociobiological Approach to Medicine.* New York: Springer-Verlag.
Henry, J P. (1990). Psychological and Physiological Responses to Stress: The Right Hemisphere and the HPA Axis. Personal Copy Gift of Author.
Hotchkiss, J. and Knobil, E. (1994). The Menstrual Cycle and Its Neuroendocrine Control In E. Knobil and J. D. Neill (Eds.), *Physiology of Reproduction,* Second Edition. New York: Raven Press.
Hrdy, S. B. (2000) *Mother Nature.* New York. Pantheon.
Insel, T. R. (1992). Oxytocin-A Neuropeptide for Affiliation. *Psychoneuroendocrinology* 17(1):3-35.
Kaider, A. S., Kaider, B. D., Janowicz, P. B., and Roussev, R. G. (1999). Immunodiagnostic Evaluation in Women with Reproductive Failure. *American Journal of Reproductive Immunology* 42(6):335-346.

Koob, G. F., Heinrichs, S. C., Menzaghi, F., Pich, E. M., and Britton, K. T. (1994). Corticotrophin-Releasing Factor, Stress and Behavior. *Seminars in Neuroscience* 6:221.

LeDoux, J. (1998). *The Emotional Brain.* New York: Simon and Schuster

Lucena, E. and Cubillos, J. (1999). Immune Abnormalities in Endometriosis Compromising Fertility in IVG-ET Patients. *Journal of Reproductive Medicine* 4(5) 458-464.

Lumpkin, M. (2002). Relationships and Biochemical Mechanisms of Stress. Presentation at Facts of Life conference, Houston, Texas.

MacLean, P. D. (1990). *The Triune Brain in Evolution.* New York: Plenum Press.

Orchinik, M. (l998). Glucocorticoids, Stress, and Behavior: Shifting the Time Frame. *Hormones and Behavior* 34:320-327.

Ridley, M. (2000). *Genome.* New York: Harper Collins Publishers.

Sagan, L. (1987). *The Health of Nations.* New York: Basic Books.

Schenker, J. G., Meirow, D., and Schenker, E. (1992). Stress and Human Reproduction. *European Journal of Obstetrics & Gynecological and Reproductive Biology* 45(1):1-8.

Scheper-Hughes, N. (1992). *Death Without Weeping: The Violence of Everyday Life in Brazil.* Berkeley: University of California Press.

Sen, A. (1993). The Economics of Life and Death. *Scientific American* 268 (5):40-47.

Steinberger, E (1987). Male Infertility. In J. Gold (Ed.), *Gynecologic Endocrinology* (pp. 553-590). New York: Plenum Press.

Steinberger, E., Steinberger, A., and Sanborn, B. (1974). Endocrine Control of Spermatogenesis. In E. M. Coutinho and F. Fuchs (Eds.), *Physiology and Genetics of Reproduction, Part A: Proceedings of the 13th International Latin American Symposium* (Salvadore, Brazil, 1973) (pp. 163-181). New York: Plenum Press.

Storey, A. E., Walsh, C. J., Quinton, R. L., and Wynne-Edwards, K. E. (2000). Hormonal Correlates of Parental Responsiveness in New Expectant Fathers. *Evolution and Human Behavior* 21:79-95.

Stratakis, C. A. and Chrousos, G.P. (1995). Neuroendocrinology and Pathophysiology of the Stress System. *Annals of the New York Academy of Sciences* 771:491-511.

Suomi, S. (1999). Attachment in Rhesus Monkeys. In J. Cassidy and P. R. Shaver (Eds.), *Handbook of Attachment: Theory, Research and Clinical Applications* (pp. 181-197) New York: Guilford Press.

Trevathan, W. (1987). *Human Birth.* New York: Aldine de Gruyter

Wassar, S. and Barash, D. (1983). Reproductive Suppression Among Female Mammals. *Quarterly Review of Biology* 58:513-538.

Chapter 11

The Impact of Cutoff in Families Raising Adolescents

Anne S. McKnight

INTRODUCTION

Adolescence is a period of transition into new responsibilities that has few equivalents. The child develops the social, intellectual, and vocational skills that are necessary for the future while remaining dependent on his or her family. Adolescence is a period of conflicting directions in which a young person strives to gain some autonomy in decision making and life tasks but is not ready to function independently in society.

Every culture has traditions, norms, and role expectations for this transition. Among nonhumans, young male mammals are often excluded from the social group in which they were raised. Male elephants, whales, and chimpanzees band together in roving groups as adolescents until each is able to form a strategy for acceptance into a new social unit. In human societies adolescence is often marked by formal rituals for initiation into adulthood, signifying the shift from childhood to maturity. In some traditional societies, the young men live together until they find a reproductive partner. They are trained in the skills of hunting and warfare that are essential for adult survival. In the twenty-first century, the training has evolved into apprenticeships, the armed forces, or advanced schooling (Konner, 1982).

In the nineteenth, twentieth, and twenty-first centuries, industrialized societies hold challenges for adolescents, including socially, financially, and physically separating from the family in the transition to adulthood. As the roles and tasks of adolescence have evolved, so have the composition and organization of the family. In traditional societies, the nuclear family is a part of a larger functioning family unit. Families raising children often live in proximity to the parents' families, who may become a social, emotional, and physical resource in time of need. Children are not exclusively the responsibility of their parents but are cared for and trained by grandparents, aunts, uncles, and cousins. A large social system allows a flexibility of support for parents raising children (Konner, 1982).

In contrast, modern Western society has experienced an erosion and fragmentation of the extended family unit. The nuclear family unit is often miles away from the extended family, usually due to employment opportunities. Both parents work in 65 percent of two-parent families, with over 50 percent of the mothers returning to work within one year of the birth of a child. Parents are divorcing, often leaving one parent as both the caretaker and provider. The larger social unit that provided nurturing and care is no longer available, so the family is shrinking to its lowest common denominator, usually the single mother and her children.

At the same time, another phenomenon has developed in which children who have not yet mastered the adolescent tasks necessary for self-sufficiency in the adult world have children. In some families, grandmothers have responsibility for caring for their grandchildren. The grandmother is no longer simply backup support to a mother, but has become the primary caretaker of children at a time when her health and energy levels are waning.

In developmental terms, adolescence is a transition toward individuation. In that process, the adolescent wavers between the dependency of the child and the self-sufficiency of the young adult. Those teenagers who have the most difficulty in establishing their identities and progressing toward independence often react to the parents with exaggerated stands of rebelliousness. They deny the importance of the parents' values, interests, and lifestyle by running away, leaving school, getting arrested, or becoming sexually active. Although teenagers believe this behavior makes them independent, their actions are often based on "being different" from their parents. This effort to be oppositional to the parents is an indication of how powerful the parents are in the perception of the teenager, who is basing his or her actions on the parents, rather than thoughtfully approaching the challenges of separating.

Teenagers face myriad choices regarding sex, drugs, and lifestyles at a time when less adult supervision, nurturance, and guidance is available. Drugs and alcohol are one way to appear and feel adult in a teenager's eyes. Alcohol is an adult prerogative. It cannot legally be purchased until age twenty-one in most states, although it is readily available. According to the National Institute for Drug Abuse's *Monitoring the Future Study* (NIDA, 2001), 51 percent of eighth graders and 80 percent of twelfth graders have used alcohol. Marijuana, although illegal in the United States, has been used by 20 percent of eighth graders and 48 percent of twelfth graders (NIDA, 2001). Drugs or alcohol can be an entryway to social acceptance in a peer group, either loosely organized or with the more formal structure of a gang. For some teenagers, alcohol and drugs are the social glue that binds together a friendship group which supplants their emotional reliance on a family whose emotional resources are strained (Sherouse, 1985). These broad trends form a context for understanding the families of adolescents.

A groundbreaking research paper, "Protecting Adolescents from Harm," made front-page headlines when it was published in the *Journal of the American Medical Association* on September 10, 1997 (Resnick et al., 1997). This study was unprecedented in its scope, interviewing 12,118 adolescents in grades seven through twelve from an initial national school survey of 90,118 participants from eighty high schools and middle schools (Resnick et al., 1997). The goal of the analysis was to identify risk and protective factors at the family, school, and individual levels relating to four areas of adolescent health: emotional health, violence, substance abuse, and sexuality. The variables examined included closeness to, perceived caring by, and satisfaction with relationship to mother or father, and feeling wanted by family members. The researchers measured parent-adolescent activities, parental presence in the home, and parental school performance expectations. Resnick and colleagues (1997) concluded:

> With notable consistency across the domains of risk, the role of parents and families in shaping the health of adolescents is evident . . . while physical presence of a parent in the home at key times reduces risk (and especially substance use), it is consistently less significant than parental connectedness (e.g., feelings of warmth, love, and caring from parents). (p. 823)

With the conclusions of the "Protecting Adolescents from Harm" research in mind, a study was developed that focused on a small cross section of families with a teenager being evaluated for a mental health, substance abuse, or behavior problem. The theoretical framework for the study was Murray Bowen's family systems theory. This theory conceptualizes the family as an interdependent and interactive unit, the function of which is the raising and successful launching of children. Although one family member, such as the adolescent, may be experiencing difficulties, the emotional context for the problem is the family relationship system. The behavior of the teenager both influences and is affected by the patterns of interaction in the family (Bowen, 1978).

Bowen began to develop his idea that the family was an emotional unit through his research on families with a schizophrenic member at the Menninger Clinic in Topeka, Kansas, in the 1950s. His observations there and later at the National Institute of Mental Health supported the premise that the functioning of each family member is interwoven through patterned responses to other members of the family. While an individual has a genetic and physiological makeup, he or she also has a functioning position in the original family that replicates itself in the relationships of adult life and with his or her own children. The family, positioned in a web of culture and society, is also vulnerable to the anxiety and disruptions that permeate the modern world.

Bowen theory describes the interplay of processes in a family without viewing one as the "cause" of an emotional condition. A person's constitution, his or her genetic makeup, the family's emotional life across generations, the level of stress in the environment, the disruptions in society, and the level of the person's maturity all contribute to a context for developing a problem. A symptom, such as addiction, depression, or illegal behavior, is an outcome of interweaving factors rather than a pathology.

CONCEPTS FROM BOWEN THEORY

Bowen developed a number of interlocking concepts that describe the emotional process in relationships. This research was conducted from Bowen's theoretical framework and utilized several of his concepts.

Differentiation describes the variability in human functioning that is indicated by an individual's capacity to meet the tasks of adulthood in a thoughtful and self-directed manner. One's level of differentiation is measured by one's ability to establish an autonomous identity while staying connected in a personal way to important relationships.

Families and individuals function on a continuum of levels of differentiation. In some families a person individuates in adult life while in a cooperative connection with other family members. In other families, members have difficulty in becoming self-sufficient. Contact in the family is intertwined with dependency, resulting in the development of social, emotional, and physical symptoms. Those with lower levels of differentiation react, rather than act, having less ability to think through their life direction.

Cutoff is a term used to describe a reaction to intense emotion in which an individual severs contact in a familial relationship. Kerr (1980) describes the concept as follows: "cutoff can be accomplished by physical distance, keeping contacts with family brief and infrequent and/or through internal mechanisms such as withdrawal and avoidance of emotionally charged areas while in the presence of family" (p. 232).

A person cuts off by becoming emotionally or physically unavailable to family members. This can result in isolation from meaningful and supportive family relationships. One way to manage dependency in a family is through distancing or cutoff from other members. Bowen (1978) writes: "The person who runs away from his family of origin is as emotionally dependent as the one who never leaves home. They both need emotional closeness, but they are allergic to it" (pp. 282-283).

Dependency on family members is managed by the denial of the importance of the connection and the severing of the relationship. The isolation resulting from the cutoff focuses emotional dependency on the remaining family members, often the nuclear family, making them crucial to the emotional well-being of the individual.

Bowen (1978) writes:

> The life pattern of cutoffs is determined by the way people handle their unresolved emotional attachments to their parents. All people have some degree of unresolved emotional attachment to their parents. The lower the level of differentiation, the more intense the unresolved attachment. The concept deals with the way people separate themselves from the past in order to start their lives in the present generation. . . . (p. 382)

Unresolved attachment is handled by denial and the isolation of self while living close to parents, or by physically running away, or by a combination of emotional isolation and physical distance. The more intense the cutoff with the past, the more likely the individual is to have an exaggerated version of his parental family problem in his or her own marriage, and the more likely his or her children are to cut off in the next generation.

Fusion is a process in which family members are emotionally reactive to one another to the extent that it compromises an individual's ability to function autonomously. The term signifies a degree of dependency that interferes with a person's mature functioning. The dependency may take the form of a severely impaired child who never leaves home or of an adult who relies on his or her marital partner to manage day-to-day life. In a contradictory way, the level of fusion or dependency provides a context for a person's desire to cut off a relationship in order to maintain a sense of his or her own identity. The severing of contact is an unspoken recognition that the relationship will overwhelm the person if he or she chooses to remain in it.

Multigenerational transmission process is the repetition of relationship patterns from one generation to the next. These emotional patterns may take the form of repeating a particular symptom, such as addiction, or by patterned emotional responses. Bowen (1978) identified four emotional patterns in human relationships. Each is a reciprocal interaction in which both partners play a role in creating the outcome, although the interplay can be subtle and evolve over time.

Over/underfunctioning is a relationship process in a family in which one member becomes overresponsible for another's emotional, physical, or social functioning, while the other is less responsible for his or her life and appears dependent.

Distancing/pursuit is the process in which one partner pursues the other for emotional closeness only to have the other become more distant, thus setting the first up to pursue again.

Conflict is the overt or covert discord between two people used to resolve their differences and to manage the connection between them.

The *projection process* is a pattern in which family members focus their worry or anxiety on a family member. At times, the tension between two people can be resolved when they focus on a third person. When a child is an identified problem in a family, the child is viewed as the recipient of the parents' projection.

The *triangle* is the building block of all relationship systems. The most basic definition describes a pattern in which tension develops between two people and one or the other turns to a third person. The primary triangle in every family is between the two parents and a child.

Sibling position can influence the functioning of a child in a family. The roles of each position are examined by Walter Toman (1969) in *Family Constellation*. The oldest is often responsible and goal directed, and the youngest may be creative and dependent.

The concepts of Bowen theory describe aspects of the complexity of family relationships. No single concept can be utilized to account for events in a family, nor can one concept be separated from the others in understanding family process.

OUTLINE OF A STUDY

Family systems ideas influenced the author's work as a family therapist in a suburban community mental health center. The author consulted with families whose teenagers were identified as having behavioral and emotional difficulties intertwined with a substance abuse problem. In these consultations, the author observed that parents with emotional ties to their own families were more resilient and capable of coming to the aid of struggling teenagers than parents who were isolated from family ties. She saw this population as offering an opportunity to understand better what family connection, or its absence, brought to the capacity to raise functional adolescents.

The author formulated the following questions (McKnight, 2001): If connectedness between parents and adolescents is the most important protective factor against risky behavior, what promotes parents' ability to connect? Does the presence or absence of viable family bonds and support for parents from their own parents affect their ability to provide the structure and guidance that the teenager needs to chart a path to adult independence? Is protective connection a quality that is passed from one generation to the next? Conversely, does lack of connection between grand-parents and parents lead to children who are more apt to choose risky and harmful behavior?

Research Study

With these questions in mind, I planned a research study to measure whether cutoff of parents from the previous generation had an impact on their parental functioning and the well-being of their teenage children. The underlying hypothesis was that those parents who had a more distant, superficial relationship with their own parents would have less capacity to meet the challenges of raising adolescents than those parents who had a more connected relationship with their own parents. Observations indicated that some parents of teenagers never reached the maturity level necessary to leave home and make a life of their own. Often living in the family home, these parents were dependent on, but emotionally distant from, their own parents.

Over eighteen months, the author studied sixty families who came to the mental health center for an assessment of emotional, behavioral, or substance abuse problems in their teenagers. For the purposes of this study, a definition of cutoff developed by Kerr (1981, p. 274) was used: "Emotional cutoff describes the way one generation cuts off emotional contact in order to avoid potential relationship problems."

The questions investigated were:

- Did cutoff of the mother and/or father from their parents affect their level of functioning?
- Did cutoff of the mother and/or father from their parents affect the level of impairment of the teenager?
- Did cutoff of the mother and/or father from their parents affect the cutoff of the teenager from each of them?

As these questions investigate only cutoff and self-functioning of the parents and teenager, they are not intended to explain the behavioral problems of the teenager.

Methodology

The study was designed to interview the teenager and the parents in an initial meeting when a teenager was referred for an assessment at the mental health center. In a one- to two-hour meeting, the family was first seen together, and then the parent(s) and teenager were interviewed separately. For the purposes of the center, an assessment was made on the nature and extent of the difficulties of the teenager as well as the dynamics of the family. This assessment led to the referral of the adolescent and his or her parents to the most appropriate services at the center or in the community.

While this assessment was taking place, the family was offered the opportunity to participate in the research study. This study was designed to measure the degree of cutoff of the parents from each of their parents and the degree of cutoff of the adolescent from each of his or her parents. At the same time, the level of functioning of each parent present and the adolescent was assessed.

Three instruments were used in this study. The Emotional Cutoff Scale (ECS) (McCollom, 1991) is a ten-question scale administered to parents and adolescents to assess their self-perception of the cutoff with parents of both generations. Five questions asked about the participant's relationship with his or her mother and five asked about the relationships with his or her father. The Global Assessment of Functioning (GAF) measured functioning in the parents. This is a scale from 0 to 100 developed for use with Axis VI in the *Diagnostic and Statistical Manual of Mental Disorders,* Fourth Edition (DSM-IV) (American Psychiatric Association, 1994). The Child and Adolescent Functional Assessment Scale (CAFAS) (Hodges, 1990, 1994) is an eight-part multidimensional scale that was used to evaluate the functioning of adolescents.

Profiles of Families

Cutoff was conceptualized by Bowen as an emotional mechanism to handle unresolved emotional attachment with the previous generation. But families with high degrees of cutoff can look very different. Before describing the outcome of the study, the author will introduce several families typical of those interviewed.

Emotional Cutoff in the Midst of Family

Ms. O and her son Trevor exhibited one face of cutoff. Ms. O was the younger of two children who grew up in the area where she now lived. Her father worked in a government agency; her mother was a housewife. Ms. O became pregnant at sixteen, and the child was given up for adoption. Eight years later, she again became pregnant, the father disappearing when she told him about the pregnancy. This time she kept the baby and raised the boy in her parents' home. Her father died when Trevor was five.

When she called to ask for social services for Trevor, who had recently come home drunk after school and was with a group of boys who were arrested for possession of marijuana, she asked that whoever returned the call not identify himself or herself to her mother.

In discussing this request in the first interview, Ms. O related that her mother became so distraught over Trevor's behavior that she did not want her to know they were going to counseling. Ms. O worked an occasional part-time job, but had been financially dependent on her mother throughout Trevor's lifetime. Although she lived with her mother, Ms. O did not discuss her personal thoughts or dilemmas with her, as she feared this would interfere with her ability to make decisions about Trevor. Her emotional withdrawal was an effort to handle her dependence on her mother, to feel more separate and mature.

In this example, cutoff was expressed by the emotionally dependent but distant parent who lived in the midst of family, yet felt isolated from family support.

Preservation of Well-Being by Severing Contact

Another face of cutoff is the person who chooses physical distance to handle the attachment. Ms. L was one of seven children who grew up not far from her present home. When she was a child, she was molested by her father. Her mother never acknowledged that reality when Ms. L broached the molestation with her. In the discussions about her relationship with her parents, she stated that she "had nothing to say" to her father, and she felt her mother blamed her for the childhood sexual abuse by the father.

Ms. L chose to distance from her family, raising her three children close to her parents but rarely being in touch. The cutoff had profound effects in her life. She drifted from partner to partner, having children with three different fathers, two of whom were drug addicts. At the time of the assessment, she was living in a shelter with one of her sons, and was out of contact with all but one of her six siblings, all of whom worked regular jobs and had families.

Ms. L was an outcast in her family—as are many who are cutoff. The physical distancing in the cutoff looks quite different from Ms. O. It is an active decision to avoid family relationships by avoiding contact. From Ms. L's description, this distance was necessary to survive the judgmental criticism of her mother and her brothers.

Cutoff can be an effort by a person to preserve his or her sense of identity. The person cannot see himself or herself surviving the relationship process with the family and so ends contact to gain relief. This may be quite useful for the person in the present, but in the long run the person pays a price for this isolation from important others.

Ms. L could not discuss her childhood abuse with her father or her mother, so she spent her adulthood alone, often looking for acceptance from men who were incapable of intimate relationships. In the assessment interview, she stated how frustrated she was with her son, who was then fifteen and a straight-A student. She said she wanted to kick him out of her room at the shelter, repeating the cutoff with the next generation. Ms. L was an example of a person cutting off for emotional survival and then being profoundly affected by the isolation which results.

In the course of several months of consultation, Ms. L discussed the childhood events for the first time. She began to contact her siblings, particularly one brother, and discuss the childhood abuse. She moved from the shelter to an apartment, and began a daytime job that allowed her to see her son when he returned home from school in the evenings. As Ms. L came to better understand her place in the family as the black sheep, she increasingly was able to make contact with family members in a less angry way.

Geographical Distance As Cutoff

A third example of cutoff is the T family. This family moved to the United States from the Middle East six years ago. The father, who was a Muslim, had previously been married and had four children. Subsequently, he married his second wife, a Christian, and had four more children. He reported that he had moved to the United States when his business collapsed in his country.

Mr. and Mrs. T reported great love and connection with their mothers and fathers, whom they had not seen for six years. Each scored 25 on the ECS, which is the highest level of connection for that scale. Mr. T had also not seen his three oldest children in that time. The striking question in interviewing this family was how to interpret their lack of contact with their families. Was this a move to better their lives or was the move to the United States an attempt to settle some of the unresolved issues with their families?

Whatever the cause of the move, the outcome was problematic. The father was physically and emotionally abusive to the oldest son, who was sent to long-term incarceration for a rather small offense at the request of the father. The mother was isolated, unable to work or drive, depressed, and had many physical symptoms. The second brother, age fourteen, began to skip school, use marijuana, and stay away from home for several days at a time. The eight-year-old brother began acting violent at school. The chaos of this family absorbed a variety of agencies for many months. How much of this move was an effort to separate from families who disapproved of this second marriage to a spouse of a different religion? How much of emigration is an effort to flee unresolved problems in a family, cutting off from the problems at home?

These families illustrate three profiles of cutoff. The first is the family in which the parent never leaves home but emotionally distances from the parents. The second is the family in which the parent runs away from her family, explaining the cutoff as a means of managing difficulties with the parent generation. The third is the family who physically cuts off but denies or cannot see the distance as a means of coping with family tension. These profiles are variations of cutoff and connection that all families experience.

Outcome of the Study

Sixty families participated in the study. This included sixty adolescents, forty-seven mothers, and twelve fathers. The demographics of the teenagers included twenty-four Caucasian, eighteen African-American, twelve Hispanic, four "other," and two Asian. The ages ranged from thirteen to seventeen, with thirty-six males and twenty-four females.

Cutoff as measured by the ECS (McCollum, 1991) was calculated for the mothers and fathers with their mothers and fathers. Cutoff scores for mothers and fathers ranged from 5 to 25, with 25, indicating the highest degree of cutoff. The mean for cutoff of the mothers from their mothers was 6.8 with a standard deviation of 3.4; cutoff from their fathers was 10.5 with a standard deviation of 6.3, indicating the cutoff from their fathers was significantly higher than from their mothers. The cutoff of the fathers from their mothers was 6.0 with a standard deviation of 2.2; cutoff from their fathers was 5.5 with a standard deviation of 0.9.

The cutoff of the mothers was positively correlated at .38, $p > .05$ with their level of functioning as measured by GAF. This indicated that the more cut off the mother was from her mother and father, the less well she functioned. On the other hand, the cutoff of the mother did not correspond to the impairment of the teenager ($-.20, p < .05$), as measured by CAFAS. This reverse correlation would indicate that the less cut off the mother, the more impaired the teenager. Some ideas on this result are discussed more extensively in the conclusions of this chapter.

The cutoff of the mother from her parents also did not correlate significantly with the cutoff of the teenager from her. One consideration in this result is that the scale for cutoff asks about the person's perceptions about the relationship with the parent. Children who had highly problematic lives still felt connected to their mothers despite their difficulties. This is probably developmentally appropriate for them, as they are rebelling but still feel and describe themselves as connected to their mothers.

Significance was not found between the degree of cutoff of the fathers from their mothers or fathers and their self-functioning, the degree of cutoff of the teenagers from them, or the level of impairment of the teenager. However, the number of fathers was so low (twelve) that statistical significance was difficult to determine.

An interesting pattern was observed in the research data that was not one of the principal questions asked in the study. As explained previously, the mothers' cutoff with their fathers was 40 percent higher than with their mothers. The higher the cutoff between the mother and her father, the more likely her child, whether male or female, was to be cut off from his or her father. So a relationship pattern developed in which a woman cut off from her father was more apt to have a child who was cut off from his or her father.

In looking at that result, the profile of Ms. L comes to mind. This mother did not speak to her father as an adult, and then engaged in a series of relationships with men who were unavailable to her emotionally. These fathers had little contact with their children, as the pattern of cutoff with the father continued in the next generation.

SOME CONSIDERATIONS AND CONCLUSIONS

These results bring up myriad questions and ideas about further research with families with adolescent children. In evaluating the results of this research a number of considerations are important for future investigations of cutoff in families.

The Complexity of Bowen Theory

One of the central organizing principles of Bowen family systems theory is that the family is a system with complex regulating mechanisms. Cause-and-effect thinking has little relevance in evaluating families. In this study important variables not considered in the outcome included the relationship between the two parents, the style of parenting, the level and nature of stresses on the family, and the functioning of other siblings.

The Difficulty in Defining and Measuring Cutoff

As Kerr (Kerr and Bowen, 1988) defined cutoff for the purposes of this study, one generation distances from the previous generations in order to moderate tension in the relationship. Defining the nature of the distancing is. however, very difficult. Does the researcher measure the amount of contact of individuals, the perception of the relationships, or even the amount of knowledge that individuals have about the extended family? Individuals who are in more emotional contact may know more of the facts and history of their family.

Cutoff is subtle and complicated but can be of extraordinary significance in a family's life. Often a person understands cutoff only after thinking about relationships in depth. Some of the parents in this study claimed they did not want to communicate the facts of the adolescent's problems to their own parents so as not to "worry" them, but this reluctance often was out of fear of being judged by them. Their ability to evaluate the quality of the relationship with their own parents materialized only after a period of reflection and examination.

The Preservative Quality of Cutoff

An assumption of this research study was that cutoff is deleterious to families and children. Bowen's writing (1978) indicated that individuals who sever relationships with their parents and extended families as a way of resolving difficulties between the generations replay those emotional patterns in their adult lives and with their own nuclear families.

However, in the short run cutoff can be a relief for individuals from intrusive, critical, or difficult parents. A parent wants little to do with a substance abusing grandparent, a father who is incarcerated, or a mother who is experienced as domineering. The parent feels better when he or she does not experience the tension with the previous generation. The parent can feel judged, abused, or unloved. Yet in the long run the cutoff does not change the emotional patterns that brought about these tensions, so they tend to reoccur in the next generation.

Other Research Outcomes

Several other research outcomes from the data are interesting, including those that do not stem from the original research questions. The degree of cutoff of the teenager from the father was significantly correlated (at .29, $p > .05$) with the level of impairment of the teenager with problems at home (.39, $p > .05$), and with depression (.36, $p > .05$). The degree of cutoff of the teenager from the father was significantly correlated (at .35, $p > .05$) with cutoff between the mother and her father. A significant multigenerational pattern emerged in which mothers who were cutoff from their fathers produced children who were cutoff from their fathers.

Limitations

Families have layers of complexity. This research study focused on a specific area of the family—the connections between three generations, the level of functioning of the parents, and impairment in the teenager. Many other factors that were not controlled for nor studied could also influence the outcomes, including the relationship between the two parents, the stresses on the family, and other emotional issues in the family. Families who come to a public mental health center at the request of a court or school official may be guarded and defensive at the initial interview, so as to skew the answers to questionnaires on cutoff. Some fathers who were the most cut off did not participate in the interviews and so were not included in the study.

Family therapists trained to examine the big picture of family anxiety and the family emotional patterns that cascade through generations often take note of how isolation and cutoff go hand in hand with symptoms. As important as these clinical observations are, empirical research adds depth and subtlety to understanding a concept such as cutoff. The author is convinced that severing relationships to mediate tension with the previous generations will manifest in symptoms in another part of the family, but for some families this may not happen in the short run. The evidence in this study is that cutoff did affect the functioning of the parents, particularly the mothers, but that it did not translate directly into impairment in the children.

Studies on cutoff become building blocks to examine different facets of emotional process in families. This study serves as one of those blocks.

REFERENCES

American Psychiatric Association (1994). *Diagnostic and Statistical Manual of Mental Disorders* (Fourth Edition). Washington, DC: American Psychiatric Press.
Bowen, M. (1978). *Family Therapy in Clinical Practice.* New York: Jason Aronson
Hodges, K. (1990, 1994). *The Child and adolescent functional assessment scale.* Ypsilanti, MI: Department of Psychology. Eastern Michigan University.
Kerr, M.E. (1980). Family system theory and therapy. In A.S. Gurman and D.P. Kniskern (Eds.), *Handbook of Family Therapy* (pp. 226-264). New York: Brunner Mazel.
Kerr, M.E. (1981). Cancer and the family emotional system. In J.G. Goldberg (Ed.), *Psychotherapeutic Treatment of Cancer Patients* (pp. 273-315). New York. Free Press.
Kerr, M.E. and Bowen, M. (1988). *Family Evaluation.* New York: W.W. Norton.
Konner, M. (1982). *The Tangled Web.* New York: Holt, Rinehart and Winston.

McCollum. E. (1991). A scale to measure Bowen's concept of emotional cutoff. *Contemporary Family Therapy* 13(3):247-254.

McKnight. A. (2001). An examination of cutoff and self-functioning in three generations of families with a substance abusing teenager. <http://scholar.lib.vt.edu/theses/available/etd-05042001-134210/>.

National Institute of Drug Abuse (2001). *Monitoring the future study.* <www.nida.nih.gov/PDF/overview2001.pdf>.

Resnick. M.D.. Bearman, P.S.. Blum, R.W.. Bauman, K.E.. Harris, K.M., Jones. J. Tabor. J.. Beuhring. T.. Sieving. R.E.. Shew. M.. Ireland. M.. Bearinger, L.H.. and Udry. J.R. (1997). "Protecting adolescents from harm: Findings from the National Longitudinal Study on Adolescent Health." *Journal of the American Medical Association* 278(100):823-832.

Sherouse. D. (1985). *Adolescent Drug and Alcohol Handbook.* Springfield, IL: Charles Thomas.

Toman. W. (1969). *Family Constellation: Its Effects on Personality and Social Behavior* (Second Edition). New York: Springer.

Chapter 12

The Continuum of Emotional Cutoff in Divorce

Stephanie J. Ferrera

Must divorce mean emotional cutoff? Our society tends to equate the two, and to promote cutoff with the attitude: "Get over this and get on with your life." The language of divorce has the ring of finality. Terms such as "cast asunder," "uncoupling," "dissolution," "irreconcilable differences," and "going our separate ways" describe the ending of a relationship.

At the most painful points in the process, divorcing spouses and family members understandably wish to be rid of the pain and may well believe that the only way to do that is to be rid of one another. Yet the reality is that divorce does not sever many of the ties that have been forged between the spouses and their families, especially when there are children.

In her study of ninety-eight postdivorce couples, Constance Ahrons (1994) found a range "from one extreme of caring and supportive friends all the way to the other extreme of hostile and bitter foes" (p. 6), with almost half of the couples reporting that their relationship one year after the legal divorce was civil and cooperative. Looking beyond the couple to the broader, multigenerational family, we see a continuum from families who emerge from the divorce process stable and whole to those who suffer serious damage. What makes the difference?

The striking range of outcomes in divorce is best understood by looking at what is involved in the divorce process. Divorce is a complex, emotionally intense, multidimensional, multigenerational process. This chapter addresses the complexity of divorce by looking first at the emotional intensity involved and second at the multiple dimensions of change and adaptation that divorcing couples and families undergo. With this background, the chapter then explores divorce from the perspective of Bowen theory, with special interest in the ideas and principles this theory offers to those who are interested in modifying losses and minimizing emotional cutoff in divorce.

THE COMPLEXITY OF DIVORCE

Emotional Intensity in Divorce

Although divorce has become commonplace in our society, less stigmatized and better accepted than it was a few decades ago, it remains a serious, life-changing event with an impact that goes far beyond the divorcing couple to their families and future generations. Given the nature of what is happening in divorce, it is bound to be an intense experience, though not equally so for all divorcing families. This can be understood if the nature of, the marital relationship is considered, which can be done by starting with the nature of basic human attachment.

Human attachment is rooted in the biological imperatives to survive and reproduce. We can do neither alone. Relationships are our lifeline. The parent-child attachment is the prototype for all attachments. The human infant is at once powerless and powerful: powerless in being utterly dependent on others, powerful in the ability to evoke a nurturing response in others. The parent-child relationship is the arena in which one first experiences self vis-à-vis other, first gains a sense of effectiveness and security as a person, and first works out a balance of individuality and togetherness. Ideally, the child finds a way to be close enough to parents and family to have a sense of belonging and connection, yet separate enough to establish and maintain autonomy and a solid sense of self. The dependent child is, of necessity, attuned to the emotional state of the family and sensitive to any disruption that might threaten security. Closeness taken too far is experienced as crowding or encroachment. Distance taken too far is experienced as abandonment. Both extremes create intense anxiety leading to the development of protective defenses. The child who grows up in the emotionally intense climate of a highly anxious family experiences more of the extremes and less of a comfortable balance. Life energy is devoted to searching for a level of attachment that is neither "too much" nor "too little." The child who grows up in the less intense climate of a calmer family experiences more of the comfortable balance of closeness and distance, and has a better chance to develop the boundaries that are part of being a defined self. Less energy is required to sustain relationships, leaving more energy free for growth and development.

The level of differentiation or maturity individuals develop as they grow up in their families goes with them into adult life and into selecting a life partner. A marriage begins with the way the partners meet, are attracted to each other, court, and establish the relationship. There are hundreds of questions to think about, hundreds of choices to make. Some will think their way through the process, with awareness of the questions at stake, while others will be propelled by emotional forces. The challenge for courting partners is to maintain clear thinking in the face of emotional intensity. The longing for togetherness, fueled by the chemistry of romantic attraction, may leave them with less than their best thinking powers at the very time they are making one of the most important decisions of their lives.

Most marriages begin with a mix of fantasy, hope, expectation, and optimism. Then, as people experience the realities of married life, the relationship is tested. Partners are called upon to replace some of the fantasy and expectations with reality-based knowledge of each other, to accept each other as real, struggling human beings, to take responsibility for self in the relationship, and to cooperate in establishing a home and family.

Key factors influencing the emotional climate that will evolve in a given marriage are the number and seriousness of the stresses the couple encounters, the level of emotional reactivity between them, the quality of their attachments to families of origin, and the emotional stability of the larger systems in which the marriage is embedded. Understanding the depth of the attachment, investment, and interdependence in the marriage allows us to appreciate the emotional intensity involved in the ending of the marriage.

In many cases, the decision to divorce follows months or years of ambivalence, with one or both partners seriously troubled about the marriage and torn between staying and leaving. Rarely do both partners agree that divorce is necessary. More often, one partner makes the decision to leave while the other is in the position of being left. Both have fully participated in the way the marriage has evolved, but often one is considerably more dissatisfied with the results than the other. The one leaving typically will experience guilt, self-doubt, and defensiveness as he or she faces the other's pain, opposition, and efforts to reconcile. The one being left will often express disbelief, mistrust, and anger, while still trying to hold the marriage together. Once the decision to divorce has been made, reconciliation is unlikely. The goodwill and trust that it would take, from both partners, to understand the problems and make the needed changes is not there.

In clinical work with divorcing couples and families, a therapist sees emotional intensity expressed in many ways. Some people talk about the abject loneliness of going through such a difficult time yet not being able to turn to their "best friend" for understanding and support. Many go through a period of time when it is unthinkable and unimaginable to face the future without their spouse. People vacillate between holding on and letting go, recognizing, and perhaps being advised by others, that they really must let go but feeling emotionally compelled to hold on. The roller coaster of emotion goes from fear to elation, from shame and regret over one's own failings to anger and blame of one's spouse, from relief at getting away to missing one's spouse and feeling painfully empty with the loss.

The Six Dimensions of Divorce

The disruption that accompanies divorce can be appreciated by looking at what is being disrupted. Marriage encompasses romance and sex. friendship and companionship, economic interdependence, and raising children, all within the larger systems of extended family and community: divorce changes every one of these dimensions. Anthropologist Paul Bohannan (1970) offers a helpful way of looking at the issues and tasks that divorcing couples and families face. He states: "The complexity of divorce arises because at least six things are happening at once" (p. 32). The six overlapping areas he identifies are emotional, legal, economic, coparental, community, and psychic. In the following descriptions of the six dimensions of divorce, I have taken Bohannan's framework and expanded on it from a family systems perspective.

The Emotional Divorce

Bohannan views the emotional divorce as the first visible stage of a deteriorating marriage. The couple may continue to work together as a social team, but the quality of the relationship is strained as ambivalence and negative emotion gain over the once-positive connection. People may be married for a long time with a sense that things are not right, sometimes with a lack of clarity about what it is that is not right, often with fear of surfacing their doubts and risking conflict.

Family therapist Carol Moran notes that intrapsychic cutoff. described by Bowen (1978) as "the intrapsychic process of denial and isolation of self" (p. 382), is commonly seen in marriages and is almost always present for some time prior to separation or divorce. A few examples follow:

- The spouse who is sexually unsatisfied but never lets the other know
- The spouse who accumulates heavy debt but hides the evidence from the other
- The spouse who keeps emotional reactivity suppressed to the point of developing a life-threatening illness
- The secret sexual affair or series of affairs

Moran concludes. "For each of these examples there is a spouse who is either oblivious to what is happening or who suspects that things are not well but does not have, does not seek, or is not given necessary information about chronic distress in the partner" (Moran, personal communication, 2002).

The sexual dimension of marriage is interwoven with the emotional relationship. For some couples, the sexual connection is of primary importance, and for other couples it is secondary to other things they value in the marriage. One partner may consider sex more primary than the other.

Neuroscientist Robert Sapolsky (1994) describes the intricate interplay between the physiology of the stress response and sexual desire, and provides scientific undergirding for a fact that most people discover from personal experience: stress is not conducive to sexual desire and arousal for either the male or the female. As a marriage progresses and people deal with the multiple stresses of living together, working out differences, and taking on responsibilities, the nature of their sexual relationship changes, usually in the direction of less quantity, if not less satisfying quality.

To live in a state of emotional divorce, with the erosion of the positive connection that stabilizes and sustains a marriage, is a wearing stress—one that is often accompanied by decline or complete severing of the sexual connection. Celibate marriage is not an oxymoron; it is a reality for a significant percentage of couples, at least those who confide in a therapist. It seems that, under stress, sex is the first thing to go, although in exceptional cases it may be the last thing to go. Bohannan (1970) found, among hundreds of divorcing partners he interviewed, a few for whom the sexual connection was the strongest bond.

Bowen's concept of the individuality/togetherness balance is helpful for understanding how a marriage moves toward emotional divorce. The start of emotional divorce could be defined as the point at which one or both partners cannot see a way to be an "individual"—whatever that means to him or her—within the "togetherness" of the marriage as he or she experiences it. People have different ways of talking about this, and focus on different problem areas, but the underlying theme is: "I cannot stay in this marriage without compromising myself in ways that I cannot live with." When partners encounter repeated frustration and impasse in their efforts to negotiate the changes that are needed in their relationship to accommodate their growth as individuals, emotional divorce is likely to follow. If the ultimate test of a marriage is the ability of the partners to make room in the relationship for the growth and development of two separate individuals, then divorce can be seen as the ultimate remedy when partners are unable, despite honest efforts, to find the kind of room that the two separate individuals require.

The Legal Divorce

Marriage makes an intimate relationship "legal." The marriage is usually celebrated with a ceremony of some kind, conducted by an authorized representative of the state, such as a minister or judge. The state issues a marriage certificate. However, the fact that they are entering into a legal contract is not uppermost in the minds of most couples as they plan their wedding. If and when the marriage ends in divorce, the spouses will need to pay far more attention to the legal aspects of their relationship than they did in the beginning.

Ahrons (1994) asks: "Why does breaking the contract take so much more time, money, and emotion than did making the original contract?" She offers two answers:

> One answer is that it's because our marital contracts are unwritten, ambiguous, and undefined, growing over years into a patchwork of implicit agreements. Marriage is a contract based on romantic attachment, and unlike entering a business partnership, the rules for ending the contract are not spelled out in advance. It's only when we want to break that contract that we realize even unwritten agreements are in fact real contracts with legal implications. . . . Another answer is that the legal system has a stake in keeping the business of divorce in its own hands. Today, divorce is big business. (p. 167)

Many helping professionals who work with families, including some attorneys, seriously question whether the legal system is an appropriate arena for the resolution of marital and family conflict. Family therapist Betty Carter (Carter and Peters, 1996) states: "The legal system is set up to defend individuals from their enemies, not to mediate disputes among family members" (p. 267). An attorney is an advocate for his or her client, and defines success in terms of a satisfactory outcome for that individual. In contrast, from a family perspective, a well-designed divorce settlement is one that carefully considers and protects the long-term interest of the whole family.

For this reason, probably the most important question about the legal divorce is: whose divorce is it? Decisions are best made by the people who will live with the decisions. The divorcing partners and their children and families are the ones who will live with a divorce settlement. Decisions regarding child custody, support, visitation, property, and finances will be a daily reality for the family, affecting their quality of life and their relationships with one another well into the future. Ideally the divorcing partners will "own" the divorce. They will construct their own settlement and it will represent the best that they can do to define a set of terms that is right for them, uniquely suited to the way their family functions. Attorneys, mediators, and other helping professionals will be resources operating in the service of the family, providing information and guidance without overly influencing the outcome.

This ideal outcome will happen only when divorcing families and their attorneys draw clear boundaries regarding who is working for whom, and who is in charge. The boundaries must keep the emotional issues and legal issues as separate as possible. There is no legal solution to an emotional problem. To expect lawyers and judges or mediators to resolve hidden agendas or emotional impasses is to expect the impossible. To expect them to provide enlightened guidance about rights, responsibilities, and options for mutually beneficial terms and, when needed, to set limits on unrealistic expectations or unfair demands, is within reason.

In our society, as Ahrons (1994) points out, divorce has become something of an industry. The legal divorce system has a life and a culture of its own. With its unfamiliar procedures, obfuscating language, crowded court calendars, multiple lawyers with busy schedules, and seemingly endless delays and fees, the system can be frustrating and intimidating. For a family that is already stressed, the challenge of dealing with the legal system can be daunting. The legal system, after all, is a human system. When the reactivity of the divorcing couple meets the reactivity of the legal system, the emotional level can escalate quickly. Differences that seemed negotiable in a prelegal stage of divorce often become polarized beyond reason after lawyers are consulted and an adversarial, defensive climate is created. Emotional cutoff is operating when divorcing partners no longer talk to each other and communication is routed through their attorneys.

Divorce mediation offers an alternative to a purely legal contest. Mediators are lawyers or therapists, or a team of both, who function as a neutral third party. The mediator's client is the whole family, not one individual. Mediators work with both of the divorcing partners in a structured process that respects the emotions that both bring to the table, but keeps the focus on the issues, with the goal of seeking terms of settlement acceptable to both. Mediation at its best moves the conflicting spouses to define their views and priorities more clearly, to identify common ground, and to find trade-offs and middle ground between opposing positions. The emotional process in mediation is significantly different from that in a litigated divorce, as explained by mediator Mark H. Zweig (1996):

> Mediators do not hand down formal opinions or decisions. Most importantly, in mediation the parties collaborate to determine the outcome jointly, rather than being told by a third party (e.g., a judge or jury) what will happen. Consequently, the parties do not "plead" their case to establish the validity of their respective positions or claims. This feature tends to reduce polarization and may contribute toward enhancing current and even future relationships. It is confidential and generally faster, more flexible, less formal, less adversarial and less expensive than traditional adjudicative processes. (p. 160)

For divorcing couples who take charge of the process, engage in negotiating their own settlement as responsibly as possible, use legal services selectively for information and ideas, and, most important, understand and deal with the emotional divorce as separate from the legal divorce, the role of the legal system can be minimal. The law need only provide the official granting of the divorce and ratification of the settlement.

The Economic Divorce

Humans are territorial creatures. People become attached to "things," especially their homes and personal property. Possessions are an extension of the self, a measure of one's success in the world, a reflection of one's tastes, values, and heritage. The family home reflects the individual and collective personalities of family members and tangibly represents the way of life they have created. Multigenerational history is embedded in the belongings that have been passed down, and the stories and memories those treasures hold.

Divorce calls for a major reorganization of the economic life of a family. To appreciate the issues that need to be faced, consider some of the economic questions married couples deal with. What is our standard of living, and how is it determined? What was the economic lifestyle of the two families of origin, and how does that influence our approach to money? Who has brought what assets into the marriage? Who earns income and how much? How does each partner help the other produce income? How have we supported each other's education and careers? Who runs the household? How is the workload divided up? Who manages the money? How are decisions on spending and saving made? Are nonmonetary contributions recognized and valued? Two partners will not have identical answers to these questions. Their views, with areas of agreement and areas of disagreement, will be key to their negotiation of the economic divorce.

The way the partners have worked as an economic team, for better or worse, goes with them into the divorce. In some cases, the seemingly insurmountable difficulties faced in dealing with the economic ties keep couples together long beyond the point of an emotional divorce. It is not uncommon to see partners work out an in-house arrangement of separate territories without getting a legal or economic divorce.

While the economic decisions in divorce call for careful thought, planning, and flexibility, they also trigger emotional reactivity. The emotional polarities range from demanding everything to walking away from everything. Pain and anger may be played out in aggressive demands for more than a fair settlement; guilt, sympathy, or exhaustion may lead to giving in to such demands. As money is often a battleground in marriage, so can it be, with added intensity, in a divorce.

At the high-cost end of the continuum of economic divorce are the partners who engage in a prolonged win-lose contest, usually resulting in heavy losses, steep legal fees, and emotional cutoff. The extreme case was captured in the film *The War of the Roses* (1989). In one scene, the husband's attorney, alarmed as he watches the escalating battle over who gets the house, cautions his client: "There is no winning here. There are only degrees of losing." At the other, less costly end of the continuum of economic divorce are the partners who find dealing with assets and finances the least difficult aspect of the divorce. Many are able to be reasonable, considerate of each other, and generous, perhaps in an effort to soften the pain and loss they are experiencing in other parts of their relationship.

The Coparental Divorce

Most parents who are considering divorce think long and hard about whether their children will be better off growing up in the current emotional climate that exists in the family or in the future reorganized family that will be created with a divorce. The current "frying pan" is a known quantity; the "fire" that the future may hold is uncertain.

The security and well-being of children rest heavily on the resources and stability of the family, and the stability of the family rests on the maturity of parents and other adults as reflected in the way they work out their relationships. One of the foremost concerns for divorcing families, and for society, is the danger that divorce may end not only a marriage but also a parent-child relationship. If not managed responsibly, the emotional polarizations activated between parents and among other family members in the divorce process can result in children losing their connection to one parent and, with that, often their connection to that parent's whole side of the family. Emotional cutoff between parent and child is arguably the greatest long-term cost of divorce.

The key decisions faced by divorcing parents are child support, custody and living arrangements for the children, and ongoing contact or "visitation" between the child and the noncustodial or nonresidential parent. The level of cooperation parents bring to these decisions is rooted in the maturity level of each and in their history as a couple and as parents. To appreciate the challenges divorce presents to parents, consider some of the questions they face: Can we work together as parents despite the breaking of many of the ties we had during marriage? How will we divide up, or share, the work of parenting as well as the joys? How much confidence do we have in each other as parents? Do we acknowledge each other's contributions to the children? How does each of us view the children's needs and best interests, and how similar or different are we in these views? How clearly can we draw the boundary that separates parenting issues from all the other issues between us? How willing and able are we to have the level of ongoing contact and negotiation with each other that will be required if both are to remain actively engaged in raising the children?

The emotional field in which divorcing partners live as they think about all of this includes the extended family, community, friends, work systems, professional advisors, and, of course, the children themselves. All will have influence on the decisions that are made. In cases where one or both of the partners is involved in a new romantic relationship, the new partner may exert substantial influence, in a number of ways, on the thinking, reactivity, and decision making of the divorcing partners. Complexity multiplies.

Marriages end but the parental relationship is lifelong. As the family undergoes the changes involved in divorce, some disruption to children is inevitable. Commitment to the children and to the long-term stability of the family unit fuels the motivation of divorcing parents and families to put forth the heroic effort it takes to function through the divorce process in ways that minimize the disruption and prevent cutoff.

The Community Divorce

Regarding community divorce, Bohannan (1970) discusses the impact of divorce on the social lives of the partners. With rare exceptions, they no longer socialize as a couple. Within the social network, people make decisions, not necessarily on a conscious level, about how to relate to divorcing partners. Some of the friends they had in common may remain friends with both but will see divorced partners individually rather than together. Some friends will maintain contact with only one partner. Relationships with married friends tend to become less comfortable, and divorced individuals often seek the company of other single people. As the boundaries of inclusion and exclusion change, it is almost inevitable that painful moments will occur when an individual finds himself or herself on the outside of gatherings and connections where he or she was once a welcomed insider.

Among the friends, neighbors, associates, churches, and organizations that have made up their social world, divorcing partners stir reactivity. The greater the difficulty and conflict in the divorce, the more potential it has to stir reactivity in others. Important social relationships can be damaged or severed for divorcing partners if the reactivity of others, as well as their own, results in emotional cutoff.

Although divorce has an impact on the social network of the couple, it has far greater impact on their families, including the parents, siblings, and extended families of both partners. Envision this larger family as a web of relationships in which every person is connected to every other person in a network of interlocking triangles. Envision the marriage as one link within the web. This image, which is an attempt to view the family as an emotional system, helps us to see that a marriage affects all of the people connected to the couple and all of the relationships among these people, and that all these people and their relationships affect the couple. Divorce will set in motion ripples, if not tidal waves, in the family emotional field.

Family therapist Roberta Cristofori (1977) points out that the state of the nuclear and extended families, their level of anxiety and stress at the time of a divorce, will be a key factor in their response.

> The divorce that occurs when the family system is stressed by other events is likely to be more difficult and more intense than one occurring in a calm system. . . . A separation that occurs during a time of low anxiety in the nuclear family can have greater potential for being workable and calm. Conversely, a separation that occurs in the context of other nodal family events can become invested with more feeling than would occur at another time. (p. 26)

As people think about divorcing, the question of what this will mean for their parents, siblings, and in-law family is probably second only to the question of what it will mean for the children. How will each family member respond? Will they support or oppose the decision to divorce? Will they take a side or will they try to understand both sides? What will all of these relationships come to be after the divorce? The ability of divorcing partners to be aware of the reactivity stirred in the family by the divorce, to manage their own reactivity to the reactivity of others, and to focus on the long-term goal of family stability even as they weather the day-to-day storms can significantly improve the chances for a positive outcome. In divorcing one's spouse, one need not divorce the entire family.

The Psychic Divorce

With the term *psychic divorce,* Bohannan (1970) refers to the emotional, psychological work involved in "becoming a whole, complete, and autonomous individual again" (p. 53). The absence of one's spouse confronts one with many discoveries, often unexpected, of the ways in which one had come to depend on him or her. How will the void be filled?

Divorce compels partners to change, to "reinvent" themselves. Becoming single again after being married is a major identity change, one that also changes one's status in the world. Divorce means taking on roles and tasks formerly carried by one's partner, making decisions on one's own, often dealing with reduced economic means, and, most challenging of all, learning to relate to one's children in the new parenting arrangement created by the divorce.

Divorce also provides a catalyst for a deeper level of self-examination and definition of self. Divorce places one at a crossroad. One avenue is an anxiety-driven fast track that goes in the direction of cutting off from one's spouse and attempting to fill the void in one's life with activity and new relationships while denying the significance of the loss. The other is a more reflective avenue that takes time to focus on self, to gain an understanding of one's own emotional functioning, and to redefine oneself in relationships. For those who choose it, this less-traveled road leads to a deeper and more complete resolution of the losses and costs of divorce. Cristofori (1977) explains:

> Absence of contact, following the discomfort of intense fusion, can produce the most profound feelings of loss in one or both spouses. An equally problematical situation, however, occurs when an individual denies emotional reaction to the separation and declares himself free of what he perceives as excess emotional baggage. This pattern denies the existence of previous or existing dependency. As such, it does not address the issue of loss, and increases vulnerability to collapsing or entering another equally problematical relationship in which the issues remain the same, and are only perceived as different. . . . Those in whom loss was minimal did not run from the discomfort of negative fusion, but found some optimal distance for self from which it was possible to work on the relationship ties while remaining in contact with the other spouse. (p. 27)

In summary, the discussion thus far has focused on divorce as a major life event—one that is emotionally intense, one that requires partners to deal with a complex set of tasks and changes, one that involves the entire family and affects future generations. As they go through the process over weeks, months, and sometimes years, divorcing partners and their families are dealing with reorganizing their lives around changed relationships and adapting to new realities in their economic, legal, and social circumstances. For some, divorce will mean profound and ongoing struggle resulting in lasting damage to relationships, a significant degree of emotional cutoff, and increased vulnerability to symptoms. For others, the initial losses will be painfully difficult, but the emotional attachments will be resolved in a way that allows partners and their families to maintain cooperative contact and to invest energy in new endeavors. These differences in outcome have everything to do with family emotional process, its intensity, and the way it is managed.

THE PERSPECTIVE OF BOWEN THEORY

In looking at the family as an emotional system, Bowen captured both the complexity of family relationships and the variation among families in the ways emotional process and patterns play out. Bowen theory offers a resource to divorcing partners and families in two ways. First, it provides an accurate, detailed, neutral way of understanding the emotional process operating in the family before, during, and after a divorce. Second, this calmer, nonblaming, nonjudging perspective provides a basis for defining a set of personal operating principles to which one can refer in the heat of the intensity generated by divorce. Principles defined at times of relative calm guide one through the inevitable times of stress and confusion. Theory, then, becomes a beacon in a storm.

Each concept in the theory has importance for divorcing families. Following are selected ideas from the concepts as Bowen defined them.

Differentiation of Self

This concept refers to the balance between emotional and intellectual functioning within the individual, and the corresponding balance between closeness and separateness individuals achieve in relationships. One of Bowen's (1978) more challenging assertions is: "People pick spouses who have the same level of differentiation" (p. 377). Michael Kerr (1989) expands on this idea:

> When two people marry, each "fuses" into the relationship to a degree commensurate with his or her "togetherness needs," the intensity of the needs being linked to level of differentiation, *which is assumed to be equal in both spouses.* (p. 6, italics in original)

It takes more than a little insight to see this in one's own marriage, given the propensity to see one's spouse as little less mature than oneself.

Level of differentiation is observed in the amount of life energy partners invest in managing their relationship. It is seen in the extent of their focus on approval and disapproval, acceptance and rejection. It is seen in their emotional dependence on each other and sensitivity to the amount of attention and support given and received. Level of differentiation is also seen in the way partners work out their differences. For people who are highly relationship oriented, differences pose a threat. Small differences may be magnified, molehills become mountains, and issues are taken more seriously and more personally than their importance merits.

The dilemma for spouses who are moving into the divorce process is that their level of fusion and difficulties in working out differences have led them, or at least one of them, to believe that divorce is necessary, yet the divorce itself introduces a host of new issues and the potential for triggering even more reactivity. The hopeful side of divorce is that it represents for many couples recognition of how much they have come to revolve around each other and how much self has been compromised in the process. The decision to divorce can be a decision to try to resolve the fusion and reclaim the self.

The concept of differentiation is rich in applications for divorcing partners. Knowledge of this concept guides the effort to keep thinking ahead of reactivity in dealing with one's partner and other family members. The upheaval involved in the early stages of divorce, especially when there are children involved, and the number and intensity of emotional triggers present when partners are in contact, frequently leaves people blindsided by their own and others' reactivity. One is dealing continuously with the competing pulls to hold on and to let go. In the midst of this, one can claim the option to stop, think, breathe deeply, rest, and take time to choose a thoughtful response rather than be pushed, by others or by one's own anxiety, into unthinking reactions.

Related to this is the effort to establish a responsible, long-term view and to keep this view clearly in focus as one makes decisions. Cristofori (1977) states:

> Whether divorce becomes defined as a serious loss to self, and whether the individual proceeds with some capacity for remaining intact, is related to whether decisions are made on the basis of immediate and expedient gain, or with a view toward long-term benefits. . . . A willingness to address the long range and to envision the consequences of actions for the future is characteristic of those who did fairly well in divorce. (p. 27)

Another aspect of the effort toward differentiation is redefining the relationship with one's partner. Clear thinking allows one to begin to distinguish between the aspects of the marriage to which one can and should hold on, and the aspects that one must let go. Between divorcing partners, the special intimacy and companionship they once knew is for the most part no longer possible, but it is still possible to consider and support each other's well-being in many ways. Above all, it is important to support each other's best functioning as parents.

Finally, the effort toward differentiation requires one to develop "I-positions." What are the principles and values most important to self? Write them down and keep them in the forefront of the brain. The I-position communicates to others: "This is where I stand; this is what I will and will not do." Knowing where one individual stands leaves others clearer about their options. Cristofori (1977) describes what such an effort can accomplish:

> If communicated from a non-anxious stance, clear statements about what self will and will not do are remarkably effective in calming an anxious system. Months of litigation and chaos, which only intensify feelings of loss, can be reduced when one spouse has the courage and control to operationalize the communication, "I shall not win over you, nor shall I permit myself to be done-in by you." (pp. 28-29)

Triangles

The concept of the emotional system recognizes the depth of the attachment and interdependence among family members. The concept of the triangle recognizes the interdependence between a two-person relationship and the larger systems that spawned it and surround it. A two-person system never exists in isolation. When two runaways get together in an "us-against-the-world" alliance, they soon discover that they stand on shaky ground. It is predictable that the reactivity and unresolved dependence in the relationships they are running from will go with them and be played out between them, most likely with more intensity than they knew in the prior relationships. When the decision to marry or live together is driven largely by partners' runaway reactivity to their parents and families, the relationship rests on an unstable foundation of interlocking triangles.

Given the stress and anxiety associated with divorce, it is to be expected that triangles will be active. Every person who is important to the couple—children, extended family, friends, community—is a potential candidate for triangling. The legal system, as previously discussed, is a prime candidate. Triangles that can threaten a marriage are created whenever either spouse invests in another relationship a substantial amount of the time and attention that had been invested in the marriage. This may be an affair, a consuming activity, a special friendship, or even increased involvement with a child or other family member. When an affair has been one of the precipitants for the divorce, and is ongoing during the divorce, this can create an especially difficult set of triangles.

A mild triangling process can have a calming effect by opening up avenues for shifting and defusing anxiety and thus keeping the original twosome from overheating. It is the spreading of the process into interlocking triangles that leads to an increase in tension, which in turn leads to side taking and divided loyalties, which in turn leads to cutoff. In the face of escalating tension, family members are hard pressed to find ways to relate to both spouses without taking a side, and those who have taken a side are hard pressed to find ways to relate to one another.

For those who would try to calm the system, knowledge of triangles is especially valuable. Every person who is a candidate for triangling is also a candidate for detriangling. With conscious effort, people can become aware of their own triangling behaviors and exercise a degree of thoughtful choice in what they say and to whom they say it. Divorcing partners can make an effort to manage their conflict, keep it between them, and avoid putting side-taking pressure on others. When tension does spill over, others can make an ' effort to modify their reactivity. The most helpful person to the family member or friend going through a divorce is not the one who quickly becomes an ally, but the one who is able to be somewhat calmer and more neutral. An ally may help one feel better for the moment, but a neutral friend may help one think better for more lasting benefit.

Nuclear Family Emotional System and Family Projection Process

These two concepts refer to the patterns of relating that are activated in response to tension in the nuclear family. Three patterns—emotional distance, marital conflict, and dysfunction in one spouse—describe the emotional process in a marriage or two-person system. The fourth pattern, projection to a child, describes the three-person system created by the triangling of a child into the parents' relationship.

Emotional distance is the outgrowth of people moving away from one another in response to relationship tensions. They may avoid one another physically, or may maintain contact but on a more superficial level, avoiding subjects known to trigger reactivity. The distance predictably becomes more uncomfortable to one than to the other, and that one will move to reestablish a comfortable level of closeness, thus becoming the "pursuer." If the partner reacts with further distancing, the two become engaged in the well-known pattern of pursuit and distance.

The pursuit-distance pattern, as well as any other area of disagreement, provides the fuel for *marital conflict*. Depending on their prior experience with conflict in families of origin and other relationships, spouses will have varying levels of tolerance for conflict. At a mild level of conflict, people are communicating and hearing one another well enough to exchange information. Better understanding of one another's views emerges and can be taken as the basis for resolving differences. Many books have been written to train people to deal with conflict in this adaptive way. Recent research in the field of the neurophysiology of relationships, particularly the work of John Gottman (1994), adds greatly to our understanding of why it is so difficult for people to do so. In his review of Gottman's work, Daniel Goleman (1995) states, in his *Emotional Intelligence:*

> Perhaps the biggest breakthrough in understanding what holds a marriage together or tears it apart has come from the use of sophisticated physiological measures that allow the moment-to-moment tracking of the emotional nuances of a couple's encounter. Scientists are now able to detect a husband's otherwise invisible adrenaline surges and jumps in blood pressure, and to observe fleeting but telling microemotions as they flit across a wife's face. (p. 130)

The lesson here is that conflict activates rapid and powerful responses that move partners into an escalating process. The original issues are often left behind in the heat of argument driven by each partner's defending self and placing pressure on the other to yield. The outcome may be violence, or it may be that partners become emotionally overwhelmed (Gottman's term is *flooding*) and withdraw from each other (Gottman's term is *stonewalling*), often in a state of serious discouragement about the viability of the relationship.

The third pattern, *dysfunction in one spouse,* offers an alternative to distance and/or conflict. This pattern appears as a reciprocal two-step with one partner in the lead, taking charge of situations, thinking and planning for both, while the other follows, yielding a portion of his or her responsibility. One partner overfunctioning and the other underfunctioning seems to be the primary way of relating for some couples, the pattern that comes most naturally, while for others it seems to emerge secondary to their going through the cycle of distance and conflict and seeking a more harmonious way of getting along. Depending on the nature and intensity of the process, one partner may become the benevolent caretaker of the other, one may become dominant and the other subordinate, or one may become overburdened with responsibility while the other retreats to a state of helpless dysfunction.

As marital tension increases beyond the level that can be absorbed within the two-person system, triangles will follow. The fourth pattern, *projection to a child,* moves the tension into the mother-father-child triangle. Parents shift focus away from their own relationship and form what Bowen called a "we-ness" to focus on a child. Because this is such an important mechanism, Bowen made it a separate concept in the theory, naming it the *family projection process.* This concept is so important because it illuminates the part that family emotional process plays in producing symptoms and impairment in a child.

A real or perceived problem in a child becomes the focal point for parental anxiety. In many cases, the mother is the first to become anxious and the father follows her lead, deferring to her view and supporting her approach to solving the problem. This cooperative effort tends to have a calming and unifying effect for the parents. In other cases, both parents focus on the child but have conflict about what is the best approach. Either way, the child is in a vulnerable position. Being the object of intensive concern and intervention significantly increases anxiety for the child, resulting in poorer functioning, which in turn results in even greater parental and family concern. The projection process is also at work when parents miss seeing the child as a child and relate to him or her as a little adult. A child may take on special importance to a parent as a kind of pseudopartner, meeting needs that are not met in the marriage or other adult relationships.

Looking at the four relationship patterns as they relate to divorce, a case could be made that distance and conflict are more likely to lead to divorce than dysfunction in a spouse or projection to a child. The latter two mechanisms operate to submerge marital conflict and bind the couple together. Bowen (1978) specifically commented on the marriage in which dysfunction in one spouse is the principal means of managing tension:

> These marriages are enduring. Chronic illness and invalidism, whether physical or emotional, can be the only manifestation of the intensity of the undifferentiation. The underfunctioning one is grateful for the care and attention, and the overfunctioning one does not complain. Divorce is almost impossible in these marriages unless the dysfunction is also mixed with marital conflict. (p. 379)

Likewise, the care of an impaired child may create a tie between the parents that overshadows other problems and precludes divorce.

Nuclear family emotional process and family projection process are concepts that have important practical application for divorcing families. The four relationship patterns described by these concepts provide a lens of observation, helping one to identify the particular responses and behaviors that led to problems serious enough to warrant divorce. One can come to know the patterns of distance and pursuit, conflict and impasse, overfunctioning and underfunctioning, and triangles with children and others as they play out in one's own marriage. More to the point, one can come to know one's own part in these patterns. Without such knowledge, it is predictable that the patterns that led to problems in the marriage will go with the partners into the divorce and the postdivorce relationship. There is no statute of limitations on the number of times former spouses can trigger reactivity and reenact old scenarios. It is an accomplishment worth working for to reach a point where some of the triggers are disconnected and old patterns are replaced by new, flexible responses.

The concept of the family projection process is especially valuable in understanding the risks for children as parents divorce. Divorcing partners who have been child-focused in marriage will most likely be child-focused in divorce. Children who have been caught up in the unresolved conflict of their parents during the marriage are likely to be so after the divorce. Decisions about custody, support, and visitation become the venue for ongoing battles. It has become part of conventional wisdom in our society that adults should not put children "in the middle" of divorce. Experts spell out the "dos" and "don'ts" for relating to children: reassure them that they were not the cause of the divorce; encourage them to talk freely about their feelings; do not speak badly of the other parent or send messages through the children to the other parent. Although such rules are useful, they are not much of a bulwark against the level of ongoing tension in which children live when their parents' conflict continues long past the legal divorce.

Psychiatrist and family therapist Edward W. Beal (1998) has worked with hundreds of divorcing families, including many that are child-focused. He writes about the position of children in these families:

> The age, gender, individual resilience, and the way the child is caught up in the family emotional patterns will determine the nature and intensity of the symptoms. . . . In my opinion, the predivorce family history is critical in determining how the divorcing family can continue its parental functioning. Spousal conflict continuing postdivorce and involving the children is the most potentially damaging triangle. (pp. 333-334)

He goes on to describe the families in which the prognosis for children is good:

> Although the marital conflict may be substantial, it infrequently involves the children directly. These children may be symptomatic secondary to family breakup but less so from family conflict. Conflicting spouses can retain good parental skills. . . . In general, these parents believe that more can be accomplished by keeping the family emotional process and decision making out of the legal system. In addi-

tion, these parents can minimize the influence of extended family anxiety on the divorce process. (p. 334)

Multigenerational Transmission Process

What is transmitted from parent to child across generations in families, and how is it transmitted? These are enormously complex questions usually addressed in terms of genes and culture. Bowen theory brings to these questions another variable, one that goes a long way toward explaining how family functioning evolves across generations. From the perspective of Bowen theory, the level of differentiation is transmitted, and the way it is transmitted is through the family emotional process—in particular he family projection process.

The level of differentiation of parents is passed on to children but with some variation. The family projection process accounts for that variation. Children most involved in the projection process develop a lower level of differentiation than their parents; children least involved develop a higher level. As this process is repeated over generations, different branches of a family move toward higher and lower levels of differentiation, and have lesser or greater vulnerability to dysfunction. Bowen took into account variables, such as stress, that could speed or slow multigenerational transmission.

Is divorce transmitted across generations? Does divorce breed divorce? Beal and Hochman (1991) answer yes to this question, stating: "Divorce seems to run in some families the way diabetes or heart disease does. . . . There is plenty of evidence that adult children of divorce are more likely themselves to become divorced" (p. 106). These authors go on to make an important distinction: "It is not the divorce that is the legacy, however. *It is the family patterns leading to the divorce that seep into future generations*" (p. 107, italics added).

Few divorcing partners ask themselves: what family patterns have led us to divorce? Even to ask the question requires a systems perspective. For those who are able to step back and look at the bigger picture, the concept of multigenerational transmission is a helpful guide. Looking at generational patterns and at the ways parents and ancestors worked out difficulties similar to one's own, and finding examples of coping and resilience, can bring one to a more objective and neutral place—a more hopeful place.

Thinking about the links between the generations often leads quickly to thinking about how one's marriage and divorce is linked to one's family-of-origin relationships. This takes one back to parents, siblings, and extended family. What was the level of intensity in these relationships? How were differences worked out? How were the patterns that one developed in adapting to the parental family replicated in one's marriage? Was cutoff a primary mechanism for dealing with relationship intensity? Is the divorce a continuation of this pattern?

Bowen believed that a motivated adult could accomplish more learning about self and growing up by going back to the family of origin and working on differentiation than in any other way. Divorce can be a catalyst for such an effort. Whether one's family supports or opposes the divorce or offers help or not, that family remains a resource for learning about oneself. Such learning at the time of divorce and after can influence one's thinking and behavior in ways that make a significant difference in the outcome.

Emotional Process in Society

Comparable to the family, the total society can be viewed as an emotional system. Bowen saw the individuality-togetherness balance as the key to understanding the way a society responds to challenge. When many of the responses within society move toward increased togetherness; when many decisions are made to allay the anxiety of the moment; when there is increased focus on rights with a decrease in the overall level of responsibility; regression is the result (Bowen, 1978).

A case could be made that the skyrocketing divorce rate is evidence of regression in our society. The divorce rate in the United States changed from about 7 percent in 1860 to almost 35 percent in 1960 and since then has increased to about 50 percent (Beal, 1998). Divorce affects every American family directly or indirectly. The family constellation of adults in today's society could conceivably include the following: their divorced or separated parents and the families of each; other spouses or partners of their parents and the families of each; full siblings, stepsiblings, and half siblings; their own current spouse and in-law family; former spouse(s) and in-law families; and their children and stepchildren from one or more marriages. For children, the picture can be even more complex. To deal with the number of relationships created by divorce and remarriage, and the network of triangles involved, constitutes a test of human adaptability.

As the divorce rate has had an impact on American society, so also has the society had an impact on the divorce rate. Increasing social acceptance and lessening of the stigma and barriers that formerly confronted divorcing couples go hand in hand with the rising divorce rate and, in turn, make it easier to divorce. A comment from Margaret Mead goes to the heart of the matter: "There is no society in the world where people have stayed married without enormous community pressure to do so" (quoted in Fisher, 1992, p. 109). Under the heading, Divorcing Society, Beal (1998) elaborates on Mead's point:

> It is doubtful that the nature of marriage changed drastically or that the level of maturity of those entering marriage changed dramatically. . . . It is quite possible that for such a rapid change to occur, societal factors regulating marriage have been a major influence on the dissolution rate. If stable marriages within society depend on extramarital controls such as religion, civil law, economic variability, and intact relationships with past generations, then it is possible to view the increasing divorce rate as a function of the influence of these extramarital controls. (p. 329)

As societal influence once was a force discouraging divorce, it now has almost become a source of encouragement. Many of society's messages, including those from the helping professions, encourage a "quick fix" for relationship problems followed by quick replacement of losses. Divorcing partners and families have choices to make about what part of the influence from the social environment they listen to and what part they reject. Those who can slow down, evaluate the various influences, and follow their own principles as they make their decisions stand on more solid ground.

EMOTIONAL CUTOFF AND DIVORCE

Bowen (1978) chose the term *emotional cutoff* to describe "the process of separation, isolation, withdrawal, running away, or denying the importance of the parental family" (p. 382) that he observed to varying degrees in families. Emotional cutoff is best understood in the light of the other concepts in Bowen theory. Following is a description of cutoff as it relates to the other dimensions of family emotional process.

The lower the level of differentiation, the more difficulty people are likely to have in working out the attachment to parents and family of origin. At an extreme, pressure for togetherness and difficulties separating from parents become intolerable, and cutoff is seen as the only way to preserve self and gain independence. Parents are seen as the problem, and getting away as the solution. It is tempting to move into a new relationship that promises freedom. However, one does not gain in level of differentiation by cutting off from one's parents, and with the cutoff one loses support and stability that contact with the family might provide.

When a new relationship is based in large part on the emotional cutoffs of the partners from their families, it is predictable that partners ultimately will replicate or increase the level of intensity they have tried to escape. As tension increases, it will play out in triangles, in the patterns of the nuclear family emotional system, and in the family projection process. At this point, people often will wonder how, despite all their effort to leave their problems behind, start over, and do better, they are having more problems than they had in their parental families. The nature of the problems and symptoms may be different, but the intensity is similar or greater. If this intensity plays out primarily through projection to a child, the chances increase for that child to cut off as his or her way of leaving home. In this way, emotional cutoff is transmitted across generations. One inherits the cutoffs made in previous generations, and one unwittingly passes on one's own cutoffs, plus the cumulative legacy of cutoff in one's family, to one's children.

Emotional cutoff is expressed in our society in many ways. The extreme result is seen in relationships that form as family substitutes, such as gangs, cults, and transient living arrangements. Milder expressions include the assumption that the generation gap is inevitable, the readiness to label families "dysfunctional," the level of anxiety people experience when a family occasion requires their attendance, and the high percentage of people whose contact with their families of origin is distant and superficial.

Emotional cutoff is costly to individuals and families. It takes a broad perspective to see this. In the initial period of relief people experience in getting away from a difficult relationship, cutoff seems like a blessing. In the longer term, as cutoffs beget more cutoffs, whole branches of families lose contact with one another and the fabric of the family is weakened.

Bowen (1978) wrote, "The more a nuclear family maintains some kind of viable emotional contact with the past generations, the more orderly and asymptomatic the life process in both generations" (p. 383). This is a guiding principle for people who undertake an effort to improve their level of functioning and maturity. Cutoffs can be bridged and reversed; contact can be reestablished; and people can reclaim to a significant extent the emotional connection and stability that has been lost through cutoff.

Divorce inevitably means there will be some emotional cutoff, but the degree is variable. The level of differentiation, the intensity of the emotional process, and the attendant degree of cutoff, are key factors in determining how costly divorce will be to the partners and their families. Cristofori (1977) beautifully describes the continuum of loss in divorce:

> Divorces at one end of the spectrum produce profound losses for one or both participants. Some include multiple losses over a period of time in which each loss creates sufficient anxiety to trigger additional loss. . . . At the other end of the continuum are divorces in which loss is minimal. In most of these, the real loss and the subjective feeling of loss are discriminated, addressed and resolved. Many of these divorces are

accompanied by intense feelings at the time of separation. However, they are also characterized by successful dealing with the feelings and by minimal negative repercussions in the relationship system. In this group, divorce becomes an event for mobilizing energy in a direction of more productive and responsible living. (p. 25)

CONCLUDING COMMENT

Divorce challenges people to function at their best even though at many points along the way they may feel close to their worst. What "best functioning" means is something to be defined by each individual within the realities of his or her situation. When differentiation of self is the goal, best functioning includes staying on task with the work of maintaining a home and family; taking responsibility for one's part in the problems in the marriage; attempting to modify patterns that have led to problems; accepting necessary losses while preserving the positive aspects of the marriage where possible; keeping a clear boundary between children and the issues that belong between adults; discovering new opportunities for open relationships with one's parents and family of origin; maintaining contact with one's in-law family; seeking support from others without asking them to take a side; using the resources of the legal system and other helpers in a responsible, principle-guided way; respecting the depth of the disruption and change divorce brings for each family member; and giving oneself and others the time needed to deal with loss and change. It is possible to emerge from divorce with a gain in self-awareness and maturity, a reorganized but stable family, and children in good relationship with both parents. Many divorcing families are proving this to be true.

REFERENCES

Ahrons, C. (1994). *The Good Divorce.* New York: HarperCollins.

Beal, E.W. (1998). Child-Focused Divorce. In P. Titelman (Ed.), *Clinical Applications of Bowen Family Systems Theory* (pp. 327-353). Binghamton, NY: The Haworth Press, Inc.

Beal, E.W. and G. Hochman (1991). *Adult Children of Divorce* New York. Delacorte Press.

Bohannan, P. (1970) The Six Stations of Divorce. In P. Bohannan (Ed.), *Divorce and After* (pp. 32-47). New York: Doubleday.

Bowen, M. (1978). *Family Therapy in Clinical Practice.* New York: Jason Aronson.

Carter, B. and J.K. Peters (1996). *Love, Honor, and Negotiate.* New York: Simon and Schuster.

Cristofori, R.H. (1977). Modification of loss in divorce: A report from clinical practice. *The Family* (5)1:25-30.

Fisher, H.E. (1992). *The Anatomy of Love: The Natural History of Monogamy, Adultery, and Divorce.* New York: W.W. Norton.

Goleman, D. (1995). *Emotional Intelligence.* New York: Bantam Books.

Gottman, J. (1994). *Why Marriages Succeed or Fail.* New York: Simon and Schuster.

Kerr, M.E. (1989). "Attachment and Bonding Revisited." Unpublished manuscript. Washington, DC: The Bowen Center for the Study of the Family.

Sapolsky, R.M. (1994). *Why Zebras Don't Get Ulcers: A Guide to Stress, Stress-Related Diseases, and Coping.* New York: W.H. Freeman.

The War of the Roses (1989). D. DeVito (Director). Twentieth Century Fox.

Zweig, M.H (1996) A view of mediation from the perspective of Bowen family systems theory. *Family Systems,* (3):160-165.

Chapter 13

Depression: A Symptom of Cutoff in Relationship Processes

Pamela R. Allen

INTRODUCTION

A characteristic of depression is the inability to experience pleasure (Sapolsky, 1994, p. 197). Not being able to appreciate sunsets, the rustle of October's leaves, or any other of life's small, daily happenings makes life formless and colorless. This can be as debilitating as a physical illness or as easily managed as a common cold. Although there is wide variation in the intensity and duration of the symptoms, the characteristics of depression are often the same. People have long sought the help of healers for dealing with this common problem. Individual cause-and-effect thinking has been the dominant view for understanding and treating this symptom, and although this view has contributed much to knowledge about depression, it is limited by seeing the problem as residing within the symptomatic individual.

In contrast, Bowen family systems theory provides a new way of thinking about the symptom of depression. The symptomatic individual is viewed within the context of his or her relationship network. From this perspective, the symptom is seen as a reflection of the way relationships are operating in the nuclear and extended families. It suggests that what goes on within an individual cannot adequately be understood without looking at what goes on between individuals.

The concept of cutoff as defined by Bowen family systems theory describes the way in which individuals separate themselves from the previous generation in order to deal with emotional reactivity and responsiveness to their families of origin. The unresolved emotional attachment between the generations is managed through the distancing mechanisms of withdrawal, isolation, running away, or denying the importance of the parental family. There is no value judgment placed on cutoff. It is neither good nor bad, right nor wrong, but serves a function for the family unit.

However, the more one employs cutoff to deal with the past, the more vulnerable one becomes to re-create the same problems in one's current relationships that one was trying to escape in the first place. Lacking outlets for anxiety and support that extended family can provide, relationships in the present generation can become more unstable. This relationship instability and the mechanisms for handling it in the present generation, coupled with the cutoff from the past, can pave the way for symptom development.

This chapter describes how the symptom of depression emerged from the way relationships were operating both in the extended and nuclear families of the author and of a client. The first section is on the therapist's own emotional functioning. The next section describes my efforts using theory to reduce subjectivity and the shifts that accompanied new ways of thinking. A vignette of a clinical case, with the presenting problem of depression, concludes the chapter.

As Bowen theory guides practice, new methods of resolving the problem also emerge. In this chapter personal and clinical vignettes describe how the symptom of depression developed within two different relationship systems and the way that concepts from Bowen theory, including emotional cutoff, were utilized to both understand and moderate the problem.

BOWEN THEORY AND THE THERAPIST'S OWN EMOTIONAL FUNCTIONING

We are all products of relationship networks called families. The position we occupied within our original families has a significant impact on the way we function in all future relationships. Bowen family systems theory provides a theoretical framework for understanding the individual within the context of his or her relationship network. A central component of learning theory and thinking systems is undertaking a study of one's own family to learn about one's automatic responsiveness in relationship systems. Since one's relationship responsiveness was molded and shaped in the family, this set of relationships provides one of the best opportunities for observing, learning, and trying to manage self. Although this is a task that is never complete, the progress one makes in this area directly affects the quality of one's relationships.

Personal Vignette

A series of events that occurred in my life provided an opportunity to learn more about systems and the impact of relationships on my own emotional, social, and physical well-being. In December 1992, my nuclear family and I moved back to my home state of Kansas. This was the state where I was raised and where my parents, younger brother and his family still resided. It had been approximately twenty years since I had lived this close to my family geographically. The move also put me closer to much of my extended family, who lived in Oklahoma. My older brother was living in Arizona (see Figure 13.1).

I had always been comfortable living at a distance from my family and they also had been comfortable with that. The unresolved emotional attachment was managed through geographical distance. This relationship cutoff allowed me the space to be myself, and potential relationship problems within the family were avoided. However, there was a cost to be paid in that my own functioning was more unstable.

Since I had participated in the training program at the Georgetown Family Center while living in Maryland, I assumed I was ready for this challenge. Over the past several years I had been working on bridging the cutoff in my family. I had been making frequent trips back to the Midwest to gather family history information and to get to know the family. I felt as if I had made some beginning gains in this area and it was reflected in my functioning. I was looking forward to having more contact with my family, being able to participate in family events without the expense and inconvenience of a plane trip, and being able to raise my son surrounded by extended family. Everyone seemed to be excited about the prospect of my returning closer

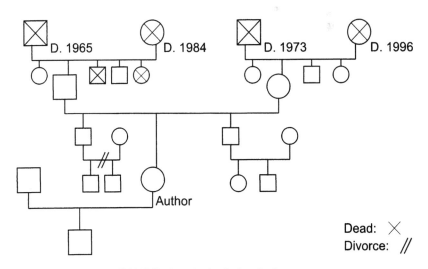

FIGURE 13.1. Author's family diagram.

to home. However, when I actually moved and started settling in, the excitement seemed to evaporate and tension took its place.

The tension was expressed in interactions between people, and relationships began to change. I first became aware of a shift in the relationship with my brothers. What had previously been a relaxed relationship with my younger brother tightened and became more competitive in the unspoken form of "Who does Mom love best? Who's doing best in the world? Whose kids does Mom love best." My older brother and I had worked out an arrangement of having weekly phone contact while I lived in Maryland. After I moved, that routine ended. He stopped calling me and my contacts with him became less regular and predictable. The relationship with both of my parents also tightened. I had always had a more relaxed relationship with my father than with my mother. He and I could talk about areas of mutual interest and I felt free to talk about myself. After the move, the "at-ease" quality of that relationship changed to distance. He seemed to lose interest in me and I also showed less interest in his life. A more constant degree of tension in the relationship with my mother developed. She seemed preoccupied with trying to make it appear that all her children were equally loved and seemed uncomfortable having two children live in the same state. My parents and younger brother had always lived geographically close to one another and they were very involved in one another's lives. My mother had developed a close relationship with my sister-in-law, in which my mother helped her out with child care and other activities. While living at a distance, my relationship with my sister-in-law was more flexible. Now, the relationship became more strained and distant as we each responded to real and imaginary threats we posed to each other. The tension was also expressed between cousins who formerly had been interested in one another. Even the contact with my aunts and uncles became less frequent, and it seemed that communication was going more through my mother than directly to me. The changes in the nature of these relationships impacted my emotional well-being, as I felt myself becoming emotionally disconnected from the family. I had not anticipated that this would happen, was caught off guard by it, and reacted emotionally by distancing from the family and blaming myself. This cutoff took the form of internally withdrawing while being in the presence of the family. This internal withdrawal was manifested by not being able to talk about what was important to me and finding it difficult to listen to others. It seemed that compromises were being made to maintain a sense of surface calm within the family.

The first couple of years of being back in Kansas were characterized by this increase in sensitivity between family members. There seemed to be a preoccupation with "who's in and who's out" and "who does what with whom." My sister-in-law was always quick to let me know how my mother had helped her out with her kids and how much she knew of my mother's daily life, likes, and dislikes that were unknown to me. My mother seemed anxious having both her daughter and daughter-in-law in the same state. Her anxiety seemed to go in the direction of providing extra love to her daughter-in-law in the form of providing favors, giving special little gifts, and siding with her children against my son.

I was miffed by these interactions. I tried to gain acceptance by becoming more like my family and hosting a lot of family dinners. Consequently, the frequency of family gatherings increased while the ability to be emotionally available decreased. There was less personal conversation, as sports, politics, and other people became the primary topics. I found myself preoccupied with relationship disturbances. Even though I was more cut off emotionally, I found myself thinking about my family all the time, neglecting personal goals. I felt as if my functioning had declined and that I was in a more collapsed position than before the move. I blamed myself for the problems in my family and pressured my husband to get me out of this mess.

From 1994 to 1996, a series of events occurred that further increased chronic anxiety and tightened relationships even more. In April 1994, my father retired, which left my parents unsure about their future and where they would live. The following year, in March, they bought a house and moved to the town where my younger brother and his family lived. One year later, in June 1996, my maternal grandmother died. My grandmother had been an important person in my life and in the life of the family. My relationship with her had been easier than the one with my own mother. My reconnecting with her over the years had seemed to give me a place in the family and to soften the relationship with my mother. Her house was also a central meeting place for the family, where aunts, uncles, and cousins gathered. I always knew I had a seat at my grandmother's table.

Following my grandmother's death, my mother's sisters started visiting back and forth more often. When my aunts would come to visit my mother, my younger brother and his family would be included in the visit, but I was not informed until after the fact. I began to feel as though I had lost my place in the family. My sister-in-law seemed to be emerging as the dominant female. She was always there to help my mother with the family gatherings and to be her "right arm." My mother did little to risk disfavor with my sister-in-law and they both seemed to be doing things to maintain the strength of their relationship. There seemed to be a growing coziness between my parents and younger brother and his family, with my nuclear family on the outside. Assuming that they had one another and did not need me, I cut off even more. This outside position was very uncomfortable, and I assumed that something must be wrong with me, my husband, or my son for this to be transpiring. All the while, the "insiders" seemed to be thriving. My father was becoming recognized in the new community; my brother was promoted; and my mother was bubbly.

My conversations with my mother were growing more sterile with an ever-present cloud of deception and pretense. I felt unable to take things up with her and would let her off the hook when her information about events did not match what had factually happened. I found myself trying to "keep peace at any price," a lesson I knew well from childhood. As a result, it seemed that tension was absorbed in me rather than being expressed outwardly in the relationship. My loss of self to the family system gave me a sense of being out of control with my own life. Daily tasks seemed more overwhelming and my world was getting increasingly narrow. I could not see my options. This sense of being out of control, not feeling on top of my own life, kept me distant from others both in and out of the family. This emotional isolation coupled with the internalized anxiety was a fertile ground for the symptom of depression to emerge. The family seemed to stabilize with my feeling depressed and in a collapsed, helpless position. However, the overall flexibility and level of functioning in the family was lower. My collapsed position also seemed to be a way of binding anxiety in my nuclear family. With my loss of self, I felt more unsure of myself and looked to my husband to be the primary decision maker. My sensing "he knew best" kept me calm and his sensing I needed him kept him calm, both familiar patterns we had learned in our families of origin.

Then, in February 1999, the course of the "emotional river" shifted again, this time with an upset in my oldest brother. He had been the one in the family to absorb the greatest amount of emotional vulnerability, although we have all struggled to varying degrees. In the recent past, he had stabilized himself with a live-in relationship with a girlfriend and in living at a distance from the family. This physical distance seemed to serve the function of providing a degree of comfort from the sensitivity and reactivity that both he and the family experienced while in the presence of one another. This cutoff seemed to minimize the potential for problems that might otherwise be present. He transferred his emotional dependence from the family to relationships with girlfriends. These relationships were difficult to maintain. After a dramatic breakup with his girlfriend he started becoming increasingly paranoid, developing some psychotic symptoms which unnerved my parents. With the loss of his girlfriend, he leaned on my parents more. My parents in turn leaned on me more, pressuring me to solve this problem. Everyone was leaning on or functioning for another, while not being responsible for self.

Now, emotional energy was going in the direction of my oldest brother. Along with his psychotic symptoms, he was having severe financial problems and his oldest son, who lived in Arkansas with his mother, was graduating from high school (see Figure 13.1). My parents got more involved in my older brother's life. My brothers have been rivals and my younger brother seemed sensitive to this shift in emotional energy. As my parents put more time and energy into my older brother, my younger brother seemed to distance from my parents and they distanced from him. Now, my younger brother seemed to move into a more vulnerable, cutoff spot in the family. This change in the balance of relationships seemed to impact his marital relationship and his emotional well-being. Each relationship was influencing every other relationship emphasizing that the family is an emotional system.

In retrospect, I think the shift in emotional forces surrounding my brother's psychotic symptoms shook things up sufficiently for me to finally start thinking about what was transpiring instead of just reacting. I also felt some responsibility for my family and I did not want things to get any worse than they already were. My parents were talking about having my brother committed to a hospital and I did not want that to happen. I also believed that if I could pull up my functioning and stay in emotional contact with the family, a hospitalization could possibly be avoided.

My own use of Bowen theory and my contacts with a consultant at the Georgetown Family Center finally helped me put together a picture of what was happening in my family. Having a way of thinking that described and accounted for how we were interacting with one another helped me to broaden my view and begin to get out of the subjective spot of blaming self or others. The next section describes how I used Bowen theory as a guide for understanding and managing myself in relationships.

Learning from Bowen Theory

Bowen family systems theory provided a way of thinking about what I was observing in my family. When I finally was able to take a step back and *see* what was transpiring between people, I began to observe the internal workings of an anxious system in operation. I was able to realize that people were not trying to be hurtful or rejecting or cut off. We were just anxious and operating in automatic, life-preserving ways. The anxiety was managed, or bound, in the pattern of interactions among people. The internal withdrawal, or cutoff, allowed us to be in the physical presence of one another without having to address the underlying relationship problems.

I puzzled over the origins of the anxiety. It seemed to be generated as much from the way that people were connected to one another as from stressors in the environment. I began to see the interdependency and intensity of attachment among family members more clearly. We were more profoundly dependent on one another than I previously had realized. This dependency seemed to create its own anxiety in the way that people leaned on and pressured one another:

> The more fused the system, the more people are leaning on each other to draw strength and a sense of well-being, but at the same time the more pressure people are feeling from each other to function in ways that will make the other feel better. This leaning and pressuring are an apparent source of chronic anxiety and relationship instability. (Kerr, 1981, p. 283)

I came to realize that what often felt like a lack of connection among family members actually was evidence of *too much* connection among family members. This idea from Bowen theory helped me to calm down.

When I got a little calmer I was able to see and observe more clearly. Patterned ways of reacting and responding were there right in front of my eyes. Anxiety seemingly had increased the activity of the togetherness force, and the balance of emotional forces in the system was disturbed. This increase in togetherness made people more sensitive to one another and more easily threatened by one another. The family was becoming more unstable as each member tried to become more comfortable. Mechanisms, or patterns of emotional functioning, came into play to deal with this instability. The two against one, distance, over/underfunctioning reciprocity, conflict, and cutoff were automatic efforts to deal with the perceived threats and changing conditions. At low levels of anxiety these patterned ways of responding worked to maintain stability, but at higher levels of anxiety the same patterns were exaggerated and contributed to problems.

Using Bowen theory as my guide, I was able to see triangles, side taking, and cutoff as part of the fabric of life, revealing the intensity of attachments in my family, not defects in me. A triangle is defined as the smallest stable relationship system (Bowen, 1978, p. 373). When one or both people in a dyad experience tension, a third person predictably is drawn in. The triangle functions as a way of managing tension in the group. I also began to see the emotional distance or cutoff between people as a reflection of the agitation in the unit rather than an indication of a lack of involvement. With this way of thinking, I was able to take things a little less personally. I was also able to see that the anxiety was a property of the entire system, based on the way everyone was functioning, and did not just reside in me, as I often felt it did. I began to realize that the togetherness force was being preserved by the way people were reacting and responding to one another and that differentiated, self-directed action was low. We were a family that was out of balance. With this new way of thinking, I thought about new ways of responding.

I tried to identify what I was doing to preserve the level of togetherness and to use that information to change my own behavior. I realized that having grown up in a family in which "peace at any price" was the motto, I was too quick to adapt, go along with, and not make waves. As a result, I had not been addressing important issues with people, letting them off the hook instead. Although this kept things calm on the surface, I was making adaptations within myself to preserve this harmony. Although it appeared that the anxiety went away with this pretense of surface calm, it was now getting disproportionately absorbed in some more than others. I had long questioned a reversal of a decision that had been made after I moved back to Kansas. While living on the East Coast I had been named executor of my parents' will. Five months after moving back to Kansas, my father told me that my younger brother was now in charge. I never questioned my father about how he made that decision, but it had long bothered me. Six years later, recognizing that this was something important to me, I decided to take this up with him in a way that was not attacking but just curious. His response did not give me a lot of information, but I felt that I was able to be more of a self with him and to do something different from my typical "collapse-withdraw-cutoff" response. The next time my mom started in with her anxiety-driven "pretense talk," I was able to say, "I don't believe it" instead of going along with her. I no longer felt as driven to function in ways to keep the other calm to avoid my own as well as her anxiety. I felt that I had more options in relating to others and that I could be myself a little bit more. I had finally been able to see how my own actions were driving the anxiety higher and decided to do something about it: "If one does not see himself as part of the system, his only options are either to try to get others to change or to withdraw. If one sees himself as part of the system he has a new option, to stay in contact with others and to change self" (Kerr and Bowen, 1988, p. 292).

I began to realize and identify things that were important to me and essential to keep me going. It was as if I had I had gotten cut off from myself while getting emotionally removed from my family. Along with taking time for self and pursuing activities to keep myself more centered, I wanted to open up relationships with my extended family. I became deeply aware of how important these people were to me. I had known them all of my life. I had shared holidays and summer vacations with them and their children. I wanted a more active, personal relationship with my aunts, uncles, and cousins. In working toward this, I encountered reactiveness from my mother. After I made a visit to her oldest sister, she told me negative stories about my aunt. I was able to see that competitiveness had been a theme over the generations and did not just start with me. This helped me to become more neutral. I was also able to see that though I came from a fairly cohesive family, in that people stayed in contact with one another, we were really quite cut off in the extent to which we knew about one another's lives. I attempted to relate in a more personal way to my aunts and cousins and found them to be receptive and open about their own lives. My mother, however, had a reaction to this and said to me, "Don't air your dirty laundry." I thought this was a wonderful opportunity for differentiation—an opportunity to be who I wanted to be in the family and not who my mother wanted me to be. This helped me to continue the process of thinking about all the myriad ways my functioning was governed by being what others needed me to be and not governed by my own thoughts, feelings, and actions. As I have worked to be more myself, relationships have opened up. I seem a little more able to be myself with others, and they with me: "The ability to be more of a self brings people into better emotional contact with the most durable and reliable support system they will ever have" (Kerr and Bowen, 1988, p. 276).

In my ongoing journey of trying to be more of a self, I have been able to see myself and others more objectively. This has been a gift. I had always been quick to undervalue self and overvalue others. This is both an anxiety-provoking and anxiety-reducing way to live one's life. Being able to see myself and others in a more neutral way has helped me to see that everyone struggles in one way or another and to recognize my own strength and resiliency. Being able to see family members more clearly has helped me to see who people are and what they are up against from their own multigenerational past. I have found that when I can see my mother's actions as reflective of her level of anxiety and level of self, I feel less angry and better able to stay in contact with the family: "The more one understands about one's family, the easier it is to reduce the reactivity and subjectivity that fuel cutoffs" (Kerr and Bowen, 1988, p. 275). The inability to see the other's reality and what they are up against had been a factor in maintaining the cutoff.

In my efforts to use Bowen theory as a guide for management of self, I have tried to use my feeling states as information about positions I occupy in relationships rather than seeing self as deficient. When I can take a moment to think about the feeling, rather than internalizing or acting it out, options reveal themselves. The options often are principles derived from Bowen theory. I have learned that it is important for me to always take things up with people. It promotes a more open versus a closed system of communication by improving person-to-person relationships and making the effort to decrease cutoff in the family. Working to maintain a broad base of family and friends that I can openly relate to about myself is another rule for living. I am now a little more neutral about the nature of the relationships my parents have with each of my brothers and feel less critical and less inclined to try to change them. They just are. With more neutrality, it is a little easier to stand alone without having to be in a triangle. Most important, I have learned that I am responsible for what I do with my own life energy and that the answers to life's dilemmas lie within myself.

Overall, it seems that the family is now a little more in balance. My brother did avoid a hospitalization and his psychotic symptoms have abated. My younger brother took some action to deal with his own emotional functioning and we have had some very open conversations in recent months. It seems that we are better able to stay in contact with each other and that there is a more cooperative and less competitive spirit. The tension between cousins has also decreased and we seem better able to recognize one another's talents without everyone needing to be the same. I now feel that my family is a resource for me.

Seeing the symptom of depression as a reflection of the way relationships are operating both in the nuclear and extended families provides not only a broader way of thinking about the symptom of depression but also alternatives for dealing with the problem. Working to bridge a cutoff between generations is an important component of symptom reduction in Bowen family systems theory.

While this involves different challenges for different people, it generally involves learning more about one's automatic ways of responding in intense relationships by going back into the family and trying to represent self in a more authentic way. Specifically, for me, this has involved learning more about how growing up in the triangle of my mother, oldest brother, and myself has had an impact on my development. Seeing how I was born to support my mother with my brother and how my efforts to keep her calm had been tripping me up, has been an important way for me to work on reducing cutoff. Assuming less responsibility for the other's welfare, I have been better able to say what is on my mind and to represent myself a little bit better. Although this has increased tension in the short run, it has worked to open up relationships and reduce cutoff in the long run. Also, making an effort to gain enough information to see how this same process has been played out over multiple generations has helped me to become more objective about the intense relationship processes in my own family.

Another way that I have worked to reduce cutoff has been to try and become neutral about triangles, without taking the "outside" position personally. For me, this has involved recognizing my own importance to the family and their importance to me without becoming critical of and cutting off from the "insiders."

The process of bridging a cutoff from one's family of origin is an ongoing process that is never really complete. However, any gains that one can make in this area can help to moderate symptoms and stabilize a life course.

CLINICAL CASE

This section provides a clinical vignette of an individual with the presenting problem of depression and demonstrates how Bowen family systems theory, including the concept of cutoff, was used to both conceptualize the problem and manage self in the clinical arena.

Mr. J. is a fifty-one-year-old married father of two children who came to the clinic with symptoms of depression. After consulting with his family physician, he was put on an antidepressant and referred for psychotherapy. When I first met with Mr. J. he spoke of having no enjoyment in life, finding it increasingly difficult to function, and feeling fatigued, irritable, overwhelmed, and hopeless. He said he was seeking help at this time because his marriage was becoming more strained, and he was feeling despair over things ever getting any better. He explained that there had been two significant stressors in the past year. His son had been diagnosed with diabetes and Mr. J. had lost his job due to organizational changes and cutbacks. Although he had been able to secure other employment, it was not as satisfying and he felt insecure about his job performance, since he was having problems concentrating. He was working in a management position in a local industry.

He described symptoms of depression occurring off and on throughout his married life and reported having been hospitalized twice previously for depression. The first hospitalization was in 1986, following the birth of their second child, and it was suggested by his wife after he talked with her of feeling suicidal. The second hospitalization was in 1991, following some family and work pressures, and was arranged by his physician for similar reasons. He had not found either hospitalization particularly useful. He had been treated with medication and supportive therapy at those times.

The initial sessions included gathering a detailed history of the presenting problem and the development of a family history. This involved placing the symptom within the broader context of family relationships and events. In the course of gathering family diagram information. Mr. J. made the connection that things seemed to be "lining up" in the family. He noted that he was now the same age that his father had been when he died of cancer at fifty-one in 1964; further, his son, who was fifteen, was now the same age Mr. J. had been when his father died. He placed some significance on this. When questioned about how he was making sense of the fact that he was having these problems at this time in his life, he saw it as both a chemical imbalance and a relationship problem with his wife. He said he felt that he could not get better until his wife changed. He also attributed his symptoms of depression to feeling overwhelmed in dealing with his son's illness and realized he had taken on too much responsibility for it. He was critical of his wife for her lack of involvement with their son's illness and blamed her for much of the ups and downs in their son's glucose levels. He was also unhappy with his new work situation but felt inadequate to look elsewhere. Mr. J. presented many areas for further investigation and discussion. Although he felt stuck and unable to see any way out, he was also interested in his situation and seemed curious to learn more.

Family History

Mr. J. has been married since 1971 and is the father of two children. He has a college degree and works in a management position in a local industry. His fifty-year-old wife is also college educated and is a schoolteacher. Over the years, she has had fewer symptoms than her husband and has been more active socially with church, family, and community activities. Their oldest child, a daughter, is twenty-one years of age, away at college, and has not been a focus of concern. Their youngest child, the son, is fifteen years of age, has a recent diagnosis of diabetes, and has been a focus of family attention.

Mr. J. is a middle child in his family of origin and has one older and one younger sister. He grew up on a farm in rural Kansas and still lives within a 100-mile radius of his mother and sisters. After his father died rather quickly of cancer in 1964, Mr. J. became the "man of the house" and assumed responsibility for the family farm with the help of his paternal grandfather. He reported feeling responsible for his mother's well-being after his father's death and described feeling somewhat sorry for his mother due to the harsh, angry manner his father had had of relating to her. His mother is still living and is in good health for eighty-five years of age. He characterized his relationship with her as distant but calm. Most of his contacts with her center on caretaking responsibilities and maintenance of the family farm. He also described his relationship with his sisters as distant and felt they were critical of him for his maintenance of the farm. Although several members of his extended family were still alive, he had little direct contact with them. However, he conveyed an interest in them as people and a respect for their lives. His mother had been one of ten children and five of her siblings were still living. His father had been the second oldest of five boys and two of his brothers were still living (see Figure 13.2).

Mrs. J. is the oldest in her family of origin and has three younger siblings. She grew up in rural Kansas and her father was a minister. Her parents divorced in 1969, while she was away at college. She lives within a 100-mile radius of her mother and siblings. She remains in frequent contact with her mother but became cut off from her dad and broader extended family after her parents' divorce. Her relationship with her siblings was described as somewhat tense in that she felt her mother favored them over her. Mr. J. described feeling blamed by his wife for the "rub" she felt with her own family.

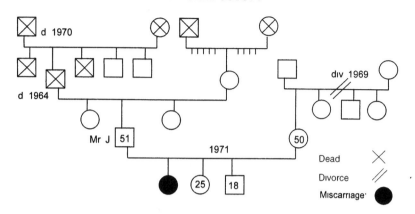

FIGURE 13 2. J. family diagram.

Nuclear Family Emotional Process

Mr. and Mrs. J. met in 1970 while they were in college. This was the same year that Mr. J.'s paternal grandfather died. and a year after Mrs. J.'s parents divorced. They had a year's courtship before they married in January 1971. They graduated from college in May of that same year. A few months later, Mrs. J. landed a teaching job and they moved to the town where they settled and reared their family.

Mr. J. characterized the courtship as intense and ideal. He described feeling sorry for his wife since her parents had recently divorced and he felt needed by her. He said he idealized his wife. viewed himself as lucky in having met her, and perceived her as somewhat better than himself. He described missing his grandfather, who had been an important person in his life, and turned to his wife to fill the void. He said his mother was happy with his marital choice and his marriage seemingly improved his standing in the family. His wife took to relating to his mother for him. In many ways this was more comfortable for him than having to deal with his mother, but it increased the cutoff in the relationship and put him in an outside position in the triangle.

In the early years of marriage, he felt pressured by his wife to be a certain way in many different areas of his life. He accommodated to his wife and tried to match himself to be what she wanted in a husband in the way he dressed and with his personal habits. They went to the church his wife chose, even though it did not fit with his own beliefs. He felt pressure from his wife to fit in with her family. Even though he made efforts to be what she wanted him to be, he still felt like an outsider with his wife's family. He said he felt somewhat looked down upon by them, especially by his mother-in-law, and felt on the outside of the triangle with his wife and her mother. He identified this as a major variable impacting his emotional well-being over the years. He felt he was not what his mother-in-law wanted in a husband for her daughter.

Mr. J. described the first six years of marriage before the birth of their first child as harmonious, despite some of the adjustments he felt he was having to make to preserve harmony. He was oriented to pleasing his wife, felt responsible for her well-being, and generally felt calmer "doing for" and having the answers for her. She frequently would turn to him for advice on how to deal with discipline problems in the classroom and he always seemed to know what to do. He felt he was carrying more than his share of the family load but did not feel overburdened by it. In fact, it seemed to provide stability for both of them.

Their first child was born in July 1978, after a miscarriage in 1977. He characterized the marital relationship as growing more distant after the birth of their daughter. The couple's level of responsibility increased along with a degree of uncertainty associated with being new parents. Mrs. J. increasingly leaned on her husband for support, and he felt more burdened by this than he had previously. Although he continued to function for his wife in many areas of family life, he said he also felt himself getting more distant from his wife. He said, "The level of responsibility I feel for her makes it harder to relate to her." He blamed himself for not being able to make emotional contact with his wife and started feeling that he was not what she wanted in a husband. He was sensitive to what he perceived as his wife "laying guilt" on him and would drive himself even harder to try to please her, to avoid a feeling of anxiety within himself. For example, he described giving in to pressure from his wife to take on the project of renovating another house after their daughter's birth, even though he felt that he was not up to the challenge at the time. He said he was feeling increasingly overwhelmed with trying to please both his wife and his mother and inept at making emotional contact with either. He started having problems with his stomach and was diagnosed with ulcers during this time.

In February 1985, a second child was born. Although Mr. J. was very happy to have a son, he felt that two children were really more than he could handle. He had not wanted a second child but went along with his wife's wishes on this issue. Their son was a difficult infant and not easily soothed. This added to the stress of having two children. With the increased level of responsibility, Mr. J. worked even harder but felt he was not getting ahead. He felt overwhelmed with responsibility and isolated from important others. In the year following his son's birth he found himself feeling depressed and suicidal. When he talked to his wife about his feelings, it unnerved her and she urged him to go to the hospital. He once again gave in to her wishes. After that hospitalization he tried to talk with his wife about feeling disconnected in the marriage. She was shocked by this information and said she wanted to spend the rest of her life with him. This reassured him. In 1991, there was another hospitalization due to a similar situation of feeling overwhelmed, isolated, and suicidal. Although there were no overt stressors precipitating this last hospitalization, it seemed to be brought on by uncertainties associated with his work situation and the continual pressures of family life and relationships.

After the last hospitalization in 1991 he said he continued his policy of maintaining harmony by avoiding subjects that might cause upset and feeling overresponsible for his wife. He described distance as being his "safety net" during those years. He put in long hours at work and his wife involved herself with the children and social activities. He said his way of coping during those years was to "get the job done" while his wife's way of coping was to "put her head in the sand and put things off." He maintained an inconsistent view of his wife as both helpless and better than himself. He held a view of himself as less-than but being in charge. These subjective perceptions of self and other coupled with Mr. and Mrs. J.'s style of operating and interacting with each other created a level of tension that was managed by internal cutoff and reciprocity. This worked well until stressors occurred that overloaded the adaptive capacity of the unit and symptoms emerged once again. In May 1998, Mr. J. lost his job due to cutbacks and restructuring within the organization. In the fall of that same year his son was diagnosed with diabetes. It was in early 1999 that I first met with Mr. J. While Mr. and Mrs. J. have been seen together on a couple of occasions, the primary contact has been with him.

Clinical Process

An essential ingredient of the therapeutic process is the therapist's own level of differentiation. This involves many variables, and a major aspect is managing one's own automatic sensitivity and reactivity to the client while keeping one's thinking alive in the face of emotional pressure from another. When I first met Mr. J. he presented himself in a fairly collapsed, helpless posture. He spoke of feeling suicidal and felt despair over things getting any better. My biggest challenge initially was to manage my own feeling responses and to monitor my automatic reaction to want to "help" him. From his history, I knew that in times past, others had responded to his collapse by putting him in the hospital. I wondered if there was a way to listen to his talk of suicide and to sit with his helpless posture without having to silence him or do something about it. Using Bowen theory as my guide, I became curious about his situation and puzzled over the degree of strength/stuckness that he brought to bear on his situation. Bowen family systems theory suggests that when anxiety is lower, people have the resources within themselves to solve their own problems (Papero, 1990, p. 83). I questioned whether there was a way to relate to Mr. J. that might allow his own resources to emerge.

Although he presented himself in a fairly collapsed position, he also brought with him an interest and curiosity about his situation. I saw this as a strength and related myself to that part of him. I found that when I remained curious and interested in who was sitting across from me, there seemed to be less pressure coming from him to "solve the problem." Both his interest in relationships and his sensitivity to relationship nuance made it rather easy to get the focus off the presenting problem and onto the relationship process that fueled the problem. He seemed to *know* what his problem was and he seemed eager to talk about it.

After several weeks of gathering information about events and the nature of relationships in the nuclear and extended families, Mr. J. came in and described the dilemma with his wife in this way: "My dependency on my wife has kept me from taking a stand with her. I have let her off the hook because I am too afraid of losing her. It has been easier to go along with her, to give in to her demands, than to say 'no' and deal with her upset." He then went on and described himself as a coward in not being able to stand up to his wife. He knew this was a major problem area for him. He had known it for a long time, but it had been easier to go along with her than to risk the threat of rejection. I thought his ability to begin to think about what transpired between him and his wife and his contribution to it was a sign of some flexibility in his thinking. I asked many questions to try to define and clarify the emotional process that transpired between Mr. J. and his wife and to generalize this process to other relationships in his life. He was able to begin to see similarities in the way he related to both his wife and his mother. He was able to see how he functioned in automatic, "instinctual" ways to relieve distress in both women and to avoid feeling uncomfortable himself. Although it created an atmosphere of harmony, he was left feeling emotionally disconnected and burdened. This way of thinking began to reveal some alternative ways of relating to important others. Through the questioning process, he was challenged to think about what it would take for him to manage and tolerate his own anxiety about the other's perceived distress without automatically having to do something to calm himself. This line of thinking also challenged his assumption that he would feel better if only his wife were different and he began to realize how he needed to be different in relationship to his wife.

At this point in the clinical process, he seemed calm enough to hear some systems ideas. I presented some ideas on emotional cutoff. Very simply stated, "the concept deals with the way people separate themselves from the past in order to start their lives in the present generation" (Bowen, 1978, p. 382). The concept describes how the unresolved emotional attachment, or undifferentiation, between generations is managed:

> The unresolved attachment is handled by the intrapsychic process of denial and isolation of self while living close to the parents; or by physically running away; or by a combination of emotional isolation and physical distance. The more intense the cutoff with the past, the more likely the individual to have an exaggerated version of his parental family problem in his own marriage. and the more likely his own children to do a more intense cutoff with him in the next generation. (Bowen 1978, p. 382)

Reducing emotional cutoff from the past is one of the most important elements of therapy (Kerr and Bowen, 1988, p. 271).

Mr. J. had a respect for and interest in his extended family and recognized that these people were important to him. He realized that the level of responsibility he felt for his mother's well-being had contributed to becoming emotionally isolated from her and from his broader extended family. I conveyed to him that the lack of connectedness to the past made him more vulnerable in the present and reestablishing meaningful contact with his family of origin would provide more outlets for his anxiety. He was interested. His own internal desire to live longer than his father had lived, and his interest in not leaving his son in the same situation he was left in at fifteen, provided Mr. J. with the motivation to reconnect with his past. One of his first trips involved visiting a maternal uncle who had been important in his life as a child. He found that moving toward his extended family seemed to be a way for him to gain a sense of control over his own life, as well as creating a larger network of relationships. This was a way to work on bridging cutoff in his extended family.

Feeling less isolated and more in control of his own life seemed to reduce his anxiety. When his anxiety was lower, he seemed to know what he needed to do. He decided to start saying no to his wife and son and to assume less responsibility for their functioning. He decided to back off and let his son take charge of his health and not to have all the answers for his wife. He worked to gain a more objective view of himself, his wife, and other family members. In doing so, he was able to see how he stabilized himself with the view that he "knows best" and that others "need" him. He was able to see the others' competence and how his self-doubt had often guided his actions. He worked to become more sure of himself and to think through his responsibilities to the family, with the idea that overresponsibility is the flip side of irresponsibility. Through trial and error, he was able to see that if he worked to manage himself and not others, it created space for others to be responsible for themselves.

As he began to become more objective about his marriage, he was challenged to think about his parents' marriage and how he fit into that triangle. He started wondering what his dad was up against with his mother. This challenged some very basic assumptions he had long held about who his parents were as people. He was able to begin to see that the level of responsibility he felt for his mother became transferred to the relationship with his wife and that the process was repeating. The theoretical idea that we marry our emotional equal was presented to him and he has tried to figure out if he believes this by looking at marriages in his own family.

On one of his trips to visit extended family, he noticed that his son's glucose levels were more erratic and less easily managed. When he returned, his wife blamed him for their son's problem, he blamed his wife, and he started to feel that they could not get along without him. It reinforced his view of his wife as helpless and he questioned whether the effort was worth it. When he talked about the family's reaction and his automatic response to give up his goals to settle things down, I conveyed to him that this reaction was predictable when someone in the family tries to do something different. If he could stay on course, good things might happen. Subsequently, he became interested in his son's glucose levels as providing information about family functioning.

At some point along the way, Mr. J. decided to discontinue his antidepressant medication. He thought it was making him more instead of less irritable. He found that when he could use his symptoms of depression as information, without feeling as compelled to "fix it," it provided him with an opportunity to think creatively about his situation. I think the particular set of circumstances surrounding Mr. J.'s life when he came to the clinic and his ascribing importance to them made him ripe for hearing some systems ideas and for making use of the ideas to pull up his functioning. He found reconnecting with his past to be most valuable in his life. Not only did it decrease his isolation but it also gave him a sense of greater control over his life. These two variables seemed important in reducing his anxiety. When he became a little less anxious, he was able to think more objectively and to see more options for himself.

Theoretical Assumptions and Questions

The vulnerability of a family system to symptom development is influenced by the level of differentiation, amount of chronic anxiety, and the degree of emotional cutoff (Kerr, 1981, p. 293). The concept of differentiation is a cornerstone of Bowen family systems theory. It is a multifaceted concept and very broadly describes differences between people in their ability to adapt to the environment. More specifically, it describes differences between people in the extent to which they are able to separate their thinking and emotional systems under stress and to guide their actions with principled thinking. It also describes differences between people in the degree of emotional fusion or separateness that exists in their relationship systems and in the degree of unresolved emotional attachment to the past. The level of chronic anxiety is a product of the multigenerational past, coupled with real or anticipated events in the present.

Mr. and Mrs. J. left their families of origin with a certain level of undifferentiation and unresolved attachment leading to the activation of cutoff as a mechanism for managing chronic anxiety. They seemingly managed this by underestimating the importance of those past relationships in their own lives while looking to each other for completion. This was a precarious arrangement and easily disturbed since it was not grounded in relationships to the past and was built on false perceptions of self and other. What had previously been a comfortable closeness during the dating period changed after the marriage. The dependency they had on each other became uncomfortable and anxiety producing as they leaned on and pressured each other to be a certain way. Bowen (1978) writes, "spouses become so involved in being the way the other wants them to be to improve the functioning of the other, and demanding that the other be different to enhance the functioning of self, that neither is responsible for self" (p. 114).

It is difficult to keep this sort of arrangement in balance and it is easily disturbed by real and imagined threats. Responding and reacting to the perceived threat of too much or too little involvement increased chronic anxiety in the system and made the family less stable. Having less inherent stability, it was harder to adapt to the real-life threats of childbirth, illness in children, and job changes. Patterned ways of interacting helped to manage this instability. This family seemed to use a combination of distance, reciprocity, child focus in the nuclear family, and cutoff from the past. When the anxiety in the system was greater than what could be managed in these patterned ways of responding, symptoms emerged.

This case has been a puzzle for me and has highlighted the level of complexity that exists in trying to tease apart and understand the mechanism of over/underfunctioning reciprocity as it plays out in a marriage. At times of heightened anxiety, Mr. J. had been the spouse who became symptomatic. Since he was in the position of the "dysfunctional spouse," I made some guesses about the position he occupied in the marriage and then proceeded with a line of inquiry to prove or disprove my initial hypothesis. My more narrow theoretical view initially assumed his symptoms emerged from a position of underfunctioning in the family; however, his verbal reports did not match that perception. He described himself as doing many tasks that were clearly in his wife's areas of responsibility, for example, renewing her teaching certificate, reminding her when things were due, giving advice, having the answers, and functioning for her in many ways. I was stumped and went down a different path of questioning, this time finding a few more clues. What was most apparent was the way Mr. J. had adapted himself to his wife to maintain relationship harmony. I began to think about the symptom as being less attached to either the overfunctioning or underfunctioning position and more attached to the one who has lost more self to the relationship system. This way of thinking seemed to lead to more clues. I looked to Bowen theory for greater understanding:

> The person most prone to becoming symptomatic is the one who makes the most adjustments in his or her thoughts, feelings and behavior to preserve relationship harmony. The one making the most adjustments may be an overfunctioning person who, feeling an exaggerated sense of responsibility about making things "right" for others, is trying to do too much, or it may be an underfunctioning person who, feeling little confidence in his ability to make decisions, is depending on others too much. In both instances the person generates and absorbs more anxiety than he can manage without developing symptoms. (Kerr and Bowen, 1988, p. 172)

I often thought of Mr. J. as a good example of what Bowen informally referred to as "being pinned down in the one-up position."

I wondered how Mr. J. had become the symptomatic one in the marriage and not his wife. It seemed that the idealized view he had of his wife; the difficulty he had fitting in with her family, sensing that she was in a more favorable position in his own family; and his cutoff in that triangle, along with his career unhappiness over the years were some of the factors that contributed to his being in the more adaptive position in the marriage. With a clearer picture of the conditions that led to symptom development, he was in a better position to see his options and to begin the process of recovering a little bit of self.

This case challenged me to try to keep my own mind neutral enough to see and learn from what was in front of me without having to make it fit with my preconceived way of thinking. In other words, I think the process of therapy becomes a joint learning experience for both the therapist and the client. When it falls short of that, I think the therapist is perceived as the change agent and the client waits for the therapist to "fix" him or her. The process of change, in essence, is a process of learning for both.

CONCLUSION

This chapter described how patterned ways of interacting lead to predictable outcomes both in the family and in the clinical arena. Feeling responsible for another and holding others responsible for one's own well-being creates one type of outcome. Assuming responsibility for self while staying connected to important others leads to another type of outcome. Although depression was the symptom that emerged in these two situations, any number of emotional, physical, or social symptoms could have developed. Although the symptoms may change the emotional backdrop of level of differentiation, degree of chronic anxiety and cutoff remain the same.

To the extent that one is motivated to take on the challenge of reducing cutoff in one's own life, one is opening up new options for dealing with the symptom of depression. This is not a quick fix, but it does allow one to begin to think more creatively about his or her situation and to tap into personal and family resources that otherwise might have gone unnoticed.

REFERENCES

Bowen, M. (1978). *Family Therapy in Clinical Practice.* New York: Jason Aronson.
Kerr, M. (1981). "Cancer and the Family Emotional System." In Goldberg, J. (Ed.), *Psychotherapeutic Treatment of Cancer Patients* (pp. 273-315). New York: The Free Press.
Kerr, M.E. and M. Bowen (1988). *Family Evaluation: An Approach Based on Bowen Theory.* New York: W.W. Norton.
Papero, D. (1990). *Bowen Family Systems Theory.* Boston: Allyn and Bacon.
Sapolsky, R. (1994). *Why Zebras Don't Get Ulcers.* New York: W.H. Freeman and Company.

Chapter 14

Emotional Cutoff and Domestic Violence

Douglas C. Murphy

INTRODUCTION

Current perspectives and hypotheses concerning the occurrence of domestic violence have been largely restricted to the individual psychological makeup of the participating individuals (perpetrator and victim), to gender perspectives, and to power and control dynamics. Although these perspectives have yielded a wealth of information and moved toward increased understanding of the phenomenon of domestic violence, they have yet to be informed by the broader relationship context in which these behaviors manifest themselves.

This lack of broader relationship context may be accounted for by several factors: the significance of the primary, violent relationship and its urgent demands for understanding and resolution; a reliance on theoretical grounds whose reach addresses only the victim-perpetrator dyad; and most important, the absence of a theoretical framework from which to gain a broader relationship perspective.

In a widely cited paper, Bogard's (1984) understanding of some "family systems theories" caused her to dismiss a family perspective of domestic violence cases for what the author conceived to be its "victim blaming," counterproductive therapeutic operational stances, and intervention techniques. Hence contributions from family systems perspectives were discarded except for a few published efforts (Goldner, 1998) that blended some systems ideas with prevailing individual and dyadic models.

Bowen family systems theory offers a unique and broad perspective of human functioning within the context of the multigenerational family emotional system. This chapter will place domestic violence within this emotional systems context and offer an additional hypothesis about its occurrence by utilizing one of the concepts of Bowen theory: emotional cutoff.

DEFINING TERMS AND PROCESSES

Emotional Cutoff

A pattern of modification of the relationship between parent and offspring from one of physical and emotional dependency at birth, through an offspring-raising phase, to the establishment of physical maturation of offspring is an orderly, unfolding process observable in all of animal life. Variations in the phases of this pattern are many, but the overall pattern is discernible.

The majority of reptiles and insects reproduce and create offspring that appear to establish near-autonomous functioning immediately after birth without further relationship with parents. In some, the caretaking function in the relationships between parent and offspring is minimally expressed as protection and it ends at a specific point of maturation. In others it is nonexistent after egg laying and/or hatching. The social insects (bees, wasps, termites, ants) represent the major exception to these patterns in insects. A relationship between offspring and other nest members begins at conception and carries on through rearing into maturation of the individual.

In mammals this relationship pattern reaches a more complex level of relationship with live birth and the dependency of the offspring on its mother's milk for its initial nourishment. Raising the offspring to physiological and emotional maturation is more protracted and the relationship between parent and offspring is extended to accomplish this process. In most mammals, when the physical and emotional maturation of the offspring has been accomplished, the parental function in the relationship with the offspring is discontinued. In social mammals a membership relationship can exist when the offspring remains a part of the parent's family, group, herd, or troop.

Higher primates (apes, baboons, chimpanzees) follow the same mammalian pattern but generally have an even more protracted relationship with their offspring before they reach physical and emotional maturation. Relationships with parents (predominantly the mother) often extend past the maturation of the offspring to form generational families of grandmothers, mothers, and daughters residing in the larger group or troop. Young males at maturation generally leave their maternal families and seek new social groups for troop membership and reproduction, thereby terminating the relationship with their parents.

In humans the parent-offspring relationship, although variable in its expression, is similar to those of other higher primates but continues after the physical and emotional maturation of the offspring to include lifelong relationship with parents, siblings, and other extended family members (grandparents, aunts, and uncles, among others).

Each variation of the pattern of relationship between parent and offspring (from no relationship, through hive, herd, troop, and family unit, to extended family) across phyla is considered to be the result of adaptive processes evolved over time in order to ensure the maturation and survival of each generation's offspring.

Murray Bowen (1978) observed these same naturally occurring relationship processes between parent and offspring in the human family in his research at the Menninger Institute, at the National Institute of Mental Health, and in his clinical practice. Through his observations he developed a theory of family emotional systems (Bowen family systems theory) to account for the variation in functioning of individuals and family units.

What he observed and later defined as the concept of emotional cutoff (one of eight interlocking concepts that comprise the theory) was variation in the outcome of the human parent-child relationship that indicated a disturbance in what was ideally an orderly and naturally occurring process leading to the mature functioning of the adult child in relationship to its family emotional system. This variation of outcome ranged from a complete termination of relationship between parent and offspring to an inability of the offspring to function autonomously outside of that relationship, a condition commonly referred to as emotional fusion.

Bowen observed that either outcome was an indication of compromised functioning for the offspring. This compromised functioning predicted vulnerability in the offspring's future areas of functioning as a competent, adult human. These functional areas included the offspring's ability to develop and maintain competent reproductive relationships and the competent functioning of the offspring's own children at the time of their physical and emotional maturation.

Bowen family systems theory states the multigenerational family and the individuals that constitute it function with less vulnerability when relationships between generations can be maintained in an emotionally mature manner. Conversely, when relationships are not maintained in such a way, the more vulnerable are members of the family emotional system to difficulties in functioning.

Domestic Violence

Domestic violence for the purposes of this chapter is defined as an act or threat of physical harm between two emotionally involved individuals who have an ongoing relationship. Such acts or threats of physical harm range from physical assaults, rape, and threats of physical assault to verbal threats of future harm.

Although there is as yet no single theory of domestic violence, certainly the prevailing causative/explanatory perspective is derived from feminist theory (Yllo, 1993). Feminist theory's basic premise is that the inequality between the sexes is intentional, with the oppression of women by men occurring through both personal and cultural means and sanctions. Domestic violence is perceived as an expression of this process, utilizing physical violence to wield power and control as the means of oppression. Since men represent the highest percentage of perpetrators and women represent the highest percentage of victims in violent relationships, this perspective has considerable validity.

Observations derived from ethology would appear to mirror this feminist perspective in that males of the majority of species are larger, stronger, and often more apt to use coercion or physical force in their interactions with females of their own species. However, variation exists. For the largest percentages of species, males and females have only significant, brief contact at the time they mate. Sustained contact between males and females, involving parenting offspring, occurs only in a small percentage of animal species. Lifelong pair bonding occurs in even a smaller sample of species.

However, nonhuman males are observed exerting physical control over females. Male baboons will use physical force when females in their harems stray away from their range. Other examples abound where the male of the species controls the female's accessibility to other males and other resources. Are these the precursors of the expression of domestic violence in humans? One evolutionary psychologist, Barbara Smuts (1992), believes that there is evidence in primate studies that can inform and instruct our thinking about the origins and expression of this phenomenon.

Bowen family systems theory is not a specific theory about the occurrence of domestic violence. It is, however, a theory about the processes inherent in family emotional systems that account for the variation in functioning of individuals and family units. Therefore, domestic violence would be considered one of a multitude of manifestations of the emotional processes in families over time. Bowen theory offers a broader view from which to understand the occurrence of domestic violence both in the violent dyad and within the context of the broader emotional system.

BOWEN THEORY AND ITS RELEVANCE
FOR UNDERSTANDING DOMESTIC VIOLENCE

The Eight Concepts of Bowen Family Systems Theory

Bowen family systems theory (Bowen, 1978) is composed of eight concepts that address the significant emotional processes in the multigenerational family emotional system. Those concepts are differentiation of self, triangles, nuclear family emotional process, projection process, multigenerational emotional process, sibling position, emotional cutoff, and societal emotional process. A full explication of the eight concepts is beyond the scope of this chapter. The reader is strongly encouraged to access the original writings about the theory (Bowen, 1978; Kerr and Bowen, 1988; and Papero, 1990) to appreciate and understand its totality.

For the purposes of placing domestic violence within the context of Bowen family systems theory, this chapter will explore two of the concepts—nuclear family emotional process and emotional cutoff— which the author believes to be particularly relevant.

Relevance of the Concept of Nuclear Family Emotional Process

The concept of nuclear family emotional process provides a theoretical structure to understand the emotional processes occurring in nuclear families as well as the manifestations of those processes. Bowen family systems theory postulates that persons forming a sustained relationship such as marriage come to the relationship with a similar degree of emotional maturity. This degree of emotional maturity is referred to as the level of differentiation, and is the outcome of emotional processes in each partner's own nuclear family. This level of differentiation provides the individuals and the relationship they form with strengths and vulnerabilities to emotional processes within the nuclear and extended families, as well as to pressures and the responses to them that occur in the larger environment.

Since emotional maturity or level of differentiation is conceptualized as always incomplete, the significant vulnerability that each relationship encounters is the emotional encroachment manifested in the relationship and the anxiety that it generates as a result of this incompleteness. This resultant anxiety is then automatically managed with four mechanisms or adaptations that constitute nuclear family emotional process (loss of functioning in a partner, projection to an offspring, emotional distance, and marital conflict).

Loss of Functioning in a Partner

As a reaction to the emotional encroachment experienced in the partner dyad and the resultant anxiety, one partner typically will begin to take a more dominant functional posture in direct reciprocity to the other partner taking a more submissive functional posture in the relationship. These functional postures can exhibit themselves in physiological, social, and emotional functional arenas for both partners, so that one partner can be healthy while the other may be sickly, or one may be more flexible and the other more rigid.

Projection to an Offspring

Another adaptive mechanism that comes into play as a reaction to the emotional encroachment experienced in the partner dyad and its resultant anxiety is projection of the anxiety to an offspring. This usually takes the form of anxiety and concern for the functioning of the child, either positively or negatively, and has an effect on the naturally unfolding emotional maturation of the offspring.

Emotional Distance

As a reaction to emotional encroachment experienced in the partner dyad and the resultant anxiety, one or both partners will attempt to achieve some level of emotional distance, either externally or internally, from the other to restore a degree of comfort. This can take the form of emotional unavailability, focus of time and/or energy on another person or pursuit, or other avenues.

Marital Conflict

The final adaptive mechanism utilized to manage the emotional encroachment and resultant anxiety in the partner dyad is relationship conflict. Anxiety experienced is responded to by conflict between the partners. Such conflict provides sufficient emotional distance for the partners while at the same time sustaining emotional contact in the relationship.

The expression and intensity of the expression of the four adaptive mechanisms in nuclear family emotional process are predicated on the level of differentiation of the partners, the degree of emotional encroachment that occurs in the relationship, the intensity of the anxiety experienced, and the broader family emotional system context in which they occur. The theory states that most families utilize all four mechanisms to varying degrees.

When the carrying capacity of each adaptive mechanism is exceeded, when it cannot manage the anxiety being experienced in the partner relationship, then the adaptive mechanism begins to manifest dysfunctional outcomes. These dysfunctions are logical outcomes of the adaptive mechanisms utilized. Emotional distance can manifest as discontinuation of the relationship. Loss of functioning for a partner can result in chronic symptoms in emotional, physiological, or social arenas. Projection of the anxiety to a child can result in his or her chronic impaired functioning. Partner conflict can manifest as physical violence.

For the purposes of this chapter, it is the nuclear family emotional process adaptive mechanism of marital conflict that is most relevant to the issue of domestic violence. The similarity that this explanatory perspective has with the feminist perspective (Yllo, 1993) is its focus on the dyad of the violent partners. Its dissimilarity is the context from which these processes originate. For the feminist theorist (Yllo, 1993), the context of these processes would be postulated as the cultural/social inequality of males and females. Bowen family systems theory places these processes within the larger context of the family emotional system, as it has evolved and developed over multiple generations.

Relevance of the Concept of Emotional Cutoff

The concept of emotional cutoff in Bowen family systems theory describes a variation of reactive responses in the relationship between parent and offspring. These reactive responses are considered to be automatic responses to manage the emotional encroachment perceived or experienced in the relationship between parent and offspring. Such automatic reactions can result in a range of responses from total discontinuation of relationship between offspring and parent at one end and the offspring's inability to achieve a functional degree of emotional, social, or physical autonomy from the parent on the other end. Bowen family systems theory proposes that the degree of emotional cutoff between an individual and his or her family of origin is indicative of the level of emotional maturity (level of differentiation) of that individual. The theory also postulates that the greater the degree of emotional cutoff between the individual and his or her family of origin, the more vulnerable the individual is to anxiety in his or her adult relationships. This in turn leads to overutilization of an adaptive mechanism and the exceeding of its carrying capacities in his or her relationships or nuclear family. Therefore, efforts to modify the emotional cutoff of individuals in a relationship or nuclear family and their own families of origin would be seen to increase the ability to tolerate anxiety in the relationship or nuclear family and decrease the intensity of reliance on the four adaptive mechanisms previously described.

From the perspective of Bowen family systems theory, violence experienced in a relationship as a fragment of a broader emotional process across generations has the potential to provide a different degree of latitude and flexibility than other perspectives for the individuals involved and the consultants working with them. Its relevance is not simply specific to the manifestation of domestic violence in a relationship but offers an outcome for addressing the processes inherent in this broader context and the potential to clarify and modify its expression.

CLINICAL CASE EXAMPLES

The A. Family: Perpetrator Moves Toward Bridging a Cutoff

Mr. A. began consultation in Bowen family systems theory-based psychotherapy three months after his wife of sixteen years had him removed
from the family home because of a display of violence in which he threw
several objects at her. This was the first time the police and criminal justice
systems had been asked to intervene in the family's difficulties. Mr. A.
stated that he had had fits of rage at his wife before, but they had been con-
fined to verbal assaults. This was the first time he had become physically
threatening. Civil charges had been taken out against Mr. A. by his wife, but
she later dropped them, and Mr. A. had been reunited with his family with
the understanding that he needed to find "help" for his anger.

Mr. A.'s family was composed of himself, Mrs. A., and their three children: two older daughters, ages fifteen and twelve, and a younger son, age
nine. Mr. A. was employed as a middle-level manager in a large corporation.
Mrs. A. worked as a housewife. The children were reported to be functioning well.

Mr. A. reported that for the past several years his wife had been more and
more intensely involved with the family's computer and the Internet. Her involvement had escalated to sitting for hours, both day and night, chatting
with persons unknown to Mr. A. This involvement had diminished her functioning in the home and had distanced her from her relationships with her
children and Mr. A. Most of the marital conflict that had occurred over the
last three years had been about Mrs. A.'s time on the Internet and her decreasing performance of what were considered by Mr. A. to be her responsibilities in the home. Mr. A. was also convinced that his wife had established
intimate relationships with men over the Internet and that she had had an actual affair with one of these men during this time. Mr. A. had no factual
proof of these convictions about his wife.

Initially Mr. A. wanted the consultant to fix his wife. Mrs. A. was not
willing to come to the consultations. Mr. A. reported that she believed he
was the "one with the problem." It was suggested to Mr. A. that an effort to
manage his own actions and reactions concerning his wife and other aspects
of his own functioning might be useful to him in the present and the future.

The following information was obtained through a thorough assessment
of Mr. A.'s family of origin by the creation of a family diagram (Figure
14.1). Mr. A. was the sixth child of seven children. His father had died ten
years previously and his mother continued to live in the family home on her
own. His relationship with his brothers and sisters was cordial, but contact

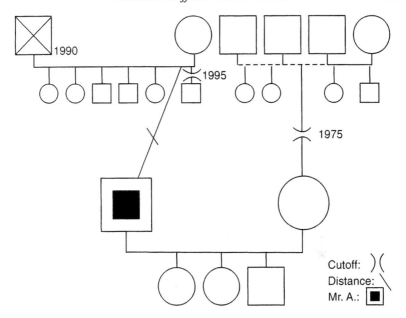

FIGURE 14.1. The A. family.

was very infrequent. One brother, the sibling younger than himself, had had no contact with family members for over five years.

Mr. A.'s relationship with his mother was one of helper and responsible son. He provided her with repair services for her home, and purchased and delivered necessities that she was unable to transport on her own. He also provided transportation for her when the destination was too far.

He was the most helpful to his mother of all of the siblings, who had infrequent contact with her even though they remained relatively close to her geographically. However, Mr. A. knew just the barest of facts about her as a person, her past life, and her extended family. The same was true for his father. To a lesser degree he had the same lack of factual information about his siblings and their families.

Mr. A. reported that Mrs. A. had been raised in a series of foster homes after her mother was unable to care for her and several half siblings. Mrs. A. had minimal contact with only one half sister.

Mr. A. found all of this "family stuff" interesting, especially because he often had thought that what he wanted for himself was to be a good father, husband, and family member. Mr. A. stated that early in his marriage his wife had often discouraged him from having more frequent contact with his family of origin because she was uncomfortable at these family gatherings. He stated that although he was annoyed by her reluctance, he went along with it and decreased his own attendance to avoid the social awkwardness of her not attending with him.

In discussion with the coach, Mr. A. began to thoughtfully lay out the facts of his family of origin, as he knew them. One fact that intrigued him and seemed to be the "springboard" for his motivation to explore his family further was his inability to recall his childhood interactions with his parents and his siblings. He could remember sitting with some of them at the dinner table each night but could not recall any other specific relationship interactions with any one of them. The reason he offered for this "lack of memory" was that he usually was absent from his family home, off playing with other children in the woods near his home. The coach challenged this explanation and encouraged him to take on the adult task of establishing substantive relationships with his siblings, their families, and with his mother.

Through the coaching consultation he began an effort to reconnect with his siblings and to have a less obligatory, more person-to-person relationship with his mother. Mr. A. found his siblings willing to increase their interaction with him and soon he was spending a considerable amount of time in contact with them.

His previous contact with his mother had always been based on his assisting her in maintaining her independence in the family home. He continued with these functions, but began to recruit his brothers and sisters to assist with these tasks, for which they willingly volunteered. He then began to have conversations with his mother about her memories of his childhood, his siblings' childhoods, and the stories of her own life and his father's. He reported that these conversations were of a quality that he had never experienced before, and he became enormously appreciative of her perspective on the family. He carried this history-gathering effort to his older siblings, three older sisters and two older brothers, and was intrigued by the variation in their perspectives.

He began to recall more of his own memories from childhood and came to appreciate how distant and out of touch he had been during this period of his life. This "distance" began to be understood as part of a functional position that he had also assumed in his marital relationship. Exploration of this idea with the coach led him to postulate the following pattern that led to his current marital difficulty: His distance in his marriage had coincided with his wife's depression, which he had rallied to "fix" by moving toward her and seeking psychiatric intervention for her depression. Once she was stabilized, he slipped back into a distant posture. His wife then began her preoccupation with the Internet, her isolation, and her functional decline. He again rallied, but his time his frustration and anger erupted into the physical expression of throwing things at her. It was then that the police had been called to intervene. These events appeared to have frozen him in place as he struggled to get her to change. He wanted her to get off the Internet, which furthered her isolation from him, the children, and the rest of the family.

It was at this time that Mr. A. decided to stop "trying to change" his wife. This was a decision that he struggled with for some time before he finally resolved to enact it in his everyday interactions with her. The desire to give her advice, to tell her that she was neglecting him and the children, to accuse her of relationships outside of the marriage was compelling, but over time he decreased these efforts, stayed in contact with her on other issues, and put more energy and time into his relationships with his family and his children.

As this process unfolded he became less concerned with his wife's involvement with the Internet and decreased his anxious concern about those with whom she was in contact. His wife in turn began to engage more in his and their children's lives and spent less time sequestered in the room with the computer. This seemed to reduce the intensity and frequency of the conflicts in the marital dyad. Mr. A. reported that he and his wife were working more often together as a team than working at cross-purposes to each other.

Each action and counteraction convinced Mr. A. that as he managed himself differently in relationship to important others, they in turn managed themselves differently in relationship to him. Mr. A. decreased his consultations to once every three months, then once a year. He finally reported in his last consultation that he was confident he would continue managing himself in the future, and that if he began to slip he would come back to seek further consultation.

The B. Family: Victim Moves Toward Bridging a Cutoff

Ms. B. had entered a domestic violence crisis shelter after fleeing several beatings from her live-in boyfriend, who resided in another state where the couple had begun their relationship. As a criterion for gaining admittance for herself and her three-year-old daughter into a long-term transitional shelter, Ms. B. began her consultation in Bowen family systems theory-based psychotherapy. Through an assessment of her own facts of functioning and her family of origin's facts of functioning it was disclosed that Ms. B. had had no contact with her parents or older brother for five years (Figure 14.2). They knew of her previous general whereabouts, but had no knowledge of her relationship with her boyfriend or the existence of her daughter. The domestic violence shelter to which Ms. B. had fled was approximately 3,000 miles closer to her parents' home than the home that she had shared with her boyfriend.

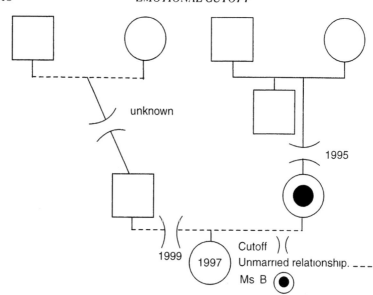

FIGURE 14 2. The B. family.

When asked about her lack of contact with her family of origin, she broke into tears, stating that they had always been critical of her. She had broken off contact and geographically removed herself by hooking up with a series of boyfriends to avoid the pain that this had caused her. She was initially adamant that she wanted no further contact with her parents or brother.

As the consultation continued. Ms. B. began to question whether she wanted to end the relationship with her boyfriend 3,000 miles away. Ms. B. had had contact with him through his mother. She had learned that he had served several months in jail for criminal activity that had occurred while Ms. B. was with him. In jail he had had a religious conversion. which he believed would change the direction of his life, and he wanted Ms. B. to return to their home to resume their family life when he was released from jail. Ms. B.'s intense emotional involvement with her boyfriend continued to make it difficult for her to keep the facts of their relationship in mind while making a decision, especially the facts of the violence between them. It was suggested by the coach that this inability to balance facts and feelings might also be part of what kept her from sustaining a relationship with her family of origin. It was also suggested that this might be an important idea for her to consider before her boyfriend was released from jail and the pressure to decide was upon her.

After further exploration of this difficulty in balancing facts and feelings at various times of decision in her life, Ms. B. decided to test her abilities by attempting to resume a relationship with her parents. She began contact with her parents by postcard and received no response. This lack of response was offered as proof to the coach that they wanted nothing to do with her. The coach then suggested that she send another postcard in five more years. Ms. B. appreciated the absurdity of her reaction and gained further appreciation of how her feelings easily dictated important life choices for her. She decided on a more protracted effort to reconnect with her parents.

This effort proceeded with letters, then telephone calls, and eventually a visit in person, which her parents made to the transitional shelter where Ms. B. and her daughter were residing. Each incremental step toward reestablishing connection with them was anxiety provoking and fraught with imagined and misinterpreted emotional land mines. In consultation with the coach Ms. B. was able to discuss these feelings, revive her ability to consider facts, and further appreciate her difficulties in staying on a decided course of action, which she had come to believe was important for herself and now for her daughter.

The connection between her and her parents was in place by the time the pressure to make the decision about reuniting with her boyfriend came due. She spent considerable energy and thought reaching the decision that she would return to the couple's home in the other state and determine if the relationship was viable for her and her daughter's future goals. She believed that her parents would now accept her decision and that their connection would continue to grow even though she would be geographically separated from them.

She was in letter contact with her therapist twice in two years after she discontinued the consultation and moved to the other state. She reported that she and the former boyfriend had married, that both were working, and that the daughter had entered school. She stated that her parents planned to visit the family at an upcoming holiday and that they stayed in frequent contact. Her confidence about her decision and her determination to continue to make a family life were apparent.

SUMMARY AND CONCLUSION

Predominant perspectives and hypotheses concerning the occurrence of domestic violence have focused exclusively either on gender issues, on the dynamic of the two-person relationship of the perpetrator and the victim, or on the individual psychological states of the perpetrator and victim. Bowen family systems theory offers a broader perspective of human functioning not limited to the makeup of the individual or to the dynamics within the dyad. Instead, Bowen family systems theory places individual and relationship functioning within the context of the multigenerational family emotional system and the emotional processes that emerge from them.

As one manifestation of individual and relationship functioning, domestic violence in this chapter has been placed within the context of this broader emotional field. Two of the concepts from Bowen family systems theory were utilized to illustrate possible emotional processes that account for the emergence of domestic violence within particular families. Those two concepts, nuclear family emotional process and emotional cutoff, were identified as two of eight concepts of Bowen family systems theory, and a thorough understanding of the interrelationship of these concepts was considered essential to the understanding of Bowen family systems theory and its applications to domestic violence.

Clinical case examples were utilized to illustrate outcomes of individuals bridging emotional cutoff with their families of origin and the subsequent outcomes in the lives of the people who took on this sometimes daunting task. It should be stated that the author considers Mr. A. and Ms. B. to be exceptional and/or fortunate in that they were curious about the broader context of their families of origin and were able to utilize these broader relationships to address their difficulties.

It is obvious to the author that further clinical understanding and research are necessary to clarify the relationship between family emotional process and the expression of domestic violence. Further clinical understanding and research are also necessary to understand why some individuals involved with domestic violence are able to consider and utilize these ideas in an effort to manage themselves more effectively in the expression of domestic violence in their relationships, while others are unable to engage or utilize them.

REFERENCES

Bogard, M. (1984). Family systems approaches to wife battering: A feminist critique. *American Journal of Orthopsychiatry* 54:558-568.

Bowen. M. (1978). *Family Therapy in Clinical Practice*. New York: Jason Aronson.

Goldner, V. (1998). The treatment of violence and victimization in intimate relationships. *Family Process* 37:263-286.

Kerr, M. and Bowen. M. (1988). *Family Evaluation*. New York: W.W. Norton.

Papero, D. (1990). *Bowen Family Systems Theory*. New York: Allyn and Bacon.

Smuts, B. (1992). Male aggression against women: An evolutionary perspective. *Human Nature* 3(1):1-44.

Yllo, K.A. (1993). Through a feminist lens: Gender, power, and violence. In Gelles, R. and D. Loseke (Eds.), *Current Controversies on Family Violence* (pp. 47-62). Newbury Park. CA: Sage.

Chapter 15

Emotional Cutoff and Family Stability: Child Abuse in Family Emotional Process

Walter Howard Smith Jr.

INTRODUCTION

Child abuse is a common problem in the United States, and it has an impact on more than 1 million children in this country each year (NCANDS, 1995). As public awareness of the prevalence of child abuse has increased over the past forty years, many treatment approaches and services have developed. These treatment approaches vary in theoretical framework and intervention strategy. The majority of them focus on individual functioning and view symptom formation and abusive behavior as manifestations of individual emotional processes and dynamics.

In contrast, this chapter describes child abuse as an aspect of family functioning. It describes how the Bowen family systems theory (Bowen, 1978) concept of emotional cutoff is an integral aspect of how child abuse develops in families. Cutoff is distance between generations of a family, and it reflects automatic relationship responses to stress and anxiety. Nuclear families in which child abuse occurs are predictably isolated and disconnected from social and extended family supports. Child abuse is not caused by cutoff. Instead, the presence of cutoff and child abuse is interrelated in family relationships that are continually changing and shifting with stresses and challenges.

This chapter discusses theoretical issues of cutoff by focusing on families with symptoms of child abuse. Studying these families provides an excellent laboratory for observing and testing theory because the relationship and family dynamics are dramatic and readily observable. The chapter views family from two broad perspectives. One perspective focuses on the

Parts of this chapter appear in an earlier essay by the author: Smith, W. H. (2001). Child Abuse in Family Emotional Process. *Family Systems* 5(2):101-126.

way family behavior explains individual variation and differences among family members. This perspective is a common focus in psychology and clinical practice. The other perspective addresses the overall functioning of a family as a single emotional system without focusing on individual behavior and specific relationship interactions. This perspective encourages the reader to view the family as a single entity that is the primary focus of observation, and discourages focusing on individual family members. These perspectives are interwoven in the chapter.

Finally, the chapter focuses on families with incidents of child abuse perpetrated by a family or household member. Children are abused in many other settings, and the described ideas must be adjusted to apply to these situations. Readers are cautioned not to interpret a focus on family interaction as decreasing the responsibility of abusing family members for their violent behavior, or spreading blame for violence to nonabusing family members. Each of us is responsible for our behavior, even if it is an aspect of a broader family emotional process. We are not responsible for the behavior of others simply because our functioning is part of a pattern of interaction that triggers abuse. Instead, this broader perspective of child abuse enlightens the complexity of how violence develops in families. The result for professionals is better clinical hypotheses and treatment interventions.

DEFINITIONS AND BACKGROUND IDEAS

Many professionals fail to recognize that child abuse reflects basic emotional processes within families. This section of the chapter defines relationships, cutoff, child abuse, and symptoms, and discusses the implications of child abuse as a symptom of basic aspects of family functioning.

Human Relationships

Relationships are a basic aspect of human functioning. They are essential to survival, maturation, and quality of life. They are more than behavioral interactions or communication among individuals. This author defines a relationship as *a condition of emotional responsiveness among people, or between a person and an object*. Emotions refer to automatic aspects of our functioning that are related to genes, hormones, instincts, the autonomic nervous system, and the relationship system. At a minimum, relationships are observed in our automatic orienting and attending responses to others, but our emotional responsiveness is reflected in many other ways. These other ways include automatic body gestures, nonverbal communications, facial expressions, physiological responses, thoughts, beliefs, and feelings.

For example, a relationship is established when we make momentary eye contact with a passing stranger and exchange smiles, even when there is no future contact. For a brief moment, there is a condition of emotional responsiveness that is mutual and reciprocal, and it triggers a cascade of automatic responses. Each person is shaping the responses of the other in ways that initiate both automatic and purposeful behaviors. For a moment, the tensions of maneuvering through busy streets ease, muscles relax, and feelings of isolation lessen. In an instant, each person assesses threat and the risks of engagement. Each person quickly assesses class status, social rank, and familiarity. As the facial muscles begin forming a smile, the other person quickly and reflexively responds with a similar nervous system response. Eye contact is established and sustained long enough to signal engagement, but not threat or familiarity. Each person assesses the level of communication to conform to social customs and cultural traditions. Not a word is spoken. There is no change in walking pace, and neither person makes an effort to sustain his or her response. Within a short distance after the interaction, each person's functioning has returned to its previous state of arousal.

This description of a short-lived relationship illustrates the great challenge in understanding more complicated ones found in social and family settings. In families individuals are highly invested in the behavior of others, and they are continually responding to one another. These interlocking relationships with family members shape perceptions, feelings, thoughts, beliefs, values, and behavior. Anxiety and stress in one family member immediately impacts others. How family members respond to the stressed member greatly shapes his or her functioning. The nature of relationships before the stressful events shapes how these interlocking relationships respond to one family member becoming stressed. Family functioning is more than a series of interactions among individuals. Family members are constantly influencing one another and shaping one another's functioning. Families have lifelong interlocking relationships and are best understood as a single emotional system.

Emotional attachment is observed when functioning and behavior are organized to sustain relationship responsiveness. In other words, we organize our lives to sustain a level of relationship response and connection. We utilize contact, distance, secrets, and closeness to sustain these connections in family and social relationships. Emotional attachment is strongest in relationships associated with surviving and maintaining the quality of our lives. Emotional attachment in family relationships is very strong, as these relationships are central to our maturation, development, management of resources for living, and quality of life. Emotional attachment does not always reflect positive responsiveness. For example, conflict, distance, stalking, and violence reflect intense attachment and responsiveness. Our strong disdain of these behaviors does not negate the fact that they reflect a high degree of relationship responsiveness and attachment.

Cutoff

Emotional cutoff is a concept in Bowen family systems theory that describes an observed condition of relationships in families. The concept is frequently misused to describe individual action and behavior. Instead, the concept encompasses unresolved conflict among generations of a family that is managed by distance, lack of contact, and avoidance. As conflict and stress increase, individuals and families reach their limits of adaptation and coping, and cutoff emerges.

Cutoff reflects high levels of relationship responsiveness and emotional attachment. Individual and family functioning are organized and shaped by efforts invested in distancing and avoiding contact. Family members often are more comfortable and less acutely anxious with cutoff. In addition, cutoff decreases family member *awareness* of attachment to and conflict with one another. Yet its presence reflects emotional attachment. Relationship conflicts and tensions are not only unresolved in cutoff but also they become quiet, persistent, and chronic. Predictably, cutoff in one generation intensifies the emotional responsiveness of family members in the next generation. Few family members associate their increased emotional reactivity and conflict in nuclear family relationships with cutoff. In this way, cutoff reflects chronic stress and anxiety, and it is an underlying relationship process in many human symptoms, including child abuse. Bowen stated: "The more intense the cutoff with the past, the more likely the individual to have an exaggerated version of his parental family problem in his own marriage, and the more likely his own children to do more intense cutoff with him in the next generation" (1978, p. 382).

The concept of differentiation of self (Bowen, 1978) is central to Bowen family systems theory and important to understanding the emotional process of cutoff in families. Differentiation of self explains individual variations in levels of lifelong functioning of family members. The depth of meaning of this concept is difficult to summarize, but it describes the overall abilities of individual family members to guide their lives with planful and goal-directed thinking and action. As stress and anxiety increase, there are greater pressures for humans to organize their lives and functioning around automatic responses to events, circumstances, and relationships. With increasing anxiety and stress, persons with lower levels of differentiation of self more readily alter their beliefs, closeness with others, and behavior. If they are fortunate to have few stresses, their level of functioning is high.

However as multiple stresses occur, their actions are directed to reducing anxiety, stress, and conflict. Bowen described persons with lower levels of differentiation by stating: "These are the people who are less flexible, less adaptable, and more emotionally dependent on those about them. They are easily stressed into dysfunction, and it is difficult for them to recover from dysfunction. They inherit a high percentage of human problems" (p. 363).

In Bowen family systems theory, one measure of family and relationship functioning is the overall flexibility of individual family members to guide and direct their actions and behavior within relationships that sustain open emotional contact. In higher-functioning families, individual members have the ability to guide their actions according to their perceived best interests and sustain open emotional contact with others, even as stresses and conflicts increase. Differences are expressed openly and managed directly. Members do not automatically respond to anxiety and conflict with distance, withdrawal, accommodation, and compromise. Instead, they hold onto or relinquish their positions in conflict based on personal beliefs, principles, and neutral assessments and observations of what is best. During conflict, differences are respected, not taken personally, and anxiety and tension are tolerated.

Cutoff limits relationship flexibility. This is not to imply cutoff causes symptoms. Some families exist with significant cutoff relationships and few significant symptoms. These families are fortunate in having few life stresses to challenge their overall ability to adapt. Other families struggle with many stresses. At their limits of adaptation, they are overwhelmed by stress and cutoff helps family members cope. But as previously stated, cutoff increases their reactivity to others, and functioning becomes guided by their automatic responses to stressful events and family conflict. Sustained cutoff in one generation of a family is one important variable to lowering levels of differentiation of children in the next generation, even when few overt symptoms are present in the past generations.

There are varying degrees of cutoff in family relationships. An extreme example of cutoff is an absence of contact between generations of a family that is sustained for decades. Less extensive degrees of cutoff include distance and lack of contact under very stressful and conflictual circumstances, but good emotional contact under calmer conditions. The extent of cutoff reflects the intensity of stresses and the family's overall capacity to adapt to and cope with challenges and stresses. There are variations in levels of cutoff among individual family members. One sibling will have little contact with parents, and another sibling will manage important emotional issues with good emotional contact with parents.

Readers are cautioned not to view cutoff as a pathological relationship process. Cutoff is an aspect of human adaptation. With enough stress and conflict, it simply emerges as a basic human relationship response to threats and overwhelming events. Cutoff sustains current functioning, even though there is a consequence to long-term functioning. In some families it emerges during a period of high anxiety and stress, and then subsides as stresses decline. In other families, cutoff is a pattern of family functioning over many generations.

Child Abuse and Other Symptoms

Child abuse is a description of a kind of family violence. This author defines child abuse as *violence directed toward a child that results in injury and has a significant impact on maturation.* Violent behavior may be verbal, emotional, physical, or sexual. It may be a single episode or a highly ritualized set of behaviors. Violence may be the omission of necessary care. In any case, abused children experience pain and harm that extends over time, limits their functioning, results in symptoms, and significantly limits social, physical, emotional, and cognitive development.

Child abuse is painful and traumatic, but many painful and traumatic experiences for children result in no injury. Injury is defined as pain that persists over time and limits functioning. Whether a child is injured by child abuse is not simply predicted by the severity and duration of aggression and violence. Some children have serious injuries after a single incident of abuse. Other children recover quickly and do well after years of abuse. Although many factors explain and predict when abuse results in injury, the role of family relationships is explored in this chapter. Cutoff is one of the notable relationship variables.

This idea is illustrated in the following example. A seven-year-old boy and his mother sought treatment when the boy showed signs of trauma within days of a spanking by his mother. The spanking took place after an incident of marital conflict and domestic violence that occurred a week before. The boy managed the incident of domestic violence by angrily withdrawing from his father and becoming sympathetic and more attached to his mother. The mother indicated that she routinely spanked her son, and this last incident was no different than previous ones. After several therapy sessions, it became apparent that the boy's perception of this last spanking shifted with his emotional response to the domestic violence. He perceived his mother's spanking as a serious threat to his safety, similar to the overheard incident of domestic violence. Until the spanking, he had perceived his only safe relationship as that with his mother.

This clinical case example illustrates the way shifting relationships in families alter family members' perception of events and circumstances. In this instance, the usual spanking resulted in injury and child abuse, though there was no apparent difference in the extent of force used by the mother. Child abuse is not simply caused by aggressive behavior. It also reflects relationships that are shifting over time, altering family members' perceptions and responses to routine events and circumstances. In the example, marital conflict and violence triggered shifting alliances that influenced the boy's later perception of his mother's anger toward him. Shifting relationships not only lead to the aggressive behavior but also shift children's perceptions and interpretations of aggressive behavior. These observations do not support a direct causal link between injury and the force of punishment and aggression. Certainly, extreme aggression injures children, but so do milder forms of verbal aggression. To fully understand the impact of aggression on children, professionals must take into account both the situational factors of parental aggression (force, duration, age of child), and they must consider the relationship context in which violent behavior occurs. Clinical observations repeatedly have shown that the quality of family relationships influences both injury and healing. Families with higher average levels of differentiation have relationships that are flexible and are better able to manage aggressive and abusive behavior. Child abuse still occurs in these families. However, it is less chronic, results in fewer severe symptoms, and is managed more responsibly.

Child abuse is a symptom of human functioning in that it reflects basic family emotional processes. The presence of child abuse predictably indicates family members have become highly responsive and attached in response to extreme conditions. As with other symptoms, individuals and families do not choose to be abusive. Aggression emerges in living things as an automatic way of adapting to threats, stress, and conflict. Stress is defined as tension, strain, and anxiety that naturally occur as our functioning adjusts to cope with change. When challenged beyond the limits of our abilities to cope, symptoms naturally develop. Aggression, violence, and child abuse are just a few possible symptoms of prolonged stress, and they will occur in some portion of all families.

Symptoms are repetitive and persistent aspects of functioning that do not readily change. As an integral aspect of coping and adapting, symptoms provide information about the basic functioning of individuals and families. For example, a husband distances from his wife when conflict and tension occur, and increases his focus and attention on his oldest son. He expects more from his son, and becomes critical and verbally abusive. These interactions trigger protective responses from the mother, and this subsequently intensifies the father's aggression toward his son. When family stresses are lower, one of the parents is able to avoid this pattern of family interaction. However during high-stress periods, the father's aggression becomes physically abusive. These parents referred their son to psychotherapy because of highly aggressive sibling conflict. In this example, marital conflict and distance are an integral aspect of violence. Violence is episodic, and occurs at points of high family stress. Even when this father made efforts to stop his aggression, he made little progress until marital conflicts and tensions were better managed.

Symptoms also promote other problems over long periods of time. They reflect an effective short-term, but ineffective long-term, adaptation to stresses. Unfortunately, child abuse is useful in reducing short-term conflicts and tensions. Aggression toward children decreases parents' tensions and conflicts. However, over a long period of time, this way of adapting to conflict becomes its own problem.

This view of symptoms and family is quite different from conventional ones. Ordinarily, families are viewed as a group of interacting individuals, and symptoms reflect individual responses to family relationships and stressful events. From this broader perspective, symptoms are an integral aspect of the way families struggle to adapt to challenges, stresses, and shifting family relationships. In addition, symptoms are not just negative behaviors. Symptoms are observed when children do what is pleasing and expected by parents and others. Many abused children excel in school and become quiet and "perfect" as a way of managing fear and violence. These behaviors are also ways of binding and managing stress and anxiety.

Family As a Single Emotional Unit

One way to view a family emotional system is by tracking the gradual shifts and changes in family relationships that occur over many generations. One observes relationship patterns of individual and relationship behavior that have sustained themselves for many decades. This historic perspective illustrates the way major events, such as births, deaths, and marriages, combine with other stressful events and circumstances, such as disease, accidents, and household moves, to shape family functioning and the development of symptoms. For example, parenting practices in the current generation of a family are shaped by cutoff relationships in previous generations. The unresolved conflict between parents and their parents influences how they perceive and behave toward each of their children. The ways chronic anxiety and long-term patterns of relationship functioning influence parental decisions, values, and behavior becomes visible. What is conventionally viewed as individual parental behavior and decision making is instead viewed in the context of broader and larger relationship processes that extend over generations of a family. Professionals gain a broader perspective to better explain multigenerational factors that account for individual variation and nuclear family functioning.

Another way to view a family is by observing it as a single, living, emotional unit composed only of living persons. Family members are related through marriage, birth, adoption, and strong continuous emotional attachment. In this view of family, there are no generational boundaries. The family emotional unit functions and adapts as a single interlocking set of relationships among living persons, guided by relationship forces that have automatic responses to threats and stresses. Some members share a household, and others live thousands of miles away. Some members are dying, and others are just born. Some have strong affiliation and constant contact, and others are distant and isolated. Some are functioning well, and others are not. Yet all of these behaviors fit together into a single, functioning, emotional unit that is continuous over centuries of time. Relationships within the family emotional unit are constantly shifting and adapting to stresses. The unit dynamically responds and interacts with its environment to sustain itself. Information and patterns of relationship functioning, viewed as transmitted over generations from a family emotional system view of family, are present in the long-term, continuous functioning of the living family emotional unit.

Viewing the family as a living emotional unit reveals its interlocking relationships that are constantly shifting to adapt to stresses and challenges. For example, a husband's conflict at work leads to his wife distancing after he arrives home irritable. The wife becomes more critical and strict with their teen daughter. The teenager distances and visits her maternal grandmother. The teen engages her grandmother in complaining about her parents. The grandmother becomes sympathetic with the teen and angry with her daughter (the teen's mother). Hours later, the husband is calmer, his wife less irritable, and the daughter returns home. Initially, there is no conflict. However, later that evening when the wife calls her mother, she receives a lecture from her about parenting that triggers conflict and frustration. After the phone call the wife complains about her mother to her husband and daughter. The mother receives support and agreement from her husband. The teen daughter spouts angry criticisms toward her mother. The father intervenes to protect his wife, and he and his daughter engage in a ferocious argument that leads to threats and physical aggression.

This example illustrates the continuous nature of family interactions, and the way generations of a family are tied together into a single functioning emotional unit. The influence of past generations in nuclear family functioning is continuous. Child abuse and family conflict are an integral aspect of escalating anxiety and tension throughout the entire family emotional unit. Aggression in the father-daughter relationship reflects continuous, long-standing, unresolved conflicts among three generations of family members.

While child abuse is a *problem,* it occurs within a relationship context of distancing and cutoff that manages chronic conflict and acute stresses.

These perspectives of family are important to understanding child abuse because they describe the relationship context in which violence occurs. Child abuse reflects both the current functioning of the entire family emotional unit as well as the way families function over long periods. These are two perspectives of the same family emotional unit. Cutoff is one concept in Bowen family systems theory that describes both current family emotional unit functioning and chronic unresolved conflict over long periods. The most accurate clinical hypotheses are derived from understanding both perspectives of individual and family functioning.

The next section describes how aggression is one automatic response to threats. The link between acute circumstances and broad relationship patterns is illustrated by how individuals and families perceive and respond to threats.

THREATS AND FAMILY STABILITY

Violence in family relationships follows a predictable course. Overwhelming stresses push family members beyond their coping abilities. The nuclear family isolates and withdraws from social and extended family supports. Stresses from events and circumstances are attributed to the actions of family members, and blaming occurs. As blaming escalates, family members perceiving one another as controlling and threatening. As stresses continue to escalate, slight differences and minor tensions are taken personally and perceived as serious threats. In this emotional environment, some family members use aggression and violence to control the behavior of others to minimize and manage threat and control. In some instances, abusive family members become violent with children that they directly blame for their stress, tension, and emotional intensity. In other instances, abusive family members are aggressive with children to manage their blaming of other family members for their tension and stress. In either instance, aggression toward children is a way for abusive family members to manage threat, stress, tension, and anger. Child abuse is a part of the way family relationships shift and change over long periods.

A key idea in understanding when shifting family relationships head toward violence is the emergence of aggression as a response to a perception of threat. This author defines a threat as *an event, action, or behavior that triggers a perceived risk of impending challenge to role, or risk of harm and injury.* A threat may be real or imagined; it can be obvious to all, or subtly communicated to a single person (Smith, 2001, p. 107). Real threats reliably result in aggressive and defensive responses by any person. Real threats are universal throughout our species. An attacking animal or the sudden critical illness of a parent are examples. These experiences challenge our safety—even if only for a moment. Identifying and responding to threats are basic characteristics of living things. Common responses to threats include withdrawal, freezing, distance, aggression, and flight. We are required to mobilize a response and adapt in ways that assure our optimal survival and sustain the quality of our lives. Individuals and families are constantly adapting to routine threatening events and circumstances.

Other threats are highly subjective and imagined. They are perceived under specific relationship conditions in a family or social group. Perceived threats are related to emotional and relationship factors. Smith (2001) illustrates this idea in an essay on child abuse and family emotional process.

> For example, during periods of conflict in a marriage, a husband perceives his wife's emotional withdrawal as threatening—despite recognizing that it is her way of managing tension in their marriage. The husband knows that his own mother's distance is a major area of unresolved conflict that he has with his parents. Yet, his wife's distancing continues to trigger strong and automatic angry responses. He withdraws when she distances, and finds he has little patience and control over his temper. (p. 107)

Poor adaptation to real threats triggers future perceived threats. For example, a recently unemployed father begins expressing irritation and anger toward his four-year-old son's habit of sitting between him and his wife. His wife defends the son. The more she defends her son the more the husband's anger escalates. Another example involves a woman who was raised in a family in which her father was verbally abusive. She is quite attentive to her husband's temper outbursts. She constantly monitors her husband's mood. If he seems to become upset or tense, she confronts him and pushes him to change. During these times, she becomes critical and controlling of her children, with frequent temper outbursts. Her perception of threat is tied to the way family relationships shift and change, and her experience of past real threats.

Aggression and violence makes sense only after understanding subtle aspects of relationship conditions of families. Frequently, what family members perceive to be threatening behavior is not perceived as such to outside observers. For example, a teenager revealed in psychotherapy that, even though her father's sexual molestation occurred only once when she was seven, she perceived reabuse was about to occur whenever he had certain facial expressions and became depressed. She responded to perceived threats of reabuse with high level of fear and anxiety. She managed these perceived threats with alcohol and drug use. The father's facial expressions and depressed moods triggered sympathetic responses in other family members. Alcohol and drugs helped the teenager manage her intense responses to him, and decreased criticisms of her by other family members whenever she had strong negative responses to her father. Family and school officials identified her problem as drug usage, unaware of its role in managing the threats of reabuse. Her father was very supportive of her drug treatment. The teen entered psychotherapy when she refused to cooperate with drug and alcohol services. This example illustrates the importance of professionals identifying child abuse and carefully examining perceived threats across the entire family.

There are not only individual responses to threats but also the family responds to threats as a single unit. Smith (2001) described this process

> [As with] a herd of zebra or colony of ants, threats trigger highly coordinated family relationship responses. Anxiety, fear and stress travel rapidly through the family unit. Roles of family members change to aggressive and defensive postures. Some family members become aggressive and engage threatening people or circumstances. Others withdraw and manage the needs of the family. Leaders and followers emerge. The level of relationship cooperation and coordination increases. Resources and plans needed to manage threats are assessed and implemented. Family members become highly attuned and alerted to slight changes in each other and their environment. Family members become vigilant, and constantly scan their relationships and physical environment for threats. Whether a parent becomes unemployed or a family member dies, threats are managed by spontaneous, and highly coordinated relationship responses. Even when threats occur to a family member who is at great physical distance from other family members, individual and relationship functioning shifts and changes in a coordinated response to threats. These coordinated responses reflect the way family adaptation is central to guiding and shaping individual and family functioning. This kind of coordination is readily observed in families with symptoms of child abuse. (p. 108)

An example is a nuclear family in which the wife sustained frequent contact with her mother and had little contacts with siblings. The husband had had little contact with any members of his family of origin since leaving the family household at age eighteen. For many years, this couple's nuclear family functioned with few symptoms and problems. This changed with the death of the wife's mother. The mother was diagnosed with cancer in late

1993 and died the following May. The wife was the oldest of three daughters and a lifelong caretaker of her mother, particularly since her parents divorce in the 1965. The death triggered the wife's withdrawal and depression, and her oldest child, a teenage daughter, became more responsible for care of younger siblings and household chores. The husband had been a distant family member, but he asserted a leadership role with his wife's depression. The family remained stable for several years. The husband's diagnosis of cancer, three years after his mother-in-law's death, triggered more shifting of relationships. The wife's depression worsened; the daughter asserted leadership of the nuclear family; and overt conflict erupted in the father-daughter relationship. Declines in the social functioning of the younger children were marked by serious school problems and drug usage. The husband's cancer treatment was successful, and this acute crisis was followed by another stable period of family functioning. Two years later the oldest daughter announced her plans to marry and leave the family household. This triggered improvement in the mother's depression, increased marital conflict over dominance in decision making, and overt physical and verbal conflict between the husband and his two younger teenage children. On several occasions, the husband/father would lose his temper and physical altercations would occur with his wife and teenage children. The oldest daughter broke off her engagement twice during this period. She married within a year of her parent's marital separation. The separation was temporary, with the parents reuniting shortly after their daughter's marriage. The family experienced another period of stable functioning.

The example illustrates the way events trigger shifts in family relationships that are highly coordinated. These shifts and changes reflect family adaptation to stresses and threats and lead to symptoms and problems. Aggression between the husband/father and his wife and younger children was an integral aspect of the process of relationship shifts over time. It occurs, and then subsides, as an aspect of marital conflict, stressful events, and shifting relationships.

The extent of nuclear family cutoff and social isolation greatly influences family management of real threats and increases the prevalence of perceived threats. The increased cutoff and isolation result in short-term relief from stress and threats. Distancing becomes a useful way of coping, and families become more focused on sustaining comfortable relationships. Successful threat management becomes defined as short-term relief and comfort instead of long-term conflict resolution. It is ironic that a family which focuses on comfort triggers an increase in perceived threats. Yet this is the repeated observation in thousands of families. In this way, child abuse occurs in families in which family members reported earlier strong positive feelings in parent-child relationships, and it predictably occurs in highly attached parent-child relationships. Child abuse has little to do with how much parents love their children and everything to do with how well families manage and resolve conflicts and adapt to stressful and challenging events.

The shift in relationship conditions, along with cutoff and distancing responses to threats, underscores the self-reinforcing aspects of cutoff. Increased cutoff intensifies the family's focus on sustaining stability and comfort, and this further increases the use of cutoff and distance as more stresses and threats occur. Families with severe symptoms of child abuse experience frequent, multiple, stressful and threatening events. This reciprocal relationship between cutoff and stressful events pushes some families to greater levels of isolation, intensity of responsiveness with nuclear family relationships, and risk for violence.

In the previous example, the husband's cutoff and distance from his family of origin decreased conflict and tension early in the marriage. His parents were critical of his choice of a partner, and there was open conflict between his mother and wife. His parents viewed the relationship distance and cutoff as leaving their son responsible for his life choices. His wife was his sole source of family support, and he was very sensitive to changes in her mood and behavior. He perceived her later depression and withdrawal as a threat.

The following is another example of the process described.

> Ed married after a long, stormy relationship with parents that he perceived as rejecting and emotionally unavailable. He always thought he was fortunate to marry a woman who was very giving, accommodating and considerate of others. His wife, Sally, viewed Ed as immature, like a child, and she enjoyed taking care of him. Their reciprocal roles with Ed underfunctioning, and his wife compensating and accommodating, developed as a chronic way of managing conflict and stresses. This pattern of marital functioning was very effective, and their roles became more polarized as stresses increased. However, when both of Sally's parents died within two years of each other, she emotionally distanced and took care of Ed less. This triggered considerable marital conflict and arguments that led to distance and avoidance. Ed's temper with their three children became unmanageable and there were moments of violence and physical assaults. Typically, Ed complained about Sally not doing enough, marital conflict ensued, and the couple distanced. While distance calmed marital conflicts, Ed became more angry and abusive with his children. Their children had numerous symptoms of trauma that neither parent associated with Ed's aggres-

sion. Sally insisted that her husband would never really hurt her or the children. and she was never afraid of him. (Smith, 2001, p. 109)

The focus of clinical intervention in this family was increasing the flexibility of spousal functioning and decreasing cutoff in social and extended family relationships. Although Ed was the most abusive family member, he was also the most stressed and uncomfortable, and experienced himself as out of control. He quickly ceased his abusive behavior, and gained more self-control with increased contacts and supports with friends and siblings.

Initially, the idea of reconnecting with his parents made little sense to Ed. He distanced as a teen, and perceived his distance as a way of minimizing and managing strong negative emotional reactions and conflict. The idea became palpable when he observed similarities in his intense emotional reactions to his children, wife, and parents. Furthermore, he recognized his violence as a parent as similar to what he experienced as a child. Sally was relieved to understand Ed's violence was rooted in his family of origin and not their marriage. Although advised to remain neutral about Ed's visits, she was clearly supportive.

During early visits, Ed was coached to observe his emotional reactions and the interactions of all family members. He began to perceive his mother's distance with him to be based on her perceiving that he and his father formed a coalition against her. He was comfortable with his maternal grandmother, and engaged her to gain other perspectives on his parent's marriage. Her view was negative toward his father, but she gave enough information to assist Ed in gaining a different view of his parents and their marriage. He began to understand that complaining about his mother not doing enough for him was his father's complaint about his wife and parents. During visits with his parents, he stopped being sympathetic with his father, and connected with his mother. Over several months, more conflict developed with his father. and he and his mother developed more open and personal communication. He took a stand against his father's use of aggression to control family decisions and other's behavior. The use of aggression with his children declined proportionally.

Sally perceived Ed's connection with his family and friends as a threat. She withdrew and became openly critical of Ed to him and their children. Over long periods, he was able to withstand Sally's threatened responses and sustain his level of contact with his parents. Sally's responses calmed, and she made substantial changes in her functioning with Ed and her family of origin. As she better managed unresolved tensions and conflicts with her family of origin, she improved her recognition and management of threats with Ed. She began setting limits and boundaries with his temper and angry outbursts. These changes increased marital conflicts and their children displayed more symptoms, but Sally sustained her changed responses and the overall level of family functioning improved.

This example illustrates some of the complexity of understanding threats in a single family. This family was comfortable and stable for long periods but this was based on inflexible roles. When Sally was overwhelmed by stresses in her family of origin. Ed was not able to accommodate and shift his functioning to take care of her. This pattern of marital functioning, even though pleasurable, set the stage for a poor response to real threats. Ed perceived his wife's withdrawal as a threat. Sally failed to recognize high risks of injury to herself and her children. The underlying relationship conditions set the stage for child abuse. Intertwined and reciprocal marital interactions intensified the perception of threat, and the failure to recognize it. Each spouse shaped the behavior of the other. As each spouse acted, his or her behavior reinforced the actions of the other. As this reciprocal and self-reinforcing process continued over time, the spouses became more isolated from family and social relationships. This isolation and distance further intensified the self-reinforcing interactions in their marriage. The entire reciprocal process was progressive, and influenced the perception and denial of threat. It triggered escalating aggressive and violent behavior.

As Ed and Sally made changes in their functioning, their ability to assess and manage threats shifted and changed, but not without considerable challenges. As each spouse functioned better, the other spouse became threatened and challenged the change. This illustrates how threat assessment and management is not only an integral aspect of violence but also integral to sustaining relationship conditions that are part of the violence.

The next section describes emotional processes observed in the most violent families. These families are violent for long periods of time, and children are severely injured. Cutoff predictably occurs in family relationships, and it is an integral aspect of both family stability and violence.

CUTOFF AND FAMILY EMOTIONAL REGRESSION

The younger the child and the more severe the violence, the more difficulty professionals have comprehending and remaining neutral about child injury because of violent physical, neglectful, and sexual behavior. Similarly, family members struggle to understand their own behavior. Abusing parents experience bewilderment at their aggressive and violent acts. Victims are confused by their various responses to abuse. Some children wonder why they did not do more to stop the abuse. Others minimize its impact on their functioning. Nonabusing parents wonder what kept them from realizing child abuse was occurring, and blame themselves for not intervening.

This section describes how cutoff is an important aspect of overall family emotional processes that lead to severe incidents of child abuse. Some families who are confronted with continual stresses resort to very primitive and aggressive behavior. Starvation, sexual assault, physical torture, and homicide are extreme forms of child abuse. These forms of abuse have an impact on the functioning of all family members and greatly alter their ordinary ways of behaving. Later, when stresses lessen, they are bewildered and traumatized by the violence and their responses. These forms of abuse greatly challenge professionals' ability to remain neutral and helpful.

Severe cases of child abuse occur in families that experience similar emotional processes and conditions. By clinical observation, these characteristics include the following:

1. Overall, level of differentiation of family members is low.
2. Nuclear families are socially isolated and have extensive cutoff in extended family relationships. When overwhelmed, they further isolate and withdraw from important relationships outside the nuclear family. Some of these families appear disorganized and overtly conflictual. Others are highly organized and are a model of appropriate social behavior.
3. Nuclear families face numerous, prolonged life stresses and challenges that demand adaptation and change. This increases relationship pressures for close, comfortable relationships within the nuclear family.
4. As stresses are prolonged, parents increasingly control and limit the actions of others in order to sustain closeness and manage conflict. Perceptions of threat increase within the nuclear family.
5. Marriages and partnerships have chronic conflict and polarized roles. Typically, the violent spouse is highly dependent, controlling, and demanding. The other spouse is accommodating, parental, and emotionally distant.
6. The use of aggression and violence is progressive, and increases with sustained stress and poor adaptation.
7. Cutoff is routinely observed over multiple generations of extended family functioning. The nuclear family with severe incidents of child abuse is proportionately more cutoff within extended family relationships.

As nuclear family cutoff and social isolation increase, family members become increasingly guided by primitive and basic emotions. These relationship conditions greatly distort perception and thinking. Children are perceived as adults and caretakers of parents. Behavior that others find aggravating and threatening is viewed as intentional and purposeful. Adults and children witness violence and ignore or minimize it. Adults have increasingly more difficulty perceiving the needs and best interests of children separate from their emotional reactions to them and others. As emotional attachment builds and family members become highly dependent on one another, they readily perceive threats in small changes in the functioning of others. Differences in ideas, feelings, and behavior trigger perceptions of threat, which in turn trigger aggressive and distancing behaviors. These conditions foster secretive behavior, impulsive acts, coalitions to manage conflict and threat, and blaming. Family members feel trapped and controlled by others. This justifies their using aggressive, withdrawing, and distancing behaviors to manage threats. Violent behavior is blamed on the people triggering it, not on the actor.

These emotional conditions in families describe emotional regression. Bowen (1978) developed the idea of emotional regression in a family as a response to sustained anxiety and stress. He stated, "Regression occurs in response to sustained anxiety, and not in response to acute anxiety. If there is regression with acute anxiety, it disappears when the anxiety subsides. Regression occurs when the family, or society, begins to make important decisions to allay the anxiety of the moment" (p. 277). Prolonged stress triggers family members to push others to change in order to increase comfort and ease threats. If these pressures win out and are sustained over time, a new norm is established in the family. There is an overall decline in each family member's ability to assume personal responsibility for his or her own functioning and take action based in his or her own best interests. There is increasing relationship pressure to function in ways that sustain relationship stability and decrease tensions. Children and adults relinquish self for the stability of the family. The regressing nuclear family unit increasingly perceives its safety in sustaining a high level of involvement and agreement. This process is complemented with more cutoff and distance from extended family and social relationships.

Nuclear family emotional regression does not occur without high levels of cutoff between the nuclear family and other branches. The regressing nuclear family begins functioning like a pressure cooker. As stresses heat up family relationships, pressures increase toward more involvement, contact, and attachment. Family members previously relied on their interdependency to relieve stress and anxiety. Now, they blame other family members for their own tensions, anxiety, and problems. In families that sidetrack violence, this increased pressure results in nuclear family members distancing and engaging extended family and social relationships as a way of coping. In regressing families with severe incidents of child abuse, increasing relationship pressures toward fusion in the nuclear family are mirrored by increasing relationship cutoff and distance in extended family and social relationships.

This tightens the lid on the pressure cooker. It is as if the family is continually banding together to fight external threats. The banding together increases a perception that the threat is external, and this drives more togetherness pressures and blame within the nuclear family. In addition, it drives more perceived threats within the nuclear family. All of the many stresses and threats of life have to be managed by a small set of family relationships that are already overwhelmed and taxed. These families have little capacity for self-correction and leadership, as they make decisions and act as if there are few, if any, important differences in experience and thinking among them. Aggression is used to control the threatening behavior of others, and family members are so regressed and sensitive to threat that any slight difference triggers perceived threat and aggression. These conditions set the stage for chronic and severe child abuse.

As the family heats up with more stresses and real threats, infantile and primitive behaviors emerge in family members. Abusive family members engage in patterned sexual and physical violence with children. Nonabusing members ignore signs and indicators of violence or overtly and covertly sanction it. Abused children develop severe symptoms, and their maturation is greatly limited. Children emotionally distance in family and social relationships in efforts to gain some self-regulation. Some children overfunction and become what parents and others expect. Some become aggressive with siblings and other children as a way of managing their own pain and injury. Others may have their social, cognitive, emotional, and physical functioning greatly limited and suffer long-term consequences at great cost to their growth and development.

In all of these ways, emotional regression reflects high levels of chronic anxiety and stress, although family members early in a regressive process experience comfort and calm. There are high levels of unresolved conflicts among generations in the extended families and between spouses. Distorted thinking of family members is evident in their normalizing abusive and violent behavior. Children are blamed for the violence and dehumanized. Sometimes they are perceived as self-sufficient adults who require no parental nurturing and protection. Other times they are objectified and treated as if they existed merely to help parents manage their lives. Parents' personal values and principles are suspended in an emotional regression. The family is highly stuck together, and functions as a single undifferentiated unit, with little individuality. There is little room for individual members to act in their own best interest. There is a great deal of relationship pressure to function in ways that sustain relationship stability and comfort, and avoid conflict. This increases perceived threats. Stressful and threatening events trigger more cutoff and distance, increasing emotional regression.

This is one irony for parents in these families. Parents made significant efforts for their children not to experience the pains, tensions, and conflicts of their own childhoods. They distance and cut off from their families of origin to cope. Yet cutoff increases the likelihood that patterns that led to violence in the past generations are replicated. Cutoff in family-of-origin relationships merely mirrors the ongoing family emotional process for many generations. Commonly, their parents managed past conflicts with their own parents in the same way.

Differences between the family's view of itself and the view of outside observers are dramatic. The disclosure of child abuse in regressed families triggers very strong emotional responses from family members, and they respond to disclosure as a serious threat. Disclosing children are blamed for family and legal problems. The intervention of professionals and legal authorities disrupts stability, and new professional relationships are pressed into the family. Often, children and adults are removed from households and the traditional patterns of family contact change dramatically. Nonabusing spouses protect and defend abusive family members. Children blame themselves for the violence and for disrupting the family by disclosing. They experience strong pressures to recant disclosures of abuse. Anxiety, previously managed by cutoff and social isolation, escalates and new symptoms emerge. Marriages and partnerships become either highly conflictual or more fused, and couples band together against authorities. Some families remain regressed and oppose interventions by professionals. Other families develop sharp relationship polarization, in which some family members oppose interventions and others become dependent on professionals. Both responses trigger strong emotional responses from professionals. Many professionals become frustrated with the family's reluctance to receive help. Others take sides in the polarized family relationship field.

This process is illustrated by a family referred for psychotherapy after four years of sexual abuse between the father and three of his daughters. All five of the couple's children were removed by child welfare authorities and taken to foster home and group home placements after the mother supported her husband's denial of the abuse allegations. The husband was arrested and faced serious criminal charges. Child welfare authorities were very angry at this mother's refusal to support her children. All of the children, except the child who disclosed, wanted to return home and resume previous family life. Therapists and helping professionals became angry and frustrated with the parents' resistance to clinical services and the mother's support of her husband. At their first visit, the couple described a long period of harmonious early family life that was disrupted by allegations of abuse. They reported more than fifteen major stressful events over the past decade that triggered increasing cutoff and social isolation. Since disclosure, the couple was in physical contact constantly. She went to work with her husband each day, and they had no friends and very occasional contacts with family members. The early sessions of psychotherapy were almost entirely focused on their allegations of child welfare authorities conspiring to take their children.

Personal reactions to the severity of the child abuse and the reactions of other professionals and the legal system challenged establishing a nonblaming professional and clinical relationship with this couple. However, conflict between the couple and professionals sustained the couple's functioning. A nonblaming clinical position with the family triggered criticisms by other professionals and legal authorities and increased the couple's perception of treatment as a threat. At one point the couple complained about the treatment to legal authorities, who encouraged them to seek other services. Simultaneously sustaining open, neutral, and well-engaged relationships with the couple and all professionals involved in their life led to better management of shifting relationship coalitions and alliances throughout the treatment.

Sustaining a clinical position of not taking sides in the family and social service system led to open discussions about the abuse and the couple's roles and responsibilities. Marital conflict increased as levels of cutoff and regression gradually declined. Although these children were never returned from foster home and group home placements to their parents' care, the mother was able to reestablish relationships with each of them. Her ability to better manage her and her husband's responsibility for the abuse greatly improved the children's ability to cope with the abuse and its aftermath.

Ironically, the longer regressing families focus on sustaining comfortable and stable relationships, the more instability these families experience. Cutoffs limit relationship flexibility, and continuing stressful events heat up family relationships. The family's automatic response is more nuclear family fusion, extended family cutoff, and social isolation. It is striking to observe the extent to which these families lack the ability to self-correct and try alternative strategies of coping. They appear to *lock in* to fixed patterns of relationship functioning. In the most severe cases of child abuse, this downward cycling process ultimately results in the death of a child.

MANAGING CUTOFF AND FAMILY EMOTIONAL REGRESSION IN PROFESSIONAL SETTINGS

Emotionally regressed families with symptoms of child abuse are common in many professional settings. Professionals are quite challenged by the family's emotional intensity and resistance to engaging in clinical relationships. This section briefly discusses general clinical strategies for managing emotional processes of cutoff and emotional regression.

The first responsibility for professionals is assuring safety of family members, particularly the most vulnerable ones. The most vulnerable members usually are children, but not always. Protecting these individuals can be done without taking sides in family conflicts and tensions. It is important that professionals recognize that the symptoms and problems children experience because of violence in families are not pathological. Children are supposed to struggle and have symptoms when raped or assaulted by family members. Treating children and families for symptoms and problems of vi-'olence without managing safety concerns is unethical. poor clinical practice, and ultimately blames children for their symptoms. This does not mean professionals are to assume full responsibility for creating safety in families, but it limits the circumstances in which families are accepted into helping services. Child welfare and other legal authorities must lead professional interventions and services when there is imminent and high risk for domestic violence and child abuse.

Although these families have numerous problems, the challenge for professionals is managing their own emotional responses to the family. Professionals must respect the usefulness and importance of cutoff and emotional regression in managing a host of continuing stresses and threats. To an outside observer, the problems and challenges the family confronts often appear simple and straightforward. However, under regressed emotional conditions, family member perceptions, thinking, problem-solving abilities, and judgments are greatly distorted by high levels of anxiety in relationships, low levels of maturity, strong emotions. isolation and cutoff, and chronic stresses and threats. Banding together and distancing assist families in managing stresses and problems. Professionals are well advised to not strengthen cutoff and regression by trying to take control of the family, unless safety and loss of life are at stake. Failing to respect the usefulness of cutoff and regression results in overly simplistic hypotheses and plans for services, and ineffective interventions. Often. the controlling behavior of professionals merely strengthens emotional regression. The family reorganizes around a perception of the professional as a threat. and the family's average level of functioning and emotional regression increase concurrently.

Professional errors with these families fall into two general categories: (1) excessive anger, frustration, and distance and (2) excessive accommodating and flexibility. It is common for professionals to feel excessive sympathy for abused children and excessive anger for abusing parents. Both of these emotional responses are problematic. and each creates specific pitfalls. Both of these strong emotional responses influence professional decision making, judgment, and clinical practice. Ironically, many professionals make the same mistake as regressing family members: assuming positive and compassionate feelings for others must result in positive relationship outcomes. Excessive positive and sympathetic responses to family members result in professionals failing to identify their errors. There is a decline in self-correcting activities, and clinical relationships are less well managed.

Families with severe cases of abuse test the professionals' level of differentiation of self. The emotional intensity of these families is contagious, and many professionals take sides for or against certain family members. Although overaccommodating professional behaviors result in higher levels of family cooperation and engagement in services, they also foster immature, regressed, and less responsible family behavior. Successful clinical management of these families requires professionals to engage with the family without trying to change (control) the way it functions. Such successful efforts usually trigger the family's initial perception of the professional as a threat. A professional sustaining a neutral stance challenges the family's isolation and emotional withdrawal. Yet professionals who maintain a consistent neutral stance with families will be successful in engaging them, and they have a high probability of offering resources and services that the family values. Professionals remain clinically neutral with emotionally regressing families when theory, clinical hypotheses, and neutral observations guide their professional practice.

A most difficult clinical challenge for professionals is managing their relationships with other professionals and colleagues. Often, families with symptoms of child abuse have multiple mental health and social service professionals involved with various family members. A common problem is professionals banding together against some family members. High levels of agreement among professionals trigger threats in families. This family behavior further triggers professionals perceiving family members as a threat, which triggers aggressive professional behavior. Professionals show aggression by removing children from families, taking control of services, and terminating services early. Agencies and organizations that exclusively serve these families are at risk of finding themselves emotionally regressed. In regressed organizations, burnout is high, professionals are aggressive with *uncooperative* families, and there is little professional accountability. Professional responses to individual families become more shaped by a drive to manage professional threat than by the work of managing child abuse in families.

Ironically, professionals are challenged to better manage their behaviors in emotionally regressed work settings in the same ways family members are challenged by regression in their families. Professionals and family members who make efforts to guide their individual functioning by solid thinking, principles, and beliefs that provide a less reactive and more steady course can be very helpful to others during a family or organizational regression. In his writings about societal regression, Murray Bowen (1978) describes the process of a person disrupting regression by improved individual functioning:

> Increasing individuation is slow and difficult and it takes place only with a disciplined decision to stay on principled course in spite of the urge to return to the togetherness. A successful attempt usually comes after several failures. When he is finally able to maintain his course without getting angry with the opposition, the opposition does a final intense emotional attack. If he remains calm with this, the opposition becomes calm and pulls up to his level of individuality. Now the family is in a bit more harmony with a bit more individuality. (p. 278)

Professionals who establish clinical relationships that do not oppose the family or overaccommodate the family, and who guide their clinical behavior by theory and clinical hypotheses that enable respect for the family's struggles, are very useful to emotionally regressed families and organizations. Family members and colleagues will eventually appreciate the neutrality by initially expressing some opposition and resistance to services, but over longer periods of time seek out the clinician as a caring, concerned, and thoughtful resource for learning and growth. Clinicians can openly express their opposition to abusive behavior without opposing the family and taking sides. Professional colleagues can disagree with one another without threat or taking it personally. Gradually some family members will begin to make their own moves toward individuation. Often, these moves create intense conflicts and family anxiety soars again. However, the clinician remaining steady and self-defined serves as an effective guidepost for continued family growth and maturity.

SUMMARY

This chapter described how child abuse is violent behavior that emerges in families under certain relationship conditions and processes. The described emotional processes do not cause child abuse. Stressful events, perceptions of threat, and aggressive responses to threats that are directed toward children combine with these broad conditions to create violent behaviors. Broad conditions that set the stage for child abuse are present for long periods of time in families. Often, professionals assume these broad conditions are negative and conflictual behaviors and circumstances. This chapter described these behaviors as both problematic and useful. Distance and cutoff in family relationships reduce overt conflict and anxiety, and many nuclear families have years of pleasurable family life under cutoff conditions. Yet cutoff reduces flexibility and adaptability, and with acute stresses these families are at risk of resorting to primitive behavior to manage stresses and threats.

The overall broad conditions that are an integral part of child abuse are best understood as an emotional regression of the nuclear family emotional unit. During emotional regression, nuclear families are socially isolated, and cutoff exists in extended family relationships. Cutoff increases emotional attachment and this is observed as less contact with extended family relationships and increased responsiveness and emotional reactivity among nuclear family relationships. When professionals fail to understand how emotional regression has an impact on the functioning of the family unit, the result is overly simplistic hypotheses and interventions in an effort to *change* the family. The risk of child abuse reoccurring is strongly related to the presence of emotional regression and cutoff. Successful clinical interventions must address both immediate concerns of injury and violence and long-term risk factors of social isolation and cutoff.

Although this chapter focuses on child abuse, cutoff, emotional regression, and violence are common in many human social groups, organizations, and families. Stalking, school shootings, and violence in businesses and sports teams are illustrations of how violent persons manage perceived threats under similar, broad emotional conditions. It is the way combined, broad relationship processes and specific factors occur that predicts the occurrence of violence. This view of violent behavior shifts from a focus on violent individuals to a focus on persons becoming violent under specified relationship conditions.

REFERENCES

Bowen, M. (1978). *Family Therapy in Clinical Practice*. New York: Jason Aronson.
NCANDS (1995). Child Maltreatment 1993: Reports from the States to the National Center on Child Abuse and Neglect. April. Washington, DC: U.S. Government Printing Office.
Smith, W.H. (2001). Child Abuse in Family Emotional Process. *Family Systems*, 5(2):101-126.

PART IV:
SOCIETAL APPLICATIONS

Chapter 16

Emotional Cutoff and Societal Process: Russia and the Soviet Union As an Example

Katharine Gratwick Baker

INTRODUCTION

This chapter explores the interlocking relationship between Bowen's concepts of emotional cutoff and societal process. Emotional cutoff has generally been discussed as a process and a mechanism for managing anxiety in multigenerational family relationships. However, there are aspects of the concept that may also be relevant for understanding societal process and the relationships between large social units over time.

The chapter is divided into four sections following the introduction. The first section briefly defines the concepts of emotional cutoff and societal process, as developed by Murray Bowen (1978). The second section focuses on the relationship between the two concepts at a theoretical level, describing the links between cutoff within an individual, within families, and in larger social groups. The third section presents an example of emotional cutoff at the societal level in the Soviet Union and postsoviet Russia. The fourth section discusses emotional cutoff as providing a generic perspective for understanding societal disruptions.

Russia was chosen as a focus for this study because the author had an opportunity to travel there frequently during the 1980s and 1990s as a neutral observer of a society going through political, economic, and social transitions as the Soviet Union came to an end and this new Russian Federation emerged. There is no assumption in this chapter that Russia has been more regressed than any other society over the long span of its recorded history, although cutoff seems to have been associated with many of Russia's domestic and international relations during the twentieth century.

Concrete manifestations of societal cutoff in the soviet system (1917-1990), such as governmental policies of secrecy, denial of the historical past, press censorship, and limitations on travel and communication across national borders, are discussed. The potential connection between these soviet policies and contemporary difficulties in postsoviet Russia is also considered, but without the assumption of a cause-and-effect relationship. In other words, cutoff as a mechanism for managing anxiety does not *cause* problems, but is often associated with them, both in the family and in larger social groups.

This chapter also speculates on a number of societal issues that may be related to patterns of societal cutoff, such as human health, life expectancy, and environmental stewardship. In addition, the chapter discusses ways in which Bowen theory and the concept of cutoff may provide a useful framework for understanding the fluctuations of societal process over long periods of history.

DEFINITIONS OF THE CONCEPTS

Emotional Cutoff

Murray Bowen developed the concept of emotional cutoff over a twenty-year period, as he observed patterns of relationships across several generations of human families. Bowen was searching for a concept that could be applied to a broad range of behaviors and responses between parents and their offspring over time, including multigenerational patterns of unresolved emotional attachment. He observed that these behaviors and responses naturally reflect the level of differentiation or maturity of the individual and his or her family.

At the higher end of the scale of differentiation, families are able to keep in "some kind of viable emotional contact with the past generations" (Bowen, 1978, p. 383). Viable emotional contact with the parental generation occurs when both parents and offspring are respectful and open with regard to expressing thoughts and feelings, as well as sharing significant life experiences with one another. It also permits adequate breathing room for the younger generation to develop mature, intimate adult relationships, create new families, and raise children.

In the middle range of the scale, parents and offspring may have regular and friendly contact, but this contact often is fairly formalized and usually does not include significant emotional openness with regard to the ups and downs of daily life.

At the lower end of the scale, such behaviors and responses as isolation, withdrawal, running away, or denying the importance of the parental family can be observed in the face of stress and anxiety.

Cutoff is an emotional relationship process in which parents and their offspring respond to anxiety in the relationship by automatically shutting down their emotional connections. Mutual sensitivity continues to be intense, but behavior is distant. Emotional distancing can be observed as a decrease in the ability to share thoughts and feelings. Physical distancing, such as a geographic move, may occur at an automatic level or it may be consciously chosen in order to avoid regular contact. Usually physical distance will reinforce emotional distance, but it is not an essential aspect of the concept, since people can live together and still be cut off from one another. Cutoff behaviors and responses are reciprocal between parents and offspring, and either generation can be the initiator.

Kerr (Kerr and Bowen, 1988) notes that "people cut off from their families of origin to reduce the discomfort generated by being in emotional contact with them" (p. 271). He observes that cutoff can reduce acute anxiety in the short term, but that over the long term cutoff will lead to an increase in chronic anxiety because of the absence of stabilizing relationships with the family of origin. If cutoff recurs over a number of generations, individuals in these families are more vulnerable to developing emotional, physical, and social symptoms. Kerr also writes that "the more complete the cutoff with the past, the more likely it is that a more intense version of the past (or its mirror image) will be repeated in the present" (p. 272).

Societal Process

Murray Bowen began to think about the apparent parallels between emotional patterns in the family and in society during the 1940s (Bowen, 1978, p. 269). He believed that "man is an evolving form of life, ... more related to lower forms of life than he is different from them, ... and that the instinctual forces that govern all animal and protoplasmic behavior are more basic in human behavior than most theories recognize" (p. 270). He was searching for commonalities in human functioning that were not culture-bound but would apply to all members of the species to some degree. It seemed logical to Bowen, therefore, that any description of societal process would have to be "in basic accord with man as a biological-instinctual animal" (p. 270).

For many years Bowen searched for an explanation grounded in the natural sciences that could account for the cyclical fluctuations of social adaptation over long historical periods. He also searched for a baseline for describing the ups and downs of societal process and came to the conclusion that some version of his descriptive "differentiation of self scale" (see Bowen, 1978, pp. 472-475) could be developed for describing the observable variation in societal process. The components of this societal scale of differentiation would have to be drawn from natural facts rather than cultural facts about larger social systems observed over time. These natural facts would be linked to natural sources of anxiety in social systems, such as changes generated by the human population explosion, the disappearance of new habitable land, the approaching depletion of raw materials necessary to sustain life on earth, and natural disasters such as earthquakes or tidal waves (p. 272). Cultural facts would be linked to a more subjective process within the society and would include such phenomena as religion, politics, and economic systems.

In 1972, Bowen was invited by the Environmental Protection Agency to present a paper for a symposium on the environmental crisis of that period. Preparation for that symposium led him to develop a new concept that he first referred to as "societal regression" and then later modified to become "emotional process in society." With this concept and through the application of systems thinking, including observations of emotional triangles, Bowen began to develop a logical bridge between what he described as "emotional process" in both the human family and in larger human social systems.

For example, Bowen (1978) observed patterns of response in parents of delinquents and noted that these parents tended to "give in to their [children's] demands to allay the anxiety of the moment, hoping this will solve the problem. This sets the stage for new and greater demands and threats" (p. 275). At the societal level, Bowen observed that public officials had also become increasingly "permissive" in the way they responded to pressures from clamorous social groups. He noted that, "operationally, the vocal segment of society is in the position of the anxious teenager who is driven by anxiety and who is demanding rights, and the public official is in the position of the unsure parent who gives in to allay the anxiety of the moment. . . . Societal pressure is directed first at those who are most unsure of self, and most vulnerable to pressure. Then it extends to others" (pp. 275-276), and can become a prevailing response to social problems. The parallel in parental and societal responses to the demands for "rights" was striking to Bowen, and led him to a beginning articulation of the concept of *societal emotional process.*

In developing this concept Bowen used the term *emotional* as it had been used by Darwin. According to Darwin, *emotional* was not synonymous with *feeling,* but referred to automatic patterns of behavior and response that were common to all living species and to all social groups to some degree. As Bowen wrote, emotion

... includes the automatic forces that govern protoplasmic life. It includes the force that biology defines as instinct, reproduction, the automatic activity controlled by the autonomic nervous system, subjective emotional and feeling states, and the forces that govern relationship systems. . . . In broad terms, the emotional system governs the "dance of life" in all living things. [In contrast], a "feeling" is considered the derivative of a deeper emotional state as it is registered on a screen within the intellectual system. (Bowen, 1978, p. 305)

Bowen's use of the term *emotion* in larger social units referred to the automatic forces within social groups that drive such natural processes as the survival and perpetuation of the species, protection of the social unit, kinship connections, the search for food, and conflicts relating to territoriality. He described social groups as emotionally "regressed" when the anxiety generated by these automatic forces is predominant.

Bowen (1978) noted that

... there are striking analogies between regression in a family and regression in larger social groups and society. Regression occurs in response to chronic sustained anxiety, and not in response to acute anxiety. . . . Regression occurs when the family, or society, begins to make important decisions to allay the anxiety of the moment. (p. 277)

He also observed that a balance of togetherness and individuality forces operate both in the family and in larger social systems.

As chronic anxiety increases and the social unit moves in the direction of regression, decisions are driven more by togetherness forces than by individuality forces. According to Bowen, extreme societal regression or

... the endpoint of too much togetherness [on the societal level] comes with viable members leaving to join other groups and the others huddled in impotent fear, so close they live in "piles" and so alienated they still clamor for togetherness which further increases the alienation, or they become violent and start destroying each other. (1978, p. 278)

When "viable" or potentially responsible members of a social group leave to join other groups and the original group begins to destroy itself, that situation could be described as an end point for "togetherness," but also as an end point for emotional cutoff, as the group begins to cut off from its original definition of "self."

Togetherness "is a biologically rooted life force that propels an organism to follow the directives of others, to be a dependent, connected, and indistinct entity" (Kerr and Bowen, 1988, p. 65). Too much togetherness in the context of low levels of differentiation is an outcome of intense chronic anxiety, and can lead to distance and cutoff. Theoretically, therefore, togetherness and cutoff are mirror-image reactive processes linked to chronic anxiety, with intense togetherness usually preceding cutoff. As the togetherness force grows stronger, both the need for and the allergy to the relationship grow stronger. Responses to intense togetherness could include both implosion (collapsing inward or fusion) and explosion (exploding outward or fragmentation). Cutoff is one of a number of mechanisms for managing these responses.

In contrast to the togetherness force, individuality "is a biologically rooted life force that propels an organism to follow its own directives, to be an independent and distinct entity" (Kerr and Bowen, 1988, p. 64). In addition, in Bowen theory, it "refers to the capacity to be an individual while *part of a group*" (Kerr and Bowen, 1988, p. 63). When individuality is discussed in the context of societal process, it usually refers to the functioning of individual members of the society, particularly those in leadership positions who define a direction for larger social units. To the extent that a critical mass of societal leaders functions with self-definition and independent thinking, while also maintaining a responsible connection to the wider social group, the society might be said to be less regressed.

A full explication of the concept of societal process requires the development of a scale of differentiation for social groups. Such an undertaking is beyond the scope of this chapter; however, some assumptions can be made about such a hypothetical scale:

1. The scale must be grounded in observable, natural phenomena.
2. All human societies will fluctuate along this scale throughout their histories, regardless of culture or other differences.
3. Variations along the scale will occur in response to chronic societal anxiety generated by real or perceived threats to the viability of the social unit.
4. The scale will reflect a continuum in the balance of the forces of togetherness and individuality.
5. The scale will also reflect a continuum of societal harmony or disharmony with nature.
6. In order to assess the basic level of a social unit at any given moment in history, a number of components must be considered, including its political system and the nature of leadership, systems for educating the next generation, systems for caring for its weaker members, its relationship to neighboring social groups, its relationship to the natural

environment, and the institutionalization of these systems and relationships through laws and regulations.

7. Conventional definitions of "civilization," including sophisticated levels of art and technologies, do not necessarily correlate with the society's basic level on the scale; for example, a highly "advanced" society (Nazi Germany, for example) could be low on the scale and an "underdeveloped" society (India under Gandhi, for example) could be higher on the scale.

THE RELATIONSHIP BETWEEN THE CONCEPTS OF EMOTIONAL CUTOFF AND SOCIETAL PROCESS

When Bowen (1978) sought a "logical conceptual bridge between emotional process in the family and emotional process in society" (p. 414), he focused on the development of *emotional triangles* in response to delinquency in the family and in society. He observed the parallels in family and societal reactivity to this phenomenon, as anxious parents and anxious social systems tended to adapt or collapse in response to the demands of adolescent delinquent behaviors. A parallel emotional triangle was at work both in families and in social systems. In a family, the parental coalition collapses as the delinquent child becomes more demanding. In larger social groups, the authority system collapses in response to demands from its least responsible members. This adaptation to irresponsible demands can also become institutionalized over time through laws and regulations, as the social unit becomes more regressed.

This chapter seeks a similar "logical conceptual bridge between emotional process in the family and emotional process in society," with *cutoff* as the common denominator. It asks the question: does cutoff, which is clearly observable in the multigenerational human family, also exist in and between larger social groups? If so, what does it look like and how does it operate in larger social groups?

The salient characteristic of emotional cutoff is a range of emotional distancing behaviors between two contiguous generations, in response to chronic anxiety and low levels of differentiation.

The salient characteristic of societal emotional process is a range or continuum in the balance of societal togetherness and individuality forces, in response to chronic anxiety generated by natural factors at the societal level. This continuum could be referred to as a societal scale of differentiation.

Figure 16.1 is a simple drawing of how these two concepts may be reciprocally related to each other and to chronic anxiety on the theoretical level. Chronic anxiety influences emotional cutoff and societal differentiation in

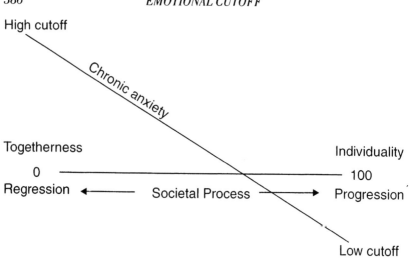

FIGURE 16.1. Reciprocal relationship between emotional cutoff and societal process.

opposite directions and is an underlying emotional process affecting both variables. It can be observed nonempirically that when chronic anxiety is low, emotional cutoff is also low and "individuality" forces predominate over societal "togetherness" forces (closer to 100 on the societal scale of differentiation). When chronic anxiety is high, emotional cutoff is also high, and societal process is driven by togetherness forces. This is what Bowen described as "societal regression" (closer to zero on the societal scale of differentiation). Undoubtedly there will always be exceptions and variations in this process, but the reciprocal relationship between these three concepts will usually vary to some degree in this manner. Although the synchrony between extreme emotional cutoff and strong societal togetherness forces (regression) may appear paradoxical, in fact both cutoff and togetherness are forms of reactivity to intense chronic anxiety, with togetherness usually preceding cutoff, as previously noted.

Common to the concept of emotional cutoff in the family and emotional cutoff in larger social groups is the relationship between generations. Some minimal degree of emotional separateness is natural and necessary both in families and in larger social groups, so that the younger generation can establish autonomous functioning, allowing for the emergence of leadership and stable adult reproductive processes.

In larger social groups, the progress of generations through time is usually described as "history." The fact that successive generations experience the world differently can be taken for granted. The passage of time inevitably creates new perspectives, new environments, and new experiences.

The relationship between two successive generations at the broad population level often is described in terms of stylistic or cultural continuities or differences (e.g., "the generation gap"). Generational differences and the behaviors associated with them (e.g., "the roaring twenties" or "the rebellious sixties") are rarely described as reactivity to chronic anxiety at the societal level. Nor are they often described as a natural process between the generations, relating to a predictable need for some degree of separateness.

Bowen's concept of emotional cutoff offers an additional dimension to understanding the historical fluctuations between generations. If societal anxiety is low, the generations can cooperate and maintain "viable emotional contact." A calm younger generation can learn from the older generation while also moving toward assuming responsible societal leadership.

But often societal anxiety is high for a variety of reasons, including territorial conflicts, depletion of resources, or epidemics, as well as natural or human-made disasters. A generation moving into societal leadership during such a period may blame the older generation for "causing" these problems. An automatic and reactive response from an anxious younger generation might be to distance from the older generation, attaching to *different* philosophies, ideologies, and solutions to societal problems simply because they are *different* and, perhaps, at least theoretically better. The chances are, however, that the greater the disconnection from the prior generation, the more likely the present leadership generation is to repeat a "more intense version of the past (or its mirror image)" (Kerr and Bowen, 1988, p. 272). This pattern is also reflected in the observation of the philosopher, George Santayana (1905), that "those who cannot remember the past are condemned to repeat it."

An automatic and reactive response from an anxious older generation might also be to distance, to "wash their hands" of current problems, and to disengage from collaborative decision making with the younger generation. The supportive "viable emotional contact" between generations that Bowen described in relation to the family is very difficult to sustain during periods of intense societal anxiety. Extreme versions of cross-generational distancing can lead to a situation in which "decision-making ability is lost, viable members desert the group, and there is overwhelming emotional reactivity, violence, and chaos" (Bowen, 1978, p. 278) at the societal level, leading inevitably to cross-generational cutoff.

With intense anxiety, cutoff can extend outward into other arenas for social polarization—between political groups, kinship groups, social classes, and religious groups, for example—and can be rigidified in institutions through laws and regulations that are difficult to change, even when the prevailing societal emotional process begins to change. An example of this rigidity can be seen in the United States in its regulatory approach to gun control. Although in this author's view a strong majority of Americans in the early twenty-first century might prefer to have stricter laws with regard to gun ownership, the legislative process has not been able to catch up with this prevailing social preference.

In fact, *change* itself can also be an arena for observing emotional cutoff in social groups. At the lower end of the scale, change would tend to be violent (revolutions, for example), disruptive, or coercive and would lead to a disconnection between the generations associated with both sides of the change. At the higher end of the scale, change would occur in an orderly and gradual manner. with sustained connection between the generations associated with both sides of the change.

This chapter proposes that the "logical conceptual bridge" between family cutoff and societal cutoff includes the following:

- The relationship between generations and its reactivity to chronic anxiety are central; other forms of societal cutoff, such as those between political, social, religious, or ethnic groups or nations may be significant but are secondary to generational cutoff.
- At the higher end of a societal scale of differentiation. change is orderly and gradual: the generations are able to maintain some kind of viable emotional contact, working together to create continuities that are in the best interest of the society; this end of the scale reflects balance in the forces of togetherness and individuality.
- At the lower end of the scale, change is disruptive or violent; both generations can manifest distancing behaviors, such as blaming, separation, and denying the importance of the past; at this end of the scale distancing and cutoff behaviors occur in response to an intense togetherness force.
- Family cutoff and societal cutoff can be reciprocal and interactive. In other words, the more that cutoff is a deeply ingrained response to anxiety in a large number of families in the general population. the more that cutoff will then become an automatic response to anxiety in larger social groups. Conversely, the more that cutoff is a predominant response to societal stress, the more families in that society will rely on cutoff to manage their own internal familial relationships; there are, however, many exceptions to this reciprocity among families that function at a higher level on the scale of differentiation and are not so vulnerable in adapting to societal process.
- Extreme societal cutoff can lead to a denial of the historical past (for example, book and archive burning in Nazi Germany or the destruc-

tion of ancient statues by the Taliban in Afghanistan), concurrent with the reappearance and acceptance of patterns from the past that are unrecognized by the younger generation.

• Societies that have significant long-term cutoff between generations are vulnerable to a wide variety of health, social, and environmental problems.

AN EXAMPLE OF EMOTIONAL CUTOFF
AT THE SOCIETAL LEVEL:
RUSSIA AND THE SOVIET UNION

The emergence of emotional cutoff at the societal level is linked to the intensity of the forces of togetherness operating in the society, and to the pervasiveness of chronic societal anxiety, usually triggered by natural phenomena. This section explores those factors as they have operated within the Slavic social groups that have inhabited the central Eurasian landmass for more than 1,000 years.

There have been roughly four periods in Russian history: Kievan Rus and the subsequent era of Mongol domination (the tenth to the fifteenth centuries); the Muscovite era (the fifteenth through the seventeenth centuries); the time of the czars (the eighteenth century to 1917); and then the soviet and postsoviet period (Hosking, 2001). Throughout all of these periods, adaptation to the geographic environment has been a primary factor in societal emotional process.

Although there are many regional differences across Eurasia, the social behaviors and strategies that the Slavs developed for managing the geography and climate of the area have been remarkably effective (Keenan, 1986, p. 122), and viable contact across generations has been traditionally continuous until approximately the past 100 years. In recent Russian and soviet history, however, cutoff has increasingly become a solution for managing togetherness and anxiety in larger social groups and has been manifested through political, economic, and social class differences. The evolution of this process is described and discussed.

The Interaction of Geography and Social Organizations

Every country in the world has a unique geography that defines the way human social organizations have developed in that specific region. Diamond (1999) summarizes his extensive exploration of this question with the observation that "history followed different courses for different peoples because of differences among peoples' environments, not because of biological differences among the peoples themselves" (p. 25).

The central Eurasian landmass provides an excellent example of the way humans discovered unique strategies for survival in a stressful environment. Russia's geography and natural environment have shaped the way human groups there have behaved and interacted for as long as the region has been inhabited. In preindustrial times the natural environment affected human behavior most profoundly:

> Men living in the pre-scientific and pre-industrial phases of history had and continue to have no choice but to adapt themselves to that nature which provides them with all they need to sustain life. And since adaptation implies dependence, it is not surprising that the natural environment, the subject matter of geography, should have had a decisive influence on the mind and habits of pre-modern man as well as on his social and political institutions. It is only when he began to feel emancipated from total subordination to nature that man could fantasize about being master of his own fate. (Pipes. 1992. p. 2)

The predominant characteristics of Russia's geography are its climate (hot in the summer and very cold in the winter), its patterns of precipitation (with rain falling most heavily in the second half of the summer, usually during harvest season), and its waterways, which run in a north-south direction with many lateral branches that create a network of navigable rivers and streams throughout the country.

Farming has traditionally been the primary occupation of nonnomadic humans. For the ancient Slavs, as for modern Russians and all other human social groups, agriculture has defined their relationship to nature and has determined the evolution of social systems in their geographic region. However, most significant for developing the sustainable agriculture necessary for human survival in Russia has been its extreme northern location. Its northern regions of tundra, taiga, and forest lands are not readily cultivatable. The southern region, or grassy steppe, is where most farming takes place. But the majority of even this fertile land lies at latitudes more northerly than the southern tip of Hudson Bay.

The most significant consequences of Russia's northern location have been a short growing season for crops and a long hard winter, with the necessity of keeping livestock indoors for two months longer than Western European livestock. Thus, with generally poor soil, unreliable rainfall, a brief farming season, and on average a major crop failure every seven years, Russian agriculture has traditionally had very low yields—enough to provide its own population with food, but not enough to produce a significant surplus that could potentially have led toward the development of trade with its neighbors.

The chief social consequence of Russian geography has been that successful individual farming is almost impossible. The growing season is so short (four to six months) that farm workers have had to pool their resources and labor together in order to harvest enough food to sustain the larger population through the winter. This necessity led to the development of cooperative social units that have continued in a variety of forms up to the present time: tribal communities among the ancient Slavs; a system of communal land ownership that developed into a feudal system of serfdom during the czarist period; and then coercively established, state-owned collective farms during the soviet period.

As Keenan (1986) writes:

> The East Slavs prospered in this marginal and forbidding environment— indeed their experience provides a stunning example of demographic dynamism and viability. Somehow the culture that they developed in this new home generated a combination of agricultural, social, and political adaptive techniques, based upon a cautious, non-innovative, but tenacious subsistence agriculture. (p. 122)

Keenan goes on to observe that in this harsh environment, individual peasant farmers could not sustain themselves, and even family units were not viable in surviving natural calamities or rampant disease. Therefore the dominant sustainable social unit that evolved was the village, or a collection of related and nonrelated families that supported one another in managing the environment successfully. In the end, all individual and family interests were subordinated to the interests of the village.

Emerging from a pervasive anxiety with regard to survival, the fundamental features of the Russian village included "a strong tendency to maintain stability and a kind of closed equilibrium; risk-avoidance; suppression of individual initiatives; informality of political power; the considerable freedom of action and expression 'within the group'; the striving for unanimous final resolution of potentially divisive issues" (Keenan, 1986, p. 128).

Another characteristic of Russian society in the context of subsistence agriculture has been a continuous population expansion eastward in search of new arable lands. As Pipes (1992) notes, "as long as the frontier remained infinitely expandable, the Russian peasant pressed outward, leaving behind him the exhausted soil and seeking soil that no human hand had touched" (p. 14). This migration began almost 1,000 years ago and continued through the soviet period, to the extent that individuals and families were politically free to move:

A major secular process in progress for hundreds of years has been carrying the Russian population outward from the central forest zone, mostly toward the east and south, causing them to inundate areas inhabited by nations of other races and cultures, and producing serious demographic dislocations in the path of their movement. (Pipes, 1992, pp. 15-16)

Others have described this eastward advance as "remorseless," but driven by the economics of hunting:

They set out across the continent as other nations embarked over the ocean, and just as spices or silver tempted European empires into being, so Russian Siberia was the creation of the sable. A few pelts from this glossy tree-marten could make a man's fortune. Their revenue poured into the czar's hands. The invading Cossacks exacted an imperial fur-tribute from natives crushed by their firearms, and spread like a disease along the rivers, spiking their passage with log forts. (Thubron, 1999, p. 32)

This eastward population movement may have provided a release from the togetherness forces of village life left behind and provided new opportunities for space, natural resources, and (temporarily at least) more autonomous functioning. When the settlers hit the Pacific Ocean, the frontier closed and there was no more open space to explore, inhabit, and develop. This ultimate geographic limitation led to the necessity for finding new strategies for responding to the forces of togetherness in village life and survival anxiety.

In summary, for many centuries of Russian history, the togetherness force was strong and continuous at the village level. Fragile human social units organized themselves cooperatively in a hostile natural environment in order to produce at least the minimal food and shelter necessary for survival and reproduction. Concurrently these fragile social units generated a balancing pressure to distance or cut off through moving eastward into uninhabited lands. As the steam valve for releasing togetherness pressures gradually closed, other mechanisms evolved for managing internal stress. During the czarist period these included the development of rigid social structures such as serfdom, a centralized system of authority in the Muscovite princely court, and a strong hereditary but apolitical bureaucracy that administered the state (Keenan, 1986, pp. 136-138). These systems could be described as extremely adaptive, given the harsh nature of the environment, but they might also be described as regressive when compared with other societies that were developing more potential for individuality during the same period of history. But those other societies, of course, had different geographic environments and a different societal emotional process throughout their histories.

The Soviet Period

During the soviet period (1917-1990), additional sources of anxiety emerged that intensified the forces for togetherness in the society. These included an increasing disharmony with nature (Feshbach and Friendly, 1992), as well as intensely technologically and territorially competitive relationships with neighboring industrial nations that exploded into world wars twice during the century. Automatic instinctual togetherness forces in Russia began to manifest themselves in a political ideology that prohibited a free press, freedom of speech, and freedom to travel or explore the outside world. It created a web of secrecy within the country, cutting the government off from the vast majority of its citizens. Those who protested against these constraints or presented even minor alternatives to the soviet system were removed from further participation in the society, tortured, shot without trial, or sent to prison camps in the far northeast, regions too bleak for habitation even by the eastward expanding populations of previous centuries. This political process could not be described as "emotional" cutoff within the families affected, since it did not stem from unresolved attachment across generations, but its impact could be described as "circumstantial cutoff," since it led to severe disconnection in those families.

There was, however, a move toward cutoff from prior generations at the societal level. The previous political system, czarism, was not only repudiated but blamed by the soviets for all social, economic, and political problems in the present. In the 1930s there was also a repudiation of the "Old Bolsheviks," those who had led the revolution of 1917. In addition, cutoff from neighboring nations was concretely imposed through setting up a barbed wire "iron curtain" between Russia and its immediate neighbors. The iron curtain was gradually extended to a large part of the rest of the world through jamming radio broadcasts, limiting travel, and prohibiting the import of "foreign ideas." Although the Soviet Union joined with the Allied Powers for four years in World War II to defeat Hitler, the same cutoff from neighboring nations was reimposed after the war. These restrictions became reciprocal in the later 1940s, as a "cold war" developed between the Soviet Union and those nations perceived as adversaries. This international cutoff lasted with some fluctuations until the dissolution of the Soviet Union in 1990.

In other words, soviet totalitarianism could be conceptualized as an extreme manifestation of automatic togetherness forces in response to multiple sources of chronic societal anxiety that were grounded in natural, political, and social "facts": human survival in a harsh environment, reduced reproduction, the closing of the eastern frontier, violent territorial border conflicts, limitations on access to mineral resources locked under the permafrost of the tundra (Daniels, 1985), and modern technology run amok (Feshbach and Friendly, 1992).

The legacy of societal cutoff in the Soviet Union included reduced life expectancy, reduced birth rate, high infant mortality, and serious damage to the natural environment. As noted by Feshbach and Friendly (1992),

> When historians finally conduct an autopsy on the Soviet Union and Soviet Communism, they may reach the verdict of death by ecocide. For the modern era, indeed for any event except the mysterious collapse of the Mayan empire, it would be a unique but not an implausible conclusion. No other great industrial civilization so systematically and so long poisoned its land, air, water and people. None so loudly proclaiming its efforts to improve public health and protect nature so degraded both. And no advanced society faced such a bleak political and economic reckoning with so few resources to invest toward recovery. (p. 1)

This author would not propose a direct cause-and-effect relationship among manifestations of societal cutoff across generations and the variety of health, social, and environmental problems apparent in Russia today, but the synchronicity of these factors and the vulnerability of the society are evident and observable. It remains to be seen how these challenges are managed over the long term in a society that actively and openly begins to acknowledge and grapple with its own historic past.

Figure 16.2 is a path diagram describing the reciprocal relationships among threats to survival, chronic anxiety, societal regression, and emotional cutoff in Russia and the Soviet Union. Because the society is an emotional system that has existed for over 1,000 years of history, all the variables in the diagram have reciprocal effects on one another.

Reciprocal Family and Societal Cutoff: A Research Study

An opportunity to observe the reciprocal relationship between societal cutoff and multigenerational family emotional cutoff was provided in a research study, undertaken by this author and a Russian colleague (Baker and Gippenreiter, 1996). The study explored the impact of the 1930s' soviet political purges on three generations of Russian families. The study noted that

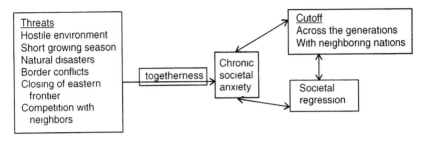

FIGURE 16.2. Path diagram showing the multifactoral reciprocal relationships among chronic anxiety, cutoff, and societal regression.

The Soviet political and social system created an environment in which abandoning connection with, or "cutting off" from, those who were purged was the "sensible" thing to do. Purge victims were physically cut off from their families through arrest, imprisonment, torture, assassination, and exile. In fact, it was a crime for the remaining family to maintain connection with these so-called "Enemies of the People." The family members themselves were cut off from the wider society through being officially labeled "Relatives of Enemies of the People." Many of these family members changed their names, went into hiding, and never again mentioned their purged relatives. Others, however, kept alive the memory of lost family members and retained a sense of pride in those memories. (p. 8)

The main hypothesis of the study was that

families who cut off physically, emotionally or socially from those family members who were arrested, deported, or purged during the late 1930s would manifest lower functioning in the grandchild generation. A related hypothesis was that families who had maintained a sense of connection with their lost family members would function more effectively in succeeding generations. (pp. 8-9)

In the study, cutoff was measured by asking fifty Russian middle-aged adults what they knew about the lives of grandparents who had been purged by Stalin. It was assumed that if they had basic information about older generations in their families, this information had been passed down through the family and would be an indicator of connectedness. In addition, they were asked if they had ever lived with a grandparent during childhood; what they knew about generations prior to their grandparents; how old they were when they found out that their grandparent had been a victim of the purge; who had told them the story; how the family functioned after the family member was purged; the quality of memories about the purge victim: the kinds of family stories or myths that developed over the years about the purged grandparents; whether the grandparents had any special talents or interests carried on by the grandchildren; whether the grandchild had any photographs, mementos, or other objects that had belonged to a purged family member; whether any grandchildren or great-grandchildren were named after purged family members; and whether anyone in the grandchild generation was said to look like the purged grandparent (p. 15).

The major finding of the study relating to family cutoff was the strong negative correlation between the factors of cutoff (for both maternal and paternal lines) and basic functioning of the grandchildren (as measured by physical and psychological health, number of marriages and divorces, health of children, and several other factors). In other words, the more cutoff in the families of the midlife Russian subjects of the study, the lower their basic functioning. As noted in the study's conclusion, "this finding validates the hypothesis from Bowen family systems theory that cutoff is a relationship phenomenon rooted in basic human functioning and transmitted from one generation to the next" (p. 31).

An additional finding indicated that there was *not* a significant relationship between cutoff and the experience of the purge:

> Emotional cutoff in Bowen family systems theory has been described as a long-term multigenerational family relationship pattern that would probably have pre-dated the experience of the purge for our subjects' families. Therefore, those families that already used emotional cutoff as a mechanism for managing anxiety would have turned to cutoff at the time of the purge in order to deal with stress and anxiety. (p. 31)

Conversely, those families that had developed skills for maintaining "viable emotional contact" across the generations would have used these skills even during the intensely traumatic period of the purge, when the government powerfully discouraged contact.

The findings of the study continue to be borne out by additional in-depth interviews in 1999 and 2000 by this author with midlife Russian adults whose grandparents were victims of the purge. In the 1930s, social and political institutions encouraged families to cut off from relatives who had been purged. However, families that had not used cutoff as a mechanism for handling stress or anxiety in the past were still able to maintain a strong sense of continuity with prior generations, even purged grandparents. It was found that this ability to maintain connection with the past actually enhanced the health and functioning of grandchildren who were adults in the 1990s. For other families, social and political pressure to cut off from their grandparents fit with their traditional multigenerational pattern of managing stress or anxiety through separation, distance, and cutoff, and they went along with the pressure. Their grandchildren did not fare so well in the 1990s.

During much of the soviet period, the latter group apparently exerted some reciprocal family support for a prevailing regressive societal pressure to cut off from the historical or presoviet past. Political denunciations of family members, friends, and neighbors were widespread (Conquest, 1990) and were undoubtedly generated by fear and an instinct for self-preservation. Therefore, family and societal mechanisms for dealing with chronic anxiety interwove to produce a web of cutoff at both levels, although more emotionally balanced families apparently maintained a sense of connection across generations in spite of external pressures to do otherwise.

The Bridge Between Family and Societal Cutoff in Russia and the Soviet Union

Several components of the "logical conceptual bridge" between family cutoff and societal cutoff can be observed in Russian history:

- There have been long periods in Russian history when the generations were able to maintain viable emotional contact and work together, creating continuities in the social process and being highly effective in dealing with the harsh natural environment of the region.
- During the soviet and postsoviet periods it has been possible to observe cross-generational distancing behaviors, as the Soviets repudiated the czarist period of Russian history, and the present generation of Russians repudiates the soviet period. Blaming the prior generation for the problems of the present, while denying that there is anything to be learned from previous generations, has been characteristic of both historical transitions.
- Although traditionally Russian and soviet society had rigid political and social hierarchies and had been in conflict with or cut off from their nation-state neighbors, this form of cutoff is thought to be secondary to cutoff across generations.
- The soviet system created a concrete manifestation of secondary societal cutoff through imposing an "iron curtain" between its own geographic borders and the rest of the world. This cutoff was reinforced by shutting out the flow of ideas, jamming radio stations, censoring

publications, and limiting correspondence, as well as curtailing the movement of peoples through limiting permission to travel across those borders in either direction. This kind of societal cutoff had occurred from time to time in czarist history, but modern technology made it more effective and complete during the soviet period.

- Societal cutoff during the soviet period led not only to a denial of the historical past, including destruction of archives, but also to the reappearance of extreme versions of the milder authoritarianism and disrespect for individuals that were characteristic of the czarist period, including imprisonment of dissidents in Siberia.

- Observations about the reciprocal nature of family and societal cutoff have been noted in the previous discussion about the political purges of the 1930s in the Soviet Union and may be more broadly characteristic of societal regression.

- The significant long-term cutoff apparent between generations in Russia and the Soviet Union may be associated with a wide variety of health, social, and environmental problems and with societal regression in general.

These observations demonstrate a contrast between societal cutoff during the early Slav settlements, the czarist period, and the soviet period. Throughout the early centuries when Slavs began to inhabit the Central Eurasian landmass, they developed highly effective strategies for managing the environmental adversities of the region. They created a cooperative subsistence agriculture that provided for their survival in a harsh, infertile land. These strategies continued through many generations and their values were reflected in the conservative, centralized political leadership system of the Romanov czars that eventually developed in Moscow (Keenan, 1986, p. 128). Governmental secrecy, cutoff between societal strata (the hereditary elite versus the peasantry), and cutoff from neighboring states were also characteristic of these periods of Russian history, but combined with the eastward population expansion they probably served as balancing mechanisms in response to the intense togetherness forces necessitated by survival anxiety.

During the soviet period earlier patterns from Russian history intensified, and cutoff across generations became woven into Communist ideology. Cutoff permeated multigenerational families as well as the political, economic, and social systems of the country. Cutoff with adversarial nations intensified into a "cold war" following the World War II. The reasons for this reactive intensification and the observable consequences have been discussed. It remains to be seen whether cutoff will continue to be a societal strategy as well as a family strategy for managing chronic anxiety in post-

Communist Russia or whether, with renewed connections to the past, manifestations of cutoff will diminish. In post-Communist Russia, many societal patterns from the soviet period persist and continue to cause significant disruption as the country moves toward a market economy with more connections to its neighbors and the wider world.

CAN THE CONCEPT OF EMOTIONAL CUTOFF PROVIDE A GENERIC WAY OF UNDERSTANDING SOCIETAL DISRUPTIONS?

A basic assumption of this chapter is that cutoff as a societal relationship phenomenon can be observed to some degree in all human social groups and larger social systems. Russia was used as an example of the historical fluctuations along a hypothetical "societal scale of differentiation" between societal cross-generational connection and societal cutoff, because the author had an opportunity to spend time in that country in the 1990s, a period of political, economic, and social transition. However, at an automatic and instinctual level, the fluctuations of Russian societal process are no different from the fluctuations of societal process in other countries. The cultural, historical, and environmental details may be different, but it is assumed that the underlying process leading toward or away from cutoff would be somewhat the same in all societies.

This underlying process includes the following:

- An adaptation to the physical environment that traditionally shapes human social organizations to meet their survival needs
- A societal reaction to pressures for togetherness
- A societal reaction to chronic anxiety with regard to external threats and reduction of resources
- A societal reaction to chronic anxiety with regard to rapid and competitive technological development
- A societal reaction to disharmony with the natural environment

Any component of this underlying process may lead a society in the direction of distancing or cutting off from prior generations, and distancing or cutting off from its cultural, biological, and environmental roots. This author proposes that the concept of societal cutoff may to some degree provide a useful perspective in the analysis of disruption in all human societies.

Disconnection from the past, both internally and externally, has been found to be associated with a wide variety of health, social, and environmental problems. It is also associated with limitations in effective leadership, as leaders generally reflect the broad maturity level of the groups from which they emerge. They also are unable to utilize the lessons of past leaders if they are disconnected from appreciating them and learning from them.

The challenge for a society embroiled in social disruption is to find the objectivity necessary for discovering solutions within its own history. Only through understanding the strengths and weaknesses of historical patterns over broad sweeps of time can a society discover emotional resources that will lead both backward and forward, linking the past to the present and the future. These connections can then promote creative energy, effective leadership, and stability for the long term.

REFERENCES

Baker, K.G. and Gippenreiter, J.B. (1996). The Effects of Stalin's Purge on Three Generations of Russian Families. *Family Systems* 3(1):5-35. © 1996, Georgetown Family Center.

Bowen, M. (1978). *Family Therapy in Clinical Practice*. New York: Jason Aronson.

Conquest, R. (1990). *The Great Terror: A Reassessment*. New York: Oxford University Press.

Daniels, R.V. (1985). *Russia: The Roots of Confrontation*. Cambridge, MA: Harvard University Press.

Diamond, J. (1999). *Guns, Germs, and Steel: The Fates of Human Societies*. New York: W.W. Norton and Company, Inc.

Feshbach, M. and Friendly, A. (1992). *Ecocide in the USSR*. New York: Basic Books.

Hosking, G. (2001). *Russia and the Russians: A History*. Cambridge, MA: Belknap Press/Harvard University Press.

Keenan, E.L. (1986). Muscovite Political Folkways. *The Russian Review* 45:115-181.

Kerr, M.E. and Bowen, M. (1988). *Family Evaluation: An Approach Based on Bowen Theory*. New York: W.W. Norton and Company.

Pipes, R. (1992). *Russia Under the Old Regime*. New York: Macmillan Publishing Company.

Santayana, G (1905). *The Life of Reason; or, The Phases of Human Progress. Reason in Common Sense*, Volume 1 New York: Charles Scribner's Sons.

Thubron, C. (1999). *In Siberia*. New York: HarperCollins Publishers Inc.

Chapter 17

Migration and Emotional Cutoff

Eva Louise Rauseo

INTRODUCTION

Life on Earth is in constant motion. Humans and other species move from their place of birth to new physical and social environments, often at great risk. What is the significance of this movement?

In addition to a talent for migration, humans have evolved an amazing ability to be in contact with many generations. In society after society there is apparent effort to maintain knowledge about ancestors and a connection to their lives through oral history, pictographs, letters, journals, and volumes of recorded history. Every human life is connected to generations who went before. In families there are many ways of maintaining connections to the stream of life that is one's personal or collective past. What happens to humans when that current of contact and knowledge is cut off?

This chapter explores the role of migration and emotional cutoff in human adaptation to life.[1] First, animal studies shed some light on the conditions of life as well as innate behaviors and relationship influences that are a part of migration and dispersal in mammals. Questions about the costs and benefits of dispersal or migration are raised.

Next, the issue of emotional cutoff is introduced. This concept comes directly from the family systems theory of Murray Bowen and is described in some detail. Conditions of life that may result in cutoff both in human and other species are examined. This is followed by a summary of changes that are observed in the generations following a cutoff.

Loss of contact among family members is described in some human families along with the conditions that often precede migration and emotional cutoff. Several multigenerational family histories are used to explore situations in which loss of contact occurs across generations under different conditions. The functional adaptation in the current generation is explored briefly.

Finally, the interaction between migration and cutoff is considered in some detail. The function of both processes and their variable consequences are subjects to be explored further. Bowen theory offers a blueprint for studying the actual facts of migration and cutoff in the human family. The skill of obtaining personal and family history and making contacts across many generations are proposed as unique human abilities that can help address the questions raised in this study.

- How does migration function in the life of human families and societies?
- To what extent are the "decisions" about migration built into the instinctual nature of the human?
- Can the conditions of life that propel migration be defined more clearly by looking at the instinctual processes in other mammals?
- How and when does emotional cutoff play a role in migration?
- What are the consequences of migration under a variety of conditions—particularly cutoff?

ANIMAL STUDIES

Animal studies can provide useful models for understanding some aspects of human behavior. Although it is clear that each species has its own "rules" and ways of deciding who leaves and who stays, the objectivity possible in observing animals is helpful in formulating new ideas about humans. Relationship factors are often important in the timing and choice of the ones who leave their home territory. For example, the functional position of individuals and their type of connection to others in the family group or troop appear to play a part in the timing and selection of those who leave and those who stay (Smale, Holekamp, and Nunes, 1997). Many of these relationship factors have close parallels to human family behavior when seen from the perspective of Bowen family systems theory.

Several forces may be involved in migration and dispersal of nonhuman species. In evolutionary biology these terms have very exact meanings that are more specific than in general usage. In animal studies, the permanent and complete departure of an individual from its birthplace is called "natal dispersal" (Greenwood, 1980) or more colorfully described as "homeless travelers (vagrants) in search of a home" (Lidicker, 1975). Migration generally refers to the persistent movement of animals beyond their original habitat to another habitat—sometimes in a round-trip movement on a seasonal basis (Dingle, 1996). Finally, the terms *migration* and *immigration* refer to movement of individuals or groups from their home (emigration) to live permanently in another environment (immigration), usually in a new social group.

Forces that propel migration and dispersal are often species specific, but studies now show more individual differences within any species than were previously assumed. For example, if females generally disperse from their natal group to join a new social group at or near reproductive age, there are exceptions to that pattern that seem to be based on relationship factors (Goodall, 1986). In other situations, if most members of a group migrate seasonally, some are found that design other solutions to the demands of their environment (Dingle. 1996). The facts of variability within a species and between species are useful in thinking about human variability in response to similar forces. In human life it is easy to assume that groups of people are all responding to the same forces in large processes such as immigration, but some of the animal studies cited here help discover the variety of influences on individuals in a group.

The influences on migration and dispersal include:

- Reproductive opportunities and mate choice
- Environmental conditions such as crowding and habitat deterioration
- Challenges in the social environment such as competition and aggression
- Functional positions in a group
- An innate force for "exploration" or wandering which may be present in a small number of individuals who show no other pressing force for leaving their place of origin (Howard. 1982)

There also may be a number of internal and social cues for dispersal that have not been identified. In general. these all can be considered instinctual forces that are regulated in the individual and in the social group as a part of the biology of living beings.[2]

The forces that propel migration and dispersal, then, may be a mix of innate individual factors and relationship factors. In solitary mammals, individuals usually emigrate alone. In social mammals, dispersal may take place as group fission under certain conditions, with the less dominant individuals more likely to emigrate. For example, when competition is present in certain female hyenas, the least dominant hyenas are the most likely to emigrate (Smale, Holekamp, and Nunes, 1997). In many species, dispersal takes place before the onset of puberty or at reproductive age, with different strategies for males and females (Smale. Holekamp, and Nunes, 1997). In rhesus macaques, the less competent males emigrate at an earlier age than their more competent associates (Mehlman, Higley, and Faucher, 1995). In other groups, a male "fraternity" may emigrate together at reproductive age.

In still others, groups of both sexes may emigrate together. Finally, under conditions of declining group size, some may emigrate to produce a more viable group size (Smale, Holekamp, and Nunes, 1997). The relationship factors in these patterns are slowly emerging.

Another mechanism for dispersal has been described as "ostracism."

> Clearly migration does not occur at random following a forced expulsion, but is rather a predictable event in the life cycle of males or females and tends to occur most often within a local community of groups and frequently between particular neighbors and not others. . . . Although such adjustments are made through the process of individual "decisions" and "strategies" to optimize personal reproductive success, the net effect is to constantly redistribute individuals in relation to resources vital to reproduction. (Lancaster, 1986, pp. 69, 75)

The destinations of male and female emigrants are often quite different, with some staying close to their home territory and others moving large distances (Gaulin and Fitzgerald, 1986). Some emigrate and form an independent social unit and therefore do not "immigrate" into another social group. Frequently, animals engage in secondary dispersal before becoming settled. Some females who engage in a secondary dispersal may actually move closer to home or back into their home territory. The relationship influences in this aspect of dispersal can be seen in the literature (Dingle, 1996; Greenwood, 1980; Lidicker, 1975).

The consequences of emigration and dispersal are also varied. Movement into a new physical and social environment has a real cost. Immigrating individuals face a great deal of uncertainty about available resources and about their ability to find a niche within the new social group. Forty to 50 percent of young male rhesus macaques die in the process of emigration (Suomi, 2000). With high levels of aggression in a new group, some individuals may be required to move a second or third time before becoming established in a new setting. For those who survive, there is often a change in social dominance. For others, there are greater opportunities for mating and reproduction in spite of a loss in social position. Clearly, individuals find a range of conditions in their new settings and have to deal with life as they find it (Smale, Holekamp, and Nunes, 1997).

Mammals' earliest ancestral condition was a solitary existence, with solitary dispersal occurring consistently among males and females alike (Eisenberg, 1981). Evolution of a more complex social group probably required the inhibition of this tendency to disperse, with most individuals remaining in the social group through adulthood. The development of strong social bonds characteristic of primates and other social mammals requires an ability to live in lifelong connection to many other related individuals (Waser and Jones, 1983). Many adults, therefore, must inhibit the tendency to disperse (Smale, Holekamp, and Nunes, 1997).

Dispersal of individuals appears to have consequences for those who leave, those who remain, and those who must integrate the new individuals into their social group. In some baboon groups, the stress hormones (in residents and immigrants alike) are much higher during the time a troop deals with the entry of certain challenging new individuals (Alberts, Sapolsky, and Altmann, 1992). There also may be benefits to the individual and to the group of having both permanent residents and newcomers. Reproductive variability is considered one of the significant results of dispersal. In rodents, only one sex usually disperses. The dispersing sex shows greater development in the hippocampus, a forebrain structure related to the memory of relationship and spatial environment. This finding may be associated with the need for greater skill in managing new territory and social environments (Gaulin and Fitzgerald, 1986). The long-term value or cost of dispersal for the individual or the species may vary under different conditions.

FROM ANIMALS TO HUMANS

Migration for humans is defined as movement from one country or region to settle in another. Many of the diverse patterns and results of emigration and immigration seen in other species are also evident in humans. Mammal studies provide new perspectives and new questions, especially in regard to the instinctual relationship factors that influence aspects of emigration and adaptation to immigration. Although many sociological and historical studies address group movements in migration, some studies also address the questions of who leaves and who stays. The societal, economic, political, and cultural factors are generally addressed. In recent years, it has become clear that the process of migration and subsequent adaptation is enormously complex and does not yield to reductionistic explanations (Morawska, 1990).

Sociological and historical studies deal with many levels of explanation; this chapter suggests another level of study. The study of relationship systems in humans and other mammals suggests that migration is influenced by the biology of relationships. The study of such poorly understood instinctual processes could perhaps add new questions and new knowledge to existing approaches in the study of human migration.

One simple example demonstrates the possibility of underlying instinctual forces in a process that is primarily thought of as a cultural or societal process. Primogeniture is a factor in regulating migration in some societies in which the oldest offspring, generally the oldest male, inherits the family land or home and remains in his home territory. If necessary, other offspring look further afield for land or work. Is it possible that innate or instinctual forces actually underlie the development of cultural patterns such as primogeniture? Primogeniture seems to provide stability for some portion of the future generations along with requiring a different adaptation in other branches of the family, possibly including migration.

If human migration is partly a response to instinctual forces, it is reasonably addressed as a part of the family system that operates at the level of emotion or instinct. Facts from evolution, biology, and the study of family systems describe aspects of such automatic behavior. In addition to looking ˙ for the influences on the timing and selection of emigrating individuals, other factors in the emotional system can be studied that address an individual's adaptation to immigration. The emotional system can be studied as it influences the immigrant's response to the level of aggression in new territories, his or her potential for reproduction, and the success of his or her search for essential resources.

Studies of other species' migratory processes can help formulate more precise questions and predictions for human studies. In addition, the study of emotional processes using Bowen theory retains the focus on the human as an evolving form of life. The concepts in Bowen theory offer variables for the study and prediction of outcomes based on family emotional process, especially the process of emotional cutoff. This variable, emotional cutoff, may not have been studied explicitly in other mammals, but its importance in humans can be broadly observed.

EMOTIONAL CUTOFF

What is the interaction between migration and emotional cutoff in human family adaptation and functioning? Emotional cutoff, a theoretical concept, is introduced into this discussion of migration to address a relationship process primarily observed in human families. Initial evidence is presented here that emotional cutoff may also be present, in some form, in other social mammals.

Defined first in the family systems theory of Murray Bowen, the term has several levels of meaning. Emotional cutoff describes one way that people deal with unresolved relationships in the past in order to start their lives in the present. It is an automatic emotional process of separation, withdrawal, running away, or denying the importance of the original family. Bowen noted that this means of managing relationships is more common in intense and less emotionally mature families. Emotional cutoff can take the form of geographic distance or may simply exist as an automatic internal process whereby the facts and feelings in the relationship are not openly addressed or even formulated in the awareness of the individuals. Often, both types of cutoff are combined (Bowen, 1978).

Several generations of geographic cutoff are often evident in the history of families with more difficult adaptations to life in the present (Bunting, 1982). Lack of knowledge or connection with the important facts of family history is associated with a greatly increased difficulty in basic functioning (e.g., finding a suitable mate, establishing a stable family unit) (Baker and Gippenreiter, 1996; Rauseo, 1996). In contrast, there are many reports of individuals who separate from a difficult configuration of relationships and find more life energy for individual functioning in a new environment. In a pilot study conducted in a prenatal clinic in El Paso, Texas, the women who had the least knowledge or emotional connection to the larger family had somewhat fewer complications during pregnancy and birth (Rauseo, 1996). In another study, the emigrating branch of a family leaving Norway at a time of increasingly difficult conditions of life was the only branch to reproduce (Harrison, 2000, personal communication).

The effects of emotional cutoff and geographic distance from a family are not yet clear in ways that can invite generalizations. However, many individual family histories give clear evidence of poorer adaptation after several generations of cutoff in their own families (Bunting, 1982). Frequently this cutoff is associated with emigration and immigration.

The author's clinical study of families experiencing cutoff associated with geographic distance demonstrates predictable shifts from generation to generation.[3] In the families interviewed, the generation that cuts off from personal history and family contacts often experiences a great deal of energy focused on gaining a new life. Frequently, individuals are very productive in spite of many challenges. However, information about the emotional issues propelling the cutoff is seldom passed on to the next generation. The extent to which emotions propel the cutoff and geographic distance may not be clear to those who leave.

The generation born to these cutoff parents experiences the emotional reactivity in their parents, a reactivity that often surfaces around life situations that reflect the fear or anxiety that was present prior to the cutoff. The offspring have no context for understanding or managing the apparent excess anxiety and reactivity in their relationships. They simply experience the tension as part of their environment and deal with it as an important part of their lives, often blaming themselves or their parents for the experience. When parents cut off, the next generation lacks the experience of people being "present and accounted for" in the most difficult times. Instead of maintaining a viable presence in tense but important relationships, the usual response is to automatically cut off to relieve the tension.

Without knowledge of the events or emotional challenges from the family's multigenerational past, people often look to their environment to provide them principles and values for living. These values may become a part of a "pseudo-self" or "pretend" self in an effort to adapt to the anxiety in the emotional system.[4]

Each succeeding generation lives with a level of anxiety in parents and self that cannot be understood in terms of actual life events. This excess anxiety reflects many unresolved issues from the multigenerational past and contains the experience of parental anxiety that is not easily understood in the present life situation. Such a family group trying to handle anxiety (using any or all of the mechanisms described in Bowen family systems theory[5]) is still an anxious organism without the experience of individual self-definition which could provide an anchor and reference point for the entire family. The clinical evidence connecting cutoff and poorer functioning is most convincing when someone in a family is able to reestablish effective personal contact within the larger cut off family and improve his or her own ability to define a self.[6] In fact, the impact of cutoff is better understood when the cutoff process is partially reversed.

Connecting with an Animal Model

In trying to get a clearer view of cutoff in humans, the author has begun to search for clear examples of animal studies where important relationships are cut off in the midst of emotionally difficult situations. The evidence of separation and withdrawal, running away, and denying the importance of the larger family is not easily documented in animal studies. There is, however, one dramatic example in the lives of the elephant families in the Amboseli reserve during the thirteen-year study documented by Cynthia Moss (Moss, 1988). One very stable bond group consisting of four smaller units had been one of the better-known families in the central population of the park (The T Family). One year poachers killed one of the matriarchs and her calf as well as an adolescent female from another family in the bond group. In the months that followed the killings, the same four families isolated themselves from each other and did not travel together, forage together, or socialize as in the past. In the remaining years of the study, two family groups reunited as a bond group while the other two remained less connected (Moss, 1988).

Many human family histories also involve deaths of significant individuals preceding a geographic move that divides formerly connected family members. However, some severe conditions of life that precede large migrations are often handled differently by different branches of a family, with some choosing to emigrate and others choosing to remain.

The literature on "ostracism" among animals suggests that social isolation plays a part in reproductive competition. This could be viewed as a form of cutoff.

> During periods of optimal resources, excess populations emigrate from the local groups with the richest resource base into marginal areas. The identity of these "pioneers" may be determined by their social marginality . . . Ostracism, emigration, and immigration remain as the basic social processes by which the ratio of resources to individuals shifts and balances from one year to the next. (Lancaster, 1986, pp. 70, 75)

Does emotional cutoff as a part of migration represent a similar process in humans?

In humans, social and family conditions preceding emigrations of past generations are often difficult to document carefully. However, it is possible to study these decisions in groups whose migrations are fairly recent and where clear access to family history remains. According to principles from Bowen theory, migration based on relationship issues within the family or on changes following traumatic events would be expected to have very different results depending on the level of emotional cutoff evident in the emigrating family (Baker and Gippenreiter, 1996; Rauseo, 1996).

MIGRATION AND EMOTIONAL CUTOFF

Migration and emotional cutoff may both represent instinctual processes that are poorly understood, particularly in humans. Although these processes may overlap in some instances, there is some value in considering them as possibly separate processes. Human migrations appear to show many of the patterns observed in animal studies. Relationships appear to play a part in the timing and choice of those who leave their home territory. Clearly, the challenges faced in leaving a home territory for an unexplored area or new social group can be exciting, necessary, or sometimes dangerous. Decisions to move great distances to start a new life are common in history, but it is not always clear what the cost and benefit are to the migrating individuals, their descendants, and those left behind.

Humans also face a unique dilemma in the consideration of migration. Humans can develop personal contact with several generations and branches of a family simultaneously. In addition to personal contact, humans have the ability to know the history and the facts of life of those who have gone before them. These contacts and history offer a context in which an individual, under ideal conditions, is able to define a self and begin to make a unique contribution to the life of the social group. How important is this multigenerational history and contact? The contact and history can be lost in the midst of migration, with emotional cutoff sometimes operating as a force in propelling the migration. Emotional cutoff can also be intensified by the geographic distance and other factors involved in the new life. Maintaining contact and history across the generations, then, is an additional challenge in human migrations beyond those faced in other species.

The interaction of these two forces, migration and emotional cutoff, in human life may be especially important at a time when migrations are increasing worldwide. In order to consider their importance in human life some observations about emigration and postimmigration family functioning can be useful.

FAMILY EXAMPLES

Three family histories are illustrative of a number of factors involved in emigration and emotional cutoff. Since the emigrations are somewhat recent and people can have access to family information in the form of contacts and archives, the facts are easily available to study. All three of these families illustrate relationship events and forces that are similar to processes in some of the animal studies cited above.

Family A

This family had four brothers who were adults during the Mexican Revolution of 1910 (Figure 17.1). The youngest brother was the one elected by the family to serve in the revolution, protecting the older brothers, particularly the one who acted as patriarch in the family. When this revolutionary was killed in the war, his death represented a difficult challenge for the entire family. Mother had been especially close to the youngest brother and had lived with him and his family.

Mother died shortly after the youngest brother. These deaths were followed by shock waves of emotional reactivity that fueled further changes. The youngest brother's oldest daughter (#1) suddenly emigrated to the United States with her husband and their first child. Youngest brother's oldest son died early, and his youngest daughter (#5) experienced family violence and two infant deaths. This daughter died when her last infant was

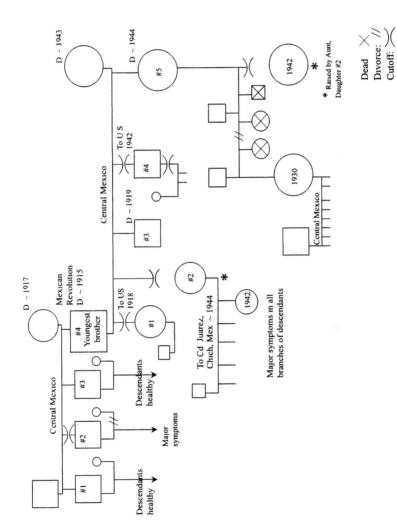

FIGURE 17.1. Family A diagram.

411

small, only a few months after the death of her own mother, the youngest brother's wife.

There was only one remaining daughter, #2, and her family. In the wake of the sequence of deaths, daughter #2 took her sister's youngest child along with her family to live at the U.S. border. The adults who emigrated knew the family history but did not talk about it. The knowledge was not passed on to the youngest family members or to the next generation who, in spite of the effort to protect them from the past, lived with great anxiety and serious symptoms.

The older brothers of the dead revolutionary and their families did not emigrate. Brother #3, the patriarch, had wanted to fight in the revolution but he was considered most necessary to the family's stability. That was the rationale proposed for the youngest brother to take his place in the fighting. Brother #3 and Brother #1 produced stable families in spite of a number of challenges. (Brother #2 cut off from the family after a difficult marriage, and his descendants are out of contact with the family history.)

Women who were born or married into branches of the family that stayed in contact with one another and with the family history were healthy and led long, productive lives. In contrast, women in cutoff branches experienced poor health and early death. In addition, the current generation of the families who stayed in contact is more stable and has fewer symptoms than the current generation of families who fled to the border or cut off from their family and history.

Before participating in this study, the family member in the current generation had little information about the facts preceding the emigration of her family from the interior of Mexico to the U.S. border. Most members of the current generation believed that the migration was related to economic need and job availability. The facts showed something different. This emigration did not take place around resource depletion as originally believed. The stories indicate that the family of the dead revolutionary was very reactive to those whose lives were less affected by the revolution. Reactions to the deaths and the issues around those deaths were difficult for people to manage. These reactions may have contributed to the dead brother's family instability after the Revolution of 1910 and later emigration.

This family situation is somewhat similar to the elephant examples in which family groups did not remain in contact after the deaths of important members (Moss, 1988).

Family B

This family is a part of a large, extended family unit that remains in the interior of Mexico (Figure 17.2). Only one female, Youngest Daughter, left

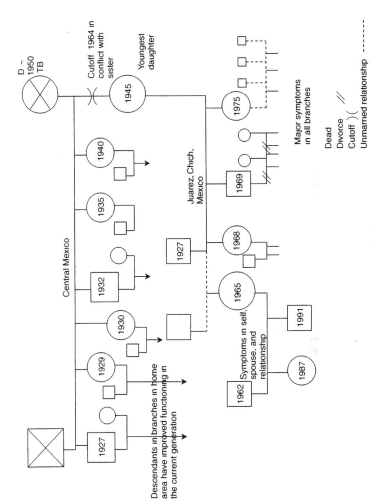

FIGURE 17.2. Family B diagram.

413

the area thirty years ago as a young, single mother. She was orphaned at age five, and she had been cared for by a succession of family members, especially her older siblings. Living with the family into adulthood, she did not find a suitable mate. Youngest Daughter's first child was conceived in an affair with a married man. In an escalating chronic conflict with a sister, she left in anger and found work about 250 miles from home. (Her first daughter later learned that the conflict often surfaced around competition between the sisters over the man who is her father.)

After migrating with her first child, Youngest Daughter later met a sympathetic man who, along with his employer, was willing to take care of her and her daughter. She and this man lived together and, after two more children, married and moved another 500 miles to the U.S. border, cutting off contact with the past. Youngest Daughter's entire large family remained intact in the interior of Mexico where they have had fairly stable lives that include general educational and economic improvement.

Youngest Daughter, who emigrated alone, has many more problems in her marriage and with her adult offspring. In recent years she has made some attempts to restore contact with the original family. Her oldest daughter, who is studying her family system, has restored viable contact with the entire large, extended family and has experienced a dramatic improvement in her own functioning. She has been able to be more effective in relating to her husband's alcoholism, in managing her limited finances, and in taking on a significant role in the community and church.

This migration took place in the context of competition among the females in an intense triangle with an important sibling. This was a solitary emigration of the youngest, least dominant female and is similar to processes sometimes seen in emigrating hyenas when competition exists between females in a family group (Smale, Holekamp, and Nunes, 1997).

Family C

A major migration in this Mexican family took place around 1910 after some family problems that are not clearly defined (Figure 17.3). In the midst of the problems and during an epidemic, one or both parents and the oldest son apparently died. Five remaining children, ages five to nineteen, migrated as a group. History of the mother in this group has been lost from family records and archives.

This family group migrated three times, moving over 1,000 miles before settling in Mexico City around 1930. By this time, some of them had married and reproduced, and all continued their migration together. The migration style of this group of siblings indicated a strong desire or need to re-

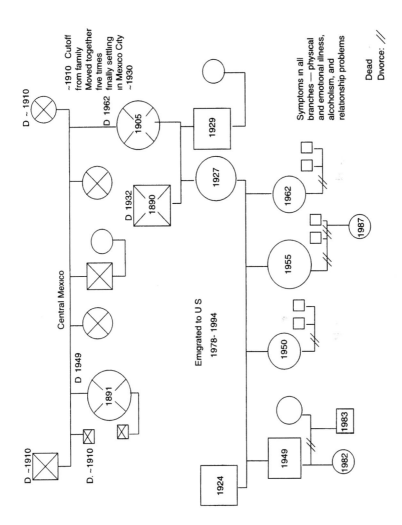

FIGURE 17.3. Family C diagram.

main together. However, they did not preserve the history or contact with the original family and these facts were lost within one generation.

The history of the family shows some instability in the first generation of migration with emotional problems and addictions evident in the younger siblings. The next generation cut off from the family in adulthood and established intense, separate nuclear units. The expectation of each nuclear unit was that they should present a united front, forget the past, and remain together. One nuclear unit emigrated to the United States, following the oldest male offspring who initially came to study and later made his home in the United States. Contacts in the broader family are still limited and mostly superficial.

The emigrations in this family took place in the wake of deaths and serious traumas. The historical and emotional contact with the past was progressively cut off. In the current family unit in the United States, which includes the parents and four adults, all four siblings have emotional symptoms, instability in their marriages, and unstable nuclear families. This generation does not possess a clear history of the past generations and does not maintain personal contact with the larger family in Mexico. The predominant characteristics of the family are the separateness from the larger family and the intensity of relationship symptoms within each nuclear unit. Each nuclear family functions "as if" the nuclear family group must be kept intact at all costs and must not depend on others in the larger family.

This family represents a style of migration in which the individual units separate from the parental unit and become a social unit somewhat isolated from the larger family group. This migration is similar to group fission in other mammals, described in an earlier section of the chapter, in which the less dominant individuals are likely to emigrate as a group (Smale, Holekamp, and Nunes, 1997).

Outcomes of Immigration

Our data suggest that relationship processes are always a part of a decision to migrate. However, the emotional reactivity or, in contrast, the thoughtfulness about that decision seems to play an important part in the outcome. The common wisdom about migration emphasizes the economic factor as primary in people's decision to migrate within Mexico or emigrate from Mexico.[7] Although the reality of limited resources continues to be a factor in many migrations, there is something important to be gained by addressing the relationship processes that also are a part of the process of emigration. The families described here show that the major forces behind the timing of their decision to emigrate and the choice of who emigrates stem largely from emotional, relationship issues. In the author's interviews with more than fifty families at the U.S./Mexico border, relationship factors are consistently present in the timing and decision about who migrates and who remains in the home territory. These factors include many of the relationship processes described in the animal literature previously cited and appear to operate alongside varying degrees of emotional cutoff. Further study will be needed to document the outcomes of those who left and those who stayed in the country of origin.

Animal research documents the risk involved in emigration and immigration (Suomi, 2000; Smale, Holekamp, and Nunes, 1997). Does human immigration pose similar risks? Recent news articles highlight the dangers in illegal immigration and the dangers of life in a new country (Jacobs and Hanley, 2001; Sterngold, 2001; Wakin, 2001). The exact number of deaths in the process of emigrating from Mexico or Central America is not fully documented, but the risk is real. In family interviews in a clinic in El Paso, most families had lost one relative, usually a young male, in the process of emigration. The impact of these losses on the family is an important part of the study of emigration.

Several new studies of humans indicate that the second and third generations postimmigration show more health problems than the first generation. The immigrant generation is generally healthier than the average U.S. population, but succeeding generations have increased physical and emotional problems (Bower, 1998; Vega et al., 1998). Although many people indicate surprise at these findings, they are consistent with the theoretical predictions of Bowen theory. The progressive loss of contact with one's multigenerational past and one's broader relationship network is associated with decreasing competence in relationships and in emotional and physical functioning. Although succeeding generations may show higher economic and educational levels, these often are not associated with improvements in emotional and physical health. In other words, the poorer health statistics may represent a deterioration in the person's ability to develop a realistic life course when cut off from a vital emotional connection to the extended family. Bowen theory describes this process as a decrease in level of differentiation of self[8] in which the development of "pseudo-self" is a way of adapting to the anxiety in the relationship system in the absence of a more certain "solid self."[9]

Sociologists write about the challenges of acculturation that can interfere with the individual's primary cultural identity. However, some older studies indicate that people with solid emotional connections to their past can manage to be fully acculturated to U.S. society without losing their identity and without symptoms often attributed to acculturation (Salgado de Snyder 1987; Buriel, 1985). The people who were well integrated in their social group before emigration appear to do better with the changes of acculturation. In Bowen theory terms, these individuals or families are thought to have more "solid self" that accompanies them through the process of migration and establishing their position in a new group. Another study emphasizes the importance of "social capital" or the connection with a social network of one's country of origin as a buffer against the stresses of immigrant life (Zhou and Blankston, 1996). Bowen theory addresses the extent to which it is possible to maintain emotional and historical connections to one's own family in a large, multigenerational network of families and acknowledges the emotional importance of these connections.

BOWEN THEORY, THE RELATIONSHIP SYSTEM, AND PATTERNS OF MIGRATION

The thesis of this chapter is that many relationship processes influencing migration are also present in some version in all mammals. The human version may require the lens of a natural systems theory such as Bowen theory to broaden the view. The human appears to have access to the many and varied strategies that are seen in a number of different mammal species.

Table 17.1 shows some of the relationship factors that are addressed in both fields of study. These are likely influences on the timing and choice of individuals who leave the home territory as well as those who stay. The main questions addressed here are: "Who emigrates?" and "Under what conditions?" and "Who stays?"

TABLE 17.1. Relationship Influences on Migration in Human Families and Other Animal Social Groups

Human Families	Other Animal Social Groups
Functional position (includes sibling position)	Functioning position (includes rank)
Triangles*	Alliances and competition
Level of differentiation	Level of competence
Tension/anxiety in family	Disturbance in system
Conflict	Aggression
Cutoff	Extrusion of individuals or groups

*A concept in Bowen theory that describes the ways in which a two-person relationship involves a third person to deal with tension in the original twosome.

There is growing awareness that habitat or environmental disturbances also are important factors in changing the *social* environment of any species. With evidence of increasing environmental crises and the mass migrations of humans that accompany great environmental changes, the evidence is growing that human social structures are profoundly affected (Kaplan, 2000). From the perspective of Bowen theory, there is no discontinuity between population pressures, environmental crises, political unrest, and the disintegration of stable social structures as seen in humans and other animals. In this context, patterns of mass migration simply fit into the human's effort to adapt to changing conditions of life on the planet. The limits of that adaptation are not yet clear, but the study of natural systems and the family may make the limits of that adaptation clearer.

Bowen theory provides a clear blueprint for studying the influence of the relationship system in important decisions about staying or leaving one's family and place of origin. Although history and sociology have always recognized that there are *individuals* who choose to stay or leave, no other theory has provided a careful study of the relationship system that can help define the specific relationship factors underlying these decisions.

Emotional cutoff highlights an important dimension in the study of emigration. Is cutoff simply one manifestation of the difficulty that mammals have in maintaining social connections under certain conditions? Does the human, then, sometimes revert to the earliest mammal condition of separating from the parental unit by permanently leaving the territory in order to begin the next generation?[10]

Evidence from clinical family studies demonstrates that emotional cutoff from an anxious system can reduce acute anxiety for individuals in that generation, but will generally leave the next generation with a very high level of chronic anxiety. Each person has to manage the anxiety that is passed on without understanding "from whence it came." Cutoff appears to leave people with behavior and feelings, values and beliefs that are not congruent. The clinical evidence shows increase in the number of mechanisms used in each succeeding generation to deal with the chronic anxiety leading to more frequent and more serious symptoms (Bowen, 1978; Kerr and Bowen, 1988).[11]

The human is clearly a "historical" animal, capable of knowing the history of many generations and connecting with many branches of relationships across time. In situations where the human cuts off from that personal historical context, individuals may do exceptionally well with their own lives while leaving the next generations with fewer relationship resources to achieve the best that is possible.

It is premature to propose a solution to a process that is still poorly understood. It is certainly unwise to propose that people "should not" cut off from difficult family situations or to propose that talking about all the unresolved issues will prevent cutoff. Those are simplistic answers to complex situations where cutoff may have both adaptive and maladaptive aspects. However, if cutoff in the person and in the family are not resolved, the person will probably be left with areas of emotional life and family emotional process that are too hidden from view to be integrated naturally into his or her life. At the same time, trying to bridge a cutoff arising from an extremely difficult emotional situation in which cutoff served a survival function may create new problems. Such actions require careful thought, an appreciation of the functional role of cutoff, and consistent efforts to increase one's own maturity and differentiation of self. Without such efforts the actions not only may increase anxiety and symptoms but also may increase the need for parts · of the family to maintain the cutoff.

From the careful study of details in family migrations, new facts may be added to Bowen theory concepts of cutoff and differentiation of self. Early work indicates that emotional cutoff not only prevents the resolution of unresolved relationships; but also leaves the new unit without an accurate *context* for defining itself and identifying facts that underlie chronic anxiety. Migration adds another barrier to regaining this personal historical context after cutoff.

Do families sometimes pay a price for migration? Do all social mammals depend on migration as a means of handling pressures within the group? When does emotional cutoff become the means of handling relationship pressures? Is cutoff one of the instinctual processes that regularly influences migration? The evidence is not yet clear. In animal populations, the ability of some individuals to leave the territory provides a safety valve against the effects of crowding and conflict.

One Mexican family with nine offspring shows fairly typical variability in the functioning of the second and third generation, with two cutoff branches having more severe emotional and social problems in their offspring. Of the five offspring who emigrated, those two cutoff branches emigrated the greatest distances—over 700 miles. The other three who migrated have stayed in close contact with the family and have had slightly fewer severe problems. Three remained relatively near the home territory where they could make contact without great expense or travel. The second and third generations of these families have the least problems. However, one male remained dependent on his parents, lived most of his adult life in their home, never worked steadily or married, and appeared to have the poorest functioning of all.

In a family with a rather modest level of differentiation, these results are not surprising. Migration and cutoff may solve some immediate problems, but the underlying relationship problems remain to be handled. In the slightly more mature branches of a family, the relationships can be addressed by remaining in contact over time. In the least mature branches, cut-off gives some relief for one generation, but the next generation is likely to show more symptoms. However, remaining dependently attached has its problems as well and can often be seen as a high level of reactivity and a life that never gets going under its own steam.

Clearly there are many factors that influence the adaptation of individuals in the midst of migration. A positive outcome to migration appears to be more likely when the family has the maturity to maintain relationships with past generations and a clear factual connection with the past. In many cases, migration provides opportunities that develop a branch of a family in ways that are impossible without new experiences and new knowledge. The thesis of this chapter, however, is that the emotional system of the family is one of the powerful influences over migratory patterns in humans and the decisions that influence migrations. That influence is still poorly appreciated and understood. Bowen theory provides one way to study the family emotional system, which we have in common with other forms of life.

CONCLUSION

This chapter presents a new perspective on the issues of emigration and immigration. While history and sociology study factual conditions of life that surround these processes, this chapter emphasizes poorly understood instinctual processes that the human has in common with other mammals. The following questions are suggested as directions for future study:

- Under what conditions do different species of mammals (including humans) regularly leave their home territories?
- Do any of these conditions have anything in common with Bowen's concept of emotional cutoff?
- What are the characteristics of individuals who leave when competition rises or of those who remain even though resources are depleted?
- What are the characteristics or functional positions in a group or family that may predispose one to leave and another to stay?
- What are the generational characteristics of migrating families that develop stable family units over the succeeding generations?
- What are the characteristics of the family emotional system of individuals and families who remain in contact with their history or with branches of the family after migration?

Animal and human studies show the importance of the relationship system in determining the timing and makeup of the group who leave the home territory to establish themselves in a new social group. In-depth studies of migrating families provide a detailed view of the variability in the circumstances in these families. From an initial study of clinical cases, emotional cutoff appears to play some part in the emigration of the small sample of families discussed in this chapter. New knowledge gained from multigenerational studies, using many of the variables proposed here with larger samples, can provide another approach to understanding the effects of emigration and immigration on families.

Finally, the importance of human connection across generations by way of history and personal contact with several generations in one's lifetime offers a counterpoint to the human talent for wandering away from "home." An important factor is the human ability both to remain connected to the past and to move into new territories and new relationship systems. The tools of maintaining history, even in the face of great trauma, and of maintaining emotional contact across many generations are proposed as unique, human abilities that draw on centuries of skills developed over generations of evolution of the human family. Bowen theory addresses this human ability[12] and provides some clues about ways to move past emotional cutoff or the barriers of time and distance to maintain one's connection to the multigenerational past and the larger family system while not being limited by it (Bowen, 1978).

NOTES

1. Emotional cutoff refers to an automatic emotional process in which individuals separate themselves from the past generation in the face of high tension and unresolved relationships.

2. Instinct is defined for this chapter as an innate tendency or response of a given species to act in ways that are important for its existence, development, and preservation.

3. See examples in later section of this chapter.

4. "Pseudo-self" in Bowen theory describes a way of responding to an anxious system without carefully defining a self in important areas of life and relationships

5. Bowen describes automatic mechanisms that are instinctual in situations of high tension in relationships: distance, conflict, over/underfunctioning reciprocity, and projection to a third person.

6. Defining a self refers to a process in which a person clearly defines life values, principles, thoughts, and decisions to important others in the relationship system.

7. Mexican immigration is not considered unusual in this regard It is simply easier to study the facts of the generations who left and those who stayed in their home territory than with immigrations from more distant locations

8. Differentiation of self refers, in part, to one's ability to be a distinct individual while remaining in emotional contact with the group.

9. "Solid self" in Bowen theory is one aspect of differentiation of self. It reflects the extent to which one is able to live by principles and beliefs in the midst of emotional forces to go along with the group.

10. See Animal Studies section at the beginning of this chapter for reference to mammals' earliest ancestral condition, where all adults emigrated.

11. Bowen theory describes several automatic processes that families use to manage tension or anxiety that is not handled directly in the relationships. These include conflict, distance, dysfunction in one spouse, and projection of the problem to a third person.

12. This ability is best captured in Bowen's concept of differentiation of self, which describes the variability in the extent to which individuals recognize profound connections to the family group, develop their own individual responsibility and autonomy, and remain in viable connection to the broad family.

REFERENCES

Alberts, S C., Sapolsky, R.M., and Altmann, J. (1992). Behavioral, endocrine, and immunological correlates of immigration by an aggressive male into a natural primate group *Hormones and Behavior* 26:167-178.

Baker, K.G. and Gippenreiter, J.B. (1996). The Effects of Stalin's Purge on Three Generations of Russian Families. *Family Systems* 3(1):1 5-35.

Bowen, M. (1978). *Family Therapy in Clinical Practice*. New York: Jason Aronson.

Bower, B. (1998). Immigrants Go from Health to Worse. *Science News* 154:180.

Bunting, A. (1982). "Emigration As Emotional Cutoff." Georgetown Family Center Conference on Children, Washington, DC, Spring.

Buriel, R. (1985). Integration with traditional Mexican American and sociocultural adjustment. In L. Martinez and R. H. Mendoza (Eds.), *Chicano Psychology*, Second Edition (pp. 95-132) Orlando, FL: Academic Press.

Dingle, H. (1996). *Migration: The Biology of Life on the Move*. Oxford: Oxford University Press.

Eisenberg, J.F. (1981). *The Mammalian Radiations*. Chicago: University of Chicago Press

Gaulin, S.J.C and Fitzgerald, R.W. (1986). Sex differences in spatial ability: An evolutionary hypothesis and test. *American Naturalist* 127:74-88.

Goodall, J. (1986). *The Chimpanzees of Gombe: Patterns of Behavior*. Cambridge, MA: The Belknap Press of Harvard University Press.

Greenwood, P.J. (1980). Mating systems, philopatry, and dispersal in birds and mammals. *Animal Behaviour* 28:1140-1162.

Howard, W.E. (1982). Innate and environmental dispersal of individual vertebrates. In Lidicker, W.Z. and Stroudsberg, R.L. (Eds.), *Dispersal and Migration*. Stroudsberg, Pennsylvania: Caldwell, Hutchinson Ross Publishing Company.

Jacobs, A. and Hanley, R. (2001). A boy's slaying resonates in a bedroom city of immigrant workers. *The New York Times*, May 24, late edition, final, section B, p. 1, col. 3.

Kaplan, R.D. (2000). *The Coming Anarchy: Shattering the Dreams of the Post Cold War*. New York: Random House.

Kerr, M.E. and Bowen, M. (1988). *Family Evaluation.* New York: W.W. Norton and Company.

Lancaster, J.B. (1986). Primate social behavior and ostracism. In Gruter, M. and Masters, R. (Eds.), *Ostracism: A Social and Biological Phenomenon* (pp. 67-75). New York: Elsevier Science and Publishing Co., Inc.

Lidicker, W.Z. (1975). The role of dispersal in the demography of small mammals. In Golley, F.B., Petrusewicz, K., and Ryszkowski, L. (Eds.), *Small Mammals: Their Productivity and Population Dynamics* (pp. 103-128). London: Cambridge University Press.

Mehlman P.T., Higley J.D., and Faucher, I. (1995). Correlation of CSF 5-HIAA concentration with sociality and the timing of emigration in free-ranging primates. *American Journal of Psychiatry* 152(6):907-913.

Morawska, E. (1990). The sociology and historiography of immigration. In Yans-McLaughlin, V. (Ed.), *Immigration Reconsidered* (pp. 187-238). New York and Oxford: Oxford University Press.

Moss, C. (1988). *Elephant Memories: Thirteen Years in the Life of an Elephant Family.* New York: Fawcett Columbine.

Rauseo, L. (1996). "Emotional cutoff and knowledge of one's multigenerational family: A study of 48 pregnant women in a community clinic." Presented at the Research Meeting at Georgetown Family Center, Washington, DC, April.

Roskies, E., Iida-Miranda, M., and Strobel, M.G. (1977) Life changes as predictors of illness in immigrants. *Stress and Anxiety* 4:3-21.

Salgado de Snyder, V.N. (1987). *Mexican Immigrant Women: The Relationship of Ethnic Loyalty and Social Support to Acculturative Stress and Depressive Symptomatology.* Spanish Speaking Mental Health Research Center. Occasional Paper No. 22 ISBN 0-918479-32-0, ISSN 0743-3-34.

Smale, L., Holekamp, K.E., and Nunes, S. (1997) Sexually dimorphic dispersal in mammals: Patterns, causes, and consequences. *Advances in The Study of Behavior* 26:181-250.

Sterngold, J. (2001). One survivor is arrested in smuggling of migrants. *The New York Times,* May 30, late edition, final, section A, p. 16, col. 6.

Suomi, S.J. (2000). "Individual variation in primate social groups." A Conference Presented at Texas Technical Health Sciences Center. El Paso, TX. March 31.

Vega, W.A., Kolody, B., Aguilar-Gaxioloa, S., Alderete, E., Catalano, R., and Caraveo-Anduage, J. (1998). Lifetime prevalence of DSM-III-R psychiatric disorders among urban and rural Mexican Americans in California. *Archives of General Psychiatry* 55:771-778.

Wakin, D.J. (2001). 12 illegal immigrants are found dead in desert. *The New York Times,* May 24, late edition, final, section A, p. 14, col. 4.

Waser, P.M. and Jones, W.T. (1983). Natal philopatry among solitary mammals. *Quarterly Review of Biology* 58:355-390.

Zhou, M. and Blankston, C L. III. (1996). Social capital and the adaptation of the second generation: The case of vietnamese youth in New Orleans. In Portes, Alejandro (Ed.), *The New Second Generation* (pp. 197-220). New York: Russell Sage Foundation.

Chapter 18

Emotional Cutoff and Holocaust Survivors: Relationships and Viability

Eileen B. Gottlieb

INTRODUCTION

The purpose of this chapter is to examine the relationship between emotional cutoff and the functioning of survivors of the Holocaust. It is the assumption of this author that emotional cutoff is a significant factor in the lifetime viability of this population. Emotional cutoff is a concept in Bowen theory that refers to the manner in which emotional process is managed between the generations (Bowen, 1978). Assuming that each individual has some degree of unresolved emotional attachment to his parents, emotional cutoff is observable in all families. Variation in lifetime functioning to some extent represents differences in the way individuals manage the process of emotional cutoff. The manner in which this is accomplished is observable across the generations of each family.

Definition of Emotional Cutoff

In Bowen's words, "The principle manifestation of the emotional cutoff is denial of the intensity of the unresolved emotional attachment to parents, acting and pretending to be more independent than one is, and emotional distance achieved through internal mechanisms or physical distance" (Bowen, 1978, p. 536).

According to Bowen theory, "there are all gradations of the emotional cutoff" (Bowen, 1978, p. 383). Many families maintain formal, distant, dutiful relationships with past generations. This usually is characterized by infrequent contact. It is believed that families that maintain more viable contact with the extended family have more orderly and less symptomatic lives. Furthermore, the manner in which a family manages the unresolved emotional attachment to the past has consequences for future generations:

One family remains in contact with the parental family and remains relatively free of symptoms for life, and the level of differentiation does not change much in the next generation. The other family cuts off with the past, develops symptoms and dysfunction, and a lower level of differentiation in the succeeding generation. (Bowen, 1978, p. 383)

Kerr and Bowen (1988) write in *Family Evaluation* that "emotional cutoff" describes the way people manage the emotional intensity associated with undifferentiation between the generations: "The greater the undifferentiation or fusion between the generations, the greater the likelihood the generations will cut off from one another. Parents often cut off from their adult children as much as their adult children cut off from them" (p. 271).

Emotional cutoff refers to the physiological, psychological, and behavioral process observable throughout nature whereby one organism separates itself from another in an effort to manage the emotional attachment between them. Paul MacLean (1990) in *The Triune Brain in Evolution* describes basic, more instinctual reactions based in the reptilian brain as well as attitudes, biases, and beliefs stored in the limbic brain. Objective, rational thought is associated with the neocortex. He believes that human functioning reflects the interaction of all three brains. Emotional cutoff is a relationship process that is presumed to express the more instinctual, reptilian, and limbic reactions. It is not associated with prefrontal cortex functions.

Emotional cutoff can occur through physical separation as well as psychological distance. It often initially results in lower states of anxiety as the organism gains comfort from the increased independence achieved through separation. It has been observed, however, that emotional cutoff heightens anxiety over time as the organism attempts to cope with environmental challenge without the protection and support gained from the emotional contact with family members (Gottlieb, 1993). When this process of emotional cutoff evolves across the generations, it weakens the capacity of the relationship system, leaving individuals more vulnerable and less viable in the evolutionary missions to survive and reproduce. Less viable emotional systems express more symptoms and lower levels of functioning.

Relationship Between Emotional Cutoff and Functioning

According to Bowen theory, functioning is the outcome of a multigenerational process comprised of chronic anxiety, established patterns for managing it, and the position an individual occupies in the relationship system (Bowen, 1978). Depending upon the degree of knowledge and objectivity one possesses regarding this process, one is more or less vulnerable to physical, emotional, and social problems. Objectivity is the outcome of clear, factual knowledge of the emotional system and one's part in it. Objective people operate from more carefully considered beliefs and principles, maintain more open, viable contact with others, and increase the possibility of relationships as resources in coping with daily life.

Objectivity concerning the intensity of emotional attachment to one's family of origin varies from individual to individual. Bowen (1978) writes "that such attachments exist in all degrees of intensity" (p. 534). He explains that the type of mechanism used to achieve emotional distance is not an indication of the intensity or degree of unresolved emotional attachment: "The person who runs away from home is as emotionally attached as the one who stays at home and uses internal mechanisms to control the attachment" (Bowen, 1978, p. 535). However, the one who runs away does have a different life course. The more intense the cutoff with parents the more vulnerable one is to repeating the same pattern in future relationships: "He can have an intense relationship in a marriage which he sees as ideal and permanent at the time, but the physical distance pattern is part of him. When tension mounts in the marriage, he will use the same pattern of running away" (Bowen, 1978, p. 535).

In *Family Evaluation* (1988), Kerr and Bowen state that people who "escape" their family of origin determined to be different from them are often the most cutoff people of all (p. 272):

> Most people who claim to be independent of their families have "broken away" from them rather than "grown away" from them. Growing away from one's family depends on gaining more emotional objectivity. More objectivity means one is able to see the ways in which he is part of the system: the ways in which he affects the emotional functioning of others and the ways others affect his emotional functioning. (p. 272)

Kerr and Bowen further suggest that if a person can gain more emotional objectivity about his or her family of origin and remain in contact rather than cut off from it, his or her amount of anxiety and emotional distance from spouse, children, and important others will decrease (p. 273).

Bowen theory assumes that depending on the ability of a person to manage himself or herself in his or her family of origin, these relationships can be more or less helpful in coping with his or her life course. Kerr and Bowen (1988) write,

> the ability to be more of a self brings people into better emotional contact with the most durable and reliable support system they will ever have. The family of origin, which includes more than just parents and

siblings, is rarely matched by nonfamilial relationship networks for
the emotional well-being reasonably active relationships can provide.
Improving emotional contact with the extended family has the potential to significantly reduce serious physical, emotional and social
symptoms in oneself and/or in one's nuclear family. A reduction in the
need to cut off to maintain equilibrium within self appears to reduce
an individual's level of chronic anxiety. (p. 276)

EMOTIONAL CUTOFF AND HOLOCAUST SURVIVORS

Bowen theory defines functioning as the interplay between emotionally
reactive and intellectually reflective brain processes. The emotional and intellectual systems operate simultaneously in the human as a response to the
environment in which he or she exists. The network of relationships of
which the individual is a part and his or her reactions to it account for his or
her behavior. The degree of objective reality about self and the broader field
is a determining factor in how the individual functions. Objectivity is comprised in varying degrees by the level of chronic or sustained anxiety, the extent of self-awareness, and the degree of self-control in the individual and
the relationship system. The less objectivity, the more behavior reflects automatic, instinctual responses. The more objectivity, the more behavior represents carefully considered beliefs and principles.

Depending on their evolved objective capacity to know self and the environment, humans are more or less able to negotiate the emotional process.
One predictable way that people negotiate their interdependency is through
a process described in Bowen theory as emotional cutoff.

As a clinician, researcher, and family member, the author has tried to observe this process in self and others by focusing her attention on variations
in response to catastrophe. She has looked specifically at survivors of the Holocaust to learn more about the impact of emotional cutoff in lifetime functioning. Six research families from a sample of seventy families are presented
and analyzed in this chapter. Each family produced at least one member
who survived the systematic Nazi genocide. Some facts are presented about
the variation in multigenerational functioning observable in these families
since the Holocaust. These facts will help illustrate the relationship between
emotional cutoff and lifetime functioning.

The author's research on variations in response to catastrophe and lifetime functioning of Holocaust survivors began in 1992 and continues. She
initially interviewed ten survivors to examine the functional facts about
three generations in each family. From 1996 to 1998, an additional sixty sur-

vivors were interviewed for Survivors of the Shoah Visual History Foundation. This organization's mission is to archive 50,000 testimonies of Holocaust survivors to be available in five libraries and museums worldwide. Included in these functional facts are the following:

- Longevity
- Health
- Education
- Career
- Financial solvency
- Marital stability
- Children
- Functional level of children
- Chronic symptoms (physical, emotional, behavioral)
- Contact with other family members
- Community service
- Lifetime achievement

This research assumes that these empirical facts represent the markers of functioning of the survivors and their families across three generations. These facts represent the data that is collected and recorded on the three-generation family diagram developed by the Georgetown Family Center in Washington, DC, for assessment purposes in clinical work. They provide a broad database about the lives of the individuals being studied which is indicative of how people behave. It is assumed that what people do is factual. Facts provide the clearest picture of how individuals and families function.

CASE HISTORIES

Bowen theory proposes that an individual's capacity to cope with the circumstances of life is the result of the family emotional process and his or her ability to be knowledgeable and thoughtful about his or her part in it. Being part of the relationship system automatically determines, to some extent, how one thinks about self and others. This process is projected from one generation to the next and influences functioning depending upon how much objectivity an individual is able to develop about it in a lifetime (Bowen, 1978). The more objective one is about the relationship process in his or her family, the greater the likelihood that he or she will be able to stay in contact with the past and manage the present effectively.

The following case histories provide evidence of the relationship between emotional cutoff and lifetime functioning. The six families represented in this sample were selected from a total of seventy survivors (ten interviewed for a paper titled "The Holocaust: Fifty Years Later" (Gottlieb, 1993), presented at the Georgetown Family Center Annual Symposium in Washington, DC, and sixty interviewed for Survivors of the Shoah Visual History Foundation from 1996 to 1998. Several of the families were also interviewed a second time for an article titled, "Holocaust Voices" (Gottlieb, 2000), which was published in *Boca Raton Magazine*. Families were not chosen to illustrate more or less emotional cutoff. This author selected those most familiar to her. However, the six families represent variation in lifetime functioning. The presence of this variation is related to the degree of emotional cutoff and the occurrence of chronic physical, emotional, and social symptoms. The families with a greater degree of emotional cutoff express more chronic symptoms.

Family Number One

Family number one is comprised of an eighty-nine-year-old survivor, S(1), his second wife of twenty-five years, his two sons (from his first marriage to another survivor, who died in 1973), and their wives and children (see Figure 18.1). S(1) was married prior to World War II. He and his wife managed to escape the Nazis by hiding first in an underground bunker and then becoming partisans in the forest near their hometown. When they went into hiding they left behind their daughter, parents, and siblings. With the exception of two older sisters and two uncles and an aunt who had relocated to the United States and Argentina prior to the war, everyone perished. Having survived the war, after returning to Belarus for several years, they were able to immigrate to the United States with their two sons and connect with family members living there. S(1) became a successful businessman. He has been honored throughout his life for his work in Jewish charitable and relief organizations. His sons married and became attorneys. His four grandchildren are all well-educated professionals. He has never suffered from any chronic illness and is robust to this day despite having surgery in the past few years. His first wife died thirty years ago, and he has been remarried for twenty-five years. He has maintained contact with his sisters and their families over time. There has been minimal emotional cutoff with his past and he is well connected with the future generation. S(1) speaks openly about the deaths of his parents, siblings, and daughter. He believes that his strong commitment to Judaism is related to his connection with these people. Bowen theory suggests that where there is viable contact with the past and present generations, both living and deceased, one is poised for a higher level of lifetime functioning. Therefore, it is assumed that an association exists between the low degree of emotional cutoff and the twelve facts exam-

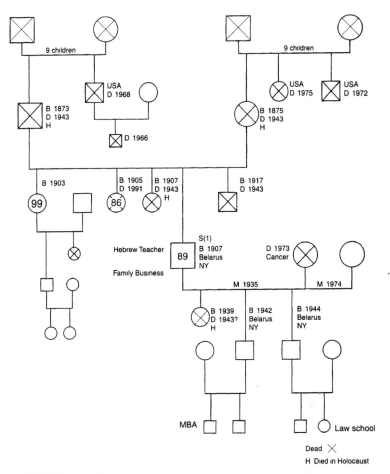

FIGURE 18.1. Family number one three-generation family diagram.

ined in this family. More contact between the generations contributes to better lifetime functioning.

Family Number Two

Family number two is comprised of an eighty-seven-year-old survivor, S(2). her three sons, and four grandchildren (see Figure 18.2). S(2) escaped to Russia with her parents, older brother, and three younger sisters during the war. After the war she met and married another survivor whose parents, siblings, wife, and three children perished in the Holocaust. After the birth

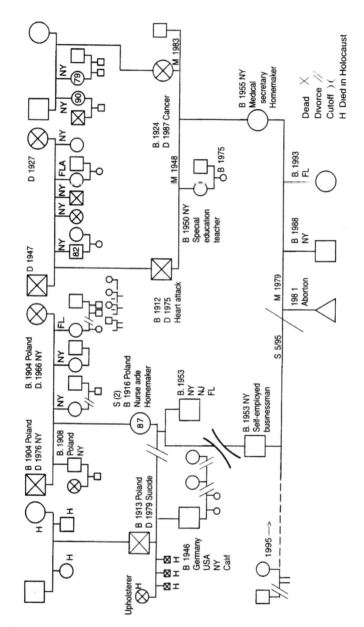

FIGURE 18.2. Family number two three-generation diagram.

432

of their eldest son in Germany, they immigrated with her entire family to the United States, where their twin sons were born in 1953. The entire extended family lived within walking distance of one another. Her husband worked at his trade until 1979, when he committed suicide at the age of sixty-six. He had been depressed for years and was treated with medication. He also had an alcohol addiction that was never addressed. He had great difficulty providing for his family. She worked as a semiprofessional to help support the family, but they always had financial problems. Her husband maintained no contact with any extended family who survived the war. She had regular contact with her extended family until the death of her parents between 1966 and 1976. Since then, although some family members still reside nearby, she has less contact with them. S(2) has always suffered from physical complications, including a chronic disorder for which she is treated with medications. Her eldest son has been married and divorced twice. He has two daughters from his first marriage whom he seldom sees. One of the twins has been married and divorced once and has been diagnosed with a psychiatric disorder. He maintains contact with his two children. One child has an emotional disorder for which he is being treated with medication and therapy. His twin has never married. The three brothers do not have much contact. Two of them have not spoken in years. S(2) has little contact with any of them. She is an observant Jew but has never been actively involved in her community. This family displays a high degree of emotional cutoff as well as a high level of significant problems. It is assumed that a relationship exists between emotional cutoff and lifetime functioning. Less contact between the generations contributes to greater difficulties.

Family Number Three

Family number three is comprised of a seventy-two-year-old survivor, S(3), his sixty-five-year-old wife of forty-nine years, two daughters, and two grandchildren (see Figure 18.3). S(3) was fourteen years old when he was deported to Auschwitz. He is the only member of his family as well as both his parents' families to survive the concentration camps. Six of his mother's siblings immigrated to the United States prior to World War II. Five of his cousins escaped during the war to Israel, China, Australia, South America, and Russia.

Having posed as a mechanic while incarcerated, his job was considered "essential" to the German war effort. He was liberated from Auschwitz at eighteen. Through the help of a Jewish American army officer, he made contact with his maternal extended family and immigrated to the United States. S(3) was a successful businessman. His daughters are both college

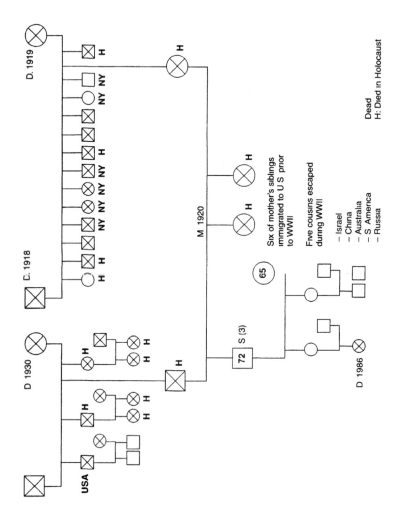

FIGURE 18 3. Family number three three-generation diagram.

434

graduates and professionals, as are their husbands. One of his three grandchildren died at age four of a birth disorder. The others are healthy and functioning well. The mother of the child who died was the president of an organization that provides support for families of children with birth defects, even long after the death of her daughter. S(3), a practicing Jew, has always been active in Holocaust education and information organizations. Neither he nor his children have had any serious or prolonged physical, emotional, or social problems. His wife has a chronic condition for which she has been treated with medication for years. He is in ongoing contact with the ninety surviving members of his extended family and is well connected to the next generation. Again, it is assumed that an association exists between the low degree of emotional cutoff and the twelve facts examined in this family. More contact between the generations contributes to better lifetime functioning.

Family Number Four

Family number four is composed of a seventy-six-year-old survivor, S(4), her four children, and four grandchildren (see Figure 18.4). Her husband of fifty-two years was also a survivor. They met after the war in a displaced persons camp. He died in 1996. S(4) survived the concentration camp with her older brother. Her parents and younger brother perished, as did her husband's parents, three older brothers, his first wife, and two children. After the war S(4) married her husband and they emigrated from Germany to Canada with their twin daughters, her older brother, and his wife. S(4) and her husband eventually moved to the United States to pursue a better livelihood. After the relocation, their second set of twins was born. Throughout the course of their lives, neither of the survivors in this family maintained any contact with the past except for a relationship with S(4)'s brother and his family. Several years before his death in 1975, they had a disagreement and stopped speaking to each other. To this day, S(4) has no contact with her sister-in-law or her nephew. Since her husband's death, she has had difficulty functioning. She has antagonistic relationships with all her children. Her three daughters and their families have all had physical, emotional, and behavioral problems. These include a daughter with diabetes, a daughter who was divorced, and a daughter with a psychiatric diagnosis whose husband died suddenly at age thirty-six. Her son never married and is not self-supporting. He is being treated for anxiety with medication. Her grandchildren have also had some significant difficulties. The eldest is married with two children. She and her husband have financial problems. One of the younger grandchildren and two great grandchildren have all been

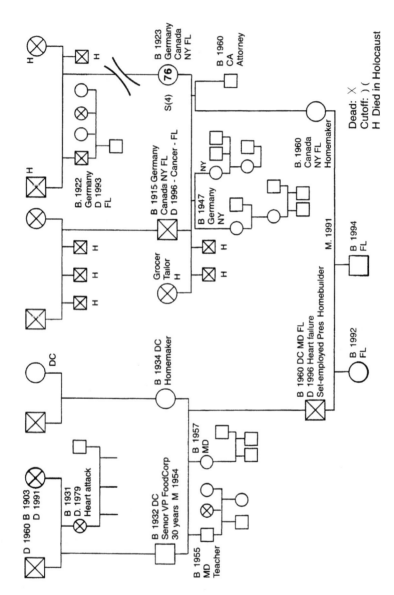

FIGURE 18.4. Family number four three-generation diagram.

436

diagnosed with emotional disorders for which they are being treated with medications. S(4) has never been active in Jewish organizations or the greater community. While she is in contact with the future generations, the relationships are difficult for everyone. This family demonstrates a high degree of emotional cutoff and a significant number of difficulties. Less contact between the generations contributes to poor lifetime functioning.

Family Number Five

Family number five is composed of a seventy-five-year-old survivor, S(5), married to her American husband of fifty years, their three sons, daughters-in-law, and seven grandchildren (see Figure 18.5). At age thirteen, to escape the Nazis, S(5) was sent from Germany with her eleven-year-old sister to live at a boarding school run by the Church of England. Her father and mother as well as her maternal grandparents and uncle remained in Germany. Her father, an Orthodox Jew, was twenty years older than his wife, who was a convert to Judaism. Although he had been deported to a labor camp at the beginning of the war, he eventually procured a visa to Cuba and left the country. His wife, considered a gentile by the Nazis, remained in Germany with her parents. S(5) spent seven years in England. After the war, upon her father's insistence, the family reunited in the United States. S(5) met her husband shortly after her relocation. They worked together at a camp for physically handicapped people. Although she had not practiced her Judaism while in England, she returned to it after her marriage. Her parents lived together for fifty-four years. Her father died at age 100 and her mother twelve years later at ninety. Her husband was a very successful professional who earned his doctorate late in his career. All three sons are college graduates in long-term marriages with children. Her youngest son lost his vision in one eye due to a childhood accident. Despite this handicap, he is a successful professional. S(5) is a healthy, strong, and very active person. Her husband has had some serious medical problems over the years, but remains very involved with his family and community. Both S(5) and her husband have been recognized for their contributions to Jewish and secular organizations. She has never lost contact with her past. She meets yearly with four survivors who were her classmates in Germany before the war. Her sister has always been in her life. She is deeply involved with her grandchildren and the next generation. This family demonstrates a high degree of emotional contact as well as a high level of functioning. Again, the association between low emotional cutoff and high lifetime functioning can be made. More contact between the generations contributes to better lifetime functioning.

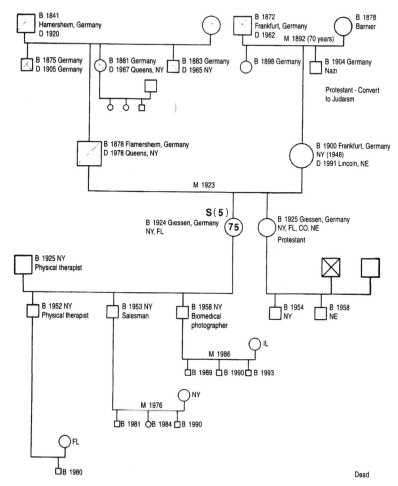

FIGURE 18.5. Family number five three-generation diagram.

Family Number Six

Family number six is composed of a seventy-one-year-old survivor, S(6), and her American husband of fifty years, as well as their two sons. who were born in the United States. At age thirteen. S(6), her parents, paternal grandmother, and siblings were deported from Hungary to Auschwitz (see Figure 18.6). With the exception of several family members who left Europe before the war, only one aunt survived with her. After their liberation. S(6) and her aunt spent time in Czechoslovakia before immigrating to the United States,

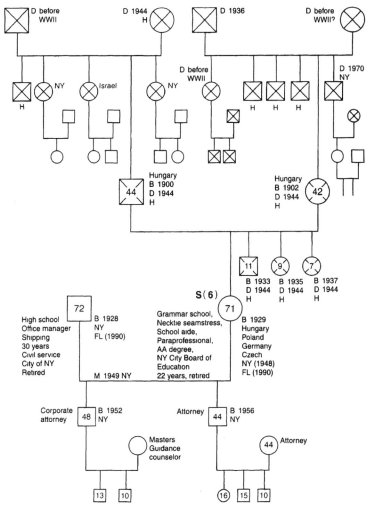

H Died in Holocaust

FIGURE 18.6. Family number six three-generation diagram

where they lived with relatives until she met her husband and married. S(6) and her youngest paternal aunt remained in close contact until her aunt died. She continues to have contact with her aunt's daughter and her family. Although S(6) did not complete highschool in Europe and did not speak English, she went to college when her sons were adolescents and completed her associate of arts degree. She was employed as a paraprofessional for twenty-two years. Both of her sons attended law school and are practicing attorneys. They have each been married for more than twenty years to professional women. Her five grandchildren are healthy, good students, and have been raised in the Jewish faith. She and her husband enjoy good health and have been retired for ten years. Recently she has become more active in Holocaust-related activities within her community and has been recognized for her contribution.She has remained connected to her past and is in close contact with the future generation. As discussed throughout this chapter, it is assumed that an association exists between emotional cutoff and lifetime functioning. With respect to this family, it would appear that more contact contributes to fewer problems.

CONCLUSION

The six case histories presented in this chapter are part of a larger sample of seventy families interviewed. The functional facts of their lives follow a consistent pattern evident among all of the families in the sample. In every case where there is significant emotional cutoff from past, present, and future generations, there are more chronic symptoms. Likewise, in families where the generations maintain more open, viable contact, there are fewer problems. The concept of emotional cutoff as described in Bowen theory helps to explain this phenomenon. When people can manage the unresolved emotional attachment that characterizes all human family relationships and remain in contact with one another, resources may exist to contend with the unpredictable challenges of life that are otherwise unavailable. These key relationships provide a foundation for family members that appear to serve them well even in the most difficult circumstances. The Holocaust and the families who lived through it provide an important opportunity to learn more about how this process works. Emotional cutoff may be one factor in the variation in lifetime functioning of Holocaust survivors and their families.

To the extent that survivors have been unable to manage the emotional process associated with the permanent and severe loss of significant family members who perished in the Holocaust, there is evidence to suggest that there will be more serious, chronic problems across a lifetime. The ability to attain some degree of objectivity about this experience, to acknowledge and remember the past while being focused in the present, appears to create a higher level of functioning as reflected in the twelve facts examined in this research. Regardless of the severity of loss, the effort to manage the reality of what occurred and make the most of whatever still exists has made a difference in the lives of some survivors of the Holocaust. Based on the facts presented in the preceding case histories, I believe a relationship exists between the degree of emotional cutoff and the functioning of these survivors and their families. To the extent that the facts presented here accurately reflect level of functioning, one may conclude that emotional cutoff is a factor in the life course of survivors of the Holocaust.

REFERENCES

Bowen, M. (1978). *Family Therapy in Clinical Practice.* New York: Jason Aronson.

Gottlieb, E. (1993). "The Holocaust: Fifty Years Later." Unpublished paper presented at the Georgetown Family Center Annual Symposium on Family Theory and Family Psychotherapy, Washington, DC.

Gottlieb, E. (2000). Holocaust Voices *Boca Raton Magazine,* January, 120-124.

Kerr, M. and Bowen, M. (1988). *Family Evaluation.* New York: W.W. Norton and Company.

MacLean, P. (1990). *The Triune Brain in Evolution.* New York: Plenum Press.

Chapter 19

Israeli-Palestinian Relations: A Bowen Theory Perspective

Fran Ackerman

INTRODUCTION

All human relations are rooted in the laws of nature. Humans tend to view themselves as unique, not only different from but also more important than any other species. In contrast, Darwin's theory of evolution presented the human as an integral part of all nature, subject to the identical evolutionary forces that govern all other living things. Bowen (1978) developed a theory of human behavior that was based on the human as part of evolution. According to Bowen, evolution explains not only the physical similarity between humans and other animals but the behavioral similarity as well (Kerr and Bowen, 1988).

The fundamental laws of nature influence the functioning of life-forms on many levels: single cells, individual animals (including humans), animal and human social groups, and entire species. One of the innate behaviors that characterizes relationships between all living organisms is the pull toward both togetherness and separateness. Many scientists have observed this phenomenon, using different language to describe it. Bonner (1988), a biologist, uses the terms *integration* and *isolation*. Bowen (1978), whose focus of study was the human family, developed several concepts that are relevant to this widespread phenomenon: *differentiation, cutoff, triangles,* and *societal process.*

The hypothesis of this chapter is that the evolutionary forces influencing humans are useful in understanding Israeli-Palestinian relations.[1] After a brief description of Bonner's concepts of integration and isolation, several concepts from Bowen family systems theory, the manifestation of these concepts and their relevance to Israeli-Palestinian relations, including an examination of their textbooks, will be presented.

BONNER'S CONCEPTS OF INTEGRATION AND ISOLATION

A universal property that affects living things, a tug-of-war between the tendency to come together and to be separate has been described by Bonner using the terms *integration* and *isolation*. This basic phenomenon influences living systems at all levels, ranging from single cells and insect societies to family systems. In human relations, including those between Israelis and Palestinians, the phenomenon manifests itself as a tendency toward "us" and "them" relationships.

The forces for integration and isolation at the level of the single cell have been described by Bonner (1988) in his studies of the life cycle of the slime mold. Within appropriate environmental conditions, a single-cell amoeba emerges from its cellulose case, consumes bacteria, and divides by binary fission. During a later stage, the amoebae aggregate, forming a multicellular organism with a front and hind end that moves in a well-integrated fashion. The forces of integration are apparent in the streaming together of the single-cell amoebae to form the multicellular organism. The forces of isolation are apparent in the existence of separate multicellular organisms; discrete slime molds do not fuse into a giant multicellular organism.

On a more complex level, the tendencies toward integration and isolation are readily apparent in colonies of social insects (Bonner, 1994). The larger colonies include different castes; each caste has a particular task. Integration is apparent in the colony's functioning as a unit. Isolation exists among colonies. Separate colonies defend their nest sites against intruders.

The prevalence of integration and isolation among many mammals is well known. One example can be observed in a wolf pack. The phenomenon of integration is apparent in the communication between the group members and their cooperation in capturing and sharing food, as well as in rearing young. Isolation is apparent in the wolf pack's separateness from other wolves. This separateness is manifested in the fact that wolves, similar to many other animals, claim territories. Claiming territories is similar to what insects do when they defend their nest sites. A wolf pack hunts in a specific area and marks off this area by periodically urinating along the boundary, a signal to other wolf packs that the territory has been claimed as a hunting preserve (Bonner, 1988).

When a phenomenon is prevalent throughout nature, it is assumed that there are evolutionary advantages to it. The tendency toward integration and its opposite, the tendency toward isolation, are both the result of identical laws, the laws of natural selection (Bonner, 1988). The integration of smaller units into larger units affords an evolutionary advantage. The larger unit is more efficient than the smaller one in its ability to feed and defend itself and in its ability to reproduce. This increased efficiency is sufficient to account for the integration phenomenon that occurs throughout nature.

The opposite tendency. isolation, is also advantageous in natural selection (Bonner, 1988). An example of isolation is the formation of discrete units of optimum size. If isolation did not occur, units would continue to integrate. They would become so large as to be inefficient and therefore would not be favored by natural selection.

Humans are subject to the same laws of nature as all other living things. People, much the same as many other living things, form groups; they integrate with certain people and isolate from others. This pattern of human relationships is related to the pattern of integration and isolation that occurs in slime molds, ants, and wolves. Among humans, this phenomenon is apparent in the tendency to form groups that are exclusionary. to relate to others as "us" and "them." Humans seem to include and exclude on the basis of many criteria, including religion. nationality. and ethnicity. The relations between Israelis and Palestinians are a clear example of exclusion on the basis of all three.

Territoriality, an example of both inclusion and exclusion, is a basis for conflicts between various groups and also is a core issue in the ongoing conflict between Israelis and Palestinians. Although "we-ness" and "otherness" may be inevitable, the forms and intensity of this phenomenon vary considerably within and between species. The variation and its manifestation will be examined in discussing relations between Israelis and Palestinians.

BOWEN CONCEPTS THAT ARE RELEVANT TO ISRAELI-PALESTINIAN RELATIONS

Differentiation of Self

A central concept of Bowen theory is differentiation of self (Bowen, 1978). According to Bowen, much of human behavior is driven by a force from the evolutionary past that humans have in common with other animals. Bowen called this force the emotional system. Behavior based on the emotional system is driven by instincts that are accompanied by feelings and subjective thinking. Functioning on the basis of the emotional system reflects an interplay of two counterbalancing forces: togetherness and individuality. The togetherness force propels people to connect with, be sensitive to, and respond to the cues of others. The individuality force propels people to be independent, to be guided by their own thinking. The higher the level of anxiety in a family and other social systems, the stronger the push toward togetherness, which includes the need to feel, think, and act alike.

Humans are also capable of behavior that is different from other animals. Their developed neocortex enables them to function on the basis of calm, objective thinking, which is based on what Bowen (1978) called the intellectual system. Differentiation is the capacity to distinguish between thinking and behavior that is emotionally driven and thinking and behavior that is based on the intellectual system. People vary in their capacity to differentiate between behavior that is driven by feelings and subjective thinking and behavior that is based on relatively objective thinking and may be informed but not controlled by feelings. The higher the level of differentiation, the greater the ability to differentiate between the influence of the two systems on one's thinking and behavior. At a higher level, functioning is based more on choice and less on "automatic pilot," that is, responding to immediate anxiety. People are more likely to have a broad perspective, to understand others' points of view and the long-term consequences of their actions. The converse applies to people with a lower level of differentiation.

As far as is known, animals other than humans do not differentiate between "automatic pilot" and thoughtful functioning; however, the variation in level of functioning that occurs in human behavior is prevalent among lower animals, as well. Kerr (1998) indicates that although naked mole-rats do not have "the well-developed intellectual system that has an important role in differentiation in human beings, . . . these rodents still exhibit some individual variation in emotional functioning" (p. 150). For example, there is considerable difference in how breeding females function in their colonies. Some neglect their pups, instead spending their time intimidating the nonbreeding females. Their functioning level is lower than that of other females who devote more time to their pups.

Among humans, according to Bowen (1978), behavior is frequently emotionally driven; nevertheless, humans have the capacity to reflect on their behavior, to be aware of their impulses and to decide on the basis of calm thinking to act differently. They can, at times, implement this decision. Although there are common patterns that characterize human behavior, the manifestation of these patterns, including their flexibility and intensity, vary. A cycle of conflict, for example, may be verbal or physical. The verbal conflict might include listening to one another and responding with mild anger, leaving the scene of the conflict, and/or screaming that is out of control. When people's behavior is based on the intellectual system, it can be flexible. In a relationship that includes ongoing conflict, for example, the participants might, at some point, function on the basis of their intellectual system, understand but not agree with the other's point of view, appreciate that they have reached a stalemate, and agree to disagree. In contrast, behavior driven by the emotional system leaves the participants with little flexibility. They have difficulty appreciating a point of view other than their own. In addition, their behavior seems to have a "life of its own" and "must" run its course.

The level of differentiation of the participants, the intensity of the relationship, and the anxiety in the system are major factors in how the behavior is manifested. Relations between Israelis and Palestinians vary considerably, reflecting at times behavior that is informed by the intellectual system and at other times behavior that is emotionally driven.

Cutoff

Cutoff, a second concept of Bowen theory that is relevant to Israeli-Palestinian relations, describes the human tendency to distance from others. Papero (1990) described this concept as the "manner in which people attempt to manage the emotional attachment to their parents and important other individuals" (p. 62). Although Bowen, in describing this concept, addressed primarily the cutoff between parents and their adult children, he noted that the term *cutoff* and its complement *fusion* also "describe the way cells agglutinate and the way they separate to start new colonies of cells" (Kerr and Bowen. 1988, p. 362).

The tendency to distance from members of the same species is prevalent throughout nature. Trees in a forest and plants in an arid area may be spaced in a nonrandom fashion. The separation allows for a more efficient access to resources, such as sun for trees in a forest and water for plants in an arid area (Bonner. 1988).

Bowen's concept of cutoff addresses the human tendency to distance emotionally. This tendency is apparent in the "us/them" polarization that characterizes relationships, including those among individuals, families, communities, and socioeconomic, ethnic, racial, religious, and national groups. The intensity of this emotional distancing or cutoff, however, varies considerably. The level of differentiation of the participants is a significant factor in the intensity of the cutoff. The more intense the cutoff, the more people relate to one another in a stereotypical pattern, not perceiving and/or relating to the complex person and/or group that the "other" is. Likewise, the "self" is presented as one dimensional. Stereotyped, narrow "self" relates to stereotyped, narrow "other."

Given the complexity of people and their relationships, it is clear that all human relationships include at least some degree of emotional distance. Although humans have developed reasons for cutoff, the basic tendency is based on the automatic processes that humans have in common with plants and other animals. The oversimplified image that is part of emotional distance is all the more likely in relating to an "enemy," as in relationships between Israelis and Palestinians.

Triangles

Another concept of Bowen theory that is relevant to Israeli-Palestinian relations is the triangle. A two-person relationship is inherently unstable because, inevitably, anxiety develops between a twosome (Bowen, 1978). This anxiety is reduced by including a third person in the original two-person relationship. The anxiety flows between the three people in the triangle. An emotional system larger than three people becomes a series of interlocking triangles. The structure of the triangle is: two or more persons form a closeness, the third person(s) is an "outsider." The relationship between the "insiders" and "outsider(s)" is characterized by distance or conflict.

Triangles occur in all emotionally significant human relationships. The membership in the triangle can readily shift or can be rigidly fixed. In a family, for example, the triangle may be fluid, with each of the parents at different times close to one of the children and with the other parent in the "outsider" position. Another form of the triangle may be a structure in which the two parents are close and each of the children is in the "outsider" position. In still another family the triangle may be rigid with a mother generally in coalition with one or more of the children against the father.

This pattern of behavior may be part of the human's evolutionary past. Bowen (1978) states: "The triangle is so basic that it probably also operates in animal societies" (p. 306). In fact, a triadic form of interaction has been observed in many primate species. The most common form of triadic relationship in nonhuman primates is a coalition or alliance of two individuals jointly opposing a third (de Waal and Harcourt, 1992). De Waal (1996) describes other examples of triadic relationships, such as when aggression between two animals is reconciled by inclusion of a relative of one of the conflictual twosome.

In humans, the triadic structure of relationships occurs among individuals as well as within and between small and large groups. Bowen (1978) states: "The emotional forces in a triangle operate the same in society as in the family" (p. 319). In very large groups or in a society, many people deal with emotional issues by choosing sides, creating either/or polarizations.

Bowen's concepts are interrelated.[2] For example, the separation that is inherent in emotional cutoff is based on emotional reactivity and is often accompanied by creating a "we-ness" with one or more individuals while separating from the other. This relationship configuration of cutoff and "we-ness" is a manifestation of a triangle. The intensity and rigidity of the cutoff and the triangle vary (Bowen, 1978). The lower the level of differentiation of the participants, the higher the level of anxiety within the system, and the more significant their relationship, the more intense and rigid the triangle and the cutoff; the higher the level of differentiation, the lower the level of anxiety in the system, and the less significant the relationship, the less intense and rigid the triangle and the cutoff.

Territorialty is one of many examples in which the cutoff and triangles between Israelis and Palestinians are manifest. This phenomenon, the maintenance of an area more or less exclusively by an animal or by groups of animals, occurs among many species. The territory is maintained by aggressive behavior or advertisement.

Many species of territorial animals respond with less aggression to their neighbors than to strangers (Langen, Tripet, and Nonacs, 2000). This interesting variation of territoriality, called the "dear enemy" phenomenon has been well documented; however, the function of this phenomenon is not clearly understood.

Humans are subject to the same natural forces that affect lower animals; however, they develop feelings and thoughts that explain, often elaborately, their basic automatic instincts. Territoriality is an example of a natural instinctual behavior about which the human frequently develops complex and intense feelings and thoughts. A major focus of the conflict between many people, including Israelis and Palestinians, focuses on territory.

Societal Emotional Process

Societal emotional process is the fourth concept of Bowen theory that is relevant to Israeli-Palestinian relations. This concept describes the manifestation of differentiation in the functioning of societies.

Societies, as do individuals and families, vary in levels of functioning. Societies functioning with a high level of differentiation maintain well-developed principles, understand the complexity of social and political phenomena, and take responsibility for their part in creating and maintaining them. They respect the legitimate rights of other societies, appreciate varied points of view, tolerate pressure, and understand the long-term effects of potential actions and respond accordingly. They develop goals based on principles and a relatively objective evaluation of their strengths, their weaknesses, and their options given the context in which they live. Societies functioning with a relatively low level of differentiation generally do not develop and maintain well-thought-out principles, nor do they accept responsibility for their part in creating and maintaining their difficulties. They function on the basis of unrealistic goals and respond to anxiety by attempting to alleviate the latest pressure with short-term solutions.

Bowen (1978) understood societies functioning with a low level of differentiation as reflecting increasing anxiety in response to "population explosion, the disappearance of new habitable land to colonize, the approaching depletion of raw materials necessary to sustain life, and growing awareness that 'spaceship earth' cannot indefinitely support human life in the style to which man and his technology have become accustomed" (p. 272). The effect of decreasing resources on the functioning of species is well documented and ranges from restlessness and emigration among ants, rodents, and songbirds to infanticide in guppies and cannibalism in many species of social insects (Wilson, 1975).

Israel, whose area is approximately 8,000 square miles (roughly the size of New Jersey), lacks natural resources, including water. The shortage of space and water intensifies the struggle between the Israelis and the Palestinians for this land. Papero (1990) points out that the more anxious the social process, the more two people or groups join together; they enhance their own functioning at the expense of a third party. Papero indicates that the increased polarization may be manifested in a "series of crises, generally resolved on the basis of restoring comfort rather than a thoughtful approach based upon principles and a degree of respect for differing viewpoints" (p. 64).

Societal emotional process is related to cutoff, triangles, and differentiation of self. Kerr (1998) describes regression on a societal level as including increased splintering of society into "we-they" factions that are characteristic of cutoff and triangles. The various subgroups adopt more dogmatic positions and are increasingly polarized from other groups with whom they disagree. The rigid factions make it difficult for people to cooperate in solving problems. The lower the level of societal differentiation, the more intense the cutoff and triangles and the more likely society responds to challenges with short-term "solutions" that alleviate the anxiety of certain segments of the population but do not address the problems within a long-term perspective.

The intensity and duration of the Israeli-Palestinian conflict reflects a relatively low level of societal differentiation that is exacerbated by the limited resources of land and water. The polarization of the two societies, which includes cutoffs and triangles, is intensifying. Many of the responses within each group are short-term solutions that attempt to reduce the anxiety of various segments of its population. The prevailing anxious and intense environment seriously limits the ability to maintain a long-term perspective that includes understanding and respecting the rights of the "other."

The author is an Israeli and American Jew living in Jerusalem. She believes that both Israelis and Palestinians have legitimate claims to the land and that each nation should have its own state.

ISRAELI AND PALESTINIAN PERSPECTIVES

This chapter addresses the relationship between Israeli Jews and Palestinians living in the disputed territories. This territory was captured by Israel in the 1967 war. The name by which this land is referred to is highly politicized. Referring to the land as Judea and Samaria, its Biblical names, implies that it should be incorporated into Israel. Referring to the land as the West Bank implies that it does not belong to Israel. Referring to the land as the "occupied territory" implies that it belongs to the Palestinians and is unjustly controlled by Israel. In the interest of neutrality, the author refers to it as the "disputed territory."

The history of the relationship of Arabs and Jews offers a perspective within which to understand the current conflict between Israelis and Palestinians.[3] This conflict is focused, to a large extent, on the land that Arabs consider Palestine and Jews consider Israel: the land represents many things to each side, including sovereignty and survival as a people with an ethnic and cultural identity. Each group's perspective presents its legitimate rights to the land.

Israeli Perspective

The Jewish claim to the land of Israel is based on the Bible, specifically God's promise to Abraham that his descendants would inherit the land of Israel. In addition, there has been continued Jewish presence in Israel throughout the centuries. The Jews' residence in Israel began approximately at the end of the second millennium B.C. Although other tribes continued to dwell there, Jews constituted a majority of the inhabitants and governed most of the country for the major part of the next millennium. The Jewish sovereignty ended in 66-73 A.D. when the Romans destroyed the Jewish temple and in 132-35 A.D. when they successfully defeated the final Jewish revolts. Most of the Jews were forced into exile.

The Arabs invaded the area that includes Israel in the seventh century. The land was not defined as a separate entity until 1920, when the League of Nations mandated that Britain should establish a homeland for the Jewish people in Palestine. Although the Jewish presence in the area between the second and twentieth centuries was relatively small, Jews retained strong ties to the land. Some came to live, to study, and to die there.

Jewish literature produced in exile is replete with references to the land of Israel. Jews prayed for the days when they would return to Jerusalem, the spiritual center of their homeland. Toward the end of the nineteenth century, when nationalism developed throughout Europe, the Zionist movement began as an expression of Jewish nationalism. Jews, primarily from Eastern Europe, began to immigrate to Israel (*Encyclopaedia Judaica*, 1972). They settled the land, establishing agricultural settlements, many of which were based on socialist ideals. They established and built cities. In addition, they initiated political and diplomatic activity directed toward establishing a Jewish political sovereignty in Israel.

In 1917, the Balfour declaration, which supported the autonomy of the Jewish people in the land of Israel, was issued. In the early 1930s, as anti-Semitism in Germany grew more intense, many German Jews immigrated to Israel. They brought professional, technical, and financial resources which contributed greatly to the development of the *yishuv*, the Jewish population in prestate Israel (*Encyclopaedia Judaica*, 1972). During World War II, Nazi genocide led to the murder of a third of the Jewish people. The Christian world, feeling compassion and guilt, offered little resistance to and some support for the Zionist cause. The Arabs, whose wartime record of sympathy for the Axis powers and hostility to the Allies discredited them in the eyes of the West, failed in their attempts to prevent the establishment of a Jewish state in Palestine. Consequently, the United Nations proposed a plan that would cede part of the territory of Palestine to the Jewish nation. Although the Arabs rejected this partition, this sharing of the land, the Jews accepted the plan and the state of Israel was established on May 14, 1948. The following day, when the British Mandate over Palestine ended, the armies of Egypt, Iraq, Lebanon, Syria, and the Arab Legion invaded the new state of Israel (Ettinger, 1976).

The survival of the Jewish state was threatened in subsequent wars as well. In the 1967 war, Israel gained land that is now disputed territory. Israeli leaders were and are willing to hand over some of the territories to the Palestinian nation, but they have never found an Arab partner willing to accept the rightful claims of the Jewish people to reside in their homeland and establish a sovereign state.

Palestinian Perspective

The Palestinians, just as the Israelis, base their claim to this territory—Palestine, or Falastin as Palestinians refer to it—on longtime residence and the belief that the territory is their homeland, to which they have deep-seated religious and cultural ties. Arabs have resided in this land continuously since the dawn of history, before there were Jews in the world. Palestinians are descendants of the Canaanite nations that resided in Palestine 4,000 years ago.

The Palestinian people include Christians and Muslims, and the land is holy to both religions. Israel is the site of many holy places associated with the life and teachings of Christ, who was born and lived in Israel. Jerusalem is the site of Christ's crucifixion, burial, and ascension (Reiter, Eordegian, and Abu Khalaf, 2001). The Koran refers to the country as the Holy Land. Hebron and Jerusalem are holy cities to Muslims. Mohammed ascended to heaven from Jerusalem to receive the principles of Islam from God (Reiter, Eordegian, and Abu Khalaf, 2001).

From the end of the nineteenth century, lands owned by Arabs were bought by Zionist groups. Following World War II, the colonial nations of the West carved up the area, ignoring the needs of the indigenous population. Since 1948, additional lands have been confiscated by the Israeli government. Following the war of 1967, more land was confiscated by Israel, and the Palestinians' freedom of movement and ability to settle the land were severely compromised. The political entity of Israel is an aggressive, colonial power that has provoked a series of wars with its Arab neighbors in order to acquire more territories. These wars, particularly the first one in 1948, have provided a cover for a premeditated plan to expel the Palestinians from their homes and have produced a substantial number of Palestinian refugees. Although many Palestinians acknowledge the suffering of the Jews during World War II, they should not be the ones to suffer for an event for which they bear no responsibility. The Zionist idea and homeland is foreign to the Middle East, primarily an Arab and Muslim region. The establishment of the state of Israel is an example of Western colonialism that brings irreparable harm to the Palestinian people. In fact, Israel's Independence Day is a day of mourning for the Palestinians, a day that they have named The Catastrophe.

APPLICATION OF BOWEN THEORY

Each group has intense feelings about the significance of the territory to its people and has difficulty appreciating its importance to the other. This bitter, ongoing conflict is built upon the same instincts that drive lower animals to define and defend territories and includes emotional cutoffs and triangles.

Using Bowen concepts to understand relationships between Israelis and Palestinians, it is interesting to note that the tendency of humans to create triangles in relationships and cut off from one another has been affecting the relationships of their ancestors for many centuries. The Bible describes Arabs and Jews as "insiders" and "outsiders" in relationship triangles and as cut off from one another (see Titelman's discussion in Chapter 1).

According to Bowen theory, relationship patterns are passed down over generations. The original difficulty between Israelis and Egyptians recorded in the Bible is present today. The factors inherent in the transmission of patterns from one generation to the next is not clearly understood and is beyond the scope of this chapter.

The intense conflict between Israelis and Palestinians that characterizes their current relationships is easily perceived as a triangle and a relationship cutoff: the "we" of two or more Israelis unites against the "other" of one or more Palestinians and, conversely, the "we" of two or more Palestinians unites against the "other" of one or more Israelis. Since the second *intifada* (uprising), which began in September 2000, Israelis and Palestinians are again engaged in ongoing, violent conflict which has exacerbated the intensity of the triangles and the cutoff between them.

Negotiations between Israelis and Palestinians are also a context in which triangles and cutoffs exist. The "we" of each group deals with the "other" of the other group. Intermediaries—including various Arab countries, such as Egypt and Jordan, the European Union, and the United States—become members of the interlocking triangles. In negotiations, the intensity of cutoff can vary from a relationship in which one perceives the other as "the enemy" with whom negotiations are a necessary evil, to a relationship in which one perceives the other as a partner with legitimate rights and obligations with whom one is ethically obligated to create a settlement that respects the rights of each of the parties. These relationship triangles, on the battlefield and at the negotiating table, have the same form—the "we" against the "other"; however, on the battlefield lives are lost, whereas at the negotiating table attempts are made to resolve differences without bloodshed.

The triangles and cutoffs involving Israelis and Palestinians take other forms as well. Less prevalent, but nevertheless significant, are groups in which Israelis and Palestinians join in projects that promote coexistence. Those opposing coexistence are the "other" whereas the group members, both Israelis and Palestinians are the "we." Examples of mutual cooperation include academic research (Scham, 2000), economic cooperation, and many dialogue groups that are established to modify the structure and intensity of existing triangles.

Triangles and cutoffs exist not only between Israelis and Palestinians but also within each group. The triangles and cutoffs within the two nations are more fluid than the triangles and cutoffs between the two nations.

Within Israeli society, there are ongoing, significant differences between religious and secular Jews. The religious, on one hand, value living within a defined, traditional framework in which people strive to function according to the dictates of Jewish law. The secular, on the other hand, value greater freedom of choice, not being bound by ancient laws. Instead of respect for the different values and lifestyles, the relations between the two groups are frequently characterized by intense triangles and cutoffs, including stereotyping and condemnation of the "other." Many among the religious view the secular as superficial, hedonistic, and lacking meaningful values. Many among the secular view the religious as parasites, taking from but not contributing their share to the nation and imposing their primitive religious practice on society as a whole. In addition, the religious and secular form separate political groups that compete against one another for government allocations. In spite of the intensity of the triangles and the cutoff between religious and secular Israelis, this triangle shifts in relation to Palestinians. Right-wing secular Jews and religious Jews, many of whom also tend to be right-wing politically, become the "we" who agree that the Israeli government should concede little to the Palestinians. Their "we" is also opposed to the Israeli Jewish left, who favor greater concessions to the Palestinians. However, differences among various groups of Israeli Jews are bridged, at least temporarily, when they experience a threat to the survival of Israel as a Jewish state. For example, there is widespread agreement among Israeli Jews against allowing the Palestinian refugees and their descendants who number in the several million to return to Israel, whose current population includes 5,200,000 Jews and 1,200,000 Arabs (Israel Central Bureau of Statistics, 2001). The potential threat of an influx of many Arab refugees to the survival of Israel as a Jewish state leads to a temporary shift in the triangles among and cutoff between religious and secular Israelis. Their conflict is temporarily bridged; however, the cutoff between these two groups is so intense that this triangle readily reappears.

Triangles and cutoffs exist within the Palestinian population as well. Within Palestinian society, there are ongoing significant differences between Christians and Muslims which parallel, to some extent, the differences between religious and secular Israelis. Many Muslims value a traditional lifestyle which adheres to the religious teachings of Islam. In contrast, the Christians are identified with the West and a modern lifestyle, which is based more on freedom of choice and less on observance of ancient laws. As in Israeli society, instead of respect for different values and lifestyles, triangles and cutoffs, including negative stereotypes, abound in the relations between the two groups. Many Palestinian Muslims view the Palestinian Christians as materialistic, hedonistic, and not willing to sacrifice themselves and their families sufficiently for the Palestinian cause. Many Palestinian Christians view the Palestinian Muslims as uneducated and fanatic. Currently, as the influence of Islam has grown throughout the world and among Palestinian Muslims, many Christian Palestinians fear that when Palestine becomes a state, it might be ruled on the basis of Islamic law.

Another triangle among Palestinians occurs between groups with different attitudes toward Israel. Groups such as Hamas and Islamic Jihad, which oppose Israel's existence, are joined in opposition to the Palestine Authority which, in signing the Oslo agreement in 1993, acknowledged its acceptance of Israel.

Since the beginning of the second *intifada* in September 2000, the conflict between Israel and the Palestinians has intensified considerably. Israel, the common enemy, has united the various groups of Palestinians despite significant and, at times, intense differences between them. It is likely, however, that the cutoff and triangles between Muslims and Christians will reappear when the relationship between Israelis and Palestinians becomes calmer.

ISRAELI AND PALESTINIAN TEXTBOOKS AND SOCIETAL PROCESS

Societal process addresses whether a nation's functioning is based on principles and thoughtful consideration of long-term goals or on a reaction to current anxiety with little, if any, consideration of the long-term consequences. In applying Bowen theory to Israeli-Palestinian relations, textbooks are a useful arena in which to examine societal process. The relationship between Israelis and Palestinians is a central issue for both societies. Textbooks are very relevant to relations between the two nations because many subjects inevitably include the interaction of one's group with others (Podeh, 2000). How does one present "us"? How does one present "them"? The educational system influences the future adult population regarding their view of their nation and others, including their neighbors.

The writing and analysis of texts are highly politicized in Israel and the Palestinian Authority, the government of the Palestinians. In Israel, school principals and teachers choose from a number of texts that represent a range of views; all textbooks have the approval of the Ministry of Education. The texts chosen by each school and the criteria for approval by the Education Ministry are strongly influenced by political views. In the Palestinian Authority, the development of new texts has been underwritten by European funding. Palestinians perceive Israel as the enemy that is occupying their land. Although the Europeans agree with the Palestinians that Israel should evacuate the settlements in the disputed territory, they nevertheless want the

Palestinians to educate for peaceful coexistence. As a result, the writing and analysis of Palestinian texts are influenced by these contradictory forces.

An analysis of textbooks can shed light on Israeli-Palestinian relations. The texts of each group reflect the societal process and the intensity of emotional cutoff.

Israeli Textbooks

Podeh (2000), a faculty member of the Department of Islamic and Middle Eastern Studies of Hebrew University, has traced the development of Israeli texts since the founding of the nation. He notes that the teaching of history represents different schools of thought that include the national, the academic, and a synthesis of the two. The national school, according to its critics, views teaching history as a legitimate tool of the nation for implementing values even if the price is the selective use of historical evidence. The dangers of the national approach include mythologizing history so that it idealizes its protagonists and demonizes those people with whom one is in conflict (Podeh, 2000). In contrast, the academic approach stresses objectivity, or at least the absence of tendentiousness.

Podeh (2000) looks at how the Arab-Israeli conflict has been presented by the Israeli educational system in general, and in its history textbooks in particular. He describes the changes in history textbooks as reflecting changes in Israeli society following crucial national events, especially the wars in which Israel has been involved. From 1920 to 1967, which Podeh refers to as the "childhood" phase, history texts were dominated by the national school. The textbooks were filled with bias and stereotypical descriptions that contributed to the institutionalization of hostile attitudes toward the Arabs. Terms typically used in the texts when describing Arabs included *savage, sly, cheat, thief,* and *terrorist.* During the period of the British Mandate (1920-1948) texts maintained the tradition of depicting Jewish history as a period of uninterrupted antisemitism and persecution. The period of Israel's War of Independence (1948) was presented so that Israel's image was not marred and there was no doubt of the right of the Jewish people to a homeland in Israel. The historical narrative was simplistic, one-sided, and often blatantly distorted. The Palestinians' leaving their land was described as flight and departure from Israel. There was no mention of the violence of Israeli soldiers. During this period, which included increasing anti-Semitism in Europe culminating with the Holocaust, societal process among Israelis was, on one hand, very productive regarding building a nation but was, on the other hand, regressive in terms of the relations between Israelis and Arabs. The rigid triangles and cutoffs which are inherent in this intense process are apparent in the simplistic and polarized descriptions of "us" and "them."

The second phase, which Podeh refers to as "adolescence," includes the period from the mid-1970s to 1992. Podeh indicates that changes in society generally predate changes in textbooks. The Six-Day War of 1967 led to significant changes in Israeli society. First, the conquest of territory previously ruled by Jordan brought Israelis into closer contact with their Palestinian neighbors, both geographically and psychologically. Interest in learning about Arabs increased. Second, serious differences in Israeli society developed over the question of the legitimacy and desirability of Israel's retaining control over the newly conquered territory, which as previously noted is referred to as disputed territory. Third, the media and the academic world presented Israelis with considerable information about the Arab world and the Palestinian national movement. Finally, Israel's swift and stunning victory over the Egyptian, Jordanian, and Syrian armies in 1967 made it difficult for some Jews to continue to think of themselves as victims.

By 1969, the desirability of teaching students about the Arab-Israeli conflict began to be addressed. The two points of view reflected the national and academic schools. The former argued that teaching the student to understand the enemy would lead to guilt feelings toward the Arabs and interfere with the functioning of Israeli soldiers when called to war. The latter emphasized the importance of "educating for truth," including facts that revealed the distortions of the official line of thinking. Pessimistic about the likelihood that the Arab-Israeli conflict would be solved politically, Harkabi, a former head of Israeli military intelligence and an expert on Arab-Israeli relations, stated:

> The wisdom is in realizing that we are destined to live with a neighbor who is also an opponent, over a long period of time, and [therefore] we have to think beyond the present day. The wisdom is not to see the opponent as a culprit . . . but to realize that there is no absolute justice . . . and that each side has its own truth. (quoted in Podeh, 2000, p. 79)

The Ministry of Education began work on a textbook that would address the Arab-Israeli conflict in a new way. During this period of "adolescence," however, textbooks were also based on the nationalist school. Nevertheless, the academic school gained ground and a new generation of textbooks was introduced. Both the Arabs and the Arab-Israeli conflict were presented in a more balanced manner, and the historical narrative was less biased and contained fewer negative stereotypes. Arabs were, for the first time, divided into separate peoples, including Palestinian Arabs. The previously held Zionist "truths" were presented in a more objective manner, contradicting myths that had, for example, negated the significant presence of Arabs in Israel when the immigration of Jews in large numbers began.

This second generation of textbooks was not, however, free of prejudice. Maps, pictures, diagrams, and caricatures continued to reflect the nationalist approach, reinforcing negative stereotypes of Arabs and the single-minded Zionist point of view rather than the more complex struggle of two peoples. Thus, the textbooks during this period reflect triangles and cutoffs that are less intense as a more complex portrayal of the "other" is introduced into Israeli texts.

Podeh views 1984 to the present as the period in which Israeli textbooks began the transition into "adulthood." Following the Lebanon War in 1982, which contributed to growing dissatisfaction with Israel's military actions among many Israelis, the trend toward the academic school of thought was strengthened. Textbooks included material on Israel's Arab citizens in an effort to teach the values of a pluralistic society with tolerance toward minorities, including the Arab minority within Israel. This was a significant step away from the nationalist school.

By the early 1990s, changes in Israeli society accelerated the changes in textbooks. The onset of the peace process brought hope that the Arab-Israeli conflict could be resolved. In addition, declassified Israeli archives were the basis of new studies in Zionist history that challenged some long-held Zionist beliefs. Several significant changes were presented in the new generation of textbooks. The narrative continues to the present rather than ending in 1948. Although the Arab-Israeli conflict is presented primarily from the Zionist perspective, an attempt is made to understand the Arab point of view. In addition, the Arabs generally are no longer described in stereotypical terms. A more complex historical narrative is presented that does not ignore the shadows in Israeli history. For example, the texts acknowledge that during Israel's War of Independence, the Arab population fled not only because it was encouraged to do so by its own leaders but that, in addition, there were acts of expulsion by the Israeli army. This depiction contrasts with the narrative of the first- and second-generation textbooks. The current textbooks are not uniform; however, according to Podeh (2000), the appearance of the more complex narrative indicates that education is no longer being used to create a narrow, historical view. Podeh indicates that Israeli society is currently more confident and is willing to confront its past, including its flaws.

In spite of the trend toward less polarization in Israeli textbooks, there are many Israelis who believe that significant problems persist in the current texts. Firer (1998) indicates that educators who wish to inculcate a strong sense of "us" and "them" continue to do so. For example, the religious Zionist section in the education ministry, dissatisfied with the more moderate texts, published its own material in 1987. The latter is replete with biblical quotations stating the Jews' unique right of possession of the land of Israel as promised by God. Although, according to this booklet, peace is desirable, it is currently unattainable because of the Arabs' claims and their not being trustworthy.

Dr. Amnon Raz-Krakotzkin (1999), another critic of the current system, notes the positive and important changes in Israeli history texts, especially the inclusion—albeit partial—of Israel's expulsion of Arabs in 1948.[4] Nevertheless, the texts' focus on past events is insufficient and, in fact, misleading because the impression conveyed is that Israel erred in the past but its current behavior is just. Thus, what Raz-Krakotzkin perceives as Israel's current unjust treatment of the Palestinians is ignored. Raz-Krakotzkin concludes that Israeli society's perception of the Arab-Jewish conflict, as reflected in the current history texts, will not permit an agreement to be reached based on the rights of the Palestinians.

Israeli textbooks have evolved from a uniform, polarized presentation of "us" and "them" to a varied set of texts which range from those that include polarization to those that teach a more complex view of "self" and "other" (Podeh, 2000). Currently, the majority of texts used reflect the less polarized view. The decreasing polarization reflects a decrease in the intensity of regressive societal process within Israel which began in the early 1970s.

With the collapse of the peace process in January 2001, there has been a shift in societal process. Most Israelis are pessimistic about the possibility of peace in the foreseeable future. The triangles and cutoffs between Israelis and Palestinians have intensified. The current government is encouraging a shift toward teaching more traditional Zionist values. However, since the minister of education changes every four years and the schools are stable and relatively independent, the textbooks being used have not been influenced by the recent changes in societal process. In spite of the current increase in the polarization between Israelis and Palestinians, Israelis know that they are outnumbered by Arabs and that their very small country is surrounded by Arabs and the sea; they must eventually find a way to live with their Arab neighbors. The new textbooks are, in fact, moving toward congruence with Israel's stated long-term goal of living peacefully with its Palestinian neighbors.

Palestinian Textbooks

An understanding of the textbooks used by Palestinian students requires looking at the background of their texts. In 1948, following the withdrawal of the British from Palestine, the current disputed territory was ruled by neighboring Arab countries. Jordan ruled the West Bank and Egypt ruled

Gaza. The textbooks used to educate Palestinian children were those of the ruling countries; therefore, Palestinians had been using Jordanian and Egyptian textbooks since the early 1950s. In 1967, when Israel's victory in the Six-Day War led to its ruling the disputed territory, Israel became responsible for the education of Palestinian children. The textbooks were amended so that overtly anti-Semitic references, including demands for Israel's destruction, were omitted.

Following the Oslo accord in 1993, the responsibility for education in the disputed territory was transferred from Israel to the Palestinian Authority. The latter continued using the Egyptian and Jordanian textbooks, reintroducing what the Israelis had censored. Adwan, a member of the education faculty of Bethlehem University, has analyzed Palestinian textbooks. Adwan (2000) states that the Egyptian and Jordanian texts are problematic for Palestinian children. The Arab states, which did not make a serious effort to help the Palestinian refugees, are uncomfortable presenting Palestinian history. In addition, Jordan, which has a substantial Palestinian population, prefers to discourage the development of national aspirations among the children of the Palestinian refugees living in Jordan. Thus, although the textbooks used by Palestinians were created within the framework of the national school, it is important to note that it is the political system, economy, society, geography, history, and national goals of the Jordanians and Egyptians that are presented, not those of the Palestinians (Adwan, 2000). Any discussion of Palestinians presents the Egyptian and Jordanian perspective. As a result, Palestinian children study from texts that ignore their own nation's narrative.

When the textbooks were written, Jordan and Egypt viewed Israel as their enemy. The texts, which reflect the national school, are replete with anti-Semitic statements, for example, referring to Jews as evil, treacherous, and deceitful. These textbooks are currently used by all Palestinian children except for those in grades one and six, for whom new texts have been written.

The Palestinian Authority has begun the process of developing texts and has thus far published textbooks for grades one and six. In the 2000-2001 school year, some Palestinian children began for the first time to study from their own textbooks, which reflect the national school. Adwan (2000) explains that Palestinians have lived under the rule of foreign authorities for many years:

> Their identity is shattered, their history is silence, their culture is oppressed and their economy is shapeless. They are alien in their land and among themselves. Texts are [intended] to challenge this. They have to start building their national identity and ethos, relating to their culture and environment not as strangers. (p. 7)

Regarding the image of Jews in the new texts, Adwan (2000) indicates that Jews are presented in a positive light. Adwan gives several examples related to the ancient past, including references to the prophet Moses, Judaism's preceding Islam, and encouraging the pupils to respect the people of the books, referring to Jews and Christians as well as their properties and religious ceremonies (Adwan, 2000). The text includes examples of ancient Jews who did and did not respect the agreements they signed and a description of the latter group of Jews allying with other tribes to fight the Prophet Mohammed (Adwan, 2000). Adwan indicates that the students are taught religious tolerance, citing an assignment to bring evidence from the Koran, New Testament, and Old Testament that advocate tolerance and oppose extremism.

Adwan's analysis of the new textbooks addresses the issue of jihad or holy war. Students are taught that all peaceful means must be exhausted to resolve a conflict. Civil disobedience is advocated, using the first *intifada* that began in 1987 as an example of Palestinian passive resistance. The students learn about Mahatma Gandhi and Nelson Mandela, leaders of nonviolent movements. As previously indicated, the Palestinians are under pressure to present their textbooks as educating for peace, according to the expectations of those funding the project. The pressure to emphasize that the texts do not educate for violence leads Adwan to a loss of objectivity. For example, during the first *intifada*, stones were the ammunition of the Palestinians. Although stones are, of course, considerably less dangerous than the bullets used by the Israeli army, they are not an example of passive resistance.

The Palestinian texts indicate that Muslims are commanded to participate in jihad only if peaceful means to resolve a conflict fail and only under certain conditions: (1) if their land and property are taken from them, (2) to rid the world of oppression and injustice, and (3) to defend Islam (Adwan 2000). However, jihad is never an act of aggression or starting wars; a defensive war is the only legitimate war. The texts cite religious leaders who commanded a military leader and his army: "Do not kill a woman, or an elderly person, or a child, do not cut palm trees or any fruit trees, if you shall find people worshiping God (Jews and Christians) leave them alone" (Adwan, 2000, p. 11).

The value of martyrdom is presented throughout the texts. Martyrs are defined as those "who are killed and sacrificed their lives in defending Islam, the people and the land and [ending] the oppression" (Adwan, 2000, p. 12). Adwan describes an example of teaching about martyrdom in a sixth grade text which directly relates to the current Israeli-Palestinian conflict. There are two black-and-white pictures, one of a martyr who died in 1935, and the other of a revolutionary group of Palestinians from 1936, depicting the struggle against the British. Between the two photos is a colored map that shows Israeli settlements in the disputed territories (Adwan, 2000). Adwan explains that the two photos indicate the method that was used by Palestinians in resisting the British. Clearly, the text draws a parallel between the struggle against the British and the struggle against the Israelis. The students are taught that martyrs and revolutionary groups were used against the British during the mandate period and should be used against Israeli settlements during the present struggle.

Maps in Palestinian textbooks generally do not acknowledge the existence of the state of Israel. Since peace between Israelis and Palestinians depends on each group's accepting the existence of the other, this is a significant issue. Adwan anticipates criticism of the textbooks regarding this issue and states that maps should not be analyzed until the borders between Israel and the future independent state of Palestine have been defined. He indicates that, until then, it is irrational and unfair to criticize maps either in texts or atlases (Adwan, 2000).

Adwan (2000) presents the dilemma of creating textbooks that teach Palestinian children to have positive feelings toward Israelis given the current situation between the two peoples. On one hand, Palestinians would like to educate their children to relate to Israelis as neighbors, as equal partners. On the other hand, the current reality includes Palestinians' experiencing Israelis as "occupiers, oppressors and victimizers" (p. 15). In order for textbooks to be relevant, they cannot ignore the reality of society. This dilemma and the pressure of those funding the development of the texts may account for some of the contradictions in Adwan's analysis of the texts. For example, he states that the books do not include even one negative stereotype of Jews or Israelis; however, he also acknowledges that Palestinians are viewed as victims of Zionist ideology and Israeli occupation.

As with the Israeli texts, different perspectives are presented by different analysts of the Palestinian textbooks. A significant group of critics of Palestinian textbooks are Israelis who use material from the texts as "proof" that Palestinians are not ready to live peacefully with Israel. In 1993, when the education of Palestinian children was transferred from Israel to the Palestinian Authority, the latter reintroduced the anti-Semitic statements, including those calling for the destruction of the state of Israel, into their textbooks (Marcus, 2001). An example of this appears in the seventh grade text, *Our Arabic Language*, which was written in 2001 by the Center for Developing Palestinian Curricula and published by the Palestinian Ministry of Education. The textbook states: "Subject for Composition: How are we going to liberate our stolen land? Make use of the following ideas: Arab unity, genuine faith in Allah, most modern weapons and ammunition, using oil and other precious natural resources as weapons in the battle for liberation" (Marcus, 2001, p. 12).

The Center for Monitoring the Impact of Peace, also known as CMIP (Marcus, 2001), notes changes in the new Palestinian textbooks from those of the Egyptians and Jordanians; however, the texts continue to be extremely negative in their portrayal of Jews and Israel. Although the new texts include positive references to Jews, an improvement over the Egyptian and Jordanian texts, many of these positive references are mitigated by negative comments nearby. For example, near text praising Jews for the role they played in transmitting knowledge in ancient times appears: "Mohammed had his personal aide learn the language of the Jews in order to be safe from their deceit" (*History of the Arabs and Moslems*, p. 133, cited in Marcus, 2000). Another change in the new Palestinian texts is that overtly anti-semitic references describing Jews and Israelis as treacherous or the evil enemy and the open calls for Israel's destruction are not present. However, according to Marcus, the change is more cosmetic than real; the shift is from an explicit to an implicit defamation of Israel. The portrayal of Israel as a colonialist conqueror that massacred and expelled Palestinians and occupied Palestine in 1948 does not require the explicit use of the term *enemy*. Marcus (2000) concludes that the new Palestinian textbooks are not educating the students for peace and coexistence with Israel.

Adwan (2000) defends Palestinian textbooks, explaining that misunderstandings are likely to occur when texts are analyzed by people whose mother tongue is different from the language of the books. Nevertheless, Adwan indicates that in situations of conflict textbooks are always used to indoctrinate students. Each group interprets events in their mutual history very differently. National ideology is legitimized and the ideology of one's enemy is delegitimized. The claims of "self" are always right and the claims of the "other" are always wrong; in fact, one's heroes are the monsters of the "other." The polarization is intensified by including little if any information that may mitigate negative feelings, such as descriptions of the others' human characteristics or discussion regarding periods of peaceful coexistence. Adwan (2000) adds that a nation should not be blamed for this approach to education.

As Adwan (2000) indicates, the new Palestinian textbooks reflect the national school. They are congruent with the Palestinians' goal of having their young develop a national identity. The texts both reflect and contribute to the intense cutoff between Palestinians and Israelis.

Textbooks and Societal Process

Examining Israeli and Palestinian texts using the concept of societal process leads to an interesting parallel. Both sets of textbooks initially reflect the national school, that is, they present information that strengthens nationalist feelings by intensifying triangles and cutoffs. Texts used by Israelis and Palestinians were totally positive regarding their own people and presented negative stereotypes about the "other."[5]

In the early years of nationhood, Israelis experienced themselves as weak and vulnerable, needing to be on constant alert lest their hostile neighbors accomplish their goal of driving them into the sea. During this period, the Israeli textbooks presented Jews as totally positive and Arabs as totally negative and did not address Palestinians as a group with a separate identity. This polarization appeals to the emotions and strengthens the feelings of closeness and unity among "us" and feelings of disdain for and distance from "them." The Israelis did not acknowledge and did not even recognize the complexity of their recent history, their part in the events that occurred, the basis for the Palestinian objection to the creation of the state of Israel, or the existence of the Palestinians as a people.

The textbooks reflected a societal process that was based on automatic responses with little if any thought to the long-term effects of simplistic thinking and polarization. Although the texts were congruent with Israel's goal of building a sense of pride and unity among its people, education that reduces complexity to "us" and "them" does not develop the capacity of its students to think objectively and independently, to evaluate situations realistically, to appreciate many points of view, and to consider the long-term effects of various options. The textbook narratives both reflected and helped to maintain the cutoff that existed between Israelis and Palestinians.

The war of 1967 had a significant impact on the Israeli people. The strength Israel experienced following its overwhelming military victory and the increased contact with their Palestinian neighbors who perceived them as "occupiers" introduced Israelis to the relatively new experience of being the "strong" party in conflict with the "weak" opponent.

> Since 1967, if not earlier, the romantic idea of the Israeli army—of armed Jews fighting to secure historic, religious, or metaphysical justice for the Jewish people—has become demystified by individual Jews' experiences of killing and being killed in wars, as well as by the moral ambiguities and ideological contradictions inherent in the encounter between a vision of liberation and the realities of conquest. (Ezrahi, 1997, p. 7)

These changes challenged the claim of the Zionist-Israeli epic of liberation as the only valid account of Israel's experience and turned the state into an arena for fiercely competing voices (Ezrahi, 1997). As a result, Israel's national story began to accommodate not only the Palestinians' narrative from without, but also the alternative narratives of Israeli individuals from within.

The shift in societal process and emotional cutoff is apparent in the textbooks that began to appear in the early 1970s. The Palestinians were acknowledged as a separate group and some of the myths regarding Zionism were contradicted. As a nation that strives to be democratic and ethical, many dilemmas were experienced and aired in Israel's free press. Simplistic polarization was replaced with a somewhat more complex portrayal of "self" and "other" as a significant number of Israelis were able to think with more objectivity. Societal process was based less on emotion. The intensity of the triangles and the degree of cutoff was reduced somewhat when the two groups began to have some contact with each other and a growing number of Israelis began to perceive the Palestinians as people rather than a distant, unknown group of the "other."

The gradual shift in societal process that is based less on instinct and more on objective thinking was accelerated in the early 1990s. Factors contributing to this change were the onset of a peace process between Israelis and Palestinians and the declassification of archives, which replaced several Zionist myths with a more complex narrative that portrayed the Israelis and Palestinians in somewhat less polarized terms. These changes are reflected in many Israeli textbooks.

The collapse of the peace negotiations in January 2001 contributed to a greater polarization in societal process in Israel. The textbooks, however, have not changed and continue to reflect, for the most part, Israel's understanding that it must find a way to live peacefully with its Palestinian neighbors.

In contrast to Israel, which has existed as a nation for more than fifty years, Palestinians are still struggling to become a nation. Between 1948 and 1967, Palestinians were discouraged from representing their own cause. Their interests were represented by Arab states, especially Jordan, Egypt, and Syria (Lewis, 1994). However, inter-Arab politics took precedence over concerns for Palestinians: "As far as the Arab regimes are concerned, the Palestinian cause is, and has been, a pawn in inter-Arab rivalry" (Kazziha, 1979, p. 17). Following the 1967 war, the Palestinians embarked on their own political action. The Palestine Liberation Organization, set up by the Arab League in 1964 to represent the Palestinians, became a skilled, diplomatic group that by the late 1980s had diplomatic relations with more countries than did Israel. However, these political accomplishments did not translate into gains for the Palestinian people. Although following the Oslo accords in 1993 Israel transferred some of the land captured in 1967 to the Palestinians, the amount of land is a fraction of what the Palestinians aspire to claim as a state. In addition, they have not received formal recognition as a nation.

The Palestinians currently are engaged in a struggle to become a nation. They continue to use Egyptian and Jordanian textbooks that depict Israelis in explicitly negative terms. Although the new texts that the Palestinians have created are slightly less negative, including some positive descriptions of ancient Jews, they continue to describe Israelis in negative stereotypes, as oppressors and victimizers. A major goal of the Palestinians, at this stage of the historical process, is to build a nation, a strong and proud identity. The difficult circumstances within which many Palestinians live have been exacerbated significantly since the beginning of the *intifada* in September 2000. Societal process among the Palestinians has intensified. Hatred of the enemy is a readily available "solution" to the challenge of building an identification with one's nation during a time of suffering.

The textbooks reflect the fact that societal process is based on emotional reactivity. Although the current Palestinian textbooks are congruent with society's goal of building a national identity, the portrayal of Israeli-Palestinian relations purely from the Palestinian perspective does not develop Palestinian students' capacity to think with complexity about human relations or the ability to think about peacefully living with their Israeli neighbors. The textbooks reflect and promote the continuation of an intense cutoff regarding Palestinians' perception of Israelis in the stereotype of colonialist occupiers.

Israeli and Palestinian society are at very different stages in their historical development. Their societal process, and their textbooks as an example of that process, reflect the difference. The textbooks of each nation reflect the current goals of each society. In fact, current Palestinian societal process and their textbooks are, to some extent, similar to those of Israel, before and in the early stages of its nationhood. In Israel, the varied goals of society are reflected in the fact that although to some extent children are still taught that "we" are wonderful and "they" are our enemies, a significant shift is apparent in the presentation of the Israeli-Palestinian conflict, with more complexity that includes, in some instances, the Palestinian point of view and negatives regarding Israelis. The Palestinians are aware of the fact that they are inculcating their youth with anger toward their Israeli neighbors; however, they argue that this reflects the current reality. In addition, as with the Israeli texts before and during the early stages of the state, the Palestinian texts are a means to promoting a sense of national identity by glorifying their own past and vilifying the "other."

CONCLUSION

The tendency to relate to others in terms of "us" and "them" is apparent to all observers of the human condition and clearly derives from evolutionary history. Thus, the fact that Israelis and Palestinians view each other as "us" and "them" is predictable and may be impossible to change. However, the inevitability of this tendency does not preclude variability in how it is manifested. As the previous discussion indicates, several concepts of Bowen theory are applicable to an analysis of Israeli-Palestinian relationships. What does Bowen theory offer in understanding the relationship between these conflicting groups?

Applying Bowen theory concepts can broaden one's perspective. The concept of differentiation describes the humans' ability to distinguish between thinking and behavior that is driven by instincts that humans have in common with other animals and thinking and behavior that is based on relative objectivity. An appreciation of the fact that the tendency to relate to others in terms of "us" and "them" occurs at all levels of nature may have a sobering influence on participants in "us/them" relationships. Realizing that ants, for example, also relate in terms of "us/them" can be humbling. Optimally, the perspective that the same instincts that influence other species also have considerable influence on humans may enable people to perceive that polarization is based on automatic reactions and the subjective thinking that is part of emotionality. If people could begin to identify when their reactions are triggered by their emotions, they might be able to use this self-awareness to draw upon their calm, objective thinking, distinguish between their emotional and objective thinking, and understand the point of view of the other. This thinking might influence participants in "us/them" relationships to be aware of the influence of subjectivity on their assumption of what "should" be and enable both groups to modify the feeling of certainty that "we" are justified and "they" are wrong. With a broader perspective people may respond on the basis of choice rather than on the basis of automatic reactivity.

The concept of differentiation also describes a range of adaptation among individuals, families, and societies. There is considerable variation in the manifestation of emotional cutoff, which is one aspect of adaptation in relations between Israelis and Palestinians. Both nations include groups that perceive the other as the "enemy" as well as groups that perceive the other with more complexity.

Israeli attitudes toward Palestinians range from very intense to little, if any, cutoff. Israelis were, for the most part, extremely cut off from Palestinians until after the war of 1967. Before 1967, the existence of Palestinians as a separate group was, to a large extent, ignored by Israelis. They considered the Palestinians part of the Arab population of the region and did not appreciate their distinct identity.

Another example of Israelis' intense cutoff from Palestinians occurs in the Israeli army, an institution that involves considerable contact between Israelis and Palestinians. Given that the army's major function is to protect the state of Israel and its people from their enemies, it is inherently based on cutoff between Israelis and Palestinians since the latter are perceived, particularly during periods of violence, as one of Israel's enemies. The soldier's realistic fear of being killed and the permission, if not the directive, to kill and impose closure on the "other" is based on and obviously intensifies cutoff. Although individual soldiers might, at times, appreciate the tragic nature of the situation and optimally, in imposing the closure, relate with as little disrespect as possible, functioning as a soldier requires and promotes intense cutoff.

A different type of extreme cutoff exists within a small group of the Israeli population. This group believes that Palestinians do not have an identity separate from other Arabs, should be transferred from the disputed territory to one of the many Arab lands, and should not have a state of their own. The number of Israelis who support this position has grown as the second *intifada* has persisted for more than two years. Within this group, a very small minority manifests a more extreme cutoff, committing violent acts against Palestinians. For example, in the early 1980s a group of twenty-seven Israelis functioned as a terrorist underground. They murdered three Palestinian college students and injured dozens of Palestinian civilians. The entire group was arrested by Israel and served time in prison. In addition, there are individual and small groups of Israeli terrorists who murder Palestinian civilians. However, even among Israelis who are extremely cut off from Palestinians, the vast majority do not advocate the use of force outside of the framework of the army and/or police.

A substantial majority of Israelis is less cut off from Palestinians. The attitudes of this group fluctuate in response to events that affect Israeli security. With the collapse of the peace process in January 2001, many Israelis have become pessimistic about the possibility of peace in the foreseeable future. They readily blame the Palestinians for initiating and maintaining the escalating cycle of violence which began with the second *intifada* and have difficulty understanding the Palestinians' use of violence as a response to their frustrations with the policies of Israel. Nevertheless, this group continues to acknowledge the right of Palestinians to a state of their own (Lavie, 2001).

Finally, a small group of Israelis works seriously at bridging the emotional cutoff between Israelis and Palestinians. These Israelis generally have considerable contact with Palestinians and present the latter's point of view to the Israeli public via the press, academia, and political demonstrations. As the second *intifada* has persisted for more than a year, the size of this group has grown smaller and the political demonstrations occur infrequently. Nevertheless, they present a Palestinian perspective to the Israeli public and their visibility in the press and in academia continues to be significant.

Among Palestinians, there is also a range in intensity of emotional cutoff toward Israelis. The most extreme form exists within groups who define all Israelis regardless of gender or age as legitimate targets of Palestinian violence. Among this group are suicide bombers and their supporters. As the *intifada*, which includes an exacerbation of Palestinian suffering, entered its second year, most Palestinians expressed support for suicide attacks against Israelis (Harel, 2001). Although the fear and wish for revenge of many Palestinians contribute to their support of random killing of Israelis, at the same time, most Palestinians support conciliation on the basis of two states for two peoples (Eldar, 2001).

Palestinians who are less cut off from Israelis view the latter as "the enemy" but are influenced less by the automatic reaction of lashing out against the "other" and instead consider the cost of revenge to their own people. Deborah Sontag (2001) reports on questions being raised by some Palestinians about the benefit of continuing the violence of the second *intifada*. Many Palestinians believe that the uprising was effective in motivating Israel to offer them a better deal than previously (which Arafat nevertheless rejected). However, some are questioning whether they have reached a point of diminishing returns. Although militants continue to promote an escalation of the violence, others are suggesting that the protest against the Israeli occupation should become nonviolent.

The group with even less intense cutoff from Israelis promotes contact because of the practical benefits accrued. They are aware that there are advantages in replacing the enmity and negative stereotypes that characterize relationships between Israelis and Palestinians with positive experiences; however, they see this as a secondary gain and not the goal of the cooperation. This group is able to analyze the conflict dispassionately in spite of the emotionality of the situation (Kirshner, 2001b).

Sari Nusseibeh, president of Al Quds University and PLO commissioner of Jerusalem affairs presents a point of view that attempts to bridge the cutoff between Palestinians and Israelis (Kirshner, 2001a). He acknowledges the Jewish people's historical connection to Jerusalem and the need for both sides to compromise in order to reach a two-state solution. Although currently Nusseibeh remains a lone public, government voice, his positions have not precluded his presence in the Palestinian Authority.

The range of emotional cutoff of each group from the other was presented separately; however, the relationship between the two groups is clearly a unit, each group affecting and being affected by the other. Lives of Israelis and Palestinians have been and continue to be inextricably intertwined. Each appreciates that it is affected by and affects the other; however, the perception of the cycle is significantly different. What Israel sees as its legitimate protection of its people and its homeland is seen by the Palestinians as land expropriation, oppression, and victimization. What Palestinians see as their legitimate attacks against the colonial oppressor of their people, Israel perceives as unjustified terrorism related to an unwillingness to accept Israel's existence. The emotional response of each group is to justify its position and negate that of the other. There is a considerable range of emotional cutoff between the two groups; however, among the majority of Palestinians, the cutoff from Israelis is more intense than vice versa. This difference is apparent in the textbooks of each nation.

The escalating cycle of violence and increased suffering of the Palestinians since September 2000 has led to an intensification of the regressive societal process. The Jerusalem Media Center, a Palestinian research center, has reported a significant increase in Palestinian support of suicide bombers (Schiff, 2001). In March 1999, before the onset of the second *intifada,* 26 percent of Palestinians supported suicide attacks against Israelis. In June 2001, eight months into the second intifada, 68 percent of Palestinians supported the suicide attacks.

The difference in the range of emotional cutoff from the "other" manifested in each of the groups is related to the difference in their stage of national development and to the effects that each nation has on the other. Israelis feel that their nation has accomplished a great deal in recent history. After two thousand years of homelessness, they achieved nationhood within their historic homeland. Although they are well aware of significant problems in their government, institutions, and society, Israelis are nevertheless proud of the accomplishments of their relatively young nation.

The *intifada* seriously affects many Israelis. Although they have a strong military relative to the Palestinians, the memory of the Holocaust, the overwhelming number of Arabs in neighboring countries, the growing strength of radical fundamentalism, and the reality of suicide bombings contribute to an acute sense of vulnerability. In addition to the deaths, physical injuries, emotional trauma, and anxiety caused by the ongoing conflict, Israel's economy has deteriorated significantly, thus causing damage that is felt, albeit indirectly, by thousands of Israelis beyond the tragedy to the families directly affected. However, in spite of the widespread negative effects of the *intifada,* most Israelis are able to go about their daily lives relatively unimpeded by the Palestinians.

In contrast to the recent history of Jews regarding the establishment and development of a homeland, Palestinians perceive themselves as having lost their homeland. They were the natives in Palestine; the Jews were a minority. The gains of the Israelis are experienced by the Palestinians as their loss. Their struggle to have an independent state continues. Israel controls most of the land that the Palestinians aspire to inhabit as a nation. In the past, tens of thousands of Palestinians have been employed as laborers in Israel. Ironically, in the construction industry, many have helped to build Israel, including settlements in the disputed territory. Palestinians are aware of the significant difference in their standard of living and that of most Israelis.

Since the beginning of the second *intifada* in September 2000, hostility between the two groups has intensified considerably. In addition to the deaths and physical and emotional injuries of Palestinians, their ability to earn a livelihood by working in Israel and their movement from one part of their territory to another is seriously curtailed by Israel. Thus, tens of thousands of Palestinians directly experience Israeli power and view themselves as victims of Israeli oppression and colonialism.

Israel's achievements and strength and the more limited and, for the most part, less direct suffering of Israelis relative to the Palestinians contribute to the ability of most of its people to relate to the Palestinians on the basis of less emotional cutoff than vice versa. Palestinians perceive themselves as victims of Israel. Palestinians' being more cutoff from Israelis than vice versa is related to the power of Israel to control "their" land and their people and Israel's relative success as a nation in contrast to the Palestinians' ongoing struggle to achieve nationhood as well as their very difficult living conditions (for which they blame Israel).

Although Israelis are less cut off from Palestinians than vice versa, their mutual relationships are characterized by considerable cutoff. Resolving differences is extremely difficult in this highly emotional context. Compromise depends upon a broad perspective based on the intellectual system. It is easier to unite a group against an enemy by appealing to the emotional system. Leaders can and do utilize this emotionality. This triangle of "us" together against "them" also distracts the people from the role that their leadership plays in their difficult life and instead focuses the entire blame on the "enemy." Forfeiting some of one's goals depends on the calm, objective thinking that is activated by the intellectual system but that does not give the sense of emotional togetherness that uniting against the oppressor brings. Ezrahi (1997) points out that

> The use of armed force is often most costly to the citizens (some of whom must risk their lives), but cheap for the political leadership, that can more easily mobilize the passions of the people against a dangerous enemy. Diplomacy is often cheaper for the citizens (it spares their lives), but more costly to the leaders because it is associated with rarely popular compromises and concessions to the enemy. (p. 59)

Some areas of conflict between Israelis and Palestinians such as territory and refugee return are, in fact, a zero sum game: "the more you get the less I get" and vice versa. However, the lack of clear thinking makes it difficult for the participants in the conflict to appreciate that there are also many areas in which cooperation could benefit both Israelis and Palestinians. The ongoing struggle costs lives and drains resources that could be used to address vital needs and enhance the quality of life of each group. The efficiency of natural selection has enabled many species to develop reasonably good relations with their neighbors. There are those among Israelis and Palestinians who appreciate the practical gains that a "dear enemy" approach could contribute to the quality of life of both groups.

Using concepts from Bowen theory to view Israeli-Palestinian relations, one could hope that the participants could become increasingly aware of the differences between reactions that are driven by the emotional system and those that are based on calm, objective thinking and, in addition, respond to one another on the basis of choice rather than on the basis of intense emotionality. Optimally, each side could achieve a genuine understanding of the other's point of view and take responsibility for its own part in the problem. It is encouraging to note that within the highly emotional climate that characterizes Israeli-Palestinian relations, at least occasionally, calm thinking that addresses the complexity of the issues and considers the long-term effects of actions is apparent within both groups.

It appears that separateness is an inevitable phenomenon in relationships between humans but the type and intensity of cutoff is within human control. Seeing the "other" as a faceless enemy enables the "we" to ignore current as well as long-range problems and dilemmas. The enemy unites and distracts us. This distraction has drawbacks; ignoring problems does not lead to their being addressed and/or solved. Generally, they continue to fester and may even get worse. Seeing the other as a person with similarities to and differences from oneself decreases the intensity of a regressive societal process. If we think that each side has rights, privileges, and responsibilities, long-term issues between groups and within each group can be addressed more productively.

NOTES

1. This chapter addresses the relationship between Israeli Jews and Palestinians living in the disputed territories. In fact, a significant number of Israelis are not Jewish and the Palestinian population lives in many countries throughout the world. For the sake of brevity, however, in this chapter the term *Israeli* refers to Israeli Jews and the term *Palestinian* refers to Palestinians living in the disputed territories.

2. The interrelatedness of Bowen's concepts is presented very briefly. A more complex analysis is beyond the scope of this chapter.

3. The concepts of Bowen theory are relevant to all human behavior including relationships among large groups. In this chapter, the concepts are applied to Israeli-Palestinian relations through December 2001, when the chapter was completed.

4. This is a very sensitive issue, as the factors that contributed to many Arabs leaving Israel during the 1948 war may determine who takes responsibility for the refugees and their descendants. This is one of the major issues on which there is substantial difference between Israelis and Palestinians.

5. It is interesting to consider the advantages and disadvantages of polarization, of glorifying oneself and delegitimizing one's enemy, in the development of national pride and national identity.

REFERENCES

Adwan, S. (2000). Analysis of the Palestinian Narrative of the Israeli/Palestinian Conflict in Palestinian History and Civic Education texts. Unpublished manuscript.

Bonner, J. (1988). *The Evolution of Complexity*. Princeton: Princeton University Press.

Bonner, J. (1994). Differentiation in cellular, social and family systems. *Family Systems: A Journal of Natural Systems Thinking in Psychiatry and the Sciences* 1(1):20-32.

Bowen, M. (1978). *Family Therapy in Clinical Practice*. New York: Jason Aronson.

Eldar, A. (2001). Peace from the Bottom to the Top. *Ha'aretz*, December 24.

Encyclopaedia Judaica (1972). Jerusalem: Keter Publishing House Ltd.

Ettinger, S. (1976). The modern period. In Ben-Sasson, H. H. (Ed.), *A History of the Jewish People* (pp. 727-1075). Cambridge, MA: Harvard University Press

Ezrahi, Y. (1997). *Rubber Bullets, Power and Conscience in Modern Israel*. New York: Farrar, Straus and Giroux.

de Waal, F. (1996). *Good-Natured: The Origins of Right and Wrong in Humans and Other Animals*. Cambridge, MA: Harvard University Press.

de Waal, F. and Harcourt, A. (1992). Coalitions and alliances: A history of ethological research. In A. Harcourt and de Waal, F (Eds.), *Coalitions and Alliances Among Humans and Other Animals* (pp. 1-19). Oxford: Oxford University Press.

Firer, R. (1998). Human rights in history and civics textbooks: The case of Israel. *Curriculum Inquiry* 28(2):195-208.

Harel, A. (2001). The 100th Suicide Bomber. *Ha'aretz*, October 8, p. 9

Israel Central Bureau of Statistics (2001). Statistical Abstract of Israel #52. Jerusalem.

Kazziha, W. (1979). *Palestine in the Arab Dilemma*. London: Croom Helm

Kerr, M. (1998). Bowen theory and evolutionary theory. *Family Systems: A Journal of Natural Systems Thinking in Psychiatry and the Sciences* 4(2):119-179.

Kerr, M. and Bowen, M. (1988). *Family Evaluation*. New York: W.W. Norton and Co.

Kirshner, Isabel (2001a). Can Nusseibeh lead a return to reason? *Jerusalem Report*. December 3, pp. 24-28.

Kirshner, Isabel (2001b). Cultural revolution. *Jerusalem Report*. April 23, pp. 24-26.

Langen, T.A., Tripet, F., and Nonacs, P. (2000). The red and the black: Habituation and the dear enemy phenomenon in two desert *Pheidole* ants. *Behavioral Ecology and Sociobiology* 48(4):285-292.

Lavie, M. (2001). Survey: 61% of Israelis in favor of Palestinian state. *Jerusalem Post*, October 19, p. 35. Online news from Israel.

Lewis, B. (1994). *The Shaping of the Modern Middle East*. New York: Oxford Press.

Marcus, I. (2000). *The New Palestinian Authority School Textbooks for Grades One and Six*. New York: Center for Monitoring Impact of Peace.

Marcus, I. (2001). *Palestinian Authority School Textbooks*. New York: Center For Monitoring Impact of Peace.

Papero, D.V. (1990). *Bowen Family Systems Theory*. Needham Heights, MA: Allyn and Bacon

Podeh, E. (2000). History and memory in the Israeli educational system. *History and Memory* 12(1):65-100.

Raz-Krakotzkin, A. (1999). The textbooks debate: No significant change in the perception of the history of Zionism. *News From Within* XV(11):3-8.

Reiter, Y., Eordegian, M., and Abu Khalaf, M. (2001). Jerusalem's religious significance. *Palestine-Israel Journal* VIII(1):12-19.

Scham, P. (2000). Arab-Israeli research cooperation, 1995-1999: An analytical study. *Middle East Review of International Affairs* 4(3):1-16.

Schiff, Z. (2001). What the Palestinians think. *Ha'aretz*, June 27, Section B, p. 1.

Sontag, D. (2001). Palestinians delicately begin debate on circle of violence. *The New York Times*, March 11, Section 1, pp. 1-20.

Wilson, Edward O. (1975). *Sociobiology: The New Synthesis*. Cambridge, MA: The Belknap Press of Harvard University.

Appendix:
A Key for the Family Diagram Symbols

Males are drawn as squares, females as circles

Male = ☐   Female = ○

Dates of birth and death are written above the person's symbol. Age is shown within the square or circle. Death is indicated by an X through the symbol

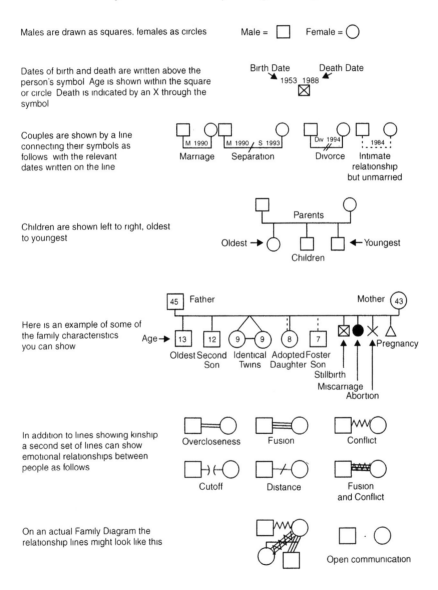

Couples are shown by a line connecting their symbols as follows with the relevant dates written on the line

Children are shown left to right, oldest to youngest

Here is an example of some of the family characteristics you can show

In addition to lines showing kinship a second set of lines can show emotional relationships between people as follows

On an actual Family Diagram the relationship lines might look like this

477

Index

Abandonment
    family issues, 188, 195
    fears, 174-175
Abraham family history, 36-38, 451
Abuse
    child. *See* Child abuse
    emotional, 282
    physical, 46, 282
    reabuse, 361-362
    sexual, 50-51, 281-282
Acculturation, 417
Ackerman, Fran, 443
ACTH (adrenocorticotrophin
        hormone), 253
Adaptation
    environment, 390
    impact of limits, 355-356
    impact on reproduction, 251
    multigenerational, 107
    overutilization of mechanism, 343
    reproduction and, 248
    societal process, 385
    stress and child abuse, 358
Adolescence of Israel, 458
Adolescents
    Bowen theory, 276-278, 284
    delinquents, 382, 385
    difficulties of research study,
        284-285
    overview, 273-276
    preservative quality of cutoff, 285
    research study, 278-284
    research study limitations, 286
    research study outcome, 285
Adrenocorticophin hormone (ACTH),
        253
Adulthood of Israel, 459
Adwan, S., 461, 462-463, 464

Afghanistan, 388-389
Aggression
    child abuse, 357-358, 369
    family stability and, 360
    multigenerational, 359-360
    threat response, 361
Agriculture in Russia, 390-391, 398
Ahrons, Constance, 289, 294, 295
Alcoholism
    adolescent, 274-275
    case vignette, 49-51
    managing perceived threats, 362
    physical dysfunction, 33
    symptom formation, 38
Allah, 463
Allen, Pamela R., 315
Allergic reaction
    emotional cutoff and triangles, 33
    emotional cutoff from family, 203,
        276-277
    emotional cutoff from family in
        marriage, 49
    family of origin, 165
    need for closeness, 140
    perceived rejection, 26
    physical symptoms, 171
    togetherness, 384
Allied Powers, 393
Allman, J., 84, 91-92, 252, 254
Alpha brain waves, 95, 96
Alternative responses, in flexibility
        development, 241
Altmann, J., 69
Altmann, S., 69
Amenorrhea, 254
Amygdala, 255
"An Odyssey Toward Science," 203
Androgens, 263, 264, 269

Anger management, clinical case
    example, 344
Animals. *See also* Mammals
    adolescents, 273
    ecological variables, 72-73
    emotional cutoff, 67-68
    evolutionary cutoff roots, 76-78
    exclusion consequences, 74-76
    migration, 402-405, 408-409, 417
    ostracism, 69-72
    relationship variables, 73-74
    solitary behavior, 68-69
ANS (autonomic nervous system),
    97-99
Anterior cingulate gyrus, 91-92, 252
Ants, 338, 362, 450
Anxiety
    acute, 20
    brain wave measurement, 96
    case vignette, 45
    chronic, 20, 389
    clinical example, 99-100
    defined, 204-205
    emotional cutoff, 408
    emotional cutoff and triangles, 33
    family contact, 53-54
    family projection, 34-35
    fear versus, 205
    impact on brain development,
        87-89, 92
    impact on child, 34
    influence on independence, 204
    level of, in self, 206
    management, 140, 223, 240-242
    in marriage, 31
    Mr. A's family, 143-144
    reproduction and, 248
Apes, 338
Arab League, 466
Arabs, 451-452, 454
Archer, J., 74-75
Assessment, adolescent research study,
    280. *See also* Cutoff
        assessment
Asymmetrical kinship, 38

Atlas, Susan, 249
Attachment
    emotional, 22, 353-354
    handling of, 203
    unresolved. *See* Unresolved
        attachment
Attraction, 251
Aunt Lee, bridging secondary cutoff,
    117-125
Auschwitz concentration camp, 433,
    438
Automatic instinctive process, 202
Automatic pilot, 446
Automatic reaction, 343
Autonomic nervous system (ANS), 97-99

Baboons
    exclusion, 76
    isolation, 69
    male control over females, 340
    migration, 405
    ostracism, 71
    parent-offspring relationship, 338
Baker, K. G., 175, 379
Balfour declaration, 452
Bates, Norman, 67
Bauman, K. E., 275
Beal, E. W., 307-308, 310
Bearinger, L. H., 275
Bearman, P. S., 275
Bees, 338
Behavioral patterns, emotional fusion,
    15, 22
Bekoff, M., 68, 74
Best functioning, 312
Beta brain waves
    clinical example, 101, 103-105
    function, 95-96
Beuhring, T., 275
Bible
    Abraham family history, 36-38
    Israelis versus Egyptians, 454
Biofeedback
    defined, 94

Biofeedback *(continued)*
electroencephalograph. *See*
Electroencephalograph (EEG)
biofeedback
function, 93-94
Biology
fusion and cutoff concepts, 21, 203
human birth challenges, 256-257
isolation and, 75-76
migration, 402
reproduction, 249, 251
use of energy, 253
Black bears, 75
Blaming process
Mr. A's family, 143, 144
threats, 360
victim, 370
Blind spots, 106
Blum, R. W., 275
Boca Raton Magazine, 430
Bogard, M., 337
Bohannan, Paul, 292, 298, 299
Bolsheviks, 393
Bonner, J., 443, 199, 444-445
Bonobos, 84
Bowen Center for the Study of the
Family, 192
Brain
autonomic nervous system, 97-99
biofeedback, 83, 88, 93-94
central nervous system, 94-97
chemistry and relationships, 245
cortex *See* Cortex, brain
development, 85-86
development and emotional cutoff,
89-91, 251
emotional cutoff and, 426
emotional cutoff in clinical work,
106-107
evolution, 84-85
factors affecting development,
86-89
functioning, 91-99
neurofeedback. *See* Neurofeedback
reactivity example, 99-106
triune, 251

Brain *(continued)*
waves, 94-97, 105. *See also*
Neurofeedback
Brainstem, 251
Breaking away, 427
Bregman, Ona Cohn, 199
Bridging emotional cutoff
brain development and, 91, 106-107
bypassing the nuclear family, 52-53
detriangling, 56-57, 304
divorced relationships, 160-164
family of origin, 164-172
Israeli-Palestinian relations, 470
nonpersonal contact, 238
observing and emotional
reactiveness control, 55
one-to-one relationships, 239-240
open versus closed system, 53-54
by perpetrator of violence, 344-347
person-to-person relationships,
54-55, 56
research. *See* Research process
results, 168-171
secondary cutoff. *See* Bridging
secondary cutoff
understanding emotional system,
238
by victim of violence, 347-349
vignette, 57-65
Bridging secondary cutoff, 111-115,
134-137
first cousin once removed, 115-117
first cousins, 125-134
theoretical principles, 136-137
with an aunt, 117-125
British Mandate, 457
Burn bridges, 26
Bygott, J. D., 70, 73, 75

CAFAS (Child and Adolescent
Functional Assessment Scale),
280, 283
Canaanite nation, 453
Cancer, physical dysfunction, 33-34

Canids, 74
Cannibalism
    animal, 71, 76
    insect, 450
Carter, Betty, 294
Case vignettes
    bridging cutoff, 57-65
    cutting off, 43, 45-51
    depression, clinical case, 326-335
    depression, personal vignette,
        316-325
    domestic violence, 344-349
    growing away to tearing away,
        39-42, 44
    Holocaust survivors, 429-440
    primary and secondary cutoffs,
        26-29
    tearing away to cutting off, 42-43,
        44
Cast asunder, 289
Catastrophe, The, 453
Catecholamines, 253
Celibate marriage, 293
Center for Developing Palestinian
        Curricula, 463
Center for Monitoring the Impact
        of Peace (CMIP), 464
Central American migration, 417
Central nervous system (CNS), 94-97
Challenging times and brain
        development, 87-89
Chicago Fire, 181
Child abuse
    background, 351-352, 374-375
    characteristics, 367
    cutoff background, 354-356
    defined, 356
    disclosure as threat, 370
    emotional regression, 366-374
    family characteristics, 367
    family emotional unit, 358-360
    intervention of, 366
    professional management, 371-374
    symptoms, 356-358
    threats, 360-366

Child and Adolescent Functional
        Assessment Scale (CAFAS),
        280, 283
Chimpanzees
    adolescents, 273
    evolution, 84
    ostracism, 71
    parent-offspring relationship, 338
    social rejection, 70
Christ's teachings, 453
Circumstantial cutoff, 393
Civilization, defined, 385
Clinical cases. *See* Case vignettes
Clinician's cutoff, 235
Closed system, 53-54
CMIP (Center for Monitoring the
        Impact of Peace), 464
CNS (central nervous system), 94-97
Coefficient alpha, 213-214
Cold war, 398
Comfort zone, 155
Communism, 398-399
Community divorce, 298-299
Conflict
    attachment response, 353-355
    defined, 278
    fusion, 21
    marriage, 304-305, 357-358
    unresolved, 358
Contact
    frequency and cutoff, 230
    maintaining, 195
Contempt in marriage, 229
Context, historical, 420
Continuum, societal emotional process,
        385
Controlled positiveness, 13
Coparental divorce, 297-298
Cortex, brain
    beta brain waves, 95-96
    emotional cutoff and, 426
    emotions versus thoughts, 202
    evolution, 84-85
    function, 91-92
    perceiving emotions, 247

Cortex, brain *(continued)*
   reproduction and, 251
   stress reactions, 255
Corticotrophin-releasing hormone
   (CRH), 252-253
Cortisol, 253-254, 260
Cousins, bridging cutoffs, 125-134,
   151-152
Covert cutoff, 221, 229, 232
CRH (corticotrophin-releasing
   hormone), 252-253
Crime rate and behavior, 77
Cristofori, Roberta
   community divorce, 299
   differentiation of self, 302, 303
   loss in divorce, 311-312
   psychic divorce, 300
Criticism in marriage, 229
Cronbach's alpha, 213
Cults, 311
Culture in societal process, 382
Cutoff
   addressing, 235-242
   assessment. *See* Cutoff assessment
   biological term, 203
   circumstantial, 393
   covert, 221, 229, 232
   defined, 25, 202, 276-277, 279
   emotional. *See* Emotional cutoff
   examples, 24-25
   expression of, 22-23
   functions, 23
   Israeli-Palestinian relations, 447-448,
      454-455, 468-470
   overt. *See* Overt cutoff
   primary, 25-29, 30
   secondary, 25-29, 30, 42
   vignette, 43, 45-51
Cutoff assessment
   broader family involvement,
      232-234
   degree of openness, 231-232
   frequency of contact, 230
   geographic proximity, 231
   involvement in family events,
      234-235

Czarism
   blame for problems, 393
   in Russian history, 389
   societal cutoff, 398
   wealth of, 392

Dahmer, Jeffrey, 67
Darling, F. F., 71
Darwin, Charles, 245, 382, 443
de Waal, F., 71, 448
"Dear enemy" phenomenon, 449, 473
Death Without Weeping, 259
Deer, 71
Defensiveness in marriage, 229
Delinquents, 382, 385
Delta brain waves, 95
Delta Nu Chapter of Sigma Theta Tau
   International, 199
Denial, 15
Depression, 336
   adolescent, 285
   case vignette, 45-47
   characteristics, 315
   clinical case, 326-335
   emotional cutoff and, 38
   family cutoff and, 164, 168, 169
   impact of, 34
   impact on reproduction, 254
   personal vignette, 316-325
   relationships and, 315
Detriangling, 56-57, 304
"Devil-may-care" attitude, 153
DHEA-sulfate, 263, 264, 269
Diabetes, physical dysfunction, 33-34
*Diagnostic and Statistical Manual of
   Mental Disorders*, Fourth
   Edition (DSM-IV), 280
Diamond, J., 389-390
Differentiation
   brain development and, 86-87
   concept of, 31
   defined, 20, 276, 446
   emotional cutoff and, 32
   emotional maturity, 341

Differentiation *(continued)*
  Israeli-Palestinian relations, 468
  levels of, 14-15, 204, 206, 341
  scale of, 20, 384
  Scale of Differentiation, 247
  of self. *See* Differentiation of self
  societal scale, 399
Differentiation of self
  Bowen theory, 301-303
  bridging emotional cutoff, 52-53
  cutoff and, 354-355
  Israeli-Palestinian relations, 445-447
  key component, 227
  scale, 381-382
Differentiation of Self Inventory (DSI),
    209-210
Digital skin temperature, 263, 269
Discriminant validity, 214
Dispersal
  animal, 76
  consequences, 404, 405
  defined, 68
  forces, 403-404
  natal, 402
Disputed territory
  defined, 451
  impact of 1967 war, 452
  in Israeli textbooks, 458
  in Palestinian textbook, 460-461
Dissolution, 289
Distancing
  attachment response, 353-354
  coping mechanism, 363
  defined, 278
  emotional. *See* Emotional distancing
  geographical, 282-283
  internal, 13
  intrapsychic, 203
  mechanisms, 203
  physical, 15
  reactive, 49, 56-57
  result of emotional encroachment,
    342
  threat response, 361
Dittrich, A., 78

Divorce
  adolescents and, 274
  background, 289
  best functioning, 312
  community, 298-299
  coparental, 297-298
  differentiation of self, 301-303
  dimensions, 292-300
  economic, 296-297
  emotional. *See* Emotional divorce
  emotional cutoff, 310-312
  emotional intensity of, 290-292
  emotional process in society,
    309-310
  family projection process, 301 308
  impact on children, 297-298, 307
  legal, 293-296
  multigenerational transmission
    process, 308-309
  nuclear family emotional system,
    304-308
  psychic, 299-300
  relationship cutoffs, 160-164
  triangles, 303-304
  vulnerability, 229-230
Domestic violence, 349-350
  background, 337, 339-340
  child abuse. *See* Child abuse
  defined, 339
  impact of nuclear family emotional
    process, 341-343
  perpetrator bridges cutoff clinical
    case, 344-347
  relevance of emotional cutoff, 343
  victim bridges cutoff clinical case,
    347-349
Donley, Margaret, 199
Drug abuse, adolescent, 274-275, 362
DSI (Differentiation of Self Inventory),
    209-210
DSM-IV, 280
Dysfunction
  physical, 33-34
  social, 33
  spouse, 305, 306, 334
Dysthymic, 45

Ecological variables, animal behavior, 72-73
Economic divorce, 296-297
ECS (Emotional Cutoff Scale), 209, 280, 283
Education and reproduction, 247
EEG. *See* Electroencephalograph (EEG) biofeedback
Egypt, 460, 461
Eichholz, Alice, 173
Electroencephalograph (EEG) biofeedback
    brain wave measurement, 94-97
    defined, 94
    function, 83
    intensity measurement of child, 88
Elephants
    adolescents, 273
    impact of leader's death, 78, 408, 412
    isolation, 72
    shunning, 70
Emigration
    animal, 71, 72-73
    consequences, 404
    defined, 402
    family examples, 410-416
    fleeing unresolved problems, 282-283
    functions, 75
    outcomes, 417
Emotion, defined, 247, 352, 382-383
Emotional. *See also* Attachment
    abuse, 282
    attachment, 22, 353-354
    cutoff. *See* Emotional cutoff
    defined, 202
    distancing. *See* Emotional distancing
    divorce. *See* Emotional divorce
    encroachment, 341-343
    fusion, 15, 21-22
    impact on brain development, 87-88
    process, in society, 382
    reactiveness. *See* Reactivity

Emotional *(continued)*
    regression, 366-374
    separation, 24, 207
    stuck-together fusion, 21
    system, 19, 238, 445
    triangles, 385
Emotional cutoff
    animals, 67-68
    brain development and, 89-91
    brain functioning and, 91-99
    concept of, 9-10, 202-203
    defined, 9, 22, 23, 90, 199-200, 425-426
    divorce, 310-312
    evolution, 16-19, 78
    family stability and, 354-356
    functioning and, 426-428
    Holocaust survivors, 428-429
    measurement, 209-210
    migration and, 406-408, 409-410
    origin, 10-16
    primary or secondary, 25-29, 30
    reasons, 106
    societal process, 380-381, 385-389
    undoing. *See* Undoing cutoff
    unresolved symbiotic attachment, 14-15
Emotional Cutoff Scale (ECS), 209, 280, 283
Emotional distancing
    behavioral patterns, 24
    Bowen family history, 16-19
    causes of, 205
    cutoff, 23
    defined, 9
    in divorce, 304
    human tendency, 447-448
    multigenerational, 35
    schizophrenia and, 12-13, 15
Emotional divorce, 292-293
    defined, 11
    marriage and, 15
    multigenerational, 35
    schizophrenia and, 12-13

Emotional Intelligence, 305
Encroachment, emotional, 341-343
Endometriosis, 254
Enemies of the People, 395
Environment
    animal social disintegration, 72
    impact on brain development, 85-86
    Russia, 390-393
    social, 419
    societal regression, 382-383
    Soviet Union, 394
Environmental Protection Agency, 382
Epinephrine, 253
Ernst, K., 78
Erwin, J. M., 252, 254
Estrogen, 252
Eurasia, 389, 390
Evolution
    brain, 84-85
    cutoff in, 202
    emotional cutoff, 16-19, 78
    human part, 443
    mammal migration, 404-405
    migration, 402
    reproduction, 249
Evolving Brains, 84
Examples. *See also* Case vignettes
    emigration, 410-412
    multigenerational reproduction
        study, 257-260
    reactivity, 99-106
    reproduction, 262-269
    reproduction research and clinical
        practice, 260-262
Excitatory response, 98
Exclusion
    animal, 71, 72-73
    causes of, 77
    chimpanzee, 70
    functions, 74-76
Explosion response, 384
Extramarital affairs, 99
Eye contact response, 353
Ezrahi, Y., 472

Falastin, 452
Family
    brain development and, 86-89,
        90-91
    bridging cutoff. *See* Bridging
        emotional cutoff
    ego mass, 15, 207
    emotional process, 33-34
    extended family and adolescents,
        273
    extended family and marriage, 229,
        232-234
    extended family and stuck-together
        fusion, 222-223
    involvement in events, 234-235
    one-to-one relationships, 239-240
    research. *See* Research process
    as single emotional unit, 358-360
Family Center, 246
"Family Concept of Schizophrenia," 14
Family Constellation, 278
Family diagrams
    bridging cutoff, 64
    cutoff and reproduction, 258, 263,
        265, 266, 268
    cutting off, 46, 48, 50
    depression symptom of cutoff,
        317, 328
    domestic violence and cutoff,
        345, 348
    Eichholz family, 175, 182, 184, 190
    Eichholz family cutoff, 181
    Eichholz family estranged siblings,
        185, 187
    Eichholz family of origin, 179, 188
    Eichholz family secrets, 177
    Eichholz multigenerational
        triangles, 180
    growing away to tearing away, 40
    Holocaust survivors, 431, 432, 434,
        436, 438, 439
    key, 477
    migration and cutoff, 411, 413, 415
    multigenerational contact, 190

Family diagrams *(continued)*
  multigenerational interlocking of
    emotional fusion and cutoff,
    18
  primary and secondary cutoff, 27
  primary and secondary triangles, 28
  primary and secondary triangles
    with cutoff, 30
  reciprocal relationship, 386
  relationship reactivity clinical
    example, 102, 104
  secondary cutoff, 113, 118, 119,
    126, 129
  tearing away to cutting off, 44
  undoing cutoff, 143, 149
Family Evaluation, 426, 427
Family History Database Project, 192,
  194
Family of Origin Response Survey
  (FORS)
  development of, 200, 207
  personal data form, 212-213
  scale development, 210-211
  scale items, 211-212
  team members, 199
  validity and reliability, 213-215
Family projection process
  in divorce, 304-308
  emotional cutoff and, 34-35
  occurrence of, 23
Family relationships. *See* Bridging
  emotional cutoff
"Family Relationships in
  Schizophrenia," 13
Family Therapy in Clinical Practice,
  10-11
Farming in Russia, 390-391, 398
Father *See also* Parents
  and daughter relationships, 359, 363
  emotional divorce, 11
  schizophrenia and, 12
Fears
  abandonment, 174-175
  anxiety versus, 205
  defined, 205

Feeling, defined, 382-383
Felix the cat, 45
Female philopatry, 68
Feminist theory, 339-340, 342-343
Ferrera, Stephanie J., 289
Fertility, male, 252
Feshbach, M., 394
Fight mechanism, impact on
  reproduction, 253
Firer, R., 459
Flexibility in responses, 241, 355
Flight mechanism
  character neurosis and, 14
  defined, 208
  distancing mechanism, 203
  impact on reproduction, 253
  measurement, 208, 211-214
  threat response, 361
Flooding, 228, 305
Follicular stimulating hormone (FSH),
  252, 254
Food supplies and animal social
  behavior, 72
FORS. *See* Family of Origin Response
  Survey
Foxes, 75
Freeze mechanism
  defined, 208
  impact on reproduction, 253
  measurement, 208, 211-214
  threat response, 361
Freud, 246
Friar, L., 83
Friendly, A., 394
Friesen, Priscilla J., 83
FSH (follicular stimulating hormone),
  252, 254
Functional
  helplessness, 14, 34
  position, 34
  posture of partner, 341
Functioning
  best, 312
  defined, 426, 428
  emotional cutoff and, 426-428
  influence of laws of nature, 443

Functioning *(continued)*
  level of, 175-176
  variability, 192-194
Fusion
  biological term, 203
  defined, 21, 277, 447
  emotional, 15, 21-22
  family ego mass, 15
  family of origin, 111, 112, 114
  function, 21-22
  intergenerational, 233
  measurement, 209-210
  parent-child, 219-223
  process of, 17, 18
  stuck-together. *See* Stuck-together
    fusion

GAF (Global Assessment of
    Functioning), 280, 283
Gandhi, Mahatma, 385, 462
Gangs, 274-275, 311
Gaza, 460-461
Gellhorn, E., 98
Generation gap, 387
Genetics
  biofeedback response, 94
  environmental impact, 97
Geographic cutoff
  distance as cutoff, 282-283
  migration, 407-408
Geographic proximity, 231
Geography and social organizations,
    389-393
Georgetown Family Center
  bridging cutoff, 165
  conference on variability, 206
  depression training program, 317,
    321
  Holocaust survivors, 429, 430
  reproduction studies, 249
  testing the theory, 160
  undoing cutoff, 145, 152
Georgetown University, 246
Gibbons, 70, 84

Gilbert, Roberta M., 159
Gippenreiter, J. B., 175
Global Assessment of Functioning
    (GAF), 280, 283
GnRH (gonadotrophin releasing
    hormone), 252, 253, 254
Goal clarification, 240
Going our separate ways, 289
Goleman, Daniel, 305
Gonadotrophin releasing hormone
    (GnRH), 252, 253, 254
Goodall, Jane, 70
Gorillas, 71, 72
Gottlieb, Eileen B., 425
Gottman, J. M., 227, 229, 305
Great Chicago Fire, 181
Green, A., 83
Green, E., 83
Growing away
  case vignette, 39-42, 44
  characteristics, 24
  emotional separation, 24
  family relationships and, 16
  objectivity, 427
  tearing away versus, 207
Growing up process, 207
Gruter, M., 69
Gubernick, David, 206
Gun control, 387-388
Guppies, 450

Hagar and Abraham family history,
    36-38
Hakeem, A., 252, 254
Hamas, 456
Hanby, J. P., 70, 73, 75
Hands, cold
  chronic level of reaction, 98
  clinical example, 101, 103
  digital skin temperature, 263, 269
  level of anxiety and, 88
  physiological reactivity and, 97
Harkabi, 458
Harris, K. M., 275

Harris, S., 75
Harrison, V., 233, 245
Hebrew University, 457
Hebron, 453
Helpless inadequate one, 13
Hilbert, G. A., 200
Hilbert-McAllister, Gail, 199, 207
Hillman, Edna, 116-117
Hinkley, John, Jr., 67
Hippocampus, 255
History
    defined, 386-387
    fluctuations between generations,
        387
    humans as historical animals, 419
    Israeli and Palestinian textbooks,
        456-467
    Russia, 389-393
    simultaneous multigenerational
        contact, 409-410
Hitler, 393
Hochman, G., 308
Hof, P. R., 252, 254
"Holocaust: Fifty Years Later," 430
Holocaust in Israeli textbooks, 457
Holocaust survivors
    case histories, 429-440
    emotional cutoff, 428-429
    functioning, 425, 440-441
"Holocaust Voices," 430
Holt, Roberta, 249
Holy Land, 453
Holy War, 462
Homeless travelers in search of a home,
    402
Homelessness, 77
Homicide
    animal, 71, 76
    child abuse, 367
Homo sapiens, 67, 77
Hormones
    impact on brain development, 88, 90
    measures of reactivity, 263, 269
    reproductive, 252
Hrdy, Sara Blaffer, 256
Human Birth, 256

Human emotional cutoff, 203-204
Hyenas, 70, 72, 403
Hypothalamus, 252, 253, 255

Illick, Hilary Selden, 199
Illick, Selden Dunbar
    anxiety and unresolved emotional
        attachment, 206
    contact information, 216
    fear emotion, 205
    focus of emotional cutoff, 203
    PFCRT development, 206-208
    symbiotic attachment, 204
    understanding emotional cutoff,
        199-201
Immigration
    animal study, 402-405
    cutoff and, 195
    defined, 402-403
    outcomes, 416-418
Immune system, 254
Implosion response, 384
Imprinting, 166-167
Independence, 204
India underdeveloped society under
    Gandhi, 385
Indirect secondary cutoffs, 114
Individuality force
    defined, 384
    emotional system functioning, 445
    function, 19-20
    societal process and, 386
Individuation, 274, 374
Infant mortality, 259
Infanticide
    animal, 71, 76
    guppies, 450
Infertility, 250-251
Information sharing, 195
Inherited secondary cutoffs, 114
Inhibitory response, 97, 98
Injury, defined, 356
Insects
    cannibalism, 450

Insects (continued)
  parent-offspring relationship, 338
  social colonies, 444
Insiders, 448, 454
Instinctual migration forces, 405, 406, 409
Integration, 443, 444-445
Intellectual system, 446
Intelligence and reproduction, 247
Interdependent triad, 11
Intergenerational fusion, 233
Interlocking triangles
  calm, 179, 180-181
  emotional cutoff compared to, 16-19
  extended family, 222-223
  intensity and extensiveness, 189
  intermediaries, 454
  marriage, 298-299
  primary and secondary, 25, 30
Intermediaries in interlocking triangles, 454
Internal distancing, 13
Internet involvement and spousal anger, 344, 346-347
Intifada (uprising)
  increase in hostility, 454, 456, 472
  Israeli cutoff, 469-470
  Palestinian passive resistance, 462
  Palestinian societal process, 467
  Palestinian suicide attacks, 471
Intrapsychic cutoff, 292, 332
Intrapsychic distance, 203
I-Position
  bridging family of origin cutoff, 166
  bridging secondary cutoff, 113
  differentiation effort in divorce, 302-303
  measurement, 209-210
  understanding client's viewpoint, 237
Ireland, M., 275
Iron curtain, 393, 397
Irreconcilable differences, 289
Isaac family history, 36-38
Ishmael family history, 36-38
Islam, 453, 462

Islamic Jihad, 456, 462
Isolation
  advantages, 445
  animal. See Animals
  defined, 443, 444
  emotional cutoff. See Emotional cutoff
  emotional divorce, 12
  functions, 73-76
  human, 78
Israeli-Palestinian relations
  Abraham family history, 36-38
  application of Bowen theory, 453-456
  conclusion, 467-473
  cutoff, 447-448
  differentiation of self, 445-447
  evolutionary forces in understanding, 443
  Israeli perspective, 451-452
  Palestinian perspective, 452-453
  societal emotional process, 449-451
  territoriality, 444, 445, 449
  textbooks, Israeli, 456-460
  textbooks, Palestinian, 460-464
  triangles, 448-449, 454-455
  "us" and "them" relationships See "Us/them" relationships
Israel's War of Independence, 457, 459

Jefferies, Susan Ewing, 199, 200, 206-208
Jerusalem, 452, 453
Jerusalem Media Center, 471
Jews
  Israeli-Palestinian relations, 451
  Muslim family history versus, 36-38
  occupation of Israel, 451-452
  relationship triangle, 454
  religious versus secular, 455
Jihad, 456, 462
Jones, J., 275
Jones, W. Thomas, 68
Jordan, 461

Journal of the American Medical Association, 275
Judaism, 462
Judea, 451

Kaczynski, Ted, 67
Keenan, E. L., 391
Kelly, Brian J., 139
Kerr, M., 199, 301
  anxiety, defined, 204-205
  cutoff and anxiety level, 381
  cutoff and triangles, 33
  cutoff concept, 276
  cutoff, defined, 279
  Family Evaluation, 426, 427
  mole-rat emotional functioning, 446
  regression, defined, 450
  separation, 207
Kievan Rus, 389
Klever, Phil, 219, 233
Kolbert, W., 78
Koran, 453
Kulkosky, P., 83

Lactation, 256-257, 259-260
Lancaster, J., 69, 73-74, 75
Lartin-Drake, Joan, 83
Lawrence, R. D., 69, 71-72, 73
League of Nations, 451
Leaning on one another, 321-322, 334
Lebanon War (1982), 459
LeDoux, J., 205, 251
Legal divorce, 293-296
Leutinizing hormone (LH), 252, 254
Level of functioning, 175-176
LH (leutinizing hormone), 252, 254
Libido, 252
Life forces, 19-20, 247
Life knowledge, 156-157
Lifelong pair bonding, 340
Likert scale, 209, 211-212
Limbic system, 95, 251-252, 255, 426

Lions
  emigration, 73, 78
  group defragmentation during
    drought, 72
  nomadic companions, 72
  population density, 72
  resident and nomad, 68
  solitary, 69-70, 75, 78
Logical conceptual bridge, 388-389,
    397
Lorenz, K., 166-167
Lovemaps, 174, 191
Low, Jane Wei-yueh, 199
Lubar, J., 83

MacLean, Paul, 251, 426
Mammals
  integration and isolation, 444
  migration, 403
  migration evolution, 404-405
  parent-offspring relationship, 338
Mandela, Nelson, 462
Marcus, I., 464
Marijuana use, 274
Marriage
  addressing cutoff, 235-242
  anxiety and, 32
  attachment process, 224-226
  beginning of, 290-291
  celibate, 293
  change and stress levels, 228-229
  conflict, 304-305
  conflict and child abuse, 357-358
  contract, 293-294
  cutoff assessment, 230-235
  dependence on spouse, 226-227
  differentiation, 20, 31
  divorce. *See* Divorce
  divorce vulnerability, 229-230
  domestic violence, 342-343
  emotional reactivity, 227-228
  emotional regression, 367, 370-371
  focus on spouse, 226-227
  interracial, 49

Marriage *(continued)*
    reactivity clinical example, 99-106
    reciprocal roles, 364, 366
    separation from parents, 219-223
    sex, 293
    undifferentiation, 31
Martyrdom, 462-463
Masters, R. D., 69
Maturity, emotional, 338, 341
McCollum, E. E., 209
McFarland, D., 68
McGuire, M. T., 69, 74, 75-76
McKnight, Anne S., 273
Mead, Margaret, 309-310
Measurement, cutoff
    instrument, 206-210
    scale development, 210-213
    validity and reliability, 213-215
Measurement, hormonal, 263, 269
Menninger Clinic, 275
Menninger Foundation, 246
Menninger Institute, 339
Menstruation
    cycle of, 252
    Society for Menstrual Cycle
        Research, 249-250
Messier, F., 72, 73
Mexican migration, 416, 417, 420
Mexican Revolution of 1910, 410-412
Migration, 421-422
    animal, 76, 78
    animal studies, 402-405, 408-409
    cutoff and, 195
    defined, 402, 405
    emotional cutoff, 406-408, 409-410
    family examples, 410-416
    function, 402
    human, 405-406, 409
    impact on reproduction, 248, 250,
        257-259
    influences, 402-403
    outcomes, 416-418
    patterns, 418-421
    preceding conditions, 401
    relationship influences, 418-419
    seasonal, 403

Mills, M. G L., 70
Mind-set, in flexibility development,
    241
Ministry of Education, 458, 463
Mirror image, 384, 387
Mohammed, 453, 462, 464
Mole-rats, 446
Molestation, 49-51, 281-282, 361
Monahan, Deborah J., 199
Mongol domination, 389
Monitoring the Future Study, 274
Monkeys, 76
Moran, Carol, 292
Mortality, infant, 259
Moses, 462
Moss, C., 70, 74, 408
Mother. *See also* Parents
    emotional divorce, 11
    schizophrenia and, 12
Mother Nature, 256
Multigenerational
    Bowen family emotional distancing,
        16-19
    family emotional unit, 358-359
    family history, 115-117
    family impact on brain
        development, 84-85, 91, 92
    process of schizophrenia, 11
    reproduction study, 257-260
Multigenerational transmission process
    cutoff in evolution, 202
    defined, 277
    divorce, 308-309
    emotional cutoff and, 31-32, 35
Multiple sclerosis, case vignette, 47-49
Murphy, Douglas C, 337
Muscle tension
    impact on reproduction, 263, 269
    reaction level and, 98, 103
Muscovite era, 389, 392
Muslims, 453, 455-456, 462

Natal dispersal, 402
Natal philopatry, 68, 75, 76

National Institute for Drug Abuse
(NIDA), 274
National Institute of Mental Health
hospitalization of schizophrenic
patient, 11, 31
relationships processes, 339
research on family as emotional
unit, 275
studying emotional cutoff, 200
National Institutes of Health
Comparative Ethology Lab
and Brain Research Unit, 255
Natural selection, 444-445
Nazi genocide, 428, 452
Nazi Germany, 385, 388. *See also*
Holocaust survivors
Nelson, Ener, 258-259
Neocortex, 426, 446
Nervous system
central, 94-97
parasympathetic, 97, 253
sympathetic, 253, 255
Neurofeedback
central nervous system, 93-97
clinical example, 101, 103-105
defined, 94
function, 83
increasing self perception, 106
Neuronal activity, 251
Neutral observer, 55-56
NIDA (National Institute for Drug
Abuse), 274
Nielson, Magnus, 257-259
Nimchinsky, E., 252, 254
Nomad
animals, 68
relationship, 38
Norepinepherine, 253
Nuclear family emotional process
bridging emotional cutoff, 52-53
defined, 33
in divorce, 304-308
dysfunctions, 33-34
impact on domestic violence,
341-343

"Nuclear Family Emotional System,"
18
Nusseibeh, Sari, 470

Objectivity, 426-427, 428, 429
Observer, neutral, 55-56
Occupied territory, 451
Olsdatter, Andrea, 257-259
"On the Differentiation of Self," 16
One-to-one personal relationships,
239-240
Open system
closed system versus, 53-54
defined, 114
detriangling, 56
undoing cutoff, 141
Openness, cutoff assessment, 231-232
Orangutan, 84
Oslo agreement (1993), 456, 461, 466
Ostracism
animal, 69-72, 73, 409
cannibalism, 71, 76
context of, 72
defined, 68-69
dispersal mechanism, 404
functions, 74-76
homicide, 71, 76
infanticide, 71, 76
"Otherness," 445
Our Arabic Language, 463
"Out-Patient Family Psychotherapy,"
15
Outsiders, 448, 454
Overfunctioning
defined, 277-278
marriage partner, 305, 334-335
Overlearning responses, 166
Overt cutoff
assessment of, 230
extended family, 223
marriage and, 225, 229
process of, 221-222
Ovulation
cycle of, 252-253

Ovulation *(continued)*
  impact of reactivity, 260-270
  reproduction and, 250-251, 252, 260
Owens, Mark and Delia, 72
Oxytocin, 255

Pain, impact on reproduction, 254
Pair bonding, 340
Palestine Liberation Organization, 466
Palestinian Authority, 456, 461, 463
Palestinians. *See* Israeli-Palestinian
  relations
Papero, D. V., 199, 447, 450
Parasympathetic system, 97, 253
Parent-offspring relationships, 338-339
Parents. *See also* Father; Mother
  as best friends, 165, 167
  coparental divorce, 297-298
  psychosis and, 13-14
  schizophrenia and, 11-16
Path diagram, 394, 395
Paul, W., 78
"Peace at any price," 320, 323
Peniston, E., 83
Personal data form, 212-213
Person-to-person relationships, 54-55,
  56
Peterson, R. O., 69, 73
PFCRT. *See* Princeton Family Center
  Research Team
Philopatry, 68, 75, 76
Physical
  abuse. *See* Child abuse
  assault. *See* Domestic violence
  distance, 15
  torture, 367
Physical dysfunction
  consequence of actions, 153
  emotional cutoff, 33-34, 38
  multiple sclerosis case vignette, 47-49
  symptom formation, 38
Physiological
  flooding, 228, 305
  linkage, 228

Physiological *(continued)*
  measures, 263, 269
  reactivity, 90
Pioneering, 75, 76-77
Podeh, E., 457, 458, 459
Polarization, Israeli-Palestinian
  relations
  intensifying of, 450
  in Israeli textbooks, 458, 459, 460
  Israeli versus Palestinian textbooks,
    465
  in modern textbooks, 466
  in Palestinian textbooks, 464
Politics, Soviet Union, 393, 394
Population density and animal
  dispersion, 72
Pregnancy, adolescent, 274. *See also*
  Reproduction
Pretend self, 408
Primary
  emotional cutoff, 25-29, 30
  triangle, 25, 28-29, 30, 222
Primogeniture, 405-406
Princeton Family Center Research
  Team (PFCRT)
  contact information, 216
  scale development, 210
  team development, 206-208
  test-retest plans, 215
Progesterone, 252
Projection process
  to a child, 305
  defined, 11, 278
  family. *See* Family projection
    process
  parent and child, 31
  from parent to offspring, 342
  Titelman family history, 112
Prolactin, 254
"Protecting Adolescents from Harm,"
  275
Pseudo self
  adaptation mechanism, 417
  growing up and, 207
  schizophrenia and, 12
  stuck-together fusion, 221

Pseudo self *(continued)*
tearing away, 15
values for living, 408
Pseudo separation
differentiation and, 32
family ego mass, 15, 207
schizophrenia and, 12
Pseudoindependence, 14
Pseudopartner, 306
Psychic divorce, 299-300
Psychosis, 13-15
Purge, Russian, 395-396
Pursuit
defined, 278
martial conflict, 304-305

Rabbits, 75
Race and cutoff vignette, 47-49
Raleigh, M. J., 69, 74, 75-76
Rape, 339
Rauseo, Eva Louise, 401
Raz-Krakotzkin, Amnon, 460
Reabuse, 361-362
"Reaction to Death in a Family," 111
Reactivity
anxiety as cause, 206
chronic level, 98
clinical example, 99-106
controlling, 55
distancing, 49, 56-57
divorce, 296, 302
impact of emotional cutoff, 407
impact on ovulation, 260-270
impact on reproduction, 245-246
influence on independence, 204
management, 240-242
in marriage, 227-228
measurement, 207, 209-210
physiological, 90
reproduction and, 248, 251
Rebellious sixties, 387
Reciprocal
cutoff process, 135
marriage roles, 364, 366

Reciprocal *(continued)*
relationship functioning, 143
societal process and emotional
cutoff, 385-386
visits by relatives, 148
Red foxes, 75
Refugees from life, 18
Regression
emotional, 366-374
societal, 382-383
societal process, 386, 450, 471
Relationship
defined, 352
family responsiveness, 354-356
human, 352-354
nomad, 38, 68
organ, 85, 107. *See also* Brain
system, 19
variables, animal, 73-74
Relatives of Enemies of the People, 395
Reproduction
A Family example, 262-263
adolescent, 274
B Family example, 264-265
Bowen theory, 249-257
C Family example, 265-269
emotional cutoff and, 245-249,
269-270
impact of cutoff, 259
infertility, 250-251
multigenerational study, 257-260
research and clinical examples,
260-262
variation, 245
Reptiles
brain, 426
parent-offspring relationship, 338
Research process
approaches, 191-192
benefits, 195-196
Eichholz family cutoff #1, 176-180
Eichholz family cutoff #2, 180-183,
184
Eichholz family cutoff #3, 183,
185-186, 187

Research process *(continued)*
    Eichholz family cutoff #4, 186,
        188-191
    guidelines, 201
    instrument, 206-210
    principles of, 194-195
    researching cutoffs, 175-176
    shift from individual to systems
        thinking, 174-175
    steps, 173-174
Research study, adolescent
    difficulties of study, 284-285
    emotional cutoff in family, 280-281
    family profiles, 280
    geographical distance cutoff,
        282-283
    limitations, 286
    methodology, 279-280
    outcome, 283-284, 285
    physical cutoff, 281-282
    purpose of, 279
Research study, Russia, 394-397
Resnick, M. D., 275
Responsiveness
    in human relationships, 352-354
    results of, 354-356
Retesting, 215
Rhesus macaques, 403, 404
Rigidity, 387-388
Roaring twenties, 387
Rodents
    emigration, 450
    emotional functioning, 446
    migration, 405
"Role of the Father in Families with a
    Schizophrenic Patient," 12
Rosenbaum, Lilian, 249
Rotherfluh, T., 78
Running away, 18. *See also* Tear self
    away
Russia
    environment, 390-393
    history, 397-398
    path diagram, 394, 395

Russia *(continued)*
    research study, 394-397
    societal process, 399
    study focus, 379-380
Rutgers University, contact
    information, 216

Safety concerns in emotional
    regression, 372
"Safety-valve" emigration function, 75,
    78
Samaria, 451
Samuel, Israel, 116
Santayana, George, 387
Sapolsky, R., 76, 293
Sarah and Abraham family history,
    36-38
Scale, FORS, 210-215
Scale of differentiation, 20, 384
Scale of Differentiation, 247
Schaller, G. B., 68, 69, 72, 73, 78
Scheper-Hughes, Nancy, 259
Schizophrenia
    emotional separation process, 9
    family relationships and, 10-16
    family roles in patients, 12
    hospitalization of, 11
    multigenerational, 11
    multigenerational process, 35
Schmitz, Mark F., 199
School shootings, 375
Schore, A., 97
Science, reproduction, 249
Seasonal migration, 403
Secondary
    emotional cutoff, 25-29, 30, 42. *See
        also* Bridging secondary
        cutoff
    triangle, 28-29, 30, 114
Secrecy, clinical example, 99
Self-definition, Mr. A's family, 150
Self-regulation, 97-99
Sensitivity, 381
Separateness, 443

Separation
  adolescent, 274
  circumstance, 248-249
  emotional, 24, 207
  parent-child, 219-223
Sex in marriage, 293
Sexual abuse
  assault, 367
  of children, 367, 370-371
  cutting off and, 49-51, 281-282
  molestation, 49-51, 281-282, 361
  reabuse perceived threat, 361-362
Shew, M., 275
Ship painting analogy, 155
Shock wave
  defined, 186, 188
  Eichholz family, 189, 190, 191
Shoulberg, Donald, 159, 160
Shunning, 70
Siamang, 84
Sibling position
  defined, 278
  emotional cutoff, 35-36
Sieving, R. E., 275
Six-Day War of 1967
  impact on Israelis, 458, 465
  Israeli recognition of Palestinians, 468
  Palestinian political action, 466
  in Palestinian textbooks, 461
Skowron, E. A., 209
Slavs
  environmental management, 389, 398
  farming, 390, 391
Slime mold, 444
Smile response, 353
Smith, Walter Howard, Jr., 351, 362
Smuts, Barbara, 199, 340
Social capital, 418
Social dysfunction, 33
Social rejection, chimpanzee, 70
Societal emotional process
  defined, 382
  emotional cutoff, 36-38

Societal emotional process *(continued)*
  Israeli-Palestinian relations, 449-451
Societal process
  bridging family and societal cutoff, 397-399
  emotional cutoff, 380-381, 385-389
  general assumptions, 399-400
  impact of geography, 389-393
  Israeli and Palestinian textbooks, 464-467
  Israeli-Palestinian relations, 456-467
  overview, 379-380
  pressure, 382
  regression, 382-383, 386, 471
  research study, 394-397
  Russian history, 389
  scale of differentiation, 384-385
  Soviet Union, 389, 393-394, 395
  togetherness, 383-384
  underlying issues, 399
  variations, 381-382
Society for Menstrual Cycle Research, 249-250
Solid self, 417-418
Solitary lifestyle
  animals. *See* Animals
  social isolation, 67
Somatic illness, 14
Songbirds, 450
Sontag, Deborah, 470
Soviet Union
  path diagram, 394, 395
  postsoviet period, 389
  soviet period, 393-394
  study focus, 379-380
Spaceship earth, 450
Spanking, child abuse, 356-357
Stalking, 353-354, 375
Starvation, child abuse, 367
Steinberger, Emil, 249
Stereotyping, 447, 455
Sterman, M. B., 83
Stonewalling in marriage, 229, 305
Stress
  child abuse and, 357, 368
  defined, 357

Stress (continued)
impact on reproduction, 254, 255
marital, 228-229
sexual desire and, 293
variations, 255
Stuck-together fusion
defined, 21
detriangling self, 56
extended family, 233
extended family influence, 223
marriage and, 225
separation from parents, 220-221
Subcortex, 91
Subscales, 214
Suicide, 77
Suomi, Stephen, 255
Survivors of the Shoah Visual History
Foundation, 429, 430
Sweat response, 97
Symbiosis
anxiety of mother to child, 31
attachment, 14
dependence, 14
infant and mother attachment, 204
schizophrenia and, 11, 12
unresolved attachment, 14-15
Sympathetic nervous system, 253, 255
Symptom formation
background, 38-39
child abuse, 356-358
cutoff and degree of, 201
cutting off vignettes, 43, 45-51
depression. See Depression
family cutoff and, 164, 168, 169
growing away to tearing away
vignette, 39-42
multigenerational cutoff, 381
stress, 357-358
tearing away to cutting off vignette,
42-43, 44

Tabor, J., 275
Taliban, 388-389
Tear self away
case vignettes, 39-43, 44

Tear self away (continued)
characteristics, 24
described, 18-19
emotional separation, 24
family relationships and, 15-16
growing away versus, 207
schizophrenia and, 12
unresolved attachment, 15
Teenagers. See Adolescents
Teitelman, Robert, 115
Termination process, 160
Termites, 338
Territoriality, 444, 445, 449
Testosterone, 263, 264, 269
Tests
adolescent research study, 280
Child and Adolescent Functional
Assessment Scale (CAFAS),
280, 283
cutoff. See Cutoff assessment
Diagnostic and Statistical Manual
of Mental Disorders, Fourth
Edition (DSM-IV), 280
Emotional Cutoff Scale (ECS), 209,
280, 283
FORS. See Family of Origin
Response Survey
Global Assessment of Functioning
(GAF), 280, 283
retest, 215
Texas Institute of Reproductive
Medicine and Endocrinology
(TIRME), 249-250
Textbooks
Israeli, 456-460
Palestinian, 456-457, 460-464
societal process and, 464-467
Therapist's Own Family, 121
Theta brain waves
clinical example, 101, 103-105
function, 95-96
Think category, PFCRT, 208, 211-214
Threats
CRH release, 253
defined, 360
domestic violence, 339

Threats *(continued)*
  family stability and, 360-366
  generational interactions, 256
  management of, 363-364
  perceived or imagined, 360-361
  real, 360-361
  sense of, 98
  survival response trigger, 140
Three-generation reproductive unit,
    84-85, 91, 92
TIRME (Texas Institute of
    Reproductive Medicine and
    Endocrinology), 249-250
Titelman, Peter, 9, 111, 199
Togetherness force
  automatic instinctual, 393
  defined, 383-384
  emotional system functioning, 445
  end point, 383
  excessive, 384
  function, 19-20
  intensity and emotional cutoff, 389
  living organism innate behavior, 443
  Russia, 392
  societal process, 386
Toman, W., 35, 278
Torture, physical, 367
Totalitarianism, 393-394
"Toward the Differentiation of Self
    n One's Own Family," 52
Transference, 160
Transient living arrangements, 311
Transmission process. *See*
    Multigenerational
    transmission process
"Treatment of Family Groups with a
    Schizophrenic Member," 12
Trees, distancing, 447
Trevathan, W., 256
Triad
  human, 448
  interdependent, 11
  marriage and emotional divorce, 15
Triangles
  defined, 278, 322

Triangles *(continued)*
  in divorce, 303-304, 305-306,
    310-311
  emotional, 385
  emotional cutoff and, 32-33
  interlocking. *See* Interlocking
    triangles
  Israeli-Palestinian relations,
    448-449, 454-455
  managing self, 150-151
  measurement, 208, 211-214
  occurrence of problems, 248
  one-to-one relationships, 239
  primary, 25, 28-29, 30, 222
  secondary, 28-29, 30, 114
  useful, 194-195
Triangling, 233
Triune brain, 251
Triune Brain in Evolution, 426
"Tuning" process, 98

Udry, J. R., 275
Uncoupling, 289
Underfunctioning
  defined, 277-278
  marriage partner, 305, 334-335
Undifferentiation
  Abraham family history, 38
  defined, 20-21
  in marriage, 31
Undoing cutoff, 139-141, 156-158
  family history in 1976, 142-143
  initial steps, 144-156
  life knowledge list, 156-157
  theoretical comments, 146-148,
    150-152, 154-155
  theory of family history, 143-144
Unemployment and child abuse, 361
Unemployment rate and behavior, 77
Universal life forces, 247
Unresolved attachment
  background, 204-206
  defined, 22
  handling of, 277, 332

Unresolved attachment *(continued)*
  link to emotional cutoff, 204
  schizophrenia and, 14, 15
  symbiotic, 14-15
"Us/them" relationships
  integration and isolation, 444
  in Israeli textbooks, 460, 465
  Israeli-Palestinian relations,
    467-468, 472
Utschig, Elizabeth, 83

Viability of Holocaust survivors, 425
Viable emotional contact, 380, 387,
    396
Viable social group members, 383
Victim blaming, 337
Vignettes. *See* Case vignettes
Violence
  attachment response, 353-354
  businesses, 375
  child abuse. *See* Child abuse
  domestic violence. *See* Domestic
    violence
  Israeli-Palestinian relations, 471
  sports teams, 375
  threats, 360-366
Volkart, R., 78

Walters, D., 83
War of the Roses, 297
Warm fusion, 21
Waser, P., 68
Wasps, 338
Water voles, 75
"We-ness," 445, 448
West Bank, 451, 460
"We-they" factions, 450
Whales, 273

White, Charles M.
  contact information, 216
  emotional cutoff, 199
  FORS development, 200
  PFCRT member, 207
White, Melanie T., 199
Wilgus, Anthony J., 67
Withdrawal
  emotional divorce, 12
  threat response, 361
Wolf, Stewart, 78
Wolves
  exclusion during mating season, 73
  integration and isolation, 444
  isolation, 69, 71-72
  solitary, 75
Woman's Hospital of Texas, 250
Woolard, T., 75
Worry
  brain wave measurement, 96
  chronic level of reaction, 98
Wynne-Edwards, V. C.
  animal dispersion, 71
  distancing process, 78
  population dispersion, 72, 75

Yishuv, 452

Zebra, 362
Zimen, E., 72
Zionist movement
  in Israeli liberation, 465
  Israeli perspective, 452
  in Israeli textbooks, 458-460
  in modern textbooks, 466
  Palestinian perspective, 453
  in Palestinian textbooks, 463
Zweig, Mark H., 295